Günter Osterloh

LEICA M

Advanced Photo School

LARK BOOKS
A Division of Sterling Publishing,Co., Inc.
New York

Layout: Michael T. Robertson
Cover Design: Barbara Zaretsky
Cover Photos: Oliver Richter
Historical Photos: Leica Archive
English Translation: Phyllis M. Riefler-Bonham
Editorial Assistance: Haley Pritchard and Delores Gosnell

10 9 8 7 6 5 4 3 2 1
Second English-Language Edition

Library of Congress Cataloging-in-Publication Data

Osterloh, Günter.
Leica M : advanced photo school / Günter Osterloh.-- 2nd English language ed.
p. cm.
Originally published in German.
Includes index.
ISBN 1-57990-637-0 (hardcover)
1. Leica camera. I. Title.
TR263.L408823 2005
771.3'1--dc22
2004019279

©2002 Originally published in German by Umschau Verlag GmbH, Frankfurt am Main, Germany (legal successor: HEEL Verlag GmbH, Königswinter, Germany) under the title: Leica M: Hohe Schule der Kleinbildfotografie
Written and illustrated by Günter Osterloh

© 2005 Lark Books—A Division of Sterling Publishing Co., Inc.
387 Park Avenue South, New York, N.Y. 10016

Distributed in Canada by Sterling Publishing,
c/o Canadian Manda Group, 165 Dufferin Street
Toronto, Ontario, Canada M6K 3H6

Distributed in the U.K. by Guild of Master Craftsman Publications Ltd., Castle Place, 166 High Street, Lewes, East Sussex, England BN7 1XU; Tel: (+ 44) 1273 477374, Fax: (+ 44) 1273 478606, e-mail: pubs@thegmcgroup.com, Web: www.gmcpublications.com

Distributed in Australia by Capricorn Link (Australia) Pty Ltd.,
P.O. Box 704, Windsor, NSW 2756 Australia

The written instructions, photographs, designs, patterns, and projects in this volume are intended for the personal use of the reader and may be reproduced for that purpose only. Any other use, especially commercial use, is forbidden under law without written permission of the copyright holder.

Every effort has been made to ensure that all the information in this book is accurate. However, due to differing conditions, tools, and individual skills, the publisher cannot be responsible for any injuries, losses, and other damages that may result from the use of the information in this book. Because specifications may be changed by the manufacturer without notice, the contents of this book may not necessarily agree with changes made after publication.

This book is not sponsored by Leica Camera AG. The following are registered trademarks of Leica Camera AG: ANGULON, APO-TELYT, CURTAGON, ELMAR, ELMARIT, LEITZ, LEICA, LEICAFLEX, LEICAMETER, NOCILUX, PHOTAR, PRADOVIT, REPROVIT, SUMMICRON, TELEVID, and VISOFLEX. Other trademarks are recognized as belonging to their respective owners.

If you have questions or comments about this book, please contact:
Lark Books
67 Broadway
Asheville, NC 28801
(828) 253-0467

Manufactured in China
All rights reserved
ISBN 1-57990-637-0

For information about custom editions, special sales, premium and corporate purchases, please contact Sterling Special Sales Department at 800-805-5489 or specialsales@sterlingpub.com.

Contents

Preface

No other camera has had such a lasting influence on photography as the Leica. It paved the way for modern photojournalism, it was the prerequisite for the candid snapshot, and—as proven by countless imitations—it served as a prototype for many camera manufacturers. Then and now, the Leica is an indispensable tool for photographers around the world. Its fast and precise focusing, its quiet shutter, and its great dependability remain unsurpassed.

New camera concepts are made possible by new technologies. The choice of auto-exposure programs and automatic focusing almost make us forget that the composition of the picture is still under the creative control of the photographer. Modern electronics may enhance the ease of operating a camera, but even the integrated circuits in the latest model do not guarantee better pictures. Technology itself can only be a means to an end. Technology should serve the photographer while remaining user-friendly—the Leica is a good example of this belief.

Every worthwhile leisure-time activity requires an investment in personal time. Typically, any golfer, mountain climber, tennis player, surfer, painter, horseback rider, musician, or skier trains and takes lessons and practices their skills. Yet, many believe that we are born with photographic skills, or that modern technology will enable us to master the art of photography. But, photography has to be learned like any other craft, both in theory and in practice.

Anyone who wishes to become a serious photographer requires a "learning period." This book is intended to be an aid for the theoretical part of the hobby. It reflects the experience with a Leica M that I have gained over 20 years. During that time, I was able to profit from the knowledge of outstanding experts. My principal mentors were Theo Kisselbach, who taught me Leica technique, Professor Stefan Kruckenhauser, whose "School of Seeing" opened my eyes, and Heinrich Stöckler, who encouraged me to write this book, which is dedicated to them.

Wetzlar, August 1985

Preface to the updated edition

Recently the continued development of the Leica M system has gained significant momentum. New technologies have permitted new designs which were considered not implementable only a few years ago. One example is the LED display of exposure-time in the viewfinder of the Leica M7, without which automatic timing would make no sense from a practical viewpoint. Other examples are new processes for manufacturing lenses, which contribute to increased imaging power, a broader range of applications, and enhanced user convencience.

In addition, the choice between different viewfinder magnifications allows photographers to adjust even better to their style of shooting. Combined with the enormeous improvements made to all films, this allows the creation of images of a quality that was inconceivable a few years ago.

In order to maximize the phototechnological options featured by current Leica M systems and implement them skillfully in the composition of pictures, the content of this edition of the book has been expanded significantly and revised. However, it still applies that, in addition to perfect product technology, the Leica photographers must endeavor to improve their skills. The joy of photography is enhanced to the same degree as the user's photographic results are enhanced by personal commitment. Good pictures are still subject to the maxim of "no pain, no gain." And that is good!

I would like to thank my publisher, Umschau Verlag, for successfully supporting the publication of my Leica books for over 20 years. My special thanks go to the employees of Leitz/Leica who supported the creation of these books with help and advice and, in particular, to my family who endured my photographic activies with great patience and assisted me whenever I needed them.

Braunfels, September 2002

The LEICA M range-viewfinder camera system

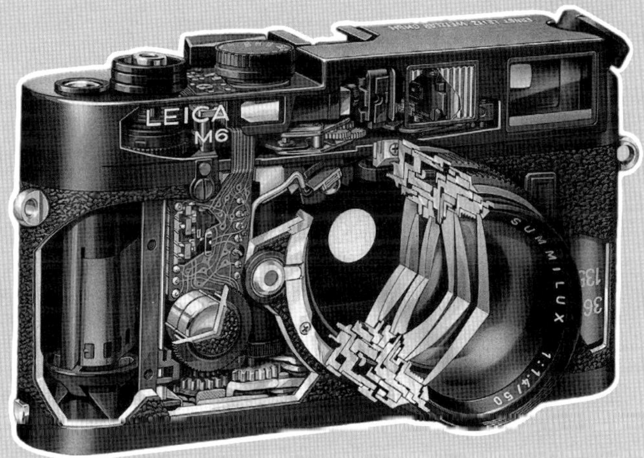

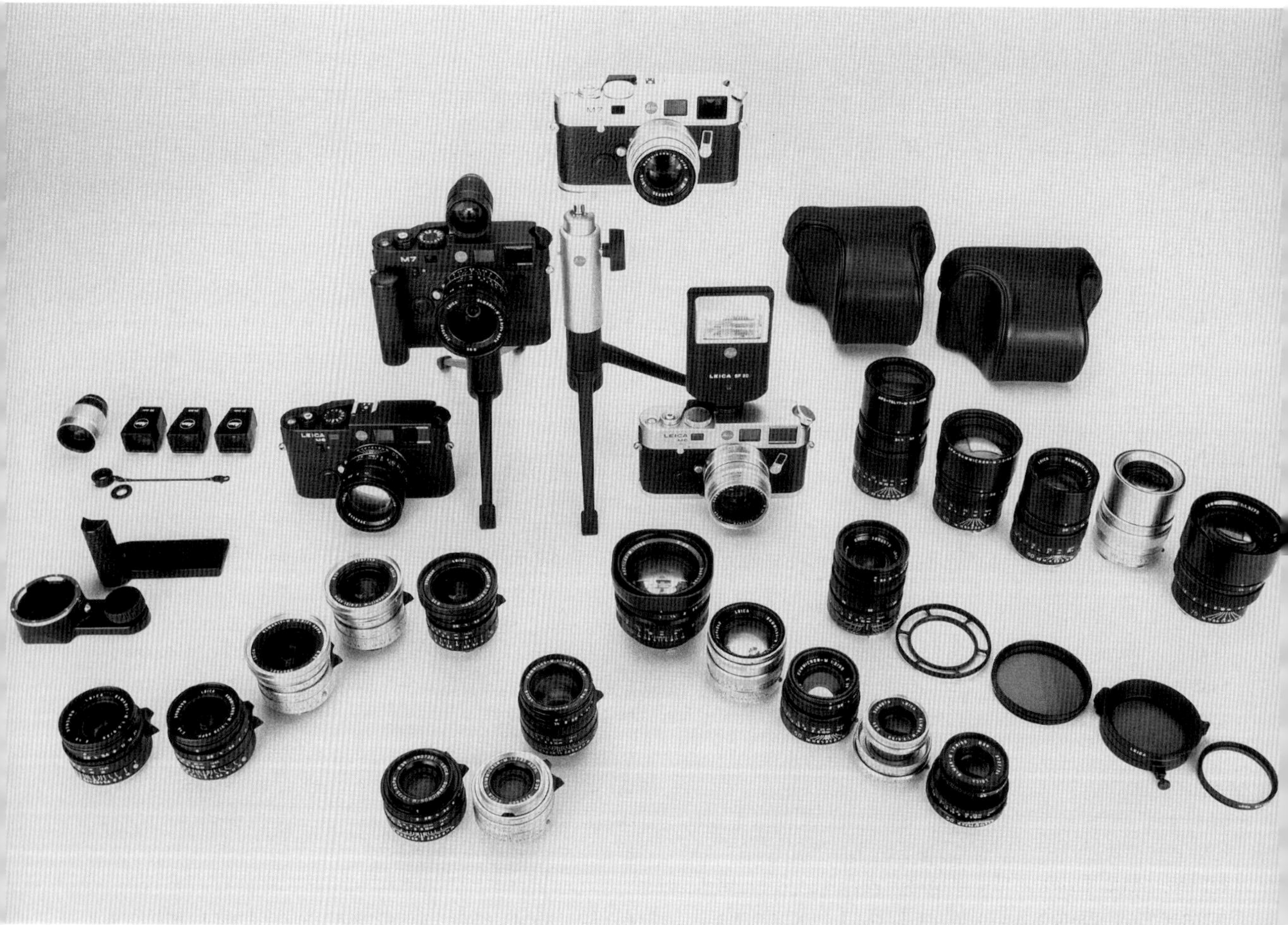

Fig. 1: *The LEICA M System*

The LEICA M Range-Viewfinder Camera System

The Leica M has been in production since 1954. It has been repeatedly modified, improved, and adapted to achieve the latest in photographic technology. Yet, in many ways, it remains essentially unchanged. It is regarded as the classic 35mm range-viewfinder system camera. Any attempt to compare the Leica M with the technical features of a modern single-lens-reflex (SLR) camera very easily leads to an erroneous assessment of the capabilities and performance of the Leica M. Therefore, we will first evaluate the Leica M without delving into technical details. We will show the reasons that the essential concept of this camera is still indispensable for many of today's photographers.

Why rangefinder cameras?

While technical descriptions of cameras are necessary, they do not convey practical essentials. Statements by experienced users are often more informative, but are limited by their subjectivity. It might seem that the best solution is to work with the camera yourself, or is it? Even when given access to a camera, does a typical photographer have the right qualifications for an accurate evaluation?

Perhaps this is best illustrated by using a violin as an example. To describe a Stradivarius, which is recognized as a superb violin, it is far from adequate to simply describe its size, weight, materials, and components. Even a brilliant virtuoso like Yehudi Menuhin might find it difficult to completely describe the tones that emanate from this instrument. One has to hear it, to experience it.

But novice testers will completely fail if they do not know how to play the violin. In other words, it is very easy to elicit sounds from a Stradivarius or to expose film with a Leica, but only masters can produce magnificent music or outstanding photographs with these superb instruments. Fortunately, both playing the violin and making great pictures can be learned.

Considering just a few characteristics quickly shows that a rangefinder camera like the Leica M continues to be technologically up-to-date. Its light weight, compact dimensions, for instance, are very important to someone who wishes to take a camera along on an airplane, or on hikes in the mountains. Those who like to take pictures inconspicuously will value the quiet shutter, and those who take photos in low-light settings will be pleased by the high focusing accuracy. But, even these and other unquestionable advantages over the SLR camera are not the only things that make the Leica M virtually irreplaceable.

Why is this camera still described, again and again, as unique? The 35mm format of 24 x 36 mm still plays a predominant role in the world of traditional photography. This applies both to its use by professionals and amateurs, as well as to its impact on the trade by photographic dealers, processing laboratories, and the photographic industry. Many diverse types of cameras—from the high-priced SLR to the compact autofocus with built-in flash and motorized advance—all use 35mm film.

All this began with Oskar Barnack's Leica. Although Mr. Barnack cannot be regarded as the inventor of the 35mm format, he can claim the distinction of having established the premise for the phenomenal growth of 35mm photography: the design of the Leica camera. The original camera very quickly evolved into a camera system, continuously meeting the growing demands of photographers by offering new improvements. From the very beginning, the wishes of those photographers were taken into account. Those who took full advantage of the increased mobility made possible by the Leica, quickly ventured into new fields in photography.

Some photographers quickly realized the new possibilities in photojournalism offered by this mobile and fast camera. They made good use of this and created a new trend in photographic style. Instead of the static, posed picture, a series of action pictures began to appear. This small, lightweight and portable 35mm camera, equipped with relatively fast lenses, permitted short, handheld exposures ideal for capturing the action.

The Leica soon displaced the large, heavy cameras, which required tripods for long exposures. This was the dawning of modern photojournalism. It distinguished itself because a photographer with a 35mm camera could now get into the event. The photo-reporter became part of the action, right in the middle of it, in direct contact with the scene. The physical distance between subjects and photographers that was necessary up to then, because of bulky and cumbersome equipment, simply shrank. Amateur photographers also were excited about the small, lightweight camera.

A candid snapshot had been only a dream for amateur photographers, but they quickly realized that Oskar Barnack—an amateur photographer, himself—had actually designed the Leica to meet their needs—and with professional-quality results!

Naturally, photography required close involvement, and, as always, a photographer with a creative eye. It is the photographer who has to approach his subject with few preconceived notions. Subjects are rarely in perfectly arranged positions waiting patiently to become part of a perfect picture.

These new progressive photographers quickly realized that they must be able to observe the subject inconspicuously. They recognized that they must work fast and confidently when the opportunity arises to capture the critical moment.

In addition to technical know-how, a successful photographer must have sensitivity. Photographers create the picture. The camera is merely the tool with which to capture, as accurately as possible, the image they have envisioned. From the very beginning, Leitz considered what might make its camera even better suited to this way of working and invited input and suggestions for new designs. To this day, feedback from photographers continues to be incorporated into new models.

One of the most important demands made of the Leica—accurate and fast focusing—was achieved in 1932 by the introduction of the Leica II, with a built-in, coupled rangefinder. When science and technology developed a need for photographic documentation and special accessories, Leica met the challenge. Advanced amateur photographers were delighted that they too could utilize all the technical tools that were available to professional photographers. Photojournalists and amateurs alike greatly appreciated the quiet shutter, the highly accurate, fast focusing, the high-quality lenses, and the excellent durability of their Leica equipment.

A significant milestone in the design of this type of camera occurred in the mid-1950s with the introduction of the Leica M camera series. A rapid-change bayonet lens mount and a combined range-viewfinder made camera operation even quicker. Around that time, it was already becoming apparent that, along with the rangefinder camera, the 35mm SLR camera was gaining popularity. Since the 1930s, Leitz had been offering the Visoflex reflex housing attachment, which converted the rangefinder Leica into an SLR camera for use in telephoto and macro photography. The 35mm SLR cameras of the 1950s offered no significant advantages over a Leica equipped with a Visoflex attachment, since advances in SLR technology such as the instant return mirror, pentaprism, and automatic diaphragm were not yet available.

The SLR camera appealed mainly to photographers who wanted to photograph with long focal lengths or macro lenses. However, the camera did not become popular until it became possible to see the subject in the viewfinder immediately after an exposure (the instant return mirror), the aperture no longer had to be stopped down manually (the automatic diaphragm), and the subject could be viewed right side up and right way around (the pentaprism).

Changing living conditions and lifestyles also had lasting effects on the practice of photography. While modern photojournalists formerly had to work very close to the subject, the improvements in long and extremely long lenses enabled them to make frame-filling photographs from greater distances. This offered protection during dangerous assignments and made it possible to fill the frame with famous personalities despite increased security requirements.

On the other hand, by using this technique, the photographer also distanced himself from the action and gradually became an uninvolved observer. Frequently this also diminished the direct contact with the action, which was so very important to the dedicated photographer. It became difficult to establish and cultivate interpersonal relationships and the content of photographs became less expressive. Photographers had reverted to an older style of shooting before the dawn of 35mm photography.

This new flexibility allowed new dramatic photographic styles to evolve, which fostered new pictorial expression. It did not, however, necessarily improve the quality of the photograph as far as content and technique were concerned. Yet, it did not mean an automatic reduction in overall quality either. Photographs were simply quite different.

In the meantime, the introduction of color photography changed photographic composition significantly and altered the consciousness of both the photographer and the viewer. Selective focus and color contrast were easier to control with an SLR camera. Variations in composition, created by changing the camera position, were easier to execute because the photographer was remote from the action with freedom to move.

Amateur photographers, who earlier had successfully mastered the professional technique of using the highly portable 35mm camera in candid photography, soon became enthusiastic about the versatility of the SLR camera and it began to flourish.

Both professional and amateur photographers started using the 35mm SLR camera and, although Leitz successfully marketed its first SLR camera, it did not shelve its Leica M models. This decision proved to be correct since, when the initial euphoria subsided, many journalists returned to the rangefinder camera without making the mistake of condemning the SLR. Practice had taught them that one system could not replace the other, rather they complemented each other beautifully.

Today, more and more young photographers are rediscovering the rangefinder camera, inspired by the elite, top photographers who use the Leica M—not

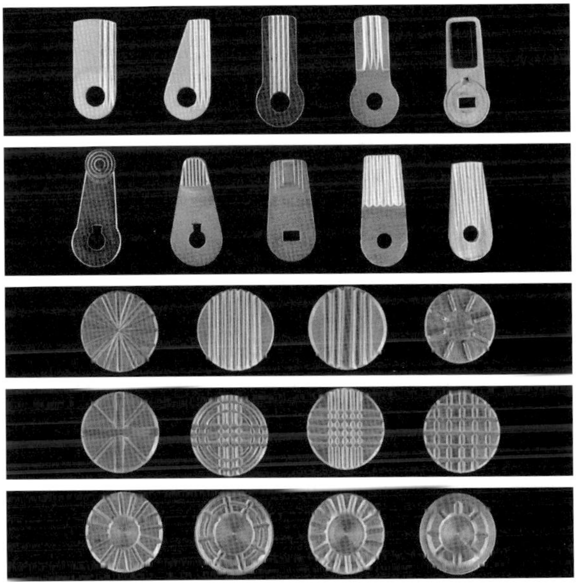

Fig. 2: *An example of the Leica design team's attention to detail, these photographs show prototypes of the field-of-view preview lever for the Leica M4, and the film-speed selector for the Leica M5.*

exclusively—but as an excellent alternative to the SLR camera. Why use rangefinder cameras? The answer is that they enable the expert to photograph during the action, and thus, be part of the action. They serve the professional's requirement for dynamic reporting and the amateur's desire for lively, candid snapshots.

The rangefinder camera entices photographers to express themselves from the center of the action, whereas the SLR camera is more conducive to observing the action from a distance. In this sense, both shooting styles are legitimate and both cameras serve those who wish to express themselves through the medium of photography.

LEICA M cameras

To this day, the fundamental characteristics of the very first Leica M cameras have been retained on all of the subsequent M models. Significant changes in size and weight occurred only once, with the Leica M5. Of course there are always some differences in the details of the various M models, as well as variations within a given model designation.

Collectors and photo-historians have been studying these peculiarities for years, but they rarely matter to the photographer. Leitz maintained product continuity through uniformity in the operation of the camera and compatibility with existing lenses and accessories.

The first two models of Leica M cameras—the Leica M3 and the Leica M2—differ mainly in viewfinder magnification and shutter advance mechanism. The magnification of the viewfinder of a Leica M3 is 0.9x and 0.72x in the Leica M2. That is why the selection of bright-line frames, which automatically appear in the viewfinder when a lens is mounted, is different in these two models.

In the Leica M3 the frame for the 50mm lens always remains visible and the 90mm or the 135mm frame is added when the respective lens is mounted. The Leica M2 is equipped with bright-line frames for 35, 50, and 90mm lenses and they appear when the respective lenses are used. With 35mm wide-angle lenses, the Leica M3 requires a viewfinder attachment in order to observe the correct field of view.

On the Leica M2 it is the 135mm lens that requires a viewfinder attachment for proper framing. Of course, a wide-angle lens with viewfinder attachment can also be used on a Leica M2. It will activate the camera's 50mm bright-line frame but the magnification of the viewfinder image will be reduced by the viewfinder attachment so that it delineates the correct field of view. Focusing continues to function properly.

The same principle applies to the 135mm lens with magnifying viewfinder attachment, which activates the 90mm frame on Leica M3 and Leica M2 cameras. Lenses that do not activate the proper bright-line frame can also be attached, and they will couple accurately with the camera's rangefinder. However, a separate bright-line finder for that lens' focal length must be inserted in the accessory shoe on the top of the camera in order to determine the correct field of view. The end of the film take-up spool in the Leica M2, unlike the one in the Leica M3, is designed to couple with a rapid film advance attachment that can be used in place of the base plate. The Leica MP, a limited special edition, corresponds to a Leica M3, but its take-up spool; permits the attachment of a rapid film advance.

There are many detailed books about vintage Leica cameras and lenses available at photo or book stores, which are of interest to collectors and historians. Also, the Leitz Wetzlar Information Service will be pleased to supply information. True experts in "Leica History" can be found in the societies that specialize in the history of the Leica. For more information visit www.leica-camera.com.
For a nominal fee, original instructions for early Leica M models can be ordered from Leica.

Only the most important models of Leica M cameras and their principal characteristics are featured in the technical descriptions that follow.

LEICA M3

Introduced in 1954

- One-piece all-metal body housing with hinged back cover and lateral carrying-strap lugs. Bright chrome-plated brass top and base plates (black enamel version in 1959). 3/8" tripod socket.
- Range-viewfinder system with automatic bright-line frames for 50, 90, and 135mm lenses (a 35mm field of view is generated by a 35mm lens with viewfinder attachment).
- Automatic parallax correction.
- Viewfinder magnification: 0.90x.
- Field-of-view preview selector.
- Shutter speed dial with click stops, which can couple to accessory exposure meters.
- Rubberized cloth focal-plane shutter for 1, 1/2, 1/4, 1/8, 1/15, 1/30, 1/60, 1/125, 1/250, 1/500, 1/1000 second plus "B" for time exposures of any length.
- Automatic flash synchronization for flashbulbs up to 1/500 second and for electronic flash up to 1/50 second.
- Separate contacts for flashbulb units (M) and electronic flash units (X).
- Variable self-timer.
- Rapid advance lever with ratcheted operation for winding the shutter and advancing the film.
- Automatic frame counter with magnified read-out.
- Film reminder dial.
- Pull-up rewind knob.
- Accessory shoe for special viewfinders and other accessories.
- Removable film take-up spool.

Note: Early versions of the Leica M3 did not have the field-of-view preview selector and were equipped with a shutter winding and film advance mechanism that had to be operated with two strokes of the rapid advance lever. In addition, the shutter speed dial was calibrated in accordance with German standards: (e.g., 1/25, 1/50, 1/100 second, etc.).

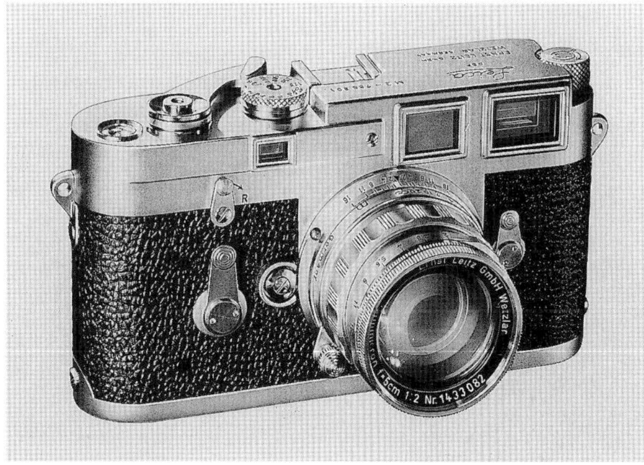

Fig. 3: LEICA M3

Dimensions: Height 77 mm (3-1/32 inches), length 138 mm (5-7/16 inches), thickness 36 mm (1-13/32 inches).

Weight: 595 grams (1 lb 5 oz.).

LEICA M2

Introduced in 1958

This camera is the same concept as the Leica M3 and therefore has similar features, with the following differences:

- Range-viewfinder with automatically activated bright-line frames for 35, 50, and 90 mm lenses (the 135mm field of view is generated by 135mm lens with viewfinder attachment).
- Viewfinder magnification: 0.72x .
- Exposure counter must be manually reset to 0.

Note: Early versions of the Leica M2 were not equipped with a self-timer and had a film rewind release button, instead of a lever.

Weight: 580 grams (1 lb. 4.5 oz.).

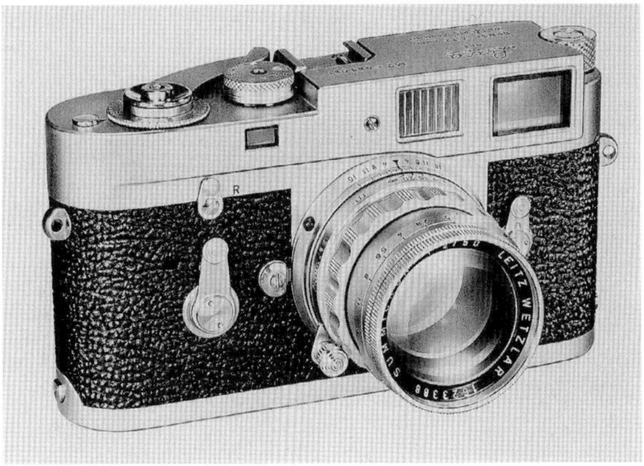

Fig. 4: *LEICA M2*

LEICA M2-Mot
Introduced in 1967

This camera has the same technical characteristics as the Leica M2, except that it does not have a self-timer.

- Equipped with a coupling for a Leica Motor.

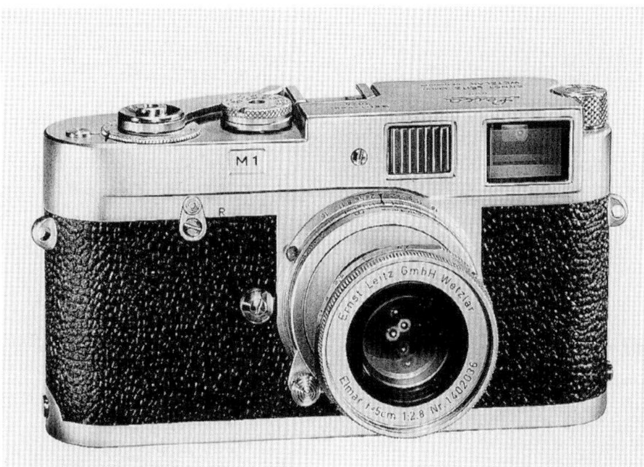

Fig. 5: *LEICA M1*

LEICA M1
Introduced in 1959

This camera's construction is generally similar to that of the Leica M2, with the following differences:

- Bright-line viewfinder with the frames for 35 and 50mm lenses permanently displayed; automatic parallax correction.
- No rangefinder.

Dimensions: Height 77 mm (3-13/32 inches), length 138 mm (5-7/16 inches), thickness 36 mm (1-13/32 inches).

Weight: 545 grams (1 lb 3 oz.).

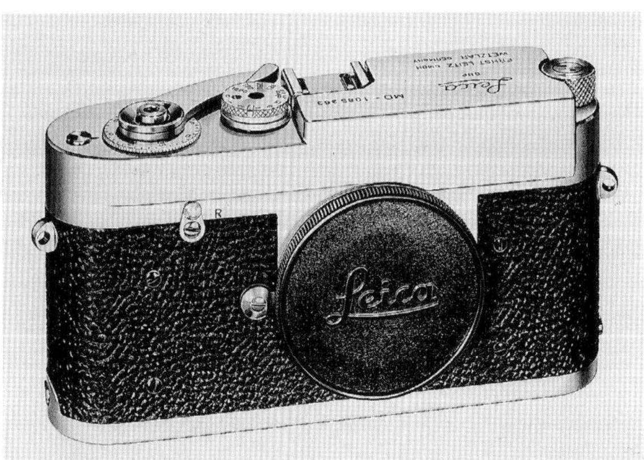

Fig. 6: *LEICA MD*

LEICA MD
Introduced in 1965

This camera body was designed for photographic documentation. Same technical characteristics as the Leica M2, except that it does not have a viewfinder or a self-timer.

- Designed to accept index strips for recording documentation directly on the film negative. This requires a special base plate with a light-tight slot for the insertion of these strips.

Dimensions: Same as those of the Leica M2.

Weight: 495 grams (1 lb 1-1/2 oz.).

LEICA M4

Introduced in 1967

- One-piece all-metal body with hinged back cover and lateral carrying-strap lugs. Bright chrome-plated brass top plate and base plate; later a black enamel finish was added to the line. 1/4" tripod socket.
- Range-viewfinder with automatic bright-line frames for 35, 50, 90, and 135mm lenses (the 35 and 135mm frames appear together).
- Automatic parallax correction. Viewfinder magnification: 0.72x.
- Field-of-view preview selector.
- Shutter speed dial with click stops, can couple to accessory Leicameter MR4 exposure meter.
- Rubberized cloth, focal-plane shutter for 1, 1/2, 1/4, 1/8, 1/15, 1/30, 1/60, 1/125, 1/250, 1/500, 1/1000 second plus "B" for time exposures of any length.
- Automatic flash synchronization for flashbulbs up to 1/500 second, and for electronic flash up to 1/50 second Separate standard flash contacts for flashbulb units (M) and electronic flash units (X).
- Variable self-timer.
- Ratcheted rapid advance lever for winding the shutter and advancing the film.
- Fast film loading system for all commercially available 35mm cameras and Leica cassettes.
- Slanted rewind crank.
- Automatic frame counter with magnified read-out.
- Film reminder dial.
- Accessory shoe for special viewfinders and other accessories.

Dimensions: Height 77 mm (3-1/32 inches), length 138 mm (5-1/6 inches), thickness 36 mm (1-13/32 inches).

Weight: 600 grams (1 lb 5 oz.).

LEICA M4-Mot

Introduced in 1967

This has the same technical features as the Leica M4, except that it does not have a self-timer. Equipped with a coupling for a Leica Motor.

Dimensions: same as Leica M4.

Weight: 610 grams (1 lb 5-1/2 oz.).

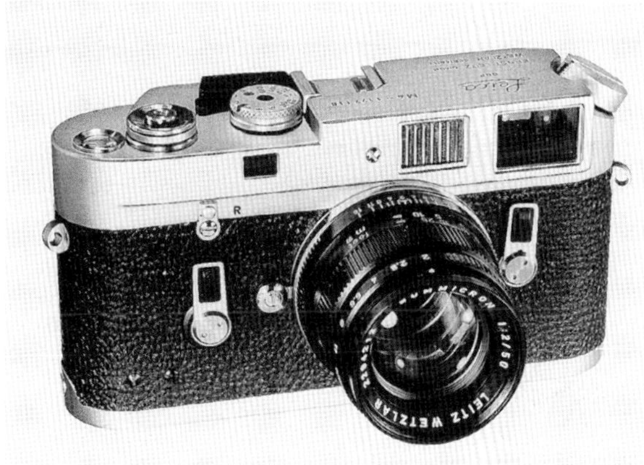

Fig. 7: LEICA M4

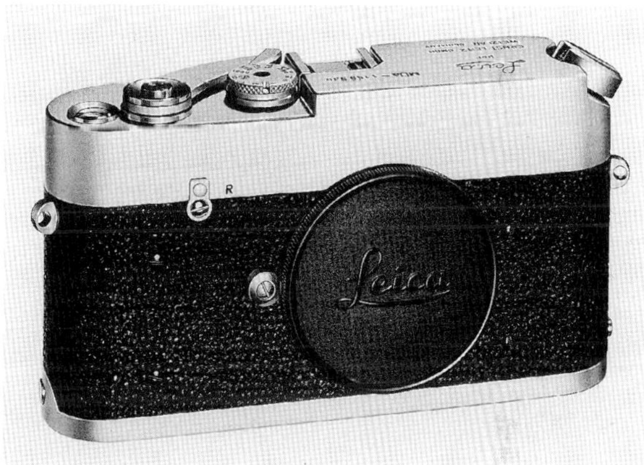

Fig. 8: LEICA MDa

LEICA MDa

Introduced in 1967

This camera body was designed for photographic documentation. Same technical characteristics as the Leica M4, except that it does not have a viewfinder or a self-timer.

- Designed to accept index strips for recording of documentation directly on the film negative. This required a special base plate with a light-tight slot for the insertion of these strips.

Dimensions: same as Leica M4.

Weight: 495 grams (1 lb 1-1/2 oz.).

LEICA M5

Introduced in 1972

- One-piece all-metal body housing with hinged back cover and carrying-strap lugs on one side (on both sides after bright chrome serial number 1355000 and black chrome serial number 1357000). Bright-chrome plated or black-chrome plated brass top plate and base plate. 1/4" tripod socket.
- Range-viewfinder with automatic bright-line frames for 35, 50, 90, and 135mm lenses (the frames for 35 and 135mm lenses appear together).
- Automatic parallax correction.
- Viewfinder magnification: 0.72x.
- Field-of-view preview selector.
- Selective through-the-lens (TTL) metering. Built-in CdS exposure meter. Light meter needle and index point (match-needle) indicators in the viewfinder.
- Film speed settings from ISO 6/9° (ASA 6/9 DIN) to ISO 3200/36° (ASA 3200/36 DIN).

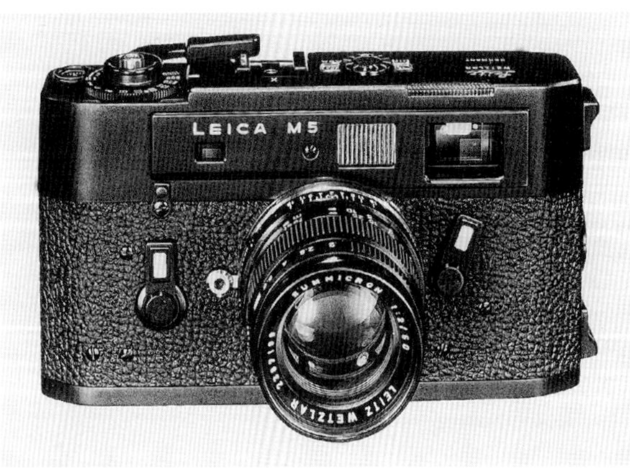

Fig.9: LEICA M5

- Button cells: PX 13 or PX 625.
- Measuring range with an f/1.4 lens: With a film speed of ISO 100/21°, from -1 exposure value to +20 exposure values.
- Shutter speeds from 1/1000 to 30 seconds; settings visible on the shutter speed dial or in the viewfinder.
- Exposure meter turns off automatically after shutter operates. (It is turned on by winding the shutter and advancing the film.)
- Battery check.
- Rubberized cloth focal-plane shutter for 1/2, 1/4, 1/8, 1/15, 1/30, 1/60, 1/125, 1/250, 1/500, 1/1000 sec (continuously adjustable intermediate times) plus "B" for time exposures of any length.
- Automatic flash synchronization for flashbulbs up to 1/500 second and for electronic flash up to 1/50 second.
- Separate standard flash contacts for flashbulb units and for electronic flash units (M and X contacts).
- Accessory shoe with X contact (hot shoe) for special viewfinders and other accessories.
- Variable self-timer.
- Ratcheted rapid advance lever for winding the shutter and advancing the film. Fast film loading system for all commercially available 35mm films (with or without tongues).
- Rewind crank in the base plate.
- Automatic frame counter with magnified read-out.
- Film reminder dial combined with circular computer for selecting equivalent shutter speed/aperture combinations in determining the exposure.
- Film plane index.

Dimensions: Height 84 mm (37.6 inches), length 155 mm (6-3/32 inches), thickness 36 mm (1-13/32 inches).
Weight: 700 grams (1 lb 8-1/2 oz.).

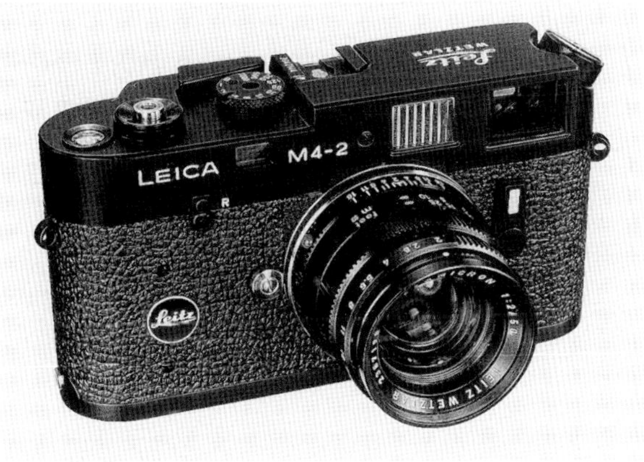

Fig. 10: *LEICA M4-2*

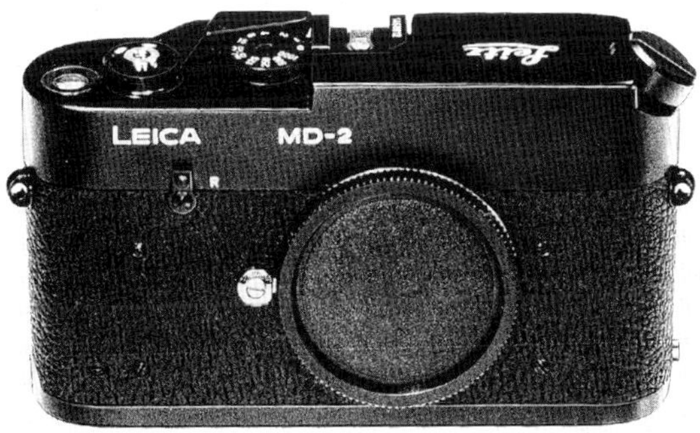

Fig. 11: *LEICA MD-2*

LEICA M4-2
Introduced in 1977

- One-piece all-metal body with hinged back cover and lateral carrying-strap lugs. Black chrome-plated brass top and base plates. 1/4" tripod socket.
- Range-viewfinder with automatic bright-line frames for 35, 50, 90, and 135mm lenses (the frames for 35 and 135mm lenses appear together).
- Automatic parallax correction. Viewfinder magnification: 0.72x . Field-of-view preview selector.

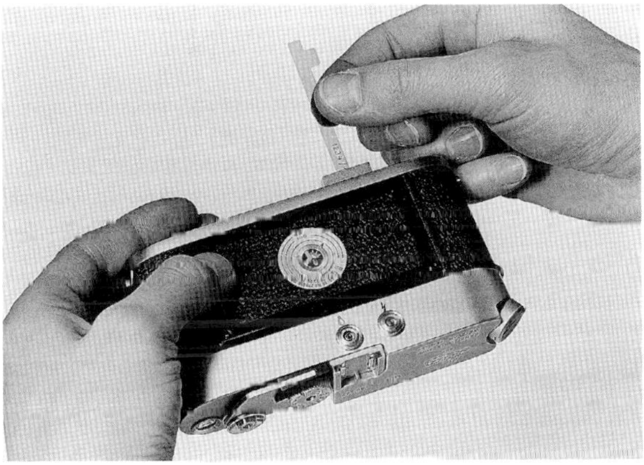

Fig. 12: Transparent recording strips for notations about the subject can be inserted into the baseplate of all Leica MD bodies (D = Documentation).

- Shutter speed dial with click stops, can couple to accessory Leicameter exposure meter.
- Rubberized cloth focal-plane shutter for 1, 1/2, 1/4, 1/8, 1/15, 1/30, 1/60, 1/125, 1/250, 1/500, 1/1000 second plus "B" for time exposures of any length.
- Automatic flash synchronization for flashbulbs up to 1/500 second and for electronic flash up to 1/50 second.
- Separate standard flash contacts for flashbulb units (M) and electronic flash units (X). Accessory shoe with X contact (hot shoe) for special viewfinders and other accessories.
- Ratcheted, rapid advance lever for winding the shutter and advancing the film. Fast film loading system for all commercially available 35mm films and for Leica cassettes. Slanted rewind crank. Automatic frame counter with magnified read-out.
- Film reminder dial with DIN-ASA conversion scale.
- Accessory shoe for special viewfinders and other accessories.
- Mechanical coupling for all Leica Winders and for Leica Motor M.

Dimensions: Height 77 mm (3-1/32 inches, length 138 mm (5-1/6 inches), thickness 36 mm (1-13/32 inches).

Weight: 525 grams (1 lb. 2-1/2 oz.).

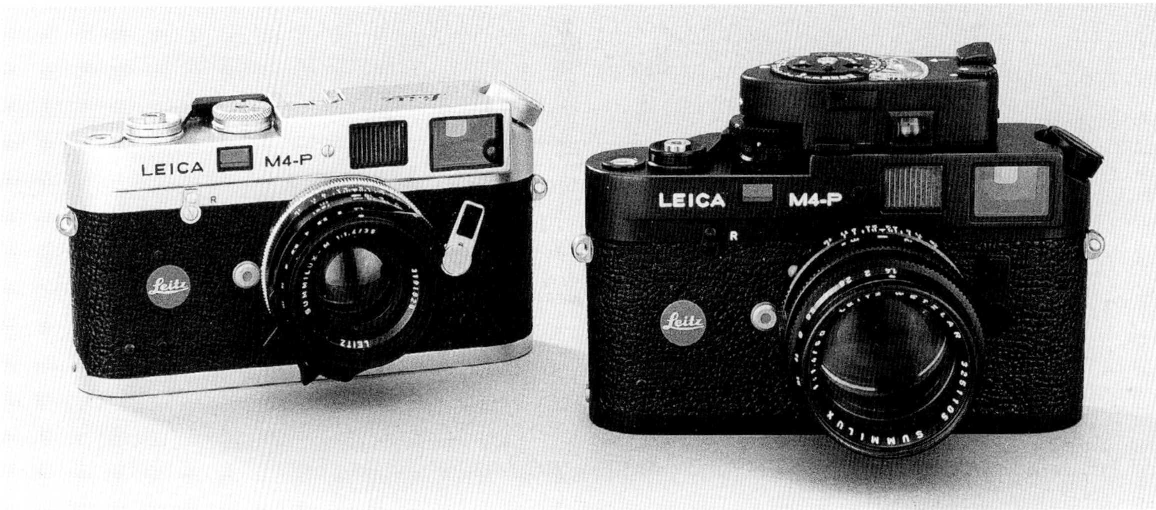

Fig. 13: *LEICA M4-P, silver and black chrome-plated versions.*

LEICA MD-2
Introduced in 1977

- Designed to accept index strips for recording of documentation directly on the film negative. This required a special base plate with a light-tight slot for the insertion of these strips.
- Mechanical coupling for use with Leica Winders.

Dimensions: Same as Leica M4-2.

Weight: 460 grams (1 lb.).

LEICA M4-P
Introduced in 1980

With the exception of the top plate and the bright-line frames. The technical characteristics are identical with those of the Leica M4-2.

- Top plate consists of 0.8 mm thick die-cast zinc, chrome-plated in silver or black; up to serial number 1620999 top plate was chrome-plated in black.
- The bright-line frame indicators appear two at a time in the range-viewfinder: 28 and 90 mm, 35 and 135 mm, and 50 and 75 mm.

Dimensions: Height 77 mm (3-1/32 inches), length 138 mm (5-1/6 inches), thickness 36 mm (1-13/32 inches).

Weight: 545 grams (1 lb. 3 oz.).

LEICA M6
Introduced in 1984

This is a compact 35mm range-viewfinder camera with:
- Long-base rangefinder.
- Bright-line frames for 6 different focal lengths.
- Selective through-the-lens (TTL) exposure metering.
- Mechanically controlled, rubberized cloth focal-plane shutter.
- Leica M rapid-change bayonet mount.

CAMERA BODY

One-piece housing of die-cast aluminum with hinged back cover. Covered with textured PVC for better handling. Mechanical coupling for Leica Winder M, Leica Winder M4-P, or Leica Winder M4-2 (Serial numbers above 10350).

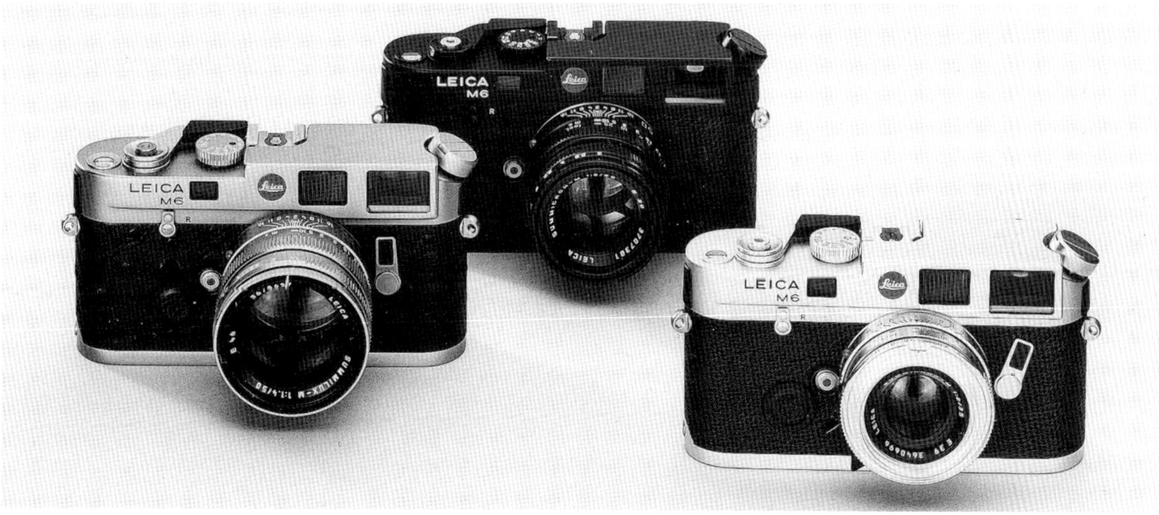

Fig. 14: Leica M6 bodies were offered with titanium plating, or in black or silver chrome-plated brass.

Top plate: 0.8 mm or 1/32" die cast zinc with thick black or silver chrome plating, or titanium plating.

Base plate: 0.8 mm or 1/32" thick black or silver chrome-plated brass, or titanium-plating.

Lens mount: Leica M rapid change bayonet mount with release button at the side of the bayonet on the camera body.

Distance from film plane to outer surface of bayonet mount on camera body: 27.8 mm (1.094 inches).

Interchangeable lenses: All Leica M lenses can be used without restrictions. The exposure meter, however, will not function with the following lenses:
15mm f/8 Hologon
21mm f/4 Super-Angulon-M
21mm f/3.4 Super-Angulon-M
28 mm f/2.8 Elmarit-M, serial number below 2314921.

Lateral carrying-strap lugs: Designed for use with special carrying strap that is 11 mm (5/16") wide at the ends, widening to 25 mm (1") at the middle, where it has an anchored 27.5 mm (1-1/6") wide anti-slip pad.

Tripod socket: Standard 1/4".

Dimensions (without lens): Height 77 mm (3-1/32 inches, length 138 mm (5-1/6) inches, Thickness 38 mm or 1-1/2 inches.

Weight (without lens): 560 grams (1 lb. 4 oz).

RANGE-VIEWFINDER SYSTEM

Bright-line range-viewfinder: The subject is not viewed through the lens of the camera.

Viewfinder magnification: 0.72x.

Viewfinder calibration: -0.5 diopters.

Visible in the viewfinder: Six bright-line frames (two at a time) for the various focal lengths. Focusing field in the center of the viewfinder image. When the exposure meter is turned on, two red triangular LEDs light up and serve as the light balance indicator for the exposure meter.

Image area covered: Indicated by two bright-line frames at a time: 28 and 90mm, or 35 and 135mm, or

50 and 75 mm. The appropriate frame appears automatically when a lens is mounted. A field-of-view preview selector may also be used for each bright-line frame.

Field-of-view preview selector: A three-position lever next to the lens-mounting flange on the camera can activate any desired pair of frames without requiring a lens change.

Parallax correction: The lateral discrepancy between the fields covered by the viewfinder and the lens, which is caused by their separation, is corrected automatically for the respective distance setting. That is, the area outlined by the bright-line frame in the viewfinder automatically corresponds to the field covered by the respective lens.

Correlation of the viewfinder image to the film image: The bright-line frames cover an area that corresponds to an image area of 23 x 35 mm on the film (mounted slide) at the shortest focusing distance of the respective lens. At the infinity setting, the image on the film will cover slightly more than the image outlined by the bright-lines in the viewfinder.

Long-base rangefinder: Split image and coincidence rangefinder delineated as a bright field in the center of the viewfinder image.

Effective measuring base: 49.9 mm (physical base 69.25 mm x viewfinder magnification 0.72 = effective measuring base 49.9 mm).

Partially silvered viewfinder window: For better visibility of the glowing LEDs with bright subjects, the lower edge of the front window of the viewfinder has been silvered.

EXPOSURE METERING

Activation: By slightly depressing the shutter release button, when the camera is wound. After the finger is lifted from the release button, the exposure meter will remain turned on for approximately 4 seconds. The exposure meter will not activate if the shutter is not wound or when the shutter speed dial is set at "B".

Exposure metering method: Selective exposure metering through the lens at the working aperture (TTL metering).

Exposure meter read-out: Two red triangular LEDs light up simultaneously and with the same brightness when the exposure is correct.

Setting the aperture: By means of the aperture setting ring at the front of the lens. Click stops at all full and half aperture stops.

Setting the shutter speed: By means of the shutter speed dial on the top plate of the camera. All settings have click stops and they can be read from the top of the camera: B, 1 to 1 /1000 sec (z = 1/50 second is the setting for electronic flash). Intermediate settings cannot be used.

Setting the correct shutter speed/aperture combination: Turn on the exposure metering system; turn the shutter speed dial and/or the aperture setting ring until both triangular LEDs in the viewfinder light up with equal intensity. If one LED lights brighter than the other or one doesn't light at all, turn the shutter speed dial or the lens' aperture setting ring in the direction indicated by the lighted triangle.

Setting the film speed: By setting the film speed selector on the back of the camera.

Range of film speeds: ISO 6 to ISO 6400 (ASA 6/9 DIN to ASA 6400/39 DIN) with click stops at 1° DIN intervals.

Metering principle: The light reflected by a round metering area on the shutter curtain is measured.

Metering area: The round bright metering area has a diameter of 12 mm and it is located at the center of the first shutter curtain. This area covers approximately 13% of the full negative format.

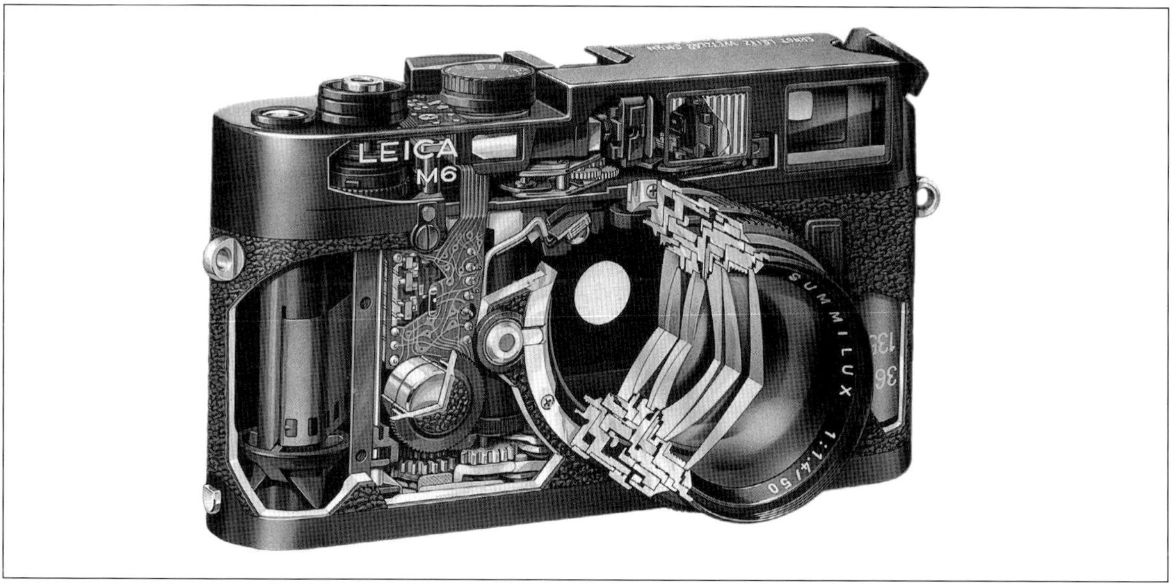

Fig. 15: This cut-away drawing shows how precisely all of the Leica M6's mechanical, optical, and electronic components are made to mesh with each other. The two batteries and the electronics of the exposure meter were accommodated in the space that was occupied by the self-timer mechanism in previous models. The round white metering area is located on the first curtain of the rubberized cloth focal-plane shutter. The silicon photodiode is situated at the upper left, behind the bayonet lens mounting flange.

Metering cell: The silicon photodiode is located behind a collector lens at top left behind the camera's bayonet flange.

Spectral sensitivity: A filter in front of the metering cell adapts it to the typical spectral sensitivity curve of a human eye.

Metering range: At f/1, from 0.125 to 125000 cd/m2 (candles per square meter).

Working range: SB ISO 100, exposure values from 0 to 20 EV, i.e. from 1 second at f/1 to 1/1000 second at f/32.

Light levels outside the meter's range: Both LEDs in the viewfinder will not light.

Location of the meter field in the viewfinder: Taking into account changes in image size as the distance setting on the lens is changed from near to distant focus, the metering area with the lens focused at infinity corresponds to approximately 23% and at the closest setting to approximately 13% of the respective viewfinder image. Still keeping in mind this change in image size, the diameter of the round measurement field at infinity therefore corresponds to approximately 2/3 of the short side of the respective bright-line frame. An outline of the various metering field sizes in the viewfinder was omitted in favor of an uncluttered viewfinder image.

POWER SUPPLY

Batteries: Two SR44, 1.55 volt silver oxide button cells (diameter 11.6 mm, height 5.4 mm) or one 3-Volt lithium battery, size 1/3N (diameter 11.6 mm, height 10.8 mm), or the equivalent batteries.

Location: The battery compartment is located on the front of the camera, to the left of the lens.

Capacity: A set of fresh batteries will last approximately 20 hours with the camera turned on continuously. At 15 seconds metering time per exposure, the battery will power about 4800 exposures or approximately 130 rolls of 36-exposure film.

Battery check: When the battery's voltage has dropped below the minimum for accurate exposure measurement, both LEDs do not light. When the brightness of the two LEDs becomes noticeably weaker than normal. The batteries should be replaced.

SHUTTER AND FILM ADVANCE

Shutter: Mechanically controlled, rubberized cloth, horizontal focal-plane shutter. Extremely quiet.

Shutter speeds: 1, 1/2, 1/4, 1/8, 1/15, 1/30, ⚡ 1/50, 1/60, 1/125, 1/250, 1/500, 1/1000 second plus "B" for time exposures of any length. Intermediate speeds are not available.

Flash synchronization: Standard X center contact for flashbulb units and for electronic flash units. All shutter speeds from 1 to ⚡ (1/50 second) plus "B" can be used for electronic flash synchronization. All shutter speeds from 1 to 1/30 second plus "B" can be used for flashbulb synchronization.

Shutter release: Release button with standard thread for the attachment of cable releases. The exposure meter is turned on (the LEDs in the viewfinder light up indicating the exposure meter is operational) by slightly depressing the shutter release.

Required depression: Depressing the release 0.25-0.4 mm turns on the exposure meter; a 1-1.7 mm depression releases the shutter.

Film advance: Angled rapid-advance lever with a hinged thumb piece. Ratcheted lever travels through 120° for winding the shutter and advancing the film. The ready position of the lever enables persons to comfortably use their left eye for focusing. Motorized film advance: Leica Winder M, Leica Winder M4-P or Leica Winder M4-2 with serial number above 10350 (3 frames per second).

Rapid film loading: Insert the extended film leader into a slot on the take-up spool, then drop the cassette into the film chamber of the camera and attach the base plate.

Frame counter: Forward counting (from –2 to 40) with magnified read-out on the camera top plate. Automatically resets to starting position when the camera base plate is opened.

Film advance indication: When the shutter is cocked, by watching the rewind lever rotate in the opposite direction of the arrow.

Film rewinding: Angled rewind lever with a hinged thumb piece on camera top plate.

Removable base plate: After rotating the lever, the base plate can be removed. Starting with models of production year 1991-92, the use of the earlier Leica metal cassettes was no longer possible.

Hinged back cover: Facilitates film loading.

Image area mask: Size 23.8 X 35.6 mm. The frame size on the film may be varied as a function of focal length.

Location of the film plane: Identified by the symbol <-o-> on the top plate of the camera (not available on titanium-plated Leica M6).

LEICA M6 – variations

Since the 1930s Leica has produced limited, special editions of standard camera models and lenses. One example was a limited edition, gold-plated luxury camera covered with select leather, engraved for a special occasion, and offered as a set in a wooden case.

A list of special-edition Leica M cameras can be found on the Internet under http://cameraquest.com under the heading "Classic Camera Profiles." The functions of these special models are the same as those of its standard counterpart, with one exception: in 1994, on the occasion of the 40th anniversary of the launch of the Leica M3 camera, 1,640 limited-edition Leica M camera outfits were produced. This represents 40 for each decade of Leica history. This special commemorative-edition included a Leica M6J ("J" for jubilee), a retractable Elmar 50mm f/2.8 lens and a matching camera case. Each camera and each lens are engraved with a special number. This includes an authenticity certificate and the wooden box.

LEICA M6J

The housing, shutter, mechanics, and exposure meter are largely the same as those of the Leica 6.

- The brass top plate and all the operating elements, such as the rapid advance lever and the frame selector, could be confused with those of the Leica M3.
- The rangefinder was completely modified. Using a magnification of 0.85x it features a viewfinder image that is almost the same size as that of the M3 viewfinder. In contrast with the viewfinder of the Leica M3, the M6J viewfinder also includes a bright-line frame for 35mm lenses. This is in addition to the 50, 90, and 135mm bright-line frames.
- The cover is genuine black leather.

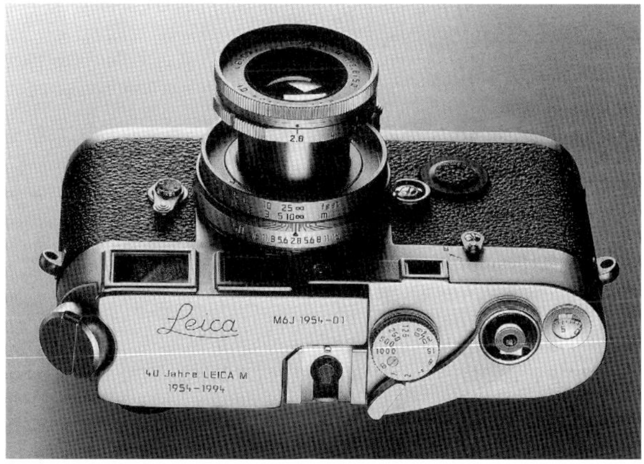

Fig. 16: *LEICA M6J*

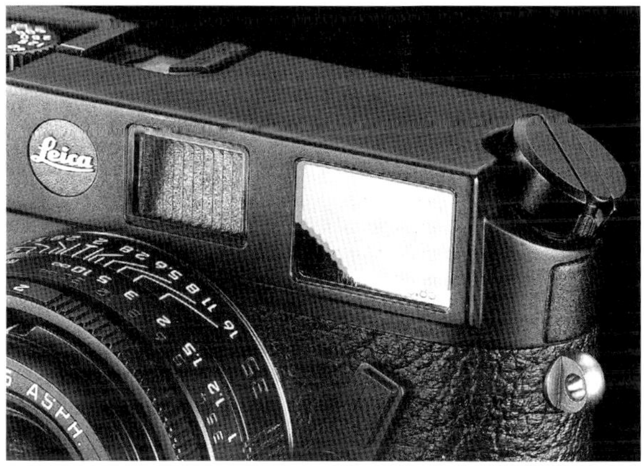

Fig. ***17:*** *Since the introduction of the Leica M6's 0.85x viewfinder, each Leica M camera includes viewfinder identification information, applied by a laser engraving, to the lower, silvered area of the viewfinder..*

LEICA M6 with 0.85x viewfinder

Following the introduction of Leica M6J, Leica offered the standard M6 with an optional viewfinder magnification of 0.85x.

This can be identified by "0.85" which is laser engraved in the lower, silvered region of the front viewfinder window. This viewfinder features five bright-line frames: four are arranged in pairs for focal lengths of 35 and 135 mm and for 50 and 75 mm. The fifth bright-line frame for 90mm lenses is featured by itself.

The subject, the bright-line frames, and the rangefinder field are viewed approximately 20% larger and, thus, the effective measuring base increases by 9 mm to 58.9 mm.

The Leica M6 0.85x is offered in black chrome. All other technical details are identical with those of the Leica M6, which features a 0.72x viewfinder.

LEICA M6 TTL

At Photokina 1998 Leica introduced new M6 models with new, fully updated, electronics. The metering system, which used to be based on C-MOS technology, now also uses a modern micro-processor. This allows flash exposure metering through the lens (TTL). To provide flash status information in the viewfinder, a flash symbol appears to the right of the newly designed LEDs for exposure balance. Starting with this Leica M camera, the direction of rotation of the shutter speed button corresponds to the directions indicated by the triangular LEDs in the viewfinder. In addition, the shutter speed button features an off position, which protects the batteries of the exposure meter against inadvertent use.

The camera housing is about 2.5 mm (1 inch) higher and 40 g (1.41 oz.) heavier. The camera's hot shoe features additional contacts for control of system-compatible flash units. Furthermore, in addition to the serial number, it is also engraved with the abbreviation "TTL" and a flash symbol. Camera models featuring the "standard" viewfinder magnification of 0.72x also are marked 0.72 in the lower, silvered area of the front viewfinder window. The film plane is not indicated on the top plate.

With the exception of technical characteristics listed below, the Leica M6 TTL features the same specifications as the former Leica M6 models.

EXPOSURE METERING

Exposure meter display: Uses red LEDs in the viewfinder (▶ • ◀). Only the central round LED lights when the exposure meter has been adjusted correctly. The two triangular LEDs located to its left and right light up alone, or with the round LED, to indicate various levels of over-exposure or under-exposure.

Setting the correct shutter speed/aperture combination: With the camera turned on, turn the shutter speed dial on the camera and/or the aperture ring on the lens. The exposure is set "correctly" when the central round LED lights. The two triangular LEDs to the left and the right of the round LED indicate under-exposure or over-exposure, as well as the direction of rotation of the shutter speed dial and/or the aperture ring for making corrections.

Switching off the system: Turn the shutter speed dial to "Off."

TTL flash exposure: Center-weighted TTL metering with system-compliant flash units and SCA 3501 M1 adapters.

Meter cell for TTL flash exposure: a Silicon photodiode in the camera bottom measures light reflected by the film through a convex lens.

Flash-ready indicator: Blinking flash symbol in the viewfinder.

Flash success check: Indicated in the viewfinder for approx. 4 second after a successful flash exposure.

Additional viewfinder options: Starting in 1999, the Leica M6 TTL with 0.85x viewfinder was also manufactured. In 2001, a 0.72x viewfinder model featuring titanium plating was introduced.

Leica M6 TTL: Special edition

In 2000 a special edition of the Leica M6 TTL was released to commemorate the introduction of the first Leica at the 1925 Leipzig Spring Fair. Limited to 2000 cameras, the edition's serial numbers were issued consecutively starting with 2,500,000.

Its deep-black lacquer finish harkens back to earlier Leica camera models. In contrast with today's typical black chrome plating, the lacquer surface is more vulnerable to wear from scratches or abrasion. This characteristic is considered desirable by many photographers and collectors because it provides the camera with a vintage patina after extended use, when the brass of the top plate shines through heavily used or worn areas.

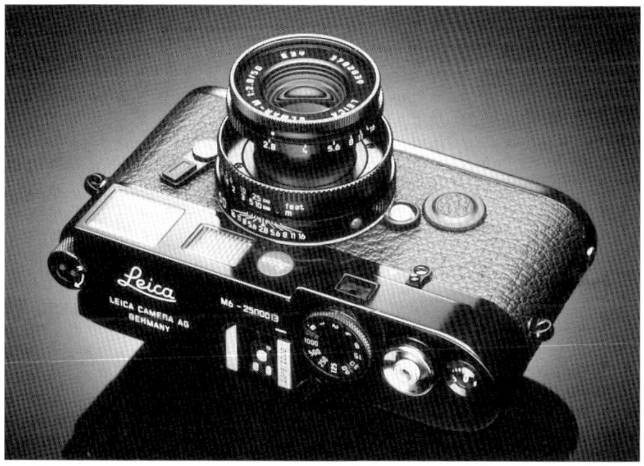

Fig. 18: LEICA M6 TTL with black lacquer finish.

Individual components of this model such as the rapid advance lever and the rewind knob have been borrowed from the classic Leica M3, while the camera technology corresponds to the Leica M6 TTL. Additional special features include the fine-line Leica signature on the upper side of the top plate, a black anodized frame counter with white numbers, brass carrying-strap lugs, and the engraving "open – auf/close – zu" at the shutter lever on the base plate. A special engraving starting at 0001/2000 on the accessory shoe documents the limited number of this edition.

LEICA M6 TTL
with 0.58x viewfinder

At Photokina 2000 another viewfinder was added to the Leica M6 TTL line. This 0.58x viewfinder is well suited for wide-angle photography and for people who wear eyeglasses. With this viewfinder the frames for focal lengths of 28 and 35mm are easier to see. Five bright-line frames are included, four of which appear in two pairs: 28 and 90mm, and 50 and 75mm. There is an additional separate frame for 35mm lenses.

The notation, "0.58" is inscribed in the lower, silvered area of the viewfinder window. All the other technical features correspond to other Leica M6 TTL models.

LEICA M7
Introduced in 2002

Compact 35mm range-viewfinder camera with:
- Long-base viewfinder.
- Bright-line frame viewfinder and choice of viewfinder magnifications of 0.58x, 0.72x, or 0.85x.
- Bright-line viewfinder frames for six different focal lengths (0.72x) or five different focal lengths (0.58x and 0.85x) are included.
- Selective through-the-lens (TTL) exposure meter.
- Flash exposure metering through the lens (TTL).
- Automatic aperture priority and manual exposure modes.
- Electronically controlled, rubberized cloth, focal-plane shutter with two mechanically controlled shutter speeds.
- Leica M rapid change bayonet mount.

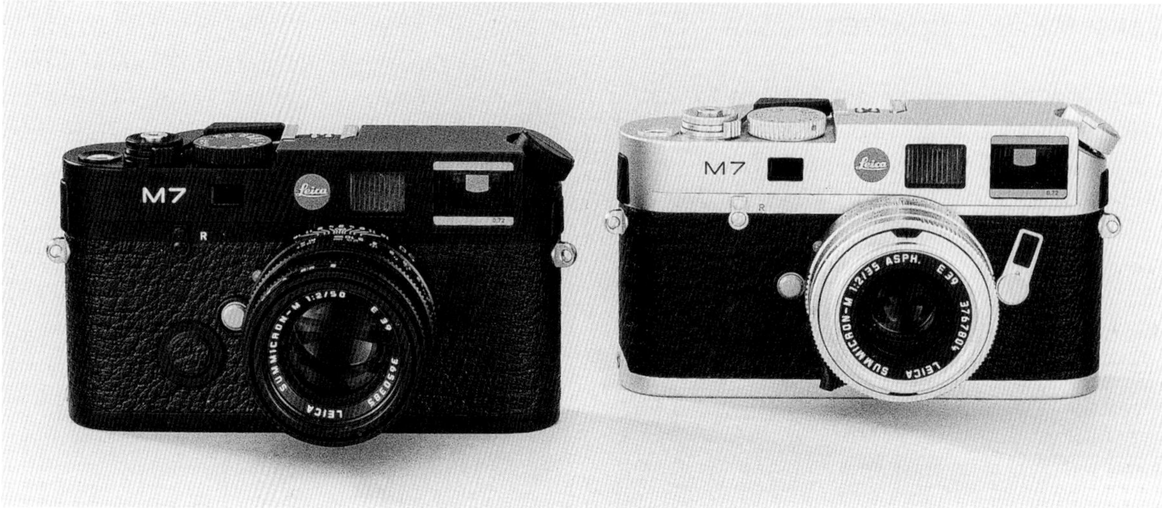

Fig. 19: LEICA M7, chrome-plated in black and silver.

HOUSING

Camera body: One-piece aluminum die-cast body with hinged back cover. Covered with textured PVC for better handling.
Mechanical connection for Leica Motor M, Leica Winder M, Leica Winder M4-P, and Leica Winder M4-2 (starting with serial number 10350).

Top plate: Milled brass, chrome-plated in black or silver.

Base plate: Consists of 0.8mm thick brass, chrome-plated in black or silver.

Lens mount: Leica M rapid-change bayonet with release button at the side of the bayonet on the camera body.

Distance from film plane to outer surface of bayonet mount on camera body: 27.8 mm (1.094 inches).

Interchangeable lenses: All Leica M lenses can be used. The exposure meter, however, will not function with the following lenses:
15mm f/8 Hologon
21mm f/4 Super-Angulon-M
21mm f/3.4 Super-Angulon-M
28 mm f/2.8 Elmarit-M, (serial numbers below 2314921).

Lateral carrying-strap lugs: Designed for use with special carrying strap that is 11 mm (5/16") wide at the ends, widening to 25 mm (1") at the middle with a 27.5 mm (1-1/6") wide anti-slip pad.

Tripod socket: Standard 1/4".

Dimensions (without lens): Height 79.5 mm (3-1/6 inches), length 138 mm (5-1/6 inches), thickness 38 mm (1-1/2 inches).

Weight (without lens and batteries): 560 grams (1 lb. 4 oz).

RANGE-VIEWFINDER SYSTEM

Range-viewfinder with bright-line frames: The subject is not viewed through the camera lens.

Viewfinder magnification: 0.58x, 0.72x, or 0.85x.

Viewfinder correction: -0.5 diopters.

Visible in the viewfinder: Depending on viewfinder magnification, five or six bright-line frames for various focal lengths. Focusing field in the center of the viewfinder image. LED indicators are in the lower viewfinder area.

LED viewfinder indicators: 33 indicator segments in an area of 0.7 x 2.3 mm are magnified 15x in the viewfinder. Automatic adaptation to the brightness of ambient light. Appropriate indicators become visible as required:

- Two triangular LEDs and one central round LED are used to set the exposure manually.
- In aperture-priority automatic exposure, the camera-selected shutter speed is displayed by four seven-segment LEDs.
- A warning appears with exposure compensation in aperture-priority auto.
- A warning appears when light readings fall outside the meter's measuring range.
- A warning appears in auto exposure of shutter speeds exceeding 2 seconds.
- There is an indication of stored exposure.
- Display of set ISO film speed, when settings are wrong, or compensation is set (appears for two seconds every time the camera is switched on).
- Self-timer display when remaining countdown time is more than one second.
- Display of elapsed exposure time in "B."
- Flash-ready and flash exposure verification indicated by the LED flash symbol
- Low battery warning.

Image area: Indicated by automatic activation of the appropriate bright-line frame when a lens is mounted or by viewing any bright-line frame with the aid of the field-of-view preview selector.

- With viewfinder magnification of 0.58x in pairs for 28 and 90mm or 50 and 75mm focal lengths. The bright-line frame for 35mm lenses is separate.
- With viewfinder magnification of 0.72x in pairs for 28 and 90mm, 50 and 75mm, or 35 and 135mm focal lengths.
- With viewfinder magnification of 0.85x in pairs for 35 and 135mm or 50 and 75mm focal lengths. The bright-line frame for 90mm lenses is separate.

Field-of-view preview selector: A three-position lever next to the lens mount flange on the camera activates insertion of a desired pair of frames without requiring a lens change.

Parallax correction: The horizontal and vertical discrepancy between the field covered by the viewfinder and the field covered by the lens is corrected automatically for any distance setting. That is, the area outlined by the bright-line frame in the viewfinder automatically corresponds to the field covered by the lens.

Correlation of the viewfinder image to the image on the film: The bright-line frames cover an area that corresponds to an image area of 23 x 35 mm on the film (mounted slide) at the shortest focusing distance of the respective lens. At the infinity setting, the image on the film will cover slightly more than the image outlined by the bright-line frame in the viewfinder.

Long-base rangefinder: Split image and coincidence rangefinder delineated as a bright field in the center of the viewfinder image.

Metering area: 40.2 mm with viewfinder magnification 0.58x; 49.9 mm with viewfinder magnification 0.72x; 58.9 mm with viewfinder magnification 0.85x.

Partially silvered viewfinder window: For better visibility of the glowing LEDs against a bright subject, the lower edge of the front window of the viewfinder has been silvered. Also, the identification for viewfinder magnification is laser-engraved in this silvered area. A sensor that controls the brightness of viewfinder LEDs is hidden behind the upper silvered area.

EXPOSURE CONTROL

Operating modes

- Aperture-priority automatic—the photographer sets the aperture and the camera automatically selects the shutter speed for best exposure.
- Manual exposure—both the shutter speed and aperture are set by the photographer (with the assistance of LEDs in the viewfinder).

TTL flash exposure: Center-weighted metering with system-compatible flash units.

Exposure lock: With aperture-priority automatic exposure, by maintaining pressure on the shutter release.

Switching on the camera: Pivot the On/Off lever located below the shutter release to activate the camera's electronics and unlock the shutter release.

Selecting the operating mode: Turn the shutter speed dial to "AUTO" for aperture-priority exposure or select a shutter speed for manual exposure.

Activation: By slightly depressing the shutter release when the camera is cocked. After releasing the shutter release, the exposure meter remains switched on for approximately 14 seconds. When the shutter has completed its travel and an exposure is made, the exposure meter is switched off.

Shutter speed display:

- With aperture-priority auto, the camera-selected stepless shutter speed is displayed in the viewfinder by a four-digit, seven-segment LED.

- With manual exposure, the light meter indicators (▶ ● ◀) become visible instead of the shutter speed. Only the round LED lights up when the exposure is "correct."

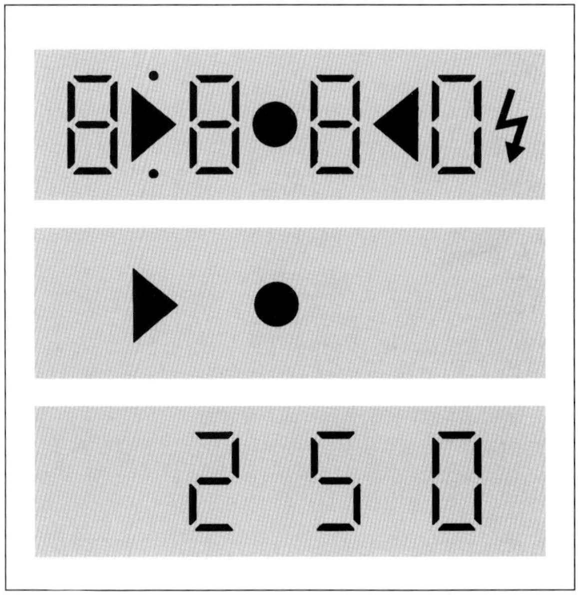

Fig. 20 a – c: The combined viewfinder display of the Leica M7 at a glance (top). In a given situation, only the appropriate display will be active, such as: the light meter indicators (center) in manual exposure, or the camera-selected shutter speed in aperture-priority auto (bottom).

Setting the aperture: By adjusting the aperture ring at the front of the lens. Click stops at all full and half apertures.

Setting the shutter speed: By rotating the shutter speed dial on the top of the camera. All settings have click stops and they can be read from the top of the camera: B, 4, to 1 /1000 second (ϟ = 1/50 second for electronic flash). Intermediate settings cannot be used.

Exposure compensation: Adjustable ± 2 EV in one-third steps on the film speed dial.

Setting manual exposure: Activate the exposure meter and turn the shutter speed dial and/or the aperture ring until only the central round LED in the viewfinder lights. The triangular LEDs to the left and right indicate under-exposure or over-exposure, as well as the suggested direction of rotation for the shutter speed dial and/or the aperture ring:

- ▶ = Under-exposure of one stop or more. Direction of rotation to the right is required.
- ▶● = Under-exposure of 1/2 stop. Direction of rotation to the right is required.
- ● = Correct exposure.
- ●◀ = Over-exposure of 1/2 stop. Direction of rotation to the left is required.
- ◀ = Over-exposure of one stop or more. Direction of rotation to the left is required.

Setting the ISO film speed: Set automatically with DX-coded films, or manually by rotating the ISO dial on the back of the camera.

Range of film speeds: With DX-setting of ISO 25 at 5000. With manual setting of ISO 6 to ISO 6400. By additionally setting an exposure correction of ISO 1.5, up to ISO 25000 is possible.

Meter function: The light reflected off a measurement area that has a diameter of 12 mm and it is located at the center of the first shutter curtain. This area covers approximately 13% of the full negative format.

Metering cell: A silicon photodiode is located behind a collector lens at top left, behind the camera's bayonet flange.

Spectral sensitivity: A filter in front of the metering cell adapts it to the typical sensitivity curve of a human eye.

Meter range: At f/1, from 0.0.03 to 125,000 cd/m2 (candles per square meter). With aperture-priority automatic, the shutter speed display will light if the settings are within the meter's range.

Working range: At ISO 100, exposure values from 4 seconds to 20 EV, or at f/1 to 1/1000 second at f/32.

Light levels outside the meter's range: In aperture-priority automatic, the shutter speed display in the viewfinder will blink.

Location of the metering area in the viewfinder: Taking into account changes in image size as the distance setting on the lens is changed from near to far focus, the area measured at the infinity setting of the lens corresponds to approximately 23% and at the closest setting to approximately 13% of the respective viewfinder image. Still keeping in mind that change in image size, the diameter of the round meter area at infinity therefore corresponds to approximately 2/3 of the short side of the respective bright-line frame. (An outline of the various metering areas in the viewfinder was omitted in favor of an uncluttered viewfinder image.)

POWER SUPPLY

Batteries: Two lithium cells, type DL 1/3 N, 3 Volt, ∅ 11.6 mm – 10.9 mm high.

Operating voltage: 6 Volts.

Location: The battery compartment is located on the front of the camera, to the left of the lens.

Capacity: At room temperature and 10 seconds metering time per exposure, a set of fresh batteries will last approximately for 65 rolls of 36-exposure film, or for approx. 2,340 exposures.

Battery check: When the battery's voltage is low "bc" appears on the viewfinder, or the viewfinder LEDs fail to light. Pulsing LEDs in the viewfinder also indicate that the batteries should be changed promptly.

TTL FLASH EXPOSURE

Flash synchronization: Standard (X) contact for both flashbulb units and electronic flash units. Center contact (X) in the hot shoe. The two contacts can be used simultaneously.ϟ 1/50 second for flash synchronization. All shutter speeds from 1 to ϟ (1/50 second) plus "B" will sync with electronic flash. All shutter speeds from 1 to 1/30 second plus "B" can be used for flashbulb synchronization.

With applicable SCA 3000 flash units and an SCA 3502 adapter, synchronization can be selected for the first or second shutter curtain.

All shutter speeds from 1 to ϟ (1/50 second) plus "B" can be used for electronic flash synchronization. All shutter speeds from 1 to 1/30 second plus "B" can be used for flashbulb synchronization.

Flash synchronization speed: The fastest electronic flash sync speed is 1/50 second and is indicated by ϟ = 1/50 second.

HSS = High Speed Synchronization: With appropriately equipped SCA 3000 flash units and an SCA 3502 adapter, manually set shutter speeds of 1/250, 1/500, and 1/1000 second may be used.

TTL flash exposure measurement: Center-weighted metering of the flash exposure with system-compatible flash units and SCA 3501 adapters.

Flash measuring cell: The silicon photodiode is located behind a collector lens at bottom right behind the camera's bayonet flange.

Film speed range for flash operation: With TTL flash exposure metering, from ISO 12 to 3200. Automatic transfer of ISO film speed and exposure compensation setting on the camera with system-compatible flash units.

Flash override: Can be set on Leica SF20 (± 3 EV in one-third increments).

Flash-ready indicator: Constant blinking of the flash symbol in the camera viewfinder.

Flash success check: The flash symbol continues to light up following exposure and temporarily blinks rapidly. If the symbol does not light, the flash exposure was not successful.

Strobe flash operation: With appropriate System 3000 flash units and SCA 3502 and 3501 adapters, the flash will fire repeated bursts during one exposure. Automatic adjustment of the shutter speed is possible with aperture-priority automatic.

SHUTTER AND FILM-ADVANCE

Shutter: Electronically operated, rubberized cloth, focal-plane shutter. Extremely quiet.

Shutter speeds: Stepless speeds from 32 second to 1/1000 second are selected by the camera in aperture-priority automatic. With manual exposure the photographer can select speeds from 4 second to 1/1000 second in full stops, "B" for time exposures of any duration, ϟ (1/50 second) = the highest speed for electronic flash synchronization.

Mechanical shutter speeds: 1/60 second and 1/125 second.

Shutter release: Release button features a standard thread for the attachment of cable releases. It operates electromagnetically with all shutter speeds and "B." When the camera is switched on, indicators in the viewfinder light up. The exposure meter is activated by depressing the shutter release 0.5 mm (1st pressure point). In aperture-priority mode, exposure lock occurs at 0.95 mm depression (the 2nd pressure point). The shutter is fired when the release is depressed 1.6 mm.

Film-advance system: Angled ratcheted, rapid advance lever with a hinged thumb piece. Lever travels through 120°, winding the shutter and advancing the film.

The ready position of the lever enables persons to use the left eye for focusing.

Motorized film advance with Leica Winder M, Leica Winder M4-P or Leica Winder M4-2 with serial number above 10350. No base plate or rapid winding.

Rapid film loading: Insert the extended film leader into a slot in the take-up spool, "drop" the cassette into the film chamber, and attach the base plate. Close the base plate or attach the rapid film loading device or the motor drive.

Frame counter: Located on the camera top plate. Counts forward from –2 to 40. Magnified display. Automatically resets to the starting position when the base plate is removed.

Film advance indication: When the film is advanced, the rewind lever rotates in the opposite the direction of the arrow.

Film rewinding: Angled rewind lever with a hinged thumb piece on camera top plate.

Removable base plate: After rotating the lever, the base plate can be removed.

Hinged back cover: Facilitates film loading.

Image area: Size 23.8 X 35.6 mm. The frame size on the film may vary slightly.

Typical characteristics of a Leica M

Over the past fifty years, every proven feature on Leica M cameras has been retained, and everything that could be improved, as a result of technological innovation, has been modified. Because of this philosophy, a Leica M7 hardly differs from earlier Leica models in external appearance. Its weight and size are practically identical to those of the M6 and M6-TTL, which immediately preceded it, as well as those of its early ancestors, the M2 and M3.

The operation of a Leica M7 is also largely the same as all other Leica M models. However, this latest model differs from the Leica M5, which featured TTL exposure metering but was considerably bulkier. This is due to the fact that criticism of the M5's size led to the discontinuation of its larger body style and a return to bodies that are similar to the more compact M models. Through intensive development work conducted by Leitz in conjunction with a team of specialists from the Technical University of Munich and ETA (a company in Nuremberg), the M6's electronic components were designed so that they were small enough to be accommodated in the traditional compact camera body. As a result, the creation of the Leica M6 was an important step in the development of current Leica M models.

Except for a few enhancements such as: the film rewind crank in 1967 (Leica M4), the correlation of the direction of rotation of the shutter speed dial with the viewfinder's triangular LEDs in 1998 (Leica M6 TTL), and the automatic setting of DX-coded ISO film speeds in 2002 (Leica M7), all typical features of all Leica M models of 1954 are still available in today's models. One unique feature that sets the Leica M apart from all other 35mm cameras is its range-viewfinder. It offers an extremely user-friendly combination of a bright-line viewfinder and a long-base rangefinder. To this day, this range-viewfinder is considered a unique masterpiece of precision mechanics and optics. This feature is a prime component of all cameras in the Leica M series.

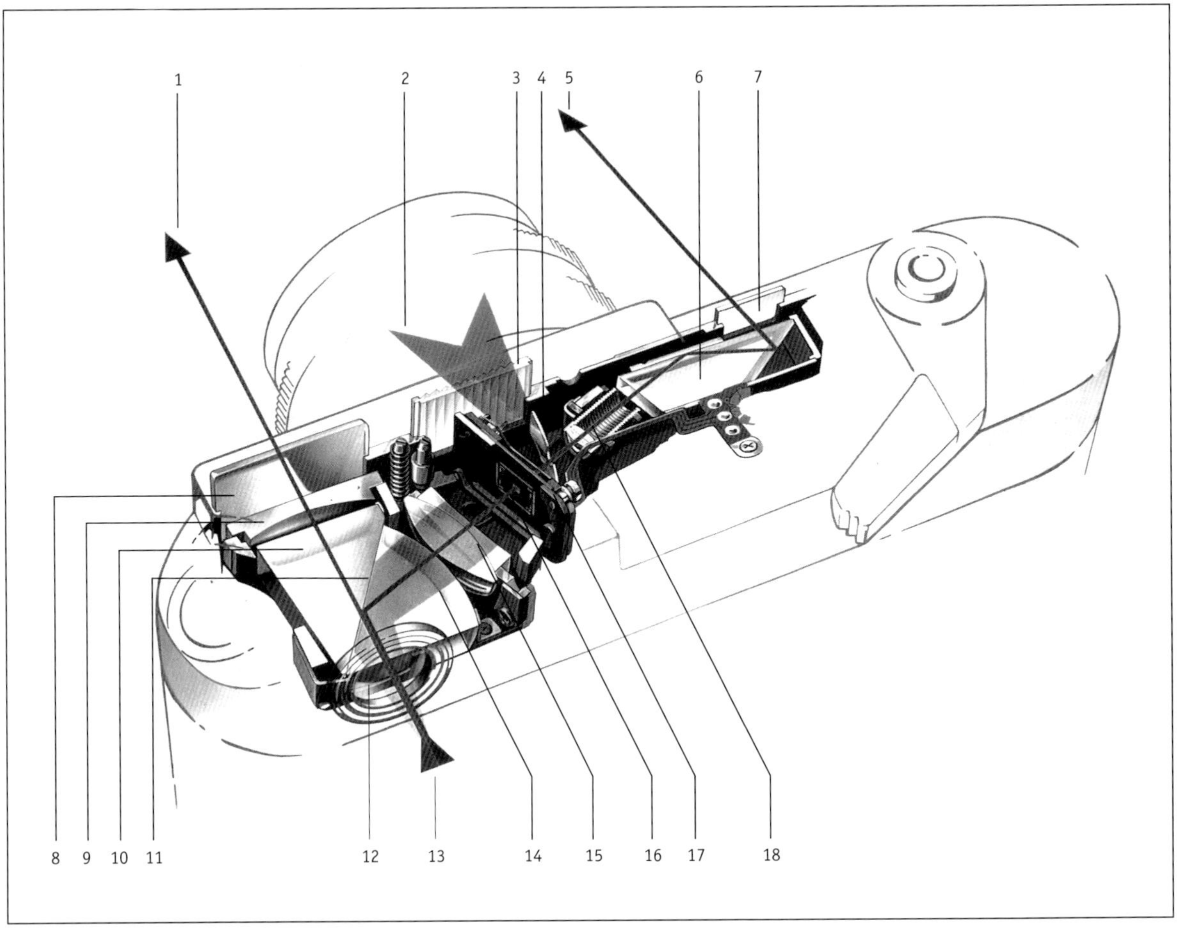

Fig. 21: *The range-viewfinder of the Leica M6. This view shows the complex assembly of lenses, prisms, mirrors, and masks: 1 = viewfinder light path; 2 = light that illuminates the bright-line frames; 3 = window for the illumination of bright-line frames; 4 = mirror for the illumination of bright-line frames; 5 = light path; 6 = pentaprism for deflecting and reversing the image; 7 = rangefinder window; 8 = viewfinder window; 9 = lens; 10 = prism; 11 = beam splitting layer; 12 = ocular lens; 13 = combined light from 1, 2, and 5; 14 = lens prism; 15 = achromat; 16 = LED light balance of the exposure meter; 17 = bright-line frame masks (which can be shifted diagonally), automatic parallax compensation, and rangefinder image plane; 18 = swiveling rangefinder lens (achromat).*

This continuity, which is maintained in development of model enhancements, allows nearly all of the models to operate identically. This is a huge advantage to photographers because once they have mastered the use of one Leica M model they will understand the operation of all other M models.

The bright-line viewfinder

Photographers who are used to using SLR cameras will first have to get used to the M camera's viewfinder image. Not only is it extremely bright but also it is always sharp from the foreground to infinity. The sizes and the variety of subject details visible in the viewfinder do not change when a different lens is mounted on the camera, so viewfinder magnification remains constant. The change in the field, caused by the use of a different lens, is indicated by a change in the luminous outline visible in the viewfinder. This is accomplished by bright-line frames, which are activated automatically when a lens is mounted. Every Leica M lens has a special cam on its bayonet mount for this purpose.

Rangefinding takes place only in the center of the viewfinder. To prevent the obstruction of rangefinder windows during focusing, the photographer's left hand should hold the lens from below, so that the left thumb is at the left side of the lens. Distance and aperture can be adjusted conveniently in this manner (see pages 229 and 230).

An SLR photographer should be aware that the actual photograph generally will include a little more of the subject than is indicated by the frame in the viewfinder of a Leica M. This is due to the fact that the lens' angle of view becomes slightly smaller if the lens is focused at distances closer than infinity. To focus at closer distances, the focusing mount of the lens moves the lens elements further away from the film. This has virtually the same effect as using a lens with a slightly longer focal length. In effect, a smaller subject area is covered (see Fig. 25). Since the lens extension for focusing at a given distance is always greater for long focal length lenses than it is for short ones, the rate of change in subject area (or, angle of view), caused by focusing at various distances, is thus, different for various focal lengths. While that change is less than 10% for a 21 or 28mm lens set at its closest focusing distance (0.7 m or 27-1/2 inches), and thus hardly noticeable, it amounts to nearly 20% for a 135mm lens set at 1.5 m (59 inches). With a normal 50mm lens set at 0.7 m (27-1/2 inches), the change is about 15%.

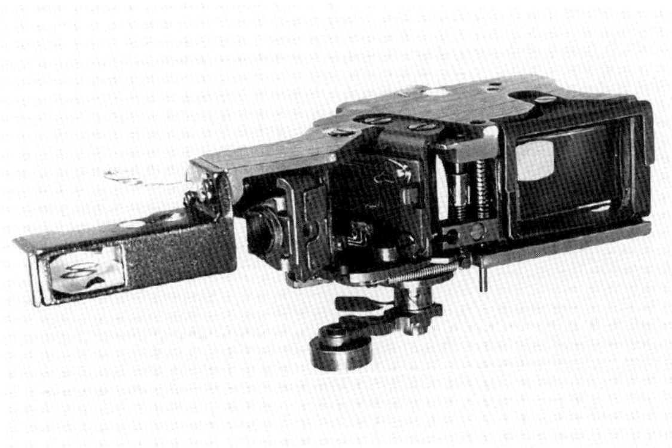

Fig. 22: *The range-viewfinder of the Leica M6 is a precision mechanical and optical masterpiece. Comprised of a total of 150 parts, it is much more expensive to manufacture than finders in single-lens-reflex cameras. The optics of the rangefinder include four lens elements in two groups, one beam-splitter consisting of two prisms, one with a lens surface, and a roof prism for vertical and lateral image reversal. The two masks for the viewfinder frames work together to generate the respective frames in the viewfinder and to correct the parallax. These are only 60 and 80 µm or 39 millionths of an inch thick. In addition, the two light-balance LEDs are positioned on one of these masks.*

The bright-line frame in the viewfinder of a Leica M6 is designed to outline the subject area covered by the respective lens, set at its minimum focusing distance. The frame also compensates for the fact that a slide mount covers up a small portion of the image around the edges of the transparency. Therefore, a lens set at any distance greater than its minimum focusing distance will always record a little more of the subject within the full 24 x 36 mm format on the film than outlined by its frame in the viewfinder. This ensures that, regardless of the distance at which the lens is focused, at least the portion of the subject area indicated by the respective bright-line frame will always be recorded

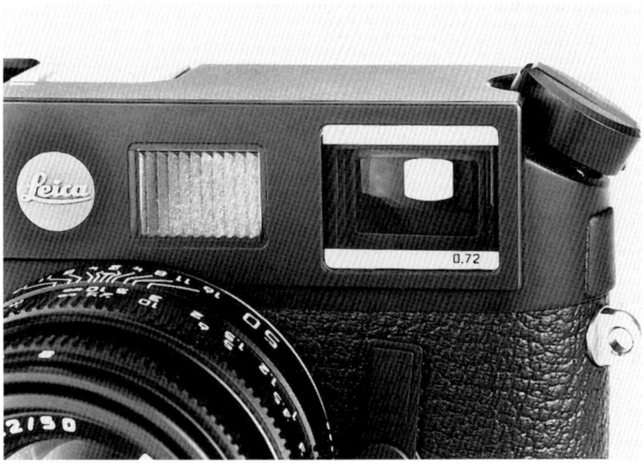

Fig. 23: *: In the Leica M7 and M6 models, the windows of the range-viewfinder are flush with the top plate of the camera and are therefore easier to clean than those of earlier models.*

In the Leica M7 and M6 TTL, the protective glass of the viewfinder window has upper and lower silvered strips; the Leica M6 has only a lower one.

The upper strip covers a Silicon photodiode, which controls the brightness of the LEDs in the viewfinder of the Leica M7. In addition, this strip—as in the Leica M6 TTL—covers a slit, which would otherwise be visible on the inside, between the splitter prism of the viewfinder and the top plate. As in the Leica M6 and all models before it, the top plate covers this slit.

The lower silvered strip ensures that the viewfinder LEDs are visible even with light subjects. This strip is also laser engraved with the viewfinder's magnification.

on film and, in the case of mounted transparencies, that area will be visible in projection.

It is possible, to estimate the additional area covered by the lens simply by using the thickness of the frame lines. In the case of a 50mm lens on the Leica M7 and M6 models, the picture area covered at the infinity setting is greater by about three thicknesses of a frame line all around the outer edge of the viewfinder frame (see Fig. 27).

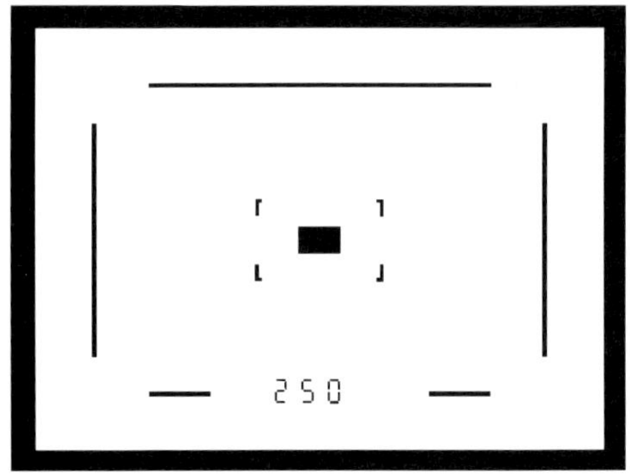

35 and 135mm

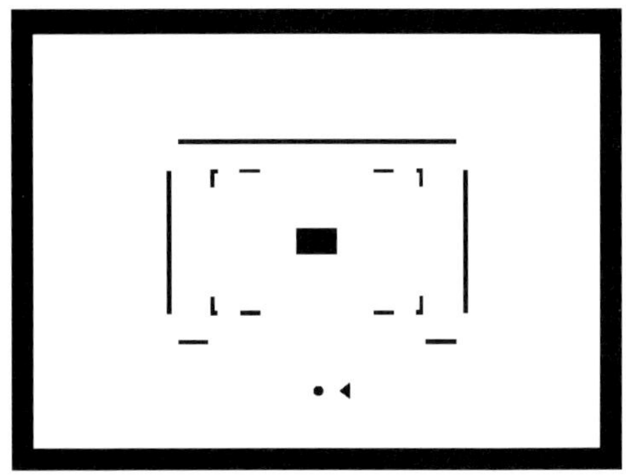

50 and 75mm

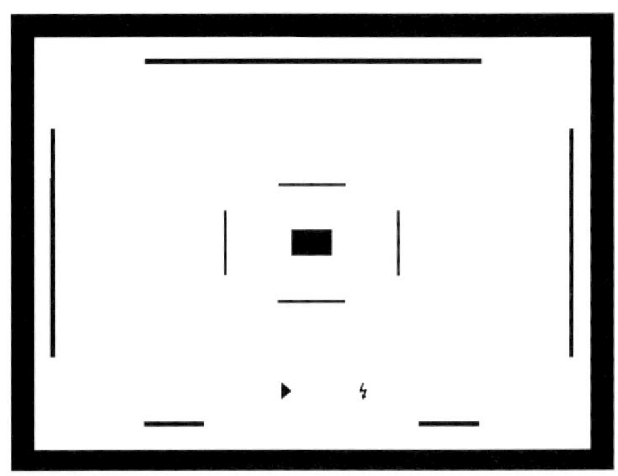

28 and 90mm

Fig.24 a – c: *The M7's .72 viewfinder is a good all-purpose choice. It features six bright-line frames, which present in pairs. Each bright-line frame outlines the area covered by the lens at its minimum focusing distance. The rangefinder focusing masks appear in the center of the frame. At the bottom of the viewfinder is the LED display, which automatically adjusts to the brightness of the ambient light. This includes, (a) the camera selected shutter speed in aperture-priority automatic, the manual exposure correction indicators (b), and the flash symbol (c).*

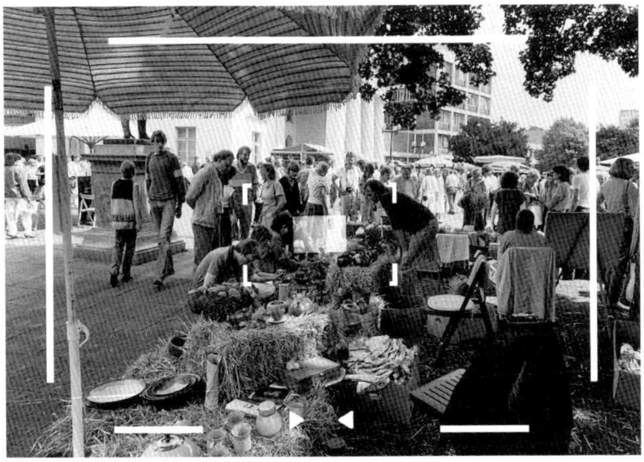

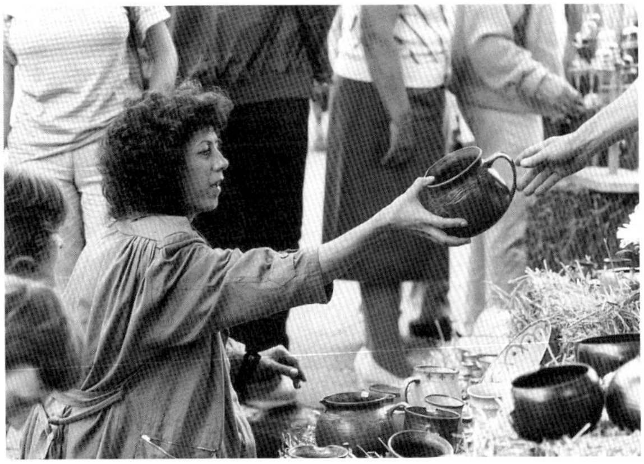

Fig. 25 a and b: *The Leica M6 viewfinder shows more of the subject than the area outlined by the bright-line frame. The advantage of this becomes apparent with use. The illustration on the left shows a market scene as seen through the viewfinder by a photographer with a 135mm lens (without viewfinder attachment) on his camera. That lens will only cover the area outlined by the smaller bright-line frame. All of the vendors movements are visible in the viewfinder, even if the customer is all that will be recorded by the telephoto lens. This enables the photographer to remain aware of the activities in the scene so that he or she will not be surprised by an arm suddenly jutting into the picture as the vendor hands an object to the customer. This also makes it easier for photographer to wait for just the right moment to release the shutter.*

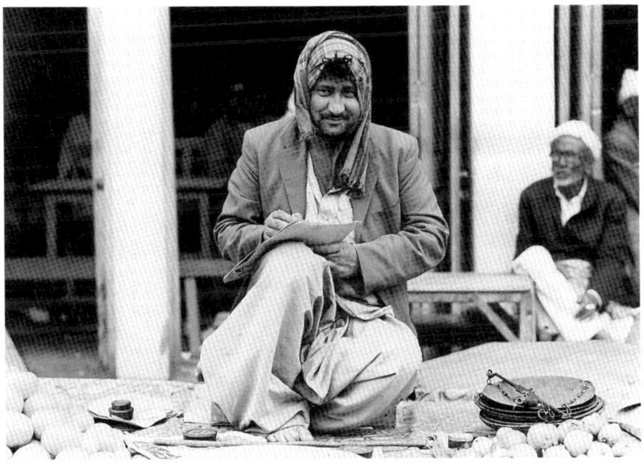

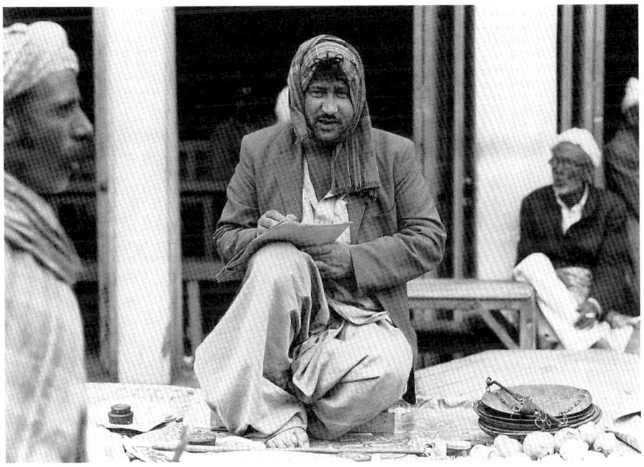

Fig.26 a and b: *With a Leica M, it is easy to anticipate what will be included in a scene in the very next moment. Experienced photographers use the concept behind the bright-line frames to their advantage. Photographers can choose the shot that tells the story the way they want it to be told—for example, whether or not to include the person passing in the foreground, in this example.*

In all M models a lens set at infinity always covers a little more of the subject than is outlined by its bright-line frame. In a Leica M3, for instance, the subject area for a 50mm lens is outlined with a rather thick line, and the subject area covered at the infinity setting is greater by about the thickness of this line around the outer edges of the bright-line frame.

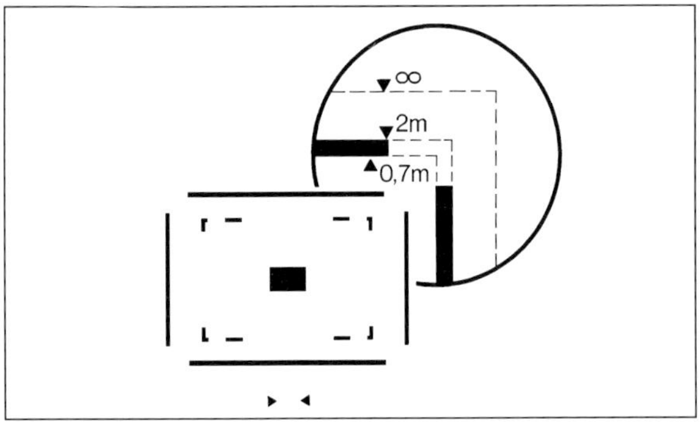

Fig. 27: *Unlike the viewfinder of a single-lens-reflex camera, which only shows the picture area covered by the lens, the bright-line frames in the viewfinder of a Leica M6 show the picture areas covered by the respective lenses at their closest focusing distances. For example, the bright-line frame for a 50mm lens corresponds to a focusing distance of 0.7 m (or 27.5 inches). The outer edge of that 50mm frame corresponds to a focusing distance of 2 m (or 6 feet 7 inches). At the infinity setting, the picture area covered by the 50mm lens is larger than that shown by its bright-line by about three thicknesses of the frame line.*

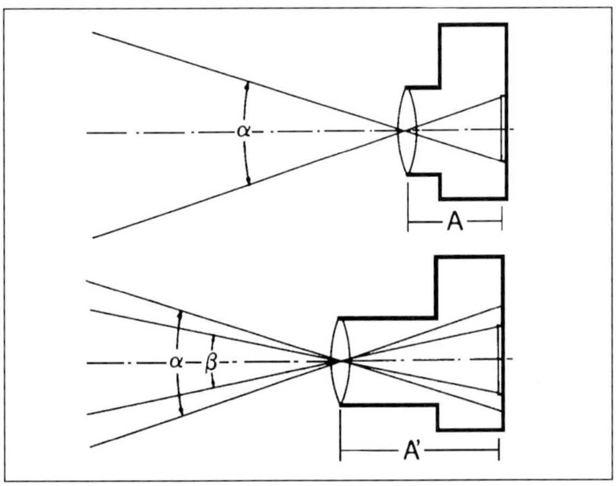

Fig. 28: *As it focuses on distances that are closer than infinity, a lens moves farther away from the film plane. At the same time, the original angle of coverage at infinity (α) is reduced to a smaller angle (β) (i.e., the angle of coverage of the lens decreases as the lens is focused at shorter distances). Top: Lens focused at infinity. Bottom: Lens set at its minimum focusing distance.*

Viewfinder magnification 0.58x

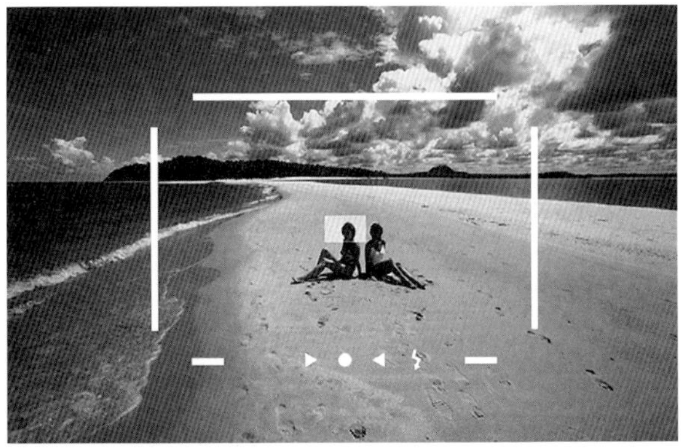

(a) 35mm

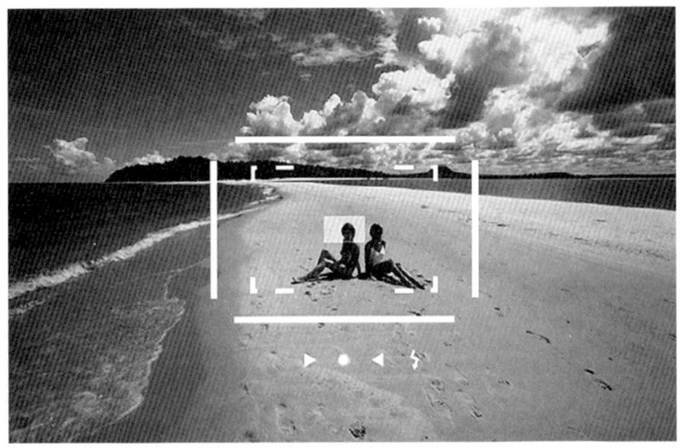

(b) 50 and 75mm

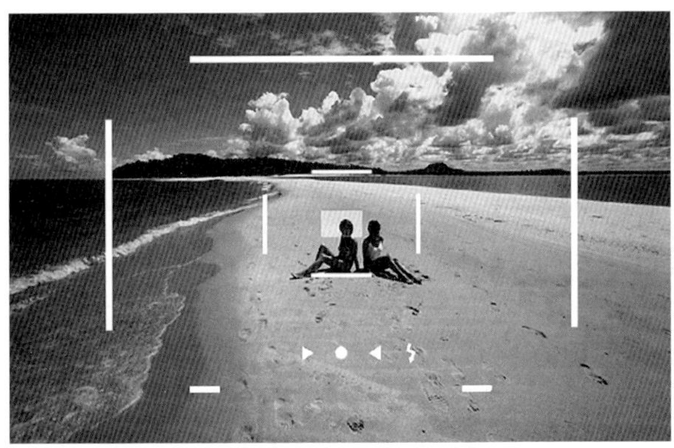

(c) 28 and 90mm

Fig. 29 a – i: *By offering different viewfinder magnifications, Leica adapted the M cameras to work well in different photographic applications. For example, photographers who work predominantly with wide-angle lenses or wear eyeglasses should select a 0.58x magnification, because it improves*

Viewfinder magnification 0.72x

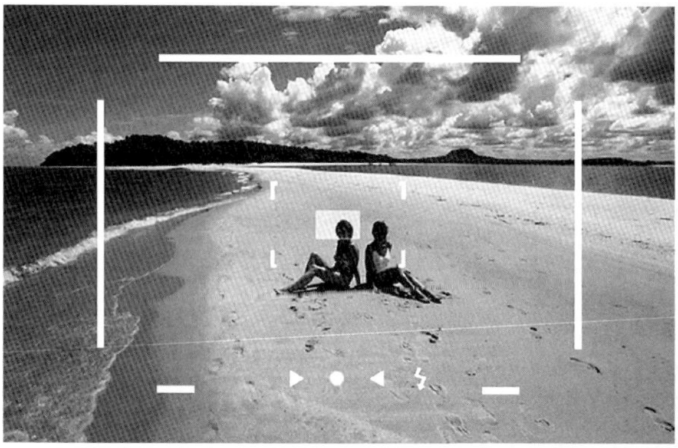

(d) 35 and 135mm

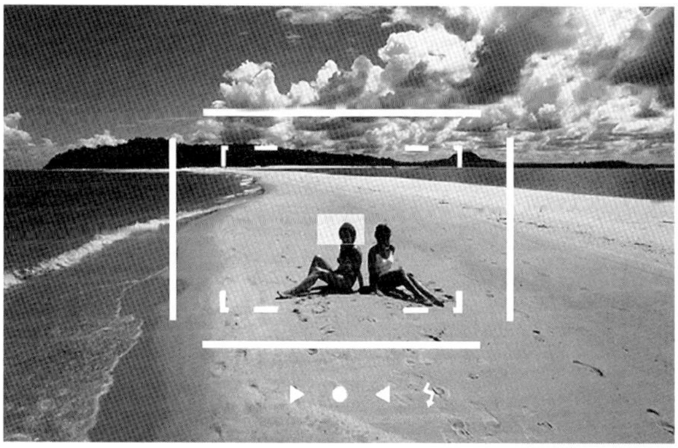

(e) 50 and 75mm

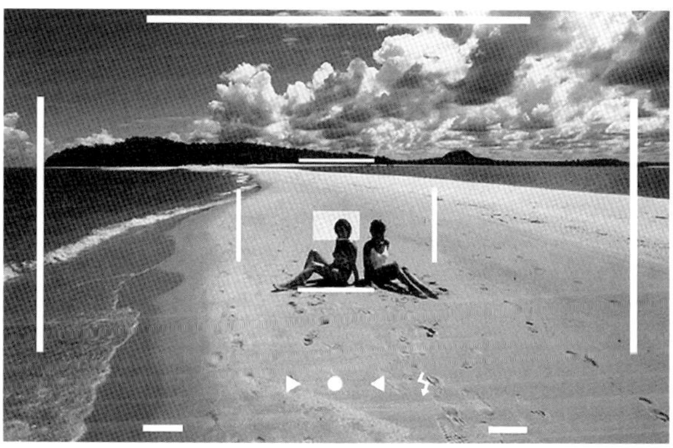

(f) 28 and 90mm

Viewfinder magnification 0.85x

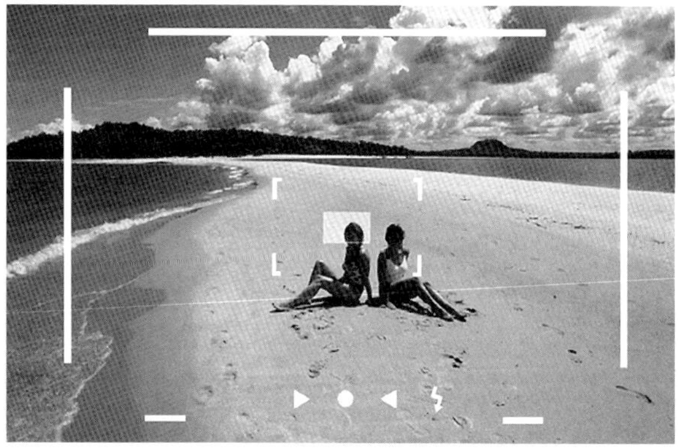

(g) 35 and 135mm

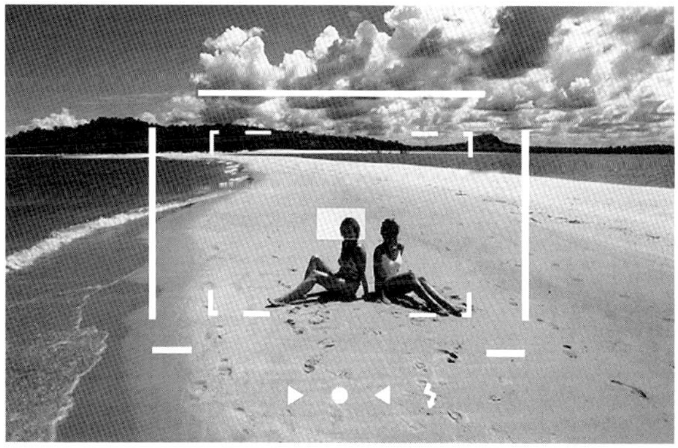

(h) 50 and 75mm

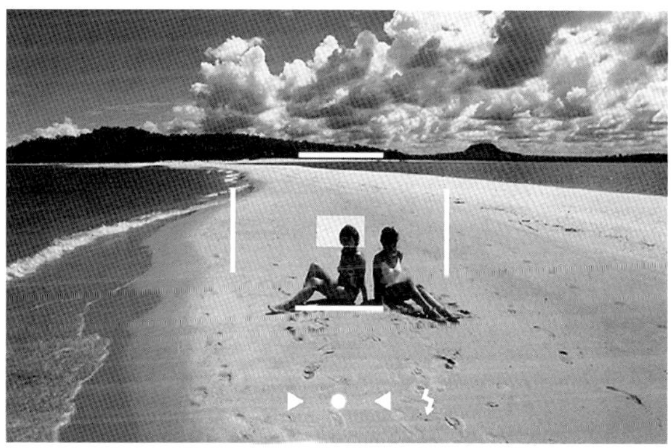

(i) 90mm

the viewfinder for use in wide-angle photography. However, those who frequently use longer focal lengths will prefer a 0.85x magnification. A viewfinder magnification of 0.72x is usually considered best overall for general use with the standard focal-length range of the Leica M system. Even though these pictures clearly illustrate the differences in a scene viewed with various finder magnifications, it is recommended that you experiment with each viewfinder at your photo-dealer before deciding which to purchase.

A unique advantage of the Leica M cameras is the option to activate the bright-line frames for various focal lengths without having to actually change lenses. By using the field-of-view preview selector lever, one can very easily check whether or not a different focal length might yield a better rendition of the subject and, thus, whether it is worthwhile to change lenses. Thus, the bright-line viewfinder of a Leica M camera is an ideal aid for composition. The M's viewfinder shows subject areas outside the bright-line frame, which makes it possible to anticipate events and changes before they enter the field covered by a lens. For example, the photographer can see that a person is about to walk into the picture area. If this will interfere with his composition, he can quickly release the shutter or wait until the person is out of the way. If, on the other hand, he wants that person in a specific place in his picture, he will be able to plan accordingly (see Fig. 26 a and b).

Action photography is also easier because the subject is fully visible in the viewfinder, even during the actual exposure. Thus, there is no dark interlude as there is with SLR cameras. In addition, in flash photography, the subject remains clear in the viewfinder throughout the exposure, allowing us to see the split second when the flash freezes the fast-moving subject.

Viewfinder parallax—the displacement between lens and viewfinder—is compensated for automatically during focusing. To accomplish this, the bright-line frame and the metering field are shifted diagonally in the viewfinder. This compensation can easily be verified by very gently depressing the cam (located just behind the top of the bayonet lens-mounting flange on the camera body with the lens removed), while looking through the viewfinder. This design assures that the classic Leica M range-viewfinder camera is well suited for action photography. Applying this concept to full advantage means consciously taking into account the special design characteristics of a Leica M camera during the execution of a photographic task. It should be used, not as a replacement for SLR photography, but rather, as a complement to it.

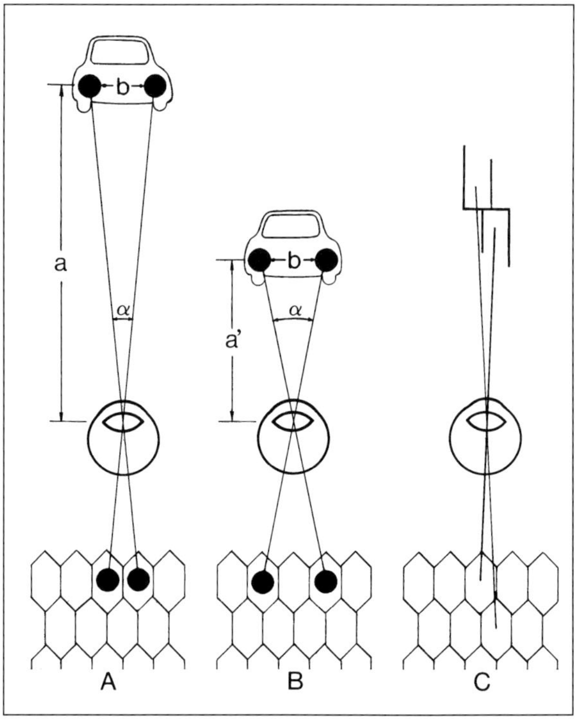

Fig. 30: *Two automobile headlights, which are two distinct bits of information, are recognized as separate light sources only when the angle they form (A) is larger than one minute of an arc. This is the angle at which two separate bits of information can be discerned by the human eye. This occurs when the two simulated photo receptors in the retinas of our eyes are separated by at least one photo receptor, which is not stimulated (B). Only in so-called "vernier seeing" when two successive photo receptors in layers, one below the other, are stimulated, as with the split-image indicator, in which two vertical lines meet (C) is the resolving power of our eyes slightly greater.*

The long-base rangefinder

With the unequalled, precise, fast focusing achieved by the long-base rangefinder, Leica M cameras occupy a very special position in relation to other 35mm cameras. Since focusing is performed with the aid of our eyes, the superiority of the Leica M range-viewfinder will only become evi-

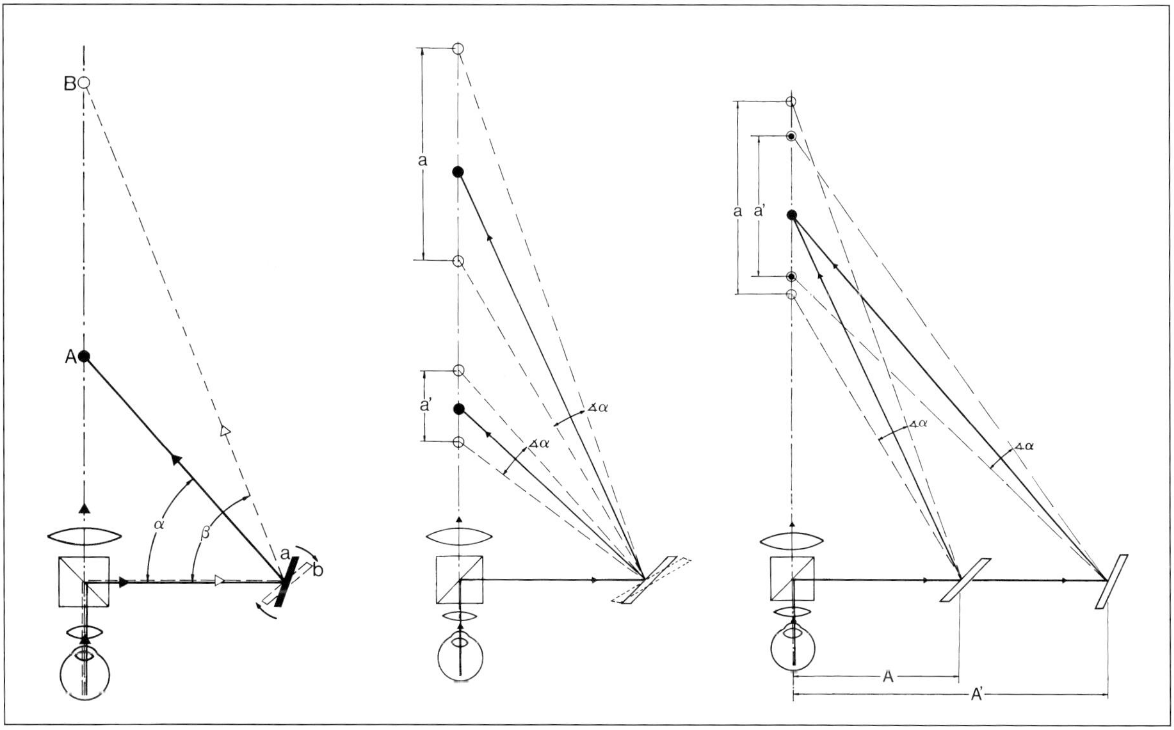

***Fig. 31:** This schematic diagram illustrates rangefinder technology. The subjects (A and B), whose distances from the camera are to be meaasured, are sighted simultaneously with light reflected by a hinged mirror, and with the light entering the viewfinder. As the lens focuses on a subject, a cam connected to its helical mount moves the hinged mirror in the rangefinder mechanism. Cam action and mirror rotation are precisely coordinated so that a sharp photograph is assured when the two identical images in the measuring field of the range-viewfinder are brought into allignment by adjusting the lens' focusing ring.*

The Leica M features a much more complex arrangement of prisms and lenses in place of the mirror, enabling it to perform the same function with even greater accuracy. Because of its dependence on the human eye, focusing is always associated with a certain margin of error. This margin is represented by the angle "a" in the diagram. This angle is a function of the distance to the subject and of the size of the measuring base. The greater the subject's distance (center) and/or the smaller the rangefinder base (A and A',), the greater the focusing error (α and α').

dent by examining the capabilities and limitations of the human eye.

Eventually everyone discovers that the resolving power of the human eye has its limits. Perhaps it was while examining a postage stamp for damage, while observing a wild deer in the woods, or while searching for life in a droplet of water. Magnifiers, telescopes, microscopes, and eyeglass lenses are but four of numerous optical aids that supplement the resolving power of the unaided eye.

You can test the resolving power of your own eyes by performing a simple experiment. Position yourself in the middle of a bridge over a long, straight highway at night, and gaze down that highway. Vehicles headlights approaching from a great distance will first be appear as a single dot of light. As they get closer, you will suddenly see two separate dots of light. Only at this point will motorcycles be discernable from automobiles. You will also observe that headlights, which are further apart, as they are on large vehicles like trucks and buses, can be recognized as two distinct light dots earlier than headlights that are closer together, such as those on compact cars. Therefore, the separation of the headlights and the distance from the viewer are significant factors in recognition.

These two dimensions enable us to calculate the angle at which we can just begin to distinguish two bits of information as being separate (the two headlights = two picture elements, or pixels), which can be resolved by our eyes. The biological explanation for this phenomenon is the fact that the human eye sees a picture that is composed of millions of individual elements. Essentially they are reproduced by a pattern of millions of photoreceptors in our eyes, much like the dots that make up a printed picture in a newspaper. The eye can only resolve individual picture elements when there is at least one unstimulated photo-receptor between two stimulated ones. This means, for example, that two picture elements at a viewing distance of 35 m (114 feet) must be separated by 1 cm (3/8"), at 3.5 m (11'6") by 1 mm (0.039"), and at 35 cm (13-3/4") by 0.1 mm (0.004") in order to be perceived as separate items.

The effect of depth of field too, can be attributed to the "inadequacy" of our eyes. The photographic image is also composed of millions of picture elements. Strictly speaking, the lens only creates a sharp image of the subject in the plane on which it has been focused. For every plane behind, or in front of, the plane of focus, points will no longer be reproduced as points. Instead they appear as greater, or smaller, unsharp areas, which are called the circles of confusion. But our eyes only begin to discern a change from a sharp (point) image, when the circles of confusion exceed a specific size, which is 0.1 mm (0.004") at a normal viewing distance (approximately 35 cm (13-3/4"). Only then will the picture appear unsharp to us.

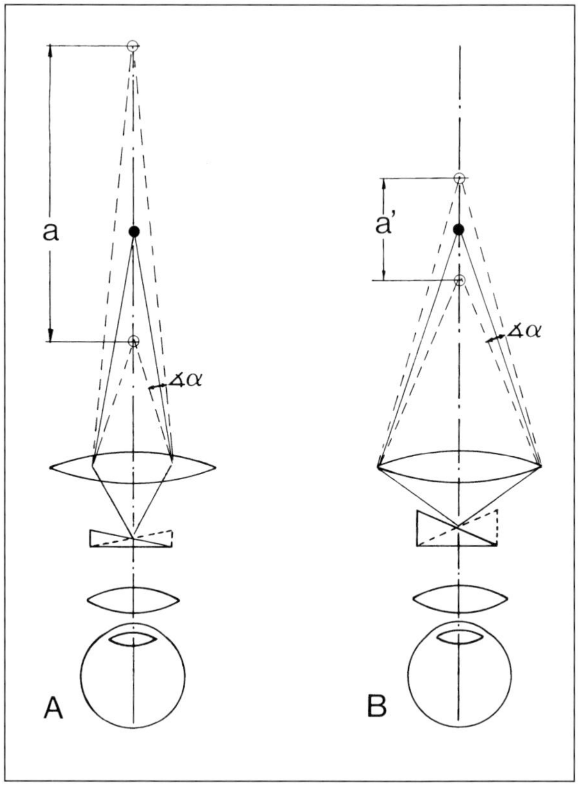

Fig. 32: *This illustrates the principle of TTL (through-the-lens) focusing. In single-lens-reflex cameras, the measuring base is determined by the geometry of the focusing aids incorporated in the focusing screen, such as the split-image indicator and/or microprisms. Flat prisms (A) reduce the base, steep prisms (B) enlarge it. Focusing errors (α and α') vary accordingly. In order to make focusing screens universally applicable in the near range too, and also with lenses of different maximum apertures, the angles of the prisms are selected in such a way that the distance between the measuring rays i.e., the measuring base, which corresponds to the diameter of an aperture of f/4 to f/5.6 (A). With the use of a plain, ground glass screen, the measuring base is determined by the full diameter of the lens, but the advantage of the reduced focusing error brought by the larger base is almost totally negated by a somewhat darker viewfinder image and by the slightly grainy texture of the focusing screen. Focusing with the aid of the split-image indicator, on the other hand, enhances the resolving power of the eye because of vernier seeing* *(see page 42)**. As a result of these conditions, the focusing error in all single-lens-reflex cameras is nearly always the same, regardless of the type of focusing screen being used.*

This means that, when there are details that are smaller than the minimum size that the eye can resolve, there is a range in focusing within which no change in sharpness is recognizable in the viewfinder—even when we turn the focusing mount, displacing the plane of focus. That applies both to rangefinder cameras and to SLR cameras. But when this "focusing error" is smaller than the depth of field of the lens, it will not be recognizable in the picture.

A determining factor in the accuracy of focusing is the effective measuring base of the rangefinder. This, in turn, is a function of range-viewfinder magnification and the distance between measuring rays at the base (see Fig. 31).

- The viewfinder magnification in most Leica M models is 0.72x. The Leica M3 magnification is 0.90x, and the viewfinder magnification in a Leica M6 is optionally 0.72x or 0.85x. The Leica M7 and M6 TTL are offered with viewfinder magnifications of 0.58x, 0.72x, or 0.85x.
- The separation between the two measuring rays as they enter the rangefinder of a Leica M, i.e., the rangefinder base, is 69.25 mm.
- In an SLR camera, viewfinder magnification is determined by the focal length of the lens in use and by the focal length of the viewfinder's eyepiece. Dividing the focal length of the lens by the focal length of the eyepiece yields viewfinder magnification.
- In an SLR camera, the separation of the measuring rays is determined by the maximum aperture of the lens being used. Thus, it corresponds approximately to the diameter of the full aperture. If focusing screens, with focusing aids like split-image indicators or micro-prisms, are used, these "measuring wedges" determine the base of the measuring rays (see Fig. 32). Depending on the type of camera, this base then corresponds to an aperture diameter of approximately f/4 to f/5.6, and in the case of the Leica R's full ground glass focusing screens # 2 and 4, it corresponds to nearly the respective aperture of the lens. The reason why split-image indicators and micro-prisms do not take advantage of the full aperture of some lenses is that these measuring wedges had to be designed to work without their surfaces blacking out when lenses with smaller maximum apertures are used, so that their application could be as universal as possible.

Since the effective measuring base of any camera can be calculated with simple formulas, it is easy to compare the different values.

Formula for the range-viewfinder camera:

Base in mm x viewfinder = effective measuring base

Formula for the SLR camera:

$$\frac{\text{Focal length of lens}}{\text{Aperture}} \times \frac{\text{Focal length of lens}}{\text{Focal length of eyepiece}} = \text{Effective measuring base}$$

For the Leica M with 0.72x viewfinder magnification, the following base is valid for all lenses with focal lengths from 21 to 135mm:

69.25 mm X 0.72 = 49.9 mm
With viewfinder magnification 0.58x = 40.2 mm
With viewfinder magnification 0.85x = 58.9 mm

For the Leica R with 50mm focal length and a universal focusing screen with split-image indicator, the measuring base is calculated as follows:

$$\frac{52}{45} \times \frac{52}{61.53} = 9.82 \text{ mm}$$

With other focal lengths the values listed below apply:

Focal length (mm)	Effective measuring base (mm)	Focal length (mm)	Effective measuring base (mm)
15	0.80	60	13.33
16	0.92	80	23.11
19	1.35	90	29.20
21	1.63	100	36.00
24	2.08	135	65.70
28	2.78	180	116.80
35	4.43	250	225.50
50	9.82		

(Rounded off values)

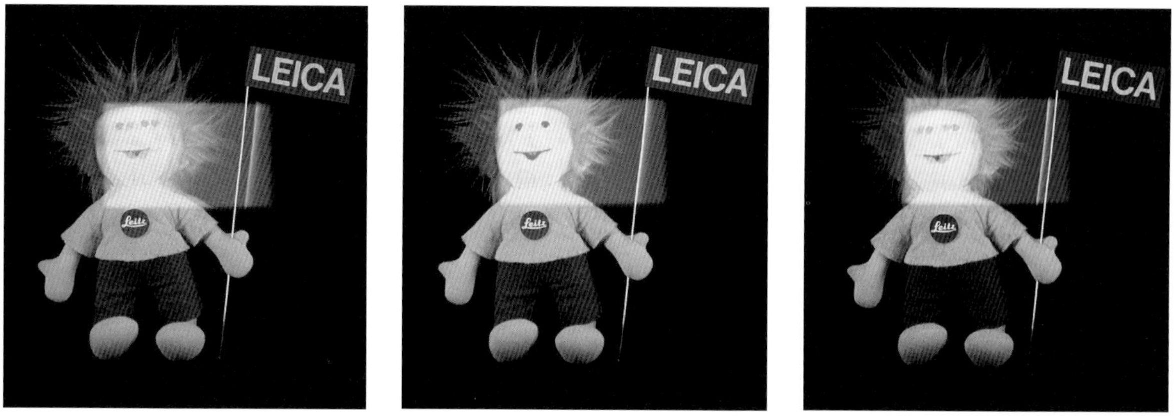

Fig. 33: *With the bright, rectangular, sharply outlined measuring field of a Leica M camera, the lens can be focused accurately on the doll using two different methods. With the superimposed-image method, double contours, such as those of the eyes or the mouth of the doll are caused to merge. Vertical lines, however, like the flagpole above, can be brought into focus more positively using the split-image method (i.e., the portion of a vertical line that appears laterally displaced is adjusted by turning the focusing ring of the lens until this line is perfectly continuous in the full viewfinder image). Left: The double image is displaced to the right of the main image, which indicates that the lens is focused in front of the subject. Center: No double image = precise focus. Right: The double image is displaced to the left of the main image, which indicates that the lens is focused behind the subject.*

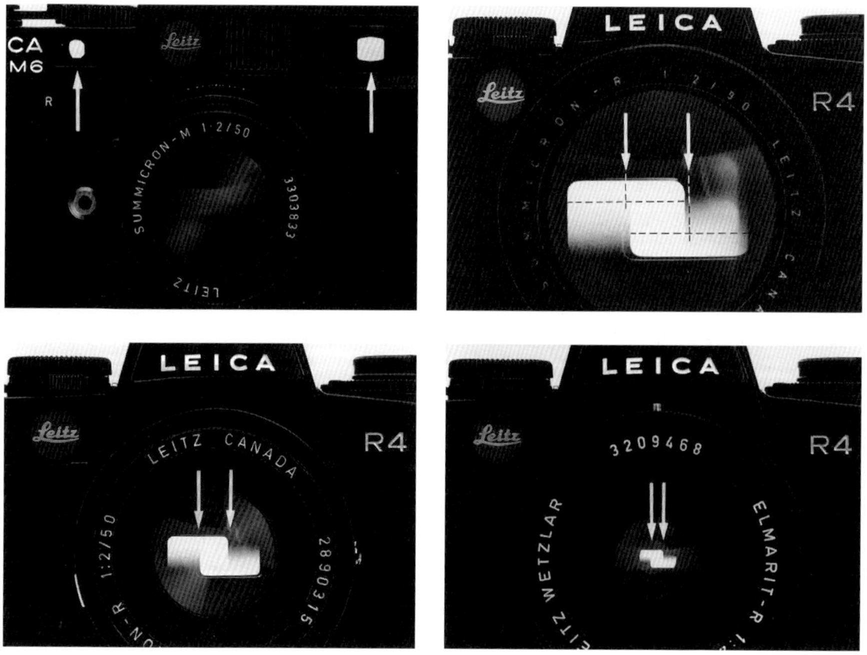

Fig. 34: *The measuring base of the rangefinder becomes visible when we look through the front of the camera's viewfinder from a certain distance. This enables us to see the separation between the light paths; in a Leica M it is the distance between the viewfinder and rangefinder windows, and in a Leica R it is visible in the lens, generated by the prisms of the split image indicator. The arrows in the illustrations indicate the different sizes of the measuring bases. In the case of a single-lens-reflex camera, they are always a function of the focal length of the lens in use. Top: 90mm focal length. Bottom: 50mm focal length (left) and 35mm focal length (right).*

Similar values apply to the Leicaflex and to all other commercially available SLR cameras. Minor changes result when fast lenses (apertures greater than f/4.5) and plain ground glass screens are used for focusing.

When we compare the measuring bases of Leica R cameras with those of Leica M cameras, the rangefinder's great superiority with short focal-length lenses is evident. The diagram (see Fig. 36) makes that clear. In actual practice, this becomes apparent in comparing the two focusing systems used with normal and wide-angle lenses. While we routinely "zero in" on the best focus with a SLR camera by turning the focusing mount of the lens back and forth several times until we have found the "best sharpness," optimal focus is achieved almost immediately and very positively with the long-base rangefinder of a Leica M camera. This works in virtually any lighting conditions.

We quickly become accustomed to the fact that focusing can only be performed in the center of the viewfinder, in the bright measuring field of the rangefinder, using the superimposed-image or the split-image principle.

Viewfinder accessories

The range-viewfinder of the Leica M is used to analyze image composition and cropping, as well as lens focus. The accuracy with which this can be done depends on the photographer's eyesight and on the magnification of the viewfinder image. Poor eyesight can be corrected by eyeglasses and contact lenses, or by a corrective lens screwed to the viewfinder eyepiece of the camera. Also, viewfinder magnification can be enhanced by a magnifier on the eyepiece.

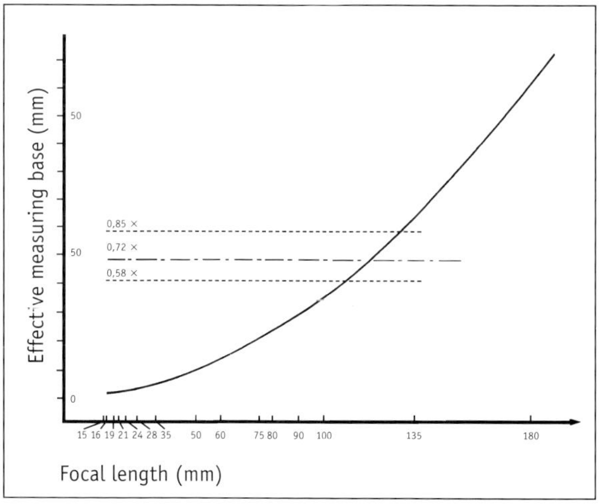

Fig. 35: *A comparison of the effective measuring bases of range-viewfinder and SLR cameras. While the Leica M has an effective measuring base that remains the same with all lenses—only the different viewfinder magnifications have an effect—there is significant variation in the measuring base of SLR cameras.*

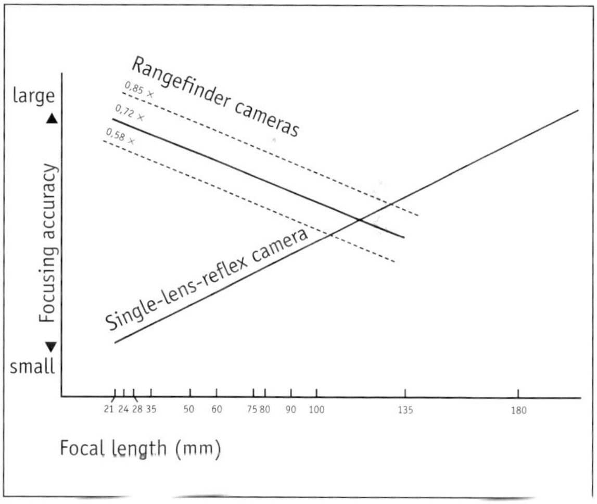

Fig. 36: *This diagram shows the focusing accuracy of range-viewfinders and SLRs with various lens focal lengths. It clearly shows the superiority of long-base rangefinder with short and medium-range focal lengths. With focal lengths of 135mm or greater, the SLR is unsurpassed.*

Corrective lenses

Many people have minor visual impairments, which are hardly noticed until they use optical equipment. The Leica M, requires excellent vision. Although the long-base rangefinder of the Leica M, in contrast with the SLR cameras tolerates minor "visual weaknesses" without negatively affecting the sharpness of the picture, for best results the eye should be adjusted to the viewfinder of the Leica M. Should difficulties adjusting the camera arise, the use of Leica corrective lenses is recommended. They are available in the following plus and minus values (spherical): 0.5, 1.0, 1l5, 2.0, 3.0 diopters.

If possible, when ordering a diopter, include a copy of your eyeglass prescription. If this not be possible, be aware that Leica M viewfinders are adjusted to –0.5 diopters. This value must be factored into the necessary correction. For example, if a person usually requires a corrective lens of +1 diopter, the Leica M should be fitted with a +1.5 diopter. Leica's Technical Service or the local authorized dealer will offer appropriate corrective lens mounts (Product No. 042-253.008). The production of the lens and the appropriate mount must be handled by an optician. Because this lens must be rotated from landscape format to portrait format when pictures are taken, it is preferable to take pictures with eyeglasses or contact lenses that correct the visual defect.

Viewfinder magnifier M 1.25x

The M 125x viewfinder magnifier is a small and practical accessory. By magnifying the viewfinder image by 25%, sections of pictures that are captured with focal lengths of 50mm and greater can be better evaluated. At the same time, the effective measuring base of the rangefinder is increased, which increases the focusing accuracy and speed. However, when the viewfinder magnifier M 1.25x is used, the bright-line frames for focal lengths of 35 and 28mm are only barely visible in the viewfinder, or are not visible at all. The black anodized aluminum magnifier mount is screwed into the camera eyepiece. Corrective diopter lenses be used with the viewfinder, which is threaded to accept them. A small chain which uses snap locks to connect the magnifier with the carrying-strap lugs on the camera, guards against loss and a small leather case on the carrying strap of the Leica protects the magnifier when it is not in use.

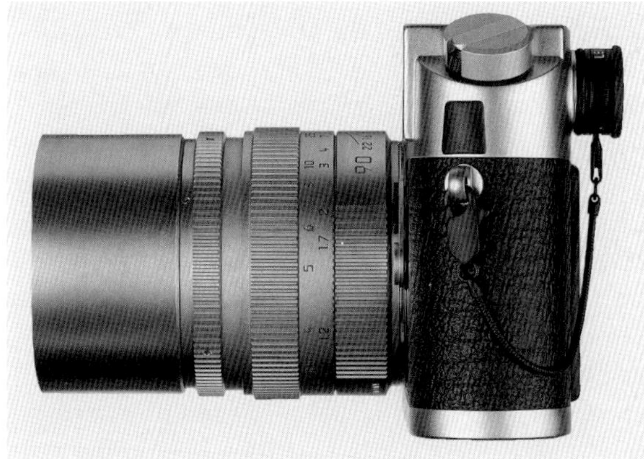

Fig. 37: *Viewfinder magnifier M 1.25x*

Fig. A1 and A2: *Colors, shapes, lines, and light provide a ready inspiration for photographers. Great pictures are made by skillful selection of the location and the focal lengths.*

Fig. A1: *By using a wide-angle lens and tilting the camera, the foreground, which complements the sea and the sky becomes dominant. The small sailboat in the foreground also increases the impression of spatial depth. 28mm f/2.8 Elmarit-M lens, 1/60 second, f/8 – 11, polarizing filter, daylight reversal film ISO 64.*

Fig. A2: *The bird's eye view and telephoto focal length eliminates the non-essentials from the composition. 90mm f/2.8 Elmarit-M lens, 1/500 second, f/ 5.6, polarization filter, daylight reversal film ISO 64.*

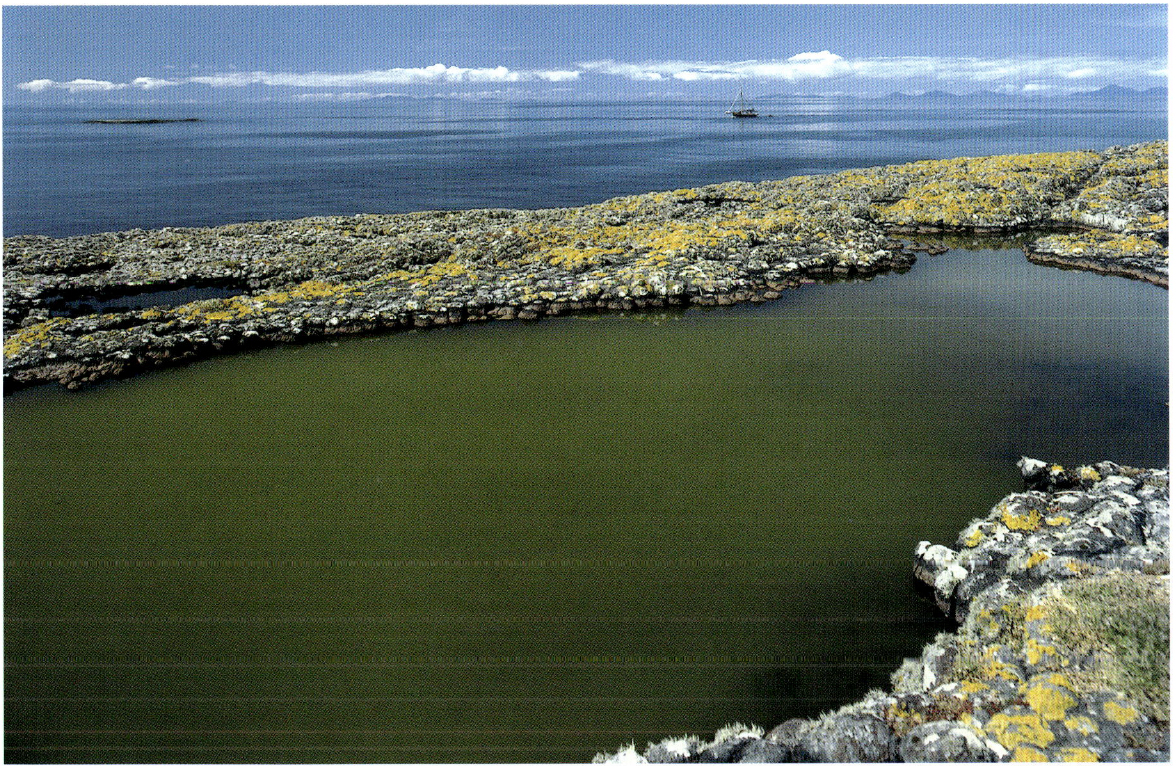

Fig. A1

Fig. A2

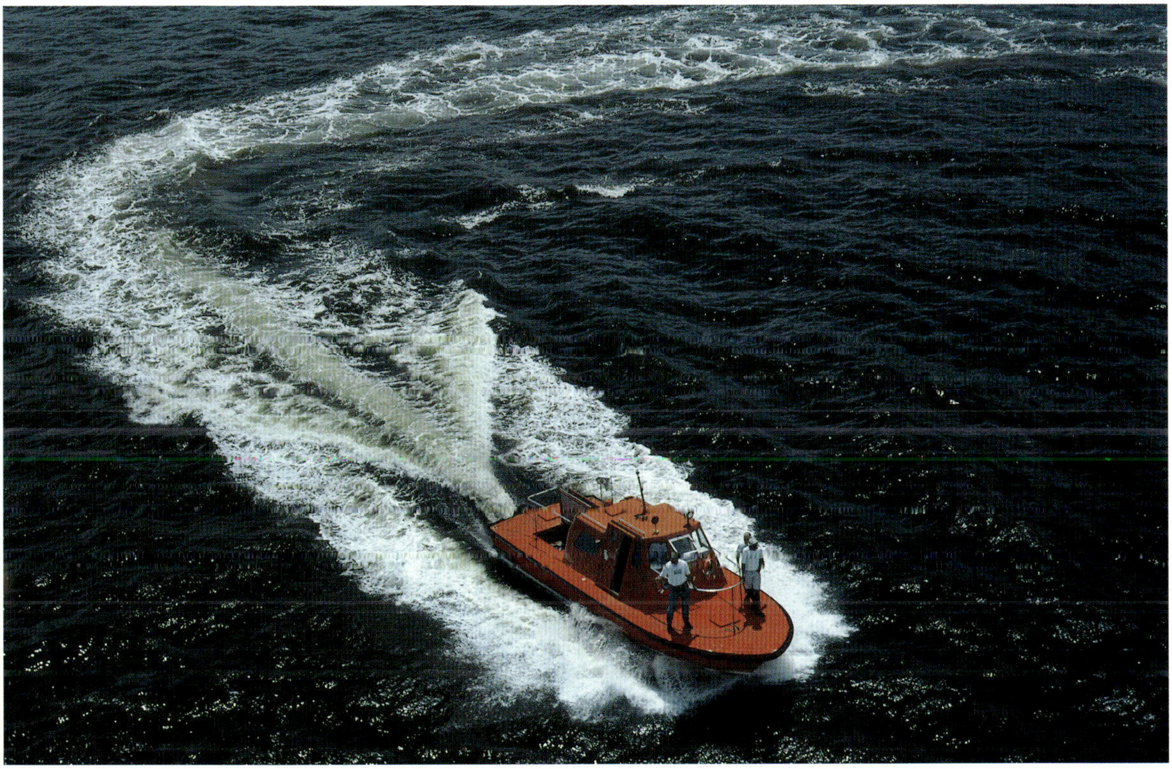

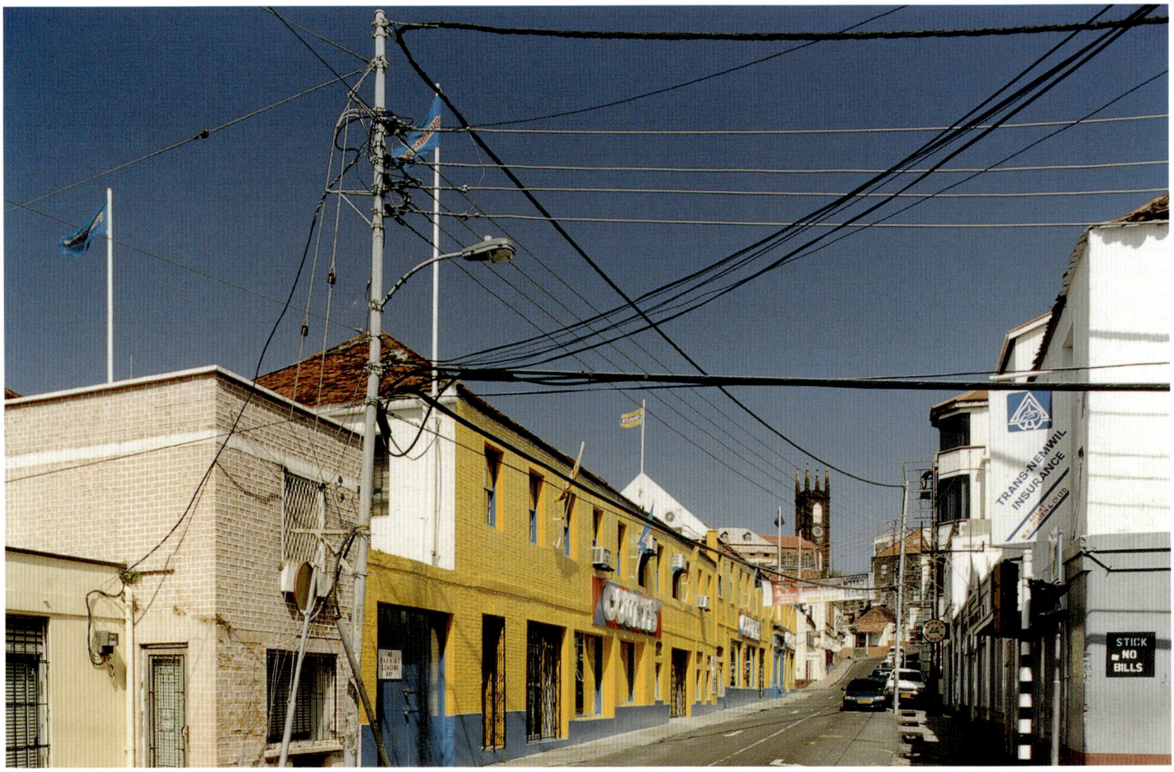

Fig. A3

Fig. A4

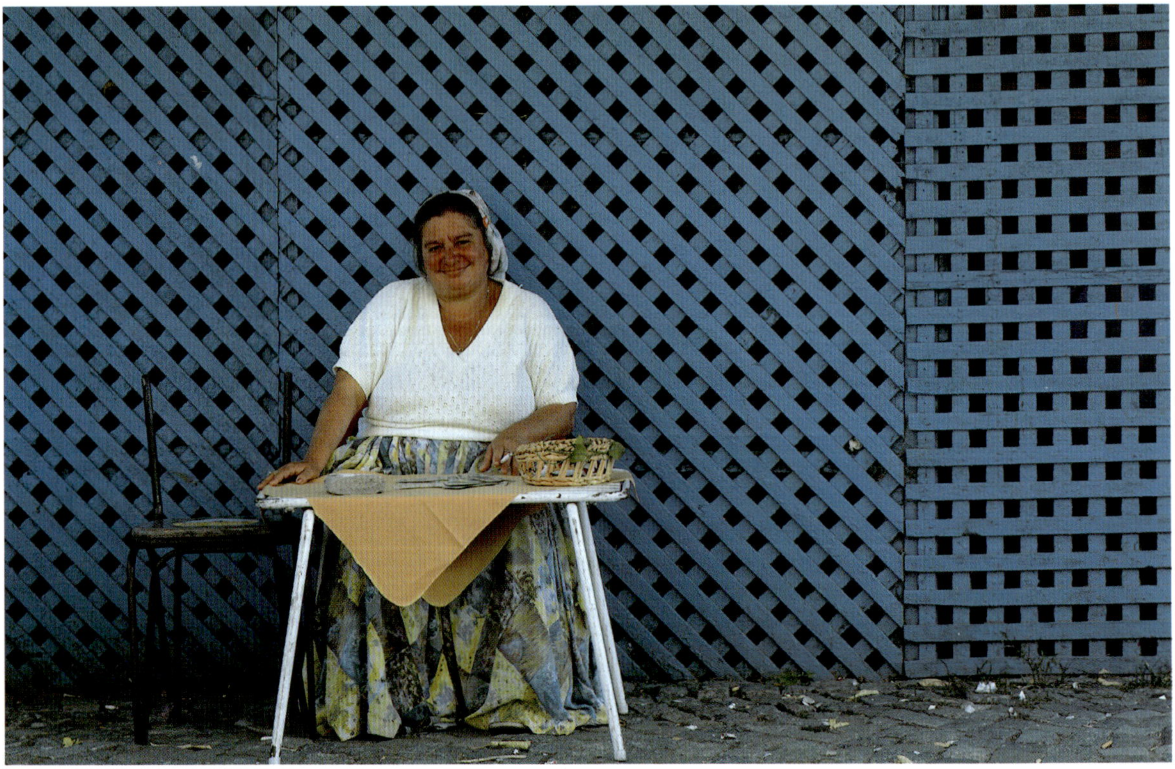

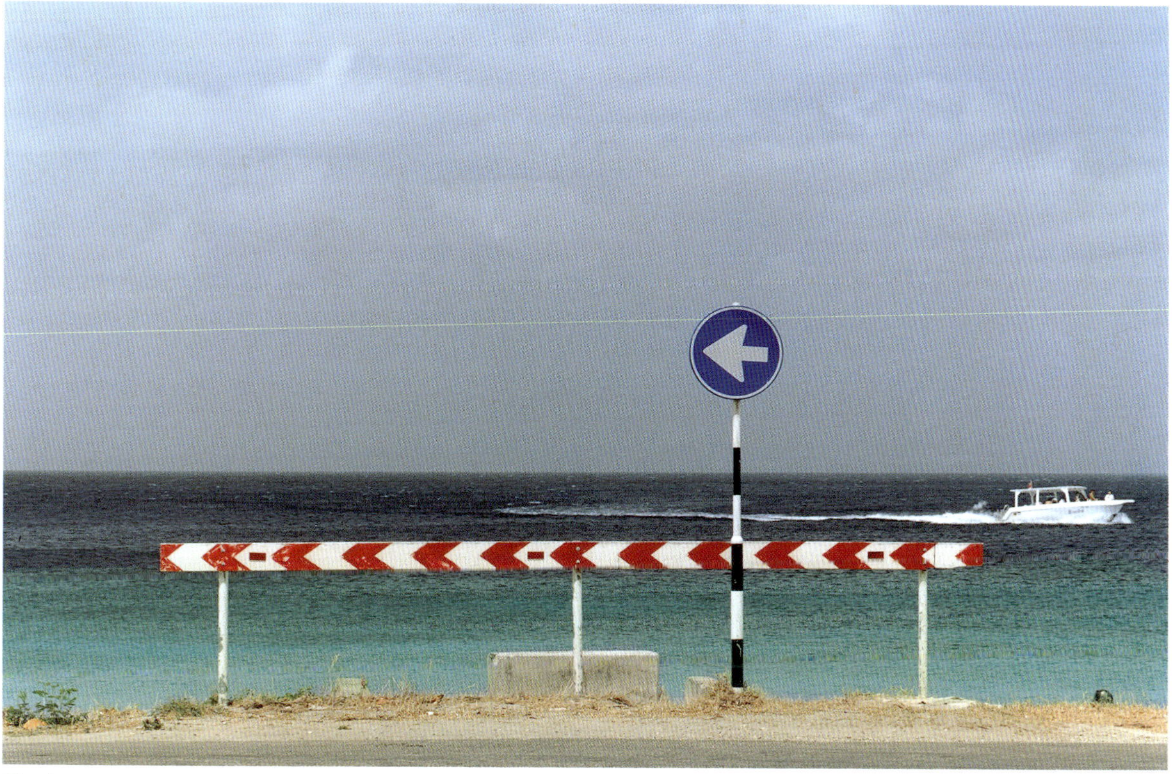

Fig. A5

Fig. A6

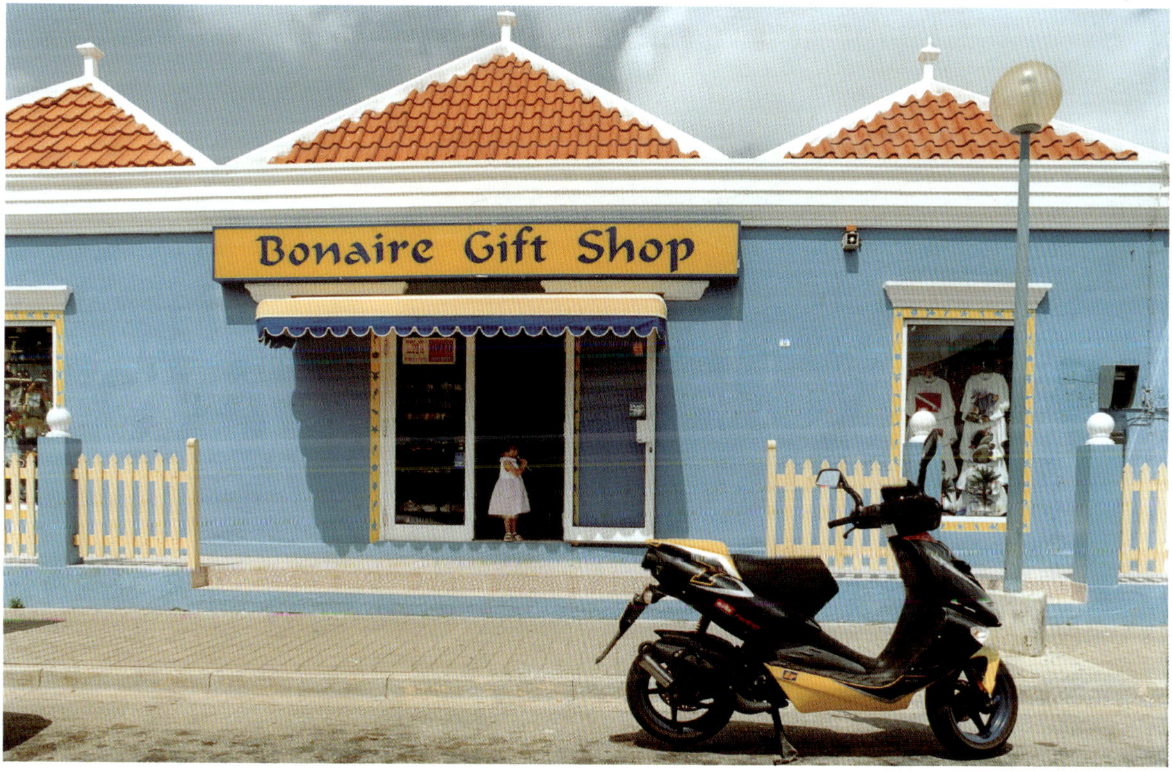

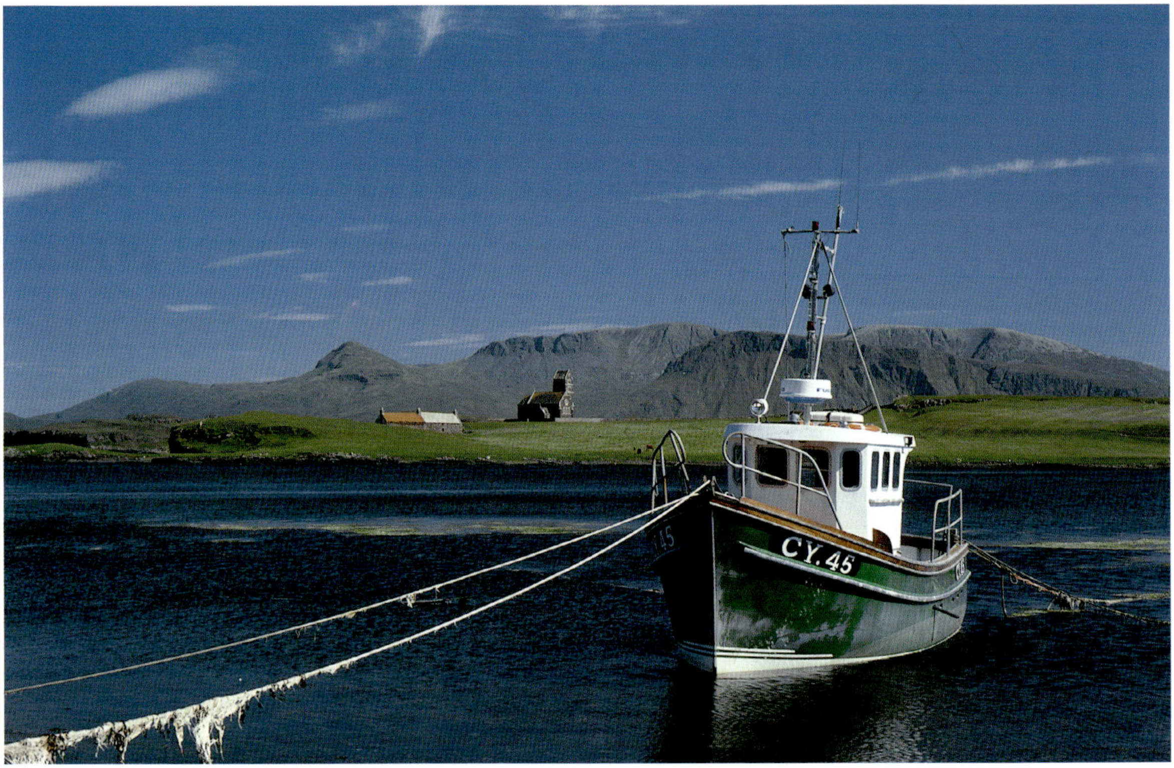

Fig. A7

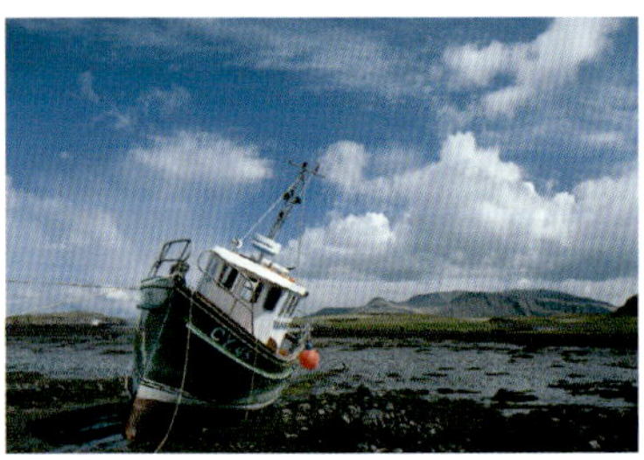

Fig. A8

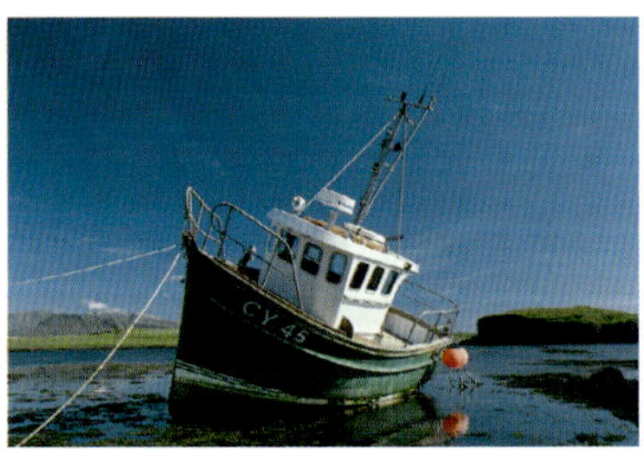

Fig. A9

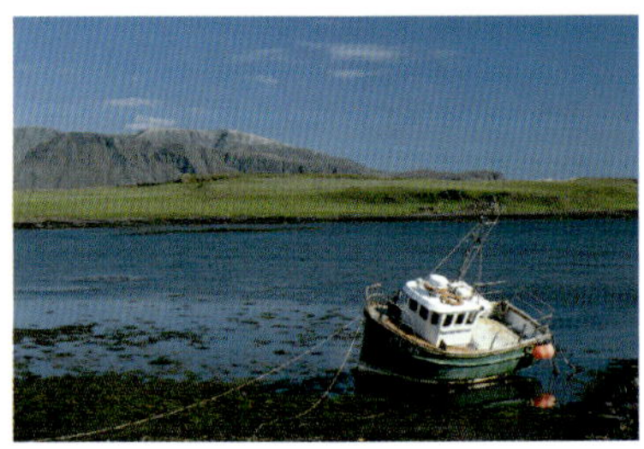

Fig. A10

Table 1: The range-viewfinder with and without viewfinder magnifier M 1.25x

Viewfinder magnifier		Visible bright-line frame *		Effective measuring basis	
Without magnifier	With magnifier	Without magnifier	With magnifier	Without magnifier	With magnifier
0.58 ×	0.73 ×	28 – 90mm	50 – 90mm	40.2 mm	50.2 mm
0.72 ×	0.90 ×	28 – 135mm	50 – 135mm	49.9 mm	62.3 mm
0.85 ×	1.06 ×	35 – 135mm	75 – 135mm	58.9 mm	73.4 mm
0.90 ×	1.12 ×	50 – 135mm	90 u. 135mm	62.3 mm	77.6 mm

* Clearly visible without eyeglasses

(Rounded off values)

Fig. A3 – A6: *Caribbean impressions. The colorful, clear composition provides an almost graphic effect.*

Fig. A3: 28mm f/2 Summicron-M lens, 1/125 second, f/8, polarization filter, color negative film ISO 100.
Fig. A4: 90mm f/2 ASPH Apo-Summicron-M lens, 1/250 second, f/4, daylight reversal film ISO 64.
Fig. A5: 50mm f/2.8 Elmar-M lens, 1/250 second, f/5.6, color negative film ISO 100.
Fig. A6: 35mm f/2 ASPH Summicron-M lens, 1/250 second, f/8, color negative film ISO 100.

Fig. A7 – A 10: *These photos of the same fishing boat photographed on two days at different times illustrates that a subject can be viewed and photographed in many different ways.*
Fig. A7: 50mm f/2 ASPH Summicron-M lens, 1/60 second, f/8.
Fig. A8: 35mm f/2 ASPH Summicron-M lens, 1/60 second, f/8.
Fig. A9: 28mm f/2.8 Elmarit-M lens, 1/125 second, f/5.6 – 8.
Fig. A10: 50mm f/2 Summicron-M lens, 1/125 second, f/5.6 – 8.
All pictures: ISO 64 daylight reversal film with polarizing filter.

Clip-on viewfinders

The design of the Leica M limits the number of bright-line frames in the viewfinder to a maximum of six. The ability to see the bright-line frame is limited by viewfinder magnification. Therefore, viewfinder frames for 21 or 24mm lenses cannot be included in any Leica M model. Also, a bright-line frame for the 28mm focal length is not available in Leica M models featuring 0.85x viewfinder magnification. In the Leica M3, which features a viewfinder magnification of 0.90x, even a 35mm bright-line frame would not be clear. This is remedied with an "optical trick": the 35mm wide-angle lenses belonging to the Leica M3 feature a permanently attached optical device, which pivots in front of the camera viewfinder when the lens is mounted. This reduces the viewfinder magnification so that 50mm bright-line frame corresponds to the image captured by the 35mm wide-angle lens.

For wide-angle lenses with focal lengths of 21, 24, and 28mm, clip-on viewfinders are offered as accessories. A separate Albada viewfinder can be used with these lenses.

Focusing is accomplished as usual through the range-viewfinder of the camera. The same applies to exposure metering.

Table 2: Comparison of clip-on viewfinders

Type	Viewfinder-Magnification	Parallax correction Indication	Eye-Relief*	Dimensions (mm)	Weight
Viewfinder for 21mm	0.30	yes	8 mm	26.2 × 30.2 × 39.2	28 g
Viewfinder for 24mm	0.30	yes	8 mm	26.2 × 30.2 × 39.2	28 g
Viewfinder for 28mm	0.50	yes	8 mm	26.2 × 30.2 × 39.2	18 g
Leica (adjustable) Viewfinder					
21mm	0.42	no	15 mm	44.4 × 37.7 × 47.8	82 g
24mm	0.48	no	15 mm		
28mm	0.56	no	15 mm		

* Distance of the eye from viewfinder lens

(Rounded off values)

Albada viewfinders

When looking through an Albada viewfinder, a bright frame outlines the image. Plus, a dotted line in the upper viewfinder area delineates the parallax for shooting distances of less than 2 meters (6 ft.).

This type of optical system corresponds to a reverse Galilean telescope. The 28mm viewfinder is comprised of four elements; the 21mm and 24mm viewfinders are each comprised of five elements.

Each Albada viewfinder displays a minimized, unreversed, and brilliant image. The housing is mounted on a foot, which is inserted in the Leica M accessory clip and can be locked in position by a small pivoting lever.

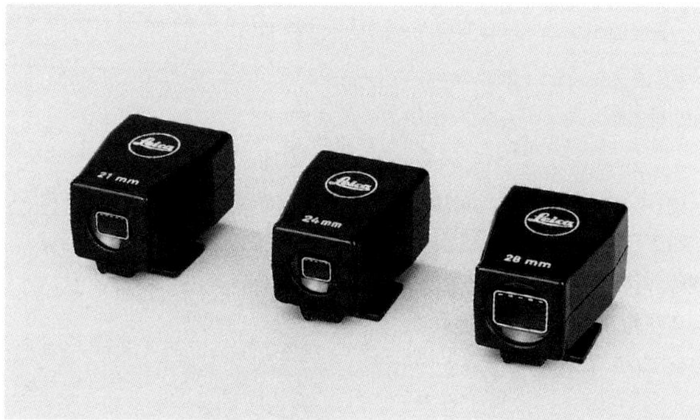

Fig.38: *Albada viewfinders for 21, 24, and 28mm lenses*

Leica Viewfinder

This viewfinder also operates on the principle of a reverse Galilean telescope. Designed for 21mm, 24mm, and 28mm lenses it features a knurled thumb ring for selecting the desired focal

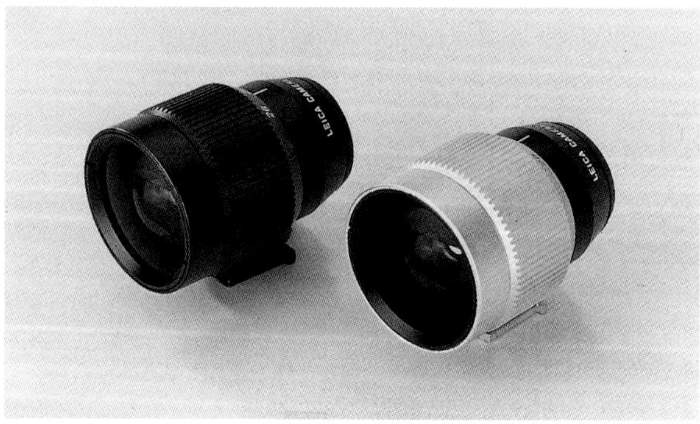

Fig. 39: *The reversible viewfinder for 21, 24, and 28mm lenses is offered chrome-plated in silver or black.*

length. As this ring is turned, each selection is denoted by a click stop, which can be felt and heard. The viewfinder's optical system consists of five elements, two of which shift to adjust the framing. The viewfinder's image is not reversed and can be easily seen even by those who wear eyeglasses because the exit pupil is located toward the back. In order to protect eyeglasses the eyepiece is provided with a rubber cup. If the viewfinder is to be used without eyeglasses, corrective lenses for the Leica M camera can be attached.

The sturdy anodized aluminum housing is available in black or silver. The viewfinder mounts in the camera's accessory shoe and is secured by a locking screw.

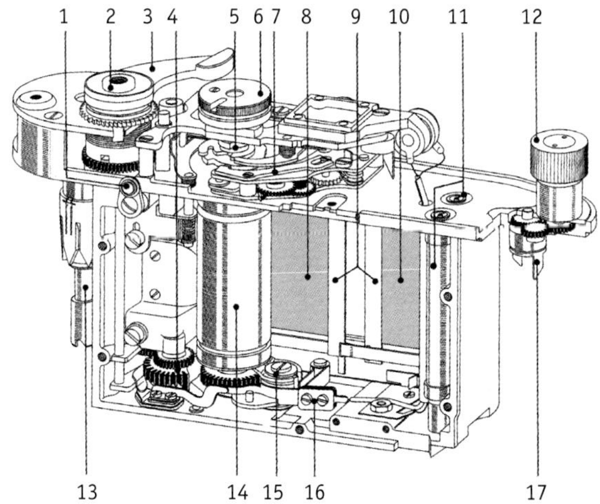

Fig. 40: *Focal plane shutter and film advance mechanism of the Leica M2. 1. The film rewind release lever, 2. The shutter release button, 3. The rapid film advance lever, 4, The winding gear (including a sector gear wheel), 5. Cams for shutter speed control, 6. The shutter speed dial, 7. The delay mechanism for longer shutter speeds, 8. 2nd rubberized cloth shutter curtain, 9. Leading and following edges of the shutter curtains, 10. 1st rubberized cloth shutter curtain, 11. Small shutter curtain cylinders with helical tension springs inside, 12. Pull-up rewind knob, 13. Shaft for film take-up spool with coupling for Leicavit or Leica Motor, 14. Large shutter curtain cylinder, 15. Cylinder brake, 16. X flash contact, 17. Teeth that engage the film supply spool for rewinding.*

The focal-plane shutter

The Leica M camera represents a combination classic design and extraordinary features that benefit today's photographer. In addition to the sophisticated opto-mechanical range-viewfinder assembly, the Leica M also features a rubberized cloth focal plane shutter, which occupies quite a bit of space within the camera housing.

More compact, metal-blade, focal-plane shutters, commonly found in today's SLR cameras would occupy less space. However, to this day there still is not a single design available that comes close to the Leica M's shutter in terms of lack of vibration and silent operation. These considerations are much less important in SLR cameras, because the portion of the sound contributed by the shutter is minor in comparison with the sound generated by the many other moving parts—such as the automatic diaphragm and the rapid mirror return mechanism. Also, shutter vibrations are more easily absorbed by the proportionately higher overall weight of the SLR camera.

Leica has retained the rubberized cloth focal-plane shutter in the M cameras because it produces a fastest shutter speed of 1/1000 second, electronic flash synchronization at 1/50 second, and is practically inaudible and free from vibration.

The shutter design of a Leica M camera offers one more advantage: the extremely short delay between pressing the shutter release button and the exposure of the film. Before the shutter can open in most modern SLR cameras, the mirror has to flip up first and the automatic diaphragm has to close down. By comparison, a Leica M camera with its 20 millisecond (ms) delay is about five times faster than one of the fastest electronic SLR cameras on the market today—the Leica R. Thus, it is much easier for the photographer to "capture" the absolute peak of an action with an M camera.

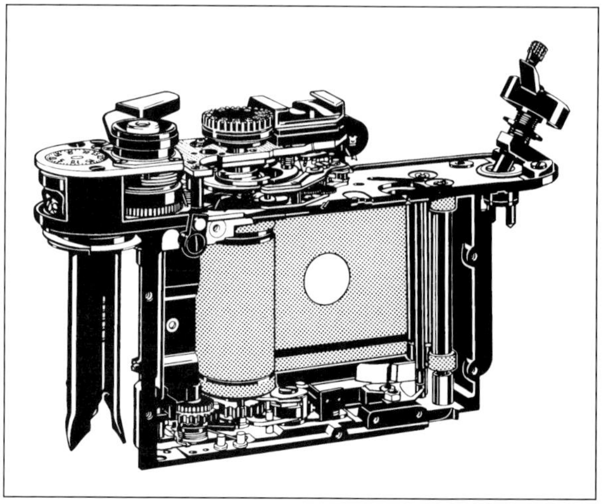

Fig. 41: *The principle of the focal plane shutter and film advance mechanism is the same for all Leica M models. The Leica M6 camera is no exception, even though numerous detail refinements have been introduced over the past 30 years. Recent Leica M models, for instance, have an angled folding rewind crank for easier and faster rewinding of the film, and the Leica M6 has a white field on the leading curtain of its focal plane shutter for selective exposure metering.*

These two rubberized shutter curtains travel in front of the film gate in the long direction (horizontally) in controlled succession. The various exposure times are produced by different distances between the end of the first curtain and the beginning of the second one.

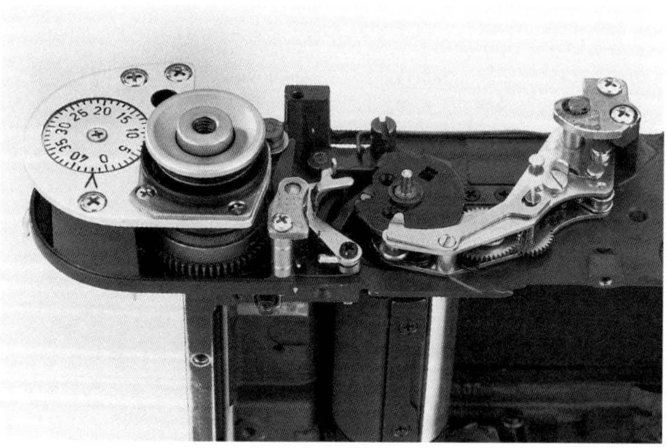

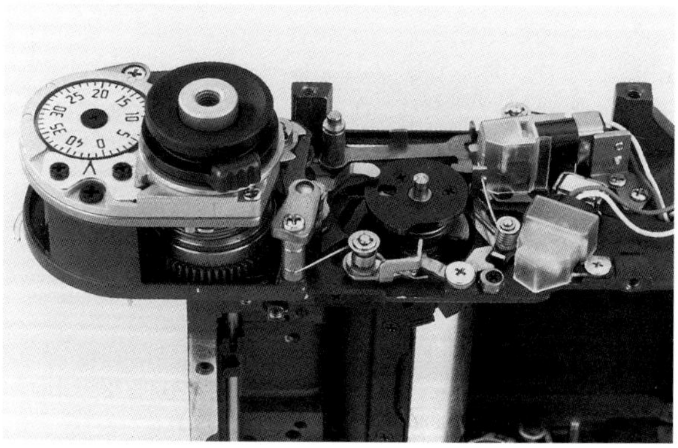

Fig. 42: *The time difference between when the Leica M's first shutter curtain begins to travel (which creates an opening for light), and the beginning of travel of the second shutter curtain (which closes this opening), is called the shutter speed. In mechanically controlled shutters, timing is controlled by cams and gear mechanisms (Fig. on left). In electronically controlled shutters, like the Leica M7's, the camera's micro-processor computes the time differences between the two operations and, ensures that they are precisely executed (Fig. on the right).*

The two curtains are propelled by tensioned springs but only a very small part of this spring tension is utilized for operating the shutter. That is why there is virtually no metal fatigue, and it makes no difference whether a Leica is stored with its shutter cocked or uncocked.

The rubberized shutter cloth has proven its outstanding dependability over the past decades. It operates safely in the tropics as well as frigid climates. The danger of damaging the shutter with the "burning effect" of a lens is remote. For example, one would have to leave a Leica M camera with its lens uncapped, stopped down, and exposed to head-on sunlight for a considerable length of time before any damage occurred.

Because the rubberized cloth curtains do not come in direct contact with the camera body's film gate at any point, and since they operate without touching each other, caution is advised when changing lenses in bright light.

HINT: Fogging the film can be prevented changing lenses rapidly in the shadow of your body.

Earlier instruction booklets for Leica M cameras referred to the option of setting intermediate shutter speeds in the ranges from 1 to 1/8 second, 1/15 to 1/30 second, and 1/60 to 1/1000 second. Leitz no longer recommends this practice, because the exposure meter is calibrated only for the speeds that correspond to the click stops of the shutter speed dial.

Coupled exposure meters

Accessory Leicameter exposure meters, which mount on the camera and couple with the shutter speed dial, have been a characteristic part of the appearance of Leica M cameras for decades. With the exception of those cameras that are equipped with built-in exposure meters, all Leica M models can be used with any of the three Leicameters.

The two-step method of coupling the meter to the camera is the same for all models of the Leicameter. Set the camera's and the mter's shutter speed to B. Pull up and turn the wheel in the direction of the arrow while inserting the meter into the accessory shoe of the camera.

When the knurled wheel of the exposure meter is turned back, its coupling pin will engage the slot between the numbers "2" and "4" engraved on the camera's shutter speed dial. The Leicameter is now coupled with the camera. Film speeds can be set with the rotating calibrated dial on the top of the exposure meter.

In addition to corresponding DIN and ASA film speeds, the Leicameter M also has a Weston scale, a shutter speed scale, and two f/stop scales.

The principle of determining and setting the shutter speed or the f/stop is the same for all models of the Leicameter. If the f/stop has already been selected on the lens, the corresponding f/stop number on the meter's dial is aligned with the channel (indicated by the meter's needle) by turning the meter's knurled wheel.

This automatically sets the camera's shutter speed, which can be read opposite the small triangular index on the top of the exposure meter. When the shutter speed has been preselected, it is set by aligning the desired speed with the triangular index. The required f/stop is read opposite the channel indicated by the exposure meter's needle and then set on the lens. Intermediate shutter speeds can also be set by using the exposure meter's knurled wheel.

Exposures that are longer than one second can be measured by lifting and turning the knurled wheel on the exposure meter so that it is no longer coupled to the shutter speed dial on the camera. Long exposure times (up to 120 seconds) measured in this manner can be obtained using the "B" setting on the shutter speed dial of the camera. All Leicameter models offer a choice of metering ranges.

Leicameter M

The first model of this attachable coupled exposure meters has a hinged metal lid over its cell that has a tiny light slit. Under normal light conditions, the Leicameter M is used with this lid covering the meter cell.

Only a small amount of light reaches the selenium photocell through the light slit. In this mode, readings are made using the black numbers on the meter's dial. When light is low, the lid is flipped up and readings are made using the red numbers on the dial. For extreme low light conditions, a booster cell can be attached to the side of the meter. In this case, the readings are still made using the red numbers, but indicated exposure times have to be increased by a factor of four, i.e., by two stops.

In addition to light readings of a subject taken at the camera position (reflected light metering), a Leicameter M also permits readings of light falling on the subject taken at the subject position. For this kind of metering (incident light measurement), the opal diffuser supplied with the lightmeter has to be inserted in the grooves on the front of the honeycomb cell.

Leicameter MC

This selenium exposure meter has an electrical switch for changing the meter's range. When this switch is set to the black dot (normal lighting conditions), the black f/stop numbers apply. When the switch is set at the red dot (for low-light conditions), the red f/stop numbers apply. A separate booster element can be slipped over the front of the honeycomb cell to increase the light sensitivity of the Leicameter MC by a factor of six. In this mode, the special index in the small hollow rectangle is used to read the required exposure times. Using the Opal diffuser supplied with the Leicameter MC makes the meter suitable for taking incident light readings.

Because the metallic collectors, which conduct the minute electrical current from the back of the selenium cell tend to oxidize and become non-conductive, Leicameters M and MC—even those that appear to be in excellent condition—are essentially useless today.

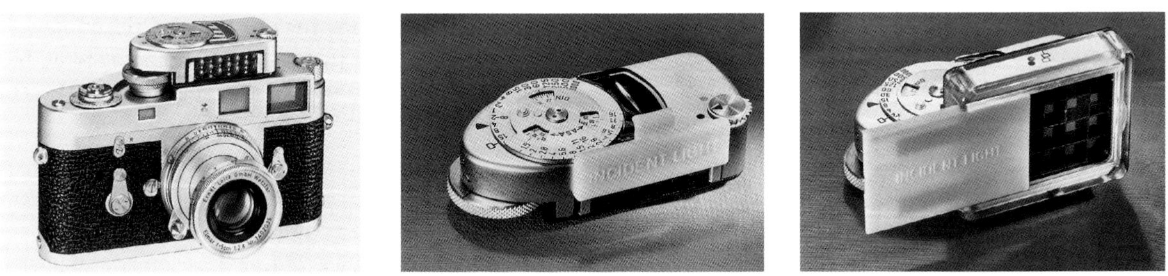

Fig. 43: *Leicameter MC mounted on a Leica M2 camera, Leicameter MC with opal diffuser for incident light measurement, and Leicameter MC with booster element and opal diffuser.*

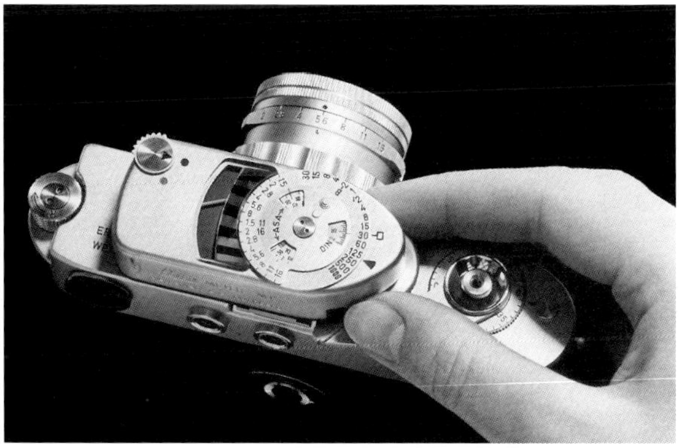

Fig. 44: *When the Leicameter is attached to the camera, the shutter speed for which the camera is set can be read an the calculator dial of the exposure meter. The aperture that corresponds to that shutter speed is indicated by the meter needle and the black or white channel to which it is pointing. In the illustration, the reading is 1/125 second at f/5.6.*

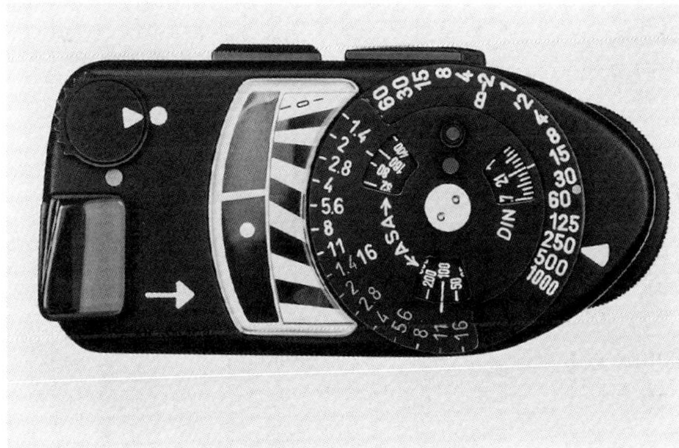

Fig. 45: *Leicameter MR seen from above.*

Leicameter MR

Unlike Leicameters M and MC, which have selenium cells, Leicameter MR is equipped with a cadmium sulfide (CdS) photo-resistor. A small mercury oxide button battery, such as a Duracell PX 625 battery or equivalent, powers this exposure meter.

In addition to a small sliding switch on its front for checking the battery, the Leicameter MC is equipped with a measurement key on the top left. The lightmeter is activated only when that key is pushed to the right. When the key is released, the needle automatically stays set at the reading that has just been taken.

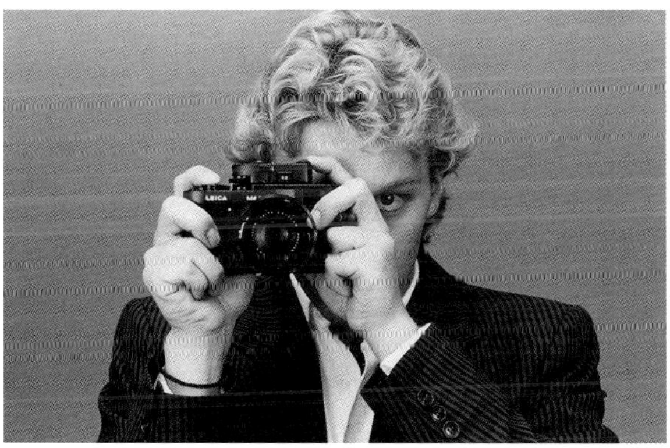

Fig. 46: *Using the Leicameter MR.*

Like the Leicameter MC, there are two sensitivity levels, which can be selected electrically. The meter's overall range, however, is considerably larger than those of the two preceding models, so that a supplementary booster element is unnecessary. Incident light cannot be metered with a Leicameter MR.

Targeted exposure metering

The field measured by a Leicameter MR exposure meter corresponds to that covered by a 90mm lens. To gauge the size of this area, the bright-line frame for a 90mm lens can be activated in the viewfinder of a Leica M camera at any time using the field-of-view preview. This shows the exact area being metered by a Leicameter MR, giving the viewfinder on a Leica M camera one more practical function.

If the middle finger of the left hand is used to push the field-of-view preview lever on the front of the camera in the direction of the lens, the bright-line frame for the 90mm lens will appear in the rangefinder. The camera can be aimed at the desired area of the subject and the required exposure can be

Table 3: Comparison of Leicameters

	LEICAMETER MR	LEICAMETER MC	LEICAMETER M
Battery	Mercury silver oxide, 1.35 V	None	None
Incident light	Cadmium sulfide meter cell	Selenium	Selenium
Reflected light	No	Yes	Yes
TTL measurement	Yes	Yes	Yes
Measuring angle, diagonal	27°	> 45°	< 45°
Measuring range 1 cd/m2	63 – 16 000	500 – 125 000	250 – 63 000
Measuring range 2 cd/m2	0.5 – 125	8 – 2000	4 – 1000
Measuring range with booster cell cd/m2	Not available.	1.4 – 380	1 – 250
Readable aperture values	1.4 – 16	1.5 – 16	1.5 – 16

measured by pushing the key on the meter with the index finger of the left hand. When the key is released, the needle remains at the reading for reference.

Shutter speeds and f/stops are set in the same manner as they are with the other Leicameter models. All Leicameters can be used as handheld exposure meters and not mounted on a camera.

TTL exposure meters

In today's 35mm cameras exposure metering is generally performed through the lens. This is called TTL or "through the lens" metering, which also indicates that the exposure meter is built into the camera.

Exposure metering with a Leica M5

In 1971 the Leica M5 was the first range-viewfinder camera in the world to feature through-the-lens exposure metering. It uses match-needle metering and the user-selected shutter speed is displayed in the viewfinder. The meter cell is a CdS photoresistor located on a hinged arm, which swings into the light path when the shutter is wound. Located in front of the camera's focal-plane shutter, it measures light through the lens. The arm with the metering cell swings out of the light path as the shutter release button is depressed—just before the shutter is fired and the exposure takes place. The meter arm also swings out of the light path when a lens is removed from the camera to protect the exposure meter.

Collapsible lenses and lenses of very short focal lengths with mounts that extend deeply into the camera body may damage the CdS cell or impair its movement. That is why the preventive measures described on page 163 should be followed.

The M5's CdS meter cell is located relatively far from the film plane and thus, measures an image that is "out of focus." A set of small concentric rings on the face of the photoresistor ensures that the readings are accurate for a variety of focal lengths and apertures. However there are exceptions. With the 50mm f/1 Noctilux and the 50mm f/1.2 Noctilux, correct exposure readings can only be made with apertures of f/1.4 or smaller.

ASA or DIN film speeds can be set on the top of the Leica M5. The range of film speeds extends from ASA 6 to 3200 (now called ISO).

With a 35mm lens on the camera, the measuring field corresponds approximately to the area outlined by the luminous frame for the 135mm lens. With a 50mm lens in place, the field corresponds to the central circular area and with a 90mm or a 135mm lens on the camera, it corresponds to the measuring field of the rangefinder. When a 28mm lens is attached to the camera, the metering field is the area outlined by the luminous frame for the 90mm lens. It could also be said that the measuring field for a given lens is the area outlined by the luminous frame that is the next smaller one to the one that corresponds to that lens.

Visible below the viewfinder image are: the shutter speed for which the camera is set, a horizontal calibration line, the meter needle, and a follower (or pointer). When the exposure meter is turned on, the needle of the galvanometer moves as the lens aperture is opened or closed. When the shutter speed dial is turned, the follower will move along the calibration line. By alternately actuating the aperture setting ring on the lens and the shutter speed dial on the camera, the needle and the follower can be aligned, which sets the correct exposure. The location of the crossing point along the calibration line gives an indication of the size of the lens aperture. Thus, opening the lens diaphragm shifts the crossing point to the right, while stopping it down moves it to the left. This is indicated by the small half circle symbol on the left, and the large one on the right side of the calibration line.

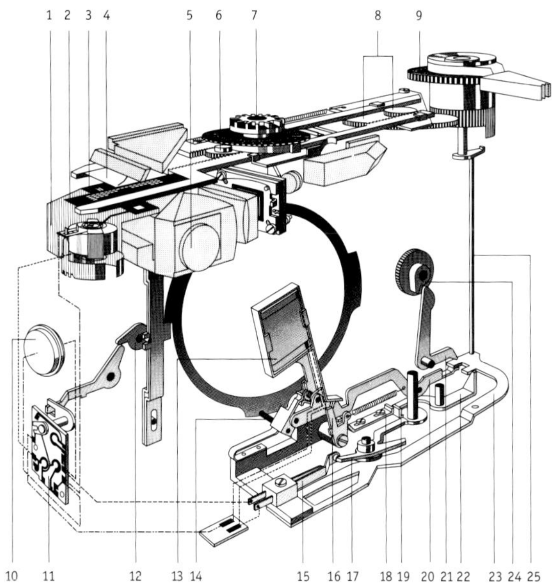

Fig. 47: *The exposure meter of a Leica M5. 1. The encapsulated galvanometer, 2. The slider for the display of shutter speeds in the viewfinder, 3. The calibration line, on which the galvanometer needle and the follower are aligned to set the correct exposure, 4. The slider and follow-pointer (with a compensating cam), 5. The viewfinder eyepiece, 6. The gear for entering the film speed in the exposure computing mechanism, 7. ASA/DIN film speed setting knob, 8. The gears for transmitting the exposure time set on the shutter speed dial (9) to the shutter speed control mechanism (1/1000 to 1/2 second). On B, the shutter speed dial is decoupled from the shutter speed control mechanism, but it continues to serve for reading measured long exposure times (1 to 30 seconds), 9. The shutter speed dial, 10. The battery, 11. The battery check switch with potentiometer for calibrating the exposure meter, 12. The battery check lever, 13. The housing for the CdS metering cell, 14. Rod that swings the metering cell assembly out of the way when the lens is removed, 15 and 17. The exposure meter switch, 16, 18, 19. and 20. The mechanism that erects the metering cell assembly, 21. The self-timer linkage, 22. The latch that releases the leading (1st) curtain of the focal plane shutter, 23. The leaf spring for the shutter release button, 24. The self timer, 25. The linkage that collapses the measuring cell assembly and releases the shutter.*

With the film speed set at ISO 100, the range of the exposure meter of a Leica M5 extends from 0.06 cd/m2 at f/1.4 to 32000 cd/m2 at f/16. So, at full aperture, exposure metering is possible even under very unfavorable light conditions. If it is necessary to close the lens down, the computation dial on the back of the camera is a useful aid. For example, if an exposure time of 1/2 second could just barely be measured at f/1.4, these two figures can be set opposite each other on the respective scales of that dial and all other correct combinations of shutter speed and aperture can be read on that dial. For instance: 8 sec. at f/5.6, or 60 second at f/16.

Note: The camera has to be held in the horizontal position in order to produce accurate exposure readings. The shutter release button of a Leica M5 must not be depressed during exposure metering.

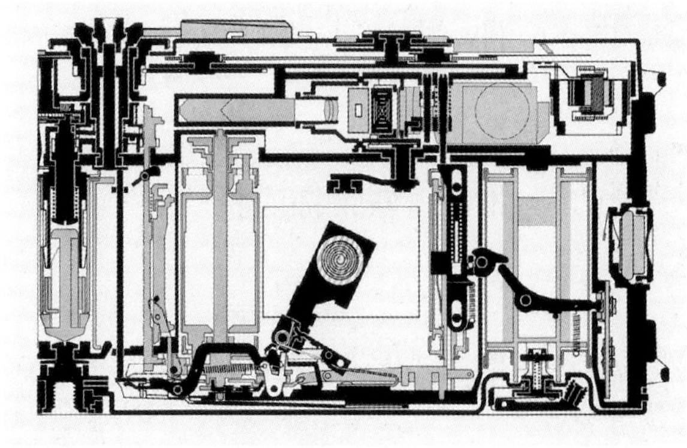

Fig. 48: *An X-ray view of a Leica M5 confirms that, in spite of its compact design, the integrated exposure meter still requires a relatively large amount of room. This dictated the exterior dimensions of the Leica M5 body, which are larger than those of other Leica M camera bodies. The hinged arm with the housing that contains the measuring cell can be seen in the erected position in the center of the illustration.*

Exposure metering with the Leica M7, Leica M6 TTL, and Leica M6

These models also measure exposure with the working aperture of the lens. A silicon photodiode (Si) equipped with a filter and a convex lens (located in the top left of the camera behind the bayonet), receives the light from a bright, round measurement spot located in the center of the first shutter curtain. This measuring spot has a diameter of 12 mm (just under half an inch). This accounts for an area of approximately 13% of the film format. The spectral sensitivity of the Si photodiode corresponds to the typical sensitivity curve of the eye.

The Leica M7 has a measuring range of 0.03 cd/m2 to 125000 cd/m2 at f/1. If an ISO 100 film is used to take pictures, the sensitivity range with a Noctilux 50mm f/1 is from -2 EV to 18 EV. Theoretically, this range would extend up to 20 EV, but the smallest available f/stop of the lens (f/16) limits the working range. Therefore, for practical purposes, the working range corresponds to aperture/shutter speed combinations of f/1 at 4 seconds to f/16 at 1/1000 second.

The Leica M6 TTL features the same metering range as the Leica M7. Since the shutter speed dial on this camera allows a maximum setting of only one second, the working range with the same lens and the same film speed is from 0 EV to 18 EV or, expressed in aperture/speed combination, from f/1 at 1 sec. to f/16 at 1/1000 second.

The Leica M6 features a meter that is 1 EV lower in sensitivity and the metering range extends from 0.063 cd/m2 to 1256000 cd/m2. With the same lens and the same film speed, the aperture range corresponds to that of the Leica M6 TTL. In practice, this lower metering sensitivity is significant only with high-speed films and very small apertures are used.

Note: While the metering range of each Leica camera model is fixed, the available apertures depend on the camera's shutter speed range. In the Leica M7's aperture priority mode, stepless shutter speeds are generated automatically depending on the selected aperture and on the film speed in use. If conditions are outside the metering range of the Leica M7, M6 TTL, or M6 (i.e. there is not enough light), this is indicated by blinking LEDs in the viewfinder.

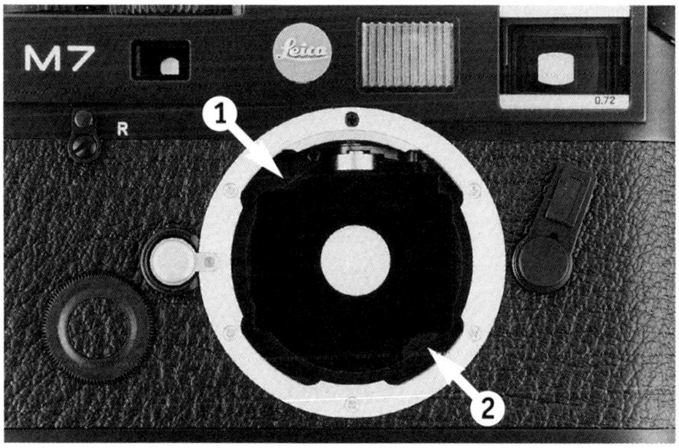

Fig. 49: The round white metering spot on the rubberized cloth focal plane shutter appears uneven when inspected closely. This, however, is intentional. Among other things, this prevents this spot from hindering the flexibility of the shutter curtain in hot or cold environments. In addition, the metal oxide color resists yellowing. The Si photodiode metering cell is located at the top left side, behind the lens bayonet (arrow 1). The cell for flash exposure metering is located on the bottom right (arrow 2).

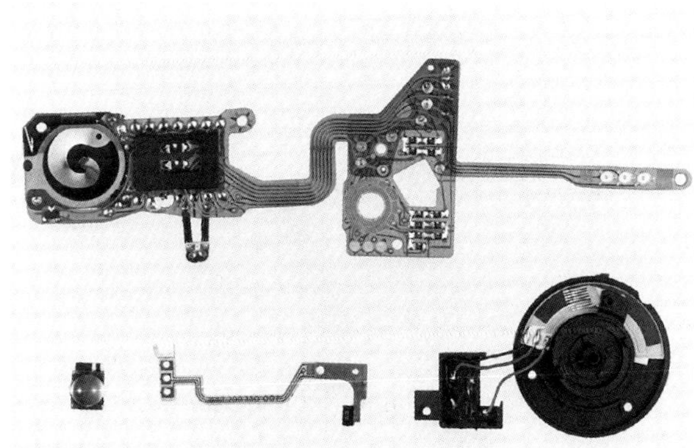

Fig. 50: Applying the very latest technologies, a hybrid C-MOS component was developed, utilizing both sides of the support substrate. This was the only way in which the electronics of the exposure meter could be accommodated within the space constraints set by the preceding model—the Leica M4-P. It also satisfied the objective of incorporating an exposure meter into the Leica M6 without increasing its physical size in relation to earlier Leica M models. The hybrid component contains 6 amplifiers, 9 transistors, 37 resistors, and 3 capacitors on two 12.7 x 16.9 mm (approx. 1/2 x 43/64 inches) surfaces. This illustration shows the conductor strip and the battery housing at the upper left, the shutter speed control resistors and, at the upper right, the connection for the film speed setting dial. The silicon photodiode is shown at the lower left, and next to it the connector strip with the two LEDs for the "light balance" display in the viewfinder. The LED chips are bonded into position within the tight tolerance of ± 5 m (approx. ± 0.0002 inches)! The extraordinarily corrosion-proof potentiometer of the film speed setting dial can be seen at the lower right corner. At Leica, this part alone is subjected to an endurance test of 5,000 cycles of changing the film-speed setting.

Applying pressure to the shutter release button when the camera is wound activates the exposure meter. In proper shooting position, the right index finger should rest on the shutter release button, while the thumb and the index finger of the left hand are used to adjust the aperture ring of the lens. In aperture-priority automatic exposure the Leica M7 generates the necessary shutter speed. If the shutter speed is set manually, the right hand is used with the Leica M7 as well as in the two M6 models. Since this means moving the index finger away from the shutter release button, the exposure meter remains on for about another 14 seconds. The exposure meter turns off once the shutter has been released or when the shutter speed dial is set to "B".

With the Leica M7 the ISO film speed is set automatically, based on the DX code on the film cassette. The sensitivity range for DX coded films extends from ISO 25 to ISO 5000. If there is no DX code, or if the ISO is to be increased by "push processing" (see page 190), the film speed may also be set manually. The hinged camera backs include a device for setting the ISO manually.

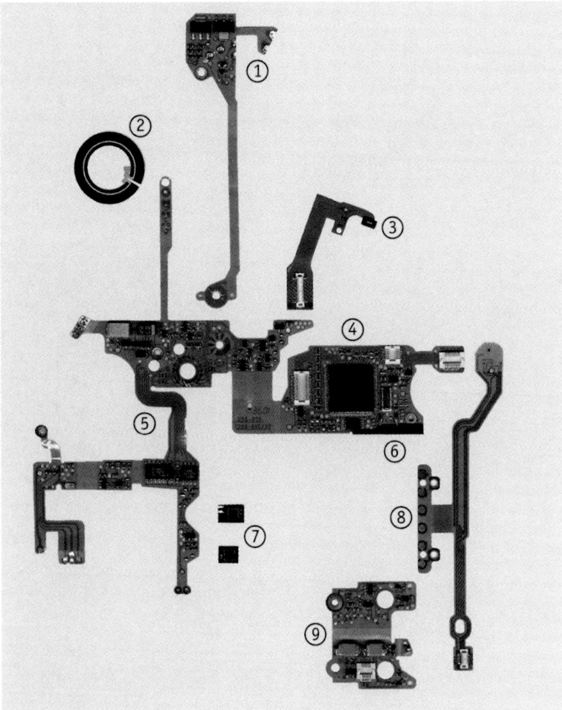

Fig. 51: *Development, design, and manufacture of the Leica M7 electronics are state of the art. A 16-bit, digital, flash processing integrated circuit monitors, computes, and controls the flash exposure, shutter operation (including synchronized shutter speeds with SCA 3000 and 3002 system flash units). It also operates the 0.7 x 2.3 mm, LED display in the viewfinder, which has a digit height of only 0.4 mm. These advanced features are possible through improved interconnection technology that allows for 80 µm conductors with laser drilled contacts having a diameter of 120 µm.*

Featured components of the Leica M7 electronics and their association with various functions of the camera are illustrated: 1 = conductor strip for flash ignition, 2 = photographer's control for film speed setting, 3 = viewfinder LED display, 4 = 16-bit digital flash processor integrated circuit, 5 = main conductor strip, 6 = light sensor for controlling display brightness, 7 = light sensors for exposure and flash light measurement, 8 = conductor strip for CX contacts, 9 = controller for shutter actuators.

In the Leica M7 and the Leica M6 models, the manually set ISO film speed range extends from ISO 6 to 6400. In the Leica M7, exposure compensation settings expand the ISO range from ISO 1.5 to ISO 25000.

After the Leica R7 is switched on, the film speed (which is set automatically by the DX-barcode or manually by the photographer) will appear in the viewfinder for two seconds. A blinking display indicates exposure compensation or erroneous settings have been made (see Table 4).

In aperture priority, when the exposure meter is activated, the automatic exposure control of the Leica M7 will set the correct shutter speed for a selected aperture. This shutter speed will be indicated in the viewfinder and may be locked by depressing the shutter-release button to the second pressure point.

If the shutter speed and the aperture are set manually, the Leica M7's and the Leica M6 TTL's viewfinder LEDs assist in determining the best combination. The "correct" exposure is set when only the central round LED lights up. The two triangular LEDs to the left and right, by themselves or in combination with the round LED, indicate under- or overexposure, as well as the direction of rotation of the aperture setting ring. With the Leica M7 and Leica M6 TTL the direction of rotation of the shutter speed dial is also indicated:

- ▶ = Under-exposure of at least one f/stop. Direction of rotation to the right is required.
- ▶● = Under-exposure of 1/2 f/stop. Direction of rotation to the right is required.
- ● = Correct exposure.
- ●◀ = Over-exposure of 1/2 f/stop. Direction of rotation to the left is required.
- ▶ = Over-exposure of at least one f/stop. Direction of rotation to the left is required.

In the Leica M6, when the speed dial and/or the aperture ring are turned, two red triangular LEDs appear with equal brightness in the viewfinder. In this camera, these triangular LEDS indicate the direction of rotation of the aperture ring, as well as under-exposure and over-exposure, as follows:

▶ = Under-exposure of at least one f/stop. Direction of rotation to the right is required.

▶◀ = Under-exposure of 1/2 f/stop. Direction of rotation to the right is required.

▶◀ = Correct exposure.

▶◀ = Over-exposure of 1/2 f/stop. Direction of rotation to the left is required.

◀ = Over-exposure of at least one f/stop. Direction of rotation to the left is required.

For manual compensation, the Leica M7, M6 TTL, and M6 require that the aperture be set in full or half f/stops. However, intermediate values should not be used in setting the shutter speed (see page 57).

In manual exposure mode the display of the selected shutter speed does not appear the viewfinder. This is not possible in the small Leica housing (M7, M6 TTL, M6).

The bright-line frames cover an area that corresponds to an image area of 23 x 35 mm on the film (mounted slide) at the shortest focusing distance of the respective lens.

In order to not clutter up the viewfinder display, lines indicating the metered area were omitted from M cameras. However, the area measured by the exposure meter can be easily assessed in the viewfinder of the Leica M7, M6 TTL, and M6. Because the bright-line frames used in all Leica M models are designed for the minimum focusing distance, at the infinity setting the image on the film will cover slightly more than the image outlined by the bright-lines in the viewfinder (see pages 37 and 40). Even though the size of the metering area always remains the same (13%) the size varies between 13% and 23% of the bright-line frame—depending on where the lens is focused. If the lens is set to infinity, the diameter of the metering area is about two thirds of the short side of its bright-line frame. When the lens is focused at its minimum focusing distance, the metered area is approximately half of the short side of the frame. In practice, it is easiest to adhere to the two-thirds rule for "infinity" as a guide for the coverage of the metering area (see Fig. 54).

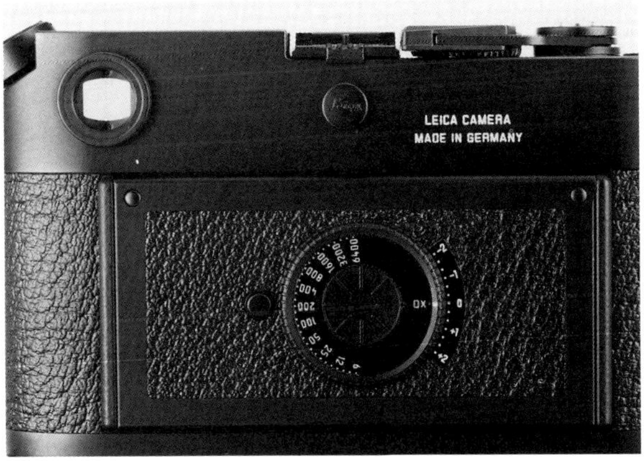

Fig. 52: *The ISO film speed is set manually using a dial on the back of the camera (starting with the Leica M6). The Leica M7 allows the choice of automatic ISO setting with DX coding or manual ISO setting using the dial on the back of the camera. This dial can also be used to for setting exposure compensation in aperture priority automatic.*

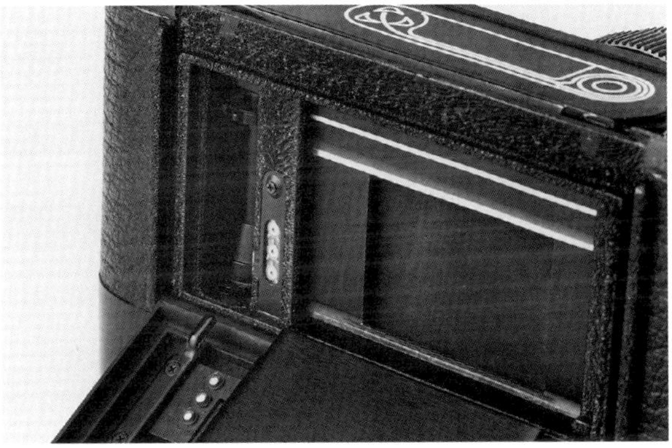

Fig. 53: *The contacts for reading the DX barcode on the film cassette are lo-cated on the back of the hinged rear cover of the Leica M6. Connections with the circuitry inside the camera are made with gold-plated contacts, which can be seen on the camera body housing and on the back cover when it is open. This system automatically sets the film's ISO based on the manufacturer's barcode.*

TTable 4: Film speed settings and viewfinder displays in the Leica M7

DX-coded film - cassette	Set film-speed	Exposure - compensation	Effective film speed	Display of the exposure meter	
				2 seconds after activation	Then for approx. 12 seconds
Yes	DX	No	The ISO/DX value	DX value	Exposure meter
		Yes	DX value +override	DX value blinks	Exposure meter below spot blinks
Yes	ISO same as DX value	No	Like ISO/DX value	DX/ISO value	Exposure meter
		Yes	ISO/DX value +override	DX/ISO value	Exposure meter lower spot blinks
Yes	ISO different than DX value	No	ISO value	DX value blinks	Exposure meter
		Yes	ISO value +override	DX value blinks [2]	Exposure meter lower dot blinks [2]
No	ISO	No	ISO value	ISO value	Exposure meter lower dot blinks
		Yes	ISO value +override	ISO value +override [3]	Exposure meter lower dot blinks
No	DX	No	ISO 100	"100" blinks	Exposure meter lower dot blinks
		Yes	ISO 100 +override	"100" blinks	Exposure meter lower dot blinks

[1] This applies also to DX-coded films for which the DX code cannot be read.

[2] Does not blink if ISO value + Override correspond to the DX value of the loaded film.

[3] Setting for high-speed film plus Override may result in a five-digit value, e.g., "12500." Because the four-digit viewfinder display is not able to represent this value, the "missing" fifth digit (always a "0") is indicated by the blinking fourth digit (also always a "0").

The shutter, the exposure meter, and the displays in the viewfinder of the Leica M7 are powered by two 3-volt lithium batteries, Type DL 1/3 N. With the exposure meter left on continuously, a set of fresh batteries lasts approximately eight hours. With a metering time of 10 seconds per exposure, the batteries are good for about 2,900 exposures, or approximately 80 rolls of 36-exposure film. In case of battery failure, exposure times of 1/60 and 1/250 second may be set manually. Of course, in this case, the exposure meter will not function. The blinking of LEDs in the viewfinder or the display of "bc" indicates that the batteries should be replaced as soon as possible. If the battery's voltage is very low or non-existent, the viewfinder LEDs will fail to light. The shutters in all other Leica M models, including the Leica M6 TTL and the Leica M6, work strictly mechanically. They do not require power. Only the exposure meters of these cameras and the viewfinder LEDs require power from two 1.55-volt silver oxide button batteries or one 3-

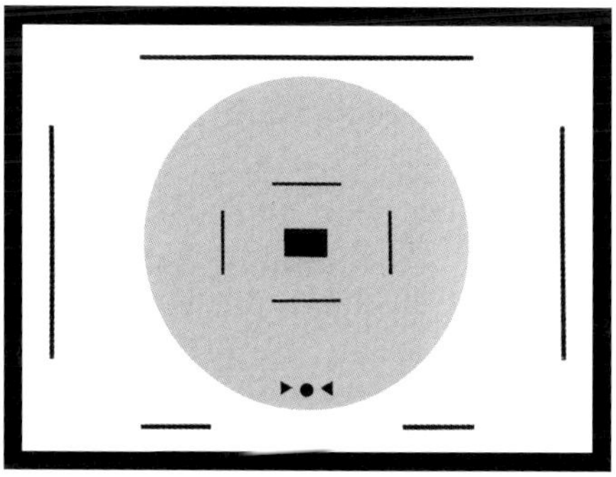

21mm

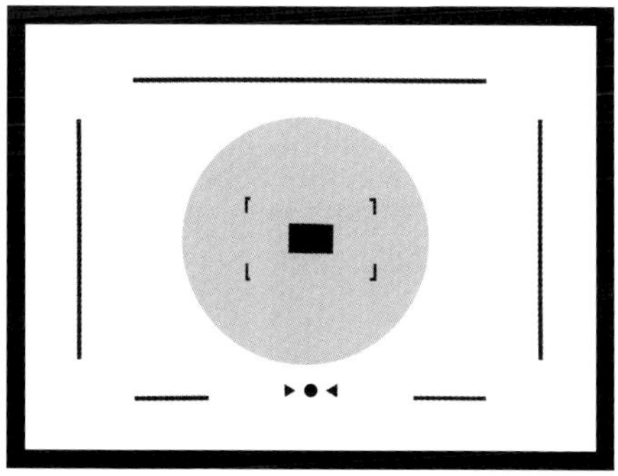

24mm

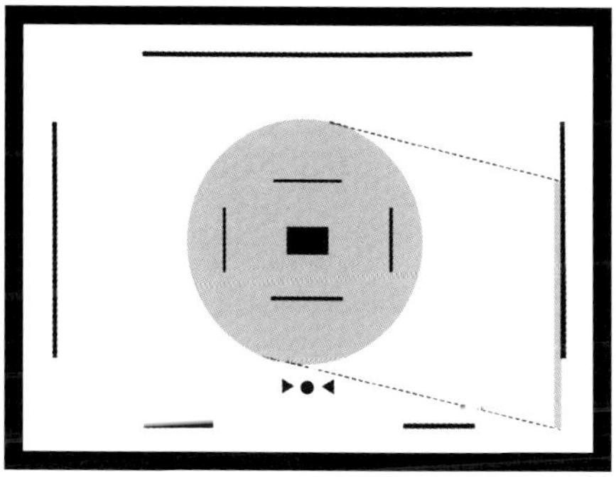

28mm

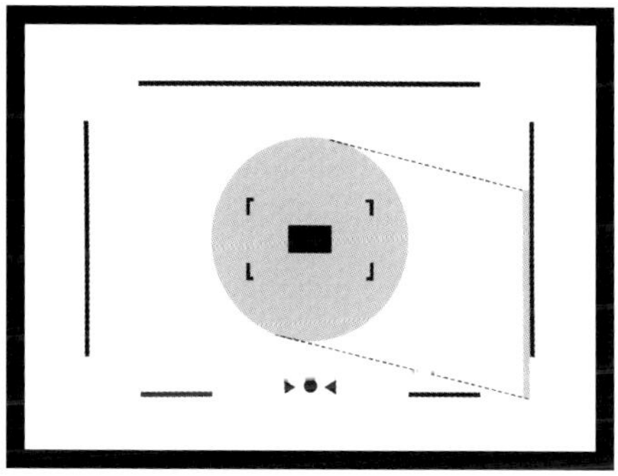

35mm

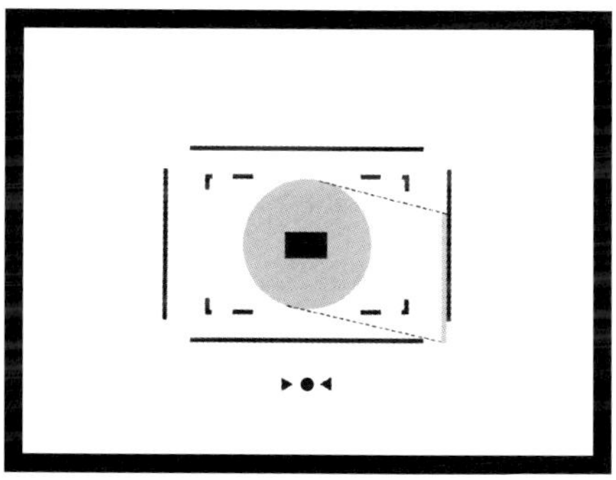

50mm

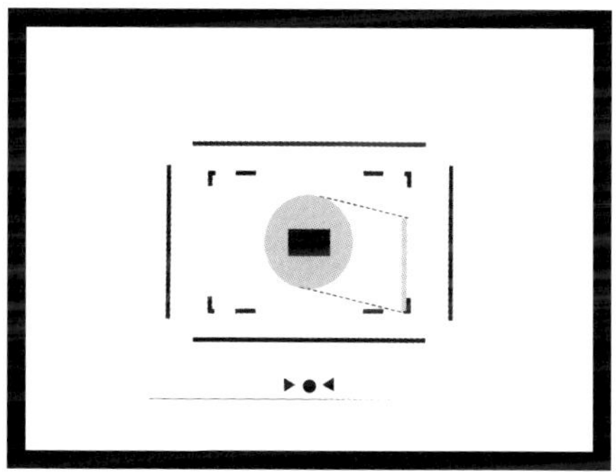

75mm

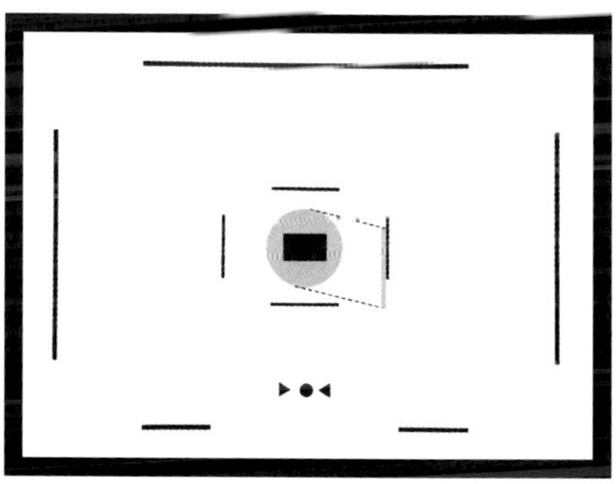

90mm and 135mm with adapter

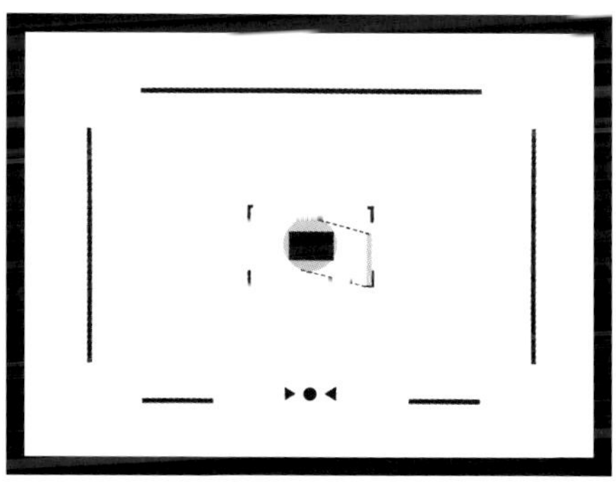

135mm

Fig. 54 a – h: This schematic representation compares the size of the diameter of the circular metering area (shaded in gray) to the height of each bright-line frame in the viewfinder of a Leica M6. Dotted lines are used to project that diameter to the right side of the frame that corresponds to each focal length. However, the round metering area is always in the center of the viewfinder. With a lens set at infinity, the respective diameter corresponds to approximately two thirds of the height of the corresponding bright-line frame. The diameter of this spot decreases in relation to its respective bright-line frame as the lens is focused on closer subjects, until it amounts to only about half the height of that frame when the lens is set at its minimum focusing distance.

Table 5: Comparison of TTL exposure meters

	LEICA M7	LEICA M6 TTL	LEICA M6	LEICA M5
Battery (quantity)	Lithium (2), 3 V each	Silver oxide (2), or 1.55V oder Lithium (1), 3V	Silver oxide (2), or 1.55V oder Lithium (1), 3V	Mercury oxide (1), 1.35V
Metering cell	Silicon photodiode	Silicon photodiode	Silicon photodiode	Cadmium sulfide photoresistor
Metering area diameter	12 mm	12 mm	12 mm	8.5 mm
Metering range cd/m^2	0.03 to 125000	0.03 to 125000	0.06 to 125000	0.03 to 125000
Exposure value (EV)	−2 to 20	−2 to 20	−1 to 20	−2 to 20
Film speed	ISO 6 to 6400	ISO 6 to 6400	ISO 6 to 6400	ISO 6 to 3200
Shutter speed Manual	4 sec. to 1/1000 sec., B	1 sec. to 1/1000 sec., B	1 sec. to 1/1000 sec., B	1/2 sec. to 1/1000 sec., B
Automatic	32 sec. to 1/1000 sec.,	–	–	–
Aperture	1 to 32	1 to 32	1 to 32	1,4 to 32

volt lithium battery. Due to the different numbers of LEDs (four in the Leica M6 TTL, two in the Leica M6) energy consumption varies. With the exposure meter of the Leica M6 TTL left on continuously, a set of fresh batteries lasts approximately eight hours. With an estimated meter use of 10 seconds per exposure, it is good for about 2,900 exposures, or approximately 80 rolls of 36-exposure film. The batteries in the Leica M6 will power the exposure meter continuously for approximately 20 hours or, figuring about 15 seconds per exposure, for approximately 4,800 exposures, or 130 rolls of 36-exposure film. Pulsing LEDs in the Leica M5 TTL or a significantly weaker illumination of the Leica M6 light balance LEDs indicate that the batteries should be replaced promptly. If the battery's minimum voltage is very low or non-existent, the viewfinder LEDs will not light.

Fig. B1: *Extremely fast lenses and high-speed films extend day into night for photography. This idyllic travel scene was taken at dusk. 50mm f/1 Noctilux-M lens, 1/125 second, f/1.4, daylight reversal film ISO 800.*

Fig. B2: *Finnish Laplanders call this time of year Kamos—when the sun no longer rises above the horizon and only illuminates mountaintops. 50mm f/2.8 Elmar-M lens, 1/30 second, f/4, daylight reversal film ISO 64.*

Fig. B3: *If no tripod is available, a house wall or, in this case, a post, can be used to support the camera. 50mm f/1.4 Summilux-M lens, 1/2 second, f/1.4, daylight reversal film ISO 64.*

Fig. B4: *The light from a window display was adequate to show the clown in action. 50mm f/1.4 Summilux-M lens, 1/15 second, f/1.4, color-negative film ISO 400.*

Fig. B5: *For exact alignment of the camera and due to the relatively long exposure time, a tripod was used for this shot. 50mm f/2 Summicron-M lens, 1/4 second, F 4 – 5.6, color-negative film ISO 100.*

Fig. B6: *With a little bit of practice even long exposure times of 1/15 or 1/8 sec. may produce good results when handheld. And even the light of a few candles can be adequate in atmospheric shots such as this. 50mm f/1 Noctilux-M lens, 1/8 second, f/1, tungsten color reversal film ISO 160.*

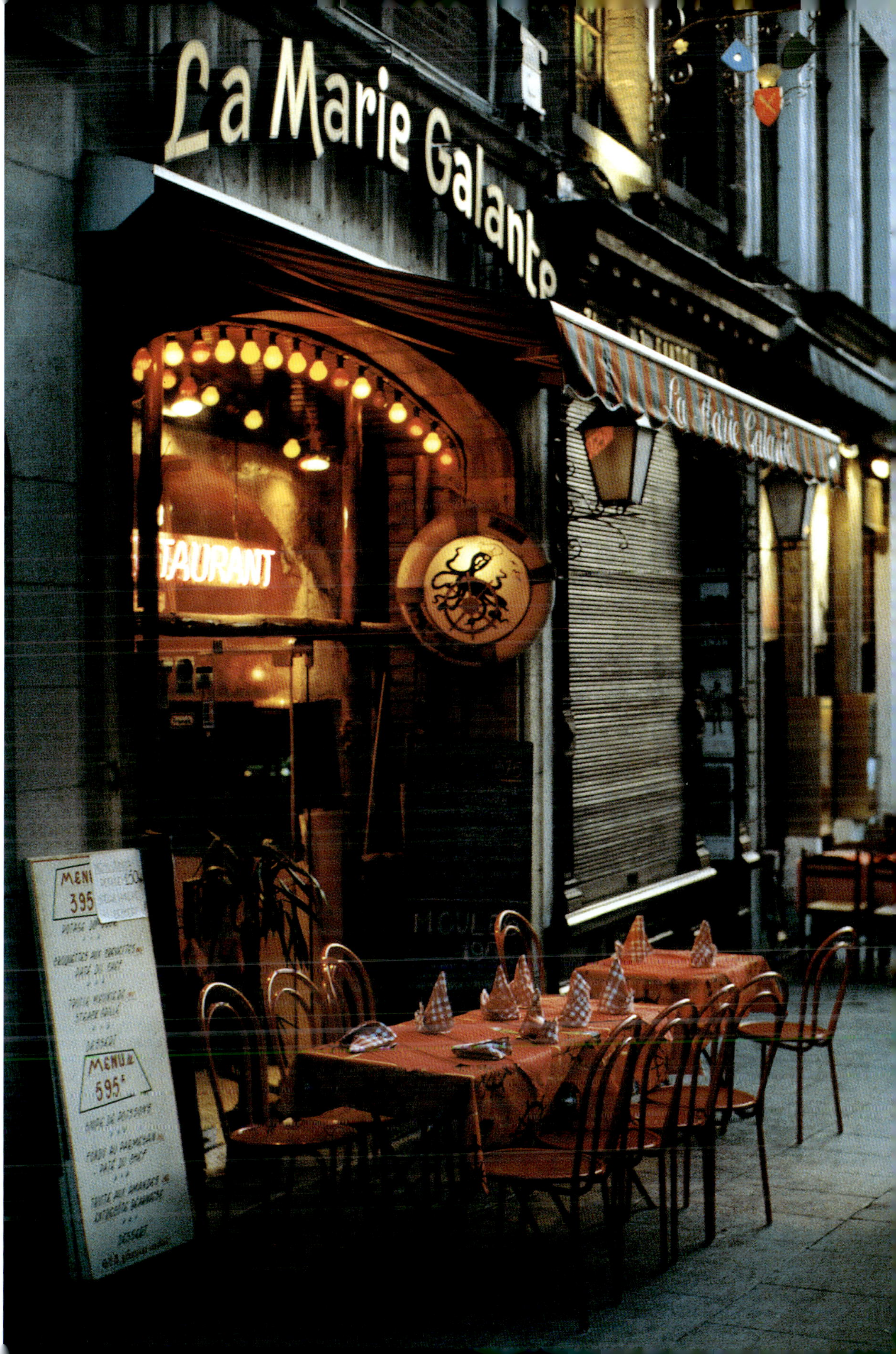

Fig. B1

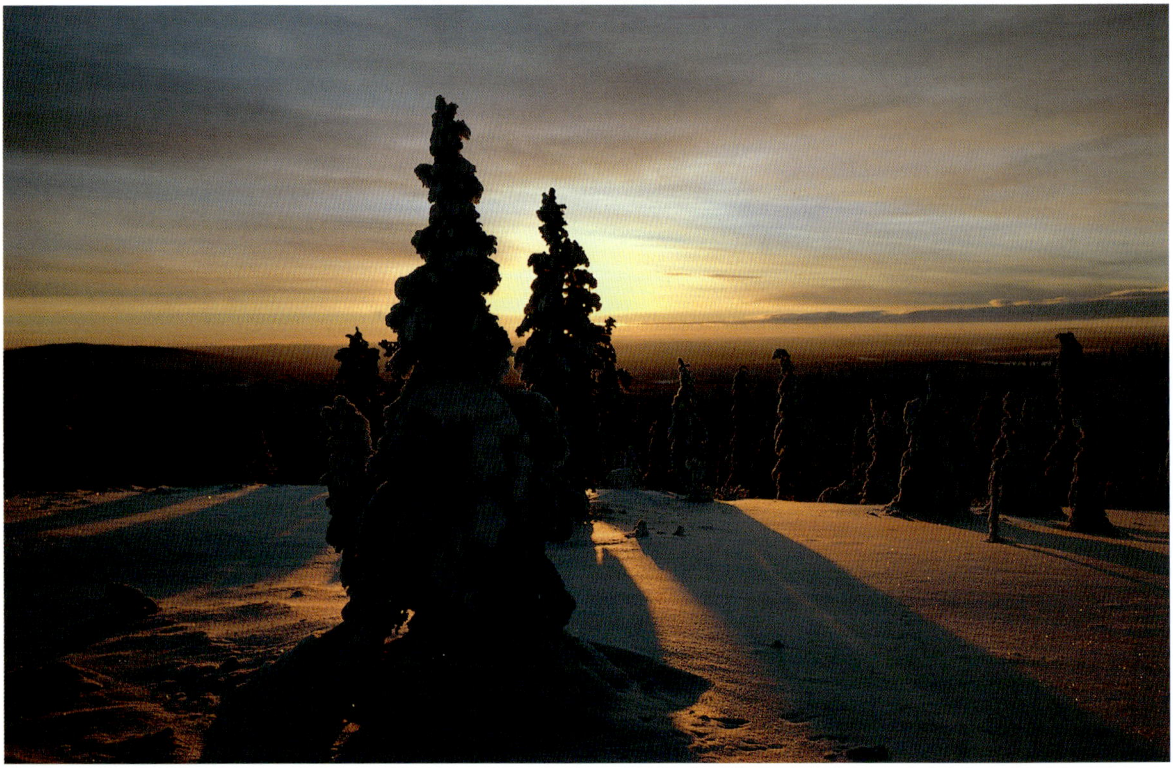

Fig. B2

Fig. B3

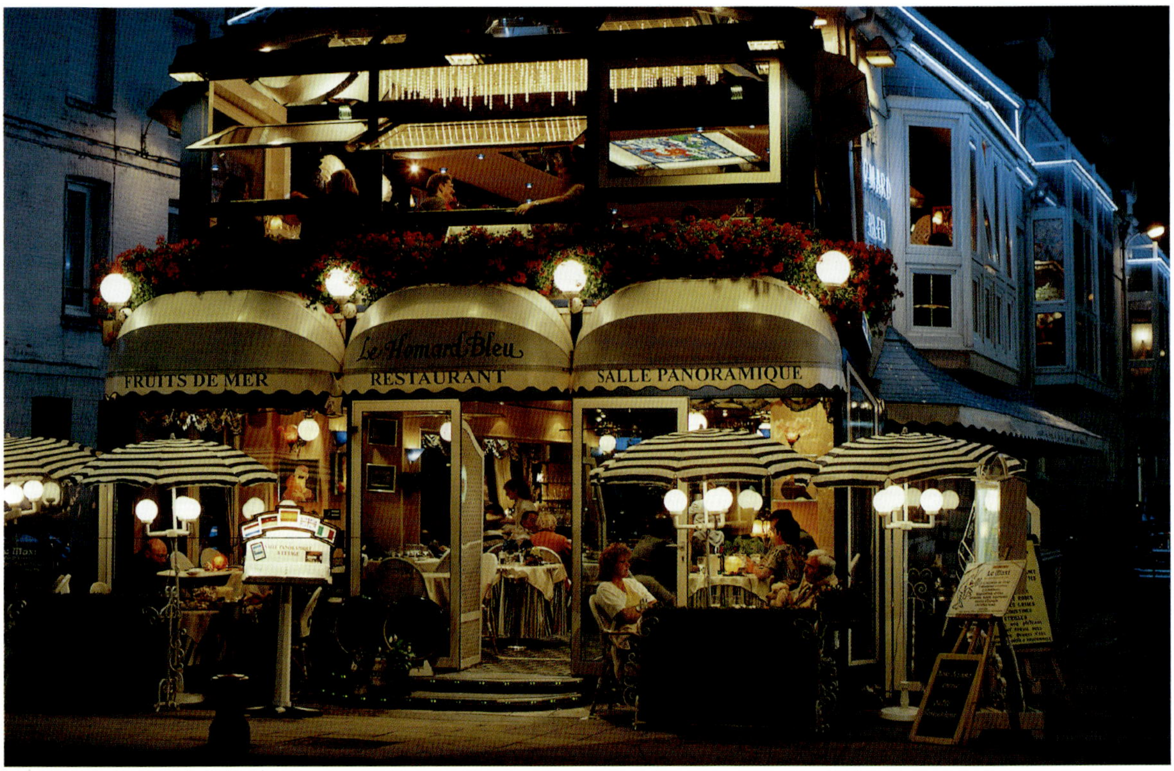

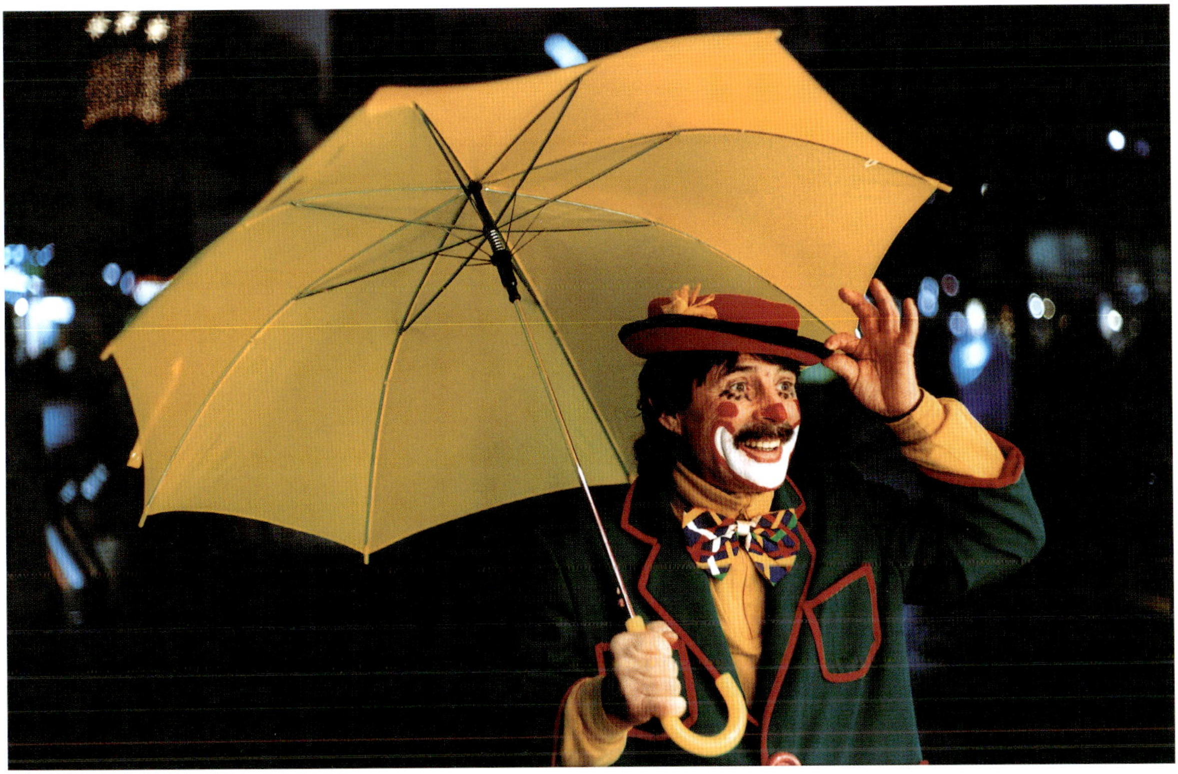

Fig. B4

Fig. B5

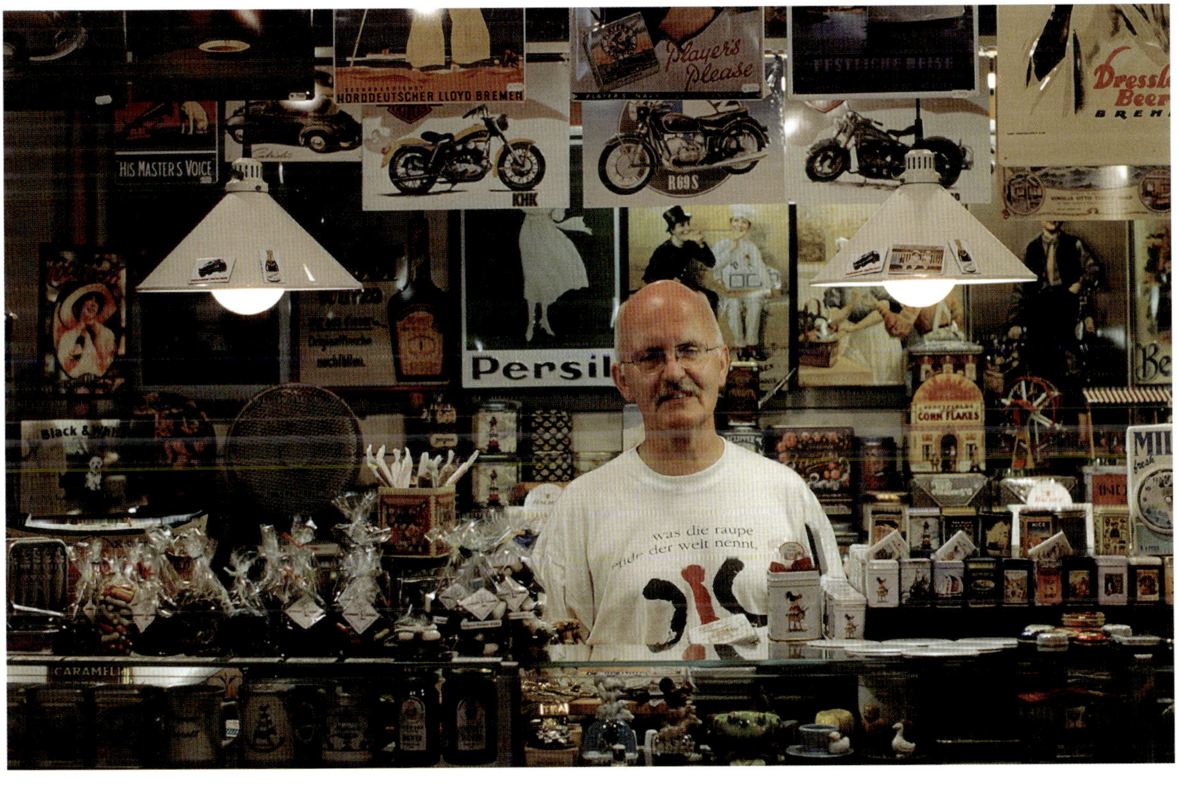
NORDDEUTSCHER LLOYD BREMEN
Player's Please
HIS MASTER'S VOICE
R69S
KHK
Persil
CORN FLAKES
was die raupe

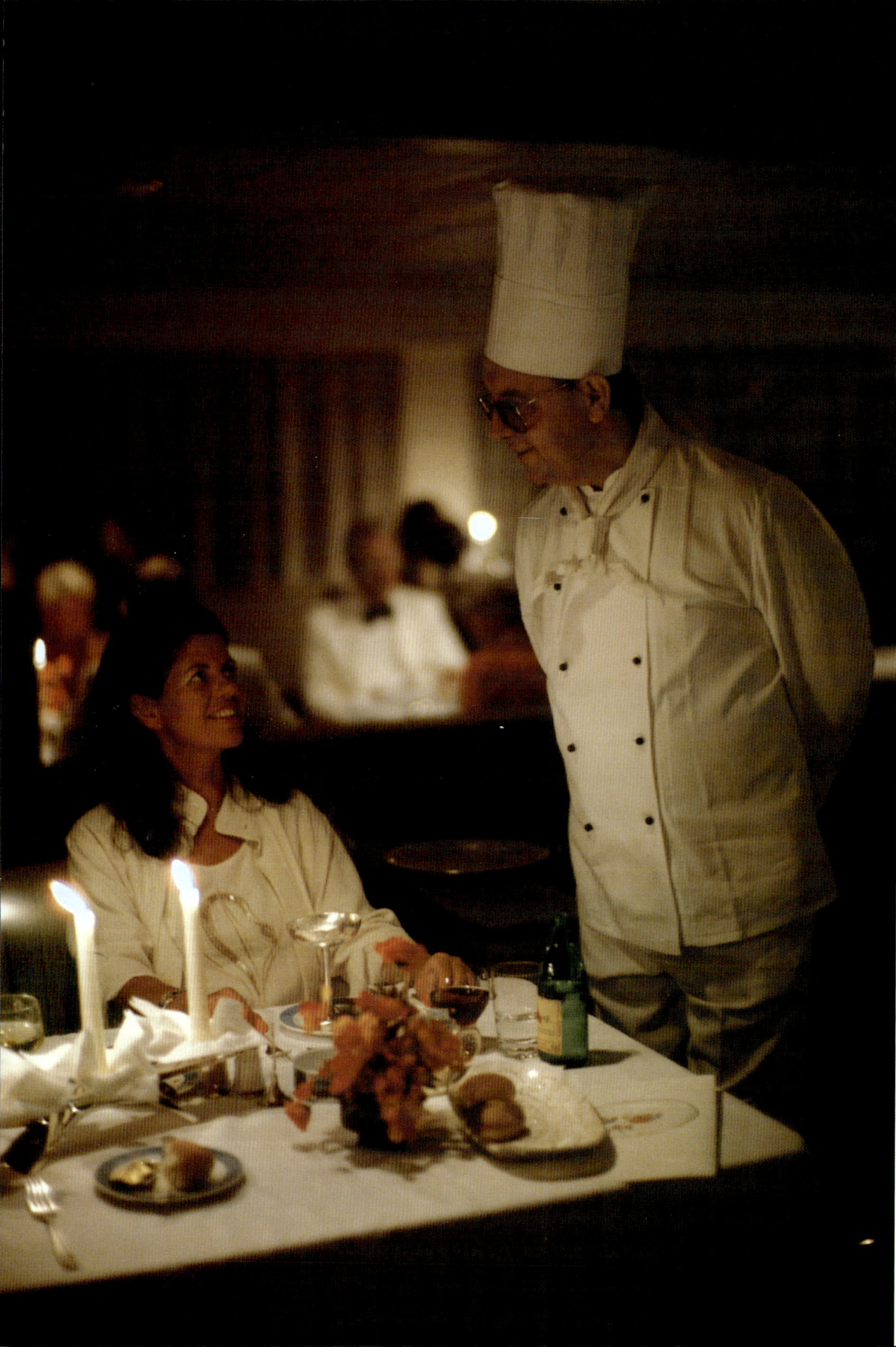

Fig. B6

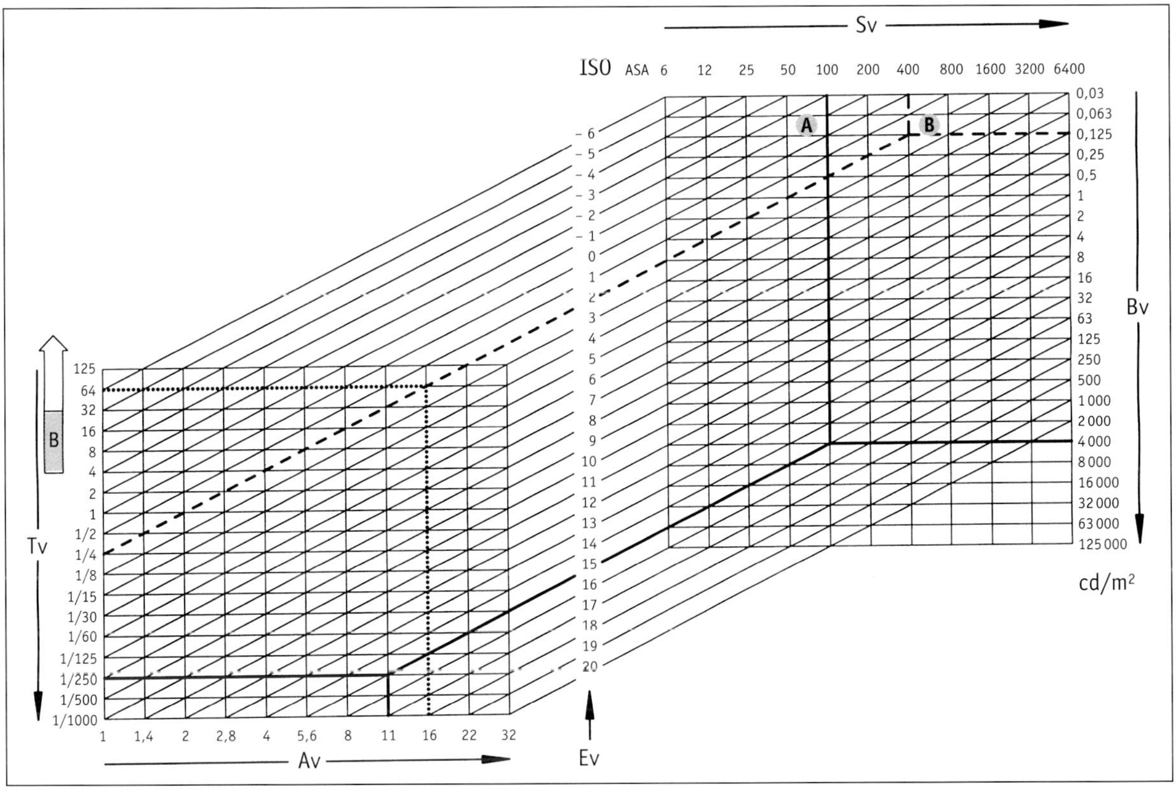

***Fig. 55:** Leica M7 metering diagram*

Values for the range of the exposure meter are indicated on the right side of the diagram; the shutter speed and aperture are shown on the left side. In between, the exposure values (Ev) can be read.

The brightness value (Bv) read by the exposure meter is shown in cd/m2 (candle power per square meter) on the right side of the diagram. Above that, the film speeds (Sv) are indicated as ISO values.

On the left side of the diagram shutter speeds appear in seconds, i.e., time values (Tv). With a "B" setting, the range is open upward. This setting is required for exposure times exceeding 4 seconds in manual exposure, or for exposure times greater than 32 seconds in aperture-priority automatic.

Using "A" as an example, the interrelationship between film speed, brightness, shutter speed, and aperture can be determined. Starting with the film speed (ISO 100), a vertical line can be followed to the point of intersection with the horizontal line corresponding to the appropriate brightness. In this example, this is 4000 cd/m2, which corresponds to the brightness generated by bright sunlight. A diagonal line leads to the perpendicular line of the aperture setting (11) and, from there, horizontally to the left to the required shutter speed (1/250 second). Along the diagonal line the exposure value (15 EV) can be determined.

Using "B" as an example, it is obvious that with the light of a candle (0.125 cd/m2) and a film speed of ISO 400, an aperture of f/1 and 1/4 second must be used for exposure. For example, if the lens is to be used at f/16, the corresponding shutter speed can neither be measured directly nor is it available on the shutter speed dial. If, in this case, a meter reading is taken with the lens fully open, the diagram can be used to determine the correct exposure time of 64 seconds, and the "B" setting on the shutter-speed dial can be used.

Metering with large apertures

Compared to an exposure meter with a galvanometer and a mechanical pointer, the LED "light balance" system is virtually shock and vibration-proof. This property is particularly important for a camera with a built-in exposure meter since, if the camera's meter malfunctions, the entire camera must be sent away for service.

However, unlike the manual setting of shutter speed and aperture, which occurs in click stops, using the light balance system has an effect, which initially, appears inexplicable to the user: The various equivalent shutter speed/aperture combinations associated with a given brightness and film speed do not necessarily generate the same display in every case.

In other words, there is a peculiar effect in connection with the manual settings of shutter speeds and lens apertures, which are made in distinct steps in accordance with the click stops, that initially puzzles even an expert. It is the fact that the various shutter speed/aperture combinations that correspond to a given lighting situation and film speed do not produce the same LED response in all cases.

With the Leica M7 and M6 TTL, theoretically, only the round LED of the "light balance" display in the viewfinder should light up for the combinations of 1/60 second at f/5.6, 1/125 second at f/4, 1/250 second at f/2.8, 1/500 second at f/2 etc. This was exactly the case when the combination was 1/30 second at f/8 or 1/15 second at f/11. However, if the lens is set to its largest aperture, only the left, triangular, LED usually lights up. In this situation, the automatic exposure control of the Leica M7 will also indicate a longer exposure time than expected.

The Leica M6 also produces this effect with its two triangular LEDs. If the correct exposure is set with the lens stopped-down, both LEDs will light up with equal brightness. However, when the appropriate shutter speed/aperture combination is set with the lens wide open only the right LED is faintly visible, or not visible at all. What might be the reason for this phenomenon?

Every normal photographic lens vignettes a little or a lot, depending on the type of lens. Vignetting is usually greater with the lens wide open than it is with the lens stopped down. As an example, if a 50mm f/1 Noctilux-M lens is used under lighting conditions that are just a little darker than required for an exact exposure with standard shutter speed/aperture combinations, the two LEDs of the "light balance" displayed in the viewfinder will indicate a correct exposure compensation at 1/125 second exposure time and f/1.4, even though the slightly lower lighting conditions, when interpreted strictly, require 1/113 sec. at f/1.34. But there are no click stop settings for this precise shutter speed and this precise aperture stop, and they would not have a noticeable effect on the results anyway, because the exposure latitude of the film would readily accommodate these small differences without any difficulty.

The following shutter speed/aperture combination could thus be chosen in our example: 1/30 second at f/2.8, 1/60 second at f/2, 1/125 second at f/1.4, or 1/250 second at f/1. Considering all of these combinations, the "light balance" should indicate correct exposure. In reality, however, when the combination is changed from 1/125 second at f/1.4 to 1/250 second at f/1 (the largest aperture), this is no longer the case. Even though the geometric aperture of the lens, i.e., the f/stop value engraved on the front of the lens, is also valid for its maximum aperture (f/1), the equivalent maximum photometric or sensitometric aperture value cannot be achieved because of vignetting and light absorption in the optical system. In these situations, this will lead to the displays or suggested changes of exposure speed generated by the automatic exposure control.
If a photograph is taken with such a setting, the

result will show an under-exposure of about 1/2 f/stop.

For the same reason, no distinct difference in the LED display will be visible when a lens is stopped down from its maximum aperture by half a stop. The results of the actual exposures show the same effect: densities will be practically the same in spite of exposures at different apertures.

Note: With single lens reflex cameras (SLRs) metered at full aperture, these effects are largely compensated by cams or the camera's microprocessor. Therefore, you will rarely see evidence of this phenomenon in the viewfinder display.

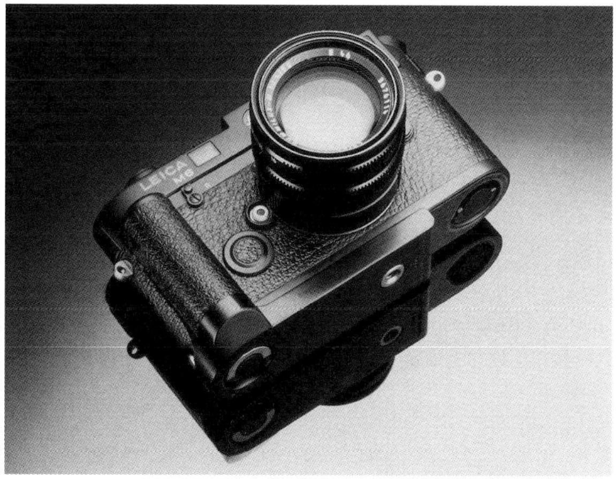

Fig. 56: Handgrip M

Displays at low light levels

If insufficient light strikes the meter's Si photodiode, the light will be too low to measure. In this case, the left LED in the viewfinder will blink. Because exposure measurement in the Leica M may occur with the working f/stop of the lens, the measuring range may be below range if there is insufficient light when the lens is stepped down.

The exposure meter remains switched on, once the finger is taken off the release, for approximately 14 seconds, even if light levels are below the meter's range. Should the light situation improve during this time, the LED display will stop blinking and light constantly.

Housing accessories

Although the Leica M was designed so that every photographic task could be accomplished without requiring additional accessories, a few practical aids expand the camera's use and/or make certain applications easier.

Handgrip M

Handgrip M improves the ability to hold the camera securely—especially with one hand. A hinged locking screw is used to attach the Handgrip to the base plate of the Leica M. The underside of the mounting rail has a screw mount for a standard 1/4-inch tripod socket so that the Handgrip need not be removed with tripod use.

For older Leica M models having a 3/8 inch tripod socket, photo dealers offer bushings that reduce the thread size to 1/4 inch. By using the busing, the Handgrip M can also be mounted to these models, with one exception—it cannot be mounted to the Leica M5.

With the Handgrip mounted, lenses with fixed viewfinder attachment such as, e.g., the 135mm f/2.8 Elmarit-M lens or the 35mm wide-angle lenses for the Leica M3, cannot be changed. However, the 50mm f/2 Summicron lens with a close-up attachment can be used without restriction.

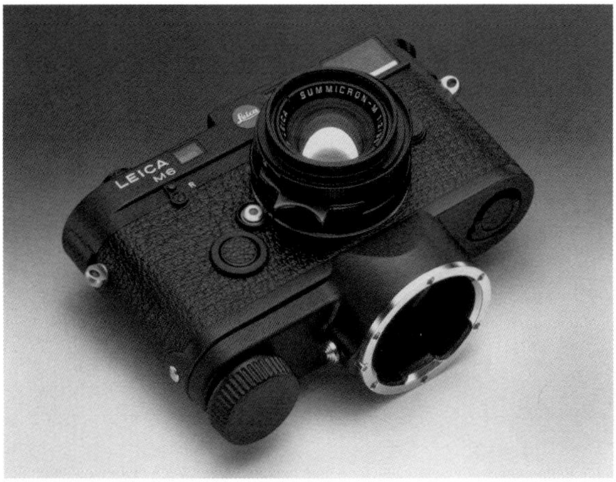

Fig. 57: The Lens Carrier M

Lens Carrier M

Lens Carrier M offers the option of carrying one Leica M body with two lenses on one carrying strap. The Carrier M is screwed into the camera's tripod socket. A second lens is then mounted to the Carrier's bayonet mount. Rapid film loading (in the case of Leica M cameras the base plate must be removed) is in no way impaired. If a lens with long focal length is mounted in the bayonet of Lens Carrier M, a "handgrip" is created. This, together with the weight of the lens, ensures that even longer exposure times may be handheld with satisfactory results. It is even possible to use the Lens Carrier M with the mounted lens acting like a small tripod on a suitable surface.

Lens Carrier M can be used with all Leica M models. However, a bushing must be used to attach it to cameras with a 3/8" tripod socket. The Carrier cannot be used with a winder or motor. In order to avoid damage resulting from vibrations or shock, it is recommended that lenses with viewfinder attachments not be carried in this manner.

Rapid winders and motor drives

To be able to shoot again, immediately after taking a picture, has always been a 35mm photographer's wish. Because of this, from early on, the Leica M system has included accessories for quickly advancing the film and winding the shutter.

Winders and motor drives are mounted to the camera in place of the usual base plate. Like the base plate, they must be removed when loading the camera.

Internal couplings for film advance, shutter cocking, shutter release, and for locking the camera are not identical on all M models. Therefore, different models work with rapid winders or motorized drives. A few cameras are compatible with limitations or not at all (Table 6).

Leicavit and Leicavit MP

The Leicavit or Leicavit MP rapid winders attach to the bottom of the camera body in place of its normal baseplate. To wind the camera, the hinged advance lever swings downward and is pulled along the baseplate as far as it will go. The shutter can be released only after the winder's spring has been allowed to snap back to its starting position. Experts can easily achieve two exposures per second (2 fps) with this winder, and the camera can be kept at eye level while in use. The Leicavit fits Leica models M1, M2, and MD. The Leicavit MP is designed to work with the Leica MP and MP 2 models.

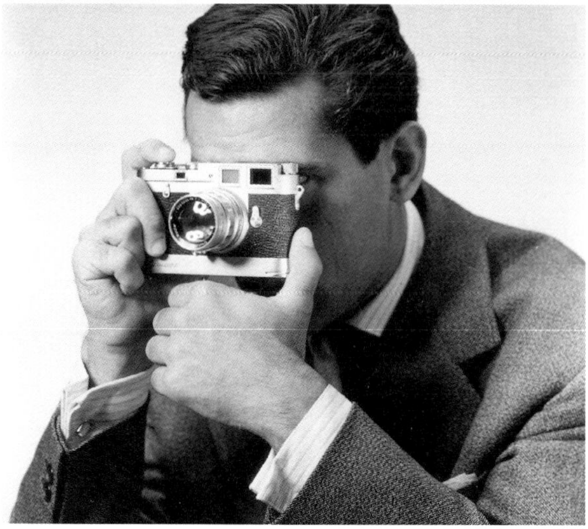

Fig. 58: *The Leica MP (P = Professional) is a special version of the Leica M3, which is equipped with the film advance and shutter-winding mechanism of the Leica M2. It accepts the Leicavit MP rapid winder.*

Leica Motor M

A motor drive is a faster and more convenient means of advancing the film and winding the shutter. Since a small amount of camera movement always occurs when the Leicavit is operated, the Motor M has the additional advantage of allowing the camera to remain perfectly steady during a fast sequence of exposures.

The Leica Motor Drive M, introduced at Photokina 2000, is an extremely small drive that is perfectly adapted to the design of the Leica M. It is convenient and comfortable to use when mounted on the camera. The Motor M has a base height of only 18.3 mm (3/4 inch)! It operates at two speeds: either 3 frames per second (fps) or 1.5 fps. The friction wheel drive allows the Leica Motor M to run very quietly, especially at the lower speed. As usual, triggering occurs via the camera's shutter release, which should be continually depressed if a series of exposures is desired. Tapered threads for standard cable releases permit remote shutter release. All shutter speeds including "B" can be used. Finally, film can be advanced and the shutter cocked manually using the camera's rapid advance lever even when the Motor M is attached.

The Motor M fits the Leica M7, M6 TTL, M6, M4-P, M4-2, and MD-2. When mounted, as in the case of the Handgrip M, the Leica Motor's grip prevents the changing of lenses that feature a fixed viewfinder attachment.

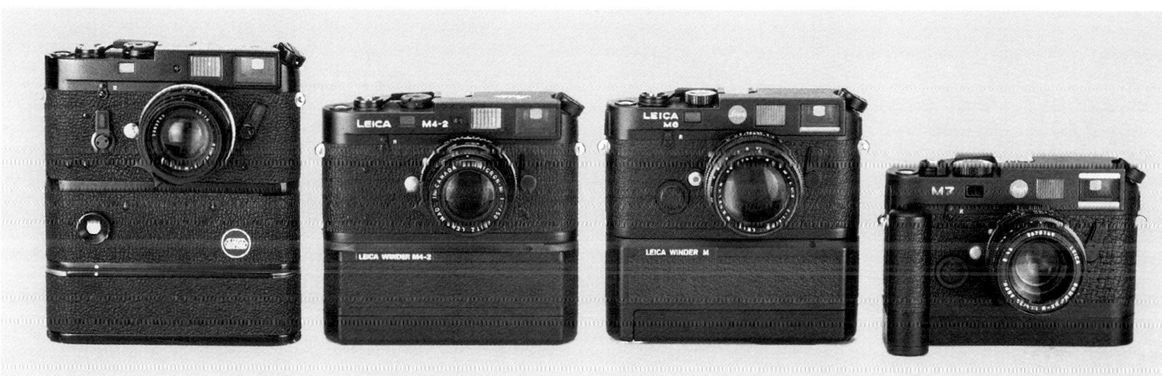

Fig. 59: *Motorized drives for the Leica M in chronological order of development. The Leica M2-Mot with the Leica Motor (1962), manufactured in the USA, is shown on the extreme left. Next to it is the Leica M4-2 with the Winder M4-2 (1976) and the Leica M6 with the Winder M (1987). The current Leica Motor M is shown on the extreme right on the Leica M7.*

Table 6: Motor Drive Compatibility

	LEICA M7	LEICA M6 TTL	LEICA M6	LEICA M4-P	LEICA M4-2	LEICA MD-2
Leica Motor M	yes	yes	yes	yes	yes	yes
Leica Winder M	yes [1)]	yes [2)]	yes	yes	yes	yes
Leica Winder M4-P	no	yes [2)]	yes	yes	yes	yes
Leica Winder M4-2, as of # 10 350	no	no	Yes	yes	yes	yes
Leica Winder M4-2, up to # 10 349	no	no	no	yes [3)]	yes	yes

1) Can be attached only if the Winder M has a flat locking plate. Leica Customer Service can easily rebuild earlier Winder M models.
2) Can be attached only to early Leica M6 TTL models. With current Leica M6 TTL models, the winder must be equipped with a flat locking plate by Leica Customer Service.
3) With the exception of cameras with serial numbers 1 552 500 - 1 552 500 884 and 1 563 000 - 1 588 536.

Body: Chassis of stainless steel clad in fiberglass-reinforced polycarbonate. The integrated ergonomic handle is made of aluminum and coated with textured PVC. The top cover of the motor housing consists of black chrome-plated brass. A 1/4 inch tripod socket is provided on the base, centered under the lens axis.

Power supply: Two 3-volt lithium batteries, Type 123A, are set in the handgrip; at 20°C (68°F) their capacity is at least 100 rolls of 36-exposure film.

Dimensions: Height to the bottom edge of camera, 18.5 mm (3/4 inch); height to top of grip, 138 mm (5.43 inches); depth, 56 mm (2.23 inches) including handle.

Weight without batteries: 225 g (7.94 ounces).

Leica Winder M

This compact, convenient winder, fits Leicas M7, M6 TTL, PM6, M4-P, M4-2 and MD-2. Single exposures with one depression of the shutter release and series exposures with normal continual pressure on the shutter release button are possible. All shutter speeds from 1/1000 to 1 second and "B" can be used. The winder can drive up to

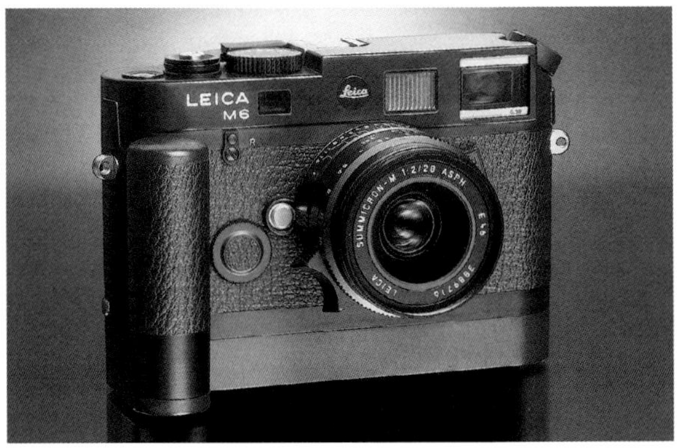

Fig. 60: The Leica Motor M

three exposures per second with exceedingly quiet operation of the gear train and motor.

Body: Sturdy, fiberglass-reinforced molded housing with covered with textured PVC for a comfortable grip. Driven by a DC micromotor with an ironless rotor, the winder is controlled mechanically by the camera. The battery housing is attached to the base of the camera. The tripod socket is 1/4 inch.

Power supply: Four 1.5-volt alkaline AA batteries fitted into the battery holder. Under Leica's testing conditions, a set of batteries lasts for about 150 rolls of 36-exposure film at 20 °C (68°F). Four rechargeable AA batteries can also be used.

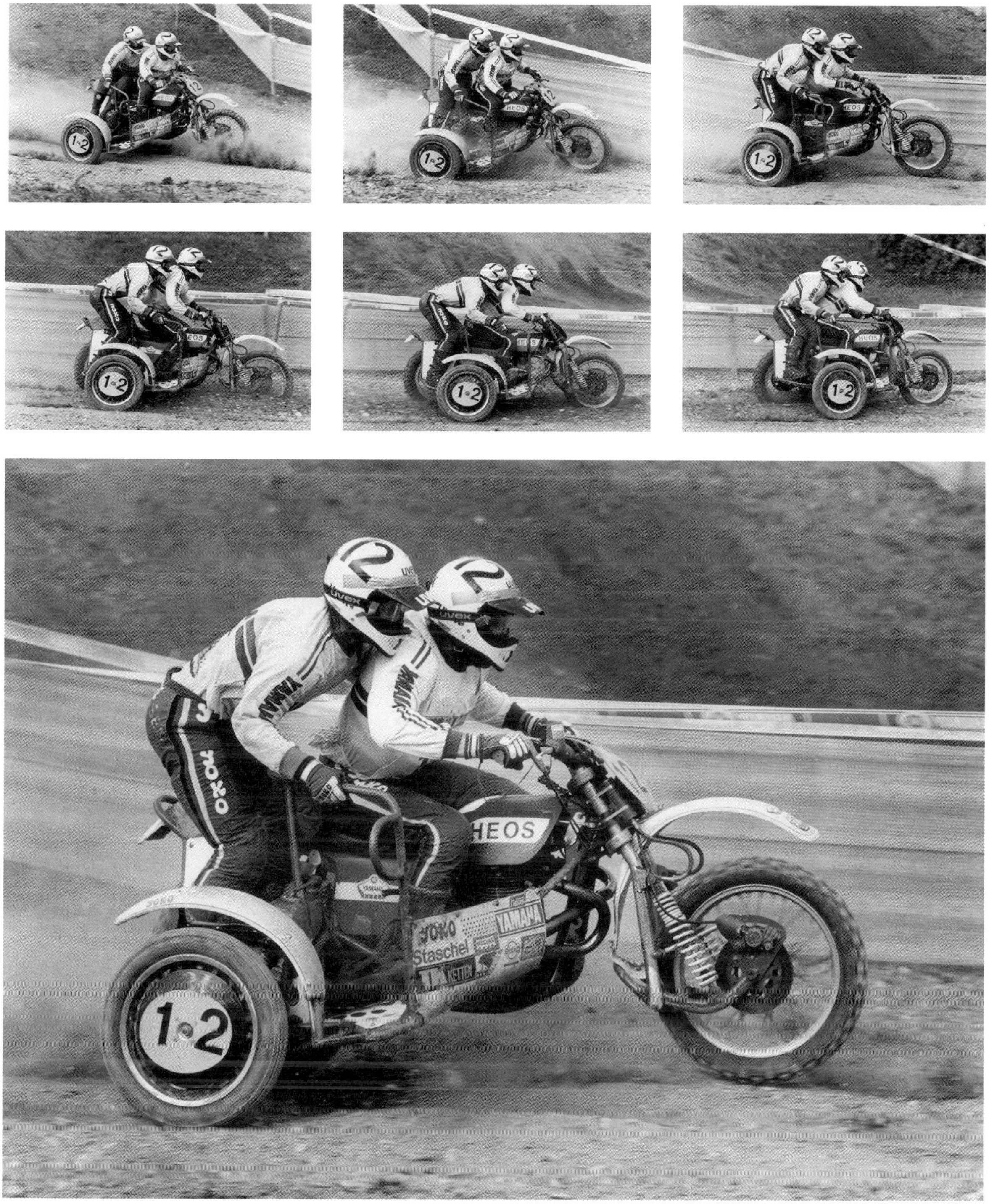

Fig. 61 a – g: *With a motor drive the Leica M is always ready to shoot. Operating at 3 frames per second, the Leica Motor M is not only a faster means of advancing the film, but it also allows the photographer to concentrate on the action and capture sequences such as this.*

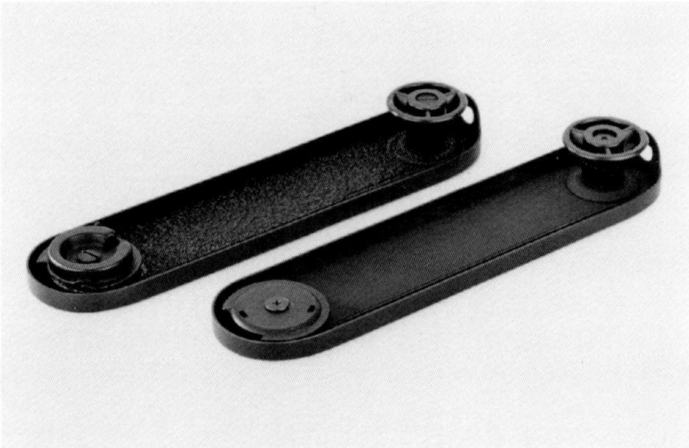

Fig. 62: The locking plates on the camera base plate and on the Leica Winder M were redesigned during the manufacture of the Leica M6 TTL and the Leica Winder M. The new, flatter design does not show the opening mechanism of earlier Leica film cassettes. If an earlier Winder M is to be attached to the Leica M7 or the current M6 TTL, it must first be equipped with the flat locking plate by Leica's technical service.

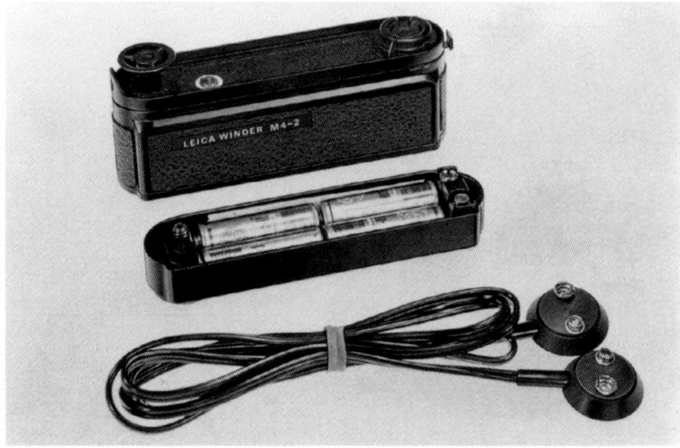

Fig. 63: In cold weather, it may be desirable to detach the battery housing from the Leica Winder M4-2 in order to keep it in a warm pocket. Its electrical connection to the winder can be maintained by using a separate cable that is supplied with the Leica Winder M4-2 for this purpose.

Dimensions: Height to the bottom edge of the camera 60 mm (2-3/8"), length 138 mm (5-7/16"), thickness 35mm (1-3/8").

Weight without batteries: 330 grams (just over 11-1/2 ounces).

Leica Winder M4-2 and M4-P

The appearance of the Leica M4-2 (1977) was soon followed by the introduction of a newly designed motor drive—the Leica Winder M4-2. Its successor models Leica Winder M4-P and Leica Winder M are very similar in design and operation.

Leica Motor

When using the Leica Motor with the Leica M2-Mot and the Leica M4-Mot cameras, single and continuous exposures can be taken with automatic film advance and shutter winding. For a continuous series, the Motor offers a choice of setting "L" (low speed) for 1 frame per second and the setting "H" (high speed) for three frames per second is possible. All shutter speed from 1 to 1/1000 second can be set.

The electric motor is operated by eight 1.5-volt AA batteries which are located in a battery housing under the motor. A set of batteries usually lasts for around 40 rolls of film.

Adaptations and modifications of Leica M housings

Since the early 1930s, Leitz has offered the option of having older camera models updated by the factory with the latest features of successor models. This re-engineering allowed the photographer to take advantage of continued developments of the Leica system and to benefit from technological and design advances. Today, Leica M models can be adapted and modified through Leica's customer service of Leica Camera AG; however, because the engineering of different camera models has become significantly more complex, there are certain technical and cost-effective limitations.

Table 7: Re-engineering and modification options offered for Leica M cameras

Camera	Modifications	Camera	Modifications
Leica M 1	• Rebuild to Leica M2 • Install standard flash socket	Leica M4-P	• Set up for adaptation to Reprovit IIa
Leica MD	• Rebuild to Leica M2 • Install standard flash socket	Leica M1 to M4 Models	• Make low-temperature resistant (temperatures below -20°C)
Leica M2	• Install viewfinder with six bright-line frames (starting with No. 1.053.312) • Install self timer • Install standard flash socket (as in Leica M4)	Leica M5	• Install viewfinder with six bright-line frames • Make low-temperature resistant (temperatures below -20°C)
Leica M3	• Covert to single-wind shutter and film advance • Install standard flash socket (as in Leica M4) • Install frame selector	Leica M6	• Modify viewfinder magnification from 0.72 X to 0.85 X • Modify viewfinder magnification from 0.85 X to 0.72 X • Install edge protector on top plate • Make low-temperature resistant (temperatures below -20°C) • Set up for adaptation to Reprovit IIc
Leica MDa	• Convert to Leica M4 • Install Leica M5 take-up spool (rapid film loading system)	Leica M6 TTL	• Modify viewfinder magnification from 0.72 X to 0.85 X • Modify viewfinder magnification from 0.85 X to 0.72 X or 0.58 X • Modify viewfinder magnification from 0.58 X to 0.72 X or 0.85 X • Make low-temperature resistant (temperatures below -20°C) • Set up for adaptation to Reprovit IIa
Leica M4	• Install viewfinder with six bright-line frames, install Leica M5 take-up spool (rapid film loading system) • Set up for adaptation to Reprovit IIa	Leica M7	• Modify viewfinder magnification from 0.72 X to 0.85 X or 0.58 X • Modify viewfinder magnification from 0.85 X to 0.72 X or 0.58 X • Modify viewfinder magnification from 0.58 X to 0.72 X or 0.85 X • Set up for adaptation to Reprovit IIa
Leica M4-2	• Install viewfinder with six bright-line frames, install Leica M5 take-up spool (rapid film reloading system) • Set up for adaptation to Reprovit IIa		

Table 7 (above) describes existing options.
Contact your Leica dealer for additional details.

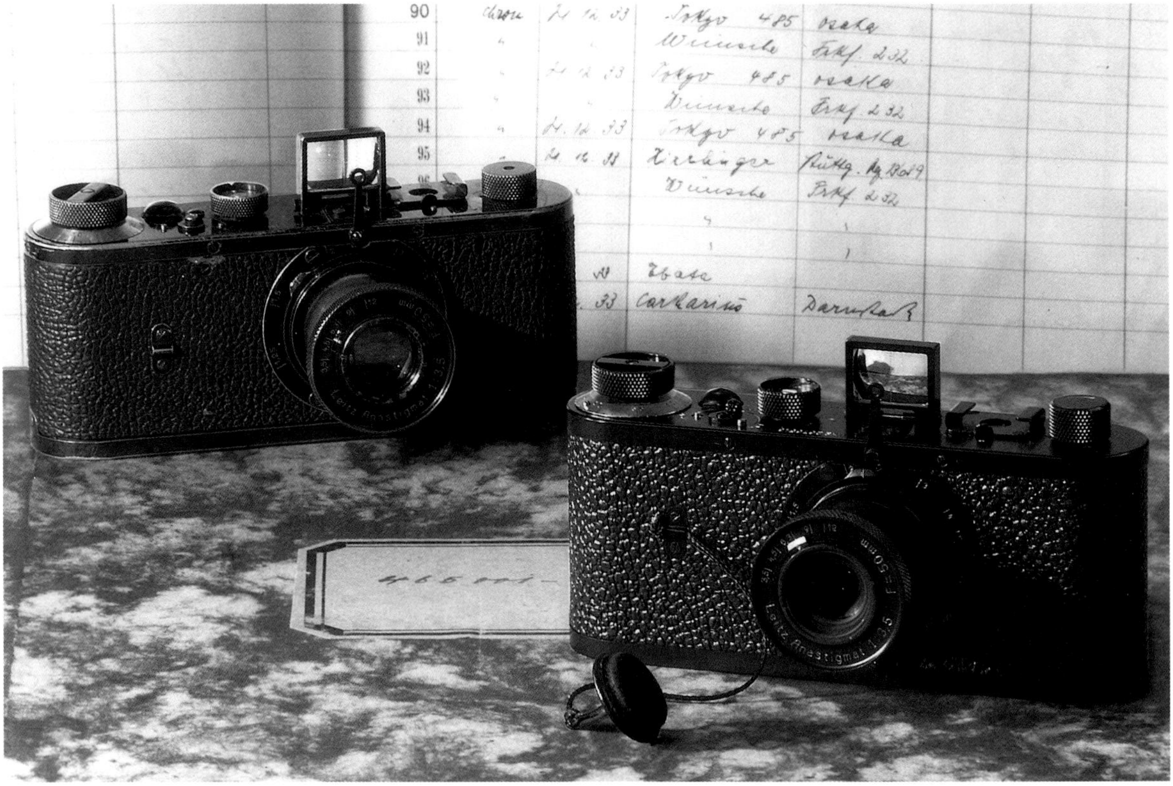

Fig. 64: *The Leica 0—old and new. The original is on the left and the replica on the right.*

LEICA 0 series

Leitz/Leica has had an on-going tradition of manufacturing special edition commemorative models. Generally, they have been modifications of cameras that are currently in production. The only departure from this was a series of 4,000 replicas introduced at Photokina 2000. Interestingly, this very special edition was a copy of Barnack's original hand-built model from 77 years earlier: the Leica 0. A tribute to Oskar Barnack—the inventor of the Leica—and to Ernst Leitz II who sponsored him and made the decision to begin assembly line manufacturing, this model was introduced to test the collector's market for replicas of historic cameras.

The reproduction Leica 0 offers all the technical features of the original including the dimensions, design, finish, engravings, and materials. The camera is fully functional. However, unlike the original, it accepts commercially available 35mm film and is equipped with a 50mm f/3.5 Leitz Anastigmat lens, which is based on its original lens, but is technically updated, including modern multi-element optical design with multicoatings.

As in the original model, the shutter curtains do not overlap during the winding operation. Because of this, a cover must be placed on the lens when the shutter is cocked and the film advanced to prevent light from entering. A small cord is used to fasten the lens cap to the front of the camera. Like the original, shutter speeds are selected using five adjustable slit widths (1,000 divided by the slot aperture = actual shutter speed):

Slot width/mm	50	20	10	5	2
Shutter speed/sec.	1/20	1/50	1/100	1/200	1/500

Long exposures (B) of any duration are possible as well.

The optical finder consists of a foldable lens with cross hairs with a movable indicator needle in front of it. This is called a Newton viewfinder. The viewfinder image is viewed at pupillary distance of approximately 30 cm (11-3/4 inches); therefore, the camera must be held at this distance in front of the face. This Leica 0 special edition includes a genuine cowhide case and carrying strap that are designed in a style reminiscent of the 1920s.

LEICA 0 Commemorative Edition
Introduced in 2000

Camera type: 35mm viewfinder camera with integrated telescopic lens.

Viewfinder: Hinged Newton viewfinder.

Body: Aluminum die-cast covered with artificial leather; internal housing of deep drawn chrome.

Shutter: Horizontal, mechanically controlled, rubberized cloth focal plane shutter. Curtains do not overlap during winding and film advance.

Shutter speeds: 1/20, 1/50, 1/100, 1/200, 1/500 second and time exposures of any length ("B"). A lever is used for shutter speed selection, and a selector knob is used for adjusting the shutter slit width.

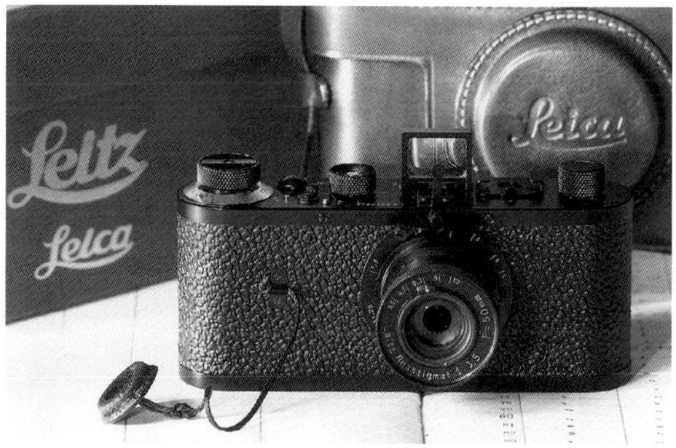

Fig. 65: The Leica 0 series includes a brown, genuine cowhide camera case and presentation box with retro, 1920s styling

Frame counter: Automatic forward counting from 0 to 40. Must be reset to 0 after film has been loaded.

Lens: 50mm f/3.5 Leitz Anastigmat, integrated and extendable. 4 elements in groups of 3.

Aperture setting: Continuous.

Apertures: 3.5 / 4.5 / 6.3 / 9 / 12.

Focusing range: Infinite to 1 m.

Leather lens cover: Is fastened firmly to the camera body by means of a cord.

Film loading: Insert individual film spool after removing base plate. The film must be cut to a length of approximately 10 cm.

Tripod socket: A 1/4", DIN 4503 (1/4").

Dimensions: Height, 65 mm (with folded down viewfinder); length, 133 mm; depth, 39 mm (with retracted lens).

Weight: 470g.

Camera case: Brown genuine cowhide with carrying strap.

A brief history of the Leica 0 series

The exceptional importance of the early models in the creation of today's Leica camera resulted in the decision of Leica Camera AG to offer a replica of the first Leica camera to photographers and collectors.

The small camera used frequently by Oskar Barnack and Ernst Leitz II for taking pictures is today known as the "Ur-Leica," i.e., the original Leica. Today this is kept at the Leica Museum. Other early cameras from this time period, which were lost, were described by Oskar Barnack as Prototype No. 1 and Prototype No. 2. It is not known whether or not they possessed the same technical features as the Ur-Leica.

It is likely that even at that time Mr. Leitz was considering the commercial manufacture of the camera because, in May 1914, a patent to protect a few of the most important technical components of these early cameras was filed. However, the application was rejected and Leitz had to contend with a utility model protection.

Because of this experience, Oskar Barnack, an engineer and hobby photographer, began to recognize the problems with his camera design but World War I prevented him from immediately revising it. Between 1918 and 1920 an improved model was developed. Oskar Barnack named it Prototype No. 3. This camera is also at the Leica Museum, however, without its lens.

In addition to many changes and improvements, compared with the "Ur-Leica," Prototype No. 3 had a very special design feature. While the "Ur-Leica" had a focal plane shutter with constant slit width, the shutter integrated in Prototype No. 3 featured several silt widths. As a result, six different shutter speeds between approximately 1/20 and 1/500 second could be selected. In addition, time exposures were possible. This was an improvement on the "Ur-Leica" which offered only two shutter speeds achieved with different spring tensions for cocking the shutter. (These were the same as shutter speeds used in motion-picture cameras—1/40 and 1/20 second.)

In the early 1920s, the idea of manufacturing Barnack's invention as a camera for use by photographers took shape. Contributing factors may have been the generally poor economy and the desire of Ernst Leitz II to provide job security for his employees. He recognized the benefit of creating new products, which could be successfully sold. The 0 Series was designed and built in 1923-1924 to see if the manufacturing process was viable and to test the market.

Unfortunately, there is no reliable documentation regarding the actual number of 0 Series cameras manufactured. According to current knowledge 22, or possibly 25 cameras having serial numbers from 101 to 125 were built. Basic features of the 0 Series were later incorporated in the Leica I. The viewfinder of this latter model was even simpler. The 0 Series cameras were subsequently equipped with a telescopic viewfinder (like the Leica II).

Like the "Ur-Leica" and Prototype No. 3, the 0 Series featured a focal plane shutter design without overlapping curtains. Because of this light could strike the film when the shutter was wound. To solve this problem a cover—fastened to the camera by a cord—had to placed on the lens when the shutter and film were wound. As in Prototype No. 3, a choice of five adjustable slit widths permitted shutter speeds of approximately 1/20, 1/50, 1/100, 1/200, and 1/500 second. However, the film was no longer advanced from one spool to another but from a cassette designed specifically for the camera. The invention of this cassette made it possible to load and unload the camera in daylight. This principle is still in use in 35mm still cameras to this day.

These "production" cameras were given confidentially to employees, sales staff, and customers in order to obtain solicit their views regarding the

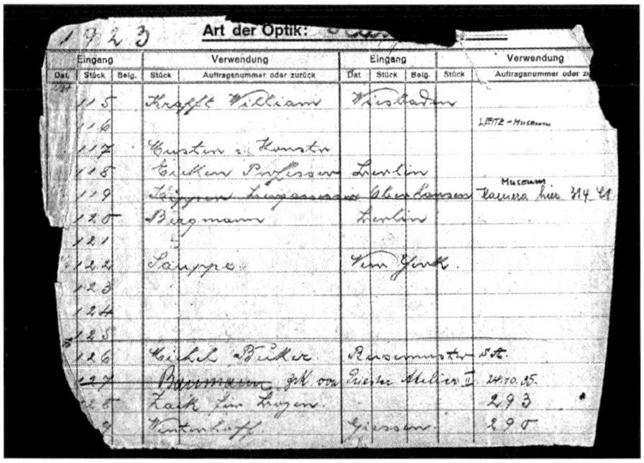

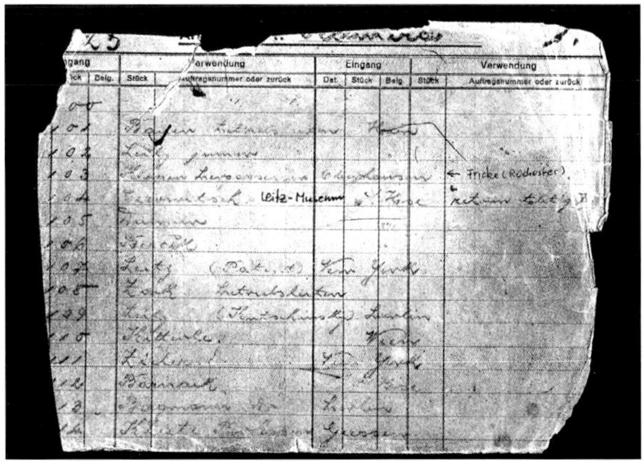

Fig. 66 a and b.: *This worn sheet of paper has barely intelligible hand-written camera serial numbers on its front and back. Also noted are the names of people who were given test cameras. For a long time, there was the belief that these serial numbers referred only to Leica 0 cameras. However, we now know that Leica I cameras with the serial numbers 126 and 128 were produced, and the numbers from 101 and 122, and possibly through 125, were used for the Leica 0. Reproduction on orthochromatic film. Strong yellow filter (Kodak Tungsten Filter No. 12).*

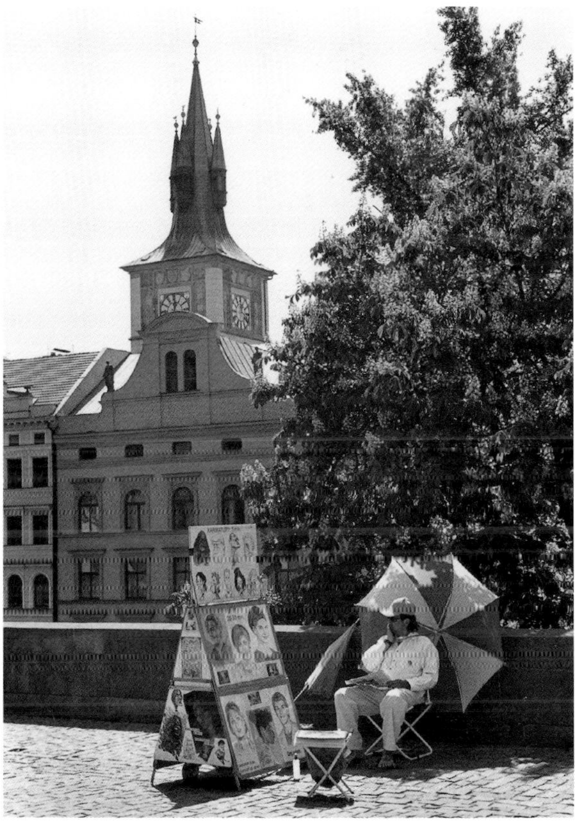

potential of such a camera for future sales. The opinions of experts regarding this completely novel camera design were by no means all positive. A majority rejected the planned project. Stories have it that an extended and controversial discussion as to whether or not a camera should be commercially manufactured was ended by Ernst Leitz II with the words, "That's it! I am making the decision. Barnack's camera will be built!" According to these stories, the time was 12:30 p.m.—the only time Ernst Leitz II was ever late for his noon lunch!

During the subsequent year, the production line model—the Leica I was introduced to the public at the 1925 Leipzig Spring Fair.

Reminescent of another day, this picture was taken with a Leica 0. Both distance and exposure were estimated. The photographer had to be careful to cover the lens when the film was wound because the shutter curtains do not overlap on this model. f/12, 1/500 second, ISO 400 film.

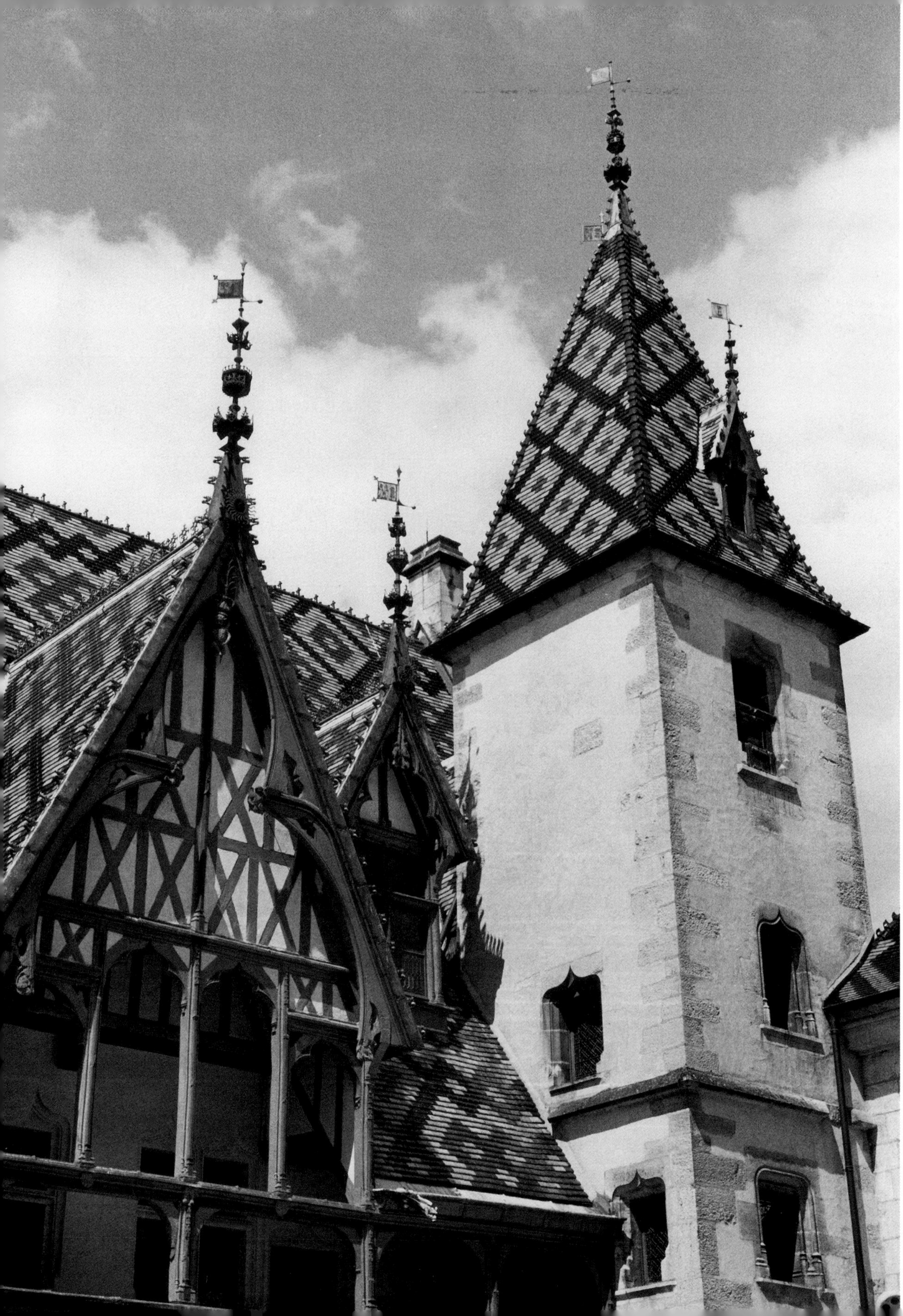

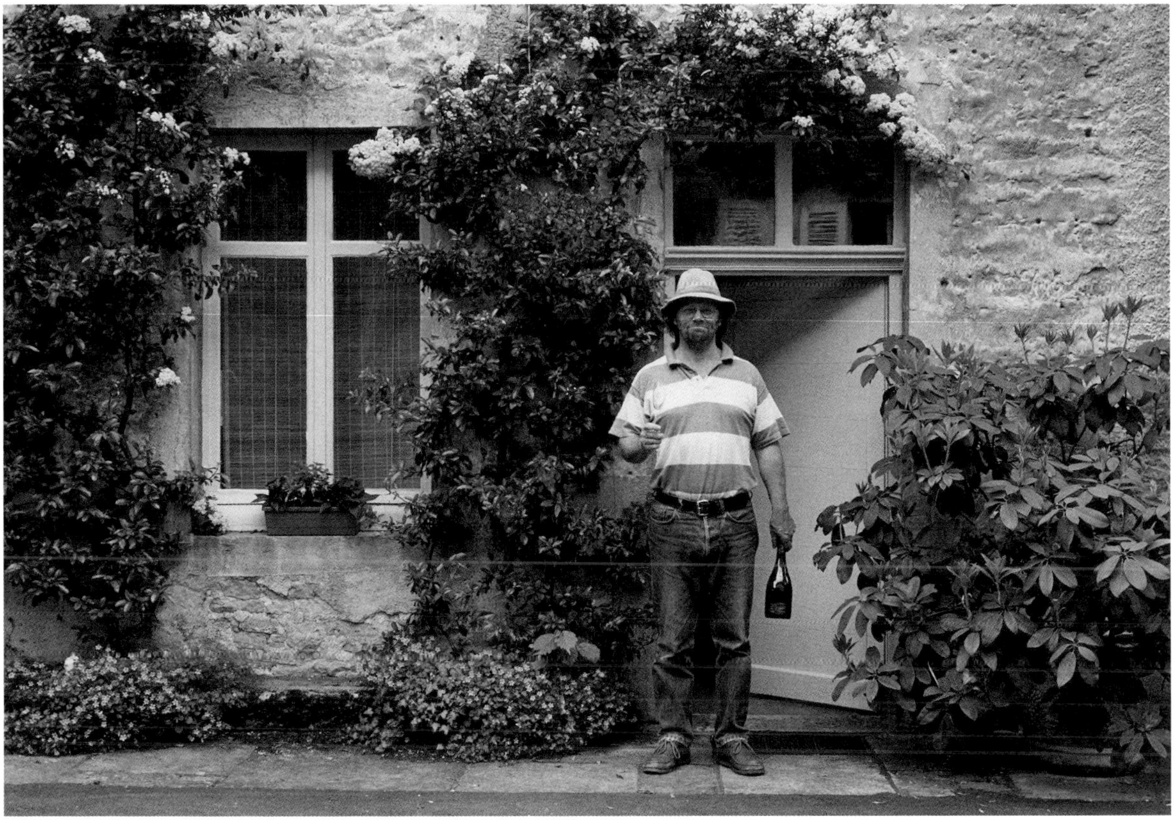

Fig. 67 and 68: *: "Estimate—but correctly!" was the motto of photographers who took pictures with the Leica 0. The fact that exposure and focus could be mastered and that the 50mm f/3.5 Leitz Anastigmat lens had excellent optics is illustrated by these two pictures. The colorfully glazed roof tiles of the Hospice de Beaune are photographed with 100-speed film, at f/9 and with a slit width of "5" = 1/200 second. This picture of vintner Alain Georger was taken at f/6.3 and a slit width of "20" = 1/50 second in the courtyard of his winery in Savigny-les-Beaune using high-speed ISO 400 film.*

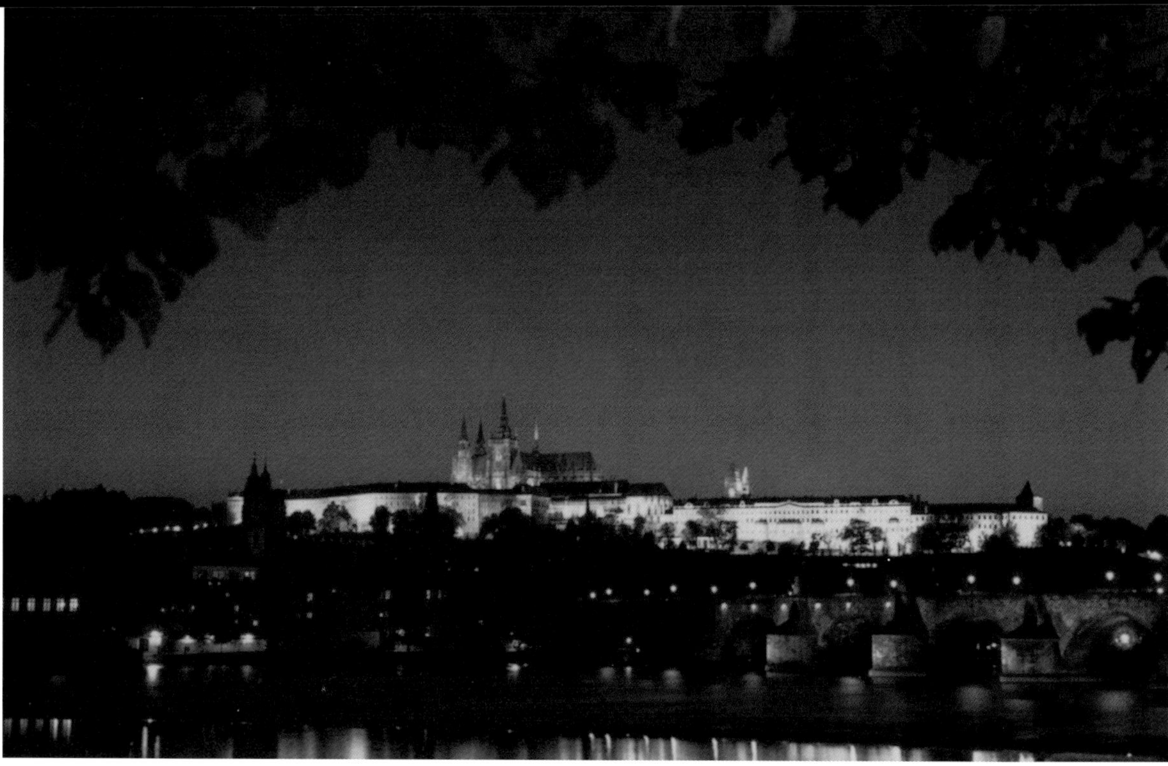

Even though it did not accept a cable release, the Leica 0 could make successful time exposures, as is evidenced by this night shot of Prague. Exposed at f/3.5 with a setting of "Z" = approx. 4 seconds, film speed ISO 400.

Fig. C1: *In particular, 35mm lenses allow relatively quick, inconspicuous photography because it is possible to conveniently estimate what the lens will capture. 35mm f/1.4 Summilux-M ASPH lens, 1/60 second, f/2.8, daylight reversal film ISO 25.*

Fig. C2: *People will usually ignore you once you tell them you are just taking pictures. 35mm f/2 Summicron-M ASPH lens, 1/250 second, f/5.6, daylight reversal film ISO 25.*

Fig. C3 – C6: *The classic Leica lens line-up includes the 35mm wide angle. And, not without reason! This is an extremely versatile focal length, as is shown with these examples:*

Fig. C3: *35mm f/2 Summicron-M ASPH, f/8, polarizing filter, daylight reversal film ISO 64.*
Fig. C4: *35mm f/1.4 Summilux-M ASPH, 1/2 second, f/2.8, daylight reversal film ISO 64. The camera was supported on a pillar.*

Fig. C5: *The contrast of the bright snow in the background and the deep blue sky are enhanced by the use of a polarizing filter. This along with the photographer's framing of the scene with the expansive foreground adds drama to this mountain snow scene. 35mm f/2 Summicron-M ASPH, 1/60 second, f/5.6, polarizing filter, daylight reversal film ISO 25.*

Fig. C6: *A self-portrait with an interesting perspective was captured with a wide-angle lens with the camera only about 1.5 meters (5 feet) from the subject. 35mm f/1.4 Summilux-M ASPH, 1/250 second, f/2, daylight reversal film ISO 25.*

Fig. C7 and C8: *Whether the picture is an action photo of hot air balloons or a calm portrait, a 35mm lens is often the right choice for vacation photography.*
Fig. C7: *35mm f/2 Summicron-M ASPH, 1/250 second f/5.6, daylight color film.*
Fig. C8: *35mm f/2 Summicron-M ASPH, 1/125 second f/2.8, daylight color film.*

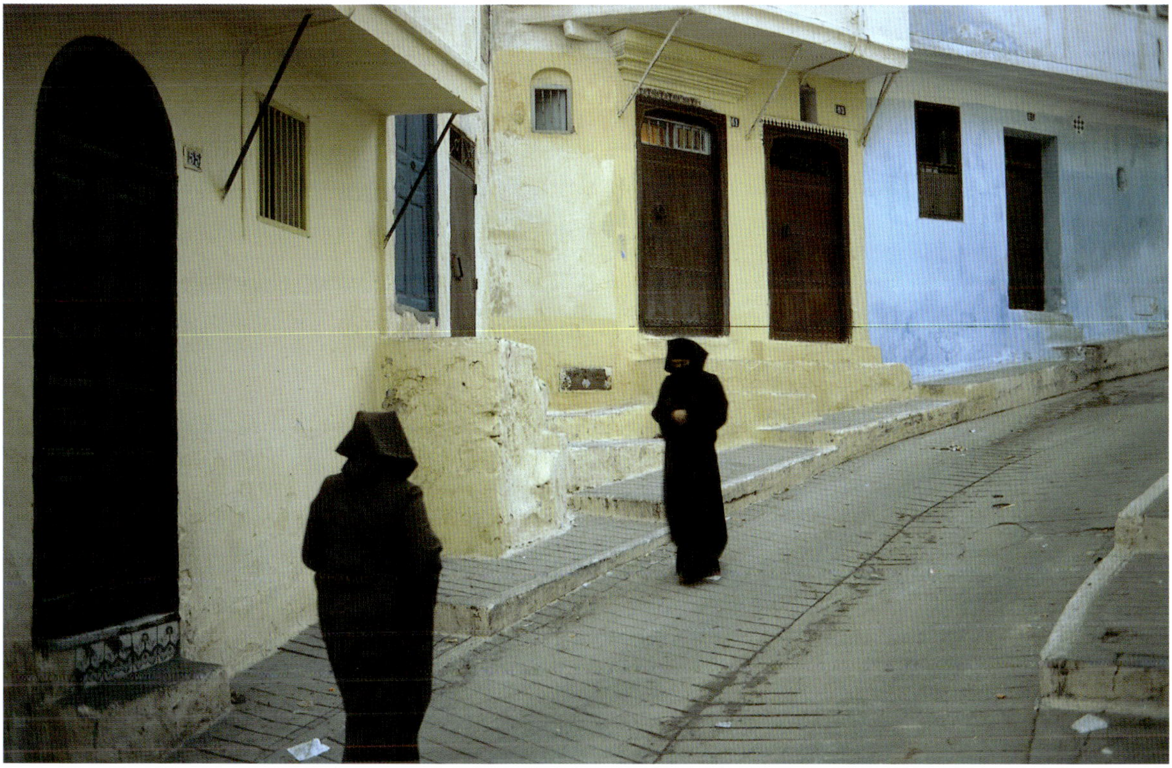

Fig. C1

Fig. C2

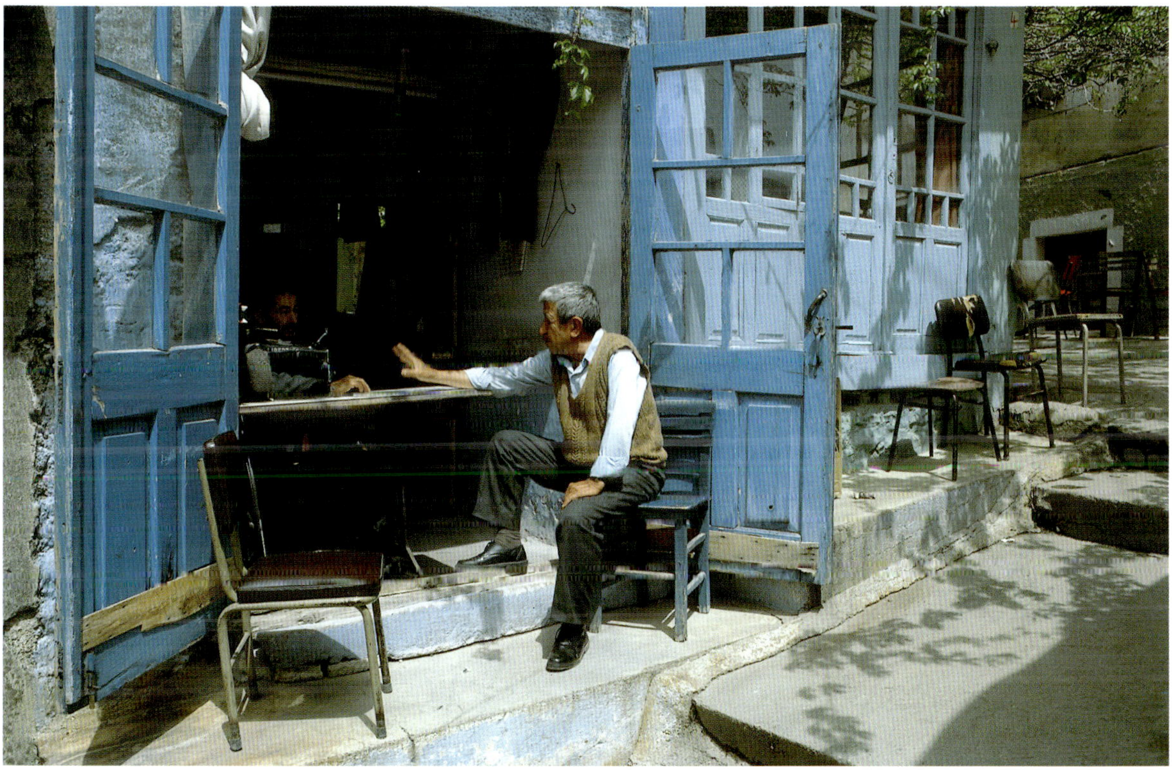

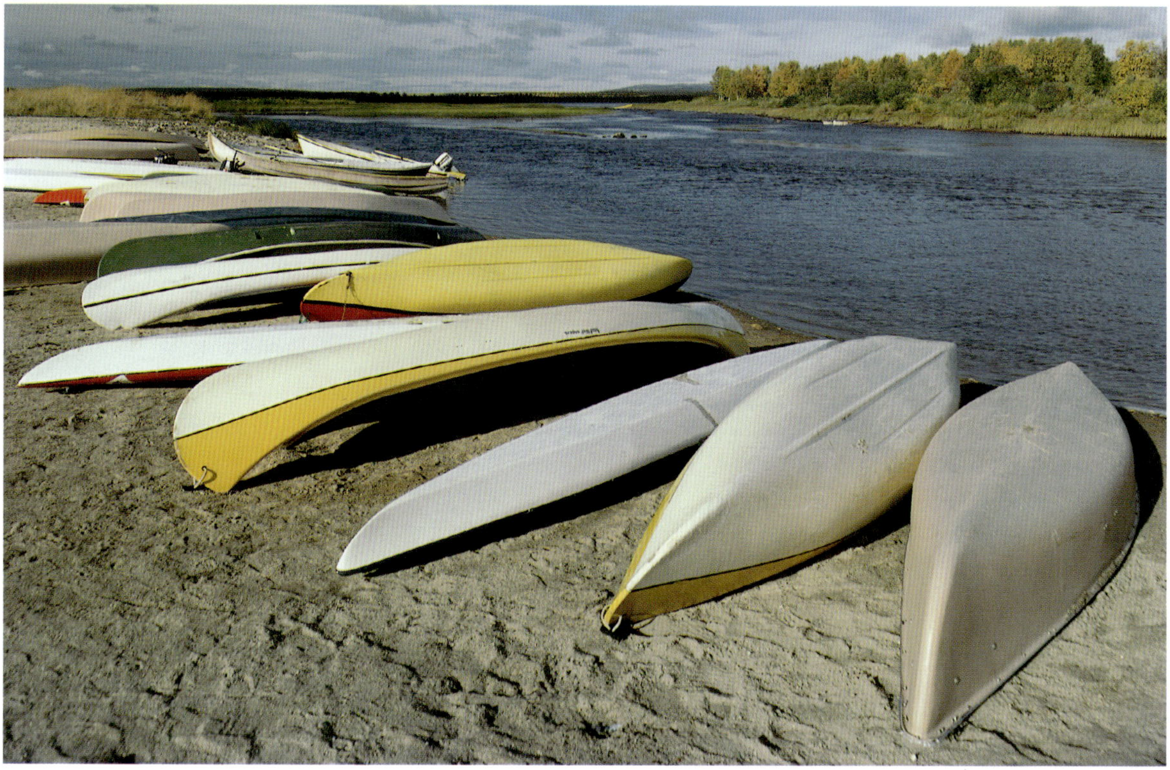

Fig. C3

Fig. C4

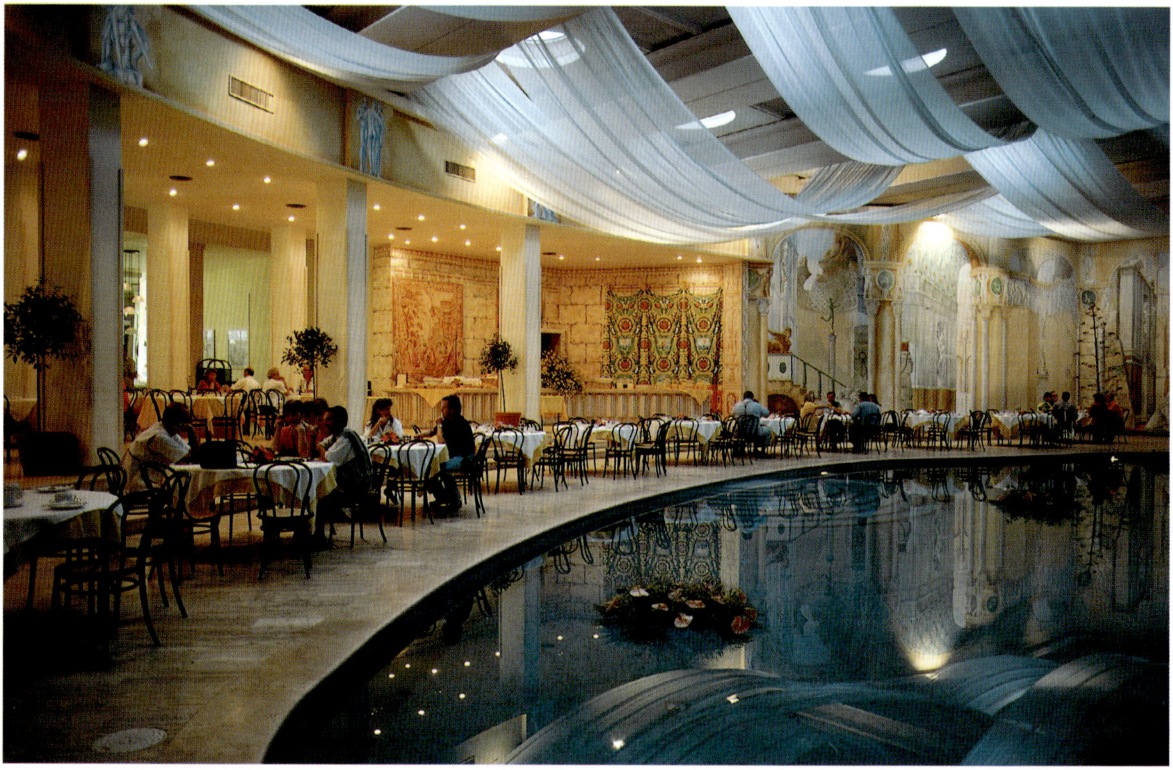

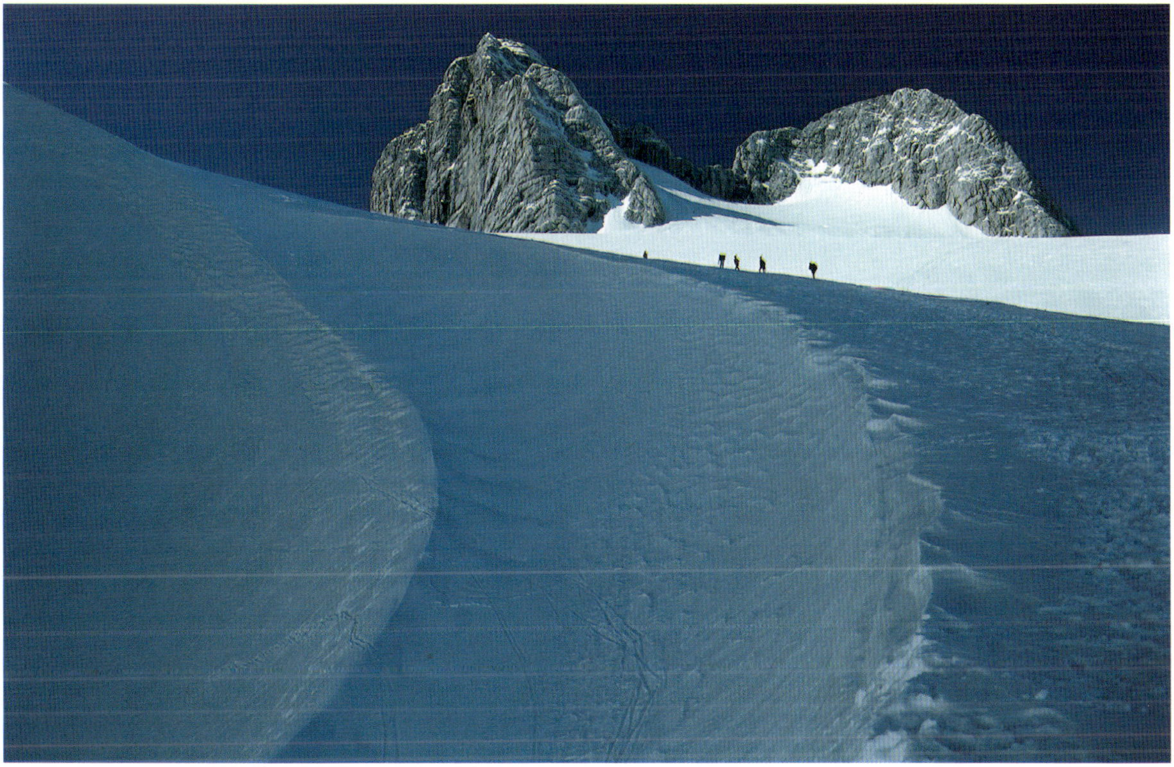

Fig. C5

Fig. C6

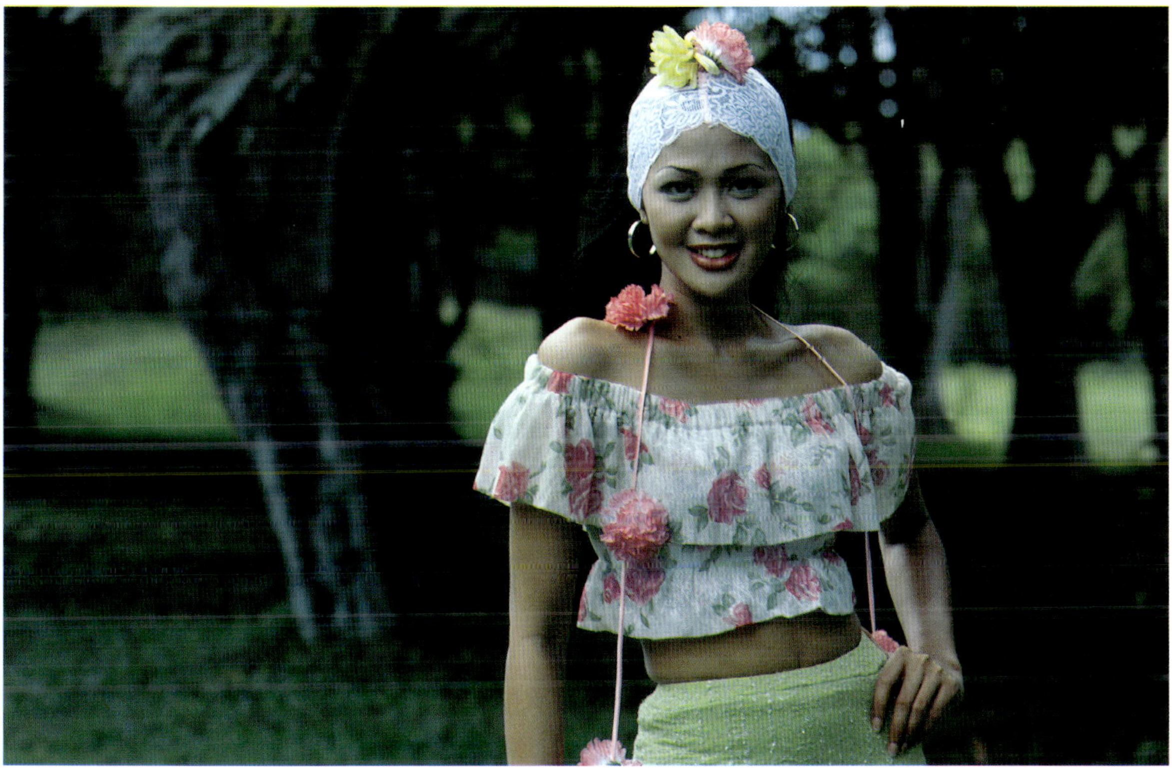

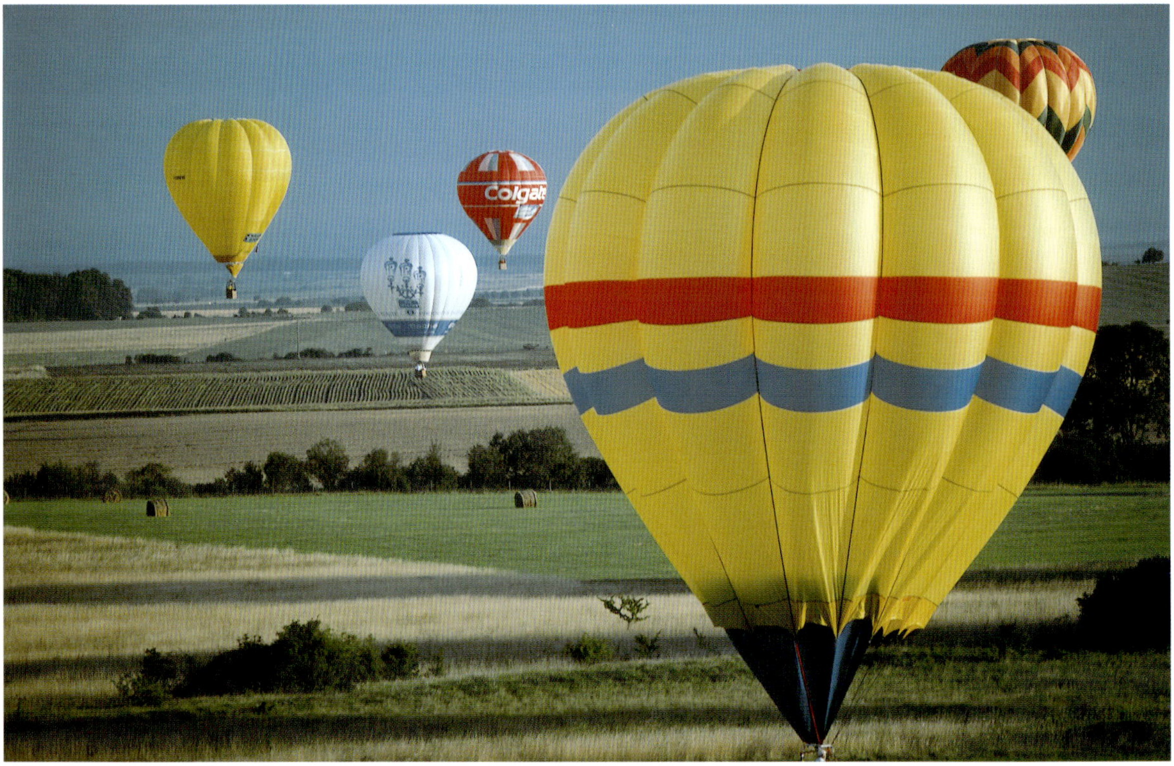

Fig. C7

Fig. C8

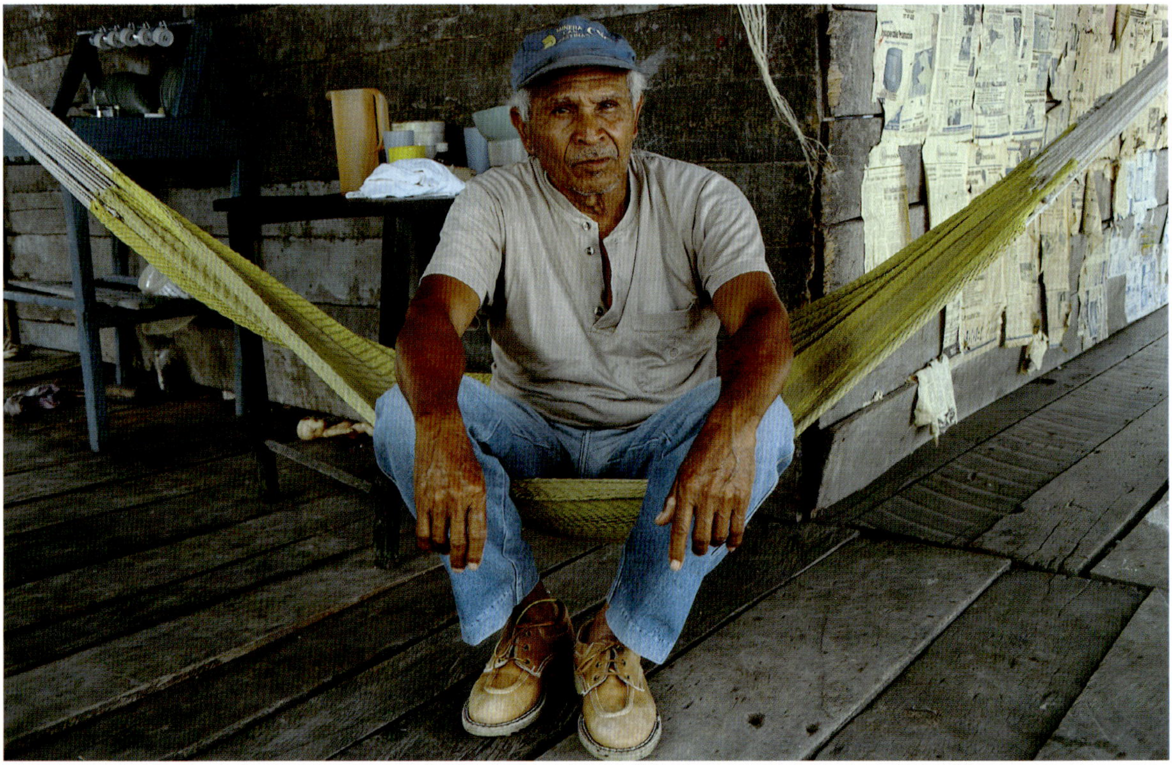

LEICA M lenses

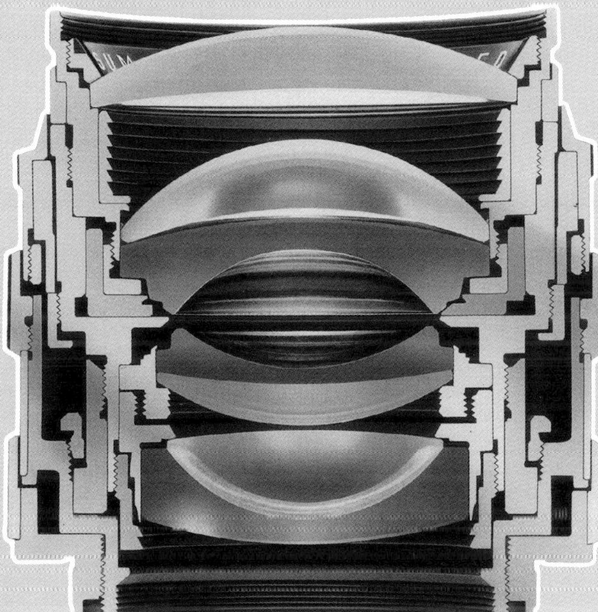

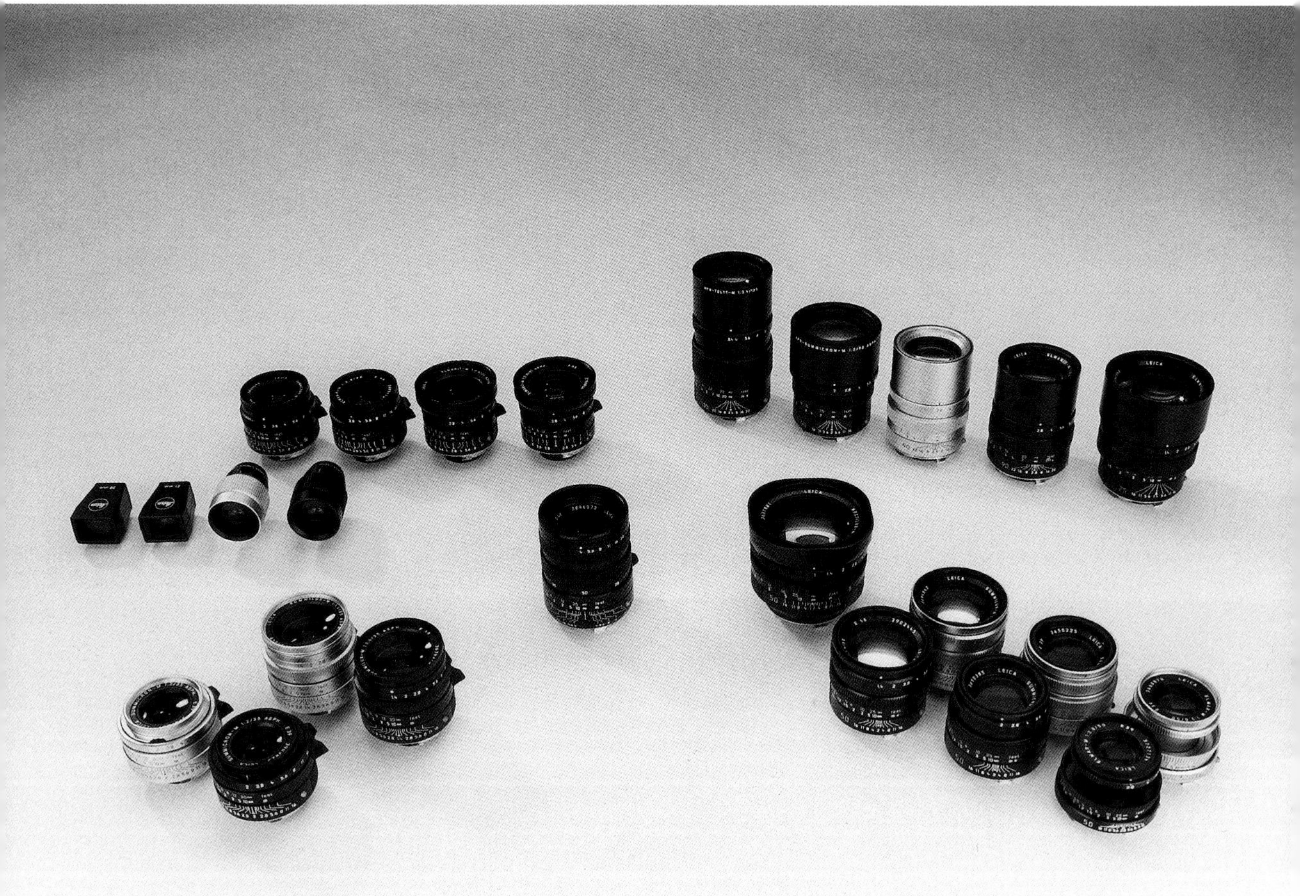

Fig.69: *Leica M lenses at a glance.*

LEICA M lenses

It has been said that the history of the Leica camera is also the history of 35mm photography. Certainly no one would argue with the fact that Leitz/Leica has influenced camera design and photographic style around the world. However, as impressive as this is, the history of Leica also includes the history of high-performance lens technology.

Today it is widely recognized that Leitz was the first optical company to utilize computers for lens design. Leitz's in-house glass research laboratory also created thorium-free high-refraction lanthanum optical glass, and designed the first machine to grind and polish aspheric lenses on a production basis.

Without the continuous research into new types of glass, new manufacturing technologies, and sophisticated computer programs, combined with the exceedingly meticulous care in the manufacture of Leitz products, the fabled success of the Leica would not have been likely to occur.

For decades, Leitz lens designs have been known for their extraordinary performance characteristics. They set the standards for lens manufacture and image quality in 35mm format photography. This is still true today.

How well do Leica M lenses perform?

There are photographers who claim that picture sharpness depends exclusively on the quality of the camera and its lenses. There are others who believe that the cameras and lenses of today are all very good, so that, at least in practice, the film and processing determine the sharpness of the photograph.

Then there are the proponents of tripods, who insist that they are indispensable for sharp pictures. Seasoned photographers, of course, know from experience that every one of these factors contributes to a sharp image.

Experts agree that there are many other influences that affect the quality of an image, which include: the lack of sharpness due to movement caused by shutter speeds that are not fast enough, focusing that is not quite accu-rate, the type of lighting, and others.

One thing that is an essential prerequisite for sharpness in a photograph is the lens. If it is not sharp all other efforts to achieve sharpness are doomed to failure. This explains why the interest in information about lens performance is so great. And since optical systems can be evaluated electronically, it is not difficult to compare the performance of various lenses using numbers and curves or by photographing test charts.

While technically minded photographers like to discuss the graphs that result from these measurements, pragmatists, prefer to test their lenses by photographing a newspaper taped to a wall. Beginners in the field of photography willingly tend to select their photographic lenses on the basis of published test results, where the reader is often given the impression of absolute infallibility of this type of evaluation.

But are such tests truly objective and are they the best way to judge the optical performance of lenses (including those for the Leica camera) without reservations? Answers to these questions are best sought from Leitz experts Dr. W. Vollrath, manager of the Optical Design bureau, and his successor at Leica Camera AG, L. Kölsch, or from Dr. H. Thomas, manager of Optical Measurements Technology and, his colleague in quality assurance, J. Konrad, who have

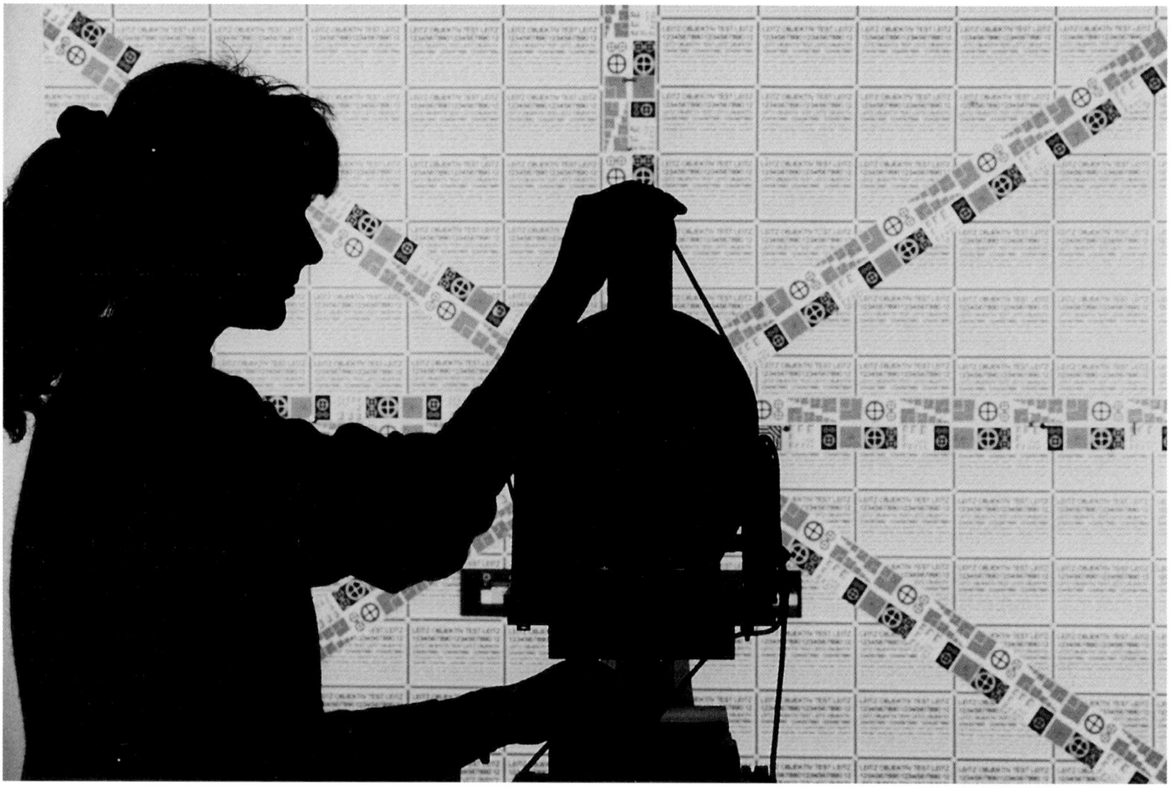

Fig. 70: *Testing begins with the examination of materials and components used before lenses are actually assembled, including mounts, helical mounts, and lens elements. Then, the individual assemblies are tested and, if necessary, corrections are made. The imaging performance of the finished lens is determined by opto-electronic measurements and documented in numerous diagrams and graphs. One of the best-known measurements is the Modulation Transfer Function (MTF). In addition, visual inspection methods like the projection test are indispensable. Among other things, this is used to evaluate spherical and chromatic errors, as well as field curvature, and centering. Finally, the compatibility of the lens with the camera and the optical performance are tested photographically.*

researched this subject for many years. Because of the complexity of this topic a brief answer is not possible and the following represents an overview of their viewpoints.

Occasionally, lens tests published by a magazine cause some readers to question Leica quality while others compare test results with their own experience. Some readers also question if the testing method was the correct one. It is quite understandable, therefore, that photographers have asked Leica to publish appropriate curves for Leica lenses. And why not, since experienced photographers constantly praise Leica lenses? Indeed, it is the preservation of this reputation for perfection in its cameras and lenses, which Leica regards as one of its most important corporate goals.

It is the Leica photographer who benefits most from this credo since it means continuing refinement of manufacturing technologies and tolerances, on-going research for new materials such as new improved optical glass, plus new designs for improved handling and greater versatility. This adds up to a constant effort to satisfy the many needs expressed by photographers. Leica is guided by the knowledge that its cameras and their lenses are generally used for the photographic reproduction of three-dimensional objects, such as landscapes, people, animals, houses, flowers, and the like. This has a direct bearing on the design of Leica lenses.

Since Leica lenses are not optimized for the photography of flat test patterns, those who attempt to evaluate their performance with the help of test charts and MTF curves will easily get the wrong picture. That is also the reason why test results published by respected magazines and institutes do not always agree with the experience of photographic experts and photographers. Lens tests have always been controversial. That also goes for the interpretation of so-called MTF measurements (MTF = Modulation Transfer Function). Still, MTF measurements are definitely significant in the evaluation of optical systems. To assure its high standards Leica Camera AG in Solms maintains modern testing facilities.

As straightforward as the principle of MTF measurement is, the equipment it requires is costly, and the measurements themselves require great care and experience. Although the experts argue about how these curves should be interpreted, they do agree that a great many measurements are necessary for a valid evaluation. The number of these measurements that popular publications use for their evaluations is generally far from adequate.

In addition, the MTF is only part of the OTF (Optical Transfer Function), whose other component is determined by the PTF (Phase Transfer Function). Among other characteristics of a lens that the PTF serves to evaluate is the coma of a lens, which is considerably more difficult to interpret than the MTF. An MTF curve also reveals nothing about color correction, unless MTF curves are generated for all the different wavelengths of light. But that would mean an unmanageable number of tests.

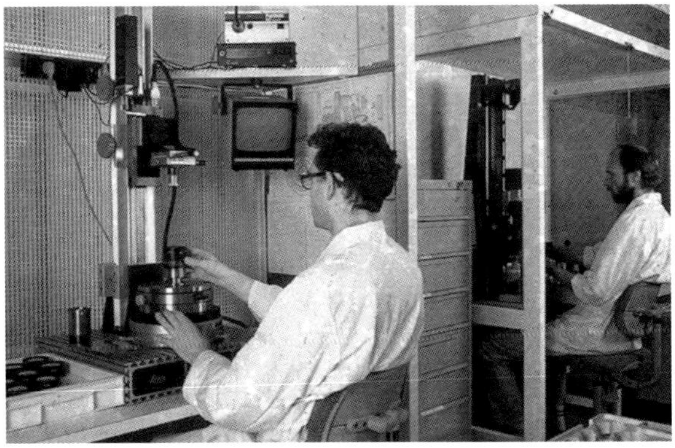

Fig.71: *The monitor at the test bench indicates the accuracy with which the lens elements have been aligned relative to the optical axis of the system. The optics expert describes this as testing the reflected image of the (lens) surfaces in auto-collimation.*

In the background is a laser interferometer, which is used to test the centering of the assembled lens or to perform corrections.

An additional problem is that only exceedingly costly apparatus can virtually eliminate measurement errors inherent in any testing system. The majority of the testing installations inadvertently introduce system-inherent errors into the final test results, which cause inaccurate evaluations of the imaging performance of different lenses. MTF curves measured with different instruments are often not comparable. Even when the measurements are accurate, generally for reasons of economy, they represent a mere fraction of what is essential for a thorough evaluation of the imaging performance.

Isolated results are thus published out of context, claiming to present an objective analysis of imaging performance that is not necessarily valid. The path of the MTF curve depends considerably on the plane of focus that has been

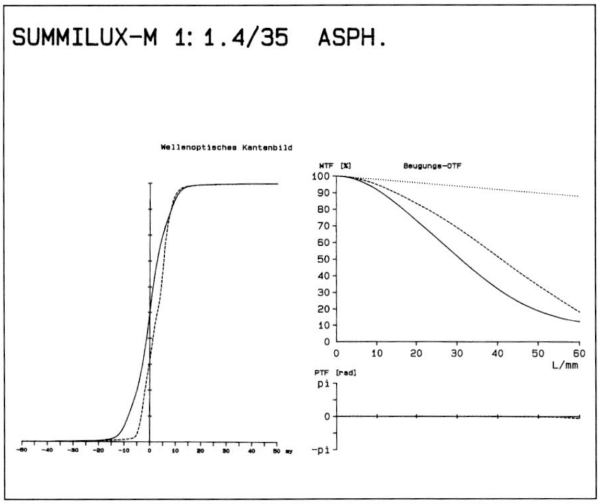

Fig.72: This is one in a series reports generated when a lens is tested. It refers to a specific point in the image area, at a specific shooting distance, with a specific aperture opening, and a specific focus. Each diagram shows pairs of graphs: the solid line graph represents the radial lens slit orientation, the broken line represents the tangential lens slit orientation. The dotted line in the upper right diagram shows the refraction limit. Left: brightness distribution in the picture of a light/dark edge. Top right: modulation transfer function (MTF). Bottom right: phase shift. Together, modulation transfer function and phase shift always represent the optical transfer function (OTF).

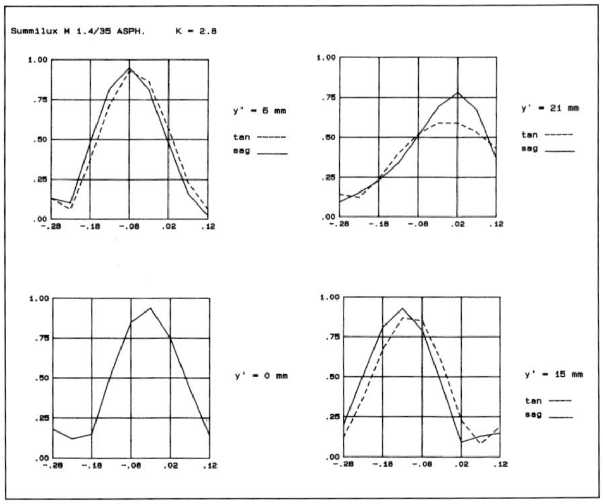

Fig.73: This computer-generated diagram shows the modulation (for 20 lines per millimeter) as a function of focusing for five different image points. Each of the four diagrams belongs to image points, which are at a distance (y') of 0, 6, 15 and 21 mm from the optical axis. The elevation of each strip represents the modulation range from 0 to 100%. These measured data directly indicate field curvature and astigmatism. From the viewpoint of Leica Camera, this evaluation of all this data, without reference to photographic practice, is questionable. Therefore, in addition to comprehensive measurements, all Leica lenses are subjectively evaluated in practice by taking photographs and by projecting test originals, as well as by a variety of tests.

selected, i.e., whether the image plane (measurement plane) that produces the highest contrast in the center of the image was selected, or whether an image plane was chosen that yields the best overall contrast across the field. Measurement of contrast as a function of focusing is critical, yet this is rarely mentioned in publications. Leica lenses generally perform even better in practice than they do on test charts and in MTF measurements.

This does not denigrate MTF measurements. It must be taken into account, however, that MTF is merely one of several considerations in the evaluation of a lens and that MTF applies to flat object or image planes. Lens tests should also include an evaluation of the mechanical components of a lens. Mechanical precision should receive proper emphasis during the evaluation, because mechanical performance is as important to the user as optical performance. Yet, has any test report ever mentioned that Leica lenses in many cases even satisfy military specifications for highest demands under the severest conditions? And which lens tester has ever noted that a finished lens is inspected by Leica Camera AG

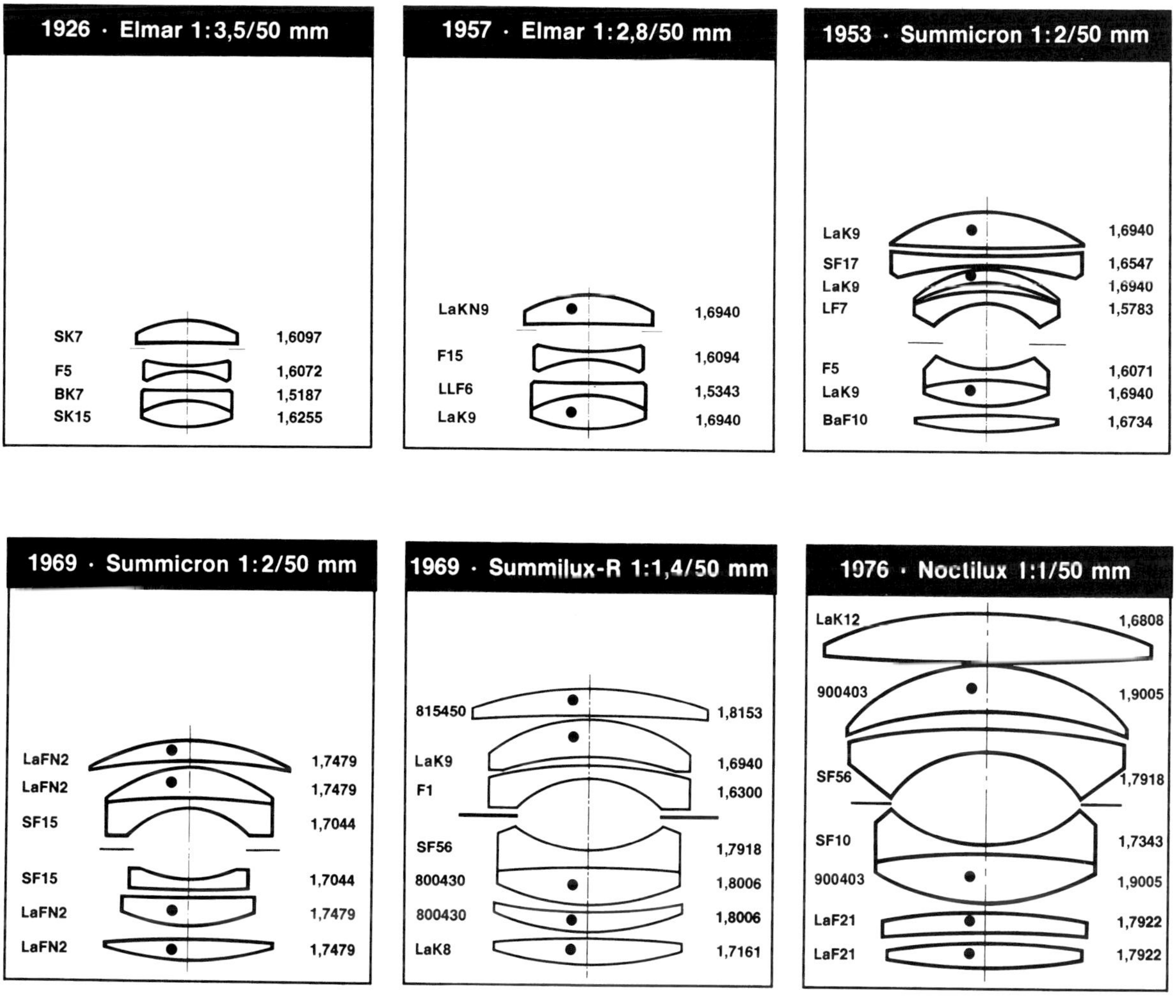

Fig.74: *These diagrams of the evolution of 50mm lenses for Leica M came-ras shows that optical progress led to more complex lenses with improved qualities. The lens elements in these diagrams that are marked with a dot are made of Leitz glass.*

for no less than 75 points, including photographic tests in hot and cold environments, with temperature gradients from +20°C (+68°F) down to -20°C (-4 °F) and back again? Other features ensure steady dependability and performance capability, even under extreme climatic conditions, for many years.

At this time, there still is no satisfactory means of achieving an objective evaluation by applying simple tests. In the final analysis, photographers must therefore draw on their own experi ence, or on the recommendations of recognized photographic practitioners. This book will clarify the performance capability of Leica M lenses by delving into the particular characteristics of each lens.

Living with image aberrations

In describing the imaging performance and the characteristic features of lenses, it is not always possible to avoid the use of terms from the science of optics and from the theory of light. The ones most frequently mentioned are various aberrations that affect the capability of a lens to produce a faithful image. In spite of optical correction programs for photographic lenses, elaborate computer installations, special optical glasses, and sophisticated methods of fabrication, optical errors cannot be entirely eliminated from photographic lenses. However, they are usually only minute vestiges of errors that visibly affect very specific regions of the image, under specific picture-taking situations.

In correcting optical aberrations, Leica strives to manipulate any residual aberrations so that they will have little or no effect as possible on the intended field of application of the lens. Often this is possible only with an exceedingly large investment in materials and expertise and nearly always affects the price of the lens.

Unfortunately a high price is not a guarantee that the lens will provide peak performance in applications other than those for which it was designed. Since this is a consequence of the laws of physics, references to characteristic features of Leica lenses that limit their application in certain types of photography, or that require additional measures in certain situations, should not be regarded as product deficiencies by the user. When other manufacturers do not mention such limitations in the descriptions of their lenses. There are probably good reasons.

A lens' imaging performance is generally expressed on the basis of three requirements: (1) a point should be reproduced exactly as a point, (2) a straight line should be reproduced as a straight line, and (3) a flat object plane should appear flat in the image plane. The fulfillment of these simple conditions is difficult primarily because of seven aberrations. Two of these are chromatic (i.e., color) aberrations, and the remaining five are monochromatic (single color) aberrations.

Chromatic aberrations

Chromatic aberrations are comprised of focus difference (also called longitudinal chromatic aberration) and chromatic magnification difference. These two color location errors occur when light rays of different colors do not converge at the same focal point. When a ray of white light passes through a collector lens (positive lens), its colored components emerge at different angles (dispersion). Red rays are refracted the least and violet ones the most. The violet focal point is therefore closer to the lens than the red focal point. This is called focus difference.

In a diverging lens (negative lens), violet rays are also refracted more strongly than red rays. The sequence of focal points, however, is the mirror image of that of a positive lens. If a positive lens element with low dispersion and a negative lens element with high dispersion are combined in one lens, the two colors can be made to converge at the same focal point. Such an arrangement, which is called an achromat, still retains the focus difference for the remaining colors that do not converge on the same focal point. This residual error is called the secondary spectrum. If three or more colors are to be made to converge simultaneously, appropriate lens elements made of special glasses have to be combined. A lens that meets these requirements is called an apochromat.

The difference in the refraction of different colors results in images with color fringes. Since violet rays are refracted more strongly than red rays, the chromatic difference of magnification causes the image to have violet to red fringes from the inside to the outside. Residual errors of chromatic longitudinal aberration and the

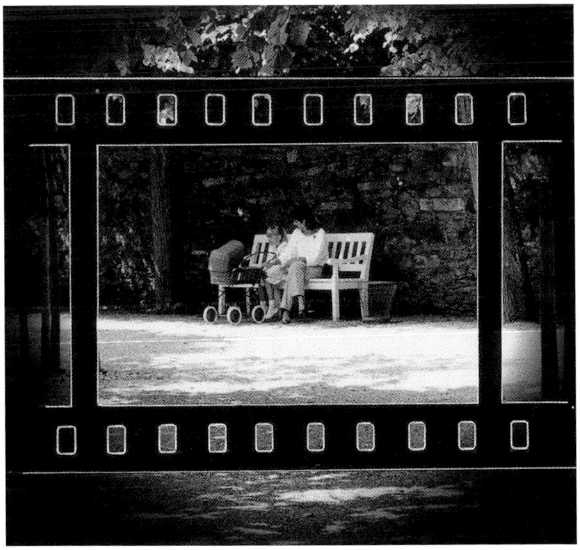

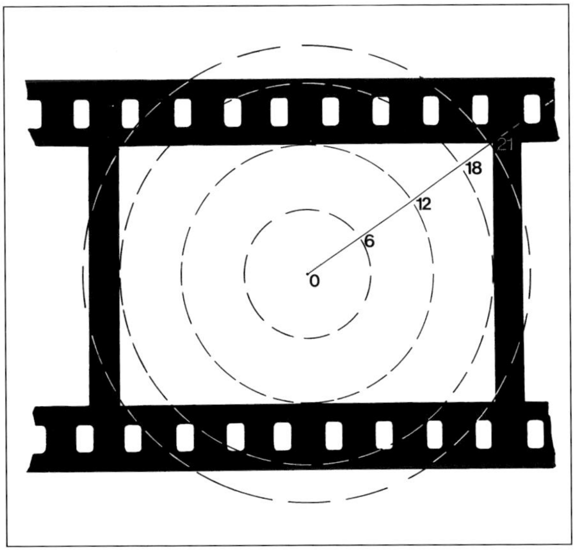

Fig.75: *Every photographic lens creates a circular image whose diameter must be at least as large as the diagonal of the picture format. However, in reality that diameter has to be considerably larger than this diagonal, because the image becomes darker and less sharp near the edge of the circle.*

Fig.76: *The point at which the effects of aberrations begin to appear can be indicated by the image radius. An image radius of "0" corresponds to the center of the image, and an image radius of "21" represents the far corners of the standard 35mm format.*

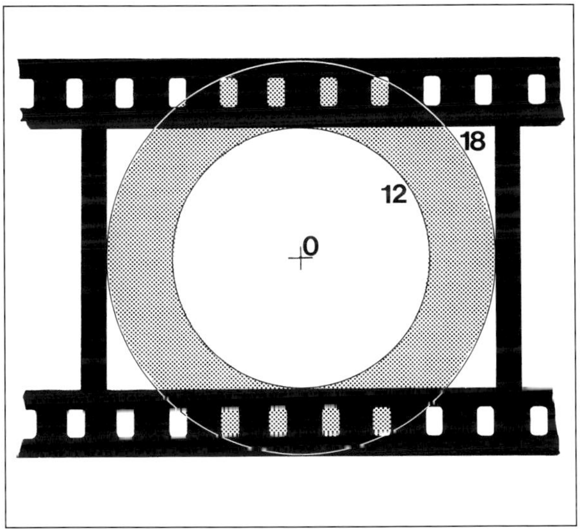

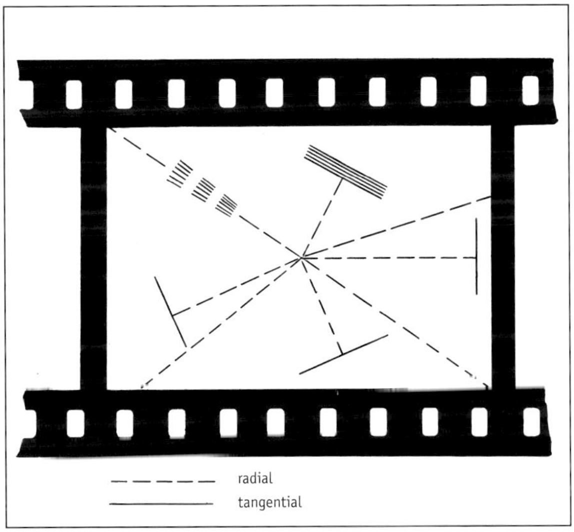

Fig.77 (above): *The term "zone" corresponds to the area between the circles of image radii "12" and "18," which are the two outer limits of the standard 35mm format.*

Fig.78 (right): *An evaluation of optical performance often includes references to the orientation of certain structures such as, test patterns in the object to be photographed. A radial orientation refers to lines that emanate from the center of the image (the broken lines). A tangential arrangement is based on lines that are at a right angle to those radial lines (the solid lines).*

difference of chromatic magnification are more noticeable in normal (achromatically corrected) long focus lenses and in strong retrofocus wide-angle lenses than in normal wide-angle and standard lenses. Contour sharpness and image brilliance are affected the most by the two chromatic aberrations.

Monochromatic aberrations

The further away a ray of light is from the optical axis, as it passes through and is refracted by a collector lens, the closer that ray's focal point will be to that lens. One could also say that the focal length of the outer part of the lens is shorter than that of the center of the lens. This creates images of different sizes, depending on the zone of the lens. This aberration increases with the size of the relative aperture, which is the ratio between lens diameter and focal length. Therefore, this aberration is called aperture aberration or, because this effect is also related to the spherical shape of normal collector lenses, spherical aberration.

With a diverging lens the farther from the optical axis that a ray of light enters the lens, the closer to the lens will be that ray's virtual point of convergence. But the sequence of convergence points is the mirror image of the sequence of a collector lens (as it is with chromatic aberration). With the aid of appropriate optical glasses and lens surface radii it is therefore possible to create a combination of collector and diverging lenses where the convergence points of rays that enter that optical system far away from the optical axis very nearly coincide with convergence points of rays that pass through the system close to its optical axis. A complete correction of spherical aberration is possible by the addition of aspherical surfaces. The fabrication of such surfaces is very complex and therefore costly. The early 50mm f/1.2 Noctilux was the first production-line photographic lens in the world to incorporate lens elements with aspheric

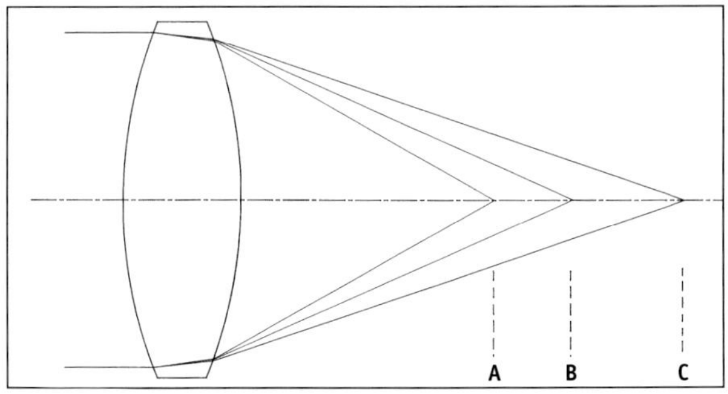

Fig.79: *Longitudinal chromatic aberration (focus difference), showing different focal points for violet (A), green (B), and red (C) light rays.*

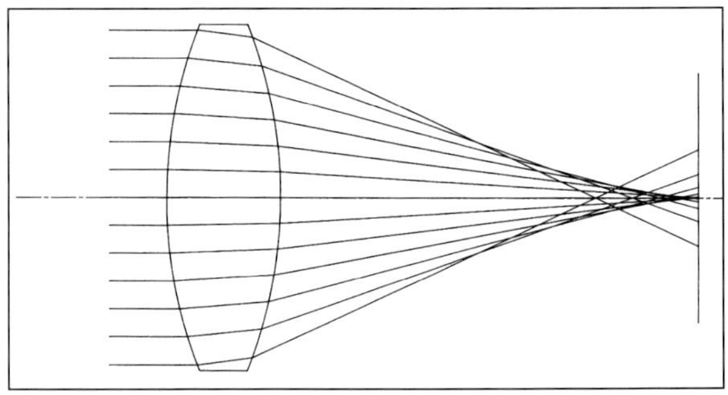

Fig.80: *Spherical Aberration*

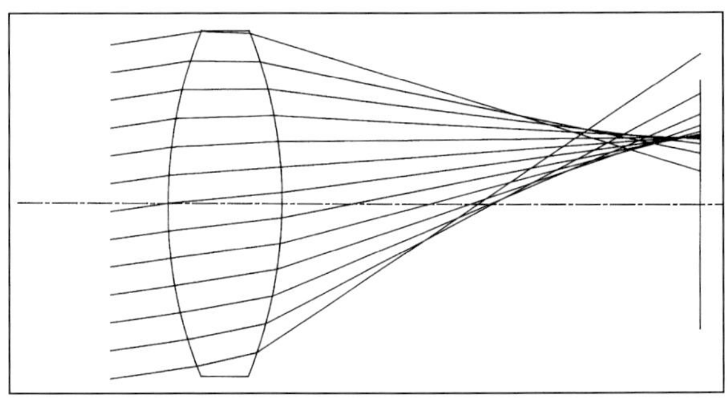

Fig.81: *Coma*

surfaces. Today the production of aspherical lenses represents one of Leica's key technologies (see page 107).

When incoming rays of light do not enter the lens parallel to the optical axis, i.e., when they

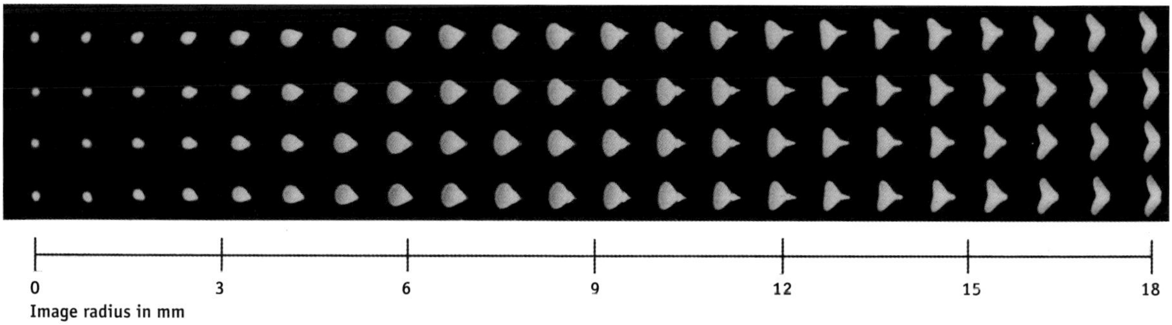

Fig.82: *Coma causes individual points of light to be reproduced as butterfly-like images. The further away the point is from the center of the image, the more pronounced is the effect.*

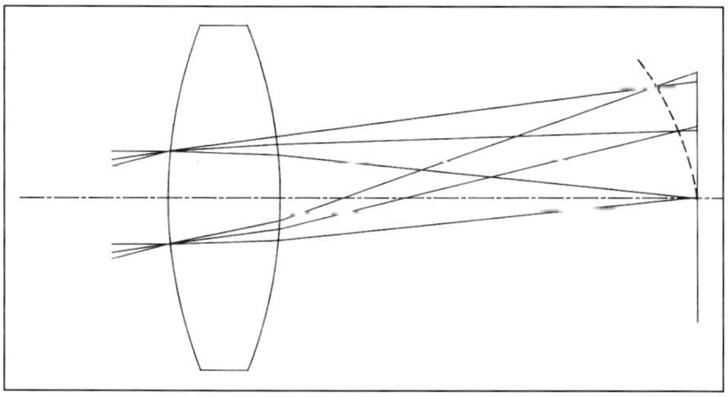

Fig.83: *Curvature of field.*

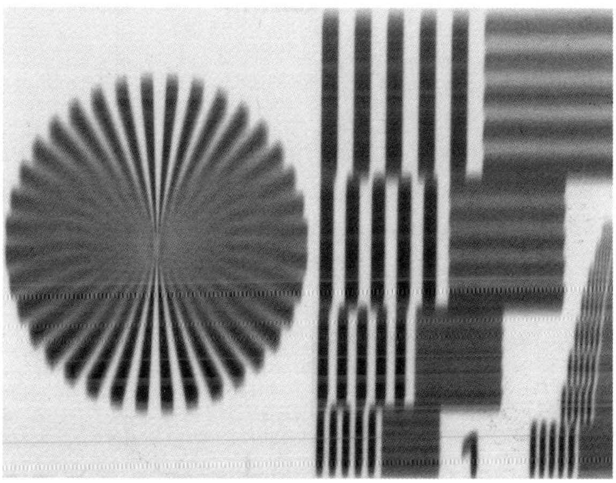

Fig.84: *The differences in sharpness in the reproduction of vertical and horizontal groups of test lines and the uneven reproduction of the individual segments of a starburst pattern as they radiate away from the center of the image, are characteristic of astigmatism.*

emanate from an object point that does not lie on the optical axis and enter the lens as oblique rays, the corresponding image point is formed towards the edge of the image plane. Spherical aberration has an asymmetrical effect on such bundles of oblique rays. A group of oblique parallel rays that enter the lens in a vertical plane that includes the optical axis (i.e., the meridional plane) will reproduce off-axis object points, not as points, but as distorted, butterfly-like images towards the edges of the image plane. This aberration is called an asymmetry error, better known as coma.

The plane that is perpendicular to the meridional plane, but does not contain the optical axis, is called the sagittal plane. When the rays in the meridional plane do not converge in the same focal point as the rays in the sagittal plane, another aberration occurs, which is called astigmatism. Astigmatism can be recognized when vertical and horizontal lines that lie on the same object plane can only be made to focus on separate image planes. If the astigmatism has been corrected, i.e., when the meridional and the sagittal rays converge on the same focal point, the lens system is called an anastigmat.

If rays of light impinge on a lens at different angles of incidence, the respective points of convergence no longer lie on a flat image plane. This so-called curvature of field has an effect that even a system corrected for astigmatism will not reproduce a flat object plane as a flat image plane, but as a dish-shaped image plane. If the optical system also has astigmatism, there

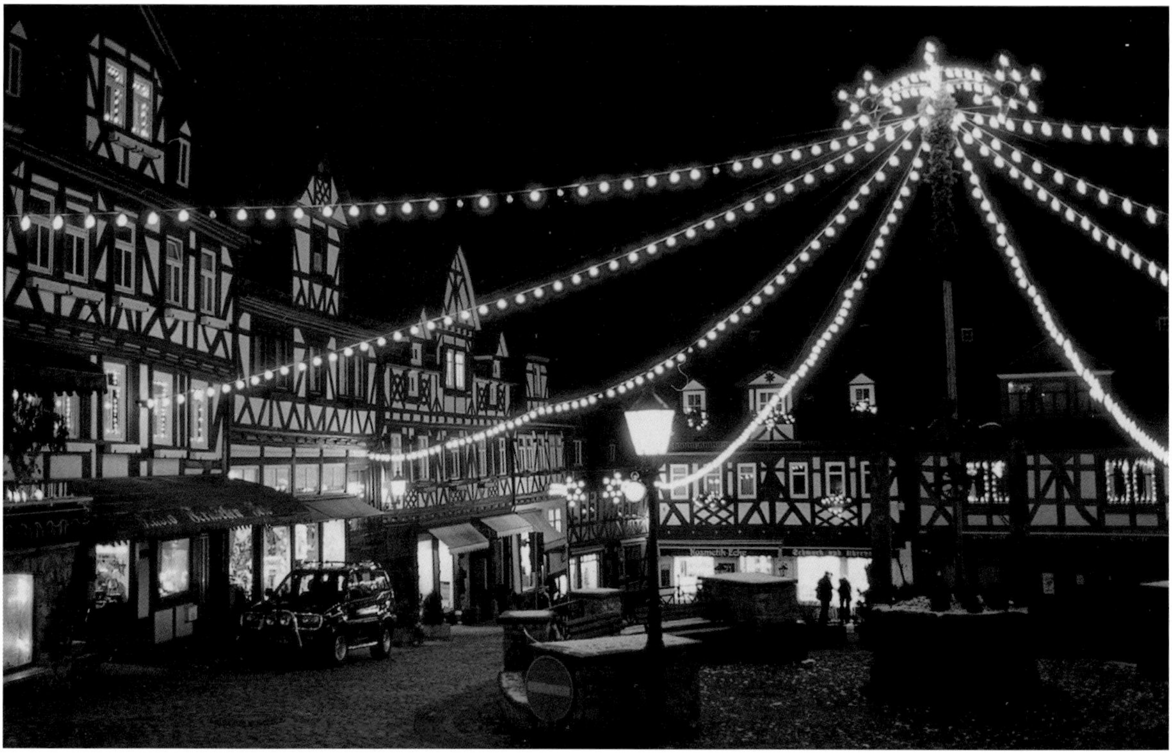

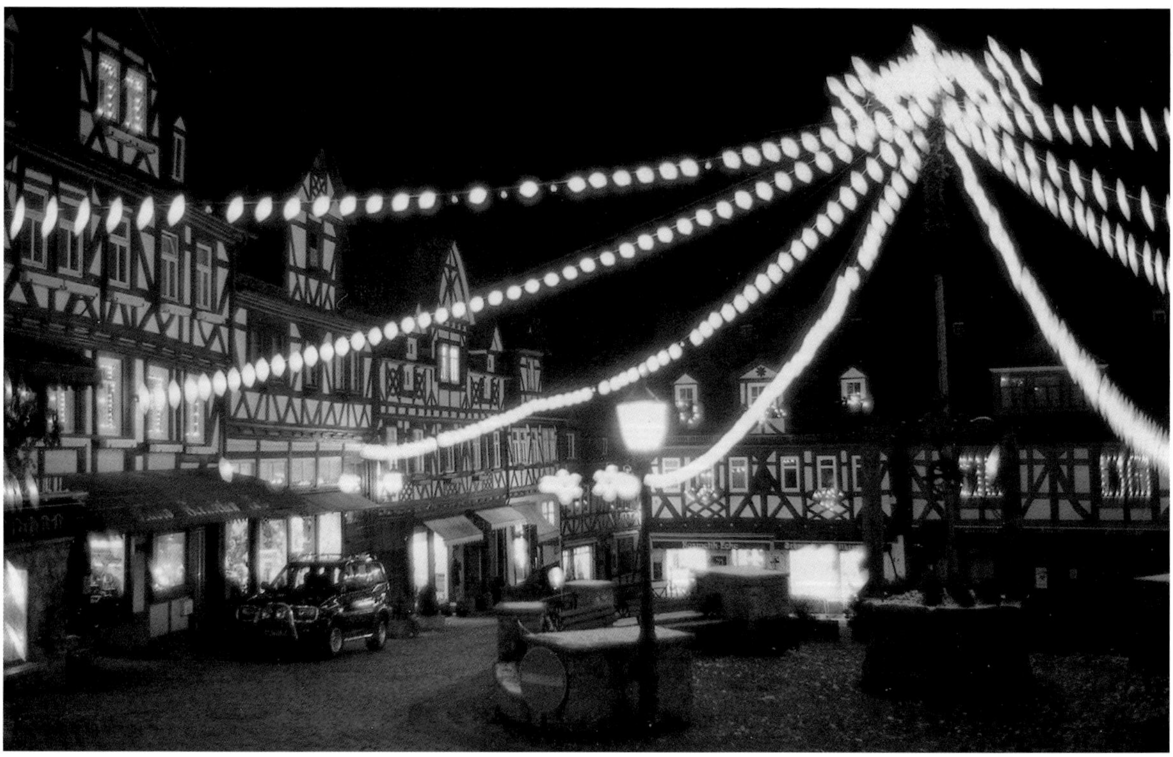

will even be two such planes: one for the rays in the meridional plane, the other for the rays in the sagittal plane.

When an image is formed with a lens, the magnification ratio does not remain constant across the image field. This causes another aberration called distortion. If the magnification ratio decreases towards the edges of the image, it causes barrel distortion; if the magnification ratio increases towards the edges of the image, the result is pincushion distortion. As a rule, the degree of distortion increases by a factor of two as the lens is set at its nearest focusing distance, where the nominal magnification ratio of Leica M lenses is approximately 1:10. But it is also possible for an inversion to occur between the opposite limits of the focusing range, from plus (+ = pincushion distortion) to minus (- = barrel distortion). A type of distortion that is especially disturbing visually is one with a sign (+ or -) that changes back and forth along the image radius. This kind of distortion causes a straight line to appear as a wavy line near the edges of the image.

Table 8: Examples of distortion with lenses set at infinity

Image radius in mm	Noctilux-M 1:1/50 mm	Summilux-M 1:1,4/50 mm	Summicron-M 1:2/50 mm
6	– 0.10 %	– 0.01 %	+ 0.05 %
12	– 0.46 %	– 0.12 %	+ 0.15 %
18	– 0.11 %	– 0.60 %	+ 0.17 %
21	– 0.13 %	– 1.20 %	+ 0.08 %

◀ ***Fig.85 a and b:*** *The through-the-lens image is frequently affected by imaging errors. Fig. 85a: 35mm f/1.4 Summilux-M ASPH at maximum aperture; Fig. 85b: lens of another manufacturer with the same specifications. In addition to being flat overall, this picture displays significant coma effects.*

The degree of distortion is stated in percent. Starting at 1.5%, distortion becomes increasingly more noticeable towards the edges of images of geometric subjects with straight lines.

With simple lenses, the type of distortion depends on the location of the iris diaphragm. When it is positioned in front of the lens, the latter will have barrel distortion. When it is located behind the lens, it will cause pincushion distortion. If two such lenses are combined and the iris is placed between them, then barrel distortion and pincushion distortion will cancel each other. This type of lens combination is largely free of distortion (orthoscopic).

Other optical errors

In addition to the seven Seidel aberrations, vignetting also affects the image. There are two kinds of vignetting: natural and artificial. The loss of brightness towards the edges of the image (natural vignetting) is due to geometric causes and is present in every lens. The explanation is simple: the geometric relative aperture, i.e., the light-gathering power of the lens, is valid only for the center of the lens. A bundle of light rays that, by virtue of the camera angle, passes through the lens obliquely necessarily has a smaller width than a bundle of rays entering the lens parallel to its optical axis.

Therefore, a smaller amount of light reaches the corners of the image. The resulting loss of brightness towards the edges of the image can be calculated in accordance with the "cosine-to-the-fourth-power law." Since a lens consists of not just one element, but of several elements in their own mounts, an additional degradation of the image occurs when light rays enter the lens at an angle. A large portion of such a bundle, which for geometric reasons already has a smaller diameter than a bundle entering the lens parallel to the optical axis, is further obstructed by parts of the lens mount. This artificial vignetting

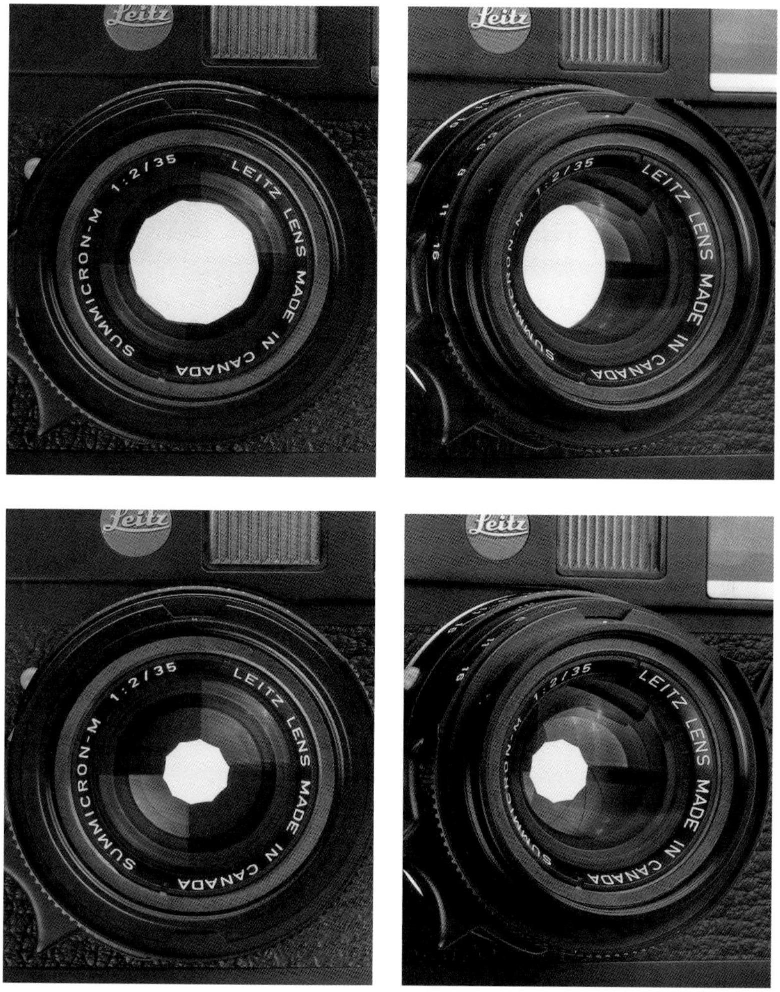

***Fig.86:** A powerful lens always consists of several elements, which are combined within the lens barrel. Therefore, if the lens aperture is wide open, artificial vignetting is inevitable. Principally, this can be demonstrated if one looks through a wide-open lens (top left) and then tilts it to obtain an oblique view. By doing this, the circular area of the lens opening becomes a circle with two corners (top right). Accordingly, this reduction of area also reduces the intensity of light in the edge areas of the image. If the lens is stopped down (bottom left), the circular area is retained even when viewed at an angle (bottom right). Therefore, reducing the size of the aperture eliminates artificial vignetting.*

can be reduced and eliminated by stopping down the aperture of the lens.

Leica designed its wide-angle lenses, from the very onset, with extra large front and rear elements so that such artificial vignetting is reduced as much as possible, even at full aperture.

Artificial vignetting can be simulated by holding any lens, with its aperture wide open, in front of a bright surface. Looking at the front element of the lens perpendicularly from a reasonable distance—thus simulating a bundle of light rays entering the lens exactly parallel to its optical axis—one can see the un-restricted aperture of the lens as full circle. Slightly turning the lens—thus looking at its front element at an angle and simulating a bundle of light rays entering it obliquely—one sees the aperture can now be seen as a figure delineated by segments of two circles, and with a noticeably smaller area. Interior sections of the lens mount obstruct portions of the bundle of light rays.

When the test is repeated with the lens stopped down, the circular aperture is unrestricted, even when the lens is turned. Thus, stopping down appropriately eliminates artificial vignetting. Natural vignetting, on the other hand, remains unchanged. Bright, even surfaces and low-light exposures nearly always make the vignetting of a lens more obvious.

In order to evaluate the performance of modern lenses, it is important to know imaging errors and their expressions and thus their influence on the image. It is also important to know where they appear. Reference is made to image center, zones, image height, and finally to the corners. Fig. 76 and 77 shows where these parts are located in the image.

Leica optical performance

In order to obtain large pictures, the small 35mm negative or slide having a size of 24 x 36 mm must be enlarged. Oskar Barnack discovered the fact that imaging errors will be enlarged and become more noticeable in the resulting image in the course of his initial tests. Therefore, upon Barnack's request, Professor Max Berek computed a special lens for the 0 Series Leica, which corrected spherical aberrations (aperture errors), chromatic errors (color errors) and astigmatism (no image points). Thus, it was an anastigmat, which was what the lens was called initially—"Leitz Anastigmat" f/3.5, F = 50 mm." For its time (1923), it delivered excellent imaging performance and was offered with the first assembly-line 35mm camera, the Leica I.

After the manufacture of approximately 200 to 250 cameras, the lens was renamed the "Elmax," a combination of the two names Ernst Leitz and Max Berek. A short time later, the C.P. Goerz glassworks offered a new, high-quality optical glass with higher refractive power and lower dispersion, so Max Berek recomputed his lens. The five-lens anastigmat with three cemented-together lenses became a modified triplet with improved imaging performance. Consisting of only four elements, two of which were cemented together, this lens became the world-famous Leica "Elmar" lens. One of the primary reasons for the success of Leica cameras was the quality of the lenses. Since Berek's time, Leica has repeatedly sought to achieve the leading edge in lens design and technical implementation and, thus, this has become the central thread through the history of lens development at Leitz and Leica.

Today's Leica M lenses are the result of 75 years of experience in the engineering of lenses for the Leica system. For many years this has been accomplished with the aid of modern computerized lens design developed by Leitz/Leica, and its ultra-modern production plants. In the past, only a few lenses were manufactured of special optical glass, which was developed by Leitz's glass research laboratory. In recent years, however, the imaging power of Leica lenses could be increased considerably due to enormous advances in the production of aspherical lens surfaces, apochromatic correction, and improved surface finishing technology. Today, Leica Camera AG possesses such competence in optical manufacturing that it clearly offers the best lenses in the photographic marketplace.

Aspherical lens surfaces

Aspherical lenses are particularly complex to manufacture. This is due to the fact that at least one of the two lens surfaces deviates from the round (spherical) form. Imaging errors such as spherical aberration and distortion, which in the past could only be remedied by adding additional lens elements, can be prevented. In photographic practice this means: asphericals permit the production of lenses of reduced volume and weight, without reducing the lens' imaging performance. Another way of looking at this is despite increased imaging performance, lenses can be produced with the same volume and weight! With the use of a profiling grinder developed by Leitz in the early 1960s, it was possible for the first time to machine lens surfaces for photographic lenses within the required narrow tolerances. The 35mm f/1.2 Noctilux-M lens, introduced at Photokina 1966, was the first

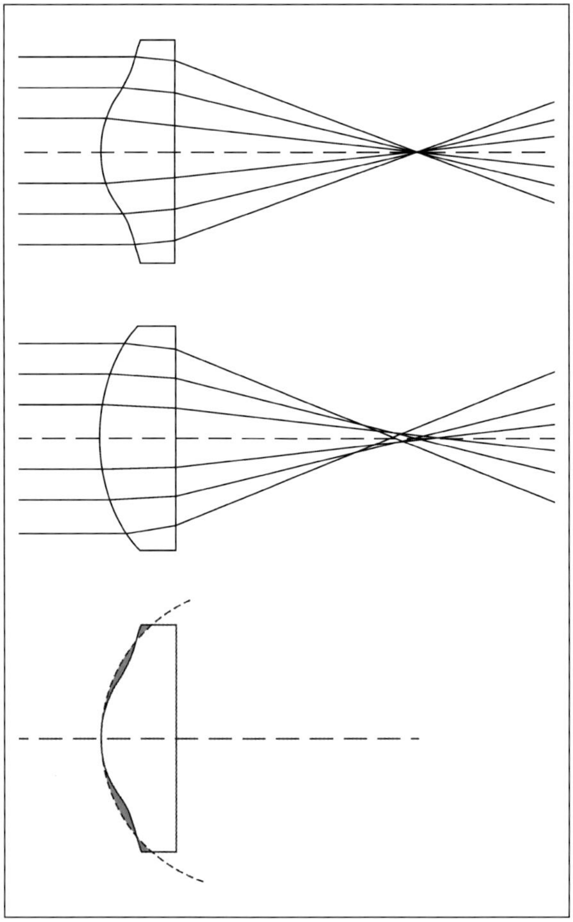

In 1990 significantly improved manufacturing technology allowed the resumption of production of assembly-line aspherical lens surfaces. This time a very powerful wide-angle lens—the 35mm f/1.4 Summilux-M Aspherical—was introduced. The description "aspherical" added to the product name characterizes the special construction features that significantly contribute to the excellent imaging performance of this lens.

Independent of its advances in grinding and polishing of the aspherical lens surface, Leica has also sought to develop less complex methods for the manufacture of asphericals. Due to the cooperation of other leading German optical companies, lenses having aspherical surfaces and a diameter of more than 20 mm could be "clear-molded" for the first time with great precision. To achieve this, a diamond-turned, point-ground and polished tool of ceramic-like material is used. The die that is created from the method corresponds in reverse to the final surface of the lens, which will be formed using it. A specifically developed mathematical model for the definition of tolerable surface deviations, as well as precise

Fig.87: *The optical paths of an aspherical lens (top) and a spherical lens (bottom). The aspherical surface curvature (bottom) deviating from the spherical form requires an extremely complex and extremely precise manufacturing process.*

assembly-line photographic lens with two aspherical lens surfaces. High production and testing costs, however, did not permit cost-effective production. Therefore, in 1977, the lens was replaced by a new computation without aspherical surfaces, but with slightly greater speed. This was accomplished with an additional lens element, which added size and weight. In 1976 it was the most powerful, mass-produced photographic lens in the world. Today's optically and mechanically updated 50mm f/1 Noctilux-M lens ranks as a special top performer in lens design.

Fig.D1: *A dominant foreground with a receding background is an especially striking feature of images made with super-wide angle lenses. 28mm f/2.8 Elmarit-M, 1/125 second, f/8, daylight reversal film ISO 64.*

Fig.D2: *The Leica M invites the photographer to take pictures in low light because the result in most cases exceeds expectations. 24mm f/2.8 Elmarit-M ASPH lens, maximum aperture, daylight reversal film ISO 64.*

Fig.D3: *Only the shortest focal length achieves the necessary overview in tight spaces. 21mm f/2.8 Elmarit-M ASPH lens, 1/250 second, f/8, daylight reversal film ISO 64.*

Fig.D4: *The slight motion blur illustrates that the people in this picture are running from the next rain shower. 28mm f/2 Summicron-M ASPH lens, 1/60 second, f/4, daylight reversal film ISO 64.*

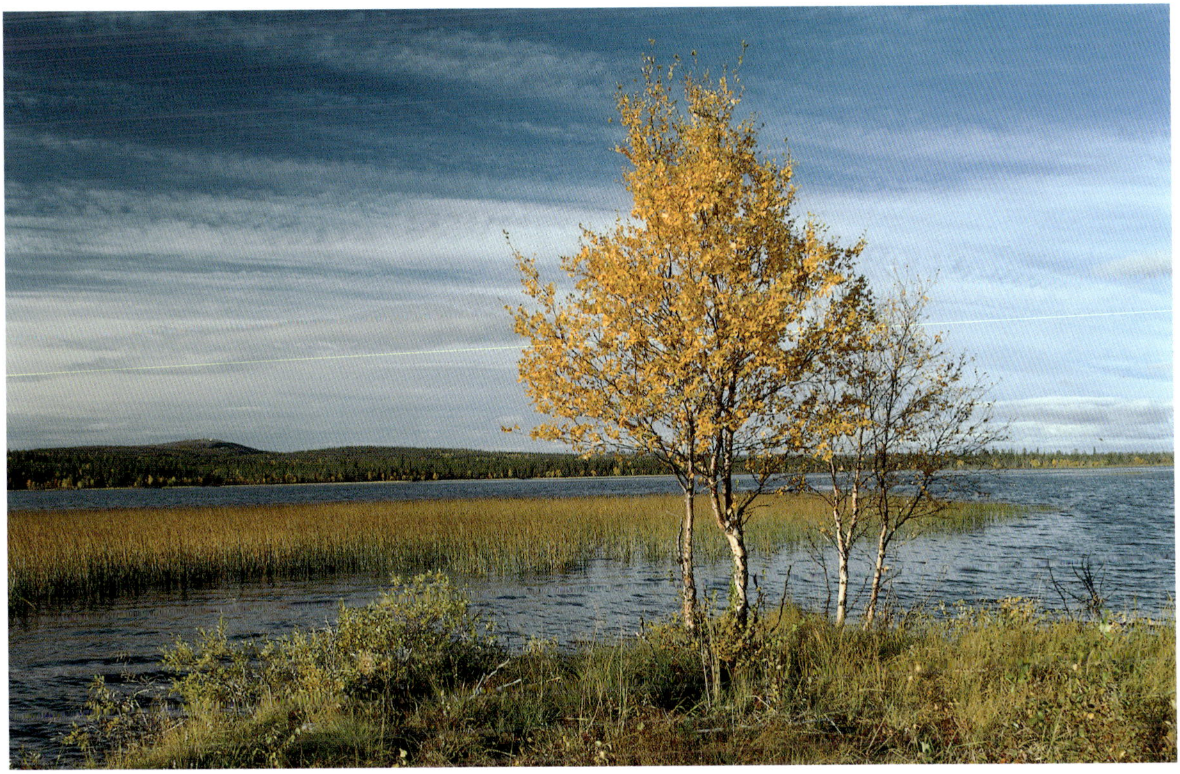

Fig.D1

Fig.D2

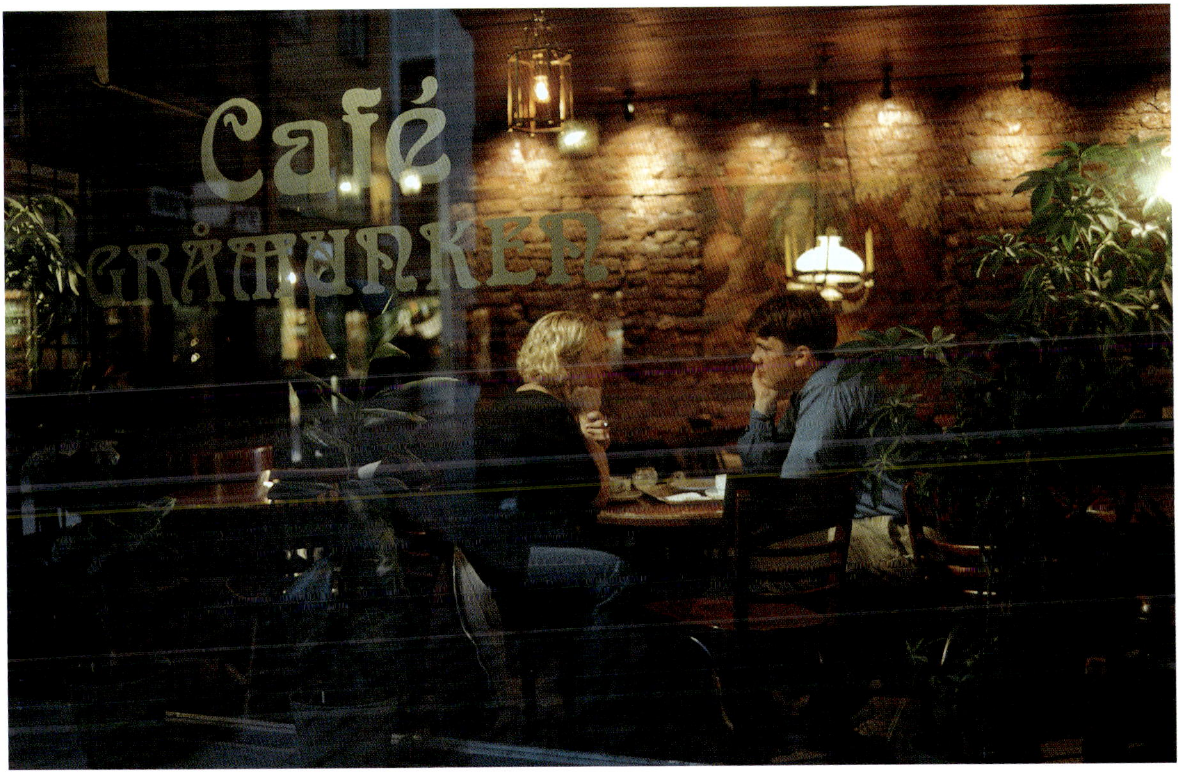

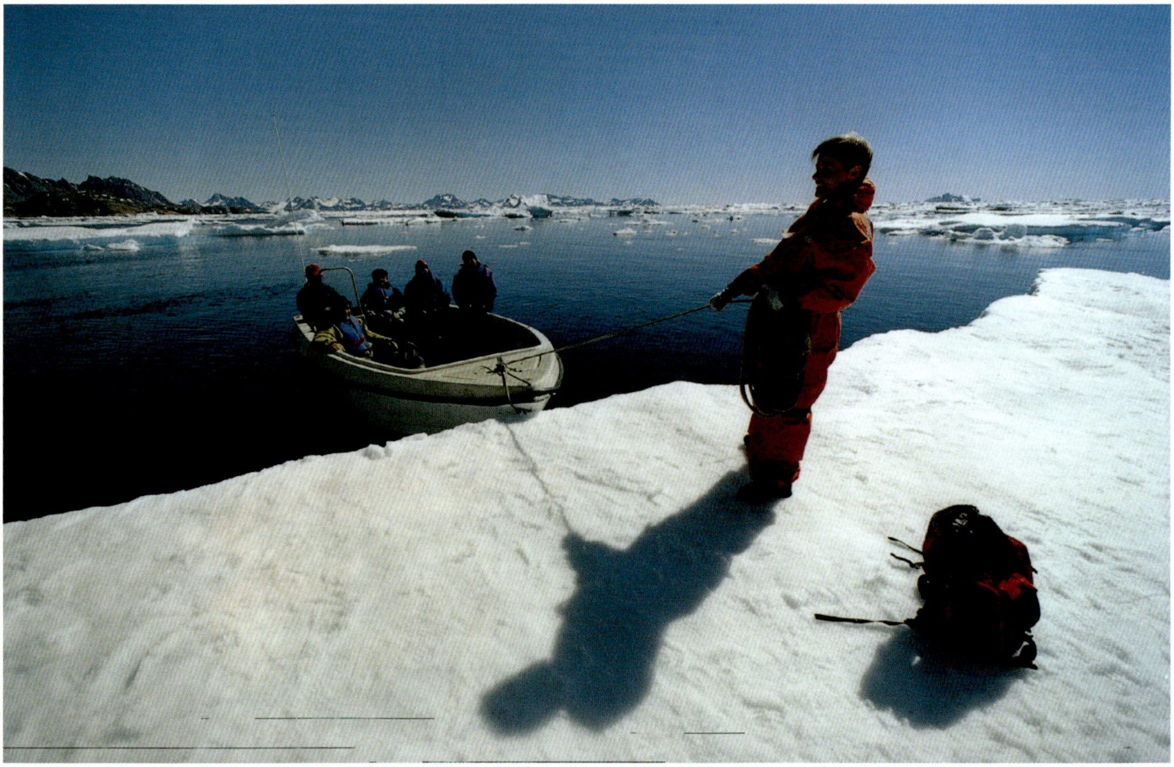

Fig.D3

Fig.D4

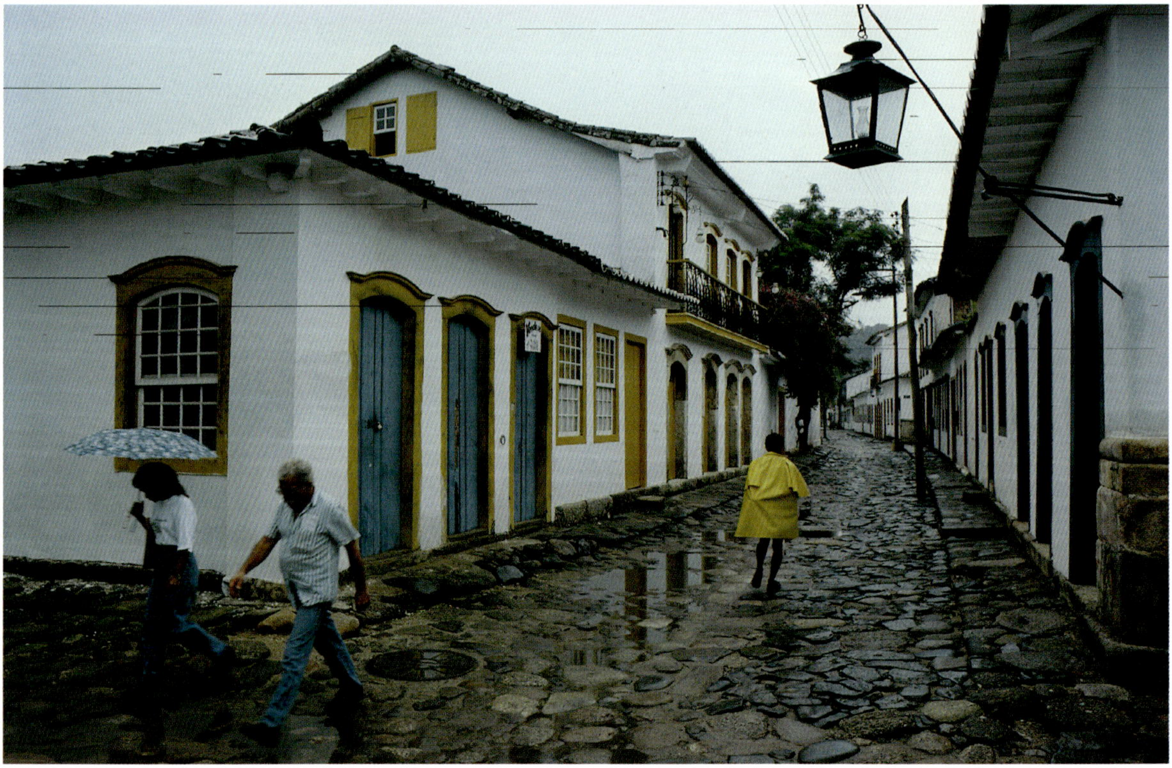

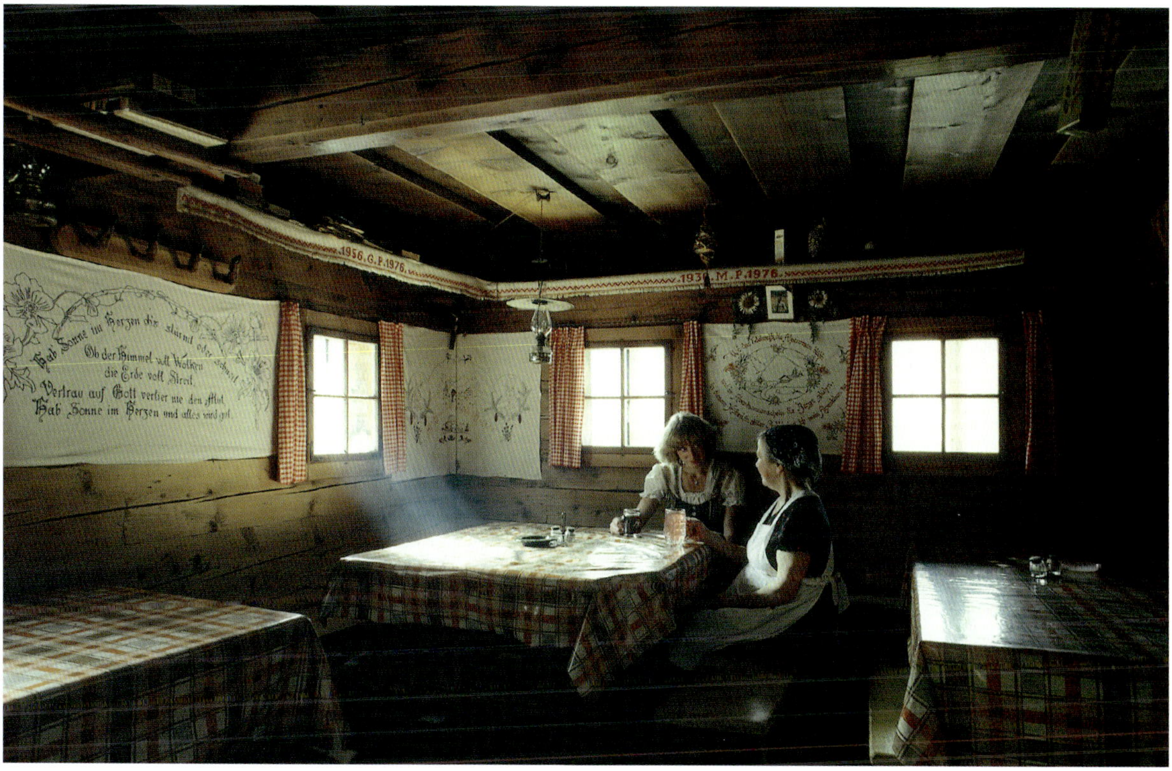
1956. G.P. 1976.
Ob der Himmel voll Wolken
die Erde voll Streit
Vertrau auf Gott verlier nie den Mut
Hab Sonne im Herzen und alles wird gut

Fig.D5

Fig.D6

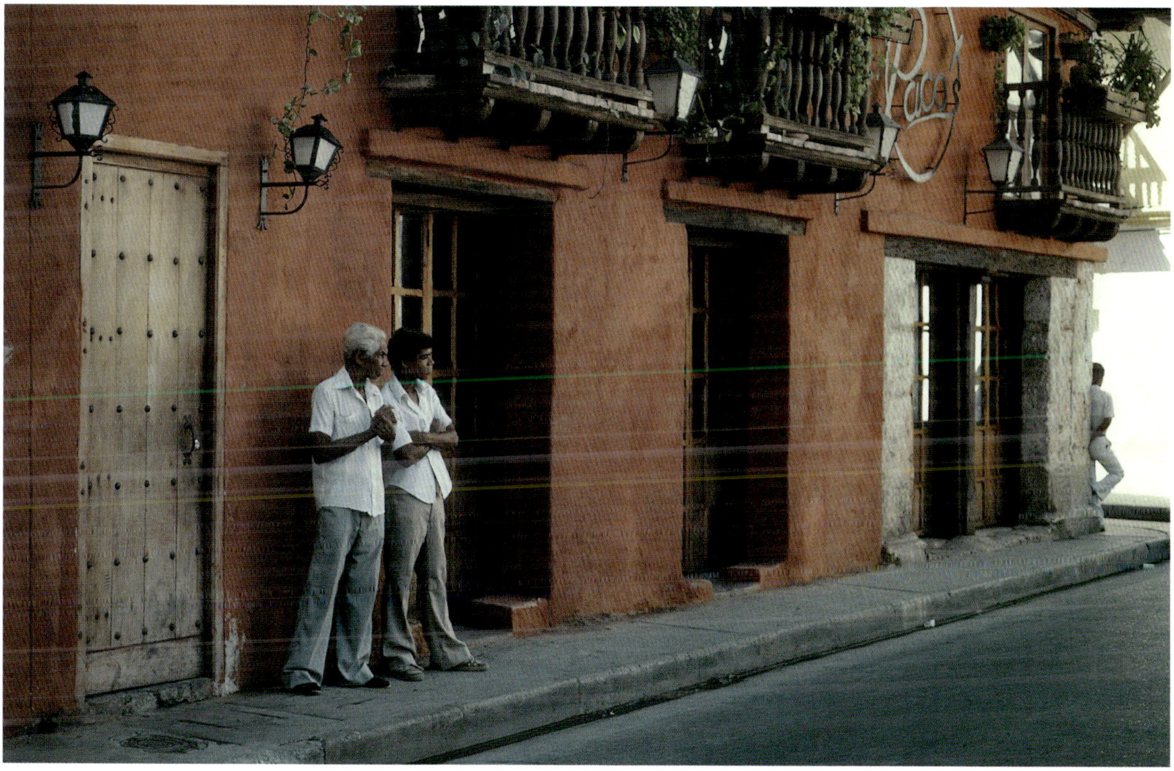

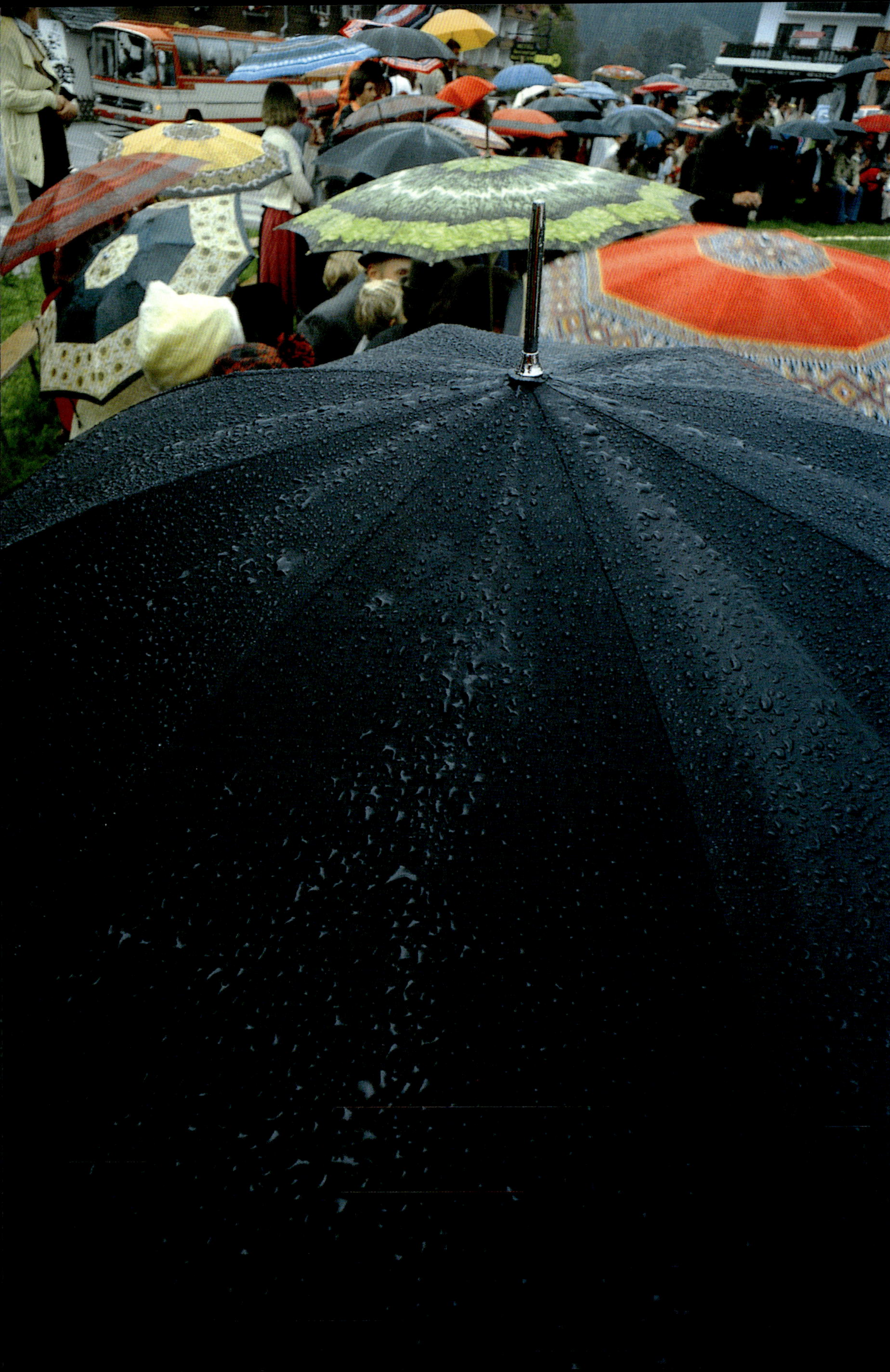

Fig. D7

optical measuring systems are used to continuously monitor results. Finally, when the lens is mounted any inevitable tolerances are compensated for throughout the system by an ingenious method—as is true of all Leica lenses. In 1994, this innovative manufacturing process resulted in the introduction of the still current 35mm f/1.4 Summilux-M ASPH lens.

In 1997 Leica Camera AG recorded another technical advance in the manufacture of asphericals, when the company succeeded in producing aspherical lens surfaces with computer-controlled CNC polishing machines. This modern production process permits greater deviation from the spherical form than was possible by precision-molding aspherical blanks. Also, significantly larger lenses and, in particular, optical glass previously unsuitable for finish molding could be machined.

In the CNC machine a diamond-polishing ring is shifted continuously by minute fractions of a millimeter (see Fig. 89). In order for the polishing process to be successful, lens blanks must be mounted in a highly precise, completely vibration-fee manner. Because of this, the finished lens includes deviations of not more than 0.001 mm of Leica tolerance. Leica participated in developing methods for testing asphericals. Quality control also incorporates the use of computer-generated holograms. With the aid of an interference image, intra-lens deviations amounting to only one tenth of a wavelength of laser light can be recognized.

Among Leica M lenses in the current line-up, fifteen feature different optical data (design, speed, and focal length). Six of these lenses have one or two aspherical surfaces. All six lenses include the abbreviation "ASPH" in their product name, which denotes the use of at least one aspherical element in the optical design.

Fig.D5: *In order to take advantage of the low light in the alpine hut, a chair had to be placed on the table and the Leica M set on it. 21mm f/2.8 Elmarit-M ASPH lens, 1/2 second, f/4, daylight reversal film.*

Fig.D6: *With its 76° angle of view the 28mm f/2.8 Elmarit-M lens, achieves the necessary overview of the narrow lane. The photographer patiently remained in the same location for quite a bit of time in order to take a picture without disrupting pedestrians and cars 1/60 second, f/5.6, daylight reversal film ISO 25.*

Fig.D7: *Even when a super-wide angle lens is used in the close-up range, the depth of field shrinks if lighting conditions mandate a large aperture opening. Therefore, exact focusing is all the more important. However, this is not a problem for range-viewfinder cameras even with dark subjects. 21mm focal length, 1/60 second, maximum aperture, daylight reversal film ISO 64.*

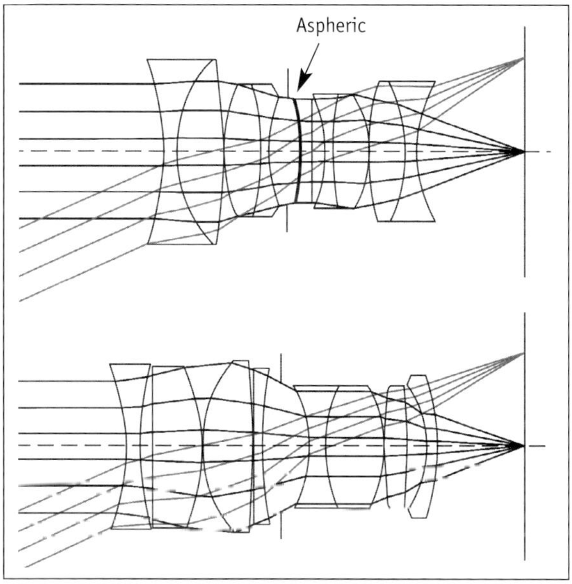

Fig.88: *This represents the optical path of a 35mm f/1.4 Summilux-M ASPH lens with one spherical surface (top). The corresponding alternative computation without aspheric surface results in a longer, heavier design. The tolerances of the individual lenses are outside what is technically feasible (bottom). Furthermore, a larger lens would obstruct more of the Leica M's viewfinder image.*

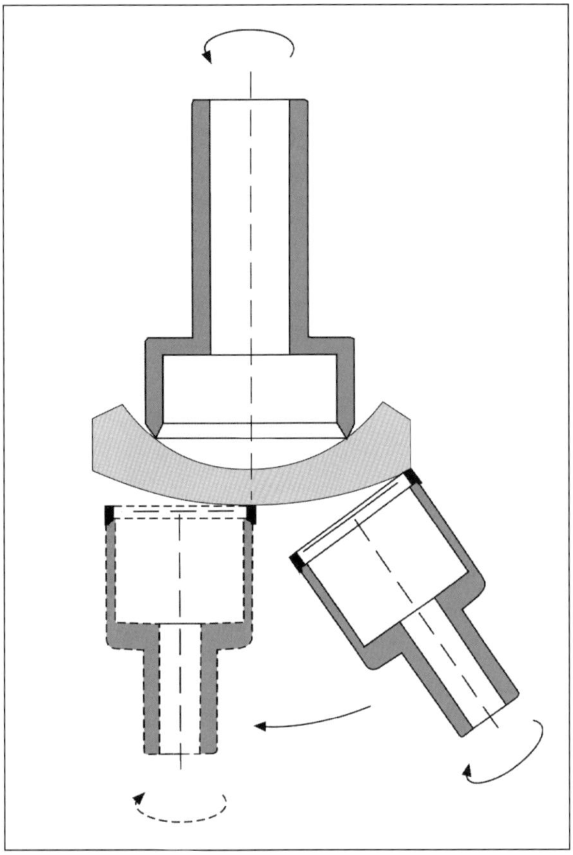

Fig.89: Schematic of the aspherical polishing process. The polishing ring machines are tangentially positioned from the edge toward the center of the lens.

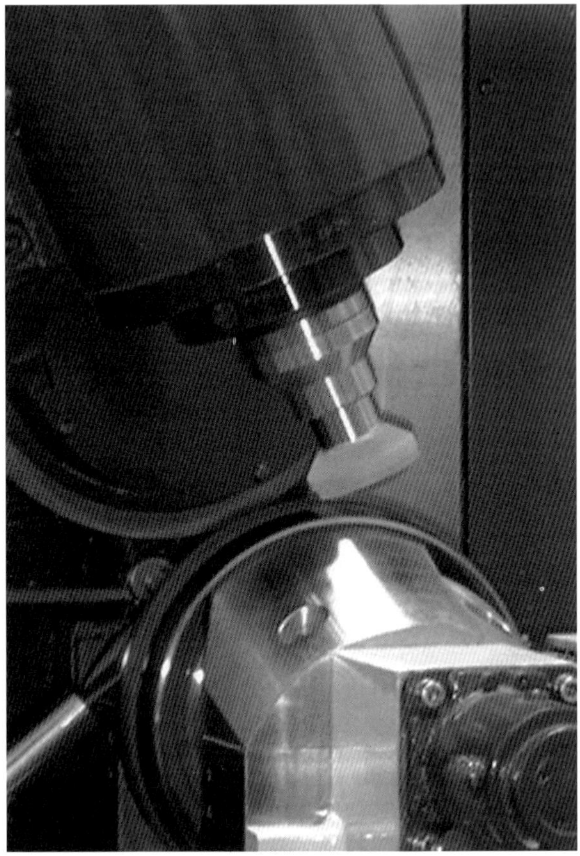

Fig.90: The aspherical lens surface is precision-machined using newly developed tools and materials. This innovative finishing technique produces brilliant surfaces.

The abbreviation "ASPH" does not provide information as to how many lenses in the lens system have such surfaces; likewise, it does not indicate which fabrication process was used for the production of the asphericals.

Table 8 provides an overview of the number of aspherical surfaces in the lens design. To produce asphericals, a process is used that is beneficial to both the manufacturing process and to consumers. By 2002 Leica produced aspherical lens surfaces in wide-angle lenses by precision "polish-molding." Longer focal lengths were produced with computer-controlled CNC polishers. The type of image errors that are predominantly minimized by the lens surface depends on the location of the surface within the optical system. Located in the center of a lens system, the surface mainly serves to correct spherical aberration, i.e., the elimination or reduction of the aperture error. When integrated in the front and/or rear of the system, the spherical longitudinal aberration (distortion), is minimized or eliminated.

The use of aspherical lens surfaces alone does not guarantee a "better" lens. Whether or not the use of these, in lens design and manufacture, makes sense depends on the requirements of those who develop, manufacture, market, and use the lens. Of course, cost and price are always important considerations. Everyone wants a Leica lens that offers maximum optical imaging performance plus, in particular, the photographer wants ease of use. Therefore, compromises are often necessary. What good is it to reduce the dimensions of a lens to minimize obstruction of the viewfinder image of the Leica M if manufacture does not allow testing of the narrow tolerances in order to guarantee optimal imaging performance? What is gained by aspehericals if the use of special optical glass (and more elements) at the same or lower cost achieves the same or even better performance, without more disruption of the viewfinder image? Conclusion: Aspherical lens surfaces are used when the user benefits from them in practical photographic applications. To Leica Camera AG it makes no sense to add "ASHP" to the lens simply to be able to use it as a marketing advantage.

Apochromatic correction

Two Leica M telephoto lenses include the "APO" description in their name. For many photographers this reference indicates that these lenses feature apochromatic correction, which guarantees exceptionally sharp, high-contrast images with excellent color reproduction. What else is implied by the concept "APO?"

As already described above, the evolution to the current state of performance of Leica lenses was never easy because every optical design created imaging errors, which require different, complex corrections. One is the use of asphericals and/or suitable types of glass with appropriate radii, as well as the arrangement of these elements relative to each other. Strictly speaking, despite every effort certain "residual errors" always remain. However, these are usually almost imperceptible. Thus, each optical design inevitably represents a series of compromises, which are designed to serve a specific application. For example, in designing a lens of high magnification and a maximum aperture, a field that is not completely flat is acceptable if the lens is not predominantly for reproduction work. Conversely, a macro lens—if it were available for the Leica M—would compromise maximum speed in the sense of an optimal correction of this spherical aberration. Considering high-speed telephoto lenses, another (uncorrected) residual error, which might not appear at all in wide-angle lenses, might even significantly impair imaging performance: pictures would then be characterized by color fringes and low contrast, as well as by a general lack of sharpness.

The reason for this is the intrinsic property of apparently uniform white light to be both refracted by each optical element and split into individual color components. The familiar play with the prism that produces beautiful light fans in rainbow colors illustrates this principle of spreading out colors, called dispersion by experts. With dispersion, the short-wave blue rays are always deflected more than the long-wave red rays.

In normal lenses and lenses with short focal length this problem is solved with an achromatic correction. By selecting appropriate types of glass and lens combinations, at least the blue and green components of light in the image plane are registered. However, because this chromatic aberration is magnified to the same degree as the subject captured by the lens, the remaining residual error resulting from the uncorrected red components, i.e., the secondary spectrum, matters increasingly in telephoto lenses. Conversely, if long focal length, high lens speed and maximum imaging quality are required, an apochromatic correction is imperative. This correction unifies the entire spectrum in one plane.

The development of new types of glass in the former Leitz glass research laboratory produced optical glass that fulfilled all of these requirements. These included high refractive power with anomalous partial dispersion. Because these types of special glass are very expensive and require an extremely precise assembly, as well as the appropriate focusing mechanism, the price for these lenses increases significantly.

It is characteristic of Leica Camera AG to develop its own criteria for apochromatically corrected photographic lens systems. These criteria cover more than the conventional definition for apochromatic correction. They include the following requirements:

1. Considering a subject point on the optical axis and rays emitted by this subject point near the axis, i.e., conditions corresponding to a small aperture opening, there are three different wavelengths (colors) for one common image point (correction of the chromatic focal distance difference; secondary spectrum).

2. Considering a light beam that is emitted by the same subject point and is at a distance from the axis, i.e., a situation that exists with large aperture, there are at lest two wavelengths for one common point of intersection with the optical axis. Therefore, the spherochromatic aberration must be eliminated.

3. The aperture error and the coma near the axis must be largely corrected (spherical correction, fulfillment of isoplanatism conditions).

In view of this definition, the description of apochromat, which was originally used in conjunction with telescope and microscope lenses, was introduced, in systems, which, in their time, were (and could be) corrected only for relatively small image fields. Consequently, the above definition provides information only regarding the chromatic and monochromatic correction for image points on the optical axis (image center) and in its immediate environment. This definition does not cover the correction in the central and peripheral areas of an extended image field, as is true of the 35mm format. The latter, however, is an absolute requirement for Leica if an "Apo" is to be used for taking pictures and the lens is not just meaninglessly labeled "Apo," even though this description is perfectly correct in accordance with the above original definition. Consequently, stricter standards apply to Leica Apo lenses: They are characterized by their already large aperture and by their apochromatic or almost apochromatic correction away from the center of the image, i.e., in the image field, and into the corners of the image.

Experienced photographers know that dark red filters may create problems when used with longer focal lengths. Inadequately stopping down may produce unsharpness caused by the above-described inadequate color correction (chromatic aberration) of the lens. This is why it is always recommended that reflex cameras be focused with the filter attached. Because focusing does not occur through the lens in the Leica M, the apochromatic correction is an advantage with greater focal lengths, even if these Leica M lenses are used for exposures with large aperture and particularly dense color filter, specifically, red and orange. Because, strictly speaking, the apochromatic correction of the Leica lenses applies only to the visible region of the spectrum, infrared exposures require that a potentially existing focal difference be determined and taken into consideration (see page 198).

In particular, the modern production of highly precise lenses made of extremely high-quality optical glass requires the very careful assembly of the individual optical components. Lens barrel component specifications refer to precise dimensional stability and the lack of incident light reflections in the finished lens system. They the lens edges must be lacquer-coated and the metal mounts and tubes must be provided with light-traps. This stops migrating light, which would lead to reflections and reduced contrast in the image. Low contrast and partial brightening (reflections) in the picture may also be caused by the lens surfaces themselves because light is reflected by each glass/light surface. Therefore, all free lens surfaces are provided with a finish.

Surface finishing

For many years anti-reflective coatings have been used on lenses, prisms, and filters throughout the Leica system. For a long time these were just called finished lenses without particular claims of single or multiple coatings. The overriding idea always was (and still is) to produce the best-possible lens. And, in truth, the performance of a photographic lens is evaluated by a number of individual features, which include contour sharpness, contrast, and color reproduction, resolution of details, as well as the absence of distortion and reflections. Lately, the technical processes used to reduce the reflection of lens surfaces have been strongly emphasized in marketing claims. The magic word is "multi-coating."

What is the significance?
When light rays pass through a glass surface, a reflection is created, whereby its intensity is a function of the refractive index of the glass. For example, window glass reflects on its front and reverse sides approximately 4% of incident light. It acts like a mirror. The same applies to optical glass which, depending on its index of refraction, reflects 4.2% to 9.6% of light. Multiple internal reflections occur in this manner in lenses with many elements. This lowers the lens' light transmission —in other words—its photometric or its sensitometric characteristics are changed and its speed is reduced. In addition, the portion of scattered light (flare) is increased; it is superimposed on the actual image and reduces the contrast. More pronounced double images of light sources or aperture spots could even occur on the film under certain unfavorable conditions.

Modern techniques of surface finishing (coating) provide the means of diminishing these interfering effects to a large extent. This involves vapor-depositing of several extremely thin layers on every free lens surface. Thus, each layer reflects a portion of the light and a portion of the light is reflected by the glass surface itself. If, for example, a single layer has the thickness of one fourth of a wavelength of the incident light, reflected light beams having this wavelength experience a phase shift (path difference) of half the lightwave length. Here a wave peak meets a wave valley and they cancel each other out. This phenomenon is called interference. Because energy, in the form of light, cannot be destroyed, the reduction of reflection increases light transmission for this wavelength. With multiple layers this interference effect is substantially more pronounced because there are different light-wavelengths.

In order to be able to achieve a uniform reduction of reflection over the entire spectral region of light (380 to 700 Nanometers), several thin layers of different thickness from a few ten thousands of a millimeter to a few micrometers are applied by vapor-deposition. In a Leica, these so-called broadband layers usually consist of six individual layers. At Leica this is called a "WeCo." In order to make them effective, these layers must be vapor-deposited with the greatest precision to achieve the desired effect. One example: In order to maintain WeCo 40 tolerance, individual layers must be coated with nanometer accuracy. One nanometer equals 1/1,000,000 millimeters!

Leica lenses are coated in computer-controlled, state-of-the-art vapor-deposition plants. The lenses to be coated are cleaned manually and ultrasonically, placed on spherical surfaces, and moved into vacuum chambers.

The substances (metal oxides and metal fluorides), which are contained in the individual layers of the anti-reflection coatings, are applied by resistance-evaporator or electron-beam evaporators. An ion source ensures compression of the vapor-deposited layers and prevents penetration of moisture to a great degree, thereby making the layers more resistant.

Due to different indices of refraction, each type of glass requires its own layer composition. In order to control vapor-deposition, the layer thickness is determined with a quartz crystal oscillator or an optical thickness-measuring device. The control computer continually compares the measured values with nominal values and completes vapor-deposition once these values have been reached. One test glass, having the same index of refraction as the lenses, will be vapor-deposited with each batch. This ensures that the vapor-deposited layer displays the required quality.

These reflection-minimizing layers assure that all Leica lenses, independent of focal length or power, exhibit similar high transmission and almost the same color reproduction characteristics. The finish is tested in compliance with environmental conditions specified by DIN and MIL standards. This includes an abrasion test (with a 50% content of pumice), as well as an exposure test (72 hours at +50°C and 40% air humidity). This assures that lens-to-air surfaces of the front and rear lenses are durable and that careful cleaning will not harm them (see page 158).

Basic components

Lenses for Leica M cameras do not require an automatic diaphragm since the subject is viewed through the camera's separate range-viewfinder. Therefore, the viewfinder image is always uniformly bright, regardless of the speed of the lens or the aperture setting. Because of the absence of an automatic aperture mechanism, Leica M lenses are generally also markedly more compact and lighter than lenses of equivalent speed and focal length for reflex cameras.

Compact design is especially important because the viewfinder image becomes obstructed when the lenses are long or have a large diameter. Leica designers therefore always seek to create an optimum design for every type of lens, while also devoting special attention to ease of use. The result is that, whenever possible, all elements that control a function are positioned in the same location. Focusing rings and aperture rings also turn in the same direction on every lens, so that operation remains identical from one lens to another. The aperture ring is located at the front of the lens, ahead of the helical focusing mount, unlike most aperture rings on lenses for reflex cameras.

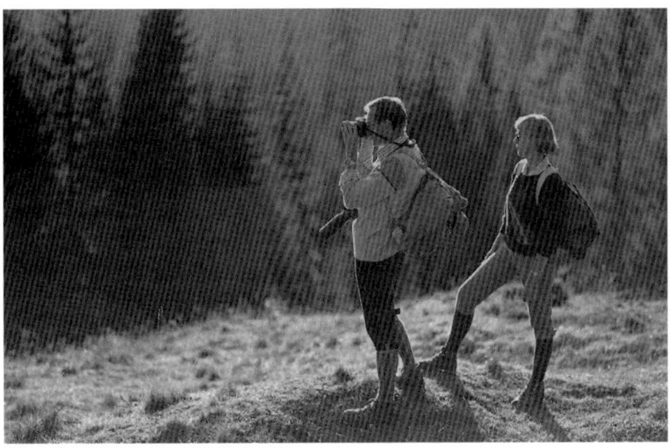

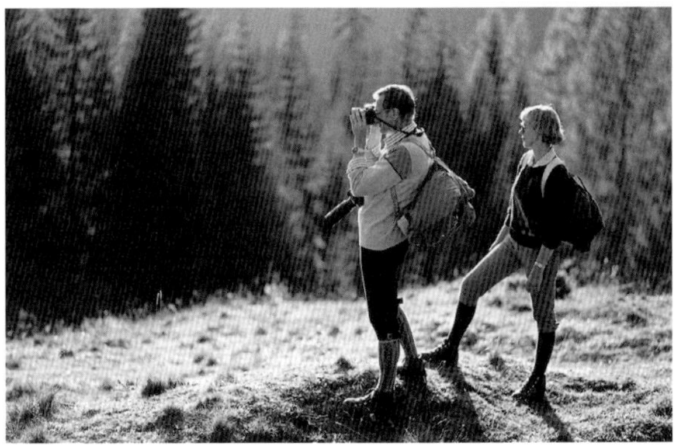

***Fig.91**: The importance of a lens hood is commonly underestimated. Often attractive lighting requires "flare prevention" for the front element. In situations when the lens hood doesn't provide enough shielding, the photographer can use his own hand, or better yet, the hand of an "assistant" to create extra shade on the lens. The photographs above were made without (left) and with (right) a lens hood. Both pictures were made with a 90mm f/2 Summicron-M lens, facing a low evening sun. 1/250 second at f/4 and medium-speed film.*

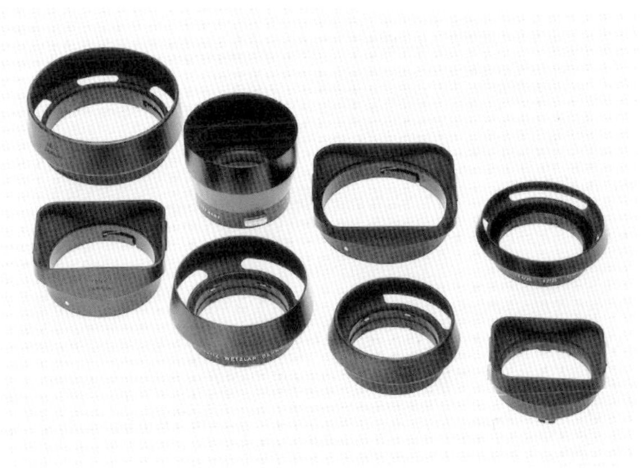

***Fig.92:** Leica lens hoods are customed designed to match the coverage of a lens while interferring as little as possible with the image through the viewfinder.*

The lens hood

All Leica M lenses are supplied complete—not only with front and rear caps but also with the proper lens hood. Leica lens hoods are custom-designed for each type of lens, to provide good protection against extraneous light while interfering as little as possible with the viewfinder image.

A lens hood is exceedingly important when the lens is ready for action. It keeps out surrounding light that would adversely affect image quality, possibly causing flare. It also largely shields the front element from raindrops, dirt, and snowflakes and keeps it from being inadvertently smeared by fingerprints.

Filter sizes

Since the use of filters and special effects attachments plays a subordinate role with rangeviewfinder cameras (no visual control is possible in the viewfinder), and because of the objective of keeping any viewfinder obstruction by the lens and its accessories to a minimum, the filter diameter of each type of Leica M lens is kept as small as possible. Therefore, filters for various Leica M lenses are not as uniform in diameter as those for Leica R lenses (see page 211).

The Leica M bayonet

All Leica M lenses can be interchanged very quickly, whether the shutter is wound or not, and regardless of focus and aperture settings. The

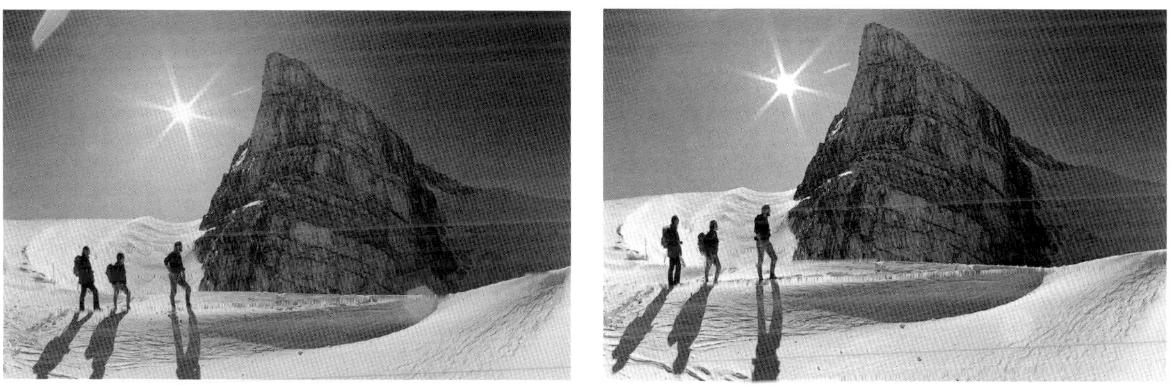

***Fig.93:** Strong light sources in the picture, like the sun in the examples below, can under certain conditions create reflections and images of the aperture (left), even when all surfaces of the lens have been multicoated. Changing the direction of the camera by turning it a little to the left or the right, or tilting it slightly up or down, can often determine whether er not such stray images will become visible. These two photographs were taken one right after the other at 1/60 second with an aperture of f/22.*

rapid change bayonet of Leica M lenses is made of sanded, chrome-plated brass. An inserted lens is seated in the camera's bayonet flange by a steel spring. A cam that absorbs heavy loads provides added protection against excessive strain on this spring. This can occur with the use of heavy (fast) lenses and/or long focal lengths. The opening of the bayonet is deliberately large, so that no artificial vignetting will occur with large apertures or long focal-length lenses.

All Leica M lenses are equipped with a rigid, knurled ring that is coupled to the bayonet mount to provide a firm grip. The lens can be handled securely by this ring to lift it out of the camera—which is accomplished by pressing the bayonet button with the left thumb to release the lens lock and then turning the lens through a short 30° to the left. The bayonet button on the Leica M3, M7, and all Leica M6 models is protected by an additional ring so that the lens cannot be released accidentally and fall out of the camera.

To attach a lens to the camera, the red dot on the knurled ring, or on the bayonet of the lens, must be lined up with the red dot on the bayonet button of the camera. With the two bayonet surfaces properly aligned and in contact, the lens can be turned to the right until it audibly locks into position. The small tactile red nub at the base of the lens enables the photographer to change lenses in the dark, as in a theater. In a crowd, or while mountain climbing, when one hand is needed for personal security, lenses can even be changed with only one hand. A Leica M lens cannot be attached to the camera incorrectly.

Even though both the front and the rear elements of Leica M lenses are generally safely recessed in the lens mounts, attention should always be paid to the glass surfaces when changing lenses. Finger prints, droplets of water and other debris should be removed immediately, because they reduce the optical performance of the lenses considerably.

Distance and depth-of-field scales

Picture sharpness is usually verified in the rangefinder field of the camera's viewfinder and adjusted by turning the focusing ring on the lens. After that, the measured distance in meters or in feet can be read on the distance scale of the lens. While the index points at the focal distance, the extent of the depth of field for each aperture setting can also be read. The nearest limit of the depth of field can be read on the distance scale opposite the left f/stop number, and the furthest limit opposite the corresponding f/stop number on the right.

Because of a shortage of space on some lenses, not every index line is identified with the respective f/stop number—only every other one. On many lenses the focal length is clearly engraved in large digits on the left side of the field scale. That makes it easier to distinguish lenses of different focal lengths that are similar in appearance, so that lens changes can be made more quickly.

Special characteristics

Experts have long asserted that the outstanding performance of Leica M lenses is responsible for visibly better results, thus making Leica M lenses world famous. Even though normal Summicron lenses were used decades ago in the navigation sensors of Surveyor's automatic lunar probes, every experienced photographer knows that Leica lenses can render their optimum performance only in applications for which they were designed. Therefore, one would not, for instance, use a super wide-angle lens for high-quality reproduction work.

All Leica M lenses are conceived for distant ranges and for the pictorial reproduction of three-dimensional objects. A photographic test that is based on photographs of a newspaper page (taken from a few meters or yards away) is practically useless in evaluating the optical performance of such lenses (also see page 95). The particular performance characteristics of a lens and the respective field of application will be discussed later in the descriptions and technical data for each Leica M lens. The following is valid for all of them:

The Optics

- Leica lenses are based on high-quality optical glass, which was often developed in the Leitz glass research laboratory, including the use of rare earth in the manufacturing process. Special Leica optical glass is remarkable because of its high indices of refraction and low dispersion, or anomalous partial dispersion, for the reduction of the secondary spectrum.
- All Leica lenses already perform at a very high degree of correction at full aperture. This means that, with Leica lenses, the full aperture is already a perfectly usable working aperture and not just a "prestige aperture."
- The image quality of Leica lenses is very uniform across the entire image field, i.e., quality does not drop off towards the corners. In addition, these lenses virtually eliminate distortion such as disturbing curves in straight lines.
- Leica lenses guarantee high color saturation, as well as fine color differentiation, which add up to a visible increase in the brilliance of the image.
- Leica lenses have virtually perfect light transmission across the entire visible spectrum, producing a high effective (photometric) aperture. The nominal f/number is purely geometric entity, which does not include light that is absorbed by the glass and by the layers of optical cement in the lens!
- The high degree of freedom from flare is achieved by the effective anti-reflection coating of optical surfaces in conjunction with sophisticated design of the interior of the lens mount, which captures stray light in blackened "light traps." Thus, the mounts for the elements in a Leica lens do more than just hold the elements precisely in place!
- All glass-to-air surfaces feature highly efficient anti-reflection coatings, which are optimized for the type of glass with the aid of computers. Double or multiple layers are utilized whenever they produce a genuine advantage but Leica does not indiscriminately apply the same coatings to all surfaces.
- Ion-based vapor-deposition coating of lens surfaces achieves a particularly dense and very uniform coating of reflection-minimizing layers. These anti-reflection layers also provide uniform color reproduction throughout the Leica lens range, independent of lens speed and focal length.

Mechanical components

- Precision-manufactured mechanical components are an important part of every Leica M lens, because, without them, the high-performance optics cannot perform properly. That is why Leitz devotes so much attention to mechanical details.
- The material for helical focusing mounts— brass on brass or brass on aluminum— is selected according to technical requirements. Whenever necessary, the mating parts of helical focusing mounts are individually matched to each other. This leads to a highly precise fit, so that only a thin film of a special lubricant developed for the Leica is needed to ensure a uniformly smooth movement of the focusing mount, even at extreme temperatures. This quality remains unchanged even with long, continuous use. Thus, Leica lenses do not have thick layers of lubricants.
- Whether the metal surfaces are chrome-plated, titanium-plated, anodized, or lacquered determines which material must be used for external lens mount components. Aluminum is easily anodized. The black anodization goes excellently with the black chrome-plated camera housings. Unfortunately, the silver look does not go well with the chrome-plated silvery camera parts. Therefore, external mount components must be made of brass that can be chrome-plated or titanium plated if the lenses are titanium-plated or chrome-plated in a silvery finish. This is why these Leica M lenses are always heavier than the black-anodized models.

- The torques required for focusing and for changing the aperture are matched to each other and adjusted so that optimum handling is assured, even at extremely high and low temperatures. The lenses can be used without limitations at temperatures ranging from -25°C or -13°F to +60°C or +141°F. All parts of the lenses are protected against corrosion, so that problem-free operation is assured under any climatic condition.
- The parallel focusing feature of Leica M lenses makes it possible to turn just the focusing ring of the lens, while the front part of the lens (front group and mount) merely moves in and out. This significantly facilitates the use of a polarization filter. Also, all lens hoods remain in the same position and the effect of the rectangular ones preserved. No additional obstruction of the viewfinder is caused with perforated hoods.
- An outstanding stability of the linear movement guides in Leica lenses has also been addressed. The lengths of the load-bearing parts of all helical focusing mounts have been designed accordingly. The results are better gliding characteristics and easy handling.
- No levers or other control linkages that could be damaged during a lens change project from the backs of Leica M lenses. Thus the lenses can also be placed on their backs on any stable support without any unusual precaution!

Quality assurance

Leica cameras are renowned for their durability. High performance over a long period of time, equipment with hard use and in extreme conditions, is a natural expectation of professional photographers. The same applies to Leica M lenses. In accordance with the overall guidelines for the many inspection departments, sophisticated testing programs and special Leica testing conditions have been developed to assure that:

- Every newly designed lens undergoes extensive testing before being released for production. Mechanical parts and the glass elements are subjected to stringent tests. The complete lens is tested for no less than 75 separate aspects. For example, photographically in cold and hot environments, as well as after a severe temperature gradient from +20°C (+68°F) to -20°C (-4 °F) and back again.
- In numerous cases, Leica lenses meet military specifications for the highest demands under the severest conditions. Their black-anodized surface, which is applied with a special Leica process, makes them look "like new" for a long time.
- The design and the fabrication techniques applied to Leica lenses assure that vibrations resulting from any kind of transportation, for instance, cannot cause any damage. Their shock and impact resistance is unusually high—up to 100 times acceleration due to gravity.
- Extremely narrow tolerances during fabrication assure high production uniformity. Individual lens elements are individually selected for assembly into an optical system with the aid of a mathematical model. This compensates the plus/minus minus tolerances that occur during manufacturing (tolerance-compensating grouping.)

Normal focal lengths

Lenses with focal lengths that correspond approximately to the diagonal of the negative format are called normal lenses. In the 35mm format of 24 x 36 mm the diagonal measures about 43 mm (1-3/6 inches). For practical reasons and for reasons of better quality, however, more than 75 years ago Leitz decided to use a standard focal length that is nearly 10 mm (just over 3/8 inch) longer. And that is still the case today. Standard lenses for Leica cameras have a focal length of 52mm (nearly 2-1/16 inches). This holds true even when the engraving around the front element of the lens reads only 50mm. Even today, most top-quality 35mm cameras are sold with a normal or standard lens with a focal length of 50mm. A total of three different lenses in this focal-length group are available for the Leica M camera. Among them are the fastest production lenses for 35mm cameras on the world market, as well as the Summicron-M lens, which is world famous for its superior performance.

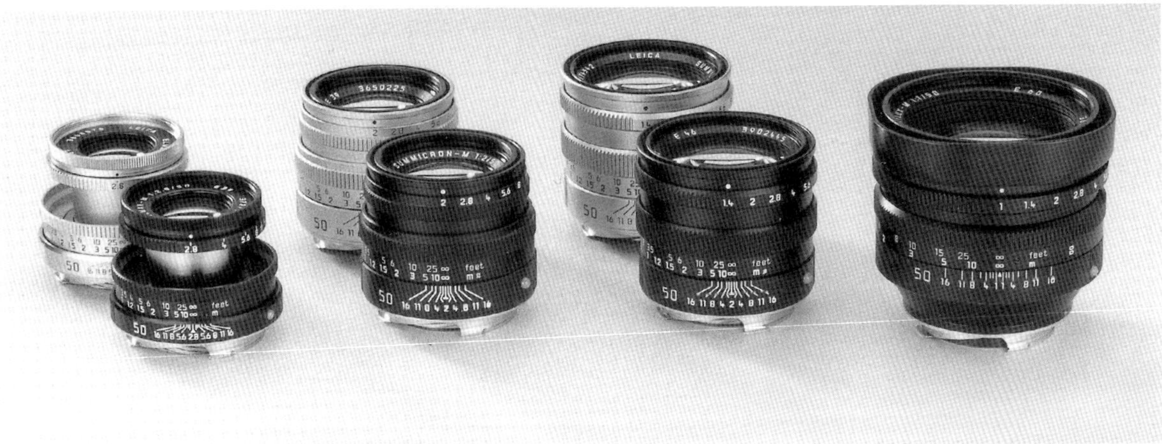

Fig.94: Standard focal lengths

Nearly every photographer started taking pictures with a normal lens. There are famous professionals who prefer this focal length, because it combines many advantages. For instance, despite their high speed, these lenses are still compact and lightweight allowing handheld photographs with outstanding image quality under poor light conditions. Those who constantly carry a Leica camera will appreciate the "ready-to-shoot" versatility of normal lenses. This use of standard lenses is uncomplicated and requires no special training.

For the novice, taking pictures with this lens is easy because its angle of view of about 45° most closely corresponds to the natural coverage of the human eye. Considering their many advantages, these lenses are certainly worth their price.

The retractable 50mm f/2.8 Elmar M lens includes a screw-mounted lens hood. The other three standard lenses are supplied with a permanently installed lens hood, which can be pulled out.

50mm f/2.8 Elmar-M

This new 1994/95 design, with its excellent technical specifications, is named after the legendary Elmar. Although, based on its design, this lens' use and imaging performance have been adapted to today's demands. It has been designed with a rectilinear focusing mount to allow exposure compensation with the lens aperture when Leica M cameras with TTL exposure meter are used, or to facilitate aperture preselection for the aperture priority automatic exposure control of the Leica M7, without inadvertently resetting the focus. This also applies when a polarizing filter is used. At the same time, lens changes become more convenient and faster.

The optical system is a triplet, i.e., a conventional four-lens system with two freestanding elements and

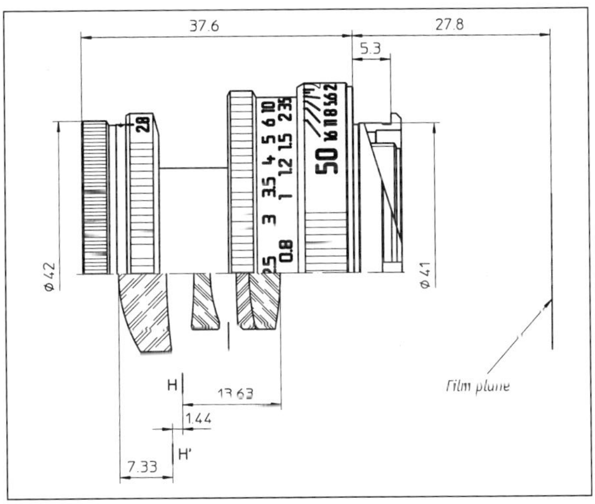

Fig.95: 50mm f/2.8 Elmar-M

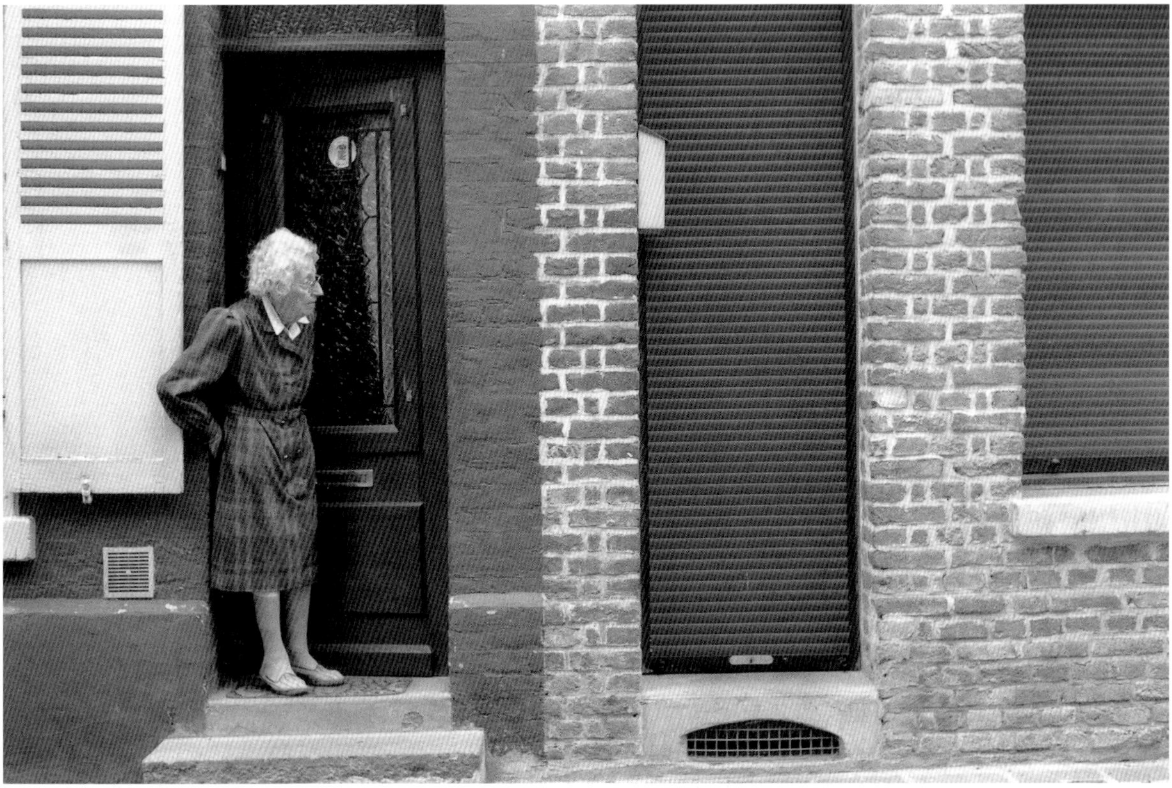

Fig.96: *A 50mm lens is compact, lightweight, and relatively fast, making it ideal for photojournalistic or candid photography. These qualities also make it an excellent choice for travel photography. This photo was taken on a trip to France with a 50mm f/2.8 Elmar-M at 1/260 second and high-speed film.*

one cemented rear element. By using glass having a high refraction index with anomalous partial dispersion (index of refraction, greater than 1.8) in conjunction with a new optical computation, the same number of lenses as used in the predecessor resulted in improved imaging performance, which is retained into the close-up range with minimal stopping down. Even at maximum aperture, the lens' performance is excellent. Curvature of field virtually does not exist; the very minor coma disappears when stopped down to medium aperture values. As is true of any optical system, the 50mm f/2.8 Elmar-M is subject to system-related vignetting. This drop in light toward the image corners becomes visible in particular with low exposure and uniformly bright image field (e.g., a full-size building wall or a cloudless sky). Starting with f/5.6 the lens is free from vignetting. When not in use, the lens may be collapsed into the camera housing. This reduces the depth of the camera by 16 mm, thereby making the Leica M compact and portable. If a picture is to be taken, the 50mm f/2.8 lens is pulled out quickly and securely locked by a quick turn to the right. This lens is sold with a very compact screw-mount lens hood, as well as with a classic silvery chrome-plated or black-anodized brass lens cap. The 50mm f/2.8 Elmar is suitable for numerous photographic applications, especially wherever low weight and compact dimensions have priority over maximum speed.

50mm f/2 Summicron-M

This six-element Gauss type lens with five plano surfaces (four of them are in the two cemented elements) is offers the best combination of features and the highest degree of performance in the class of high-speed normal lenses. It is therefore considered to be the world standard for superb image quality. Yet, it is still small, lightweight, and handy.

Its high contrast, outstanding detail reproduction, and its extraordinary sharpness all the way into the corners of the picture, are the particular performance characteristics of this lens. Even at full aperture, image quality is excellent. By stopping down only slightly, residual astigmatism present in a narrow zone disappears completely. Distortion is exceedingly minor.

These outstanding performance characteristics hardly change across the entire focusing range. That is why the 50 mm f/2 Summicron-M lens with its crisp contrast and flat field performs very well in the close-up range. Stopping the aperture down to f/2.8 or f/4 increases the performance of the lens in this range even further.

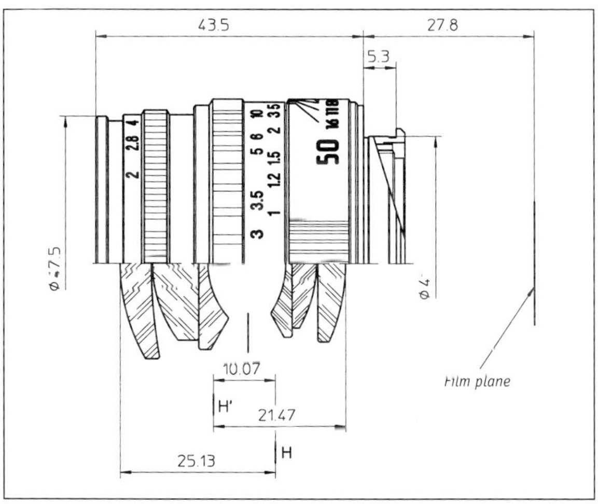

Fig.97: *50mm f/2 Summicron-M*

At full aperture the 50mm f/2 Summicron-M lens is free from coma and it shows only a negligible tendency for reflections (or repeated images) of light sources that appear in the picture. The vignetting that is inherent in the system is hardly noticeable in practice. At apertures of f/4 or smaller, the lens is completely free from vignetting and the image is very evenly illuminated across the entire field.

50mm f/1.4 Summilux-M

This lens is a modified Gauss type that has high contrast and very good correction for coma at full aperture. This meets the requirements of the application for which it was designed—available light and nighttime photography, with emphasis on high-contrast performance. Residual astigmatism is minor. Stopping down the aperture enhances performance even further. Its neutral reproduction and exact differentiation of colors are especially remarkable.

The 50mm f/1.4 Summilux-M is a lens with unusually good reflection characteristics, which means that it has practically no disturbing ghost images and no aperture reflections in extreme backlighting situations or when light sources are included in the picture.

In the close-up range, the Summilux-M shows good contrast across the entire field, even at full aperture. However it is not entirely free from curvature of field in this working range. A trace of barrel-shaped distortion may also become apparent with critical subjects that have characteristics such as straight lines near the edges of the picture.

At f/1.4, the effect of vignetting that is inherent in every optical system may become noticeable with short exposures of uniformly bright surfaces such as blue skies, building walls, and the like. However, vignetting diminishes rapidly as the lens is stopped down. At f/4 and smaller apertures, the lens is free from any vignetting that is inherent in the optical system.

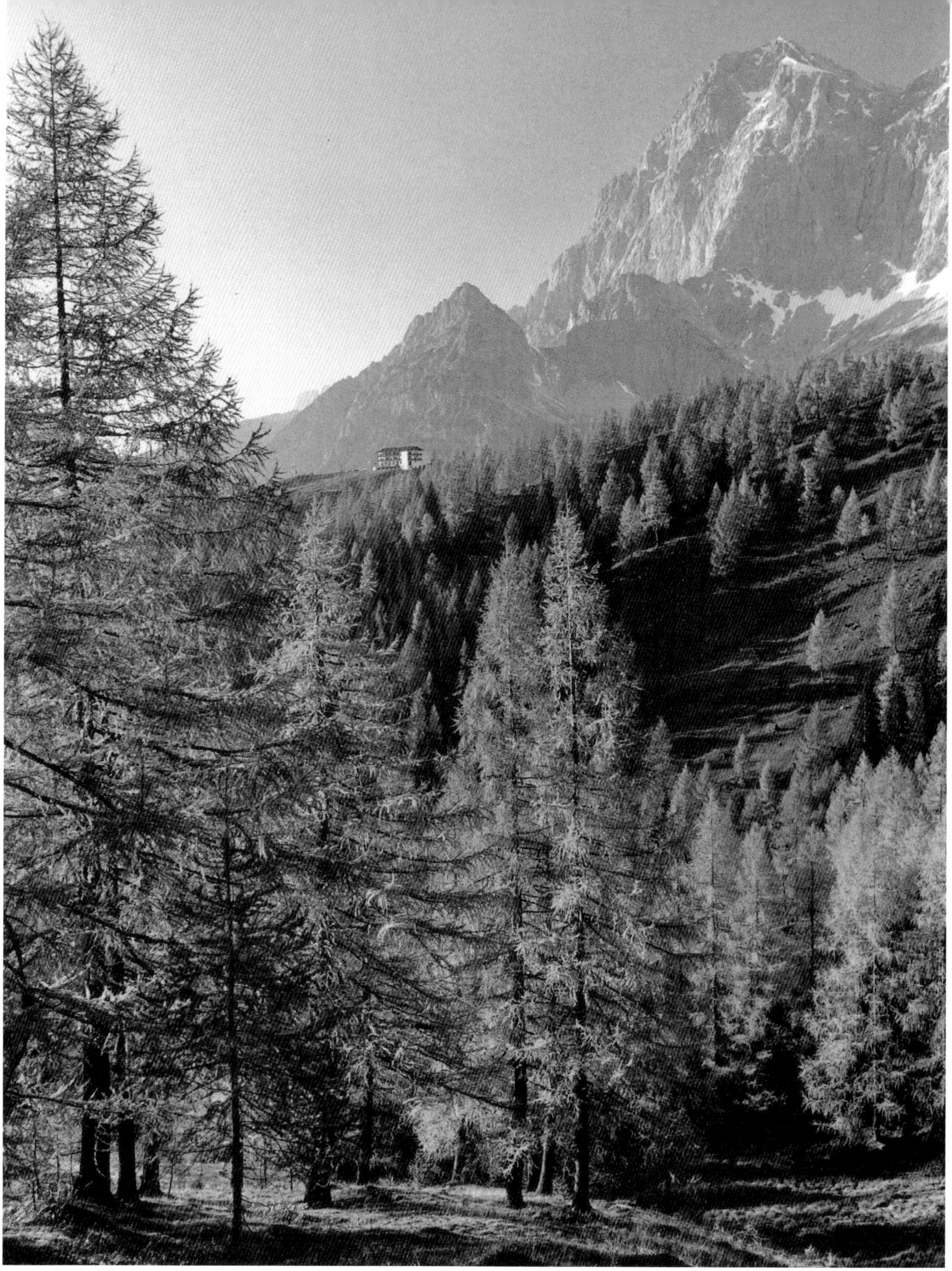

Fig.98: *Normal lenses are very versatile. The 50mm f/2 Summicron-M lens' fine image quality made it excellent choice for this scenic photograph taken with a yellow-green filter and low speed film at 1/125 second and f/5.6.*

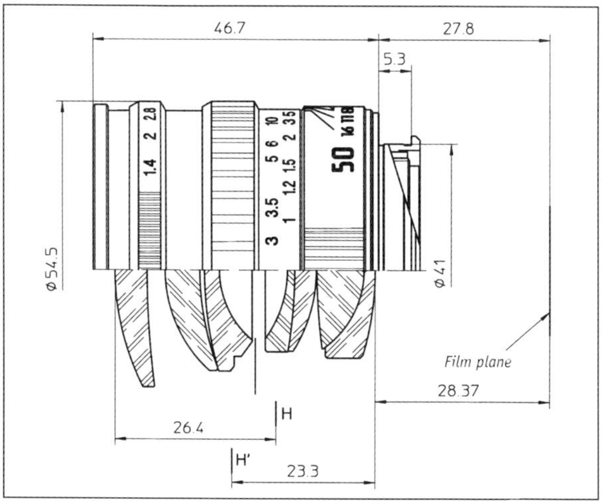

Fig.99: *50mm f/1.4 Summilux-M*

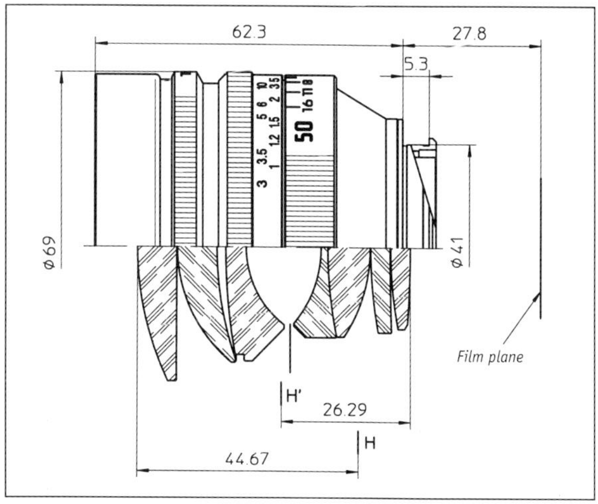

Fig.101: *50mm f/1 Noctilux-M*

50mm f/1 Noctilux-M

Wide open, the fastest lens in the Leica M system (the world's fastest lens for 35mm range-viewfinder cameras currently in production) already has good resolution and good contrast in the center of the image and in a large portion of the field. The small amount of residual astigmatism that is still present in the zone area at full aperture disappears entirely when the lens is stopped down, and then the Noctilux-M delivers very good overall performance in both near as well as distant ranges.

Thus it is also well suited for scenic photographs, where many times there are miniscule details that still have to be resolved. Then its slightly warmer rendering of colors (as compared to other Leica M lenses) even reduces unwanted blue haze in the distance. At full aperture, the 50mm f/1 Noctilux-M lens shows the strong vignetting in the corners of the image that is inherent in the optical system. As the illustrations in this book prove, this loss of brightness in the corners is not at all objectionable under extremely poor lighting conditions. By stopping the lens down to medium apertures, vignetting is eliminated and even illumination is assured across the entire image. In the near focusing range, i.e., closer than 2.5 m (8' 2-1/2"), high contrast is preserved in the center of the image.

However, as focusing distances grow shorter, curvature of field begins to appear, so that this lens cannot be recommended for certain technical applications, such as interior architectural photographs of large uniform surfaces like room walls. In practice, the 50mm f/1 Noctilux-M lens is free from nearly all reflections. Under unfavorable photographic situations, e.g., when there are light sources right in the picture, its tendency to produce distracting aperture reflections or ghost images is extremely low.

Having developed a high-refraction glass (index of refraction n = 1.9005) in its own glass research laboratory, Leitz was able to design a lens with a performance that approaches the limits of what is physically possible. Even without

Fig.100: *There is no such thing as bad weather with fast lenses and high-speed films. Quite the contrary, the soft, uniform light of a rainy day offers many advantages as far as illumination for photography is concerned. 50mm f/1.4 Summilux-M, 1/60 second at f/2, high-speed, non-silver film.*

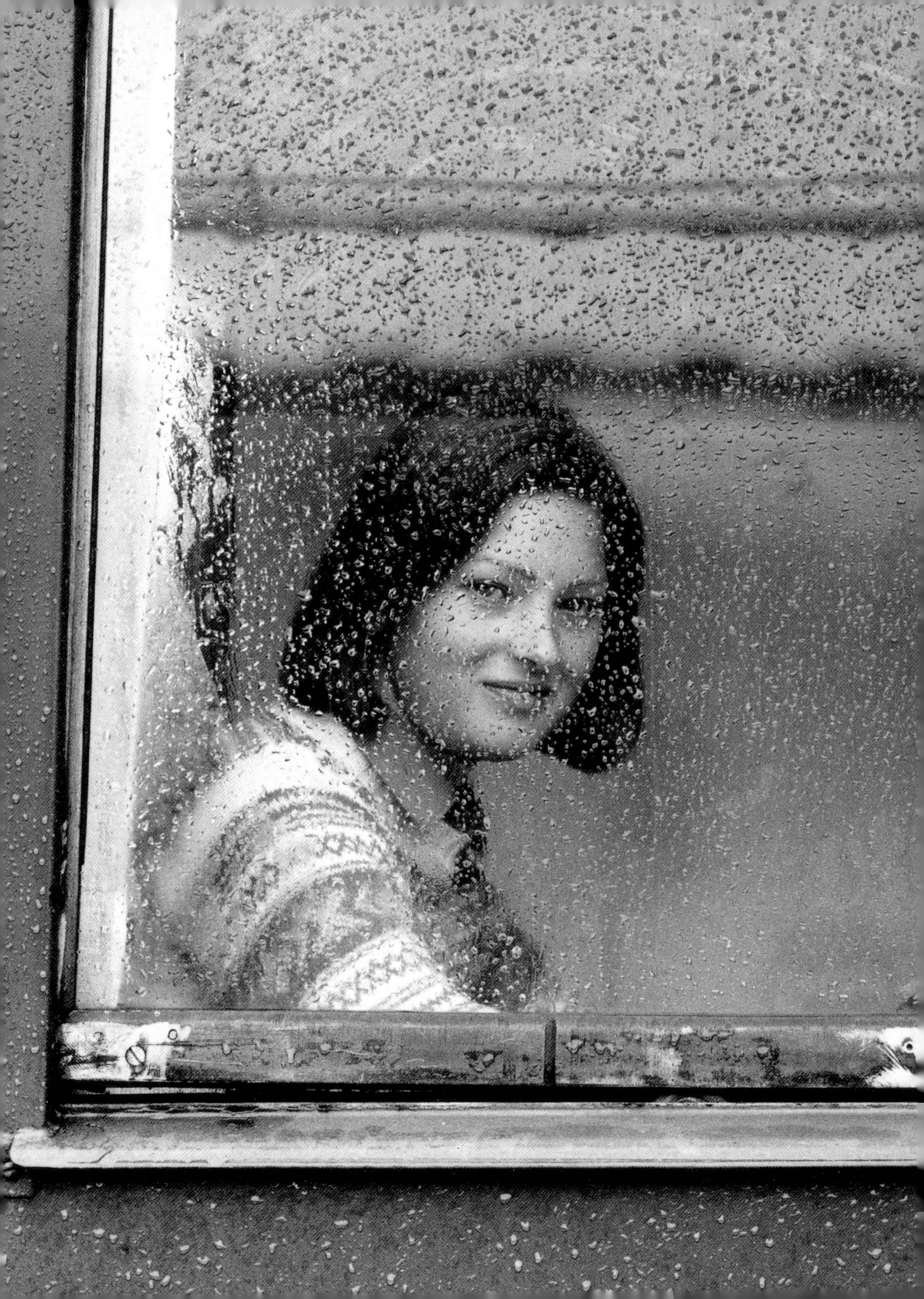

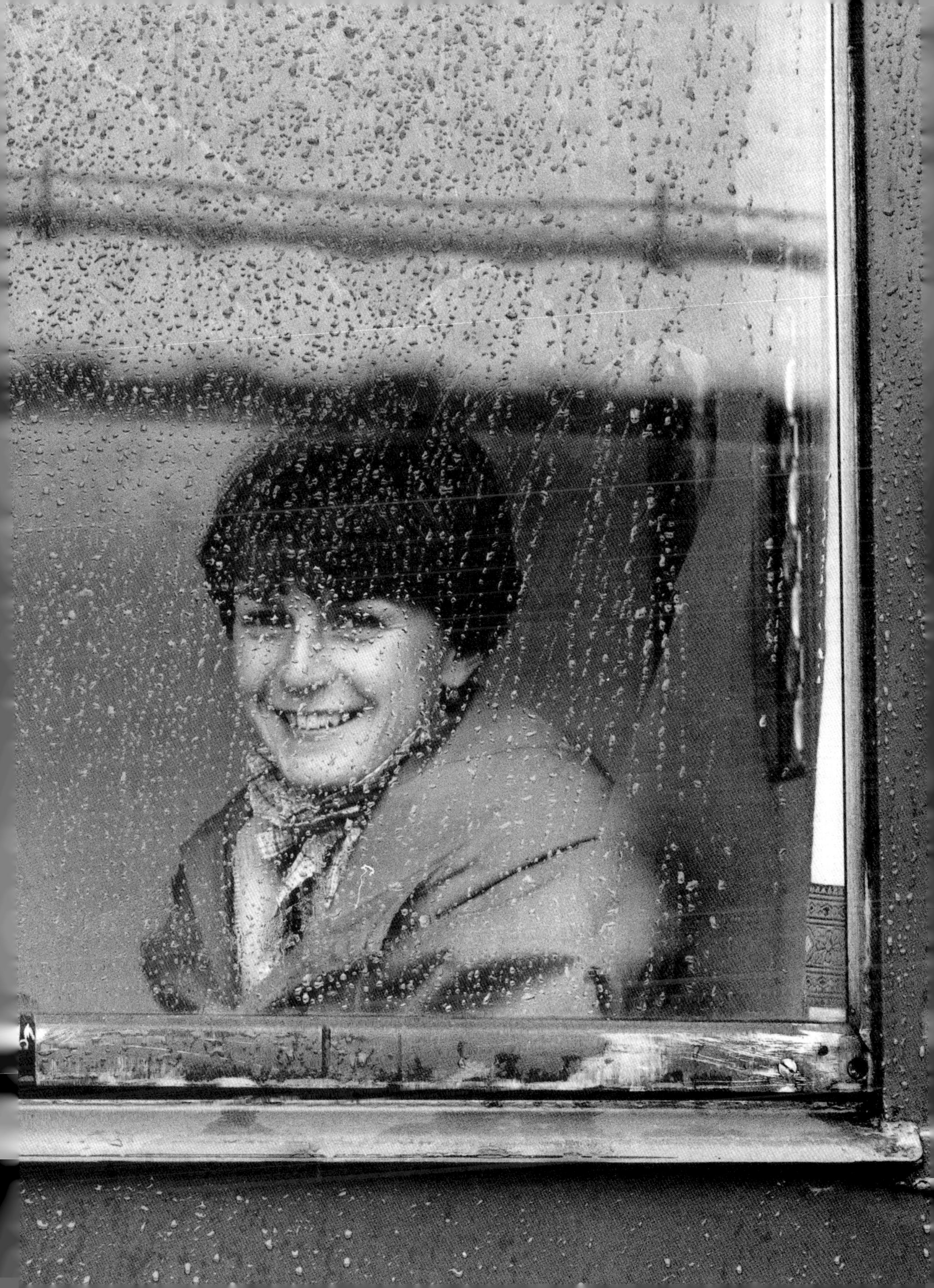

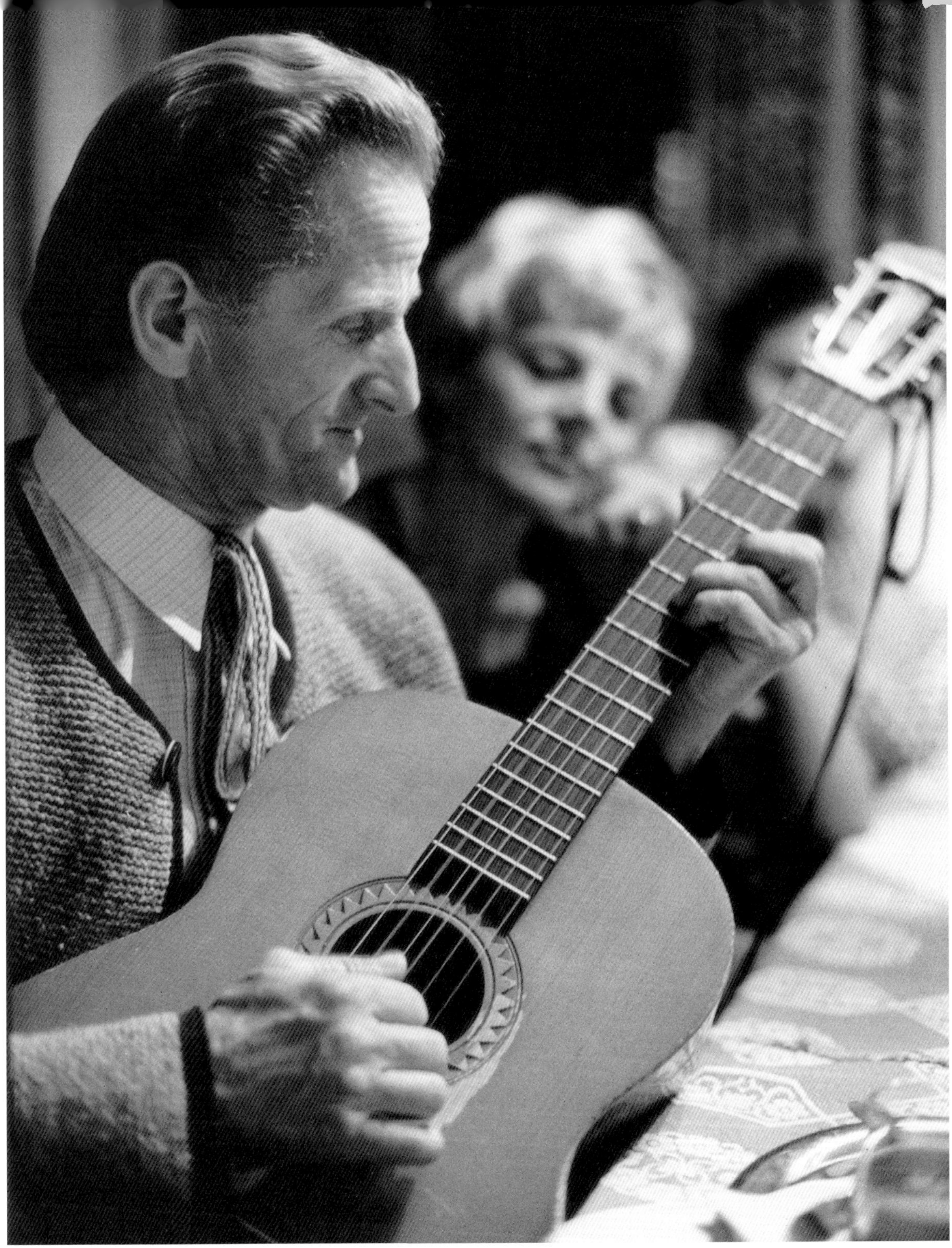

Fig.102: *With a Leica M camera, a photographer can also take pictures very unobtrusively in small, intimate groups. And since he won't need a disturbing flash, even in poor light situations, the natural mood will be preserved in the scene—and in the photograph. 50mm f/1 Noctilux -M, 1/15 second, wide open, high-speed film.*

aspheric elements. The 50mm f/1 Noctilux-M is unsurpassed for candid photography and for powerful photojournalism under any lighting conditions. It distinguishes barely visible nuances of color in the subject and it cleanly resolves the finest structures, even under extremely unfavorable lighting conditions.

Wide-angle lenses

"Wide-angle is the magic angle" is a very old photographer's axiom. And indeed, sometimes wide-angle lenses can do wonders. They can make ordinary subjects look different. When a lens with normal focal length covers just a section of the subject, the wide-angle lens shows the general overview. Taken from the same distance, however, all the details will be reproduced correspondingly smaller. A reporter surrounded by a crowd can record the overall scene by using a wide-angle lens. Interiors, as well as large buildings, can often only be covered in this manner. Just as landscapes with big skies or narrow canyons and alleys can only be characterized in a wide-angle photograph.

The properties of wide-angle lenses can be utilized in many fields of photography. With the lens only slightly stopped down, depth of field extends from the foreground into the distance. That makes these lenses ideally suited for photojournalism. And when there is not the time needed for exact focusing, one can still count on usably sharp results. From the same camera position and at the same aperture, the shorter the focal length of a lens (and/or the smaller its aperture), the greater will be its depth of field. With a lens set at f/5.6 and a distance of 2 m (6′ 6-3/4") see the examples in the following table:

Focal length of the lens (mm)	Depth of field from – to (m)	Depth of field in cm
135	1.97 – 2.03	6
90	1.92 – 2.08	16
50	1.80 – 2.30	50
35	1.55 – 2.82	127
28	1.40 – 3.70	230
21	1.15 – 8.34	719

A sharply receding background, such as a sharply converging perspective gives wide-angle pictures an especially dramatic effect. This enhanced impression of spaciousness is used as a creative tool in advertising and press photography, for instance. Typically, the foreground is reproduced "quite large," and the background "quite small." If the camera is tilted, vertical lines will appear to converge. This exaggerated perspective has nothing to do with distortion, however. A lens has distortion when straight lines, among others, appear curved near the edges of the picture. Converging lines, on the other hand, like those on a tall building, occur when that building is photographed from a short distance at ground level, so that the distance from the camera position to the main entrance on the ground floor is much shorter than the distance to the neon sign at the top of the building. Thus, due to the laws of central perspective, the more distant a subject is from the lens, the smaller will it be reproduced.

Nevertheless, a small amount of distortion is generally unavoidable in wide-angle lenses. With Leica lenses, however, this is minimal and rarely noticeable in practice. In very critical situations, the barrel distortion typical of wide-angle lenses can be disguised by the judicious positioning of irregularly shaped structures near the edges of the picture. In architectural photographs, for example, trees and furnishings can serve this purpose. The situation is similar with vignetting, i.e., a very small amount of natural fall-off of light towards the corners of the picture is inevitable. But this unavoidable phenomenon tends to become noticeable only with large, uniformly bright areas.

In photographs of landscapes with bright blue skies, the effect of vignetting—dark corners in the picture—is heightened by the fact that a blue sky is always darker at the zenith than at the horizon.

Another phenomenon causes circular objects near the corners of extreme wide-angle photographs to appear

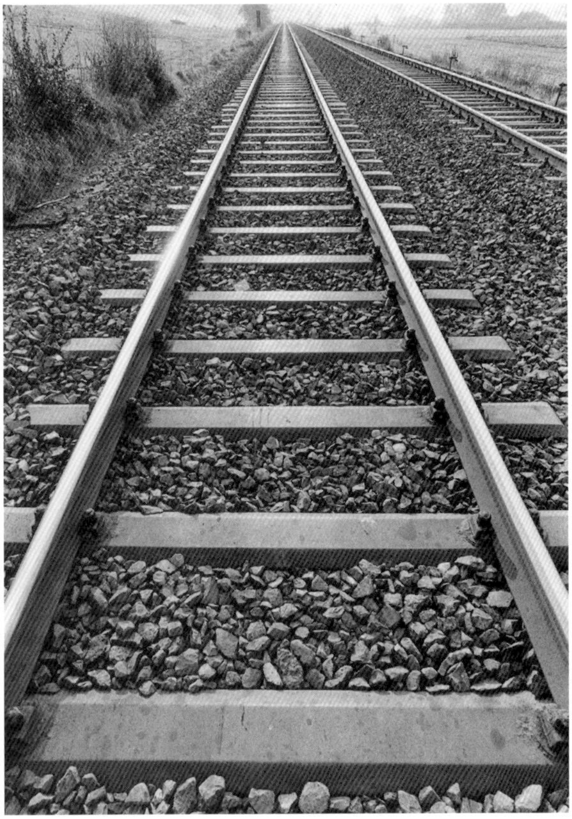

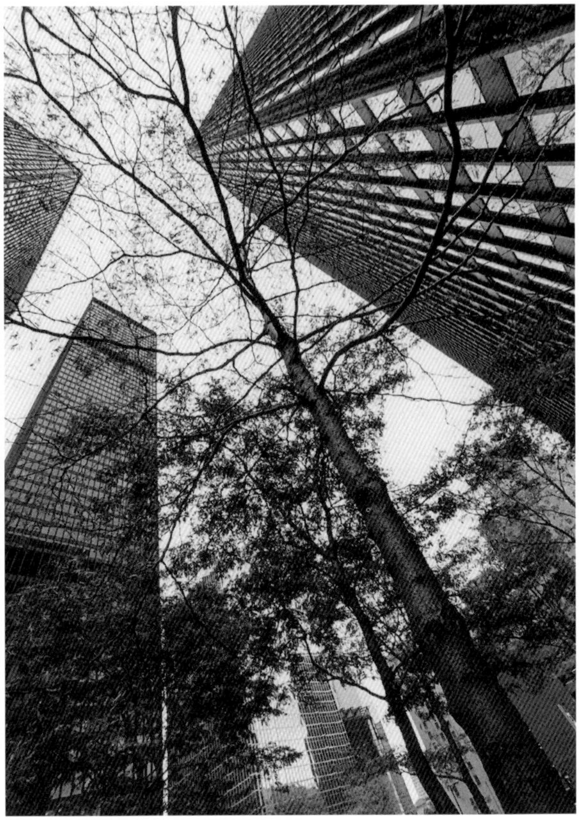

***Fig.103 and 104:** Receding backgrounds are ideal elements for wide-angle lenses. Sharply converging parallel lines in a picture convey an impression of spacious depth or height. Whenever possible, this characteristic of wide-angle lenses should be used to advantage in composing a photograph. Left: 21mm f/2.8 Elmarit-M: right: 35mm f/2 Summicron-M lens.*

elliptical. Experienced photographers photographing a group of people will make sure people are not near he edges of the frame. Instead, they will include a sufficiently ample area around the group as part of the composition.

Retrofocus lenses

The distance between the outer surface of the rear element of a lens and the film plane is usually dependent on the focal length: the shorter the focal length, the shorter this distance. To prevent wide-angle lenses from obstructing a part of the exposure measuring coverage of the silicon photodiode of a Leica M6 by extending too deeply into the camera body, or to ensure the unencumbered movement of the swinging arm with the CdS measuring cell on a Leica M5, new wide-angle lenses have been designed with a longer back focus distance.

Such retrofocus designs are characterized by a front group of diverging elements and a rear collector element—a strongly asymmetric design. This generally causes such lenses to be slightly bulkier. Typical examples of retrofocus lenses are: 21mm f/2.8 Elmarit-M ASPH, the 24mm f/2.8 Elmarit-M ASPH, the 28mm f/2.8 Elmarit-M ASPH, as well as the 28mm f/2 Summicron-M ASPH.

Floating element

Photographic lenses for 35mm cameras normally reach their optimum imaging performance when focused at infinity. The concept of "infinity" indicated by a reclining figure eight (∞), cannot be defined precisely for photographic lenses. Therefore, in designing lenses for the Leica camera, Leica applies the largest number that can be utilized in the computer, namely: ∞ = 1,701,411,834,605 x 1035 meters or 1,057,206,276 x 1035 miles.

Image quality necessarily diminishes in the close-focusing range. It can be assumed that there is no noticeable loss of performance at a focusing distance equal to approximately 50 to 100 times the focal length of the lens. Accordingly, the corresponding focusing distance for a standard lens is about 2.5 to 5 m (8'7" to 17'2"). At Leica, however, it is a matter of policy also to take into account the correction that is necessary in the optical design for proper performance at close range.

Nevertheless a clearly noticeable deterioration in image quality may occur when fast wide-angle lenses with very large angles of view and large focusing ranges are used at short focusing distances. A correction can be accomplished for such situations by varying the distances between individual lens elements or lens groups within the optical system. Such a "floating element" is coupled with the focusing mechanism of the lens, so that it is moved forwards and backwards.

The term "floating element" is often used as a synonym for particularly good image quality. However, this is not necessarily always true. To begin with, there is no need for floating elements in wide-angle lenses for Leica M cameras because the near focusing range ends at 0.7 m (2′ 3-1/2″).

Furthermore, research at Leica has shown that, as a rule, a floating element only significantly improves the image quality in the plane of focus. The space in front and behind that plane, the depth of field, does not profit from a floating element to the same degree. In some cases, more distant subjects in the corners of the picture are reproduced unsharp when the lens is focused on the foreground of the subject, even though the depth of field is sufficiently large for a sharp image. This effect is particularly disturbing in pictorial photography, because such pictures always involve spatial subjects, not flat planes.

Leica therefore looks at each case separately to determine whether or not a floating element would be advantageous and whether it is practical to manufacture it. Guided by these considerations, which are based on experience, Leica was able to justify floating elements only in a few instances involving lenses for the Leica R system but not in Leica M lenses.

The classic 35mm focal length

Lenses with a focal length of 35mm are considered to be "classic" Leica M lenses. When accompanied by a 90mm lens, they form an extraordinarily versatile outfit that is ideal for those who value compact size and light weight. There are several internationally renowned photojournalists who rarely use any lenses other than these two.

In many instances a 35mm acts like a 50mm lens. However, the 35mm lens offers greater depth of field, which is often beneficial for quick shooting and snapshot photography. Thus, these wide-angle lenses are ideal for photojournalism. Also, with the 35mm lens, the slight tilting of the camera, when photographing structures, does not produce obvious converging lines that would be objectionable in the final photograph.

Because of their focal length, these lenses are also especially well suited for taking pictures in the middle of the action, or in other words, for photographs taken at short distances. Whenever the mere action of raising the camera to the eye in itself might make it impossible to take any pictures, a 35mm lens makes it relatively easy to take pictures without raising the camera and without looking through the

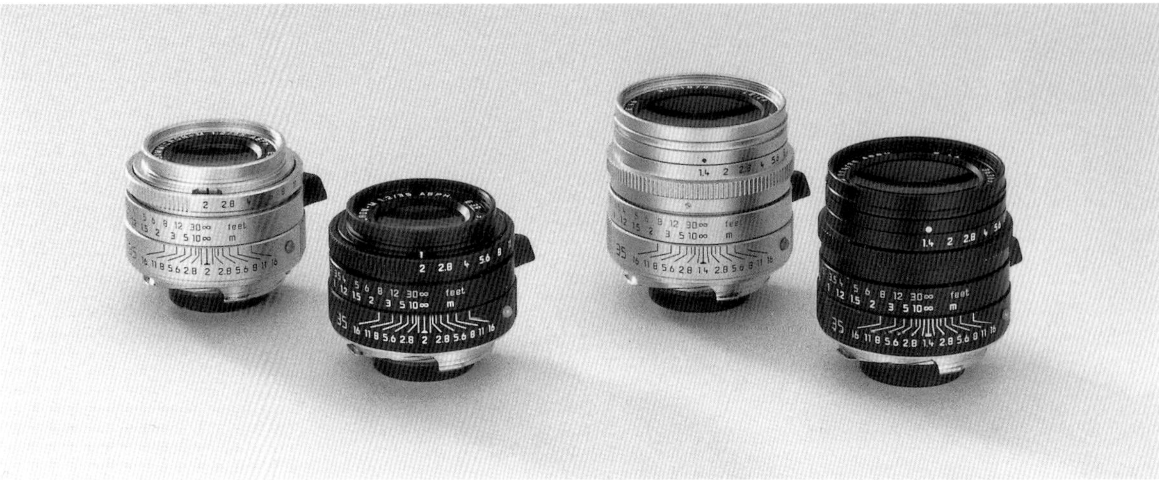

Fig.105: *Wide-angle and normal Leica lenses.*

viewfinder. In such situations, it is particularly useful to know approximately where the edges of the picture will be. For the 35mm wide-angle lens, there is a classic rule of thumb that is easy to remember: the distance to the subject corresponds to the horizontal coverage of the picture.

In practice, in order to take photographs without being noticed, all that is necessary is to aim the camera as closely at the center of the scene as possible and to estimate the field of view covered by the 35mm lens. If the distance to the subject is about 3 m (9' 10"), the following area will be covered by a horizontal photograph: largest subject width = 3 m (9' 10"), so that 1.5 m (4' 11") to the left and to the right of the center of the subject will be included. Since the short dimension of the 35mm format is always two thirds of the long dimension, the height of the subject covered in this example will be 2 m (about 6' 7"), or 1 m (3' 3-1/2") measured up or down from the center of the subject.

Since the camera is usually worn on a strap on the chest, with or without its carrying case, it is quite easy to aim the lens at the imaginary center of the subject without raising the Leica to eyelevel. But first the estimated subject distance has to be set on the focusing scale of the camera. If the camera doesn't offer autoexposure, the shutter speed and the aperture will also have to be guessed, if it is not possible to make a meter reading inconspicuously. With constant practice, it becomes quite easy to estimate these settings.

Photographers will be able to take pictures inconspicuously only they are familiar with their cameras and totally master the controls. Making settings and aiming the camera must be performed totally discreetly, and this just is not possible without appropriate practice. The photographer's movements and expressions are very important as well. They have to be appropriate for the circumstances of each picture, and they must not arouse suspicions among the people being photographed. The very quiet shutter release of a Leica M camera is a distinct advantage in these situations. The late French photographer Henri Cartier Bresson was an accomplished master of this kind of photography, and many of his world famous photographs were created in this manner.

35mm f/2 Summicron-M ASPH

This lens is distinguished by an entire absence of distortion. Coma, astigmatism and curvature of field are hardly noticeable. Combined with high sharpness and high-contrast performance, as well as its high resolving power in the center of the image and throughout the greatest portion of the image area, the 35mm f/2

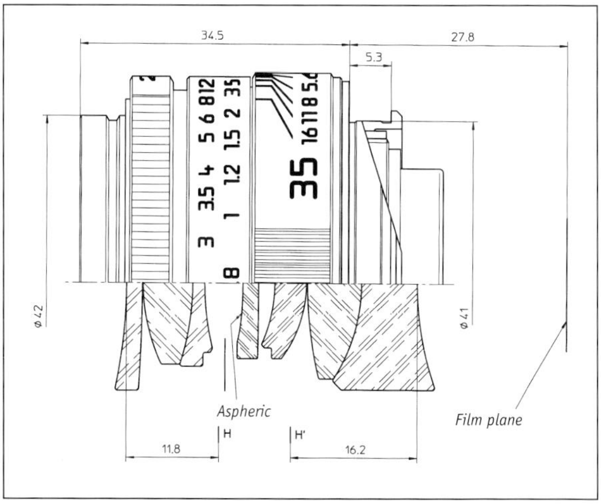

Fig.106: *35mm f/2 Summicron-M ASPH*

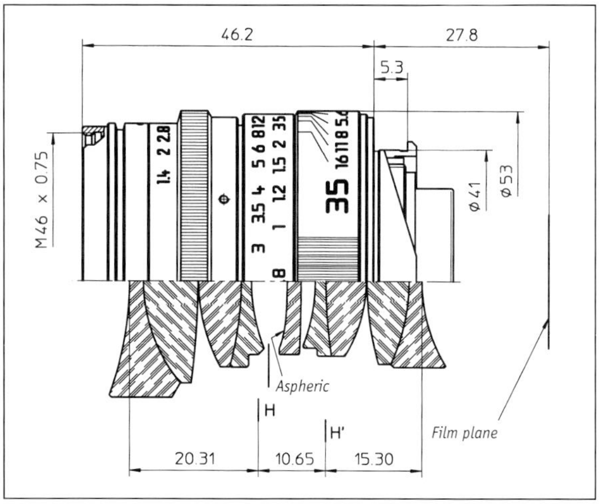

Fig.108: *35mm f/1.4 Summilux-M ASPH*

Summicron-M ASPH sets new standards for this traditionally designed series. The excellent imaging performance, which already exists at full aperture, can be increased even further by stopping to f/5.6. Even in the near-focusing range of up to 70 cm (27-1/2 inches), this excellent optical performance remains almost unchanged. The vignetting that is present in every lens is minimal but can appear with under exposures, especially in areas of uniform brightness such as building walls.

The exceptionally good imaging performance of this seven-lens system is achieved by three elements with high indices of refraction—one of them featuring anomalous partial dispersion—and by the use of one aspherical lens surface. Finally, the lens cap fits the attachable, rectangular soft-plastic lens hood. Therefore, it can be conveniently put in a pocket when pictures are taken.

35mm f/1.4 Summilux-M ASPH

A noticeable feature of this lens is its convex front lens surface. This causes a "widening" of the center portion of the bundle of light rays and, in combination with the symmetrical design of this lens and the aspherical lens surface, acts as means of compensation, which improves imaging performance. Thus, a high-contrast image up to the frame edge is obtained and the 35mm f/1.4 Summilux-M ASPH provides good contrast even at full aperture, excellent reproduction of details in the image field, and an almost complete absence of coma. This imaging performance can even be enhanced by stopping down. The slight barrel-shaped distortion is hardly noticeable in practical photographic applications.

As with any other wide-angle lens, the 35mm f/1.4 Summilux-M ASPH is subject to vignetting. This drop in light toward the image corners will be particularly visible with slight under exposures and a uniformly bright image field, e.g., a building wall or blue sky. At full aperture, vignetting is extremely minimal and practically non-existent starting with f/4.

Because all the performance characteristics of this lens remain equally good even in the near-distance range, the 35mm f/1.4 Summilux-M ASPH can be used as a universal wide-angle lens for many applications.

The rectangular lens hood is mounted to the lens in a different way than the usual spring mount used with most Leica lenses. It slides on—white dot on white dot—and secured by a textured rotatable ring. The lens hood includes a soft plastic lens cap, which the photographer can conveniently carry in a pocket.

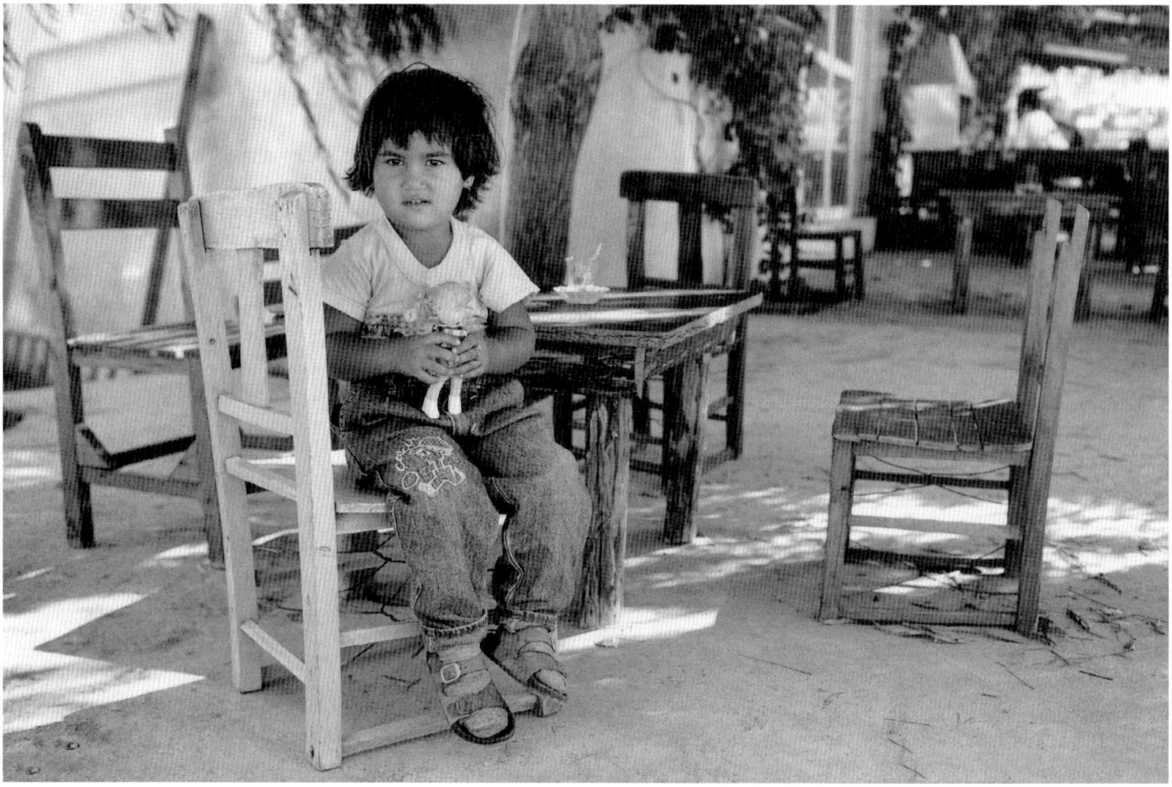

Fig.107: *The photographer best gains the confidence of he subject by dropping to the same eye level. This also produces photos of children that are natural and do not appear forced.*

Super wide-angle lenses

All of the familiar characteristics of normal wide-angle lenses are present in super wide-angle lenses but in a more pronounced form. Thus, even a slight tilt of the camera will produce disturbing converging lines. But this effect can also be used deliberately for creative purposes. Super wide-angle lenses make the foreground appear very large, thus emphasizing it, while the background appears small, creating the impression that it is further away. Therefore, the composition of the foreground requires special care. The ability to convey a large overview from only a short distance gives a certain dynamic character to pictures made with super wide-angle lenses.

The shortest focal length, which will still appears in the bright-line frame of the viewfinder of most Leica M models is 28mm. These cameras include: the Leica M6 and M7 with 0.72x or 0.58x viewfinder magnifications, and the Leica M4-P. The viewfinders of the Leica M2, M4, M4-2, and M5 can be adapted by Leica's service department. In addition, clip-on Albada viewfinders and the Leica Viewfinder for 21, 24, and 28mm lenses are available as accessories.

When 35mm lenses do not offer adequate field of view, a 28mm focal length may be the right choice. In addition, it is a good choice with flash since its large 76° (diagonal) angle of view is covered by most flash units.

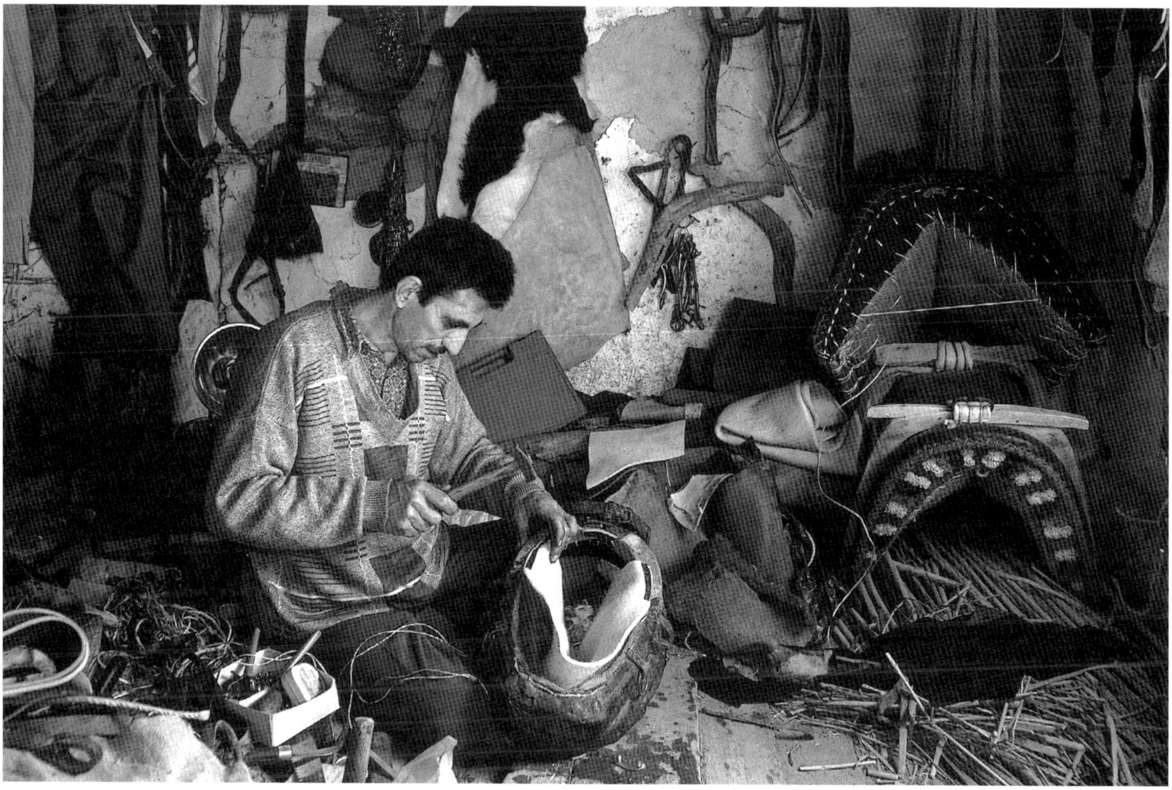

***Fig.109:** : In the Caravan route of Milas carrying frames for mules and donkeys are still made and repaired by hand. Light entering through a small window was used for the exposure with a large aperture and with a relatively long shutter speed. In order to still be able to take an unblurred picture of the saddler, the tiny moment when he aimed with a hammer at a just set nail was seized. 35mm f/1.4 Summilux-M ASPH, 1/15 second, full aperture, medium-speed film.*

28mm f/2.8 Elmarit-M

This 28mm lens is a modified retrofocus design, in which the nodal planes are moved forward in the lens. A notable feature of these wide-angle lenses is the large front and rear elements, which are plane-concave in the front and act as a dispersing meniscus in the back. Because of the large diameters of these lenses artificial vignetting is minimized significantly. However, the natural vignetting that is inherent in every optical system is present in the 28mm f/2.8 Elmarit-M lens and becomes especially noticeable with low exposures of even, uniformly illuminated surfaces. Excellent contrast and reproduction of details across the entire image field characterize these outstanding features of this wide-angle lens. Even at full aperture it produces considerable sharpness and brilliance. This reproduction characteristic is also present in the near focusing range. Due to the increase in curvature of field, however, a slightly greater loss of sharpness will occur in the extreme corners at near focusing distances, which cannot be eliminated entirely by stopping down the aperture. Barrel shaped distortion is very minimal with the 28mm f/2.8 Elmarit-M lens so that it is completely acceptable in practice.

Even backlighting or the depiction of light sources in the picture does not result in disturbing reflections and flare.

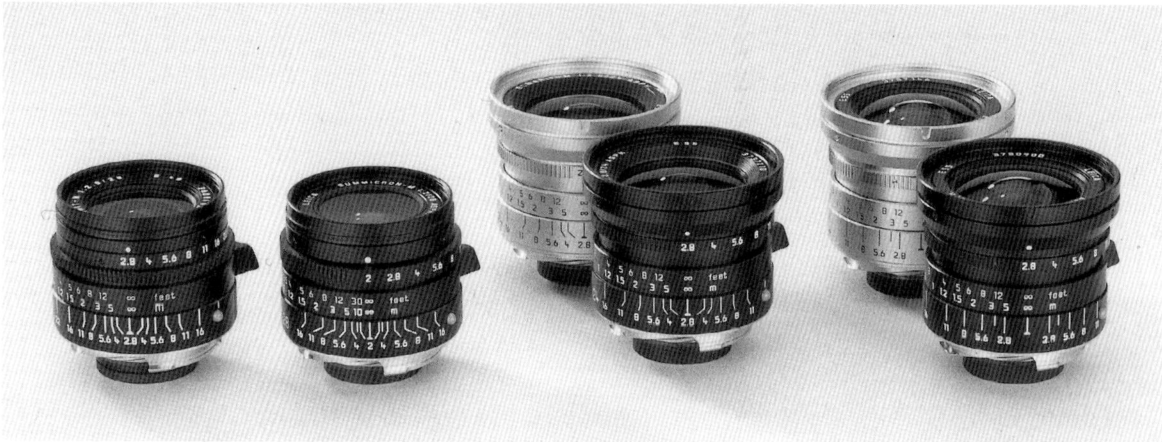

Fig.110: The super wide-angle lenses.

28mm f/2 Summicron-M ASPH

This lens is a good example for how Leica-M photographers have benefited from Leica's leadership in aspherical technology. The 28mm f/2 Summicron-M ASPH is even shorter than the Elmarit by 6 mm and its weight has increased a minimal 10 grams. Even though it is faster by one stop this lens offers excellent imaging performance. The reason for this is the new lens is designed with six groups of nine elements, three of which exhibit high indices of refraction and of three feature anomalous partial dispersion. The last lens in the system has an aspherical inside surface.

The imaging performance is uniformly high across the entire image field, even at maximum aperture. This means, that even at f/2, the 28mm f/2 Summicron-M ASPH exhibits considerable sharpness and brilliance. A slight increase may be achieved by stopping down; there is practically no coma. The barrel-shaped distortion of at most –1.1% is very minimal for a wide-

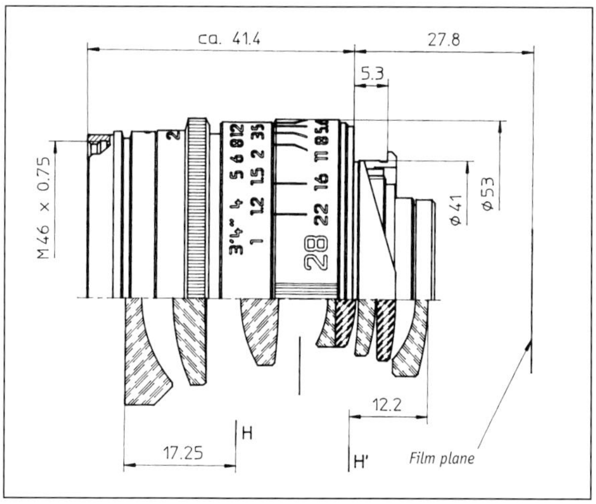

Fig.111: 28mm f/2.8 Elmarit-M

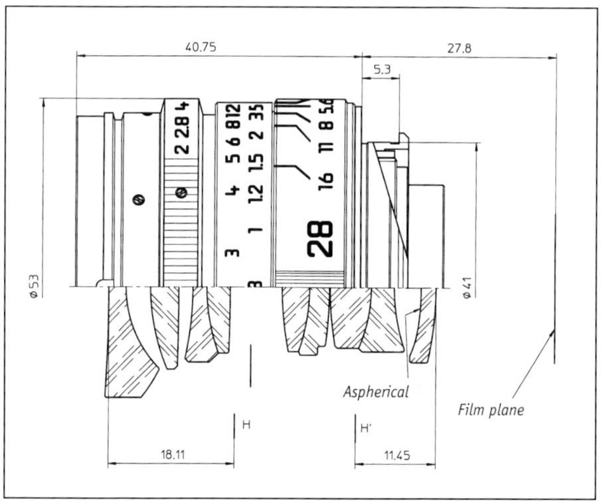

Fig.113: 28mm f/2 Summicron-M ASPH

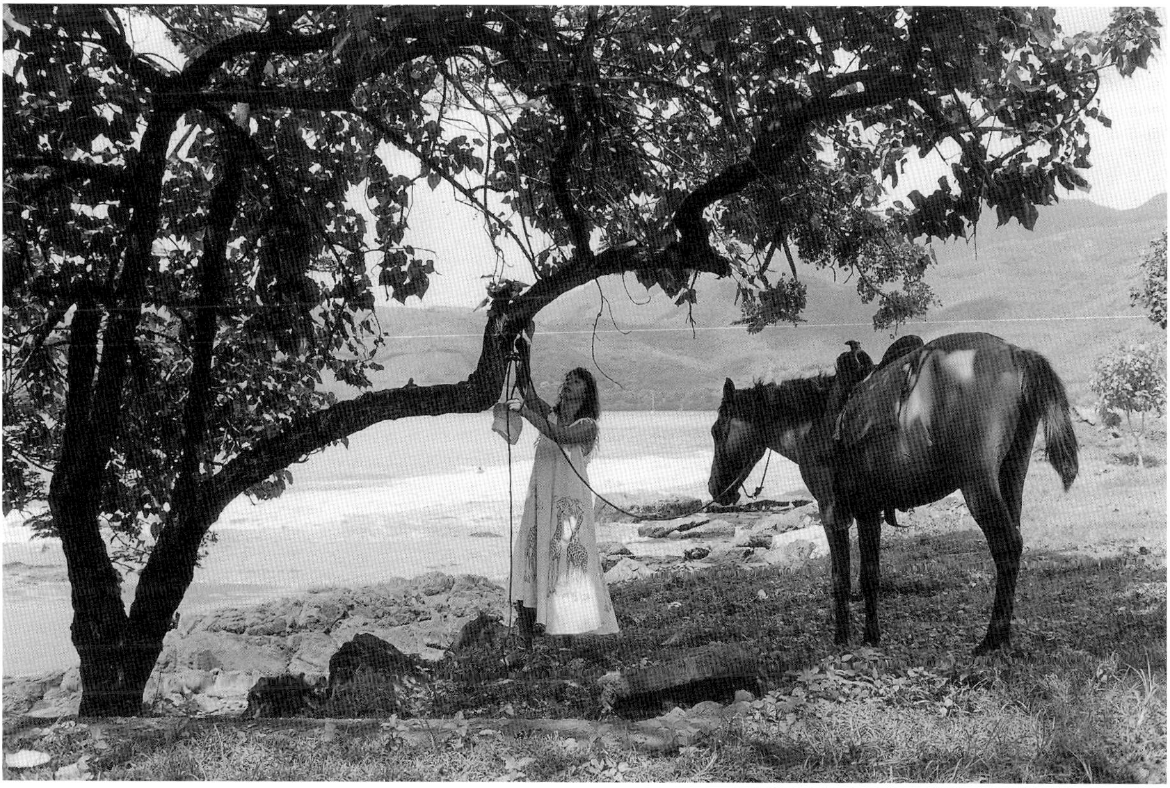

Fig.112: *A dominant foreground becomes even more impressive in a picture made with a super wide-angle lens. Light and shadows can effectively enhance this characteristic even further. 28mm f/2.8 Elmarit-M, 1/250 second at f/5.6, medium-speed film.*

angle lens and is therefore virtually irrelevant. The vignetting inherent in the optical system becomes visible in particular with under exposures and in uniformly bright areas (blue sky, light building walls), however, is minimal for a 28mm featuring this speed. Starting with f/5.6, there is minimal natural vignetting. The 28mm f/2 Summicron-M ASPH ensures finely differentiated and perfectly sharp exposures even in dusk or inadequately illuminated rooms. This is the perfect 28mm lens for use in photojournalism or anyone working in difficult lighting conditions.

24mm f/2.8 Elmarit-M ASPH

For many years many Leica M photographers have wanted an additional choice in the super-wide-angle lens category. Features on the wish list were ease of use and excellent imaging performance. The 24mm focal length is frequently used for pictures, which due to their perspective achieve a special effect without it being overly obvious that a super-wide-angle lens was used. Therefore, the 24mm lens is one of the favorite lenses of many photographers who work with a reflex camera. Unlike the Leica R, however, a Leica M super-wide-angle lens requires an extremely compact design in order to prevent lens components from impairing the optical path of the rangefinder. However, this requires that the optical and mechanical

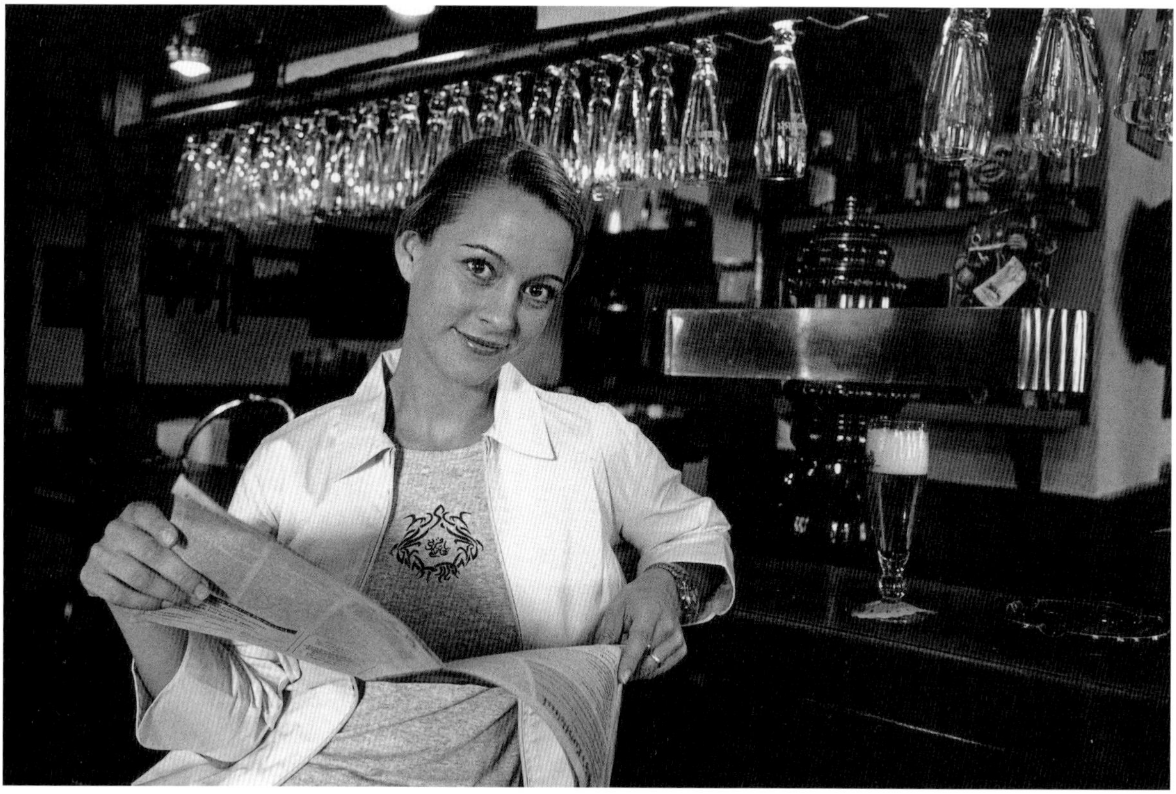

Fig.114: *Portraits are successful even with super-wide-angle lenses when a sufficiently large shooting distance (approx. 1.5 m or 10 feet) is maintained. The expressive eyes and the pretty, well-proportioned face of this young lady are additionally slightly lightened by the opened menu. 28mm f/2 Summicron-M ASPH, 1/30 second, full aperture, high-speed film.*

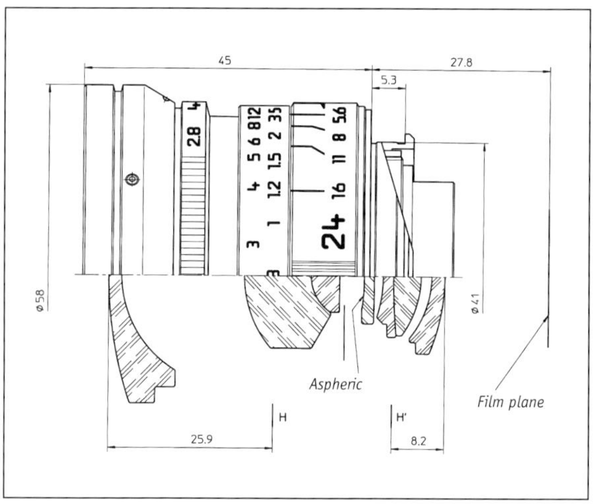

Fig.115: *24mm f/2.8 Elmarit-M ASPH*

components increase in weight as the demands on the imaging performance are increased. Optical engineers at Leica for have sought a way out of this dilemma as long as there was the wish for a 24mm lens. However, until the mid-1990s they were not able to overcome technical problems at a cost that would make sense from a marketing standpoint. Only in 1996 was it possible to finally satisfy this demand for a new focal length in the Leica M lens product-line with the 24mm f/2.8 Elmarit-M ASPH, which incorporates the latest aspherical technology. Even at full aperture, the seven-lens system exhibits excellent imaging performance with high-contrast reproduction and good field flatness. Coma and astigmatism virtually do not exist. By stopping down to f/5.6, the performance is slight-

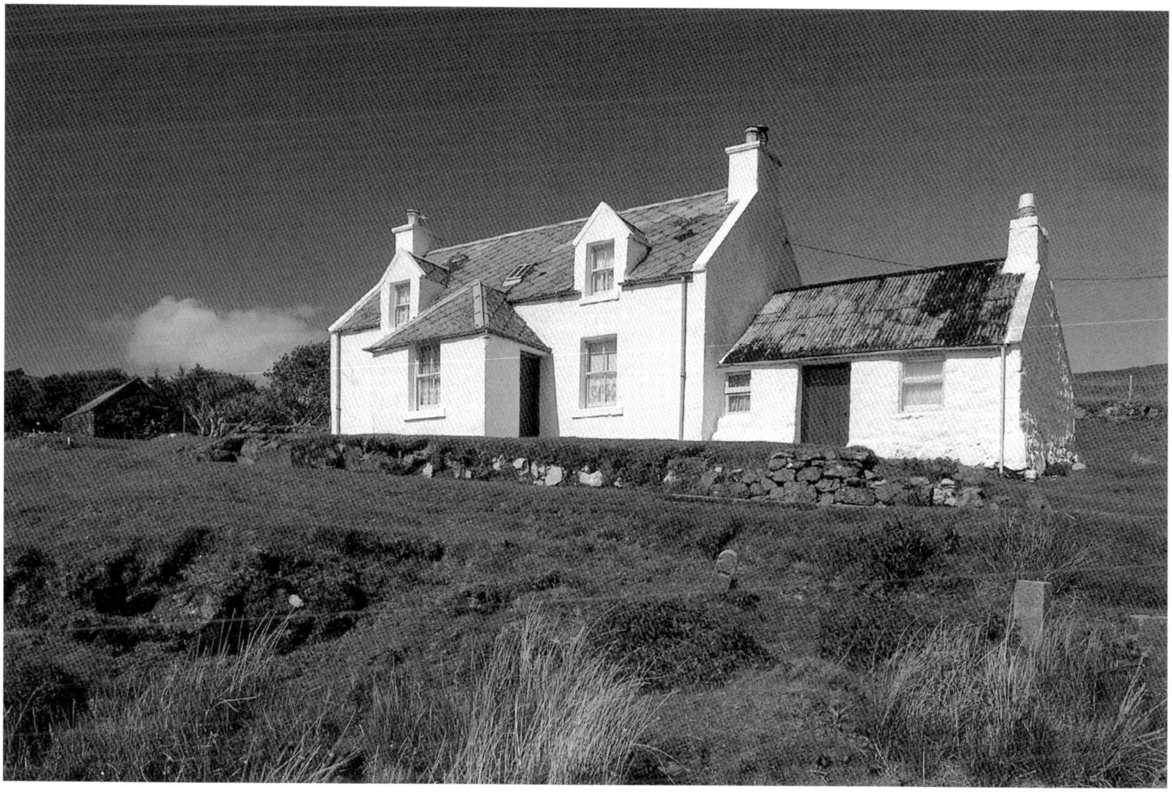

Fig.116: *Architectural exposures, as a rule, require an exactly aligned camera to prevent converging verticals. If a tripod is used, the base, side walls and the camera back of the Leica M can be used as a collimation axis. This is simpler and more accurate than any commercially available aids such as, a level. 24mm f/2.8 Elmarit-M ASPH, yellow-green filter, 1/30 second, f/8, low-speed film.*

ly enhanced. If, at close distances below 2 m (about 6 feet) quality at the corners of the image is critical, an aperture smaller than f/5.6 should be used.

The vignetting inherent in any optical system is greater in super-wide-angle lenses than in lenses with longer focal lengths. In order to minimize this with the 24mm f/2.8 Elmarit-M ASPH lens, the front and rear lenses are particularly large. Nevertheless, as in all wide-angle lenses, the 24mm f/2.8 Elmarit-M ASPH exhibits light fall off toward the image corners at full aperture. This is true in particular with a uniformly light image field, e.g., a building wall or a cloudless sky. Minimal barrel-shaped distortion is noticeable only at the outer image edges.

The separate rectangular lens hood offers good protection against flare, debris and mechanical damage to the front of the lens. When mounted, the lens hood is firmly connected with the lens due to a strong clamping effect—it will remain on the lens even if the camera or lens were to be lifted carelessly by the lens hood. The lens hood includes a flexible plastic cap, which protects the front of the lens when not in use.

The 24mm f/2.8 Elmarit-M ASPH is focused like all other Leica M lenses, by looking through the rangefinder. The image area can be determined by using an accessory viewfinder. Both the Albada viewfinder and the Leica Viewfinder for 21, 24, 28mm lenses are inserted in the clip-on shoe of the Leica M and are secured against loss.

21mm f/2.8 Elmarit-M ASPH

With an angle of view of 79°, this focal length is well suited for dynamic photo-journalism, snapshots, landscape, and architectural photography, as well as for exposures in confined spaces. Even at a small distance a large overview of a scene can be depicted. The extremely large depth of field is generally adequate even with larger apertures to reach from the foreground to the distance and, as a creative element, supports the impression of depth in a picture. If one is in a hurry and unable to focus exactly, sharp results may still be achieved. This is a significant advantage for photojournalists, for quick travel photography, or general snapshots.

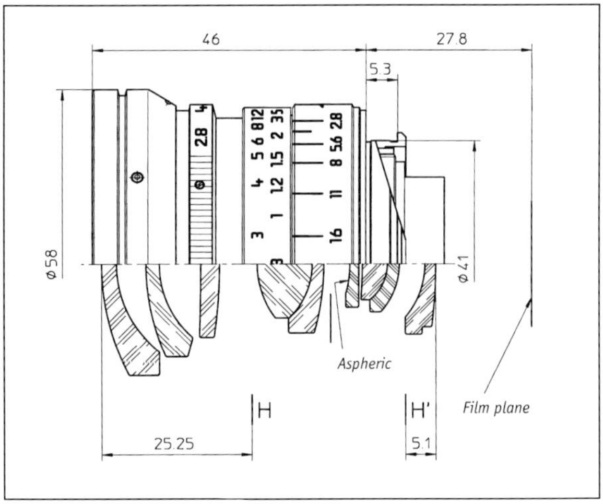

Fig.117: *21mm f/2.8 Elmarit-M ASPH*

Even at its maximum aperture, the lens is exhibits very good reproduction of contrast and details in the center of the image and in the image field. Only the extreme corners of pictures indicate a somewhat reduced performance. In addition, the very good flatness of field, as well as the reduced occurrence of reflections under extreme exposure conditions, such as, with strong light sources in the picture, should be noted. The performance of this new lens is restricted by coma on the image edges merely in the extreme close-up range of 0.7 to 0.9 m (2 to 3 feet). Closing down to f/5.6 may reduce this effect.

The 21mm f/2.8 Elmarit-M ASPH lens combines nine elements in seven groups; one of these elements has an aspherical surface. Three elements consist of optical glass having a high index of refraction and two additional ones exhibit anomalous partial dispersion. The excellent design has produced a superb, compact lens. Vignetting, which is inherent in any optical system, is more marked in super-wide-angle lens systems than in all other focal lengths. The light drop toward the image edge becomes particularly visible at wide-open aperture, low light, and uniformly light image field. Starting at f/5.6, the 21mm f/2.8 Elmarit-M ASPH is free of artificial vignetting. The barrel-shaped distortion is minimal, despite the large angle of view and is virtually unnoticeable in photographic practice.

Exact focusing is achieved with the rangefinder of the Leica M. The image section is determined with the aid of the clip-on Albada viewfinder or the Leica Viewfinder for 21, 24, 28mm lenses.

Long focal lengths

One of the techniques of successful 35mm photography is filling the frame with the subject. To achieve this, it is necessary to include a variety of focal lengths in one's own Leica M outfit. Long focal lengths help the photographer to concentrate on the pertinent part of the subject, to leave out everything that is superfluous, in order to strengthen the power of the photograph.

There is also the welcome additional effect produced by long focal lengths. Because of their limited depth of field especially at larger apertures, they isolate the main subject by reproducing the foreground and the background in softer focus. And, of course, compared to normal lenses, long focal lengths bring the subject up

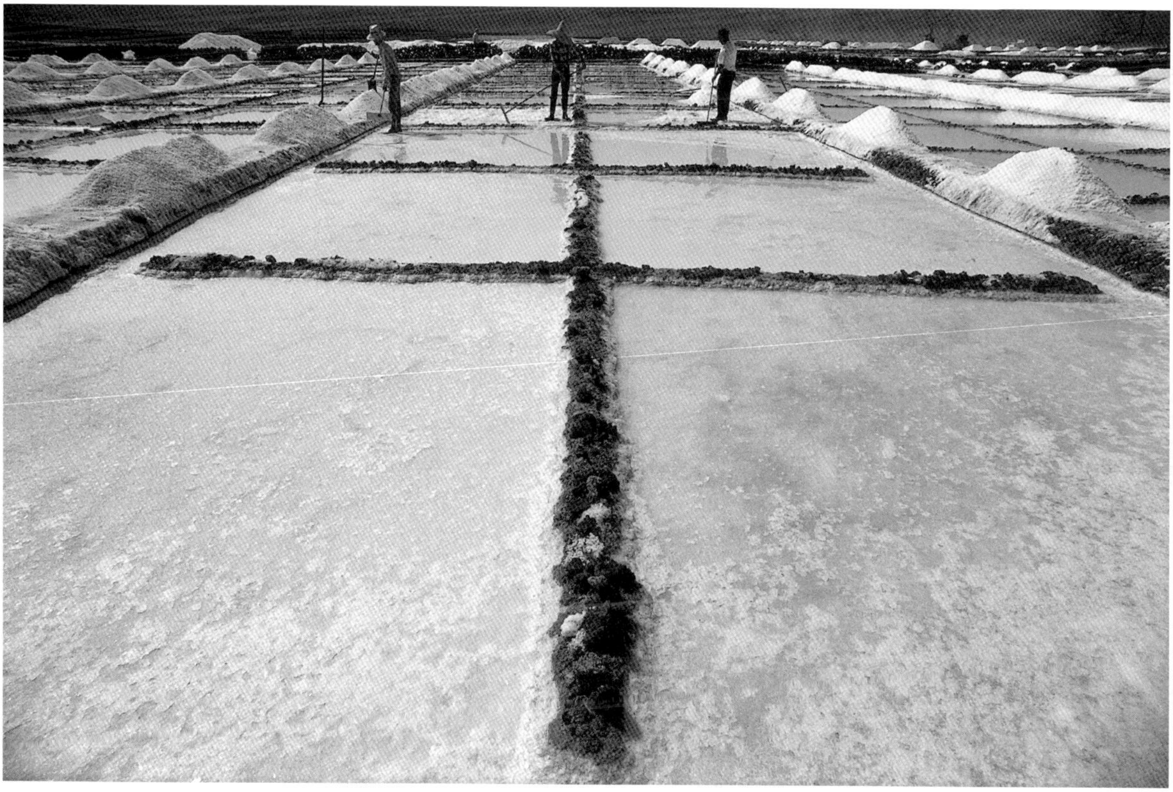

Fig.118: *Super-wide-angle lenses are also ideal landscape lenses. Here it is important that the foreground is effectively incorporated in the image composition. 21mm f/2.8 Elmarit-M ASPH, 1/250 second, f/11, medium-speed film.*

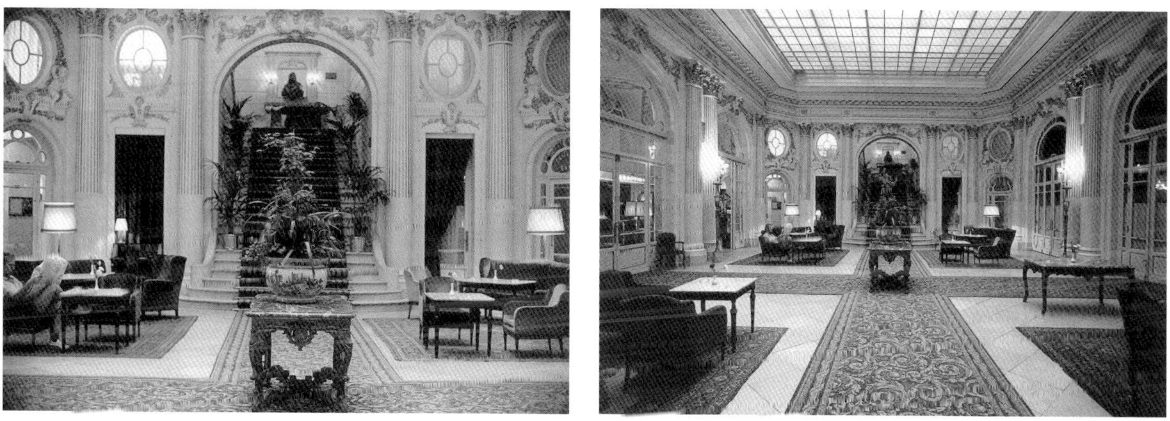

Fig.119 a and b: *Should one ever have the opportunity and pleasure of staying in a time-honored hotel like this one, the 21mm Leica must come along. Only this super-wide-angle lens reproduces this impressive overview of this space. Left: 50mm focal length. Right: 21mm focal length.*

close. At the same subject area coverage, the camera position is further away and the perspective is different—space appears tight and distance is com-pressed.

What is the magnification?

Questions about the magnification of various focal lengths often arise. However, these questions cannot really be answered without comparing the magnification of one lens with another. This can be calculated by dividing the longer focal length by the shorter one. Compared with a 21mm lens, a 135mm lens reproduces a subject approximately 6.5 times larger (135:21 = 6.45), and only 2.7 times larger than a normal or 50mm lens (135:50 = 2.7).

Frequently, the expectations for magnification that are placed on long focal length lenses are not realized. Even with the longest focal length in the Leica M system, a solitary person at a distance of 20 m (almost 66 feet) will not fill the frame. Hint: A good rule of thumb is that 100 times the focal length = 100 times the format.) For the 35mm formal of 24 x 36 mm this means that, at a distance of 13.5 m (44' 3-1/2") (100 times the focal length of a 135 mm lens), a subject area of 2.4 x 3.6 m (7' 10" x 11' 9") (100 times the format of 24 x 36 mm) will be covered. At a distance of 27 m (88' 7"), a subject area of 4.8 x 7.2 m (15' 8" x 23' 6") will be covered. In other words, at a distance of 200 times the focal length, an object area of 200 times the formal will be covered.

In order to fill a vertical format while photographing a person who is about 1.75 m (5' 9" tall), however, a subject area of only 1.2 x 1.8 m (approximately 3' 11" x 5' 11") is needed. That corresponds to 50 times the 35mm format, so that the subject distance should be 50 times the focal length of the lens being used—for a 135mm lens that would be 6.75 m (about 22' 2").

Fig.E1 – E3: *: To be able to crop without moving or changing lenses and with only with a small turn of the lens, fills many photographers with enthusiasm, especially if they value small and lightweight photographic equipment.*
28 – 35 – 50mm f/4 Tri-Elmar-M ASPH lens; 28, 35, and 50mm focal length (from the top). 1/250 second, f/8, color-negative film ISO 100.

Fig.E4: *Many bridal couples have their pictures taken by professional photographers in the Botanical Gardens of Singapore. With a Leica M it is easy to take a picture inconspicuously. 75mm f/1.4 Summilux-M, 1/125 second, f/2, daylight reversal film ISO 64.*

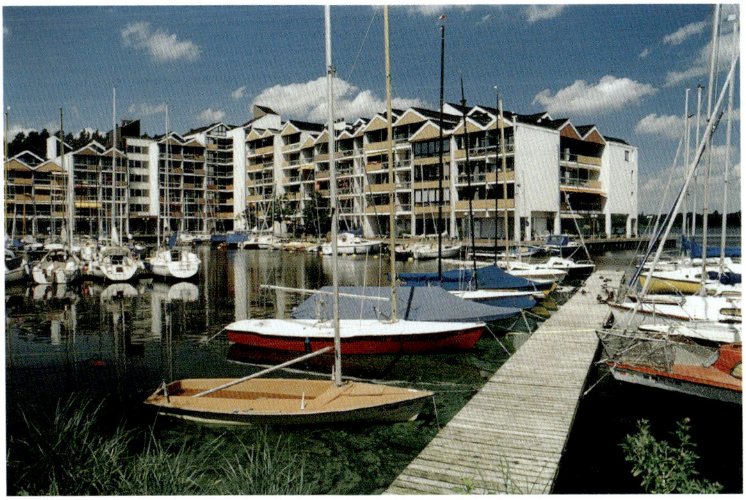

Fig. E1

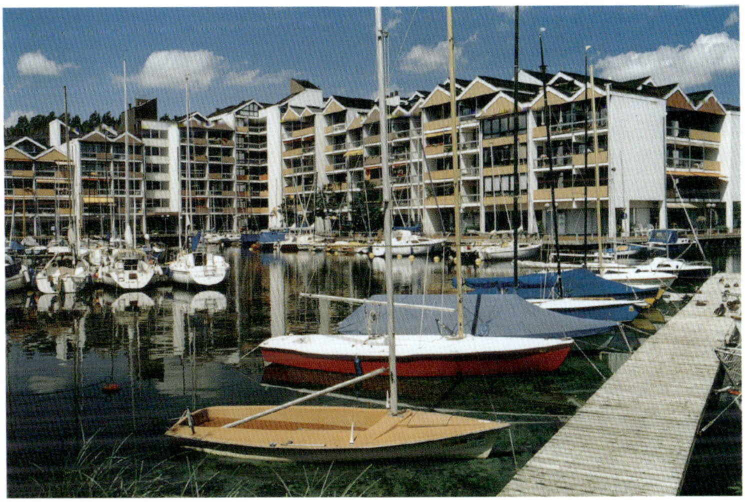

Fig. E2

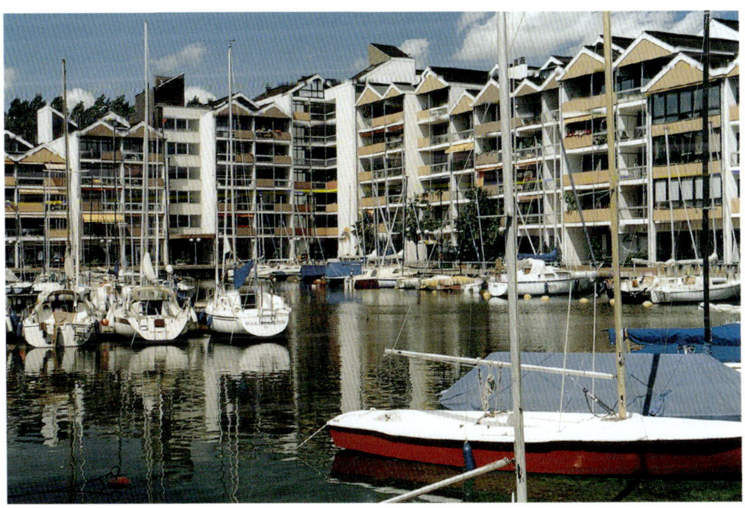

Fig. E3

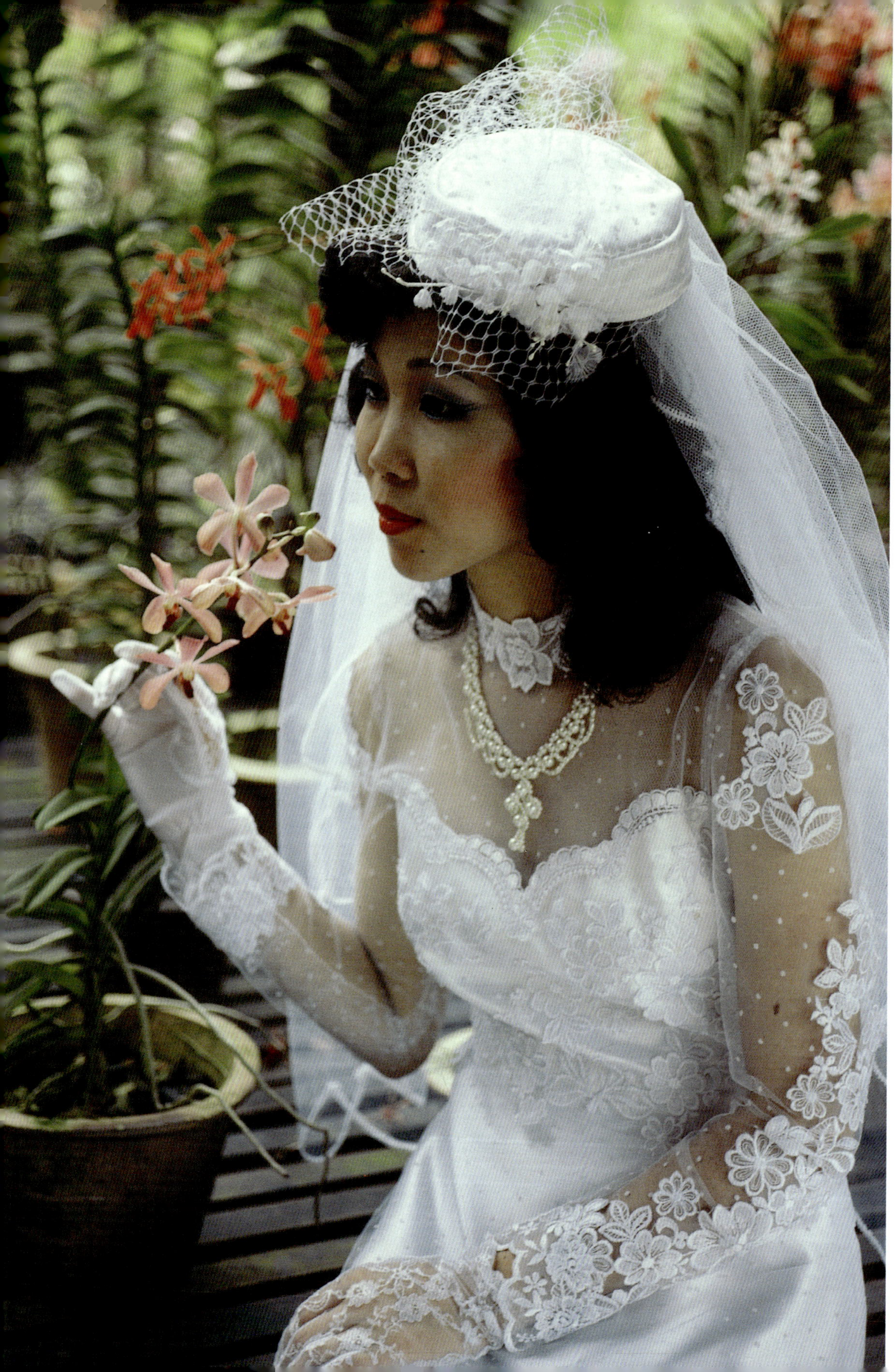

Fig. E4

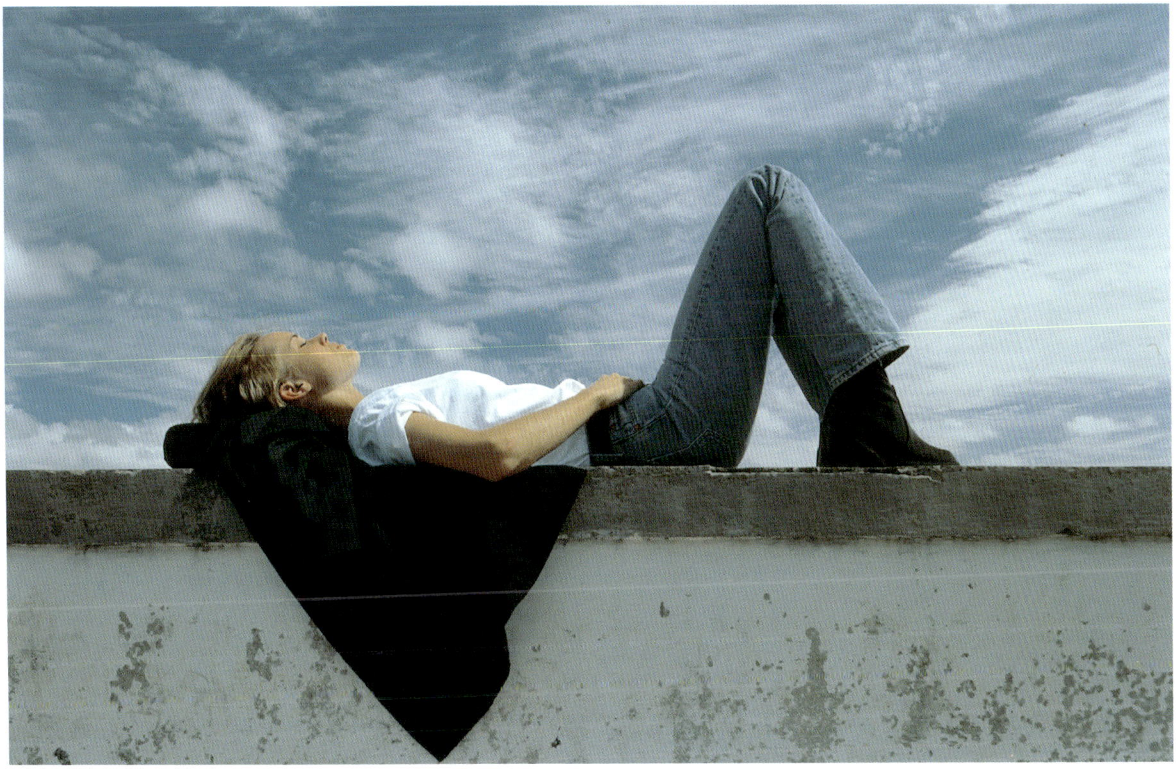

Fig. E5

Fig. E6

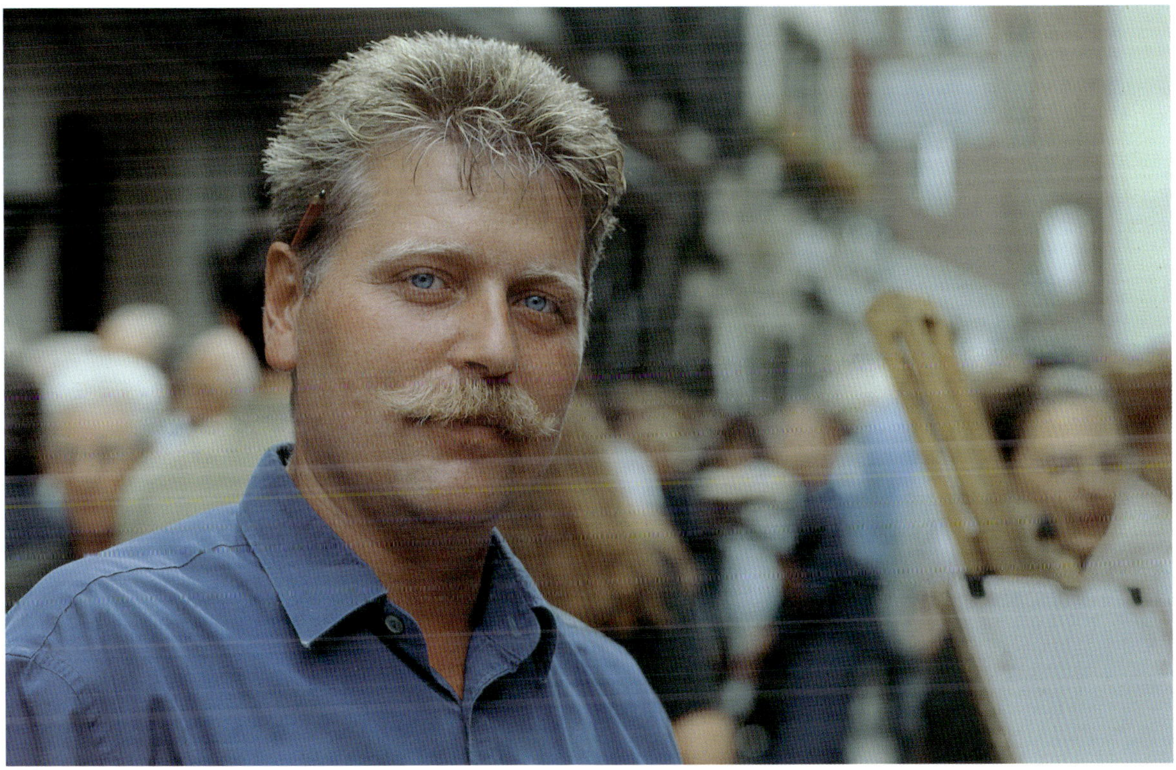

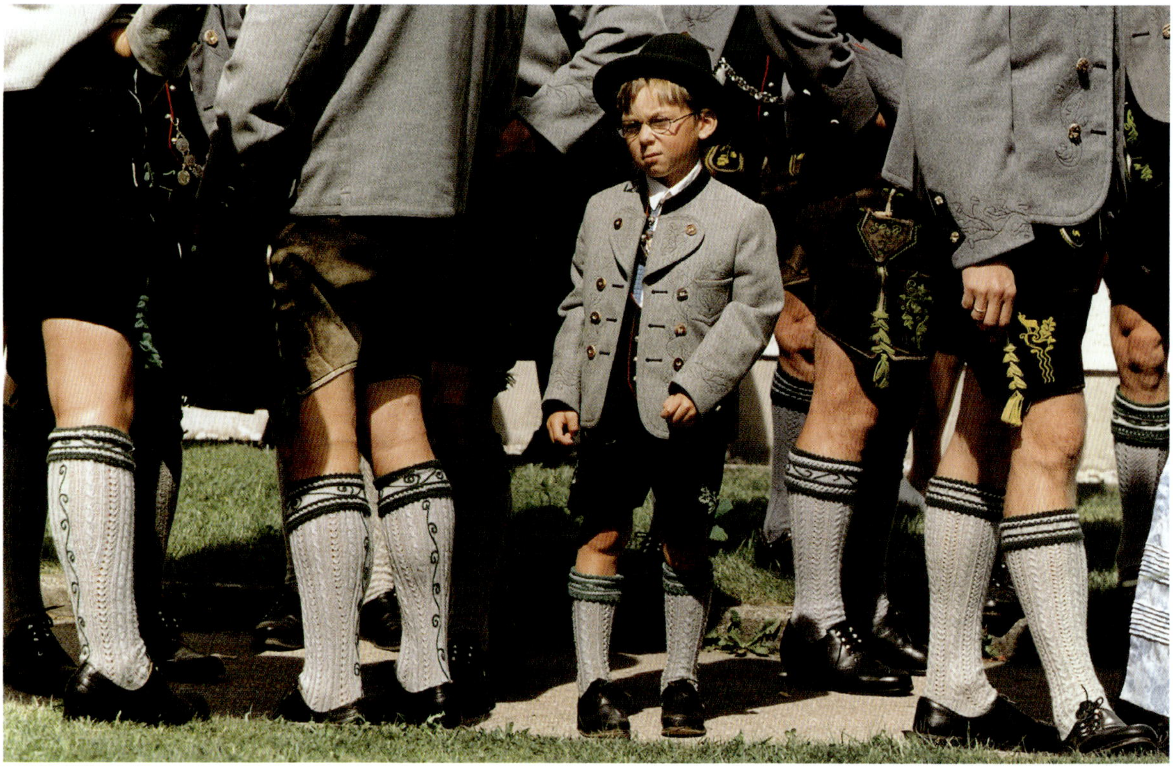

Fig. E7

Fig. E8

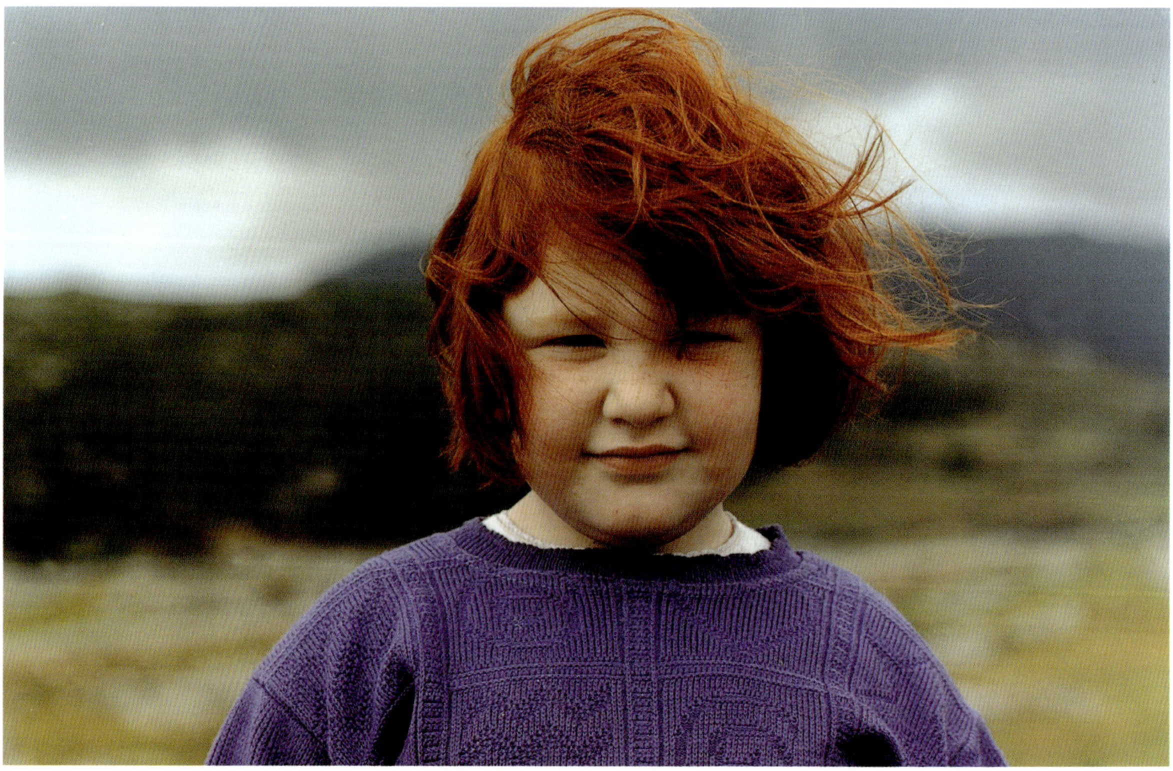

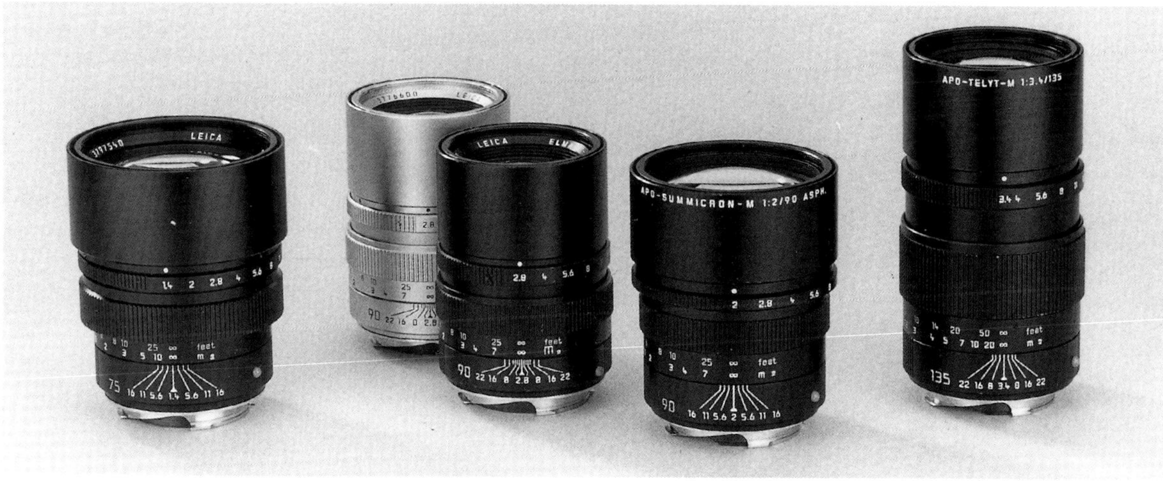

Fig. 120: *Telephoto lenses for Leica M cameras.*

Fig. E5: *A slight alteration in camera location can often make a big difference in the compositon. By crouching low to the ground, the photographer was able to eliminate a busy background and use the blue sky to set off the subject. 90mm f/2.8 Elmarit-M, 1/125 second, f/4 – 5.6, polarizing filter, daylight reversal film ISO 64.*

Fig. E6: *Flattering your subject may result in a better photo! Despite the mad rush at Düsseldorf's old-city fest, the photographer complimented a waiter, saying that he chose his shirt perfectly to match the color of his eyes. This was enough to get the waiter to stop for just a moment and pose for a picture. 135mm f/3.4 Apo-Telyt-M, 1/250 second, f/4, daylight reversal film ISO 64.*

Fig. E7: *Pay attention to the small details! The often overlooked people on the sidelines of an event may provide interesting subjects for photography. 135 mm f.3.4 Apo-Telyt-M, 1/500 second, f/8, color negative film ISO 100.*

Fig. E8: *This girl on the Outer Hebrides was proud of her sweater but the photographer was quite taken with her striking red hair. 90 mm f/2 Apo-Summicron-M ASPH, 1/250 second, f/4, color negative film ISO 100.*

Choosing shutter speeds

The requirements for dynamic 35mm photography received particular attention in the design of lenses for the Leica M cameras. Even with long focal lengths, handheld photographs can be made with ease. However, this normally requires the use of faster shutter speeds. As a general rule, the slowest shutter speed for handheld photography with a given lens can be determined with the following formula:

1/focal length in mm = shutter speed (in seconds).

With practice and good technique, even slower shutter speeds may be used for handheld photography without the effects of camera shake (see also page 229). However, faster shutter speeds are not an absolute guarantee against camera shake. Care in holding the camera is definitely essential for all photography. The camera and lens should be supported firmly whenever possible or, better yet, use a tripod. With these factors in mind, it is understandable that there are no hard-and-fast rules for choosing the right shutter speed.

Leica telephoto lenses

The greater the length and/or the diameter of a Leica M lens, the greater the possibility of obstructing the viewfinder image. In order to minimize these obstructions, steps are often taken to reduce the size of a lens. For this reason optical designs that limit the physical length of the lens are used. This is achieved by an asymmetrical optical design with the special characteristic of a rear element with a low index of refraction, i.e., a diverging rear element. Strictly speaking, the term "telephoto" only applies to this type of lens design. In common usage, however, the word "telephoto" is commonly used in place of "long focal length."

Fast telephoto lenses require more elements than slower traditional lenses. Consequently they also tend to be slightly heavier. In designing long lenses for Leica M cameras, the optical engineer has many considerations, including the need to keep the viewfinder image as unobstructed as possible, while providing fast handling and low weight.

Four small telephoto lenses

Today's Leica M System includes three long focal lengths: 75, 90, and 135mm. The 90mm and the 135mm are each represented by two lenses with different maximum apertures. All lenses in this group share the characteristic of being nearly as universal as normal lenses. Descriptions such as "small tele" and "medium-long focal length" clearly demonstrate the desire of photographers to segregate this group of focal lengths in a special category within the system. They realize how important it is to start planning the expansion of their personal camera outfits with lenses of different focal lengths as soon as they start using the Leica M system. Thus, the question arises whether it would not be wiser to choose a 75mm or a 90mm lens instead of a normal lens. Naturally the preferred types of subjects that are to be photographed with them should mainly determine the choice of lenses.
Photojournalists who use a Leica M camera have proven that a lens with a slightly long focal length, paired with a 28mm or a 35mm wide-angle lens, is often the ideal mini-outfit, suitable for many photographic situations. Of course this also applies to the combination of 50mm and 135mm lenses. It is not unusual that the lens with the longer focal length assumes the dominant role. It has the advantage that its narrower angle of view forces the photographer to concentrate on the relevant part of the subject. Often a lens with a longer focal length is the first choice in what will later become a complete photographic outfit.

75mm f/1.4 Summilux-M

The fastest long focal length lens in the Leica M system distinguishes itself by extraordinarily high performance. Even at full aperture, this modified Gauss type lens produces high contrast across the entire image area. Resolution and detail reproduction are outstanding at the same time. These imaging qualities can be improved even further by stopping down the lens. Even with the lens wide open, no coma is visible in the image area. The vignetting that is inherent in the system is exceedingly low for a lens of this aperture, and distortion is practically undetectable. Because of its superb characteristics, the 75mm f/1.4 Summilux-M lens is an ideal lens for available-light photography. Its performance remains largely uniform, even at close range.

The focal length of 75mm departs from the traditional formula of longer focal lengths for lens outfits, but its high speed of f/1.4 makes it a good addition. Even though its focal length is shorter than a 90 mm lens, in actual use, the 50% increase over a normal focal length is quite noticeable. The bright-line frame for the 75mm f/1.4 Summilux-M lens is a standard on Leica

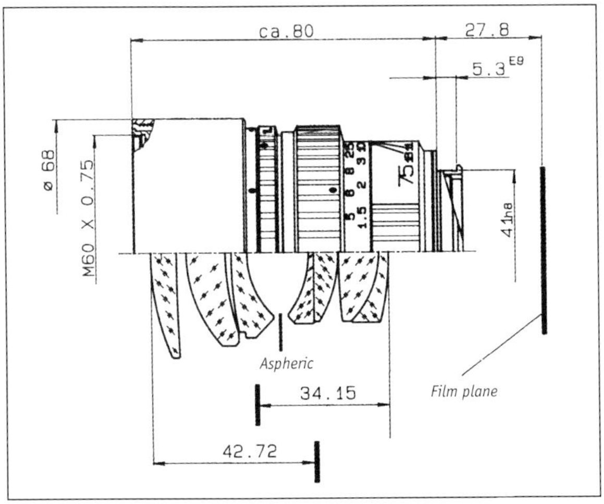

Fig. 121: *75mm f/1.4 Summilux-M*

M7, Leica M6 and M4-P cameras. Viewfinders of Leica M2, M4, M4-2, and M5 cameras can be modified by Leica's technical service to include the appropriate viewfinder mask.

90mm f/2.8 Elmarit-M

The optics and image performance of this lens are identical with the popular Leica R lens, which shares its name. And like the R lens, at full aperture, the 90mm f/2.8 Elmarit-M offers high contrast and excellent reproduction of detail. Even in extreme lighting situations, this lens does not produce disturbing reflections. It features good field flatness, i.e., the corner-to-

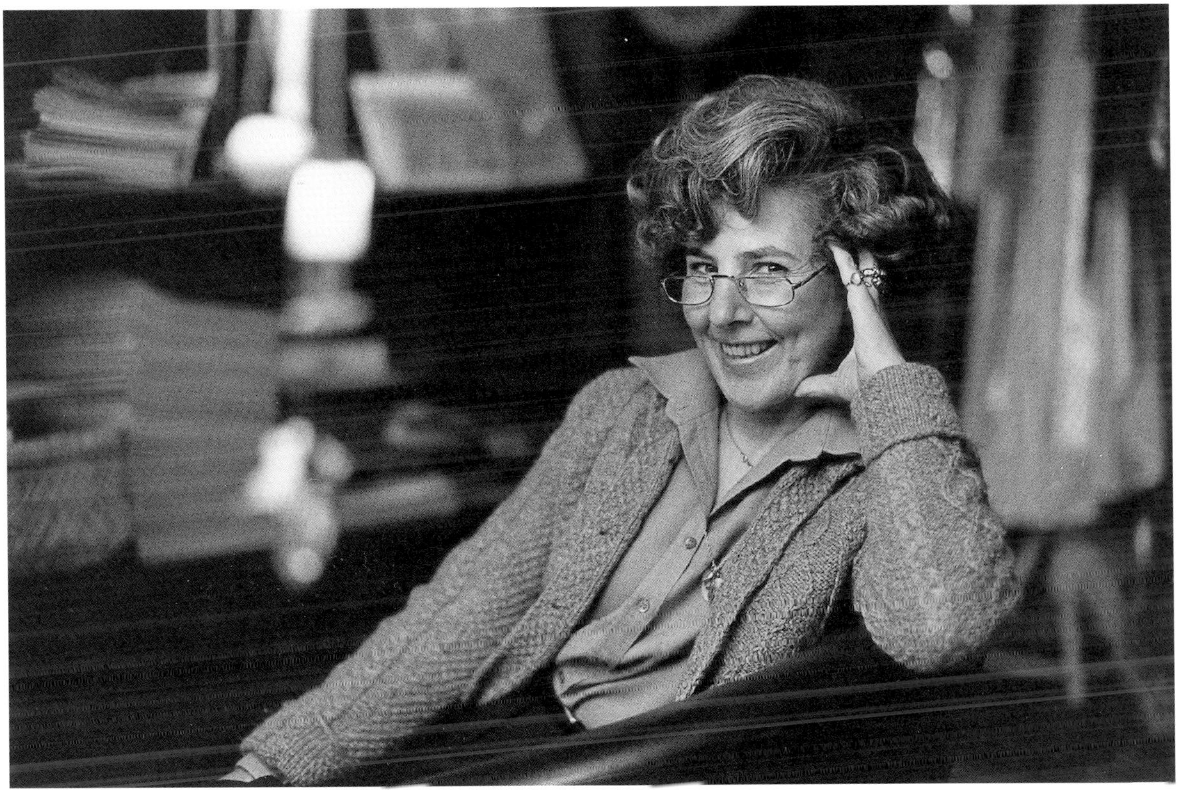

Fig. 122: *The extraordinary features of the 75mm f/1.4 Summilux-M lens are that it not only has a large aperture, but it also combines the versatility of a normal lens with the effect of a small telephoto lens. These characteristics allow photographers to be largely independent of the constraints of light and space, which encourages concentration on the most important part of the subject. 1/60 second, wide open, high-speed film.*

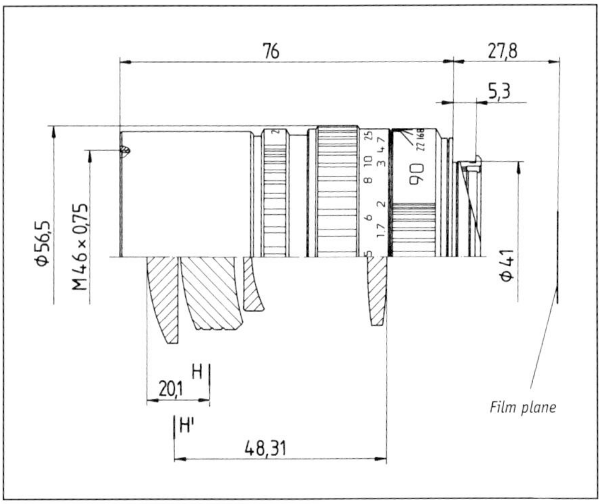

Fig. 123: *90mm f/2.8 Elmarit-M*

corner sharpness is excellent even at full aperture. Quality is improved further by stopping the lens down to f/4.

In the close-focusing range (less than 2 m or about 6 feet), this lens produces high contrast and good field flatness. Vignetting, which is inherent in any optical system and is particularly noticeable with low light, is extremely minimal in the 90mm f/2.8 Elmarit-M lens, so that it is negligible in actual use.

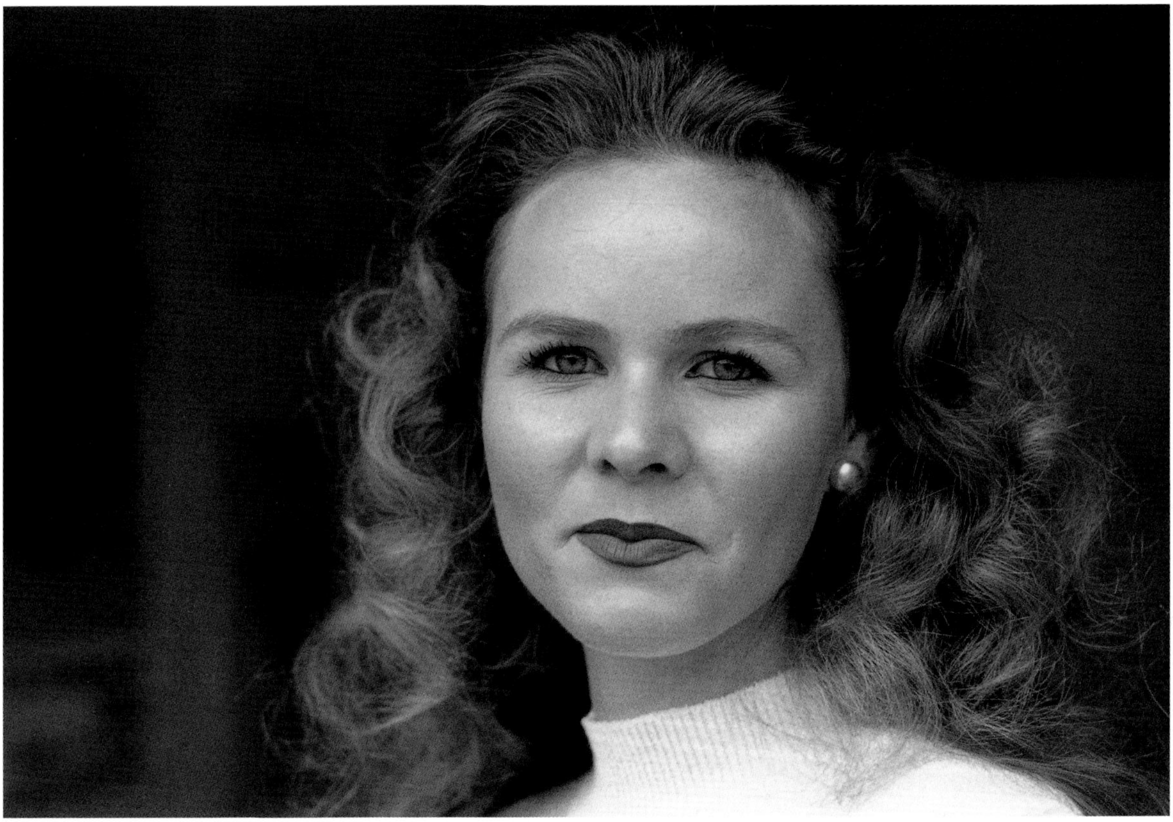

Fig. 124: *Leica lenses having a focal length of 90mm have always been considered ideal for portraits. The ease of use of these lenses encourages spontaneity, which is required to take dynamic pictures. 90mm f/2.8 Elmarit-M, 1/250 second, full aperture, medium-speed film.*

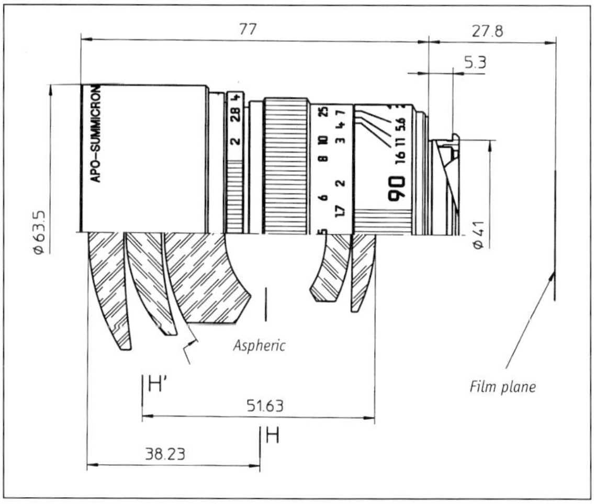

Fig. 125: *90mm f/2 Apo-Summicron-M ASPH*

90mm f/2 Apo-Summicron-M ASPH

This lens features an aspherical and apochromatic correction. Of the five elements in the 90mm f/2 Apo-Summicron-M ASPH, two are made of optical glass with a high index of refraction and two others feature anomalous partial dispersion. One lens has an aspherical surface, which, because of its size, is polished by computer-controlled CNC machines. The result is excellent reproduction of contrast and extraordinary sharpness. Residual color errors occurring with longer focal lengths and greater speed are eliminated by apochromatic correction. Even pictures with extremely fine detail do not exhibit any color fringes. Even at full aperture, the

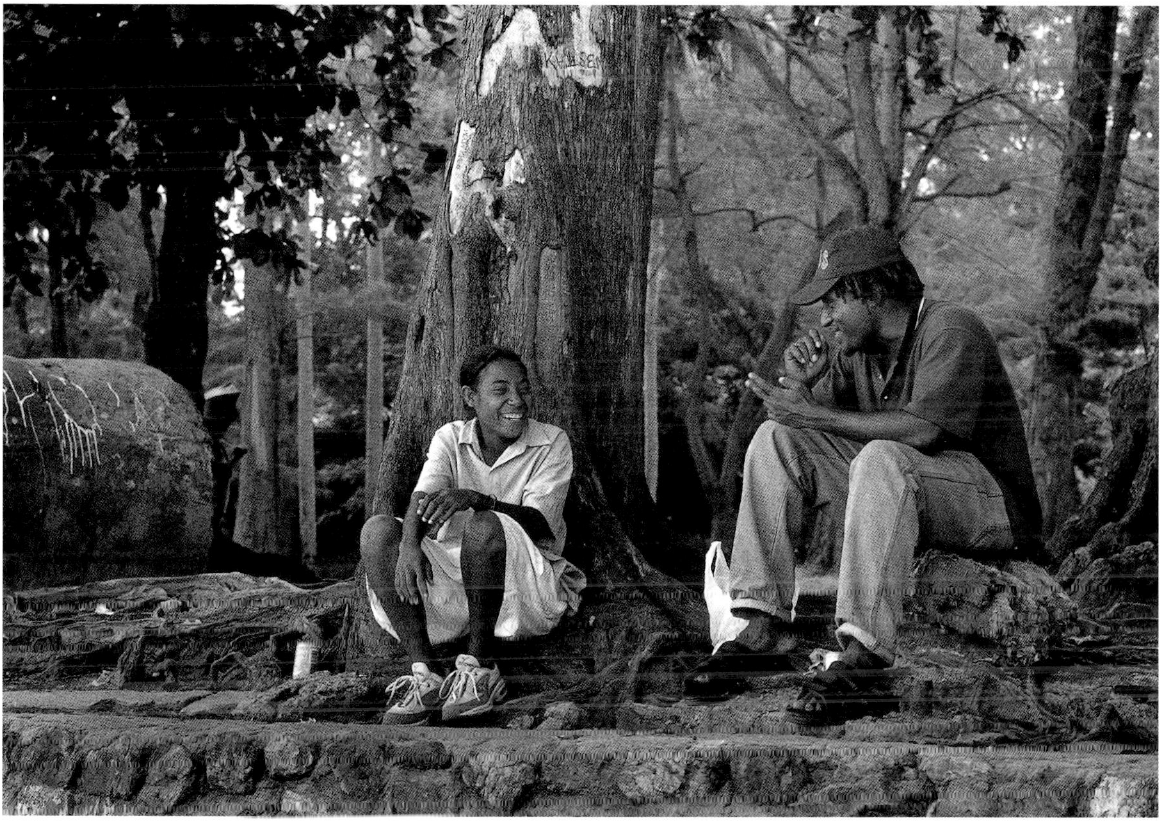

Fig. 126: *From a discreet distance—not unnoticed but almost ignored—the photographer can observe and photograph unposed scenes such as this one with a small tele-lens on the Leica M. 90mm f/2 Apo-Summicron-M ASPH, 1/250 second, f/5.6, high-speed film.*

reproduction quality is uniformly high across the entire image field. Stopping the lens down by one stop yields only insignificant additional improvement. Brilliance and resolution of the new 90mm f/2 Apo-Summicron-M ASPH are exemplary across the entire image field, even at full aperture. Even under exposures of difficult subjects such as light building walls indicate virtually no distortion. Artificial vignetting is minor and disappears completely starting at f/4. The best optical performance is achieved at medium distances and is largely retained throughout the close focusing range.

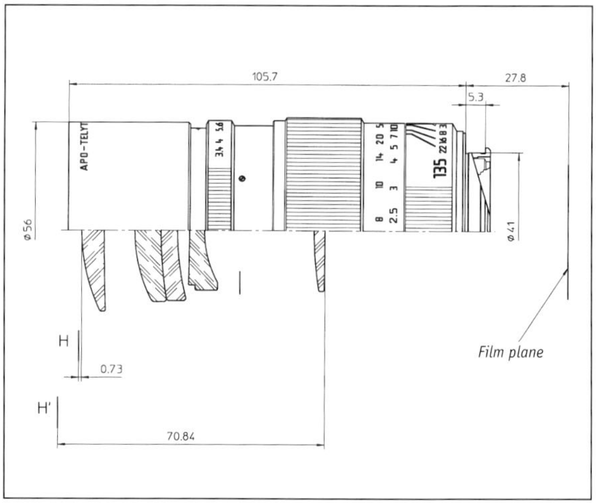

Fig. 127: *135mm f/3.4 Apo-Telyt-M lens*

135mm f/3.4 Apo-Telyt-M

This 135mm lens has a long history at Leitz/Leica because the first interchangeable lenses for Leica cameras included this focal length. Improved continuously over decades, the 135mm lens has always been considered indispensable in the Leica line up. As the longest lens in today's Leica M line-up, the 135mm f/3.4 Apo-Telyt-M is a good example of the flexibility offered by the Leica M system.

The new 135mm f/3.4 Apo-Telyt-M was the first M lens with apochromatic correction and it represents a milestone in the history of M lenses.

Compared with its predecessors, its imaging characteristics have been improved considerably, while its weight and dimensions have been reduced significantly. Together with the Leica M body this lens forms a comfortable, well-balanced compact unit.

By using several elements featuring anomalous dispersion, the secondary spectrum is suppressed effectively, so that residual color errors are practically non-existent. Contrast and resolution are excellent on the optical axis and over the entire image field. Aperture errors, coma, astigmatism and curvature of field are virtually non-existent with an infinite setting and are minimal in the closer focusing range. The freedom from distortion is another significant feature of this lens.

The outstanding imaging performance of the 135mm f/3.4 Apo-Telyt-M lens—including residual color errors, which are almost imperceptible due to apochromatic correction—is achieved even at full aperture of the lens. This performance is largely maintained even in the close focusing range (up to 1.50 m or about 5 feet). In close-up photography, an additional slight improvement of the picture can be achieved by stopping down one to two f/stops. Vignetting inherent in any optical system and which becomes particularly noticeable with even, light areas such as, white walls is very minimal and completely eliminated from f/5.6 – f/8.

The multi-layer coating developed specifically for the 135mm f/3.4 Apo-Telyt-M lens makes the lens highly insensitive to reflections and flare. In addition, the lens system has been adapted in such a manner that its color characteristics fit perfectly in the Leica M lens system.

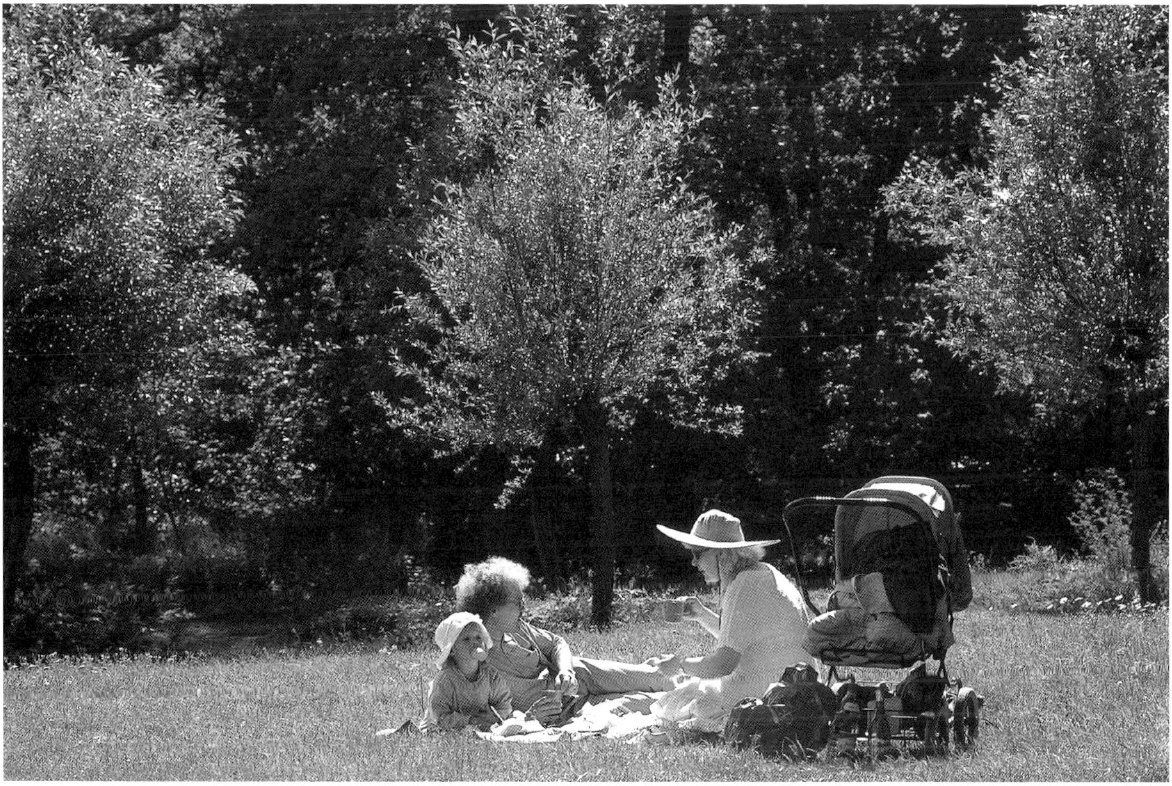

Fig. 128: *If distances are shrunk and the edge of the forest moves closer, the large meadow in the park becomes a small sunlit clearing. Three-dimensional backlighting and tight cropping remove anything that is not essential from the picture, making it easy to capture this family picnic in a picture. 135mm f/3.4 Apo-Telyt-M lens, 1/250 second, f/8, medium-speed film.*

Three focal lengths – one lens

In the true sense of the word, the development of the new Leica M lenses parallels the development of Leica M camera bodies. To ensure compatibility with various Leica M models, the bayonet lens mount—the connection with the rangeviewfinder, and the mechanical insertion of the appropriate bright-line frame—cannot be altered. In addition, Leica M lenses must not interfere with the optical path of the rangeviewfinder and should minimally obstruct the viewfinder image. Therefore, these lenses must not exceed a certain size.

These facts must be considered in order understand why zoom lenses (readily available for reflex cameras) are not available for the Leica M. Because many photographers have asked for the option of taking pictures with various focal lengths without having to change the lens, Leica's optics designers and engineers had to consider a zoom option and, again, reach the limits of the technically feasible. In addition to many minor details, three main problems had to be solved first:

- In zoom lenses, a small size, which causes the least obstruction of the M camera's viewfinder image, is highly inconsistent with high optical

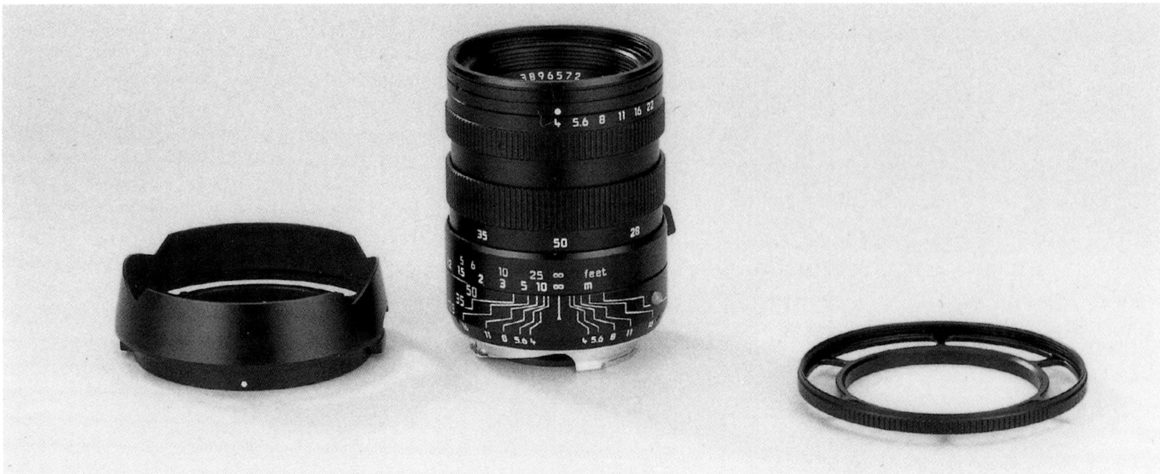

Fig. 129: Three focal lengths in one lens.

performance. In order to create a compact zoom with imaging quality that meets the specifications of the newest generation of Leica M lenses, Leica engineers incorporated two aspherical elements in their design. One aspherical element (lens 2) reduces distortion and another aspherical element (lens 4) minimizes monochromatic image errors. Furthermore, five of the eight elements in this complex system are fabricated from optical glass displaying high indices of refraction.

- The appropriate bright-line frame is usually inserted in the viewfinder of the Leica M by a flange in the bayonet mount. This varies in position, depending on the respective focal length groups, 28/90mm, 50/75mm, or 35/135mm, for example. In order to include the required bright-line frame when a focal length is selected on the M zoom lens, the flange is moved by an adjustable mount in the bayonet.

Unlike the zoom lenses for SLR cameras, which only require the movement of lens groups relative to each other, an M-series zoom lens must also move the flange, which inserts the correct bright-line frame in the viewfinder. A considerable engineering effort was required to achieve both a smooth zoom action and the ability to tactually detect when the correct bright-line frame is inserted.

- The range-viewfinder in Leica M lenses is focused by sensing the lens shift when the focusing ring is rotated. However, in zoom lenses—unlike prime lenses—the entire optical system shifts, not just the first element the system. Therefore, the transmission of the focus setting must take place from the first element group, to the second group, to the camera, with the same accuracy as other Leica M lenses.

This engineering resulted in a zoom lens with a speed of f/4 and adjustable focal lengths of 28, 35, and 50mm. These focal-length settings are fixed so it is not entirely like the usual zoom lens. As is indicated by the maximum aperture (f/4), such a lens does not really replace the prime lenses in the Leica M system. However, it can be a very useful addition. It is an ideal lens for different shooting situations while "traveling lightly."

28-35-50mm f/4 Tri-Elmar-M ASPH

One striking and distinctive feature of this lens is the sequence of adjustable focal lengths. While the central position of the zoom ring is associated with the focal length of 50mm, the wide-angle positions for 35mm and 28mm are achieved by a small 45° turn to the right or left. This unusual action is allowed by the lever construction of the camera, which acts as adjustment mechanism for including different focal lengths.

This unique design, introduced in 1954 on the Leica M3, was retained on all subsequent M cameras to ensure compatibility of all Leica M cameras and lenses.

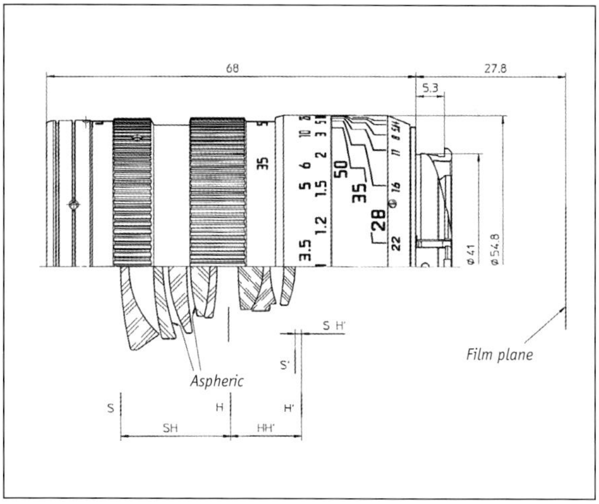

Fig. 130: *28-35-50mm f/4 Tri-Elmar-M ASPH*

The 28-35-50mm f/4 Tri-Elmar-M ASPH is characterized by good-to-excellent imaging performance for all three focal lengths. Even at full aperture, a high-contrast picture with good resolution of details is achieved. When the aperture is stopped down to f/5.6 – f/8, the contrast may even increase. The curvature of field with all three focal lengths is minimal and not noticeable in practical photographic applications.

Compared with good zoom lenses, the distortion is very slight. It is only at a focal length of 28mm that the lens does not achieve the high quality of a corresponding Leica M fixed focal length lens.

With shorter focal lengths, vignetting is more pronounced than in lenses with normal or long focal length. This drop of light toward the edge of the picture can become particularly visible with the aperture wide open, under exposure, and with light, even colored subjects.

At focal lengths of 50mm and 35mm vignetting of the Leica M fixed focal lengths is comparable, except that artificial vignetting is slightly more pronounced at 28mm. Starting at f/8, all three focal lengths of the 28-35-50mm f/4 Tri-Elmar-M ASPH lens are free from vignetting. Distance and focal length are selected in a similar manner to a two-ring zoom lens by operating two separate rings. One can hear and feel the zoom ring engage so that an incorrect adjustment of the focal length is unlikely. Unlike a true zoom lens, intermediate settings result in blurred images and cannot be used. A round, metal accessory lens hood is available. It is designed to permit a good view through the viewfinder. When not in use, this lens hood may be reversed and attached for storage. Still, even if this additional lens hood is not used, the front lens of the 28-35-50mm f/4 Tri-Elmar-M ASPH is protected against flare, raindrops, or fingerprints. The longer the focal length, the more recessed the lens hood is in the front mount of the lens. In order to prevent vignetting when filters are used, low-profile or "wide-angle" filters are recommended. Leica offers a matching UVa filter. A specially configured adapter for a polarizing filter, E67 allows control of the polarization effect by looking through the camera viewfinder. Adapters and filters ensure freedom from vignetting.

The 28-35-50mm f/4 Tri-Elmar-M ASPH was developed for use with the Leica M7 and the Leica M6 models (not for M6J). The lens can also be used on older Leica M models as correct focusing

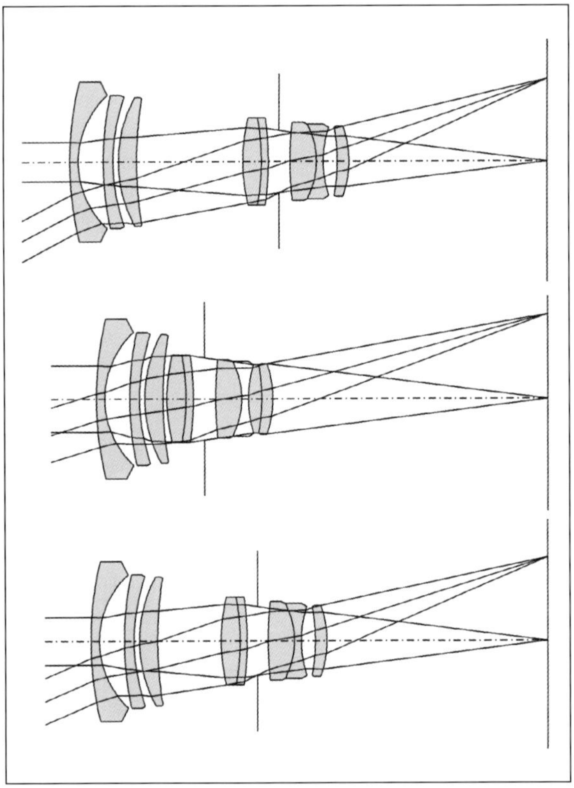

Fig. 131: *The arrangement of the lens elements and the optical path in the 28-35-50mm f/4 Tri-Elmar-M lens.*

through the range-viewfinder is ensured for all focal lengths.

A few Leica M models do not have the bright-line frame for 28mm in the viewfinder. However, some of these earlier models can be updated (see Table 7). Another option is the use of the Abada viewfinders for 28mm, which is offered as an accessory by Leica. Engineering differences in the design of the viewfinders of older models could only be given limited consideration when the lens was developed. Therefore, it may happen in some models that several viewfinder frames are included at the same time. In isolated cases this effect may also occur in newer M cameras if the adjustment mechanism of the viewfinder masks has not been serviced in a long time. In every case Leica can provide help and information.

Tips for the care of Leica M lenses

Lenses for Leica M cameras are practically maintenance-free. Nevertheless, they should be cleaned from time to time after rigorous use. Of course, that also applies to filters. Dust should be removed from exterior lens surfaces with a soft lens brush. Spots or debris can removed by using a very clean, dry, soft cloth to swab the lens gently in a circular motion, starting from the center, all the way to the edges. Leica recommends microfiber cloths (available at photoshops and from opticians), which are stored in protective containers and can be washed at temperatures of up to 40°C. Do not iron these or use fabric-softener when laundering them. Cleaning cloths that contain chemicals should not be used because they could damage the lens' multicoatings.

The portion of the microfiber cloth that is to be used for wiping the lens dry must not be touched with bare fingers beforehand. That is the only sure way of preventing perspiration or skin oils from reaching the lens surface.

To use lens cleaner, moisten a very soft, unfinished cotton fabric and gently rub in a circular motion, starting from the center to the edges. A dry cotton cloth should be used immediately afterwards until the surface is completely dry again.

Special cleaning tissues such as those used for cleaning eyeglasses are not recommended, because they are impregnated with chemicals that may damage the optical glass of coatings. Materials used for eyeglasses have a different composition than optical glass used for high-performance photographic lenses.

For easy, smooth lens changes, the bayonet is factory-coated with an ultra-thin layer of lubricant. With normal use, this coating remains for years, even if the bayonet is cleaned occasionally with care. If a solvent is used in the cleaning process, that thin lubricant layer should be reconstituted by applying a very tiny amount of acid-free vase-

a

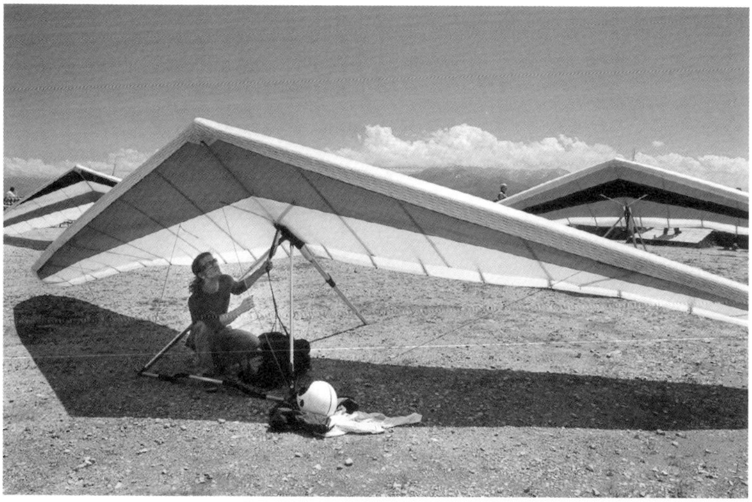

b

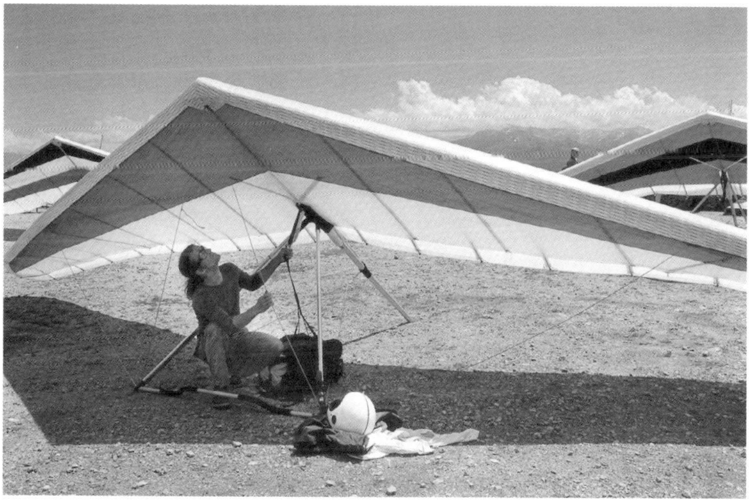

c

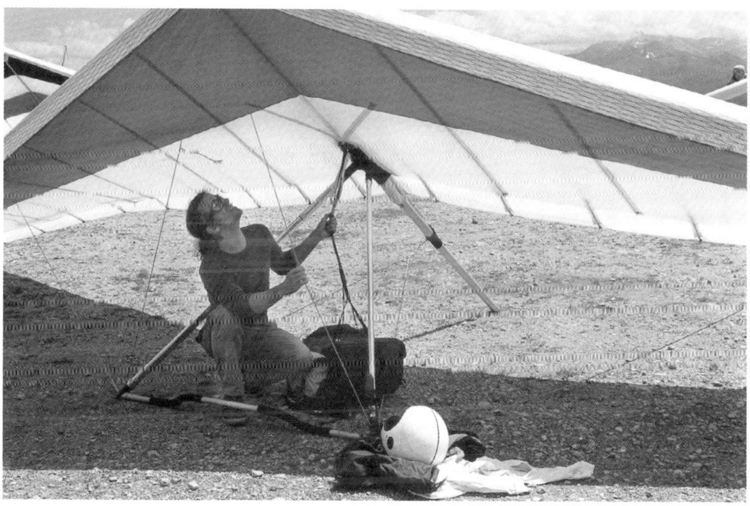

Fig. 132 a – c: *The differences between various focal length settings are shown in this comparison. The exposures, taken from the same camera position, illustrate that the captured segments vary more significantly than expected from focal-length data. All exposures were made at 1/500 second, f/5.6-f/8 on medium-speed film with focal length settings of 28, 35, and 50mm (from the top down).*

Table 9: Leica M lenses at a glance

M lenses [1]	Order Nr.	Lens speed / focal length (mm)	Field of view	Number of lenses	Number of elements	Aspherical surfaces	Smallest aperture	Minimum focusing distance (m)	Smallest - object field (mm)	Pupil enlargement	Recommended filter size	Design length (mm)	Largest ∅ (mm)	Weight (g)
Elmarit-M ASPH silver chrome plated	11 135 11 897	1:2.8/21	92°	9	7	1	16	0.7	696 × 1044	1.38	E55	46.0	58.0	300 415
Elmarit-M ASPH silver chrome plated	11 878 11 898	1:2.8/24	84°	7	5	1	16	0.7	630 × 950	1.26	E55	45.0	58.0	290 388
Elmarit-M	11 809	1:2.8/28	76°	8	7	–	22	0.7	533 × 800	1.09	E46	41.4	53.0	260
Summicron-M ASPH	11 604	1:2/28	76°	9	6	1	16	0.7	528 × 793	1.23	E46	40.8	53.0	270
Summicron-M ASPH silver chrome plated	11 879 11 882	1:2/35	6°	7	5	1	16	0.7	419 × 627	0.99	E39	34.5	53.0	255 340
Summilux-M ASPH. silver chrome plated	11 874 11 883	1:1.4/35	64°	9	5	1	16	0.7	420 × 630	1.11	E46	46.2	53.0	250 415
Elmar-M silver chrome plated	11 831 11 823	1:2.8/50	45°	4	3	–	16	0.7	274 × 411	0.85	E39	37.6[2]	52.0	170 245
Summicron-M silver chrome plated	11 826 11 816	1:2/50	45°	6	4	–	16	0.7	277 × 416	1.02	E39	43.5	53.0	240 335
Summilux-M silver chrome plated	11 868 11 856	1:1.4/50	45°	7	5	–	16	0.7	277 × 416	0.94	E46	46.7	54.5	275 380
Noctilux-M	11 822	1:1/50	45°	7	6	–	16	1.0	410 × 615	1.04	E60	62.0	69.0	630
Summilux-M	11 810	1:1.4/75	31°	7	5	–	16	0.75	192 × 288	0.96	E60	80.0	68.0	560
Elmarit-M silver chrome plated	11 807 11 808	1:2.8/90	27°	4	4	–	22	1.0	220 × 330	0.80	E46	76.0	56.6	410 560
Apo-Summicron-M ASPH	11 884	1:2/90	27°	5	5	1	16	1.0	220 × 330	0.82	E55	78.0	64.0	500
Apo-Telyt-M	11 889	1:3.4/135	18°	5	4	–	22	1.5	220 × 330	0.66	E49	104.7	58.5	450
Tri-Elmar-M ASPH.	11 831	1:4/28 1:4/35 1:4/50	76° 64° 45°	8	6	2	22	1.0	750 × 1130 620 × 930 430 × 650	1.61 1.45 1.23	E49	67.8	55	340

[1] Also black anodized.

line on the bayonet with a finger and then thoroughly spreading it just on the seating surface with a clean cloth. Of course this must be done with great care, so that the bayonet and other parts of the lens do not become smudged.

Which lens on which camera?

Earlier Leica M lenses on Leica M7 and M6 models

All earlier Leica M lenses can be attached without restrictions. However some of them reach too far into the interior of the camera, thus partially shading the silicon photodiode. Proper exposure measurements can therefore not be made when one of the following lenses is attached: 15mm f/8 Hologon, 21mm f/4 Super-Angulon-M, 21mm f/3.4 Super-Angulon-M, and 28mm f/2.8 Elmarit-M 1 with serial numbers under 2314921. But the Visoflex 1, 2 and 3, as well as most of the accessories of the past three decades, can be used.

Leica M lenses on Leica R cameras

The oft-expressed desire to use Leica M lenses on Leica R cameras can only be satisfied to a very limited extent. The distance from the lens-seating surface to the film plane amounts to 27.8 mm for a Leica M lens (28.8 mm for screwmount lenses), while it is 47 mm for Leica R lenses. Furthermore, the diameter of the Leica M bayonet is smaller than the diameter of a Leica R bayonet. This precludes any rangefinder-coupled Leica M lens from being used directly on a Leica R or a Leicaflex camera.

However, since the Leica M System includes certain lenses that have the capability of being used on Visoflex 2 or 3 reflex housings, these particular lenses can be attached to Leica R and Leicaflex cameras by means of Adapter Ring 14167. With its length of 21.8 mm, this Adapter Ring increases the distance from the lens seating surface to the film plane of a Leica R or a Leicaflex camera to the 68.8 mm lens flange to film plane distance for which lenses intended for use with Visoflex 2 and 3 reflex housings have been designed. Working conditions, such as subject distance and areas of coverage, will then be the same for a Leica R camera as they would be for the use of these Leica M lenses on Visoflex 2 or 3 reflex housings.

Since Leica M lenses do not have automatic diaphragms, the ease of use and the range of applications of these lenses in conjunction with Leica R single lens reflex cameras is noticeably more limited compared to equivalent Leica R lenses. Exposure measurement has to be made with the working aperture. The choice of exposure measurement modes and the automatic shutter speed control on Leica R cameras remain fully functional.

Leica M lenses on the Leica CL camera

For the general public, the introduction of the Leica CL in the year 1973 was the first evidence of Leitz/Minolta cooperation. The design of this camera was executed at Leitz; its manufacture took place at Minolta. Its set of lenses consisted of the 40mm f/2 Summicron-C and the 90mm f/4 Elmar-C. In addition, standard lenses for Leica M cameras with maximum apertures up to f/2 were an integral part of the Leica CL system.

Since the bayonet lens mount of this compact Leica (the designation CL stems from the first letters of the words Compact Leica) is similar to the bayonet lens mount on Leica M cameras, certain other Leica M lenses can also be used on a Leica CL. However, the short effective measuring base of that camera's rangefinder, which is only 19 mm long, has certain limitations. As a result, the measuring accuracy of that rangefinder is inadequate when fast lenses are used at full aperture.

Furthermore, certain lenses or their lens hoods extend into the light path for the rangefinder, so that it either cannot be used or is seriously impaired. Lenses that extend too far into the camera also cannot be used. The viewfinder of a Leica CL camera has bright line frames for 40, 50 and 90mm lenses. The complete field that is visible through that viewfinder corresponds approximately to the field covered by a 35mm lens.

An accessory bright line finder that can be inserted in the accessory shoe of a Leica CL is required when a 28mm lens is used. But this accessory shoe is not aligned with sufficient accuracy for use with an accessory viewfinder for a 135mm lens, so that the viewfinder image and the subject field covered by a 135mm lens often do not coincide exactly.

LIMITATIONS

- Many of the Leica M lenses can only be focused in the near range.
- When used with the Leica CL, the powerful 50mm f/1.4 Summilux-M and 50mm f/1.2 Noctilux-M lenses require stopping down to at least f/2.
- A 50mm f/1 Noctilux-M lens makes focus setting virtually impossible.
- The rangefinder of the Leica Cl has a setting range of up to 0.8 m. A few of the Leica M lenses permit setting an even closer range. In these cases, it is not possible to focus at a distance of less than 0.8 m.
- With collapsible lenses, the degree to which the lens is collapsed has to be restricted to a permissible depth by means of a "protective band." It is not necessary to send the lens to the Technical Service of Leica to have this done. Dymo International manufactures appropriate self-adhesive tapes in various widths, which are available in stationery supply and other stores. The tape should go completely around the tube of the lens except for a gap of about 1 mm (or just over 1/6"). To determine the correct length of the tape, it is helpful to make a sample band out of paper first.

For the following bayonet and/or screwmount lenses, the tape should be 9.5 mm (3/8" wide): 50mm f/3.5 Elmar, 50mm f/2.8 Elmar, 50mm f/2 Summar, 50mm f/2 Summitar, 50mm f/2 Summicron, and 90mm f/4 Elmar. A tape that is 12.7 mm (1/2") wide is required for the 50mm f/2.5 Hektor lens. 35 mm f/2 Summicron-M, 35mm f/1,4 Summilux-IM, 50mm f/1.2 Noctilux-M and 90mm f/2.8 Elmarit-M lenses

- The following Leica M lenses cannot be used on a Leica CL: lenses with a rear lens mount that extends too deeply into the camera body, like the 21mm Super-Angulon-M and the 28mm f/2.8 Elmarit-M with a serial number below 2314921.

Likewise, lenses with viewfinder attachments, like the 35mm wide-angle lenses for the Leica M3 and the 135mm f/2.8 Elmarit-M cannot be used.

Portions of the light path for the rangefinder are obstructed by powerful long focal lengths, e.g., as those of the 90 mm f/2 Summicron-M. Furthermore, the accuracy of the rangefinder of a Leica CL is no longer sufficient when that lens is used with large apertures.

All of the above is also valid for the Leitz Minolta CL camera, which was sold in Japan, the U.S.A., and several other countries. Aside from the name, this model is identical to the Leica CL.

Leica M lenses on the Minolta CLE

The Minolta CLE is the successor model to the Leitz Minolta CL (Leica CL). It has a slightly modified range-viewfinder and automatic exposure control. Even though the effective measuring base of the rangefinder on this model is a little longer than it is on a CL, similar limitations apply. Exact details of this can be obtained from subsidiaries of Minolta Corporation.

CL and CLE lenses on Leica M cameras

Early interchangeable screwmount Leica lenses, as well as lenses for Leica M cameras, have differential focusing mounts, i.e., during focusing, their contact surfaces for the roller of the rangefinder arm move parallel to the optical axis. This type of focusing mount was not used on the 40mm f/2 Summicron-C and the 90mm f/4 Elmar-C lenses for the Leica CL, however, in order to achieve lighter and more compact design. Both of these lenses have a steep cam. Even though they can be attached to Leica M cameras, it is not possible to focus them accurately by using the Leica M rangefinder. That is why Leica does not recommend the use of Leica CL lenses on Leica M cameras.

For the same reasons, the use of Minolta Rokkor lenses for Minolta CL and Minolta CLE cameras on Leica M cameras also cannot be recommended. Furthermore, when the 28mm Rokkor lens for the CLE is attached to a Leica M, it actuates the bright-line frames for 35 mm and 135mm lenses.

Early Leica M lenses on the Leica M5

All lenses with Leica M bayonet mounts, as well as older screwmount Leica lenses with corresponding bayonet adapters, can be used on a Leica M5. In general, they are suitable for full utilization of that camera's selective through-the-lens exposure meter. However, there are some exceptions and limitations:

- The amount of travel of the tubes of collapsible lenses must be restricted to the permissible depth by means of a "protective band." It is not necessary to send the lenses to Leica to have this done. Dymo International manufactures appropriate self adhesive tapes in a variety of widths, which are available in stationery supply and other stores. The tape should go completely around the tube of the lens except for a gap of about 1 mm (1/6"). To determine the correct length of the tape, it is helpful to make a sample band out of paper first.

For the following bayonet and/or screwmount lenses, the tape should be 9.5 mm (3/8") wide: 50mm f/3.5 Elmar, 50mm f/2.8 Elmar, 50mm f/2 Summar, 50mm f/2 Summitar, 50mm f/2 Summicron, and 90mm f/4 Elmar. A tape that is 12.7 mm (1/2") wide is required for the 50mm f/2.5 Hektor lens.

- Certain lenses have to be sent to the Technical Service of Leica or to the official distributor, or an authorized Repair Service for adaptation. Among them are early 21 and 28mm wide-angle lenses with rear lens mounts that extend too deeply into the camera body. By milling away a certain portion of the bayonet mount, the arm with the CdS photoresistor is prevented from swinging into the optical path. After that, these lenses can be attached to a camera, but its through-the-lens exposure measurement feature cannot be used. The following are the particular lenses that require modification: screwmount 21mm f/4 Super-Angulon (only the bayonet adapter with catalog no. 14097 needs to be altered in this instance). In this case, please state "for 21mm." Bayonet mount 21mm f/4 Super-Angulon, bayonet mount 21mm f/3.4 Super-Angulon (with serial numbers below 2473251), and bayonet mount 28mm f/2.8 Elmarit (with serial numbers below 2314921) also have to be sent to a repair service.

Lenses with removable viewfinder attachments that impact the top cover of the Leica M5 must also be sent to one of the services mentioned above in order to have their bayonet mounts and their viewfinder attachments modified: 35mm f/3.5 Summicron with removable viewfinder attachment and near-range 50mm f/2 Summicron.

Screwmount Leica lenses on Leica M cameras

Until recently, Leitz/Leica offered Bayonet Adapters for screwmount lenses. Each adapter is 1 mm (just 1/16") thick and has a bayonet on the outside and a screwthread on the inside. Since these adapters had to actuate the appropriate bright-line frames, three different versions were available. Each is engraved with the focal length of the lens with which it works.

Leica R lenses on Leica M cameras

Aside from the fact that Leica does not offer an adapter for attaching R lenses to Leica M cameras, such a combination would not be practical anyway, as exact focusing would not be possible because of the absence of a rangefinder-coupling cam on Leica R lenses.

Furthermore, most Leica R lenses are bulkier than Leica M lenses, so that they would have to be used in conjunction with accessory viewfinders, because they would obstruct large segments of the viewfinder image of Leica M cameras.

Note: More than ten years ago, Leitz offered an adapter with Catalog No. 22228 for the use of Leica R lenses on Leicina Special movie cameras. It could also be used on Leica M cameras, but it would not couple to the rangefinder. This adapter is no longer available.

Other manufacturers' lenses on Leica M cameras

Most lens manufacturers produce lenses for single lens reflex cameras. All these lenses have an automatic diaphragm mechanism that is not needed on lenses for rangefinder cameras, and they do not have the cam that couples with the long-base rangefinder of Leica M cameras. Looking at it this way, the question about the possibilities of using other brands of lenses on Leica M cameras does not even arise.

Basically, the same applies to all third manufacturers' lenses – with or without adapter ring:

- The precision of the lens seating on the camera, and consequently the calibration of the optical system for optimum reproduction, also depends on the number of coupling junctions. With Leica M cameras, as with any system camera, at least one coupling junction is unavoidable. With adapters, such as those that are generally used with other manufacturers' lenses, at least one more coupling junction is introduced. This also causes tolerances to accumulate.
- When they are not manufactured competently, bayonets can cause wear and they can also damage the mount on the Leica M camera.
- Color characteristics of other lenses are different from those of Leica M lenses. This is particularly problematic in slide projection.
- And then there is the question of where one may expect to find help if there ever is a problem with the combination of "camera + different-make of lens."

The Leica M up close

Close and distant ranges are the uncontested domain of single-lens-reflex cameras. Today, Leica R cameras easily cover both of these ranges. For decades, the rangefinder camera system included accessories for making photographs of close-up and distant subjects. The present Leica line of products no longer includes these accessories, and current lenses and camera bodies may not always be compatible with them. Nevertheless, many of these earlier accessories can still be used on Leica M cameras. Those who are used to operating modern single-reflex cameras may not readily know how to use them. Therefore, it is nice to know that instruction booklets for most of these accessories are still available from the Technical Service of Leica or H. Lindemanns Buchhandlung, Stuttgart, Germany. Of course the information service of Leica Camera AG will also be able to provide information.
It is remarkable how many combinations were possible with earlier accessories. These combinations were possible primarily because the lens head—the actual optical system—could be unscrewed from the focusing mounts of most of the older lenses. With the aid of extension tubes and small helical mounts (special focusing mounts), it was possible to adapt the lens heads to attachments for close-up and distant photography to meet the various demands. It was in those days that the tongue-in-cheek comment was made by many photographers that Leitz was also a factory for adapter rings.

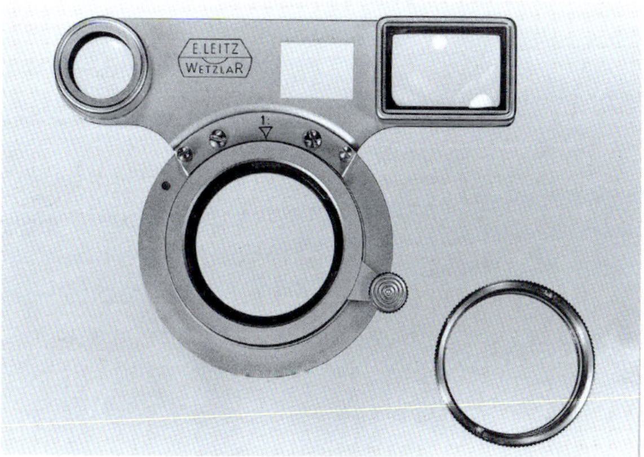

Fig. 133: Optical close-up attachment.

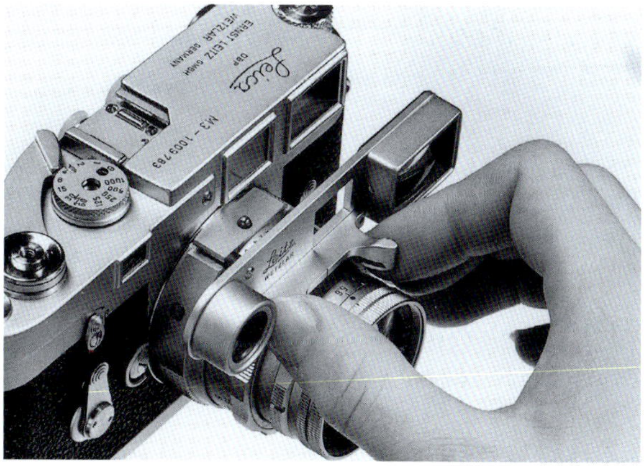

Fig. 134: 50mm f/2 Dual Range Summicron lens.

Optical close-up attachment

This accessory for 50mm lenses consists of a helical focusing mount and an integral viewfinder attachment. It can be used with collapsible 50mm f/2.8 Elmar and 50mm f/2 Summicron lenses, and also with the lens head of the earlier rigid 50mm f/2 Summicron lens (with an adapter ring). With this attachment, the camera's rangefinder is coupled from 88 to 48cm (or 34.65 to 18.89 inches). Parallax correction remains fully functional. Its working range covers reproduction ratios of 1:15 to 1:7.5. A special version of the earlier 50mm f/2 Summicron lens, called the dual range Summicron, was equipped with a double helix. When used with its slide-on view-finder attachment, it covered the same reproduction ratios.

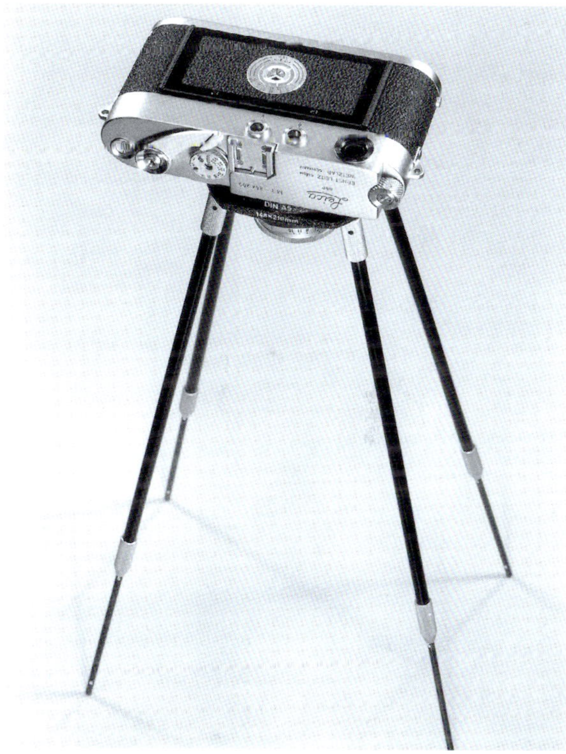

Fig. 135: The close-up device with telescoping metal rods.

Close-up device for DIN A4, A5, and A6 formats

This device consists of three collars and four telescoping metal rods. Depending on the format to be photographed, select the appropriate collar, attach the four legs and extend them to the notch corresponding to the collar being used. The ends of the rods mark the corners of the subject area being photographed and they also guarantee the correct distance. Each collar provides the correct lens extension and the proper angle for the metal rods. With the close-up device for DIN A4, A5, and A6 formats 50mm lenses are used in the same manner, as they are with the optical close-up attachment.

Close-up device for 1:3, 1:2, 1:1.5, and 1:1 reproduction ratios

This small copystand consists of a base with an adjustable column, four extension tubes for fixed reproduction ratios, three masks for delineating the subject area, a magnifier and an intermediate bayonet ring. All 50mm lenses can be used. Focusing takes place by means of a magnifier, that is attached in place of the camera body. The subject area is outlined by the masks or the inside rim of the base. The 1:1 mask has alignment guides for mounted slides, and there is a milled channel for filmstrips at the bottom of the base. The bayonet permits the use of Leica M models, as well as Leica screwmount models.

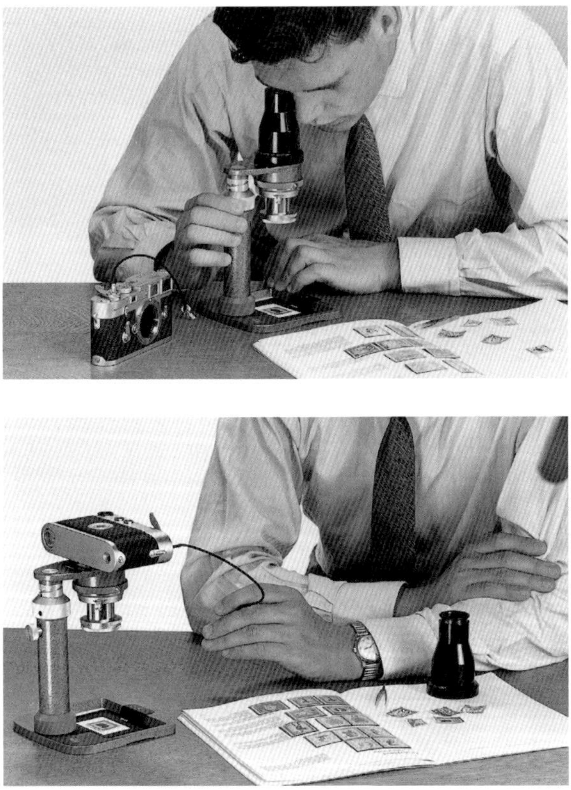

Fig. 136 a and b: *After focusing with a special magnifier the photographer attaches the camera to the close-up device.*

Reprovit IIa

As the name suggests, this device is intended primarily for reproduction work. In recent years, fast office copying machines and versatile microfilm installations have increasingly replaced documentation by means of the Reprovit IIa. And universal single-lens-reflex cameras have replaced it as a tool for close-up photographs. The Reprovit IIa, which has been discontinued by Leitz, is used primarily in conjunction with Leica M cameras without viewfinders, such as models MD, MDa, and MD-2. These cameras have a lateral stud, as do Leica models Ml, M2, and M3, which serves to position them accurately on the sliding focusing device of the Reprovit IIa. Leica models M6, M4-P, M4-2 and M4 can be retro-fitted with this positioning stud (see Table 7) by the Leica's Technical Service. The Leica M5 cannot be used on this reproduction device.

The Reprovit IIa has numerous applications. It can be used for the photographic reproduction of flat as well as three-dimensional objects, both colored and black-and-white ones. It is suitable for all kinds of subjects, such as maps, drawings, paintings, book pages, transparent subjects, templates, tools, etc. Its principal working range covers subject areas of 450 x 680 mm (or 21.6 x 26.75 inches), which approximately the DIN A 2 format (a reproduction ratio of 1:19), down to 24 x 36 mm (1.2 x 1.55 inches), which is a reproduction ratio of 1:1. Enlarged reproductions of up to 7x magnification are possible.

The Reprovit IIa is equipped with a 50mm f/4.5 Focotar-2 lens. This special lens was designed with optimum correction for the near range, down to a repro-duction ratio of 2:1. Enlarged reproductions up to 7:1 are possible with the 25mm f/2 Repro-Photar lens. Lighting by means of four lamps ensures a very uniform illumination of the subjects, which can be placed on the baseboard, positioned in a framing box (book press), or on a light box.

A Leica M camera body is placed on a sliding focusing device, which has a ground glass screen with several markings at the exact level of the film plane. It serves

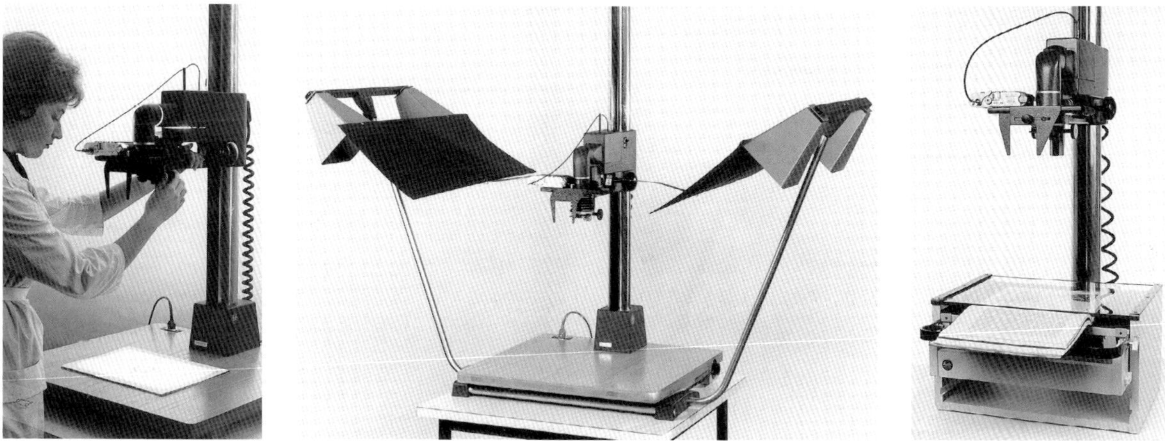

Fig. 137 a – c: *When using the Reprovit IIa, focusing is normally accomplished by projecting a ground glass that has a test pattern. A wide range of accessories, such as a framing box and a light box, make reproduction work easier.*

as a focusing aid. Quick and distinct focusing is possible by projecting a test pattern on the center of the subject field. This also delineates the exact area of coverage. The carrier arm can be moved up and down on the column and it is counterbalanced by weights suspended over ball-bearing pulleys, so that uninterrupted work over many hours is not tiring.

Focusing by projecting the test pattern is used for subject areas down to approximately 80 x 120 mm (3.2 x 4.75 inches) with a reproduction ratio of 1:3. For smaller areas, an angled 5x magnifier is used for accurately focusing the image on the ground glass screen of the sliding focusing device. To make the exposure, the sliding part of the device is moved to place the camera in the position just occupied by the ground glass housing. If focusing took place by means of test pattern projection, the action of sliding the camera into position automatically turns off the projection and activates the four-lamp illumination.

The lens diaphragm, which was wide open for focusing, is also stopped down to a preselected value. The camera's shutter is actuated by means of a vibration-free magnetic release and an electric timer. Since the illumination provided by the four lamps is always constant, the exposure values are generally determined from an exposure table. The exposure time factor required for close-up photographs can be read on the diaphragm actuator of the sliding focusing device. With a Leica M6, the exposure time can be measured through the lens set at the working aperture. In that case, the exposure factor is taken into account automatically.

Visoflex mirror reflex attachments

The ability of directly observing the image formed by the lens offers the greatest advantages and the most versatile possibilities in photography at close-up and distant ranges. By using a mirror-reflex attachment, any Leica M camera can be transformed into a single lens-reflex camera. Until a few years ago, Leitz offered the Visoflex mirror reflex attachment for this purpose.

Since the Visoflex attachment is placed between the camera body and the lens, the normal distance between the lens and the film plane is necessarily increased. The effect is the same as that of a lens extension: one can only focus on close-up subjects. In order to focus at infinity, the lens has to be brought closer to the film plane. That is the reason why the lens heads could be removed from the regular mounts of many of the older

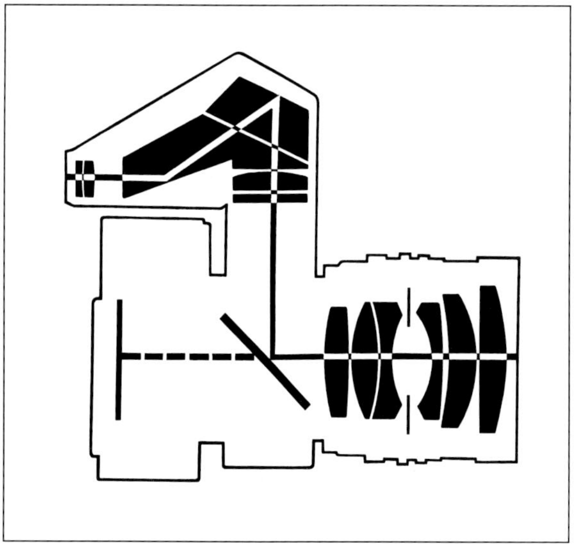

Fig. 138: *Visoflex mirror-reflex attachments can be used to convert a Leica M camera into a single-lens-reflex camera. The above diagram shows the light path through a Visoflex 3.*

lenses. By using the Visoflex attachment with special focusing mounts that are shorter, the distance between lens head and film plane can be reduced so that it is possible once again to focus at infinity. This can only be accomplished however, with lenses whose focal lengths are longer than the lens-flange-to-film-plane distance of the Visoflex housing when it is attached to a camera. On the Visoflex 1, that distance is 92 mm (camera = 28.5 mm plus Visoflex attachment = 63.5 mm). Therefore, the lens with the nearest longer focal length that can be focused at infinity is the 125mm lens. On the smaller Visoflex 2 and 3 attachments, that distance is 69.5 mm (camera = 28.5 mm plus Visoflex attachment = 41mm). The lens with the shortest focal length, that can still be focused at infinity on the Visoflex 2 and 3 attachments, is even smaller 65 mm. This is because the 65 mm f/3.5 Elmar-V can protrude slightly into the Visoflex housing without interfering with the movement of its quick return mirror.

Leica M lenses are not equipped with automatic diaphragms, so that this convenience is not available when mirror reflex attachments are used. Leitz did, however, offer certain lenses equipped with preset diaphragms designed especially for use on Visoflex attachments. On these lenses, the desired aperture stop could be preset on a special ring. The iris diaphragm itself remained wide open for focusing. An instant before the exposure, a quick finger movement stopped the lens down to the preselected aperture by flicking a second ring around to a mechanical stop.

Visoflex 1

This mirror reflex attachment was designed for use on a tripod. It has a special mount that allows the camera body to be turned conveniently for horizontal or vertical photographs. There are two different magnifiers available for observing the ground glass screen: the vertical 5x magnifier produces an upright but laterally reversed image, whereas the 45° 4x magnifier has a reversing prism that yields a vertically and laterally correct image. Both magnifiers are adjustable for individual eyesight correction.

A double cable release is used to swing the mirror out of the light-path just prior to the exposure. The cable for the mirror is slightly longer, so that it acts first, just before the other cable releases the shutter. The mirror can also be locked in the up position. This is necessary when the Visoflex attachment is used with very long focal lengths, such as 400mm. The subject can then be composed with the corresponding sports finder, which can be inserted in the accessory shoe provided for that purpose on the Visoflex 1 attachment.

Focusing is accomplished on the ground glass screen before the mirror is locked in the up position. The Visoflex 1 was available for screwmount as well as bayonet mount cameras, but it accepted only Leica screwmount lenses.

Visoflex 2

With its much flatter and more functional design, this mirror reflex attachment is also very well suited for hand-held photography. The mirror is raised and the

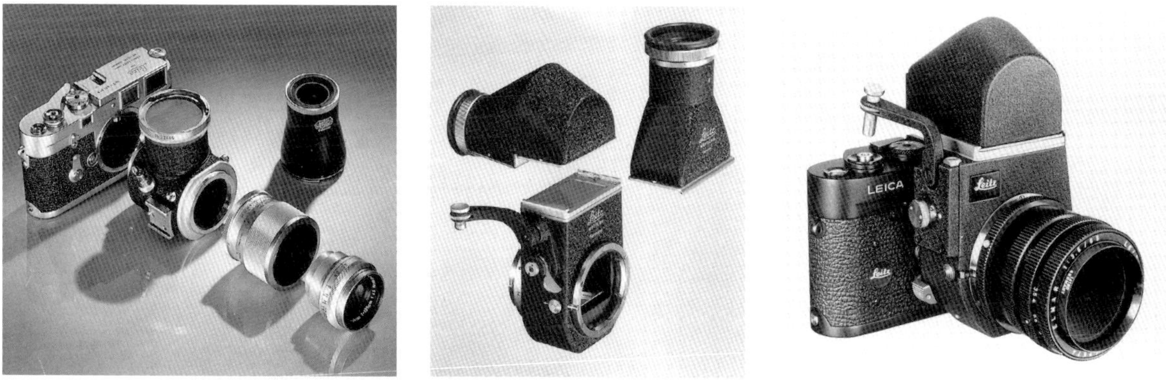

Fig. 139 a – from left to right: Visoflex 1, Visoflex 2, and Visoflex 3 with a 65mm f/3.5 Elmar-V lens in the universal focusing mount.

shutter is released in a fraction of a second by de-pressing a release lever. It is important that the gap between the touch screw in that lever and the shutter release button of the camera, which controls the timing between the mirror movement, and the shutter release, be adjusted accurately for the mirror to be completely up by the time the slit of the focal plane shutter begins to travel across film gate. That gap should be approximately 1 mm or just over 1/32 of an inch. After each exposure, the mirror has to be returned manually to the down position, where it locks into place.

A 4x prism magnifier with eyesight correction permits eyelevel viewing of an upright and laterally correct image on a ground glass, just as it is done with today's single lens reflex cameras. With the vertical 5x magnifier, conventional horizontal images appear laterally reversed, and vertical images are seen upside down. For that reason, this magnifier is used more for work on a copying stand or for photomicrography.

The Visoflex 2 housing can be attached like any Leica lens when the eyelevel magnifier is removed and when the shutter actuating lever is swung to the front of the housing. It is available with either a Leica M bayonet mount or a Leica screwmount on its camera side, and both versions have a Leica M bayonet mount on the lens side. All Leica M models, with the exception of M7, M6 TTL, and M5 can be used.

Visoflex 3

This model is equipped with an instant mirror return mechanism, so the mirror automatically returns to the viewing position after the shutter has been released. One of three modes of operation can be selected by means of a knob. The settings are identified with colored dots:

- Yellow dot = the mirror swings out of the lightpath briskly just before the shutter is released.
- Black dot = the mirror swings up gradually as the release arm is depressed, so that the shutter is released as gently as possible.

In both of the above modes, the mirror and the release arm automatically return to their starting positions after pressure is lifted from the shutter release button.

- Red dot = the mirror remains locked in the up position, so that several exposures can be made after another without mirror movement.

Unlike the Visoflex 2, the Visoflex 3 housing can be attached to the camera body directly, i.e., with the 4x prism magnifier in place and without swinging the release arm forward. The Visoflex 3 housing can also be attached to the taller Leica M5 camera body. Only the extension of the adjustable touch screw below the

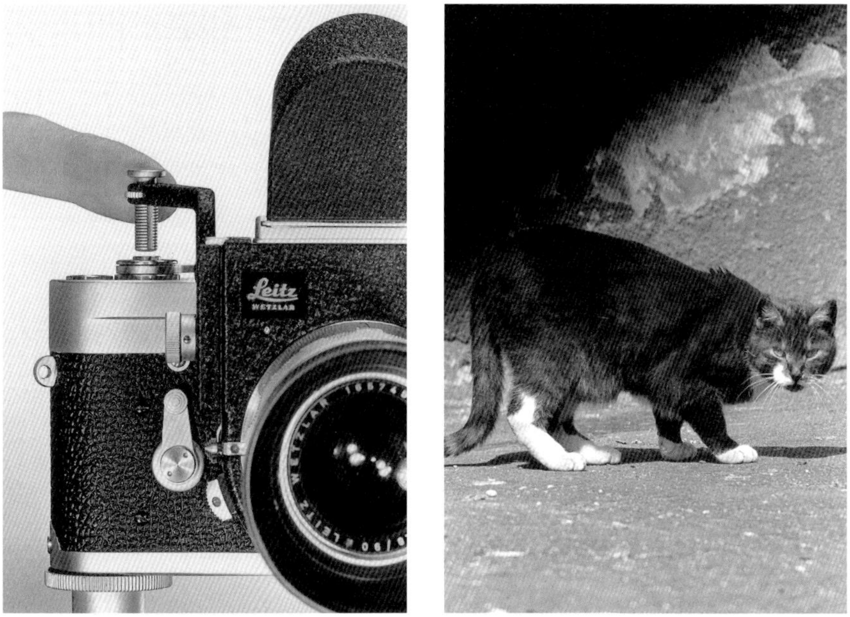

***Fig. 140 a and b:** The gap between the tip of the adjustable touch screw an the release arm of the mirror reflex attachment and the shutter release button of the Leica camera has to be at least 1 mm or just over 1/32 of an inch in order to ensure that the mirror is completely out of the light path when the focal plane shutter is released. If that gap is too small, a part of the image will be obstructed by the part of the mirror that has not yet reached the up position (right).*

release arm has to be reduced. As with the Visoflex 2 attachment, there has to be a gap of approximately 1 mm (just over 1/32 of an inch) between the tip of the adjustable touch screw on the release arm and the shutter release button of the camera. When used with Leica M5 or M6 cameras, the Visoflex 3 attachment also makes it easy to make exposure measurements through the lens. Preferably using the black dot mode of operation for this purpose, the mirror is kept in the up position and the indicators in the cameras' viewfinders are balanced in the normal manner. The measuring field of the Leica M5 camera is outlined by the ring in the center of the ground glass screen. On the Leica M6, the diameter of the measuring field is 12mm (just under 1/2") for lenses of any focal length. That is about half the length of the short side of a ground glass image format. The vertical or straight 5x magnifier of the Visoflex 2 attachment also fits on the Visoflex 3 attachment.

Eyesight correction lenses can be inserted in the front of the ocular of the 4x prism magnifier for the Visoflex 3 housing. The Visoflex 3 is equipped with a Leica M bayonet both on its camera side and on its lens side.

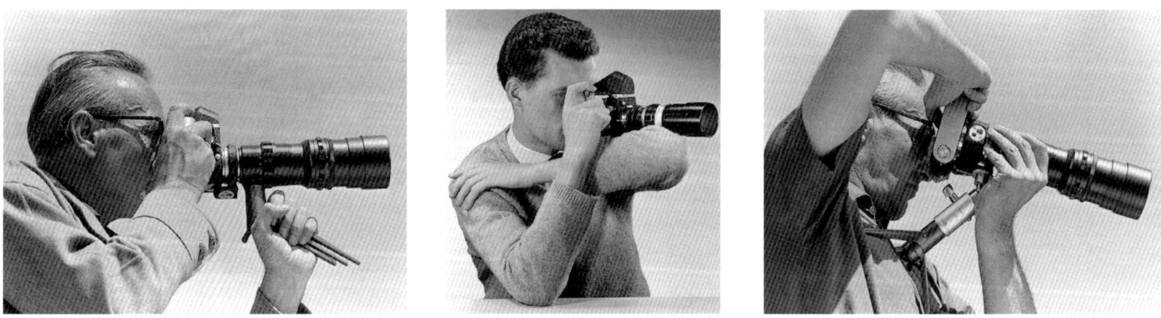

***Fig. 141 a – c:** Holding the camera properly—whether using a special grip, resting it on an arm, or bracing it against the chest—is recommended to prevent camera shake.*

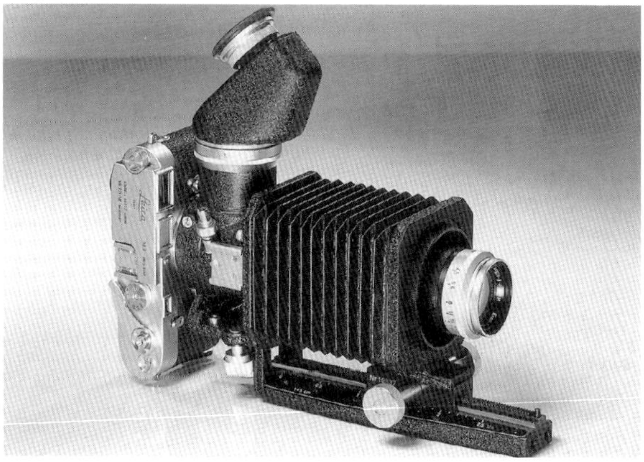

Fig. 142: Universal Focusing Bellows 1

Universal focusing bellows

Universal focusing bellows provide a variable lens extension for continuous settings for photography ranging all the way from infinity to reproduction ratios of 1:1 and beyond. There are two bellows versions in the Leica M System: the Universal Focusing Bellows 1 for use with the Visoflex 1 attachment and the Universal Focusing Bellows 2 for use with Visoflex 2 or 3 attachments.

Universal Focusing Bellows 1

Because of the long lens-to-film-plane distance of the Visoflex housing when it is attached to a Leica M camera, it can only be used with lenses with focal lengths of 125mm or longer for focusing all the way from infinity to close-ups. With 125 and 135mm lenses the focusing range extends down to a reproduction ratio of 1:1.

Lenses with longer or shorter focal lengths can also be attached to the front standard of the Universal Focusing Bellows, but they will permit more limited focusing ranges. Usually the lens heads are unscrewed from their regular focusing mounts and attached to the Bellows by means of adapters. For actual use, the Universal Focusing Bellows 1 should be supported by a tripod with a ball-and-socket head or attached to the arm on a copystand. There is a tripod socket for this purpose on the bottom of the base rail of the bellows device. Two calibrated scales along the base rail can be used to determine reproduction ratios and exposure factors for 125 and 135mm lenses.

Universal Focusing Bellows 2

This bellows unit extends the versatility of Visoflex 1 and 2 attachments. The lens with the shortest focal length that can still be focused at infinity with the Universal Focusing Bellows 2 is the 65mm f/3.5 Elmar-V. In the close-up range, this focal length reaches a reproduction ratio of 1:4:1, and thus, the image of the subject on film is now larger than the subject itself. This bellows unit should also be used on a tripod. Focusing can be accomplished by two methods:

- The front standard is moved in order to change the distance between the lens and the film plane. This also changes the reproduction ratio.

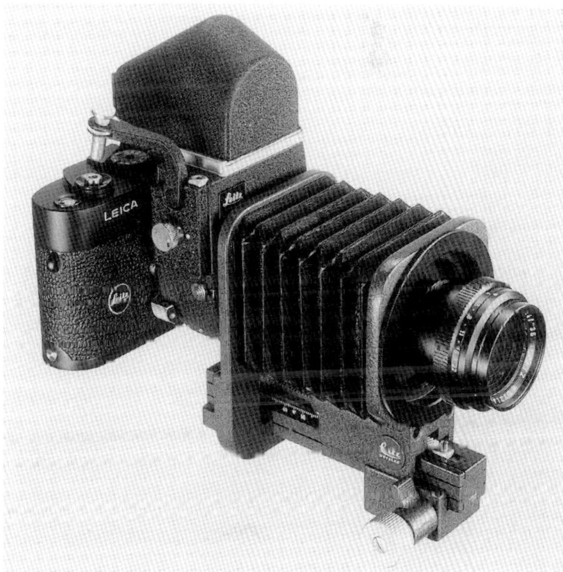

Fig. 143: Universal Focusing Bellows 2

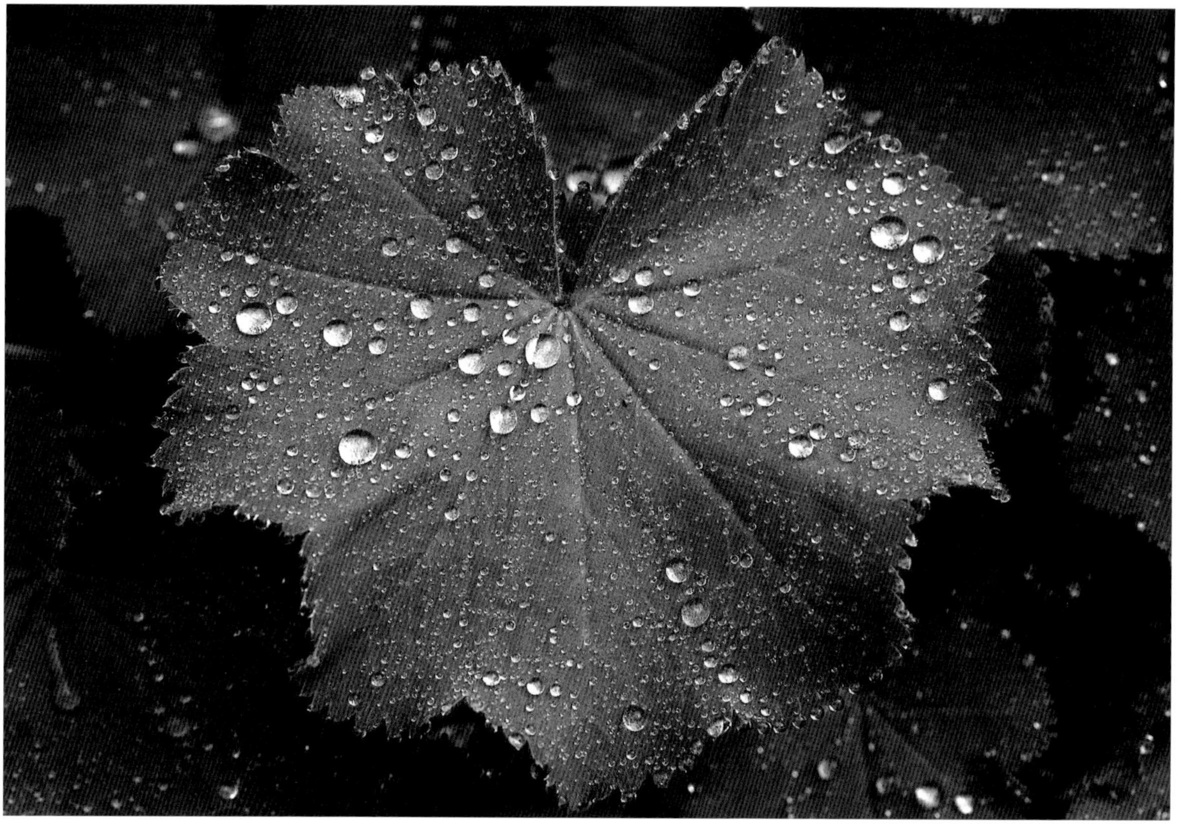

Diffuse, soft light is ideal for close-up shots so rainy days are much appreciated. Those who still have the necessary accessories to take close-ups or those who have found then in an antique shop, will be able to enter the photogenic close-up range even with the latest Leica M models. This exposure was taken with a Visoflex III, Universal Focusing Bellows 2, and a 90mm f/2.8 Elmarit lens head on a Leica M6 TTL.

Or

- The entire outfit, with a given reproduction ratio set in advance, is moved along a tripod, focusing rail without altering the lens extension, i.e., the subject distance is changed.
- To change from a horizontal to a vertical format, camera and Visoflex are simply turned after releasing a latch on the rear standard of the bellows unit.

Selective through-the-lens exposure metering with M7, M6, and M5 cameras can be used in conjunction with the Universal Focusing Bellows 2. Reproduction ratios and exposure factors for 90mm Elmar-M and Elmarit-M lens heads can be read on a scale on the left side of the base rail. Exposure factors are incorporated automatically in exposure measurements made with Leica M7, M6, and M5 cameras.

The lens extension in mm can be read on a scale on the right side of the base rail. This permits specific settings to be repeated at any time. In addition, by means of this scale and with the aid of a table, it is easy to determine reproduction ratios and exposure factors for different focal lengths. An accessory bellows lens hood can be attached to the Universal Focusing Bellows 2 unit to provide effective protection in situations with severe backlighting.

Photography is writing with light

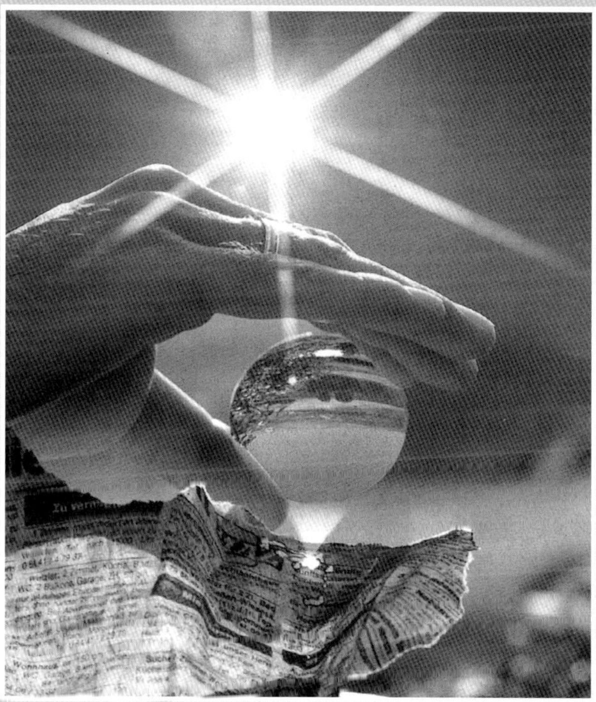

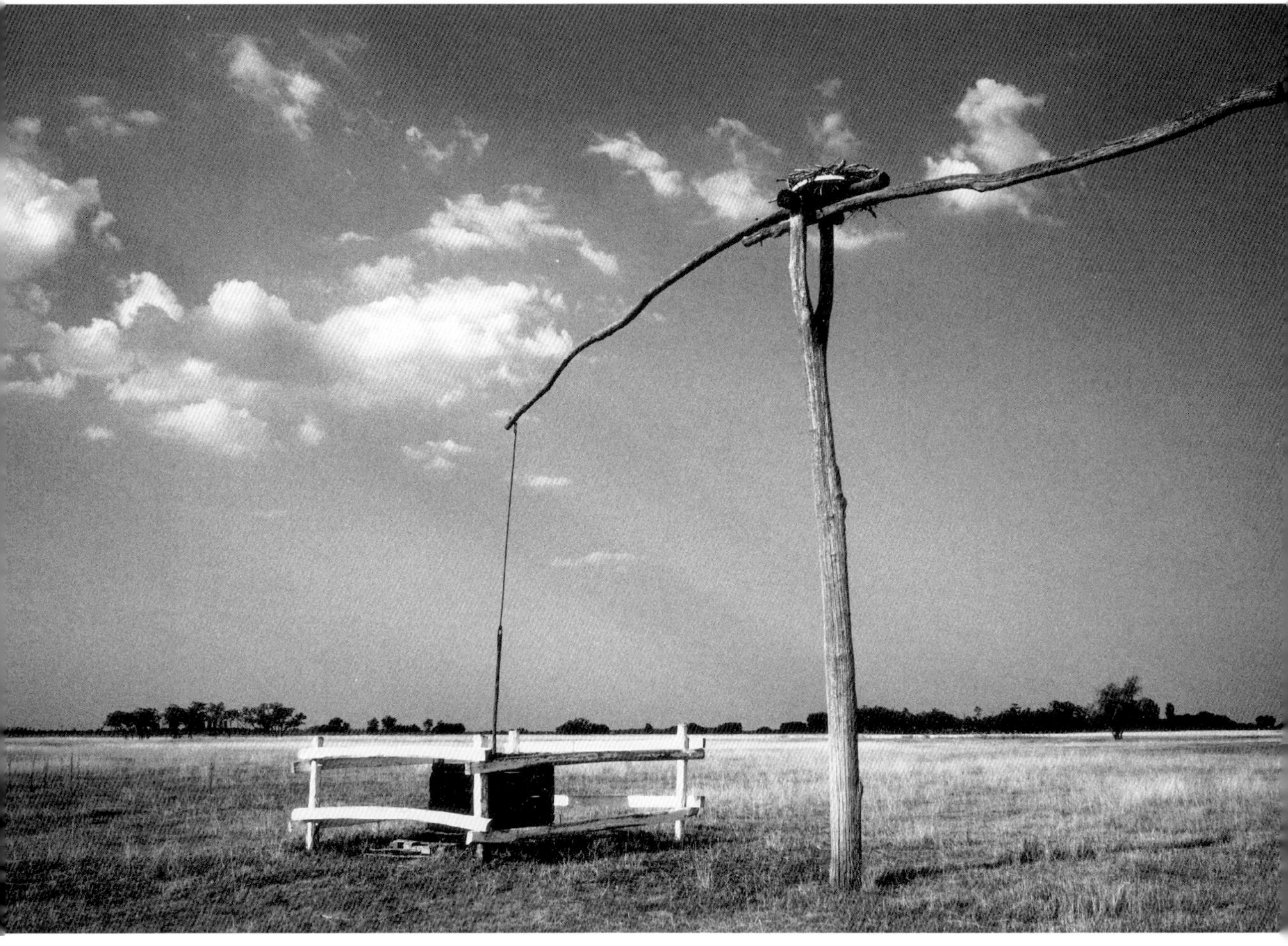

Fig. 144: *Contrast and perspective are elements the photographer considers when composing a picture. Searching for a good position, waiting for the right light, and selecting the right filter demand a little patience and experience. To achieve attractive framing, a sufficient number of different focal lengths are available. 28mm f/2 Summicron-M AS-PH, 1/125 second, f/8, orange filter, ISO 100 film.*

Photography is writing with light

The objective of researchers and designers at Leica, as well as serious photographers, has always been creating the best possible picture. With technology constantly improving the possibilities, there are always new challenges to those who are involved with photography. However, the most important tasks continue to be the responsibility of the photographer. Only photographers determine which lens will be mounted on their Leica camera, the direction in which it will be pointed, and when the shutter will be released. Photographers select the point of view and use shutter speeds and apertures as tools to control the exposure and the rendition of certain picture elements. Photographers control the illumination, and decide which film to use. Even the highest performance camera and the most expensive accessories cannot perform these tasks for the photographer, but they can make them easier.

For outstanding, creative results, photographers must know more about photography than what is printed in the instruction manuals for their cameras. That is why the following pages contain a description of the relationships and reciprocal influences of focal length and perspective, exposure and illumination, camera position and subject coverage—the mutual relationships between light and photography. Also proven aids and practical tips for successful photography are provided when appropriate.

What is light?

The word "photography" itself, (from the Greek words "phos" = light and "graphein" = to write), clearly suggests the overriding importance of light to the photographer. Those who wish to write with light must therefore devote closer attention to the phenomenon of light.

Just as a good toolmaker has to know the principal characteristics of the materials he has to work with, so must the photographers be knowledgeable about the characteristics of light if they strive to create good photographs. This is still true today, in the age of automation and high technology, just as it was many decades ago, when photography was in its infancy.

In a strictly scientific sense, to this day, there is no all-encompassing theory of light that can do justice to all of the questions. However, the description that follows may be the easiest for photographers to understand:

- Light is a form of energy that we are capable of perceiving through one of our senses: our eyes.
- Passing through the crystalline lens of the eye and on to the retina, light creates a sensation of brightness and color in the sight center of the brain. Therefore, light is a prerequisite for sight and it is also a prerequisite for photographic reproduction.

In the opinion of the English scientist Isaac Newton (1643-1727), a ray of light consists of an infinite number of minute particles that radiate like tiny missiles from a hot light source with a speed that no solid object is capable of exceeding. The particle theory can be demonstrated with the aid of many examples, among them the radiant sun.

At about the same time that Newton was creating his theory of light, the Dutchman Huygens came to the conclusion that light is transmitted in the form of waves. Two hundred years later, English physicist J. W. Maxwell was able to prove that light consists of electro-magnetic waves. His explanation is helpful for understanding the behavior of light, especially when it is refracted, diffracted, dispersed, reflected, polarized, or converted into another form of radiation. Maxwell's wave theory is probably of greatest significance to photographers.

German scientist Max Planck developed another theory—the quantum theory—in 1899. According to Planck, photons are the particles that carry light. Even though this theory and Albert Einstein's theory of relativity contributed to further clarification of the mysterious complexity that is "light," they are not yet sufficient to provide thorough answers to all the questions. This suggests that there are still some undiscovered processes in nature. Today's scientists accept the duality of light, i.e. in some cases light behaves like solid particles, but as a rule its wave-like character cannot be denied. Seen in this manner, light is a very small segment of the great range of electro-magnetic waves, which have wavelengths extending from approximately 1000 m (broadcast long waves) to about 0.2 nm (high-altitude radiation). One nm (nm stands for nanometer) is defined as follows:

$$\frac{1}{10\,000\,000}\ \text{cm or}\quad \frac{1}{1\,000\,000}\ \text{mm}$$

What we call light—that part of the spectrum of electro-magnetic waves that can be perceived by our eyes—lies between the wavelengths of 400 nm (violet) and approximately 700 nm (red). A very specific color can be attributed to every single electro-magnetic wavelength in between. Light that we perceive as white is really a mixture of light rays of all wavelengths between those two limits.

Light travels at a speed of approximately 300,000 kilometers per second (186,411 miles per second). As long as it does not strike an obstacle, it travels in a straight line. Light is reflected when it strikes an opaque (not black) object. If this object has a reflective surface, light will be reflected at a specific angle. In that case, each incoming ray will be deflected according to the law of reflection: angle of incidence equals angle of reflection. Non-reflecting surfaces, i.e. matte or grainy surfaces, produce diffuse or irregular reflections. Colored surfaces reflect only certain colored components of the incident white light. Black surfaces reflect none, and white surfaces reflect all components of light.

Light is refracted (deflected) when it enters a transparent medium of a different density at an angle: from a lighter medium (air) to a denser medium (glass). It is refracted towards the perpendicular to the surface at the point of incidence. The opposite occurs when light enters from a denser into a lighter medium. When a light ray traverses a plano-parallel glass plate, there will only be a parallel shift, because both kinds of refractions will occur. There is no refraction, however, when the light ray impinges on the glass surface perpendicularly.

A light ray will be refracted twice when it travels through a glass prism. It will then leave the prism at an angle to its original direction. This angle of refraction depends on the type of glass (on the refractive index of the glass) and on the shape of the prism. In addition, a ray of white light is dispersed by the prism and divided into its colored components. The blue-violet component of light is refracted more strongly than the red one. If a white surface is placed behind the exit side of the prism, a band of colors will appear: the spectrum of light.

In a collecting lens, which we can imagine as being composed of an infinite number of small individual prisms, the refraction of light is used to rejoin (to collect) back into a point a large portion of the light rays emanating from another point. Light is diffracted, i.e. light rays are deflected from their direction when they pass next to an edge. This phenomenon is called diffraction. The effects of diffraction can become noticeable in photography when very small apertures are used, in which case they reduce image sharpness. With grid-like special effect attachments, diffraction is utilized on purpose to create star effects or to produce a certain amount of softness by causing flare of the bright parts of the image.

Light and color

Both daylight and artificial light are usually composed of many different electro-magnetic waves, and each wavelength corresponds to a specific color. The general sequence of colors is as follows:

380 nm to 459 nm = violet
460 nm to 495 nm = blue
496 nm to 574 nm = green
575 nm to 589 nm = yellow
590 nm to 620 nm = orange
621 nm to 780 nm = red

The human eye perceives light as colorless when the individual wavelengths of this rich mixture are present in equal intensities. If a particular wavelength is dominant, the light will assume the color of that wavelength.

Certain photographic systems are based on the fact that the superimposition of red, green and blue light produces white. This mixture is possible because each of the three primary colors encompasses nearly 1/3 of the total radiant energy of the visible spectrum. When there is no balance between the wavelength segments of red, green and blue, the result is a color. When the balanced light intensity of all three primary colors is decreased uniformly, the result is a neutral color ranging from white to progressively darker shades of gray, all the way to black.

Since the three wavelengths of light in this procedure are being added, this principle is called additive color mixing. In subtractive color mixing, white light is not the end product but the startling "raw material." All colors are then created by subtracting one or more of the light components (complementary colors) cyan, magenta, and yellow from the original white. Modern color photography is based on this principle.

Color temperature

Photographically, it is particularly important that all colors in the spectrum of "white" light merge into one another with even continuity. When this is not the case, i.e. when one or more colors are missing, there will be color deviations in the color photograph, which are called color casts
While daylight, light from electronic flash units, or incandescent bulbs have a continuous spectrum, the spectrum of the light emitted by certain other sources like fluorescent tubes is not continuous. To achieve pleasing color photographs with the latter kind of illumination, special steps have to be taken (see page 209).

The continuous spectrum of daylight is also influenced by the atmosphere. Depending on the position of the sun, the atmosphere absorbs the shortwave portion of the spectrum to a greater or lesser extent. That is why red light predominates when the sun is low on the horizon and light rays have to travel through a larger portion of the atmosphere. When the sun is high in the sky, the distance that light travels through the atmosphere is shorter and less blue radiation is absorbed, so that the blue component of daylight is greater. These changes in the color of daylight are express as its color temperature, which is measured in Kelvin.

The term Kelvin (K) is defined as the temperature to which a "black body" has to be heated in order to emit light of the same color as that of the light source being described. This temperature measurement is different from conventional temperature, which is measured in degrees Celsius or Fahrenheit in that it is 273.1°C or 523.6°F higher than the latter, because it is a measurement on the scale of absolute temperature, in which zero is at approximately -273.1°C or -459.6°F. Kelvin units are the same magnitude as degrees Celsius (not degrees Fahrenheit).

Daylight and the light from modern electronic flash units have an average color temperature of approximately 5500 Kelvin. Modern photo lamps (halogen bulbs) emit light with a color temperature of 3400 Kelvin. Color reversal films and professional color-negative films are balanced for the most frequently used light sources. Daylight type films are balanced for approximately 5500 K and films for artificial light for 3200 K (normal photolamps) or 3400 K (halogen bulbs). The color temperature of subject illumination can be corrected and adapted to a specific type of color film with the use of appropriate conversion filters (see page 208 and 209).

Light and film

It may be fascinating for a theoretician to analyze the imaging performance of a Leica M lens with the aid of curves and numbers. For the practitioner, however, it is the quality of the photograph that matters. In addition to the camera body and the lens, the film that is being used significantly determines the performance capability of a photographic outfit. The type of application and the desired result should already be considered when a film is being selected. The way the film is processed can idealize or characterize the images, but it can also spot them. Different characteristics of films and their relationships with light are frequently not taken into account correctly, and this usually leads to unsatisfactory results. Often an increase in the quality of reproduction can already be achieved merely by using specific films for specific applications.

While it is well known that color films balanced for artificial illumination should be used for making color transparencies with artificial light, it is not nearly so well known that high-speed black-and-white films have greater sensitivity to red, so that a correction of the film speed setting on the light meter may be necessary for photography under artificial illumination. Exposure and illumination can only be mastered to perfection when one also knows the characteristics of films.

Film characteristics

Normal films can be grouped into four main categories: black-and-white negative films, black-and-white reversal films, color negative films, and color reversal films. Each group can, in turn, be classified according to general sensitivity, as low, medium, and high-speed films. Choosing the correct film is of decisive importance for achieving high quality in a photograph.

The first consideration, the desired result—black-and-white or color, paper print, or a transparency—governs the choice of film. An optimum black-and-white enlargement is best made from a black-and-white negative. Black-and-white transparencies can be made from black-and-white negatives or black-and-white transparency film.

Color reversal film is ideal for color slides. Good color enlargements can be made with ease if conditions are right (low contrast in the slide). Those who prefer color prints should choose color negative film, from which color slides can be made as well. The film should, of course, also be appropriate for the various characteristics of the application. What will be the type of illumination? Daylight or artificial light? Are short exposure times required? Or is it important for the film to have an especially high resolution, etc. These are questions that can be answered easily if one knows the most important characteristics of films. Here is a description of those characteristics:

General sensitivity or speed

A certain amount of light is necessary for the correct exposure of film, and that amount depends on the general speed of the film. Until about 1980, in the United States and in many other countries, ASA values were used as a measure of film speed (ASA = American Standards Association). These film speeds were determined according to prescribed standards.

In Germany, film speed was stated in degrees DIN, and it was determined according to standards set by the German Institute for Standards (DIN = Deutsches Institut für Normung). The measurement of film speed according to ASA standards corresponds exactly to the measurement made in accordance with DIN standards, except that the ASA scale is arithmetic, whereas the DIN scale is logarithmic. An ASA 100 film is twice as fast as an ASA 50 film.

In recent years film speeds have been stated in ISO values (ISO = International Standards Organization). Thus ASA 50 or 18 DIN became ISO 50. Exposure meters are set and films are exposed according to ISO, or ASA and DIN, film speeds. These values include a small reserve, which amounts to one stop or more.

This means that in general, an ISO 50 film can also be exposed at ISO 100 if processing is adjusted accordingly. In the ISO system, the doubling of the film speed with every increase of three degrees (carried over from the DIN system) does not correlate with the fact that the aperture rings on lenses at best are calibrated in half stops. This is unimportant in actual practice, because exposure differences of 30% are not clearly noticeable in current black-and-white or color films.

Graininess and grain

A granular structure erroneously labeled as grain can occasionally be observed in very big enlargements. What is actually being seen is graininess: clusters of silver bromide crystals that formed during the development stage. The individual silver bromide crystals themselves are much smaller. Their size is a function of the general film speed: as a rule, the larger they are, the higher the general film speed. In other words, the term "grain" refers to the undeveloped silver bromide crystal, whereas "graininess" applies to the developed emulsion. Although metallic silver is bleached out of color film emulsions during processing, so that the silver particles themselves are no longer visible, the "holes" that remain also create an overall impression of graininess.

Low-speed films have the lowest graininess after processing. The location of the interstices is the determining factor. The most significant improvements, especially in fine grain films, are based on the fact that emulsion makers succeeded in embedding a sufficient quantity of silver bromide crystals in a relatively small amount of gelatin, so that it became possible to coat thinner layers than before. Naturally, the sizes of individual grain particles also constitute a criterion for sharpness. A picture element that is smaller than a grain particle cannot be resolved, no matter how big an enlargement is made.

Resolving power and contour sharpness

The frequently encountered notion that these two properties are firmly related to grain size is incorrect. First of all, it is the thickness of the emulsion that is the determining factor. Since a light-sensitive emulsion is a diffusing medium, it scatters light. Light scattering within undeveloped emulsion layers is high, so that under certain circumstances, strong over-exposures can diminish the resolving power of the film. Resolving power used to be evaluated only by means of test charts (line patterns, radial grids, mired values) and results were stated in lines per millimeter. Since many unrelated factors influenced these evaluations, other methods were sought.

A new concept, called "contour sharpness," was adopted. It is an objective measure of the film's performance as far as sharpness is concerned, regardless of graininess and gradation. Diffused halation plays a decisive rote in this measurement. Contour sharpness is determined by means of a slit that is only 0.015 mm (0.0006") wide. The film is exposed in direct contact with the slit, without the use of a lens, and the resulting spread is measured after processing.

Freedom from halation

There are two kinds of halation: one is caused by diffusion, the other by reflection. The first one results from light scattering within the emulsion layer, the other one from reflection off the rear surface of the film. Both types of halation are usually present together.

A basic cause of halation is always a high contrast lighting in the scene being photographed. A spread or "halo" around a strong light source, which appears in the picture is a typical example. Thin-layer films display reduced halation caused by diffusion. Dying can reduce halation caused by reflections off the rear surface of the film. An anti-halation coating between the light-sensitive emulsion layer and the base of the film achieves even better protection.

Fig. 145 a-d: *Today's black-and-white films no longer show a significant difference in graininess in their different ISO film speeds unless the picture is enlarged greatly. To illustrate this, the photo at the right was taken with three different film speeds and the small section framed in black was enlarged to 25x. Thus, the 35mm negative, which is 24 x 36 mm (15/16 x 1-13/32 inch), was enlarged to 60 x 90 cm (24 x 36 inches).*
Below left: Low-speed film exposed at ISO 32.
Below center: Medium-speed film exposed at ISO 125.
Below right: High-speed film exposed at ISO 400.

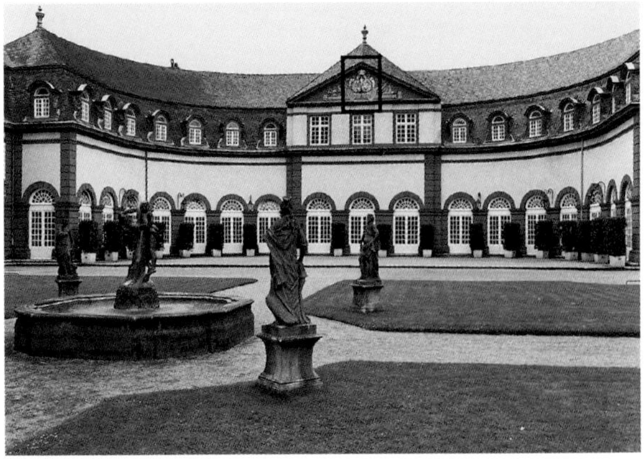

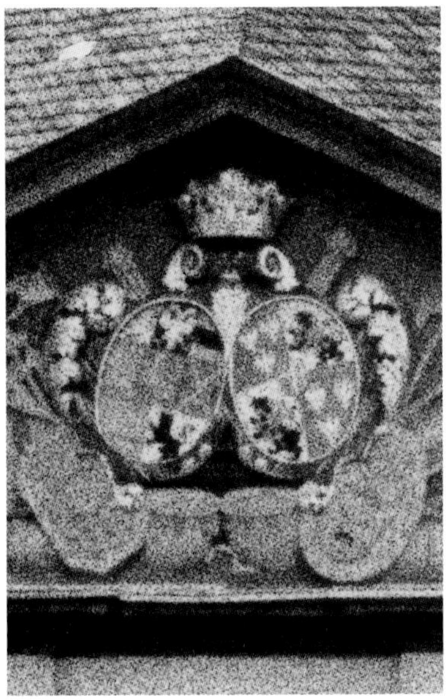

Fig. F1:: *The line screen of the instant transparency film by Polaroid is visible only during projection when the viewing distance is less than normal. The graininess corresponds to that of high-speed films having a sensitivity of over ISO 400. This portrait was taken at 1/125 second at f/5.6.*

Fig. F2 and F3: *Photographers who like to experiment will be particularly excited about the IR false-color film.*
Right: normal daylight color reversal film.
Left: IR false-color film and green filter.

Fig. F4 and F5: *If a neutral color reproduction in artificial illumination is more important than a moody warm-tone effect, pictures must be taken on tungsten reversal film. With the use of appropriate conversion filters every color film can be "adapted" to the color temperature of the recording light.*

Fig. F4: *Tungsten reversal film.*

Fig. F5: *Daylight reversal film.*

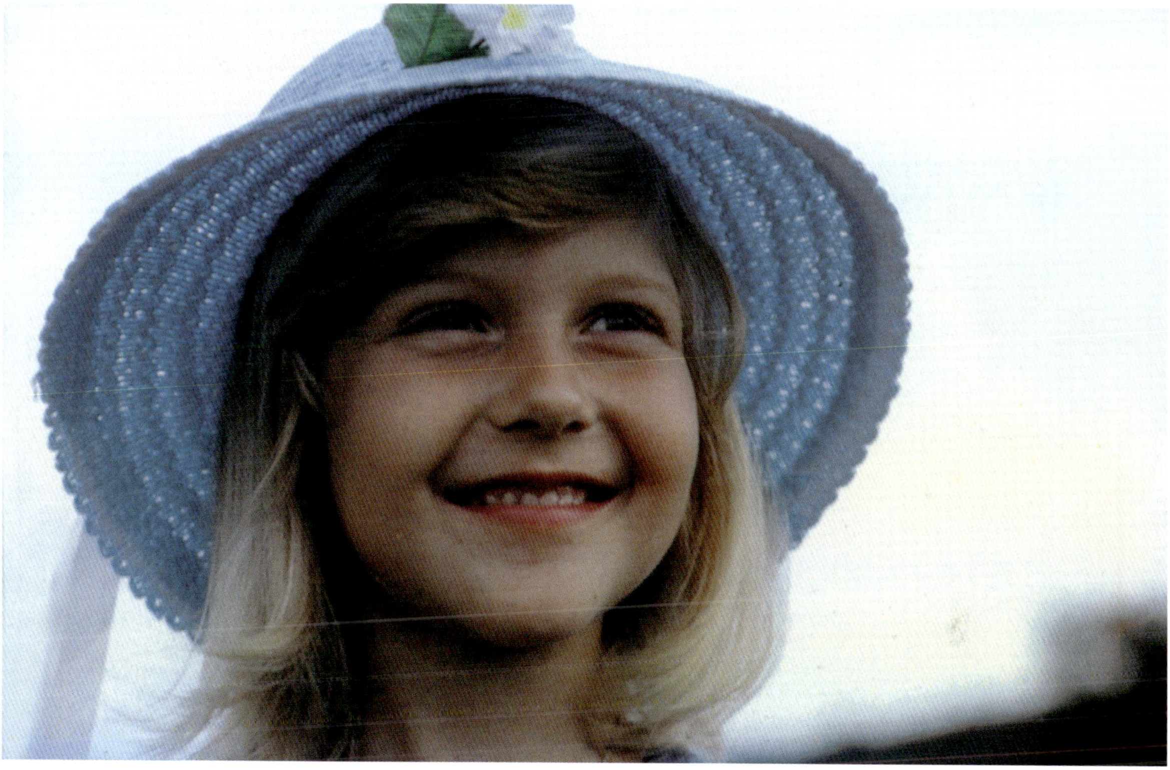

Fig. F1

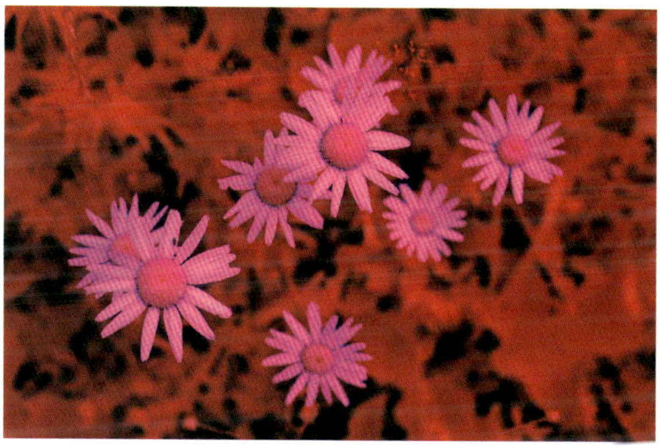

Fig. F2

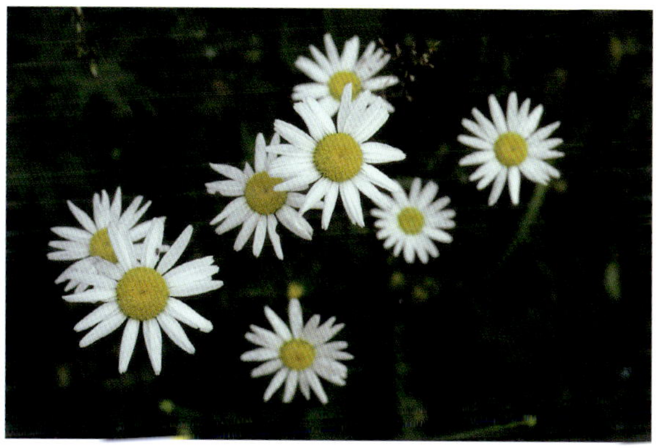

Fig. F3

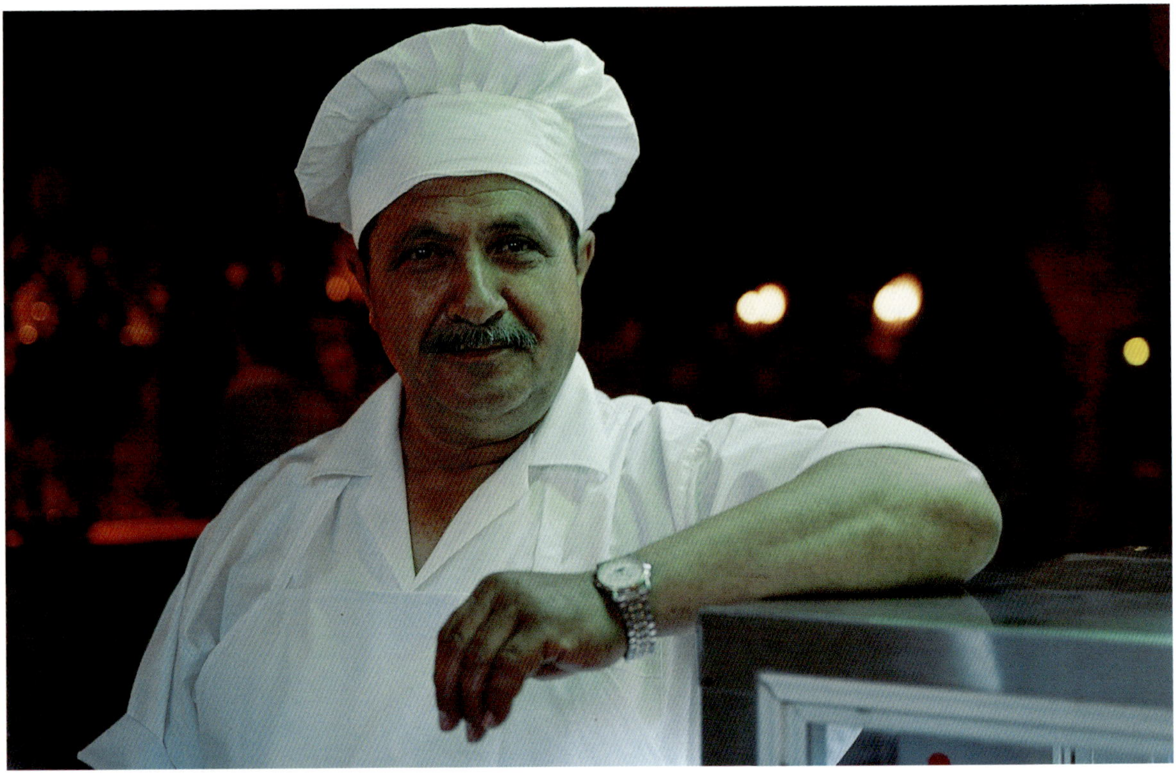

Fig. F4

Fig. F5

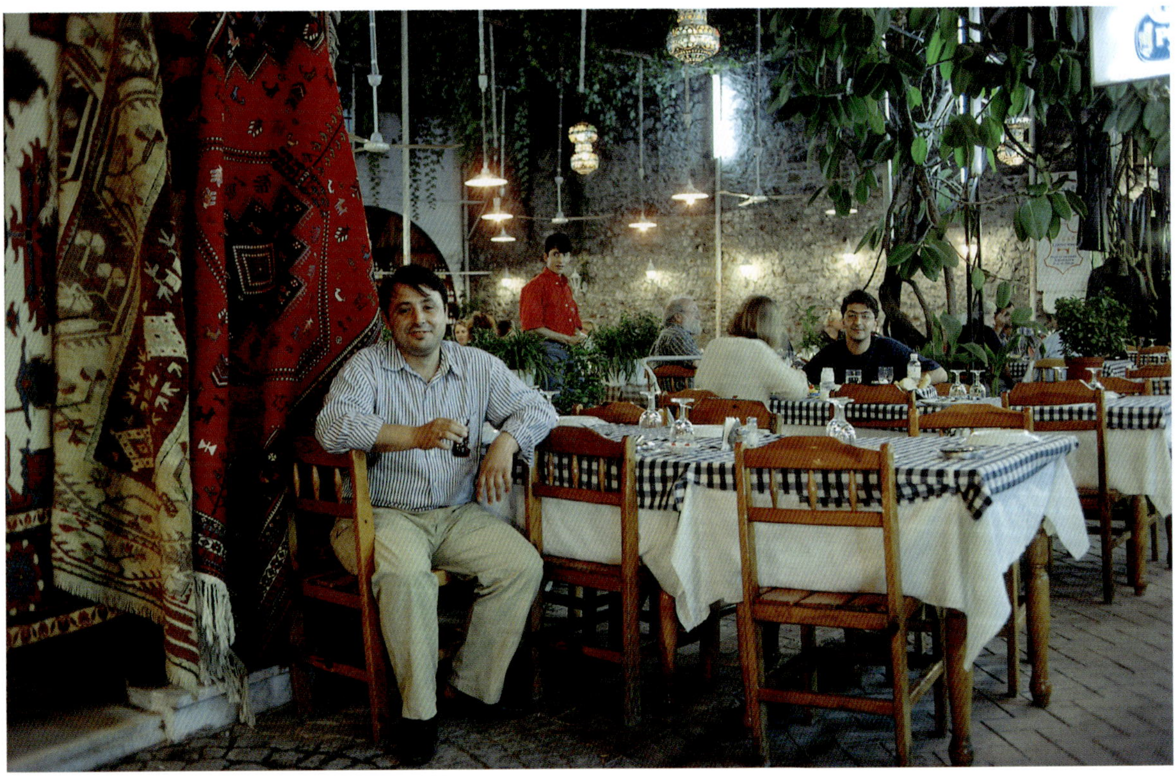

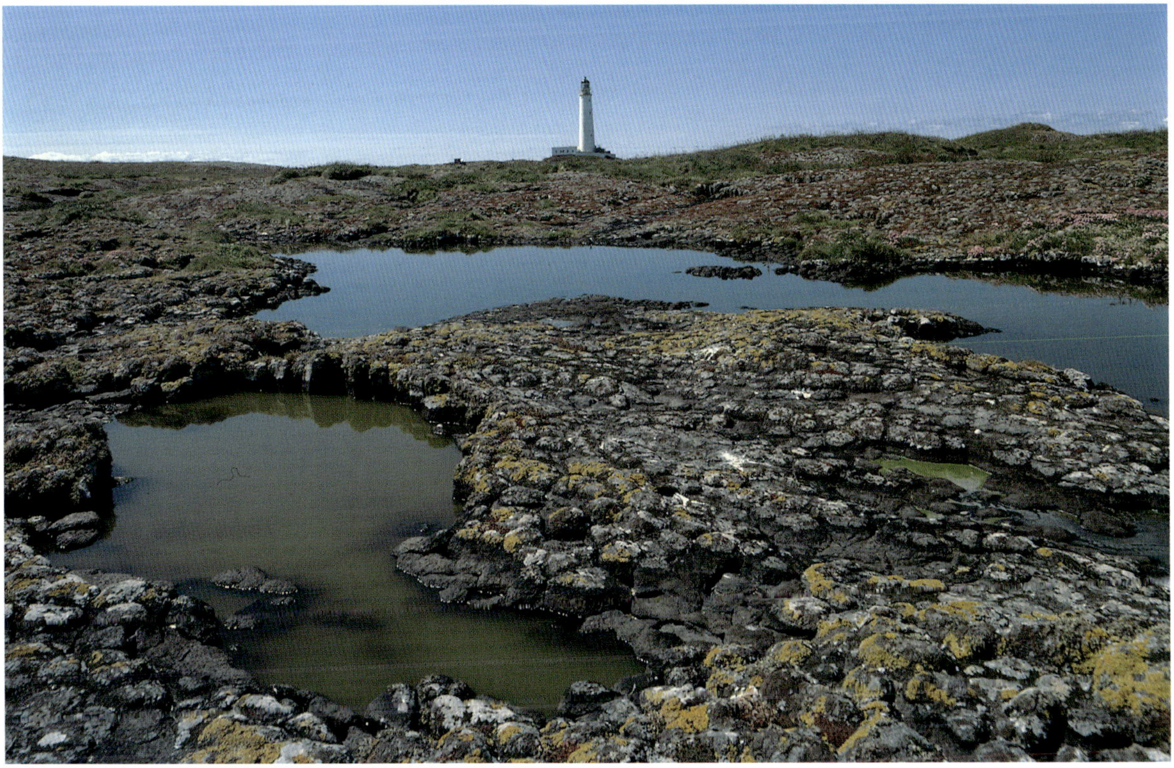

Fig. F6

Fig. F7

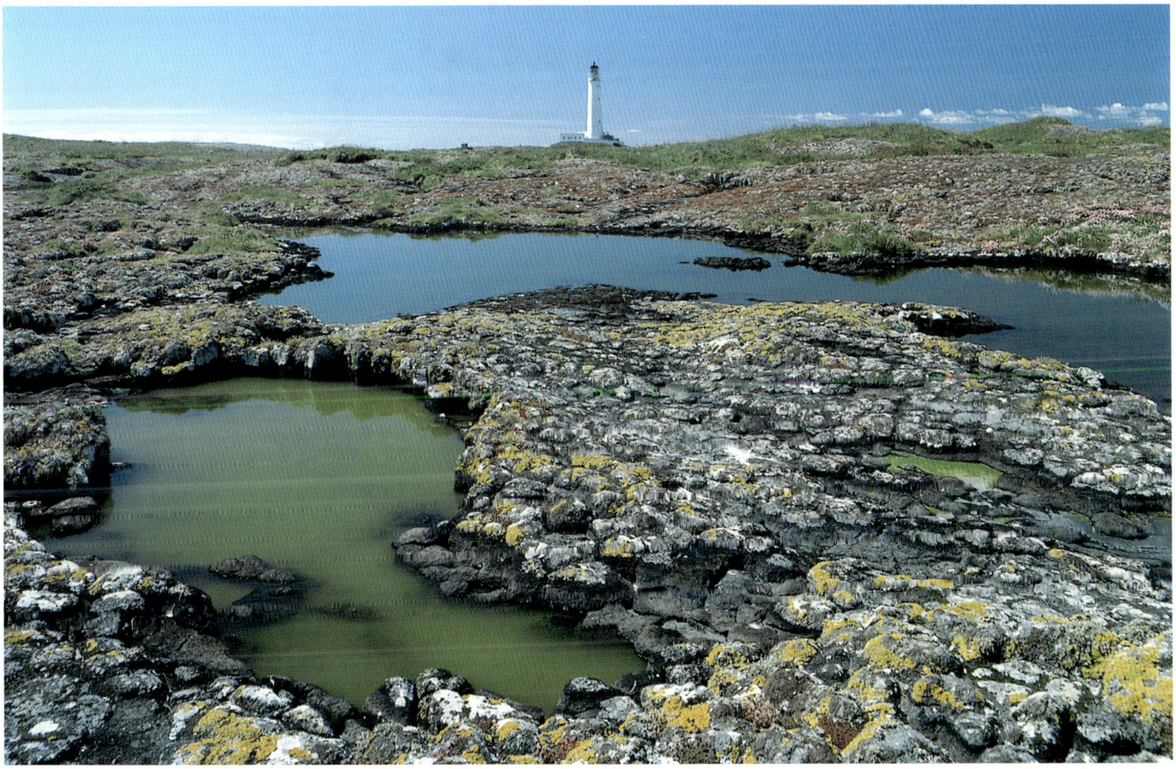

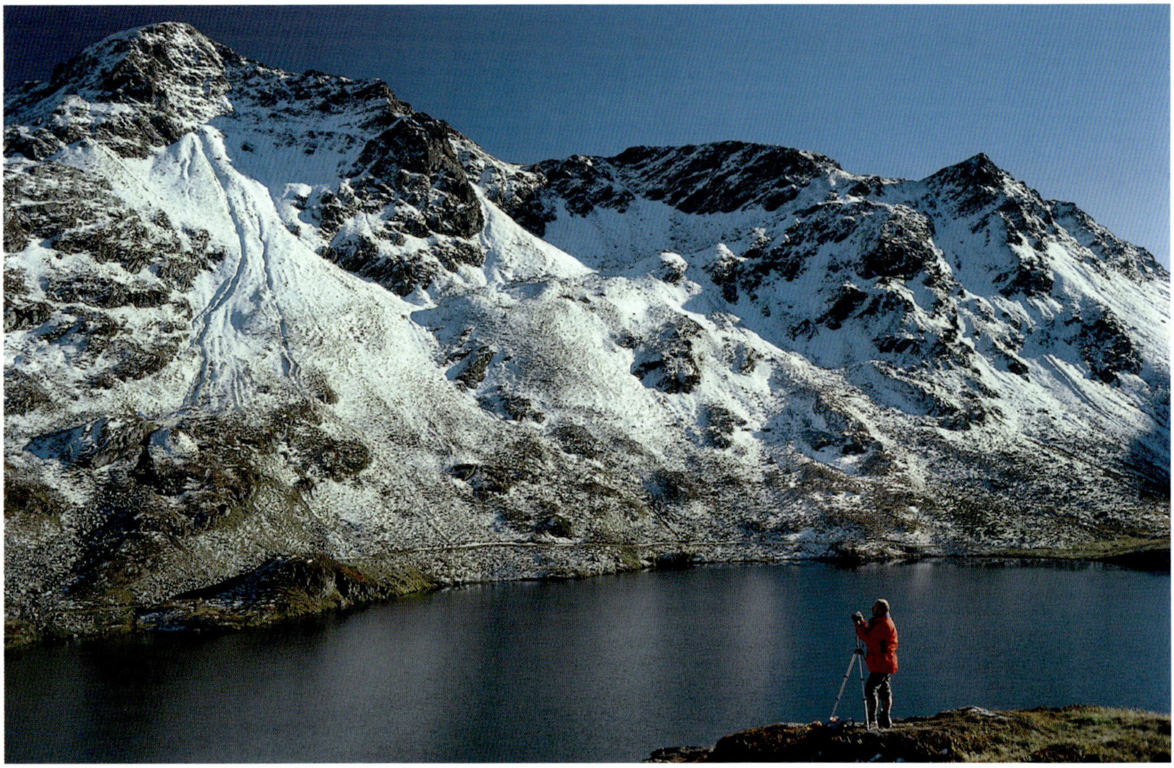

Fig. F8

Fig. F9

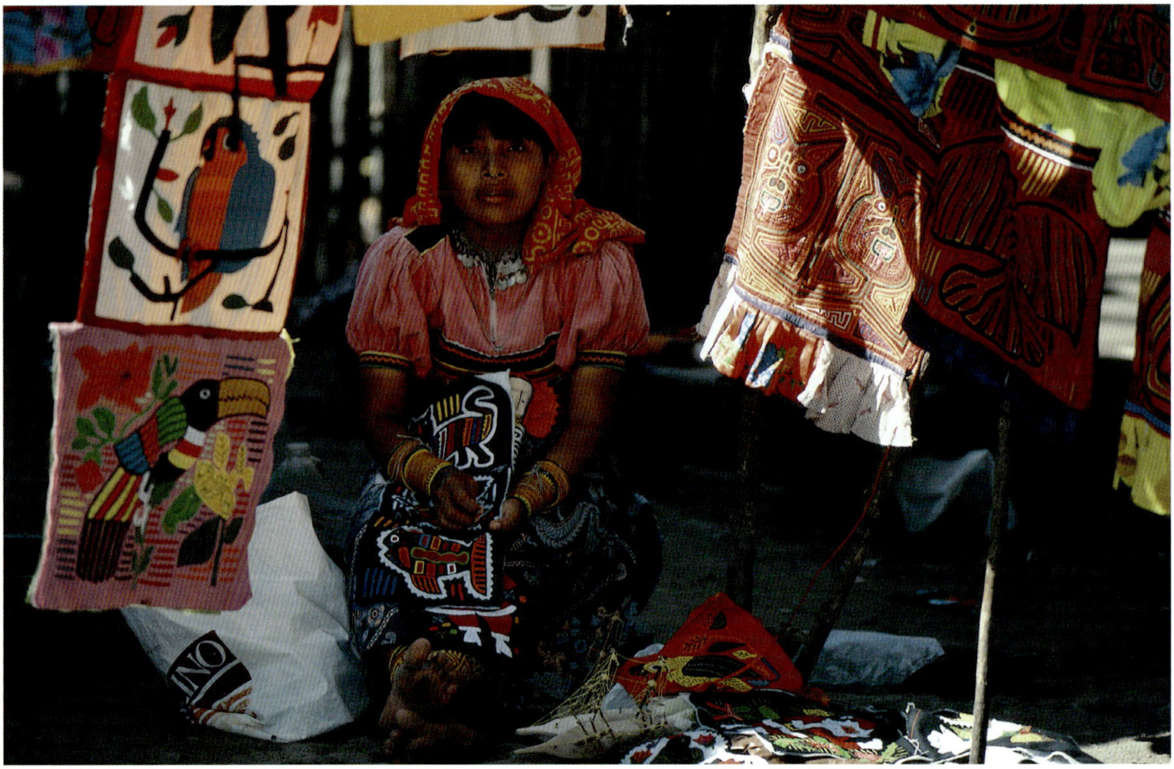

Gradation

One of the most important properties of photographic film is gradation, which means the way it reproduces different density values in the subject area, i.e. its contrast. Details in the subject area are differentiated by a variety of brightnesses and colors. They can range from the brightest white to the deepest black. But they can also be limited to delicate differences, as they are in pictures taken in a fog. If the film reproduces these differences in tones approximately as we perceive them with our eyes, it has normal gradation. If it lowers the contrast, so that large differences in brightness are bridged, the film is said to have soft or flat gradation. If, on the other hand, the film increases small differences in brightness, it has hard or steep gradation. The latter type of film cannot reproduce large brightness variations with good differentiation.

For use in copying and reproduction, films with extra hard gradation (extra high-contrast films) should be used. The basic characteristics of a photographic emulsion are largely established at the time of manufacture. They can, however, be influenced by the processing method, especially in the case of black-and-white films. But this may also alter the general speed of the film.

Fig. F6 and F7: *A polarizing filter reduces glare, enhances color, and increases the contrast betweens clouds and sky. The effect is easy to observe and adjust.*
Fig. 6: Without polarizing filter.
Fig. 7: With polarizing filter.

Fig. F8 and F9: *Using fresh, top-quality film is important so that you can maximize the quality of Leica lenses. Using the lowest ISO rating that conditions allow will assure the best possible color and sharpness. These photos were made using daylight color reversal film, ISO 25.*

Reciprocity law failure

Correct exposure is not the least of the important factors for optimum photographic results. It is the product of the intensity of the illumination and the exposure time. But results are not at all the same when the light-sensitive emulsion is exposed to a very brightly illuminated scene for a very short time or to a very dimly illuminated scene for a very long time. Under the same lighting conditions, for instance, an exposure of 1/1000 second at f/1 does not produce the same densities as an exposure of 1 second at f/32, even though in theory they should be identical.

In the United States, this phenomenon is called reciprocity law failure, and in German-speaking countries it is called the Schwarzschild Effect, named after its discoverer. As a rule, reciprocity failure manifests itself with extremely long and with extremely short exposure times (for instance, with the ultra-short exposure times produced by electronic flash units), and it results in the loss of film speed, changes in gradation and in the case of color film, the additional change of color balance. That is why modern electronic flash units have a flash duration of 1/500 second and longer, so that they are within the acceptable exposure time limits of most films.

Only color reversal films balanced for artificial light are designed for best results with long exposure times. Specific information about reciprocity law factors (exposure factors for reciprocity law failure compensation), as well as recommendations for the necessary color corrections are given in the instruction/data sheets published by film manufacturers.

Conventional black-and-white films

Black-and-white reproduction of our colorful surroundings is influenced by the sensitivity of black-and-white films to color. The wording "sensitivity to color" may be misleading in this context, since the reproduction of colors on black-and-white film takes place in shades of gray. The film records only the differences in brightness of the various colors, not the colors themselves.

Sensitizing dyes are added to the light-sensitive emulsion for this purpose, so that the film reacts to several colors. The original emulsion is sensitive only to ultraviolet (UV) and blue radiation. A film with sensitivity extended to green and yellow is called orthochromatic, and a film that is sensitive to all colors, including red, is called panchromatic.

However, the sensitivity of different panchromatic films to various colors is not necessarily identical, and it varies from brand to brand. There are considerable differences in the sensitivity to red, in particular. Sensitivity in the red range generally increases relative to the other colors as the general film speed increases. That is why exposure measurements made through red or yellow filters may not be accurate. A correction factor may be required, which can easily be required by means of test exposures. The reproduction of tonal values of different colors can be manipulated by the use of colored photographic filters.

Even though ultraviolet radiation is not visible to the human eye, all films are sensitive to it, unless it is first absorbed by a filter or by the lens itself, as it is with Leica M lenses. For long-wave infrared radiation (IR), however, special films and filters are required.

Black-and-white films and developers in actual use

The variety of black-and-white films that is available for 35mm cameras could create the impression that it is exceedingly complicated to select the right film. But since many of the different black-and-white films are made for photographic applications for which a range-viewfinder camera is not intended, the number of black-and-white films for the Leica M photographer to choose from is already reduced considerably. Besides, not every Leica M owner is likely to take complete advantage of every single one of his camera's multitude of capabilities and of every brand available for each type of black-and-white film. Thus the variety of films practically limits itself to an assortment that can be evaluated conveniently.

Aside from reasons of common sense which favor a small standard assortment of black-and-white films and developers, such a standard assortment has the special advantage that the prospects for a uniformly good crop of photographs are much greater when only a few types of familiar films are used. Of course there will always be very particular films and very particular developers, which will produce better results under very particular conditions and with very particular film and developer combinations.

Experience shows, however, that this is the case far, far more infrequently than occasionally claimed in publications. But for rare exceptions, the black-and-white illustrations used in this book were made with the films and developers described in the paragraphs and in the tables that follow.

Selecting the correct film type

Conventional black-and-white films can be classified in three categories according to their general film speed. With special black-and-white films, often the name already indicates their intended applications. Thus, the following classification presents itself for the intended range of applications of Leica M cameras:

Low-speed films

Low-speed films from ISO 16 to ISO 50 are ideal for photographs with fine details, such as landscape and architectural photographs. Low speed films are especially well suited for big enlargements because of their high resolution and low graininess.

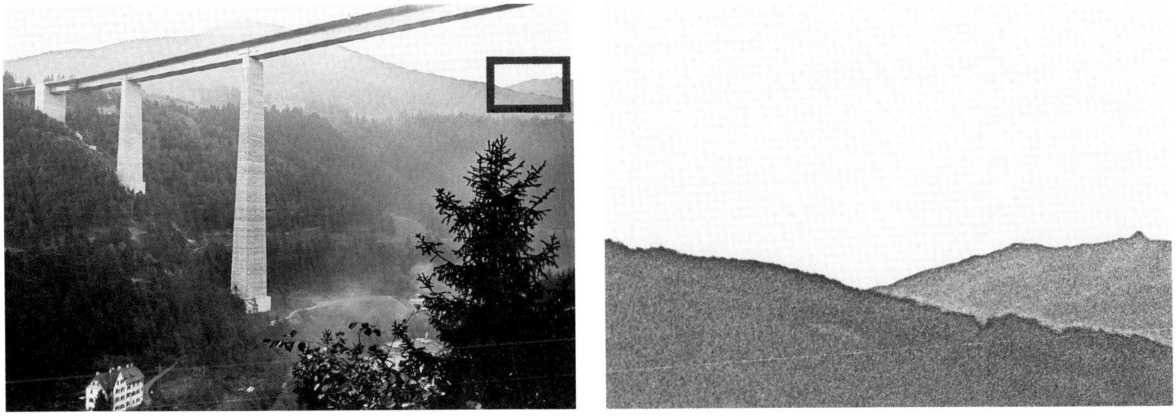

***Fig. 146 a and b:** The edge effect produced by surface developers becomes clearly discernible in big enlargements. This is evident in the section shown on the above right, which was enlarged from the photograph on the left. This edge effect can be used to enhance contour sharpness. Photo by Doris Schäfer.*

Medium-speed films

Medium-speed films from ISO 64 to ISO 200 are good all-purpose films for 35mm photography. They are a perfect choice for souvenir pictures, snapshots, and portraits, as well as architectural, sports and landscape photographs. With enlargements up to 18 x 24 cm (nearly 8 x 10 inches), their slightly higher graininess and slightly lower resolution are barely noticeable.

High-speed films

High-speed films from ISO 250 to ISO 1000 and higher are the standard choice of photojournalists and those Leica M photographers who wish to photograph without flash under unfavorable lighting conditions. Even under normal lighting conditions, high-speed films of ISO 400 are regarded as all-around films for reportage and candid photography, when fast shutter speeds and great depth of field are often required. If no custom laboratory is available for special processing, it becomes an indispensable necessity for photographers to process their films themselves in order to assure good results.

Copy films

Copy films are intended for line reproductions. There are two kinds: orthochromatic (not sensitive to red) and panchromatic copy films. When the illumination is not too contrasty, and with soft development, copy films can also be used for conventional photography, such as landscape photography. Kodak Technical Pan Film 2415 is an example of film in this category.

Black-and-white reversal films

Black-and-white reversal films provide positives without negative and are used for all above-described applications. Processing has been paid at purchase and will be handled by authorized photofinishers.

Infrared films

Infrared films are special films that are sensitive to invisible infrared radiation. Special instructions must be observed when these films are used (see page 197).

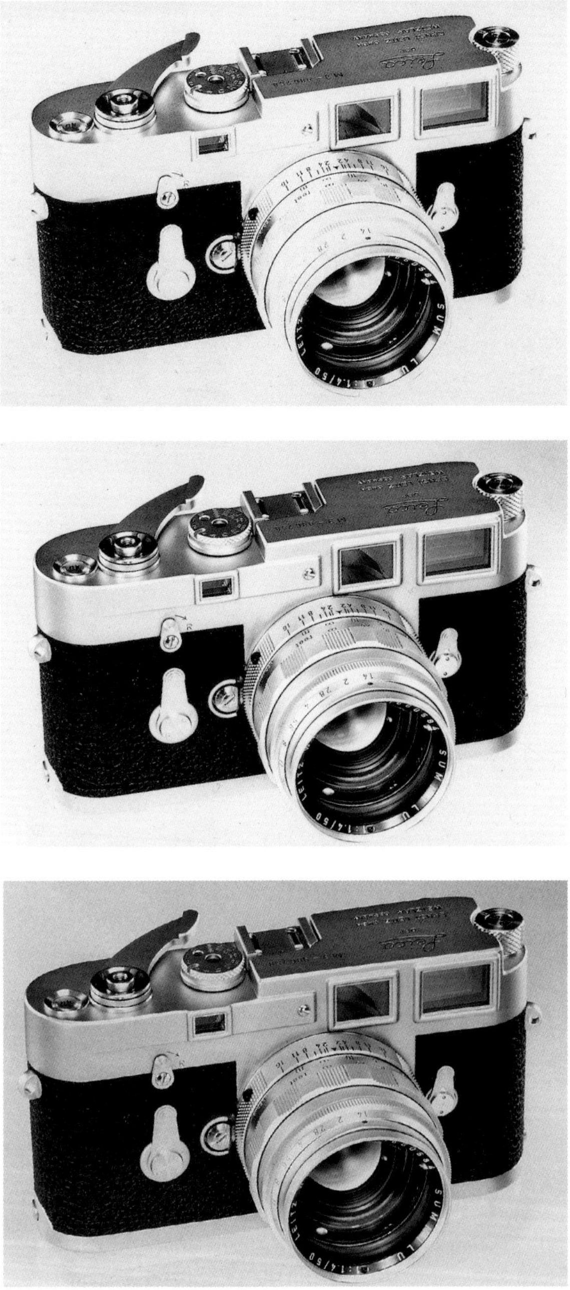

Fig. 147 a – c: Colors, the surfaces of objects, as well as light and shadows determine the contrast range of the subject. With the appropriate choice of black-and-white processing, the contrast range of the negative should be controlled in such a way that minor corrections can be made during enlarging by selecting a suitable grade of paper. Photographs of subjects with a high contrast range should receive ample exposure and short (soft) development. From top to bottom: Long, normal, and short development.

When to use which developer

Characteristics of black-and-white films, in particular gradation, are strongly influenced by development. Since the negative is only an intermediate step towards a positive, the greatest care should be taken to achieve optimum quality, so that good prints can be made from that negative. When processed correctly, negatives will have good gradation and not be too contrasty. During the development phase, silver halide crystals, such as silver bromide crystals, are reduced to metallic silver. Adjacent silver grains form clusters at this stage. When ultra-fine-grain or fine-grain developers are used, the distribution of the silver grain structure is more uniform because clumping is prevented. Light can then pass through the processed layers during the enlarging step, striking the photographic paper and creating an image of the translucent spaces. Since greatly different subjects may have been photographed on the same film, graininess may also be disturbing to a greater or lesser extent. Graininess becomes particularly noticeable in light gray areas. Whenever very fine-grain photographs are desired, it is much better to use a very fine-grain film to start with, rather than use higher speed films and process them with ultra-fine-grain or fine-grain developers.

High-speed films should preferably be processed in (ultra) fine-grain developers in order to keep the grain as small as possible. The following are examples of developers that accomplish this without building up too much contrast while still taking good advantage of the films speed: Atomal (Agfa-Gevaert), Microphen and Perceptol (Ilford), D-76, T-Max developer and Microdol-X (Kodak), Promicrol (May & Baker) and Ultrafin (Tetenal). Since the development time depends on both the film and the developer, correct times should be obtained from the instruction sheets supplied by the manufacturers of the films and developers.

Table 10: Film/developer combinations for black-and-white pictures

Purpose of use	Type of film	Make	To be exposed like	Development
For fine details, e.g., landscapes and object shots with normal contrast.	Low-speed film	Agfa-Gevaert Agfapan APX 25	ISO 25	Agfa-Gevaert Rodinal, 20 °C, 1:25/6 Min.
		Ilford Pan F plus	ISO 50	Ilford Perceptol, 20°C, 1:1/15 Min.
With high contrast, e.g., portrait shots in sunlight and deep shade		Ilford Pan F plus	ISO 50	Agfa-Gevaert Rodinal, 20 °C, 1:25/6 Min.
		Agfa-Gevaert Agfapan APX 25	ISO 12	Agfa-Gevaert Rodinal, 20 °C, 1:50/8.5 Min.
		Ilford Pan F plus	ISO 25	Agfa-Gevaert Rodinal, 20 °C, 1:50/8.5 Min.
Very high contrast, e.g., inside rooms with view from a window		Agfa-Gevaert Agfapan APX 25	ISO 9	Agfa-Gevaert Rodinal, 20 °C, 1:50/6 Min.
		Ilford Pan F plus	ISO 12	Agfa-Gevaert Rodinal, 20 °C, 1:50/6 Min.
All-round film for poor weather, sunshine and flash exposures on a film, ideal for travel, on vacation and photojournalism.	Medium speed film	Agfa-Gevaert Agfapan APX 100	ISO 100	Agfa-Gevaert Rodinal, 20 °C, 1:25/8 Min.
		Ilford FP 4 plus	ISO 125	Agfa-Gevaert Atomal, 20 °C, 8 Min.
		Kodak T-Max 100	ISO 100	Kodak T-Max, 24 °C, 6.5 Min.
Still be able to take hand-held pictures in poor weather conditions. Ideal for photojournalism without flash in rooms, for short exposure times in poor weather and for sports pictures.	High speed film	Ilford XP2	ISO 400	C41-Prozess oder Ilford XP1-Entw.
		Kodak Tri X	ISO 400	Kodak D 76, 20 °C, 8 Min.
		Kodak T-Max 400	ISO 400	Kodak T-Max, 24 °C, 6 Min.
For photographs under extremely poor lighting conditions for action shots with short exposure times.		Kodak T-Max P 3200	ISO 3200	Kodak T-Max, 24 °C, 9.5 Min.
For fine details and large enlargements with normal contrast. For fine details and large enlargements with high-contrast subjects contrast.	For copy film	Kodak Technical Pan Film 2415	ISO 50	Tetenal Neofin-Doku, 20 °C, 15 Min.

p-Aminophenol-based developers have proven themselves effective with low and medium speed films and copy films. Among them are Rodinal by Agfa-Gevaert and Paranol by Tetenal. The latter are sold in a highly concentrated form, to be diluted just before use. In practice, a dilution of 1:50 has proven to be successful and these developers are used only once and then discarded. Development time depends on the film and on the desired contrast. These are surface developers, which extract the best sharpness from the negative, and which further enhance the impression of sharpness because of the so-called adjacency or edge effect. This effect causes a dark area to have a slightly darker edge all along the line where it meets a lighter area, and the lighter area will have a slightly lighter edge along that same line. This causes fine variations in brightness in the subject to be reproduced with better differentiation on film.

By varying the development time, contrast can be controlled to a small extent with (ultra) fine-grain developers and to a considerable extent with surface developers. With surface developers, this can also be achieved by using different dilution ratios. By prolonging the development time, contrast is raised and film speed is increased. Reducing the development time lowers contrast and film speed. In practice this means that scenes with high brightness ratios should be given ample exposures, so that the resulting negatives will still have enough density after being given a soft (short) development. Low-contrast subjects, on the other hand, can be given shorter exposures and longer development. A rule of thumb states that increasing the development time by a factor of 1.4 doubles the speed of the film.

Table 11: Example of speed-affecting film development

Film: Ilford Pan F plus = ISO 50/18°
Surface developer: Agfa-Gevaert Rodinal, 20 °C

Contrast:	Development:	To be exposed like:
Soft	1:50/8.5 Min.	ISO 25
Normal	1:25/6 Min.	ISO 50
Hard	1:25/8.5 Min.	ISO 100

For soft development under 5 minutes, the concentration of the developer should be diluted from 1:50 to 1:100 so that the development time can be prolonged. Development times shorter than 5 minutes often result in uneven development (streaks). A significant increase in contrast can be achieved by developing the film in a developer for papers. The author develops all his films with speeds up to ISO 80, including copy films, in Rodinal (Agfa-Gevaert). The only exception is Kodak Technical Pan Film 2415, which is developed in Neofin-Doku. Films with higher speeds are processed in ultra-fine-grain developer Atomal (Agfa-Gevaert) or fine-grain developer D-76 (Kodak). All three developers are recognized for their good compensating action with different contrasts. Film speeds remain at the nominal values.

The above values are valid for solution temperatures of 20°C (68°F) and for agitation by inverting the tank. Kodak T-MAX films are processed at 24°C (75°F); all other films are processed 20°C (68°F). During the first 30 seconds, the processing tank should be inverted repeatedly and from then on once every 30 seconds.

With Rodinal the hardness of the water has an effect on the development time. The "harder" the water, the longer the development time. The times listed above are based on water with 18 degrees of hardness (German scale).

Since development times may lead to changed results when conditions are different—negatives may be too dense or too transparent—advance testing is recommended. It must also be remembered that, the harder the gradation of a film, the smaller its exposure latitude and the greater the need for exact exposures. If a factor of 2 is chosen for the individual steps in a series of test exposures with a normal black-and-white film, the following shutter-speed sequence can be used at the same aperture setting, for instance: 1/125, 1/60, 1/30, 1/15 and 1/8 second. The shutter speed that is expected to be the right one should be in the middle of the sequence, so that both over- as well as under-exposures will be made. On the other hand, test exposures with a contrasty copy film such as Kodak Technical Pan Film 2415, which is superbly suited for landscape photography, should be made in steps with a factor of 1.4: 1/125 second at f/5.6, 1/125 second at f/5.6 - f/4, 1/60 second at f/5.6, 1/60 second at f/5.6 - f/4, and 1/30 second at f/5.6.

High-key and low-key techniques

The drama in photographs in which all details are kept "light on light" or "dark on dark" can be enhanced by means of high-key or low-key techniques. Both techniques usually involve black-and-white photography, but the concept can also be applied to color photography.

High-key pictures consist exclusively or nearly exclusively of light tones (high key = high tones = very light picture tones). The subject must not include any strong color contrasts. An example would be a honey-blonde girl in a white blouse standing in front of a light wall, or a dozen white chicken eggs in a white porcelain bowl standing on a white tablecloth. A totally diffuse illumination effectively enhances this special photographic style; harsh shadows would destroy it. The high-key treatment can be particularly effective when a tiny detail in the subject is kept in deep black. For instance, the eyes in the portrait of the girl mentioned above. Correct exposure and slightly reduced development time—"soft" under-development—ensure delicate black-and-white negatives, which are indispensable for high-key enlargements. Unlike those in high-key photographs, the subjects for low-key photographs are all of very dark shades of colors. A portrait of a Black singer wearing a black shirt and standing in front of a dark background would be predestined for this style of photography and reproduction. For the deep tones of the face to stand out from the dense black background, only a few highlights (spotlight illumination) are permissible. With this technique "delicate" negatives should be attempted through slightly shorter (softer) development.

Chromogenic black-and-white films

(Note: at the time of publication of this edition, the publisher is uncertain whether the Ilford film described below will continue to be readily available.)

A new kind of "silver-free" black-and-white film was first introduced at Photokina 1980 by Agfa-Gevaert (Agfapan Vario-XL) and by Ilford (XP1 400). The one that still available is the Ilford film.

Today it is called "XP2" and is processed in special chemicals. Like color films, they are, after processing, free of silver. A "black-and-white negative" obtained in this manner is thus comparable with a color negative that consists only of gray tones, and which has a slight yellow-red color and is compatible with all conventional black-and-white photographic papers. The T-Max T 400 CN by Kodak works on the same basis. Both "colored" (chromogenic) black-and-white "color" films have two panchromatically sensitized layers: one is a high speed emulsion, the other one a low speed emulsion, which are coated one on top of the other and which complement each other in such a way that they produce an especially soft gradation. The exposure latitude of these films is significantly greater than that of conventional black-and-white films. Therefore, these films can be used both as high-speed as well as medium-speed films, and as super high-speed films. In the case of the Ilford XP2 the speed ranges even from ISO 50 to ISO 800; for Kodak T 400 CN T-Max from ISO 25 to ISO 1600 (when pushed, even to ISO 3200). With ample exposure (as medium-speed films), the graininess of these novel films, which is already low, is reduced even further. This is achieved primarily by virtue of the fact that these films incorporate so-called "DIR couplers," which produce the special effect in color processing that graininess is reduced in particular in the dense portions of the negative. DIR is an abbreviation of "Development Inhibitor Release."

The ecological and economical aspects of the recovery of the silver bleached out from these films are also important. From the point of view that silver reserves are gradually becoming scarcer, the new technology is in keeping with the obligation of using valuable raw materials sparingly. The silver that is dissolved out of the new kind of black-and-white films can later be recovered from the fixing and washing solutions, just as with normal color films. This creates a raw materials cycle, which is beneficial from an economic and ecological point of view.

Color-negative films

Basically, all color negative films have three superimposed light-sensitive layers: the top one is sensitive to blue light, the middle one to green light, and the bottom to red light. Because all three layers are inherently blue-sensitive, including the red- sensitive and green-sensitive layers, a yellow filter layer has to be placed under the top layer. It prevents blue light from reaching the layers below, and its yellow color is removed during the development process.

In addition to the silver bromide crystals that are sensitive to the respective ranges of color, each emulsion layer contains so-called color couplers. These are complex chemical compounds that cause colors to be formed in the individual layers during development. In the blue-sensitive layer, yellow is formed; in the green-sensitive layer, magenta is created; and in the red-sensitive layer, cyan is formed. Thus, a purely blue subject will only create an image in the layer with the yellow dye couplers, whereas a green subject will form an image in the layer with the magenta dye couplers, and the layer with the cyan dye couplers will only react to red subjects. Multiple colors will affect corresponding additional layers. If the light is white, i.e. if all colors are present, all layers will react. This produces the greatest density in the negative, which, in turn, will produce white in a transparency or a print.

The metallic silver that is reduced during the development stage and the unexposed silver bromide are dissolved by the bleach-fixing solution. Only the pure dyes will remain in the film. That is how a negative image is created. Its colors are formed by the densities of the dyes in the three individual layers. From what has been stated above, it is evident that color film must consist of more than three layers. One problem with color-negative films is that the three photosensitive layers do not each exactly cover one third of the color spectrum. In other words: the green-sensitive layer exhibits the greatest spectral sensitivity in its spectral region, however it is also slightly sensitive in the other regions of blue and red.

This color-sensitivity applies equally to the blue-sensitive and the red-sensitive layers. In practical applications this leads to undesirable effects, which manifest themselves as color-tone shifts, low color saturation and reduction of brightness. In order to reduce the photosensitivity in the two undesirable regions, i.e. in order to avoid additional densities, colored masks that filter and absorb the undesirable color portion are interposed between the respective layers of the color-negative film. The presence of these masks is obvious because of the orange coloration of the entire film.

Thus, color film must consist of more than only three layers. For reasons of quality improvement, even the three photosensitive layers are in turn subdivided in today's color negative films. In addition, there are an anti-halation layer, intermediate layers, a substrate layer, so that modern color negative films can have more than 10 layers.

Silver halide crystals, in particular, have been significantly improved in recent years. Before this, conventional emulsions contained pebble-like crystals, which Kodak, for instance, replaced with flat, tabular crystals, so-called T-crystals. While they have the same volume as conventional crystals, they offer a larger surface, which can receive more light. Fuji calls similar shapes double-structure crystals, and Agfa refers to structured twin crystals. The lower exposure requirements of these silver halide crystals resulted in higher film speeds without an increase in graininess.

In addition, thanks to new DIR dye couplers, today's color films have purer colors, lower graininess, greater exposure latitude, and a better adjacency effect, which causes the borders between two brightness ranges or between two color areas to look as if they were drawn with an extremely thin line.

Unlike black-and-white films, color films always used to be tied to specific developers, mostly because two fundamentally different dye couplers were used with different films. Agfa, for example, used water-soluble, fatty acid-bound couplers, whereas Kodak used water-repellent, oil-protected couplers.

Today, there is really only one color-negative process, and that is Kodak Process C-41. Nevertheless, it is still important to follow each film manufacturer's processing instructions faithfully. That also applies to processing kits available from other manufacturers.

The influence of the color developer on the gradation of color films is extremely small compared to the effect on gradation of black-and-white film processing. The various color processes are so complex that changes in individual processing steps do not affect one specific characteristic of the film. A reduced development time, for example, not only results in a softer gradation, but it also disturbs the formation of the mask and the color balance of the film at the same time. Professionals and amateurs alike can thus, process all color-negative films relatively easily.

Unlike the development of color negative films, which is tied to specific processes, color enlarging permits much greater manipulation than does black-and-white enlarging. Aside from burning-in or dodging certain parts of the image, the colors too, can be strongly influenced.

Conventional color negative films are balanced for the median color temperature of daylight (5500 K), so that they are suitable for photography in daylight or with electronic flash. There is still ample latitude for achieving a neutral color balance during the enlarging phase by placing filters in the light path of the enlarger. Nevertheless, a blue conversion filter is still recommended for photography by artificial light. The instruction sheet for every color-negative film contains detailed information for this purpose. Color negative films are available with various film speeds, ranging from ISO 25 to ISO 1600. Normally, they are exposed according to the ISO values recommended by the manufacturer. With strong contrasts in the subject, however, they should be slightly over-exposed, i.e. readings should be taken of the shadows. This applies to borderline situations as well, because under-exposed color negatives can only be enlarged with compromises.

Color reversal films

The configuration of color reversal films is similar to that of color negative films. In principle, they also have three light-sensitive layers. The yellow filter layer is also present. Naturally, the new emulsion and crystal technologies that evolved in recent years have raised the performance characteristics of color slide films enormously. With the exception of Kodachrome film, which does not have dye couplers incorporated in the film but, rather, in the developer, the processing of all color reversal films is based on the same process: Kodak process E-6.

In the normal color reversal process, the film first undergoes regular black-and-white development (with a special black-and-white developer, of course), so that a black-and-white image is formed in each of the three layers. In addition to these negative images that consist of metallic silver, the unexposed and undeveloped silver bromide still remains in the emulsion layers. It occupies an area that is exactly complementary to the negative image, therefore it represents the positive image. This undeveloped silver bromide is then developed through a chemical transformation, whereby, proportional to the density in the individual layers, the colorless dye components are converted into non-diffusible dyes. The metallic silver that was formed during the two developing stages is subsequently bleached out. The result is a positive color image—a color transparency.

Processing of Kodachrome film is much more complex. In this process, the color dyes in the layers are formed by consecutive re-exposures to red, green and blue light, each one followed by development in separate tanks. Each developer is chromogenic. Thus, the color dye couplers are contained in the developer, not in the individual emulsion layers. The advantages of the Kodachrome principle are well known: Because it permits the use of very pure color dyes, high color saturation is created. And its sharpness is unsurpassed, because the absence of color dye couplers makes it possible to use much thinner emulsion layers than in conventional color reversal films. An advantage of color reversal films is their low granularity. As mentioned earlier, the latter depends on the general film speed. The faster the film, the larger the silver bromide crystals. Large crystals absorb more photons, so that they become capable of being developed earlier, and thus, in reversal films, they are developed first, but the positive image is only completed during the second development, through the rest of the silver bromide crystals that still remained after the first development. And these are mostly the very small ones. Thus graininess in color reversal films is always lower than it is in color-negative films of the same speed.

Since a color reversal film always receives and records light objectively, it has to be balanced for the color temperature of light in order to reproduce white as white. Subsequent correction, as it is practiced with color negative films by placing filters in the light path of the enlarger, is usually not possible. Therefore, color reversal films, in addition to being available in a range of film speeds, are also available in two types: as daylight color reversal films and as artificial light color reversal films. The reason for this is that the composition of the light perceived as being "white" may vary. Because we are not able to perceive colors objectively, a white sheet of paper will always appear white. It does not matter whether the workstation is illuminated with artificial light or if we are outside in sunlight: the sheet of paper will appear white to us! Our eyes do not recognize the subtle differences in color characteristics, namely the yellowish-reddish reproduction of artificial light or the bluish reproduction of daylight. We all know when we select our clothes to choose lighting conditions which resemble those in which we are going to wear an outfit: Before a decision is made to purchase a coat, it is best to go to a window in order to be able to better assess its color effect in daylight

The daylight color reversal films are adjusted to 5500 K; artificial light color reversal films are adjusted either to 3100 K, 3200 K (photographic lamps), or 3400 K (halogen light). If the color temperature of the illumination is differs by more than 200 K from the color temperature for which the film was balanced, the color reversal film will react with a pronounced color cast. It is possible, however, to adapt color reversal films to light sources with different color temperatures by using conversion filters (see page 208). Color reversal films have less exposure latitude than normal black-and-white and color negative films, therefore they have to be exposed very accurately. Over- and under-exposures of more than half an exposure value (1/2 an aperture stop) will already be noticeable. That is why test exposure series are made in steps with a factor of 1.4. In cases of doubt, particularly with subjects with strong contrasts, one should preferably underexpose slightly, i.e. measure the highlights or the brighter parts of the subject. The special advantage of color reversal films is their great luminosity. Compared to a paper print, which can have a brightness contrast of 1:30 at most, a color transparency can have a brightness ratio of approximately 1:300.

Large, bright, and sharp projection shows what a color transparency can do. In addition, color enlargements can easily be made from slides that are not too contrasty. With the exception of Kodachrome film, all color reversal films can be processed by the photographer him or herself. But that is advantageous only when the finished slide is needed quickly, because the accuracy required for color reversal processing can only be achieved with a relatively large investment in equipment.

Color reversal films are available with film speeds ranging from ISO 25 to ISO 1600. Most laboratories also offer push processing for E-6 process color reversal films that are exposed at higher than recommended film speeds. However, this often entails a slight loss of color quality. Information regarding the films that can be used in this manner, as well as information as to how far film speeds can be pushed, is available at camera shops, processing laboratories, and film manufacturers.

Instant slide films

Three different 35mm slide films that do not require processing in a darkroom were introduced by Polaroid under the name "35mm Autoprocess System." Each film is supplied with a separate developer pack that contains the necessary chemicals for processing the film. All films are processed in a so-called Autoprocessor. Special accessories for cutting and mounting the transparencies are also available. All five instant slide films, whether color or black-and--white, can be used effectively in businesses where rapid availability of slides is desired or necessary. But there are countless applications for amateur photographers as well, who can also use them creatively. During parties, weddings and other family events, guests will be surprised when they see themselves in a slide reviewing scenes that took place only minutes ago.

Polachrome-CS for color slides

Polachrome-CS instant color slide film works on the same principle as other instant films, namely the silver salt diffusion process. Color mixing takes place according to the additive color system, i.e. red, green, and blue light combined produces white. This color mixture is accomplished with very narrow bands of the three aforementioned primary colors, which are coated over a black-and-white layer and which function like tiny color filters. Polachrome-CS is thus a color screen film based on the additive color system. The color screen in this film is so fine that it only becomes noticeable when the projected image is viewed from a shorter than normal viewing distance. The color screen has 180 lines per millimeter. Each of the alternating red, blue and green lines has a width of only 0.0085 mm (about 335 millionths of an inch). Naturally, the color screen reduces the speed of this film to ISO 40.

Another characteristic of color screens is the high density of Polachrome-CS slides, which becomes especially disturbing when these slides are projected along with conventional slides. The color screen requires a very unusual film configuration: Polachrome-CS consists of just a single, very thin emulsion layer, because only one black-and-white image is created. In spite of the super-imposed color screen, this film is much thinner can conventional color reversal films.

Graininess appears to be relatively high in relation to the effective film speed and it is especially noticeable in shadow areas. This can be attributed to the afore-mentioned significant reduction in film speed caused by the tight color screen. Because of the density of the color screen, the sensitivity of the emulsion, which is located behind that screen, has to be much higher—approximately ISO 800. Its color rendition takes getting used to: first impressions during normal viewing lead to wrong conclusions, as the apparently dominating purple cast is less noticeable during projection. With the aid of powerful Leica projectors, high-reflectance screens and modest projected image sizes, its colors radiate relatively naturally.

The exposure latitude of Polachrome-CS film is even lower than that of conventional reversal films. Over- and under-exposures result in color shifts, whereas long exposures of up to about 10 seconds do not. Subjects with high contrasts should be avoided. The best pictures can be made in the morning or in the afternoon with a slightly overcast sun. For flash pictures, the light should be soft and indirect. With TTL flash exposure compensation is generally used.

Tips for further applications

Polachrome-CS slides are intended primarily for projection. If they are to be used for making paper prints or for printed reproductions, they have to be handled with the greatest care, because they are highly susceptible to scratches. Positive papers can be used without hesitation for small enlargements up to 13 x 18 cm (about 5 x 7 inches). For bigger enlargements, it is bester to use internegatives. The filtering needs to be slightly corrected in both cases by a reduction of about 30 to 40 magenta units. There is also no problem in making duplicate slides on conventional reversal film.

Matters become a little more difficult when a Polachrome-CS slide is submitted to a graphic arts house to have color separations and film positives made. In that case, there are some points to be considered. A few tests will be indispensable for optimum results, because scanners are generally not (yet) programmed for this material:

- The slide has to be attached to the scanning drum in such a way that the lines of the color screen are not parallel, but at a 90° angle to the direction of scanning.
- To avoid a line structure and moiré patterns, it is advisable to defocus the Polachrome-CS slide slightly and to increase the unsharp masking.
- Setting the color tones and color correction is more difficult than it is with conventional transparencies. Both have to be executed manually.
- In order to avoid scratches during subsequent cleaning, Polachrome-CS slides should not be oiled; they should only be treated with talcum powder.

Polapan-CT for black-and-white halftone slides

Polapan-CT black-and-white transparency film is very well suited for making halftone reproductions. But its exposure latitude is large enough for very normal photographs as well, such as press pictures. Polapan-CT has a film speed of ISO 125. It is sufficiently sharp and it has a granularity that corresponds to that of conventional high-speed films. There are no problems with projection, because the base density of Polapan-CT slides is not significantly higher than that of conventional black-and-white transparency films.

Polagraph-HC for black-and-white line reproductions

Even though the current Leica M System no longer includes any accessories for copy work, it should be mentioned that Polaroid offers Polagraph-HC high contrast copy film for the reproduction of line drawings, tables, text, and similar originals. This film is also very well suited for the production of title slides that only contain text.

Processing instant slide films

All instant slide films are loaded into the camera and removed from it in the normal manner. If the tongue of the exposed film is accidentally wound into the cassette, it can easily be retrieved with the metal extractor that is supplied with the Autoprocessor. The Autoprocessor is a handy processing device, into which the film is inserted together with its respective developer pack. The film tongue that is protruding from the cassette is attached, together with the film tab of the developer pack, to the same take-up spool. After closing the lid of the Autoprocessor, the developer pack is opened by pressing a lever, and a capsule with liquid developer is ruptured. The crank of the Autoprocessor is then turned, which causes the solution to be applied uniformly to the surface of the exposed instant slide film. It penetrates the film and reduces the exposed silver halides of the negative layer to silver. After 60 seconds the film is rewound with the same crank. The cassette can now be removed and the transparency strip can be cut and mounted immediately. From exposed film to projection-ready slides, all in all a matter of only a few minutes.

Infrared photographs

For photographers who like to experiment, infrared photography is likely to be a welcome opportunity to explore a different medium. Aside from a few peculiarities that have to be taken into account, only a couple of filters or gelatin filters are needed to accomplish the first successful results. Black-and-white infrared photographs in the normal range are especially easy to take with a Leica M camera, because the subject is composed with the separate range-viewfinder and not through the lens, as it is with single lens reflex cameras. That is because there is a dark filter attached to the lens, which is a requirement for infrared photography.

What is infrared light?

Taking infrared pictures means photographing with invisible long-wave light, uncontrolled by our eyes, in a manner of speaking, because the human eye is sensitive only to a certain region of the spectrum of light. Our eyes react to various wavelengths of visible light from about 400 to about 700 nm (nm = nanometer = 1/1 000 000 millimeter). The eyes perceive different wavelengths as colors, for instance 400 nm = blue-violet, 550 nm = yellow-green, and 700 nm = red. Wavelengths shorter than 400 nm (ultraviolet light) and wavelengths longer than 700 nm (infrared light) remain invisible. They can, however, be recorded photographically.

Although special lenses are required for photography with ultraviolet light (UV photography), every normal photographic lens can be used for infrared (IR) and UV luminescence photography. But certain preparations have to be made. For example, special films and filters are needed for IR photography. Aside from certain exceptions, Leica M lenses have to be calibrated for a focus difference that depends on the film and filter that will be used.

IR photography is used in various fields of technical and scientific photography, for instance in medicine, botany and criminology. Since these fields usually require close-up photographs, for which today's Leica M system no longer offers any accessories, these applications will not be covered in this text. But photographers can still explore the broad field of pictorial photography. There are numerous possibilities for them to obtain special effects in that area. With sunlight and a cloudless sky, for example, the impression of a night photograph can be created, because the sky and the shadows are reproduced as black. In landscape photographs, meadows and trees look like they are covered with snow. A flash unit can be suitably and inexpensively prepared for undetected photography in the dark (see page 284), a feature that is also utilized by reporters and investigators. For the color photographer who likes to experiment, Kodak Ektachrome Infrared film, often also called false-color film, offers a substantial expansion of a photographer's field of activities.

Black-and-white infrared photographs

Infrared films are sensitive not only to the long-wave, invisible portion of the light spectrum, they are also sensitive to visible light. To obtain the pure effect of infrared light, special filters have to be attached to the lens or to the light source. Infrared films are relatively coarse-grained, and their resolving power is lower than that of high-speed black-and-white films. For that reason, black-and-white IR films are processed in fine grain developers. Correctly exposed and processed, they have a greater density than normal films. As in black-and-white films, gradation can be influenced by the length of the development time, which also influences the speed of these films (see page 200).

Processing takes place in complete darkness. It has to be remembered here that daylight-processing tanks made of plastic material may be transparent to infrared light. Thus, if a plastic tank is used for IR films, processing must also be executed in the darkroom.

Infrared filters

There are different infrared filters with light transmission "windows" of different widths, that is, they absorb more or less of the visible light. This prevents too much visible light from affecting the infrared film. These filters are available in optical glass or as square gelatin sheets. The glass infrared filters formerly offered by Leica M lenses correspond to "Kodak Wratten No. 25" filters, which look dark-red by transmitted light. Filters that absorb even more of the visible light, for instance Kodak Wratten filter No. 87, are also called black filters. The various filters have to be taken into account in determining the exposure and in the setting the focus.

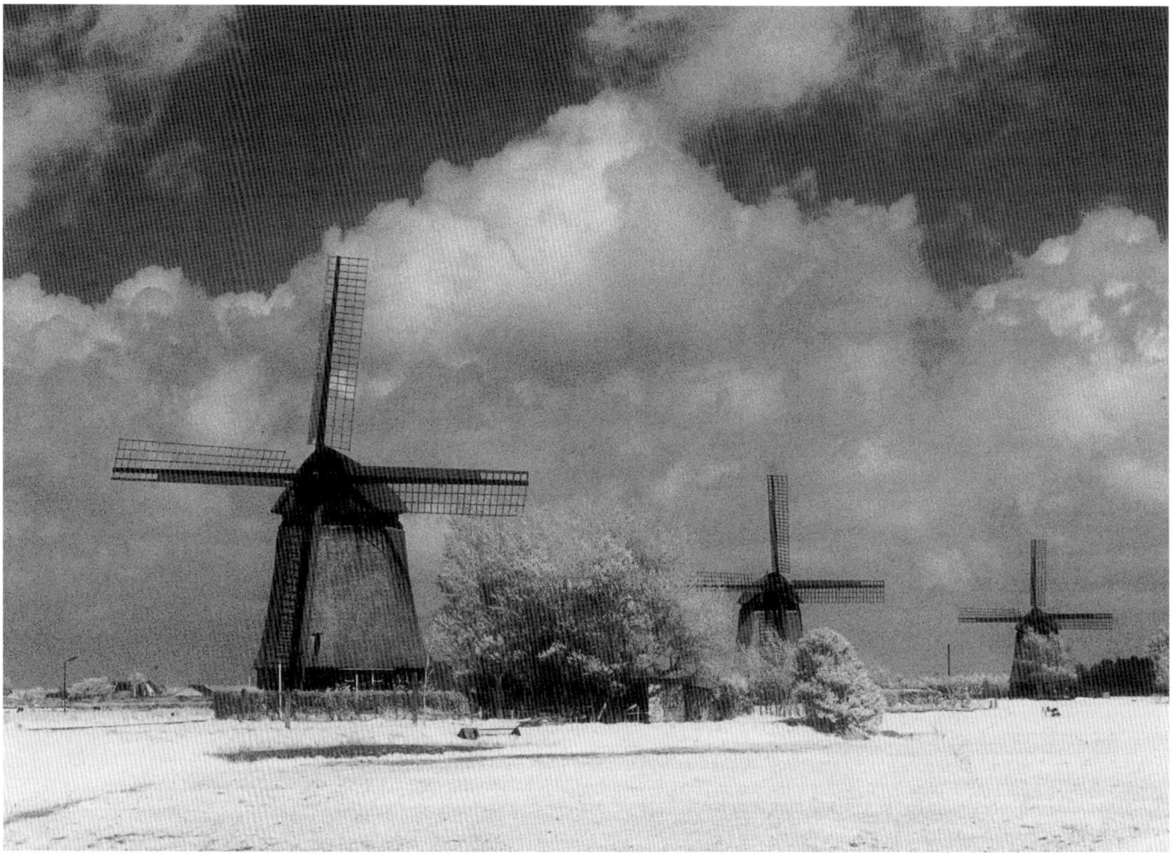

Fig. 148: *The green from the chlorophyll in plants reflects infrared radiation especially well. Thus, leaves and grass are reproduced in very light tones. A blue sky, on the other hand, appears nearly black. Clouds, if any, always look very three-di-mensional. For these reasons, landscapes with bright sunshine and scattered clouds often make the best infrared subjects. Try to avoid large shadows areas, however, because the inherent lack of detail in the reproduction of dark shadows usually de-tracts from the quality of the photograph. 35mm f/2 Summicron-M, High Speed Infrared film, Wratten Filter No 87, 1/250 second at f/8-11.*

Conventional focusing is no longer correct

Since normal photographic lenses are not corrected for infrared light, the focus setting has to be adjusted. Some Leica lenses feature infrared indexes in the form of a red dot and the letter "R". These could be used for adjusting the focus but only under certain conditions, because the mark applies to only one type of film, one type of filter, and only as an infinity setting. Leica, therefore, no longer uses an infrared marking.

As a reference value, the lens extension has to be increased by 1/200 to 1/400 of the focal length of the lens. A test has to be conducted in order to determine the best focus setting. The procedure is as follows: First find the optimum infinity setting for infrared light. Based on the premise that 1/300 of the focal length is an average value, the lens is set, not on infinity, but at a closer distance that corresponds to 300 times the focal length of the lens in use. For a 50mm lens, this amounts to 15 m (50 feet) 300 x 50 mm or 300 x 2", for a 90mm lens it amounts to 27 m (88 feet 7 inches), and for a

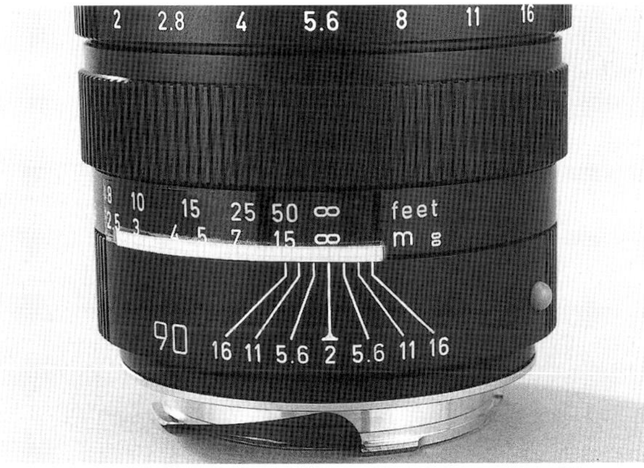

Fig. 149: *The reproducibility of settings that were determined by means of test photographs is assured with the aid of a narrow strip of graph paper affixed to the focusing mount of the lens.*

135mm lens it is 40 m (131 feet 2 inches). Now a strip of graph paper is attached to the focusing mount of the lens, so that the focus setting of the lens can be changed by one calibration step for each of the subsequent test photographs, both to the left as well as to the right. (see above).

The aperture of the lens also affects the focus; therefore it is best to make all test photographs at the same f/stop. When the lens is stopped down too much, particularly in the close-up range, the resolving power of the lens in the infrared range is reduced considerably. A working aperture of f/8 is recommended. If all the settings have been carefully recorded, it becomes an easy matter to determine the right setting based on the negative that has the best sharpness. An auxiliary index can now be applied on the depth of field scale, opposite the lens' infinity symbol. This auxiliary calibration indicates the proper correction, but only for the particular film and the particular filter used for the test photographs.

At closer ranges, or closer than 2 meters (6-1 /2 feet), the auxiliary index is shifted, because the extension increase of 1/200 to 1/400 of the focal length, plus the normal extension of the lens, have to be taken into account. The same method described earlier can be used again to establish the new index. The auxiliary index for infinity can be used as an initial approximation.

Exposure metering, lighting, and processing

Infrared light cannot be measured with the accessory Leicameter, because the latter is only calibrated for visible light. This is also the case with through-the-

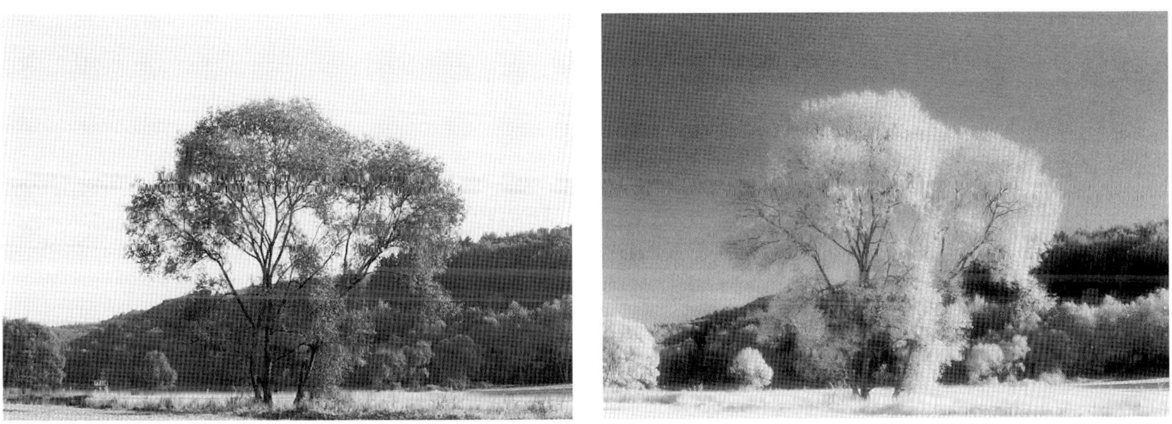

Fig. 150 a and b: *A Leica M camera is particularly advantageous for infrared photography, because the image is seen through the viewfinder and is not obscured by the dense infrared filter on the lens. This makes it even more pleasurable to use these films for creative expression. Left: Normal film. Right: Kodak High Speed Infrared film, Wratten filter Nr. 87. Both photographs were made with a 90 mm f/2 Summicron-M lens.*

lens exposure meters on all Leica M models. Also, it is difficult to perform a meter reading through a very dense infrared filter. However all exposure meters can provide reference readings (filters must be detached from the lenses on Leica M7, M6-series, and M5 cameras), but the film speed setting will depend on the type of illumination. The infrared component is much greater in incandescent or flashbulb illumination than it is in daylight or electronic flash illumination. The instruction sheets for infrared films contain the appropriate data.

If the photographs are made by artificial light, diffusion sheets, tissue paper, or other diffusing aids should be placed over the light sources. Diffuse illumination assures the even lighting that is essential for infrared photographs. Processing recommendations are also contained in the instruction sheets for the various infrared films. The author of this book has used the following reference values in practical applications:

Table 12: Sensitivity and Filtration of IR Film

Film	Illumination	Kodak Wratten-Filter	Film speed setting
Kodak High Speed Infrared Film	Daylight (sunshine)	Nr. 25	ISO 200
		Nr. 87	ISO 100
	Artificial light (halogen)	Nr. 25	ISO 800
		Nr. 87	ISO 400
Developer: Agfa Atomal, 12 minutes at 20°C or 68°F			

Contrast can be increased by extending the development time. This also increases the film speed. With a development time of 18 minutes and using the method described in the above table, the film speed setting can be raised by approximately twice the ISO value. Because this reduces the exposure latitude, test exposures should be made by varying the f/stop in half-stop intervals. The right exposure for a specific combination of film, illumination, filter and processing can be determined with such an exposure series.

Infrared photographs in color

In addition to its black-and-white infrared film, Kodak also offers an infrared color reversal film: Kodak Ektachrome Infrared Film. This film was originally used for military purposes, such as making camouflaged objects hidden in the woods become visible through photography. With an orange filter, the green color of vegetation is reproduced as red, whereas artificial green is reproduced as blue. The other colors are also "shifted." With strong infrared reflection, yellow will thus appear as white, and orange or red will appear as yellow. That is why this film is also called a "false color" film. Today, this film is used successfully in agriculture and forestry when certain diseases or pest infestations of trees are to be detected early enough to be treated. Photographers enjoy the "crazy" color effects that can be achieved with this unusual film.

Colors that surprise

Unlike regular Kodak Ektachrome films, Kodak Ektachrome Infrared Film has an infrared-sensitive emulsion layer in place of the usual blue-sensitive layer, while the layers that follow are similar to those in normal Ektachrome films, i.e. a green- and a red-sensitive layer. After processing, the three layers of this "false color" film will contain a cyan, a yellow and a magenta image. Because of this modified layer configuration, colors are reproduced incorrectly. In addition, all three layers are sensitive to blue light, so that Kodak recommends the use of a strong yellow filter (Kodak Wratten Filter No. 12) in all cases. When this filter is used, colors will be reproduced approximately as shown in the table (page 201, top).

Since the actual reproduction of colors depends on the amount of infrared radiation (sunlight or overcast sky) and on the infrared reflectivity of the subjects, the results will often be surprising. The color shifts can be influenced within certain limits by the use of color-compensating filters (page 201, bottom). Stronger color shifts can, of course, be achieved by

Original color	is reproduced as follows with strong infrared reflection	with weak infrared reflection
Blue-green (Cyan)	Magenta	Blue
Purple (Magenta)	Yellow	Green
Yellow	White to Gray	Cyan
Red	Yellow	Green
Green	Magenta	Blue
Blue	Red	Gray
Gray	Red	Gray

Desired color shift	Kodak Color Compensating Filter
from green to more magenta	Cyan (CC 10C)
from yellow to more blue	Cyan-2 (CC 10C-2)
from cyan to more red	Blue (CC 10B)
from blue to more yellow	Magenta (CC 10M)

the use of normal photographic filters, such as those used for black-and-white films. Kodak Ektachrome Infrared Film is developed in Process E-4, either in the home darkroom or in a commercial laboratory in care of your photographic dealer, and it can also be mailed directly to a lab by means of an appropriate prepaid processing mailer.

Problem-free focusing

Two thirds of the exposure of false color films is contributed by light in the visible spectrum, only one third is contributed by infrared radiation. Since the share of visible light is usually dominant, a correction for focus differences need not be taken into account. An adjustment of the focus setting may only become necessary when dark red filters are used, and it becomes a must when visually opaque ("black filters") are used.

Caution: All infrared films should be stored in their unopened original packages at temperatures between -23°C and -18°C (-10°F and 0°F). They should be processed as soon as possible after being exposed.

Proper handling of films

Loading a Leica M camera should be practiced thoroughly with an old roll of unexposed film. Practice until you can load the camera smoothly without looking. Only when you have mastered that can you be sure that the film will advance properly when it has to be loaded into the camera quickly, under strained conditions. Never load or unload the camera in direct sunlight. If necessary, do it in the shade of your own body, otherwise the first few exposures may be spoiled by light penetrating the slot of the cartridge. Rewound cartridges should never be left in bright light for any length of time. They should be returned to their film cans right away or wrapped into a light-tight package.

If part of the film is to be processed before the entire film has been exposed, it can be marked in the following manner: a blank exposure is made after the last picture and the film is advanced once more. With the shutter speed dial set at "B," the shutter release button is kept pressed, causing the focal plane shutter to remain open. With the lens removed from the Leica M camera and in subdued light (body shade), a small self-adhesive label is applied directly to the film, which is now visible in the film gate. The shutter is now allowed to close and the film rewound into its cartridge (except for its tongue).

Back in the darkroom and in total darkness, the film is then gently pulled out of the cartridge, passing between two extended fingers. This makes it easy to locate the frame marked with the label. The film is cut off at that point, so that the exposed portion can be processed. It is not advisable to open the camera in the dark and to attempt to cut off the exposed portion of the film inside the camera, because the shutter could inadvertently be damaged. The procedure described before has the additional advantage that the camera can be used again immediately and anywhere, and it does not have to be taken into a darkroom. If it becomes necessary to switch films during a picture-taking session, the film that is in the camera must first be rewound without its tongue disappearing into the cartridge.

To prevent that, one should stop rewinding immediately at the end of the strong resistance that is felt as the film tongue is pulled out from under the lugs on the take-up spool. If one is not careful at that point, the film tongue will slip into the cartridge. When that happens, the tongue has to he retrieved before the film can be loaded into the camera again to expose the remaining frames, or before the exposed part can be cut off in a darkroom. Photographic dealers have devices that perform such retrievals, including a plastic strip with small hooks, with which the tongue can be quickly and safely extricated through the mouth of the cartridge.

X-ray controls and their effects

The question whether or not the security checks at airports spoil films in carry-on baggage or in checked luggage is very relevant today. New, powerful scanning equipment, which has been used in the U.S. for examining checked luggage may be used in the future for scanning carry-on bags. This equipment uses energy that is 300 times greater than that of conventional scanners. These can damage all film, but especially the new high-speed films of ISO 800 and higher. The increasing frequency of air travel and stepped-up security at airports, has revived the question of whether or not film in carry-on bags can be damaged during carry-on security checks. As a rule, modern industrial countries employ devices that operate with an "x-ray flash." These devices subject the baggage to radiation for an extremely short length of time—only about 0.25 microseconds. The screen image generated by the x-ray flash is recorded by a highly sensitive television camera and stored by a video circuit that permits continued viewing of the image on a monitor for up to 15 minutes.

The effect of the radiation emitted by the x-ray flash is very small. At an object distance of 1 meter (about 40 inches) and depending on the power of the x-ray tube, its level generally lies between 0.18 and 0.36 mR (millirems). Actually, if these machines were used to scan passengers, which they are not, it would amount to a harmless exposure for any passenger. According to radiation protection codes, the permissible weekly dose of radiation for human beings is 100 mR (0.1 R). Even high-speed films are not affected by these low amounts of x-ray radiation, including film taken on longer trips and subjected to multiple airport x-ray security checks.

The following rule applies worldwide, though: Not all airports are equipped with modern x-ray control equipment, especially Eastern block and developing nations. Other airports employ modern security check equipment for examining passengers and carry-on baggage but not yet for examining checked luggage.

For these reasons it makes sense to carry always carry film in carry-on bags on all air travel. Today the danger of films being spoiled in hand luggage exists only in some Eastern European countries and in developing nations. In those airports, carry-on luggage should be handed over for x-ray examination only after first removing the films. As long as only a few rolls of film are involved, there should be no problem in storing them in coat or jacket pockets. Protective lead foil pouches reduce the effects of x-rays, but they do not eliminate them. Apparently the protection afforded by currently available pouches is still too low, because reports of spoiled films include both unprotected films as well as those that were transported in such pouches.

In major airports in the U.S. and in Europe, films that were packed in checked luggage have been fogged due to more powerful scanning machines. Therefore, it is still the safest way even today, always to place films in carry-on luggage.

The x-ray proof bags that are marketed to photographers are not sufficient for protecting film in checked luggage. Also, one should request a hand inspection of high-speed film in carry-on luggage. Kodak recommends visual inspection for T-Max P3200 Professional Film (ISO 3200).

Since natural aging of all sensitized materials is accelerated by unfavorable climatic conditions (high humidity or high temperatures), there is a justified desire during extended visits to tropical areas to airmail exposed films back to a processing laboratory as quickly as possible or to be periodically resupplied with fresh films by air. Today, only a fraction of airmail packages are x-rayed although this may be changing in the U.S. and other countries for security reasons. Unfortunately, information about countries that have these requirements is usually not readily available.

In view of the hazards of x-ray controls, the same precautions recommended for air travel also apply to postal shipments. With today's security concerns, there is always the danger that films may be spoiled by x-ray inspections, even when mailed. Therefore, one should only request airmail shipments when it has been ascertained that the postal authorities do not subject parcels to x-ray inspection.

Film from the refrigerator

Photographers who take a large number of pictures should always purchase an ample supply of film with the same emulsion number. This ensures uniform quality and color balance. The expiration date of the film should be at least a year away. Important: All film should be stored at the lowest possible temperature and processed as soon as possible after being exposed.

Storage in a refrigerator or better yet, in a freezer is recommended. Before stored, however, films should be protected against humidity by first being sealed in plastic containers or plastic bags. Stored in this manner, the films will remain fresh well beyond the expiration dates printed on their cartons. In the freezer, freshness is maintained practically indefinitely.

Refrigerated films should be taken out of storage well in advance of being used (many hours in the case of storage in the freezer), so that they can reach ambient temperatures before being exposed. They should remain in their sealed original cartons during the warm-up period.

Photographic filters

Filters are among the earliest and most effective photographic tools. In black-and-white photography, for example, they are very useful for achieving better contrast or for corrections in the conversion of colors into shades of gray. Filters can also be used to create effects, which alter the pictorial message of a photograph. In addition, picture-taking filters are especially important for color photography, where they can be used, among other applications, for improving the reproduction of colors.

With range-viewfinder cameras, however, the versatility of filters is limited. To begin with, Leica M cameras are generally used for photographic applications that do not require filters. Filters mounted on M cameras would encumber the otherwise smooth handling of the lens or impair the image. Furthermore, a visual assessment of the filter's effects is not possible with Leica M cameras since the photographer is not viewing through the taking lens.

Leica, therefore, deliberately limits the assortment of filters for Leica M lenses, practically reducing it to six protective filters that absorb ultraviolet radiation (protective UVa filters), plus one polarizing filter. Beyond that, certain filters from the Leica R system can also be used on Leica M lenses. Specific information about the line of Leica filters for Leica M lenses, their catalog numbers and what sizes are recommended for individual Leica lenses is contained in the tables on subsequent pages of this section. In addition an extensive selection of filters is available from a number of reputable filter manufacturers.

Even though photographic filters are not as relevant for applications with range-viewfinder cameras as they are for single lens reflex camera work, I have included all aspects of photography with filters in this text.

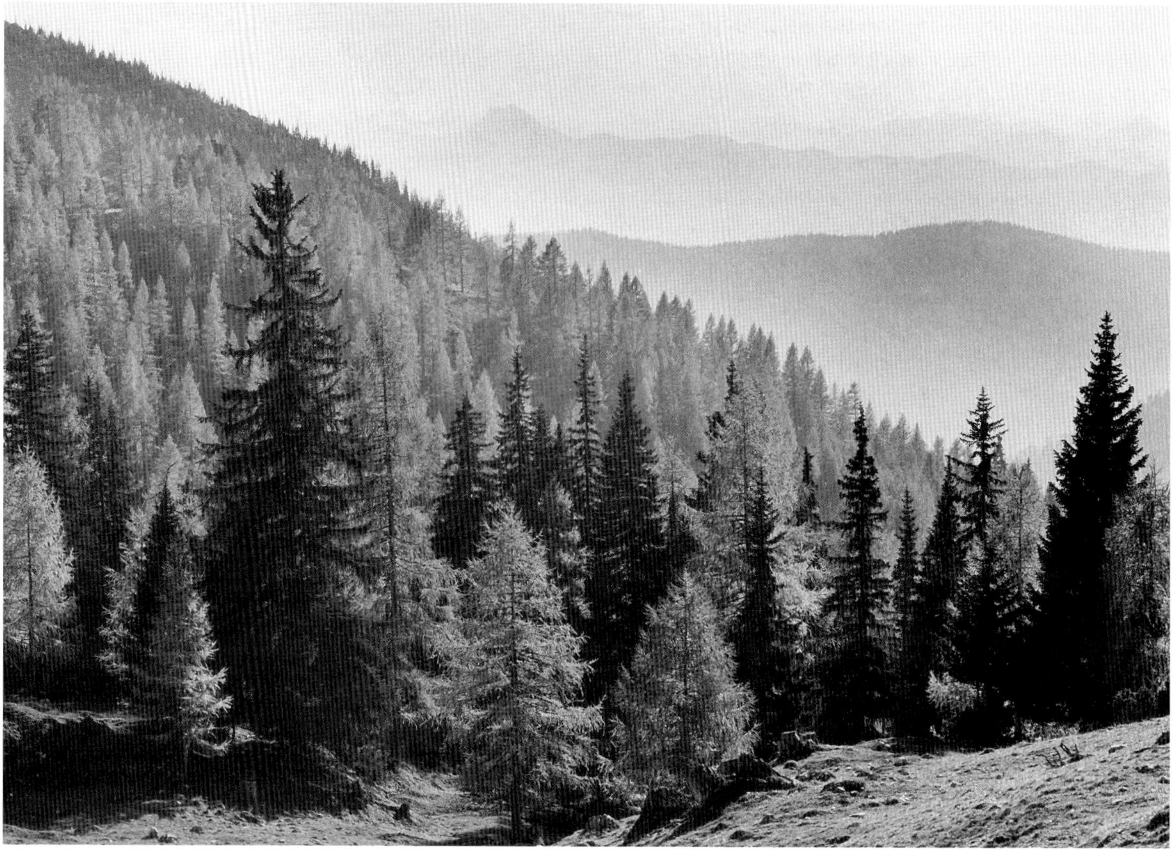

Fig. 151: *Often in black-and-white photography a strong mood is created only when a color filter is used. In the above example, the differentiation between the dark (green) fir trees and the lighter (yellow) autumn foliage of the tamaracks was enhanced by the use of an orange filter, creating a dramatic effect.*

Photographic filters are manufactured from optical glass, optical plastics, or gelatin in a variety of densities and sizes. When buying filters, one should always insist on good quality, because the sharpness of the photograph should not be degraded by the filter. Photographic filters from Leica are manufactured with the same meticulous precision as Leica lenses. They are made of solid, pure, dyed-in-the-mass optical glass, and they have ground and polished plano-parallel surfaces. This preserves the optical performance of a lens when it is used with a filter. As with lenses for Leica cameras, Leica filters feature anti-reflection coatings, which are specifically designed for each filter's field of application.

Wherever necessary, Leica assembles the optical glass disks in their mounts with a small amount of play for technical reasons. Therefore, do not be concerned about a small amount of rattle that may occasionally be heard when handling the filters. This special characteristic of Leica filters assures that the filters will be impervious to humidity and temperature differences.

Nearly all filters absorb some light. If the loss of light is substantial, the exposure has to be adjusted by increasing either the exposure time or the aperture. The amount of this increase is stated as the exposure or filter factor. Example: With an exposure or filter factor of 2, the exposure should be increased by one stop.

It should be noted here that the desired effect of a filter is often most dramatic when the photograph is slightly underexposed. This is because a slight overexposure usually weakens the effect of the filter. The exposure factor of a filter is, however, not an absolute constant, because it depends on the color sensitivity of the film and on the spectral characteristics of the illumination. For critical applications it is best to determine the appropriate filter factor experimentally with test exposures. Filter factors of polarizing and neutral density filters are not affected by the color sensitivity of the film and the spectral characteristics of the illumination.

The amount of light absorbed by filters is generally taken into account automatically by through-the-lens exposure measurement. Nevertheless, certain filters require an additional exposure factor even when they are used in conjunction with cameras designed for through-the-lens exposure measurement, such as Leica M7, M6 and M5 cameras. While exposure meter cells have a color sensitivity similar to that of most films, there may, however, be differences, which may furthermore even vary from brand to brand of film. Initial test exposures are especially recommended in black-and-white photography with red, orange and strong green filters, whereas an additional exposure factor can be neglected when yellow, yellow-green, green, and blue filters are used.

Filters can also be detrimental

Those who use filters must know that, in certain situations, even high quality filters can cause problems. With high-contrast scenes, for example, when photographing the setting sun, when photographing at night, with strong light in areas of the picture, or when photographing bright subjects from inside a dark archway, the danger of reflections is very real. This can occur even with plano-parallel, ground and polished, coated Leica filters. Double images, a general flattening of the contrast, or parts of the image that have been lightened by stray light are relatively frequent. In these photographic situations, all filters, including those that are used primarily for the protection of the front element of the lens, should be removed.

Universal photographic filters

Most filters apply to either color or black-and-white photography. However, there are a few filters that are used for both. These universal filters are ultraviolet light absorbing (UVa) filters, polarizing filters, and neutral-density filters.

Ultraviolet filters (UVa)

A colorless filter for the absorption of ultraviolet radiation. Filter factor: 1.

Ultraviolet rays are not visible to the human eye, but they do have an effect on film. They are present everywhere when the visibility is clear. They are held back, in part, by dust particles in the air, so that they are strongly absorbed, for instance in large cities. The opposite is true where the air is clean, as it is in the high mountains or by the sea, where the light is especially rich in ultraviolet rays. Ultraviolet radiation impairs the sharpness of black-and-white photographs and it also causes a bluish cast in color pictures, so that the color balance of reproductions will be cold. Therefore, it has to be filtered out.

Nearly all photographic filters absorb ultraviolet light, but usually their own colors also affect color reproduction. Because this normally leads to unusable results in color photography, colorless ultraviolet-absorbing filters were created to block the ultraviolet rays. With earlier Leica M lenses, particularly in color photography, the use of such filters was a necessity. Since the mid-1960s, in other words, with all Leica M lenses that are currently available, UVa filters are no longer needed. Because of the use of certain types of glass, and particularly because of the special technique used for cementing lens elements, current Leica M lenses absorb ultraviolet radiation, so that the use of UVa filters is generally unnecessary. Due to the use of special cement, identical color characteristics in all lenses are ensured; this, in turn, ensures uniform, neutral color reproduction. Even at high altitudes! Therefore, a UVa filter nowadays serves only to protect the front element of a lens.

With some color reversal films, Leica UVa filters also add a slightly warmer color reproduction. But this usually is only noticeable with a direct comparison (the same photograph taken with the same lens - with and without UVa filter - on the same film). In actual use, however, this is rarely obvious.

When extreme wide-angle lenses are used, filters in front of the lens may also produce inferior exposures. As a result of the greater camera angle the light rays on the edge of these lenses must travel a slightly greater distance through the filter than the light rays in the center. This may considerably diminish image quality in the corners of the picture.

Skylight and haze filters

Lightly tinted filters for the absorption of strong ultraviolet radiation. Filter factor: 1.

These filters have a mild pink tint and they are used for color photography in light that has particularly strong ultraviolet and blue components, like portraits in the shade under a clear blue sky or distant views with a light-blue haze. Skylight or haze filters should be used with caution on Leica M lenses, because these filters cause colors to be reproduced unnaturally warm.

Polarizing filters

Filter for the elimination of reflections. Filter factor: 3.

Polarizing filters are used primarily for the elimination of disturbing reflections from non-metallic surfaces, such as those that occur on water, plastic items, glass, polished wood and lacquered pieces,

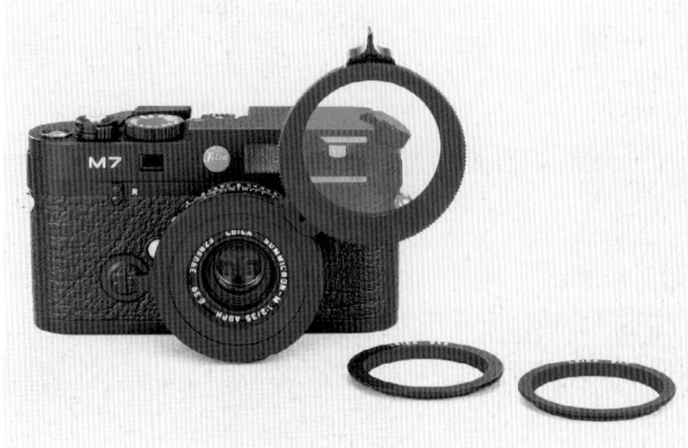

Fig. 152: *The polarizing filter for the Leica M camera includes adapter rings for different lens diameters. As illustrated in the picture, the polarizing filter can be pivoted by 180° so that the photographer can observe the filter's effect.*

but also on grasses and leaves. By eliminating reflections, higher contrast and better color separation is achieved, and this results in better color saturation. The effect is based on the fact that reflected (polarized) light vibrates in only one plane—normal light vibrates in all directions—and polarizing filters only transmit light that vibrates in one plane. Therefore, it is important to rotate the filter into position in front of the lens, namely the position in which it blocks polarized light. That position is best found by viewing the subject through the polarizing filter while rotating it.

Since maximum reduction of reflections is achieved at very specific camera angles, for instance 37 degrees with water, 33 degrees with glass, and 35 degrees with polished wood, all reflections cannot always be made to disappear completely. The effectiveness of a polarizing filter also depends on the focal length of the lens—the longer, the better. If reflections on metallic surfaces are to be eliminated, the light used for illumination must also be polarized. With artificial light this can be done by placing polarizing filters over the light sources and using a filter on the lens. In order to block the reflection, the planes of vibration of these two polarizing filters have to be at right angles to each other.

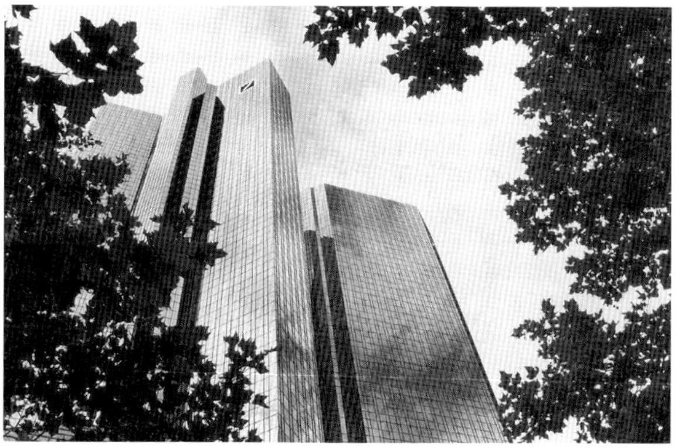

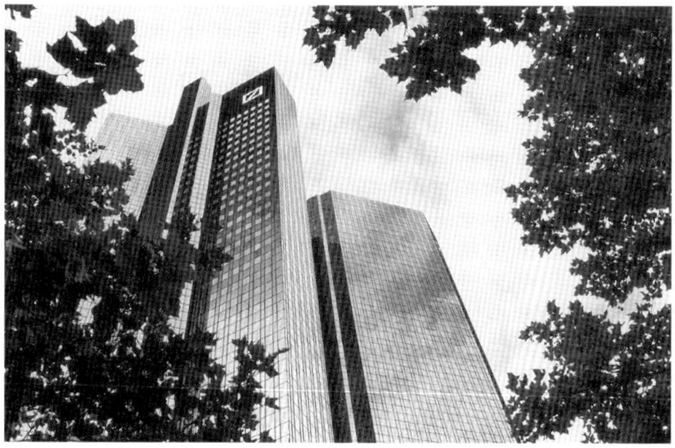

Fig. 153: a and b.: *At a certain angle, reflections on polished surfaces, such as glass, can be eliminated. By rotating and looking through the polarizing filter the effect can be observed. Left: without polarizing filter; right: with polarizing filter.*

Polarizing filters are particularly useful for landscape photography on color film. Since a portion of natural light is also polarized, it can be controlled to a certain extent by polarizing filters. The degree of polarization of light from the sky depends on the position of the sun and on atmospheric haze. The amount of polarization is greater at high altitudes. The greater the polarization, the stronger the effect of a polarizing filter. The greatest amount of polarized light occurs at right angles to the direction of sunlight. Therefore, the most dramatic polarizing effects can be achieved with lateral sunlight (usually the best illumination for photography). Also in landscape photography the effect depends on the focal length of the lens. This is easy to understand if one visualizes the following situation: A landscape bathed in lateral sunlight is photographed with a 21mm super-wide angle lens. As a result of the large angle of view of more than 90 degrees, the intensity of the polarizing effect will vary across the picture because the angles subtended by various points across the subject area relative to the sun and the camera also vary substantially. While one side of the picture is nearly backlighted, the other side is nearly frontlighted. Sunlight coming in at an angle of 90° relative to the optical axis of the lens (for the most dramatic polarizing effects) therefore occurs only strictly in the direction the camera is pointed, i.e. in the center of the picture.

A rotating polarizing filter is available for the Leica M camera. Slip-on adapters with different diameters permit the use of the universal polarizing filter on most lenses of the current Leica M program, however also on many of the earlier Leica M lenses if their filter diameter is not greater than E49.

Once the appropriate adapter has been screwed into the lens mount, the swing-out mount is attached and held in place by a lock screw. Then the polarizing filter with its rotary mount and lens hood can be swung out laterally by 180°. In that position it is possible to look past the lens and through the filter in order to observe the effect while rotating the filter. When the desired effect is reached, the filter is simply swung back over the lens (in the case of Leica M5 cameras with TTL exposure metering, exposure is measured through the polarizing filter) and the photograph is taken. Since polarizing filters always have the same effect after being rotated by 180°, the effect observed while the filter was swung out is retained completely after the filter is swung back over the lens.

The universal polarizing filter comes with adapters for filter mounts E 39 and E 46. The adapter for E 49 and special models for the 135mm f/3.4 Apo-Telyt-M lens and the (earlier) 135mm f/4 Tele-Elmar-M lens are available as accessories. Leica offers an adapter ring for E 67 polarizing filters to be used with the 28-25-50mm f/4 Tri-Elmar-M ASPH. lens. The adapter ring has an opening between the threaded mount for the lens (E 49) and the filter threaded mount. The effect of the screwed-on polarizing filter can be viewed directly through the camera viewfinder.

This equips Leica M photographers with a polarizing filter that is specifically designed for convenient use with range-viewfinder cameras and which will fit the most important lenses that are preferred for landscape photography.

Neutral density filters (ND)

Filters used to reduce light intensity. Filter factors: 2, 4, or 8.

Neutral filters are to block light across the entire visible spectrum. Until recently, these filters were used primarily in motion picture photography, but now they are also being used more and more in still photography. For example, when very long exposure times are required to achieve a creative effect, or when the camera's fastest shutter speed is not fast enough to produce the correct exposure with the lens wide open (for shallow depth of field) in bright light.

Filters for color photography

The variety of different colors and densities of these filters is enormous. In conjunction with film manufacturers, specialized filter manufacturers offer the most important filters as part of their standard product lines, but no individual firm has a complete line of every filter that exists. The many filter variations can be classified in three main groups:

- Conversion filters
- Color-compensating filters
- Special effect filters

The characteristics of conversion filters and of color-compensating filters are described below. Special effect filters are not practical for use with range-viewfinder cameras, because their effects cannot be adjusted without viewing through the lens.

Conversion filters

These filters adapt the color temperature (Kelvin) of a light source to the color balance of the film (such as daylight film or artificial light film) that is being used. Both film and filter manufacturers offer a line of reddish filters and a line of blue filters in various densities (often in the form of gelatin filter squares). The respective density, i.e. the color shift or conversion value, is not stated as a color temperature value, but in mireds or decamireds. The latter are calculated as follows:

$$\frac{1\,000\,000}{\text{Kelvin}} = 1 \text{ Mired}$$

$$10 \text{ Mired} = 1 \text{ Dekamired} = \frac{100\,000}{\text{Kelvin}}$$

The required correction (in decamireds) for lowering or raising the color temperature of a light source can be determined with the aid of a color temperature meter. Blue conversion filters raise the color temperature and lower the mired values. Reddish conversion filters produce a lower color temperature and higher mired values. To take photographs in daylight on color film balanced for artificial light, a reddish conversion filter (light-balancing amber = LA) is needed on the lens. For photographs by artificial light on color film balanced for daylight, a bluish filter (light-balancing blue = LB) is necessary. Some European filter manufacturers still use the earlier designations KR for reddish conversion filter and KB for blue conversion filters. Kodak gelatin filter squares bear the name "Wratten" followed by a number.

Conversion filters with low densities can be used to change certain lighting moods, for instance when a neutral color rendition is wanted for certain reasons in the early morning or late afternoon light. It hardly needs to be mentioned that this destroys the character of these lighting situations. Of course, these moods can also be accentuated by the use of appropriate conversion filters.

Color-compensating filters (CC)

Small shifts in the general color balance of a color film, such as those that may occur with very short or very long exposure times (reciprocity law failure), can be corrected with color-compensating (CC) filters. The latter are available as gelatin filter squares in finely differentiated densities in the colors yellow, magenta, cyan, blue, green, and red.

Corrections for light from fluorescent tubes

Fluorescent tubes do not emit light with a continuous spectrum. This leads to color casts in photographs on color film. An optimum correction is conditionally possible with the use of a combination of different conversion filters. Nearly all filter manufacturers offer a so-called FL-D filter that yields better color reproduction when daylight color-reversal films or color-negative films are used with light from today's daylight fluorescent tubes. The FL-W filter is intended for use with "white" fluorescent tubes, and an FL-B filter is available for use with Type B color reversal films balanced for artificial light. Professionals often use a magenta-colored CC30M color-compensating filter as a "universal" filter for all types of fluorescent tubes.

Filters for black-and-white photography

Black-and-white films translate colors into shades of gray. However, very different colors are often reproduced as similar tones of gray. In this case, color filters can be used to attain better differentiation between those colors. Color filters help to render certain colors lighter or darker. They can also be used for special creative effects. The way it works is that subject colors of the same hue as the filter are reproduced lighter in the color print or transparency, and subject colors that are complementary (or opposite on a color wheel) to the colors of the filter are reproduced darker:

Color	Complementary Color
Blue	Yellow
Green	Magenta
Red	Blue-green

In practical applications, this means:

Filter	Lightens	Darkens
Blue	Blue	Green/Red/Yellow
Green	Green	Red/Blue/Magenta
Red	Red	Blue/Green
Yellow	Green/Red/Yellow	Blue

Yellow filter (Y)

Filter factor: 1.5.
The Panchromatic films that are available today produce such outstandingly accurate tonal gradations that the yellow filter (yellow = Y) has lost much of the significance it once had. Yellowish, greenish, and reddish tones are lightened noticeably, skin tones are lightened and skin blemishes are slightly subdued. Clouds contrast slightly with blue sky. A yellow filter is also important in the photography of snow scenes in sunlight, because it increases the contrast in blue shadow areas. Photographs of snow scenes made without a filter tend to be rather flat.

Yellow-green filter (Y-G)

Filter factor: 2.
Its effects are similar to those of the yellow filter and it produces nearly the same rendering of clouds. Green tones, however, turn out somewhat lighter; therefore it is especially useful for photographs of landscapes with plenty of green, such as scenes in the woods and botanical subjects. It will yield accurate tonal renditions of clouds in beach scenes with-

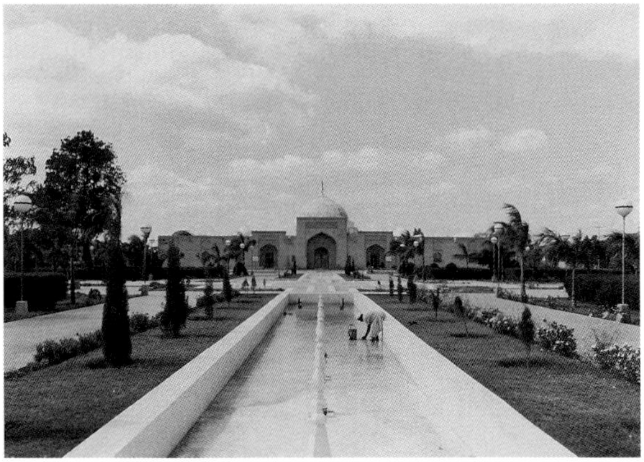 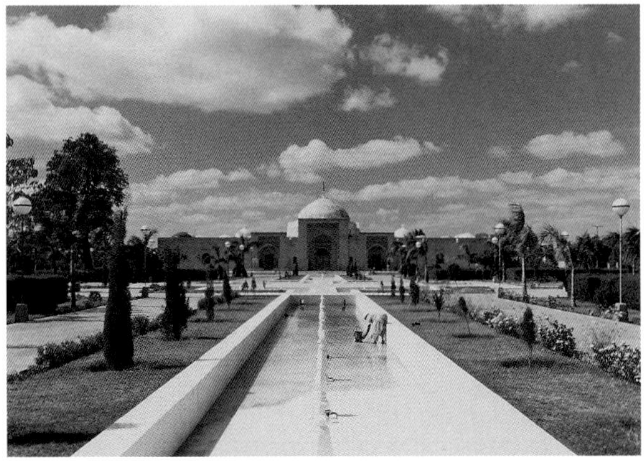

Fig. 154 a and b.: The photograph taken with a yellow-green filter (right) conveys the typical impression of a sunny, crisp day much more effectively than the photograph taken without a filter (left).

out lightening tanned skin tones. Skin tones are actually reproduced darker, but skin blemishes, red blotches on the skin, and freckles will also appear somewhat more prominently.

Green filter (G)

Filter factor 3-4.
This filter produces a decidedly stronger effect than a yellow-green filter by further lightening greens in landscape photographs. Green areas in the shade, like fringes of woods or mountain slopes, still show shadow detail. Red tones, on the other hand, are reproduced very dark. Red roof tiles in landscapes, for instance, are rendered dark gray, and freckles and skin blemishes will appear unnaturally prominent.

Orange filter (O)

Filter factor: 2-5.
Blue is recorded markedly darker, yielding particularly impressive cloud scenes. This filter is good also for winter photographs in sunshine, because it gives more depth to snow by slightly strengthening the shadows. It penetrates mild haze in landscape photography, making distant scenes appear clearer and more brilliant. Red and yellow hues are rendered very light, and suntanned skin also appears much lighter.

Red filter (R)

Filter factor: 6-25.
A red filter has an even stronger effect than an orange filter. It dramatically exaggerates cloud scenes. Since blue is reproduced as nearly black, interesting possibilities present themselves. In architectural photography, for instance, brilliant white building exteriors can be made to stand out dramatically against a dark sky. In distant views, it penetrates haze even better than an orange filter does. Fresh scars, freckles, reddened skin areas and skin blemishes disappear. Skin tones are rendered very light.

Blue filter (B)

Filter factor: 1.5.
Blue filters make panchromatic films act nearly like orthochromatic films when they are exposed in daylight or by electronic flash. Scars and the tiniest veins under the skin become clearly visible. Reddened skin areas are emphasized in relation to their surroundings. Blue filters also help to preserve the misty atmosphere of a foggy scene in daylight on panchromatic film. In artificial light, they prevent blue eyes from being rendered too dark and give more vitality to lips and skin tones.

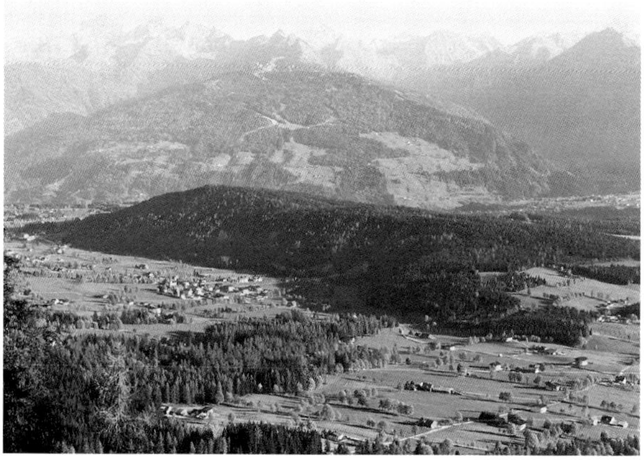 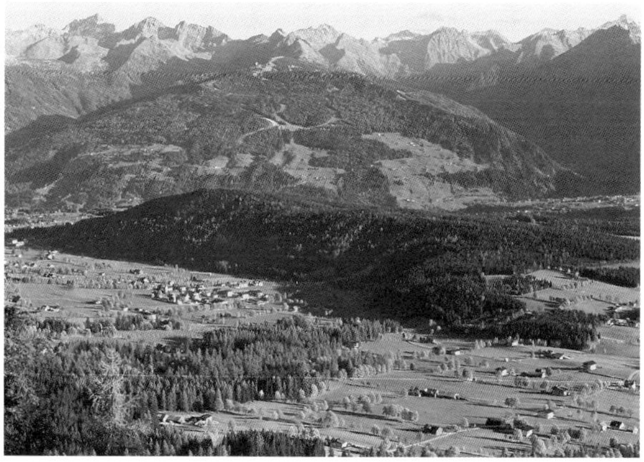

Fig. 155 a and b: An orange filter penetrates the haze and enhances the contours of the mountains (right). The green of the evergreens becomes darker and the fall colors of larch and maple trees are reproduced a little lighter, creating a more successful rendition than the photo made without a filter (left).

Gelatin filter squares and filter systems

Certain filters are available only in the form of gelatin filter squares. These filters are particularly susceptible to finger prints, humidity, and physical damage. Whenever possible, they should be mounted or better yet, cemented between two sheets of plano-parallel glass. They are mounted on the lens by means of filter holders. However, with range-viewfinder cameras, these holders are impractical because they partially obstruct or sometimes totally block the light path of the viewfinder and the rangefinder.

Adapters for photographic filters

When lenses with different filter screw thread diameters are used, larger filters can often be attached to lenses with smaller filter screw threads by means of step-up adapters. However, such adaptations entail the risk that it may no longer be possible to attach the lens hood or to extend the integral lens hood. This markedly increases the danger of internal reflections. Furthermore, larger filters may obstruct the light path of the viewfinder and the rangefinder.

Filter care

Always keep your filters meticulously clean. Take the same care of them as you do for your high-quality Leica M lenses. Several filters used together are seldom worth the effort; usually they merely impair the image quality. Information about the effects that can be attained by the use of filters is available from your photo dealer and from film and filter manufacturers.

Table 13: Leica Filters for M lenses

	UVa-Filters	
Filter size	Finish	Product no.
E 39	black	13 131
E 39	silver	13 132
E 46	black	13 004
E 46	silver	13 005
E 49	black	13 328
E 49	for Tri-Elmar (11 625)	13 329
E 55	black	13 373
E 55	silver	13 374
E 60	black	13 381
	Polarizing-Filters	
Universal-Pol-Filter	for E 39 & E 46	13 356
Adapter	for E 49	14 211
Adapter	for M 3.4/135 mm	14 418
Adapter	for M 4/135 mm	14 213
Adapter ring	for Tri-Elmar (11 625)	14 286

Table 14: Recommended filter sizes and screw thread sizes of earlier Leica M lenses

Leica M lens	Filter size	Screw thread size
Super-Angulon-M	Series 7[1]	M 48 × 0.75
21mm f/3.4	or	
up to Nr. 2 993 700	E 48	
Elmarit-M	E 60	M 60 × 0.75
21mm f/2.8		
Summaron-M	A 36	M 34 × 55 Gg
28mm f/5.6		
Elmarit-M	Series 7[1]	M 48 × 0.75
28mm f/2.8	or	
up to Nr. 2 977 550	E 48	
from Nr. 2 977 551	E 49	M 49 × 0.75
Summaron-M	E 39	M 39 × 0.5
35mm f/3.5		
35mm f/2.8		
Summicron-M		
35mm f/2		
up to Nr. 2 307 450	E 39	M 39 × 0.5
up to Nr. 2 483 503	Series 7[2]	–
up to Nr. 2 974 250	E 39 oder Series 7[2]	M 39 × 0.5
from Nr. 2 974 251	E 39	M 39 × 0.5
Summilux-M		
35mm f/1.4		
up to Nr. 2 166 700	E 41	M 41 × 0. 5
up to Nr. 3 538 211	Series 7[2]	–
Aspherical	E 46	M 46 × 0.75
Elmar-M	E 39	M 39 × 0.5
50mm f/3.5		
50mm f/2.8		
Summicron-M	E 39	M 39 × 0.5
50mm f/2		
up to Nr. 2 925 800		
Summarit-M	E 41	M 41 × 0.5
50mm f/1.5		
Summilux-M	E 43	M 43 × 0.5
50mm f/1.4		
up to Nr. 3 675 530		
Noctilux-M		
50mm f/1.2	Series 8[2]	–
50mm f/1/		
up to Nr. 2 929 656	E 58	M 58 × 0.75
up to Nr. 3 220 708	E 60	M 60 × 0.75
Summilux-M	E 60	M 60 × 0.75
75mm f/1.4		
up to Nr. 3 223 300		
Summarex-M	E 58	M 58 × 0.75
85mm f/1.5		
Elmar-M	E 39	M 39 × 0.5
90mm f/4		
Elmarit-M	E 39	M 39 × 0.5
90mm f/2.8		
Tele-Elmarit-M	E 39	M 39 × 0.5
90mm f/2.8		
Summicron-M		
90mm f/2		
up to Nr. 2 997 000	E 48	M 48 × 0.75
Exception:		
from Nr. 2 813 801		
up to Nr. 2 813 900	E 49	M 49 × 0.75
from Nr. 2997 001		
up to Nr. 3 177 200 and		
from Nr. 3 177 201	E 55	M 55 × 0.75
Hektor-V	E 58	M 58 × 0.75
125mm f/2.5		
Hektor-M	E 39	M 39 × 0.5
135mm f/4.5		
Elmar-M	E 39	M 39 × 0.5
135mm f/4		
Tele-Elmar-M	E 39	M 39 × 0.5
135mm f/4		
up to Nr. 3 658 440		
from Nr. 3 658 441	E 46	M 46 × 0.5
Elmarit-M		
135mm f/2.8	Series 7 with	M 54 × 0.75
up to Nr. 2 788 926	Adapter 14 161	
from Nr. 2 788 927	E 55	M 55 × 0.75
Tri-Elmar-M	E 55	M 55 × 0.75
28-35-50mm f/4 ASPH.		
Elmar-V		
65mm f/3.5		
up to Nr. 2 378 900	E 41	M 41 × 0.5
from Nr. 2 378 901	Series 6	M 44 × 0.75
	with Adapter 14 160	
Telyt-V	E 48	M 48 × 0.75
200mm f/4.5		
Telyt-V	E 58	M 58 × 0.75
200mm f/4		
Telyt-V		
280mm f/4.8		
up to Nr. 2340 592	E 58	M 58 × 0.75
from Nr. 2 340 953	Series 8	M 66 × 0.75
	mit Adapter 14 169	
Telyt-V	Series 7	M 72 × 0.75
400mm f/6.8	filter slot	
Telyt-V	Series 7	M 85 × 0.75[3]
400mm f/5.6	filter slot	
Telyt-V	E 85	M 85 × 0.75
400mm f/5		
Telyt-V	Series 7	M 88 × 0.75[3]
560mm f/6.8	filter slot	
Telyt-V	Series 7	M 113 × 1[3]
560mm f/5.6		
filter slot		
Telyt-S	Series 7	–
800mm f/6.3	filter slot	

1: Filter is held in place by the lens hood.
2: Filter is placed in a two-part lens hood.
3: Engraved front ring must first be unscrewed.

Note: The above table includes screwmount lenses that were still available from Leitz at the time the Leica M System was introduced in 1954, and which could be used an Leica M cameras with their respective bayonet adapters. In the above table, all lens names were given the suffix "M" or "V", even though that suffix may not have been in use when some of these lenses were available.

Leica

Practical photographic techniques

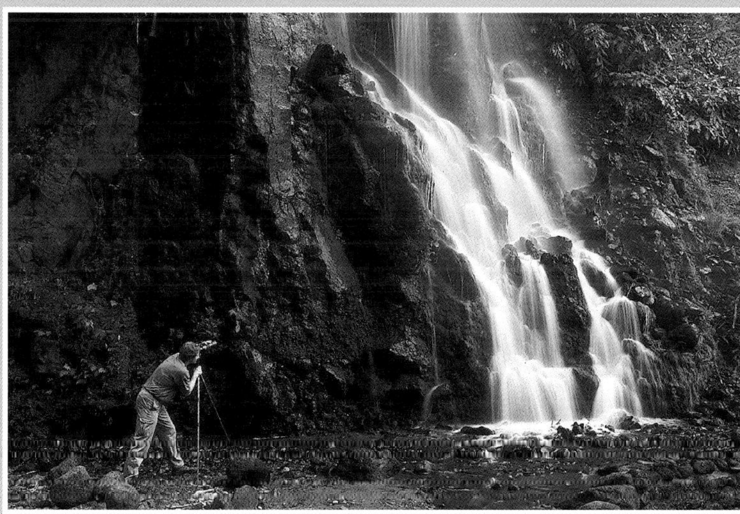

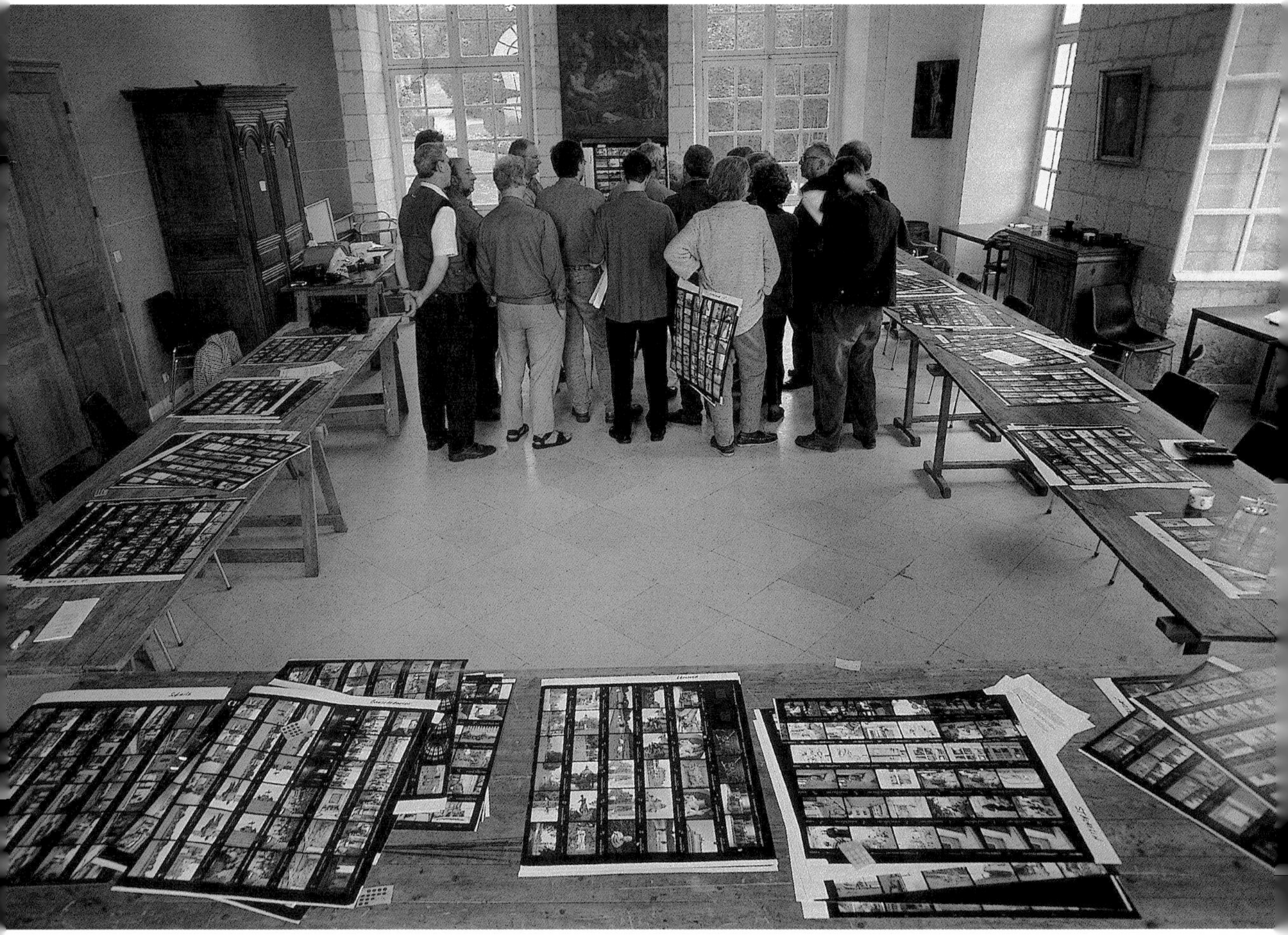

Fig. 156: *At the Leica Academy photographic techniques for better pictures are taught in seminars and workshops – in theory and in practice. Once photographs created during exercises are available, participants find the discussion of the pictures with experts particularly helpful.*

Practical photographic techniques

"You press the button—we do the rest." With that slogan and his first easy-to-use, simple camera of 1888, George Eastman transformed photography into a popular hobby. Since then, technical advances have automated the photographic process. The quality of the materials and reproduction has also improved enormously. Nevertheless, photographers who wish to express their personal creativity by creating compelling images still need to master the basic skills. They cannot rely on technical improvements, in the hope that technology by itself will assure great pictures. Good photographers know that it is primarily their skill that determines whether or not a photograph will be successful. The best photographers constantly strive to improve their skills. Leica M cameras can help to make this easier.

Design features that have proven themselves successful in various models of Leica M cameras are carried forward in subsequent models. The handling of all Leica M cameras remains virtually unchanged, so that there is no difficulty at all when one switches to another M model or uses two different M models. That is quite important, because certain manipulations are necessary for even the simplest of photographs, for example in setting the aperture stop or in focusing. The more creativity a photographer exercises in a photograph, the more equipment functions are used. If these settings can be performed on all camera models with the same hand, are set in the same place, and in the same sequence, photographers do not have to worry when reaching for another M body. This helps them to work faster and with more confidence.

This book does not provide specific operating instructions for the use of the various Leica M cameras and related accessories. Instead, you should read the instruction manual carefully. If you do not have the instruction book for your equipment, for a nominal fee, instruction sheets for currently available equipment can be obtained from Leica Camera or off the Internet. Since detailed descriptions of specific equipment handling requirements can be found in the respective Leica and Leitz user manuals, they are not presented in this book. This leaves all the more room for photographic techniques. While operations are described in general terms, they are based on the practical and technical application of Leica M photography. All serious photographers have to adhere to the rules of photographic technique, if they wish to achieve technically flawless photographs. It does not matter whether they are beginners, advanced photographers, or experienced experts, or whether they are amateurs or professionals. Technically perfect and highly creative photographs are often "merely" the result of superbly mastered photographic technique. Therefore, it is best to learn good technique in order to derive maximum benefit from it.

Basic photographic concepts

Operating a modern camera such as the Leica M7 or M6 TTL does not require special technical training. With a bit of intuition and a number of "dry runs," in which the camera is operated without film, anyone will soon gain the necessary dexterity in handling the camera. But more than just perfect handling is needed for photography. Cameras, lenses, and accessories are only tools to record the photographer's concepts on a visual medium. However, they can only do that if their user, the photographer, becomes familiar with and respects physical realities. The following pages are intended to convey information about such realities from the point of view of an experienced photographer.

Focal length

Most everyone remembers how collector lenses bundle rays of sunlight, producing so concentrated an image on a piece of paper placed in the plane of focus that it would burn a hole in that paper. Under the very same conditions all objects at an infinitely great distance are also imaged sharply on that paper. That distance from the lens to the paper is called the focal length (f). For nearby objects, the distance from the lens to the image plane has to be greater than the focal length. In other words, this distance has to be adjusted (focused) for closer objects (the object plane).

Unfortunately the image created by a collector lens has several aberrations, which manifest themselves very disturbingly in photography (see page 102). By combining several lenses with different curvatures made of different types of glass, collector systems can be created that produce significantly better image quality. This is the basis of photographic lenses. The focal length of a photographic lens is stated in millimeters and is engraved on the front of the lens mount as part of the identification of the lens.

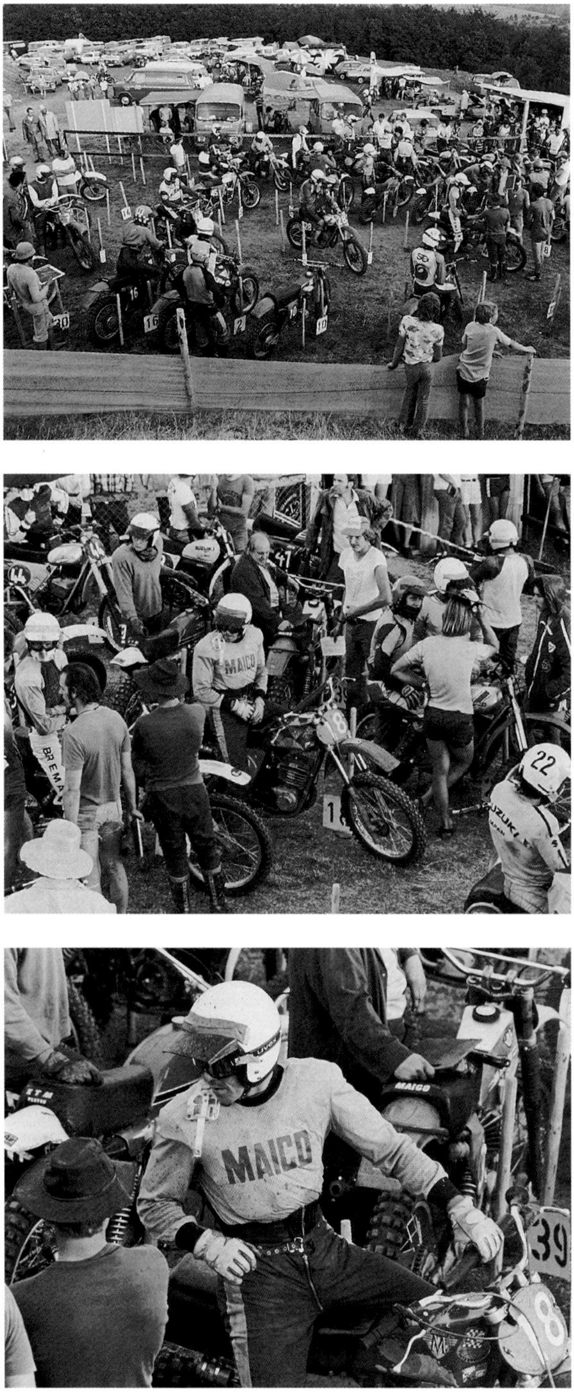

Fig. 157: *From the same camera position, different focal lengths cover different views of the same subject.*

Fig. G1 – G4: *When pictures are taken in snow, a substitute meter reading most frequently produces the best exposure (top). This is how it is done (bottom row of shots): Due to the snowy mountains, the glaciers, and the bright reflections in water, which are within the area measured by the exposure meter, the film will be underexposed by 1.5 EV (left). Underexposure is even greater (-2 EV) if the snowy area alone is measured (center). If the aperture is opened two f/stops (2 EV) more than indicated by the exposure meter, the exposure is correct (right). Now the picture can be reframed with the desired cropping.*

Fig. G5 – G10: *A few examples of subjects that are best metered up close. If this is not possible, a substitute reading can be taken.*

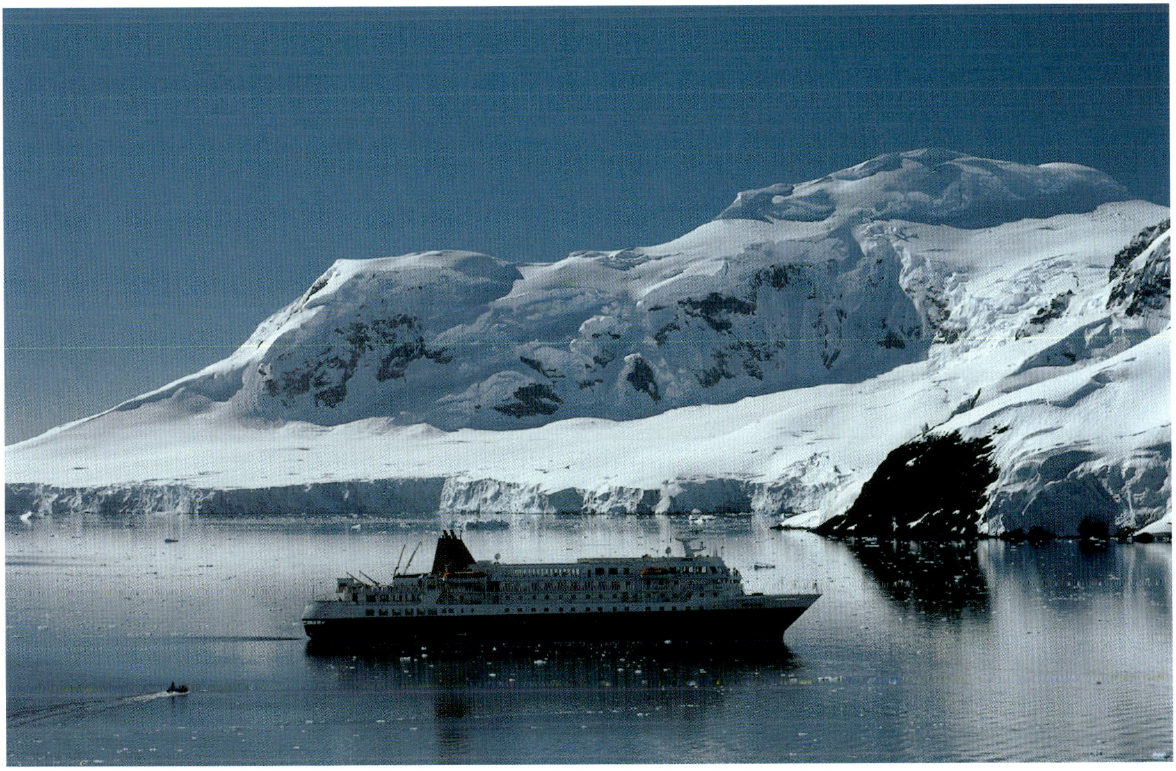

Fig. G1

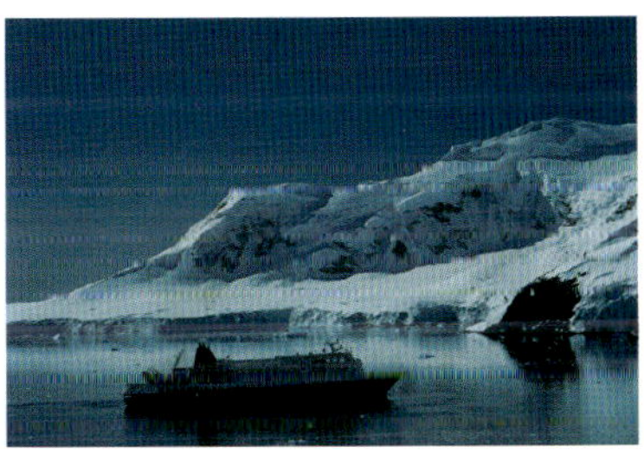

Fig. G2

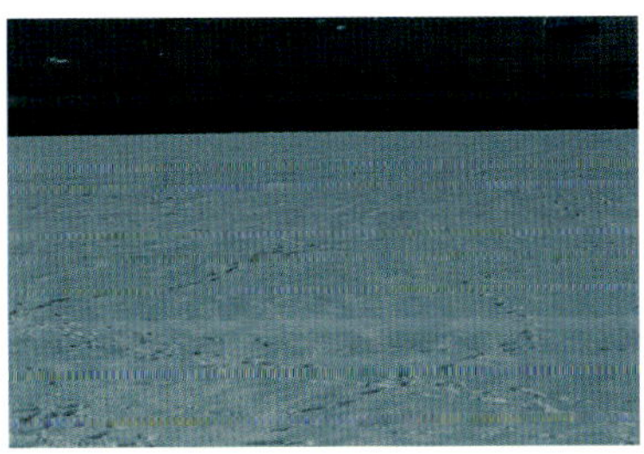

Fig. G3

Fig. G4

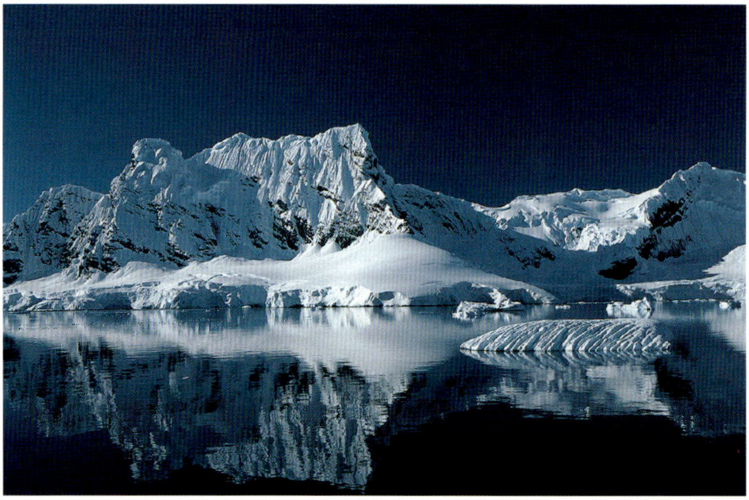

Fig. G5

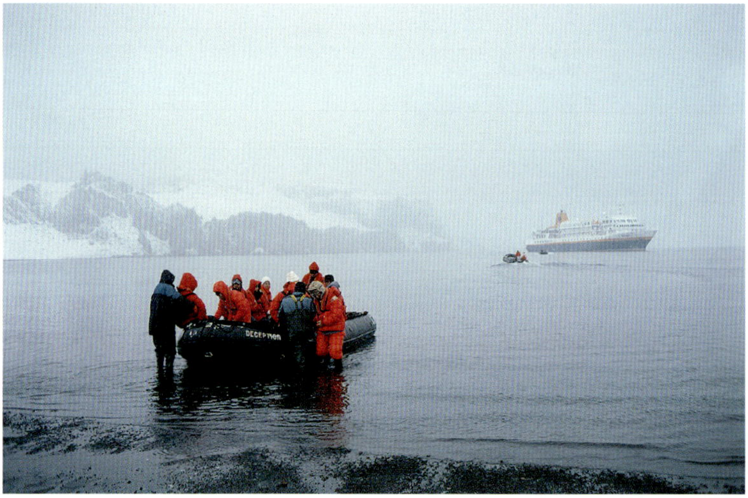

Fig. G6

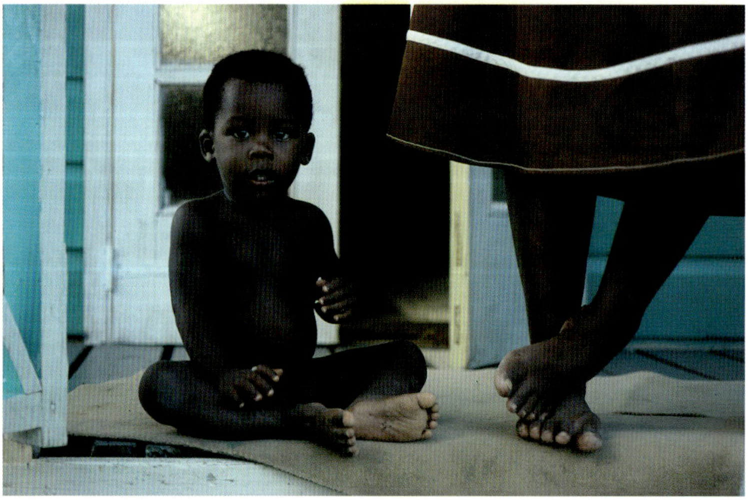

Fig. G7

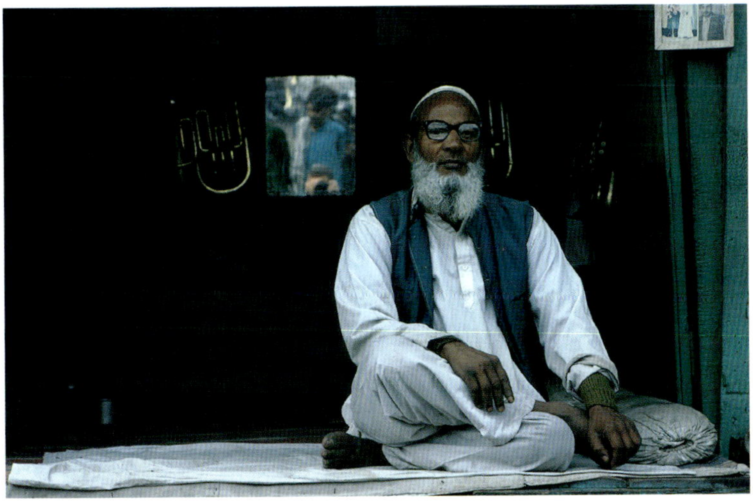

Fig. G8

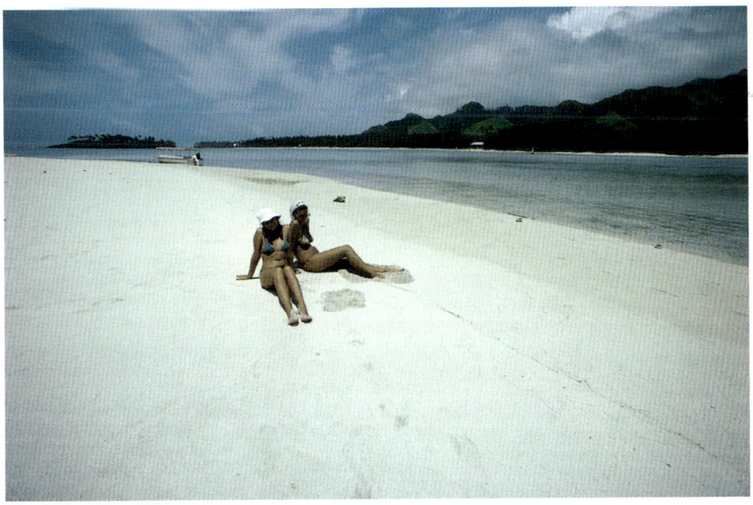

Fig. G9

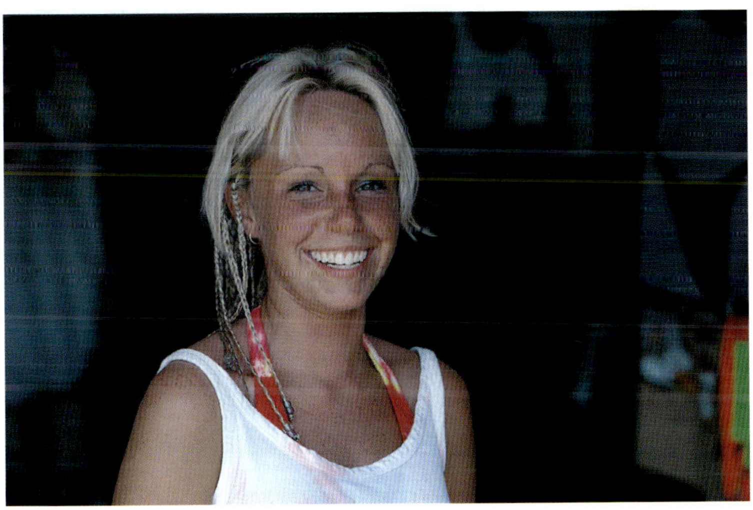

Fig. G10

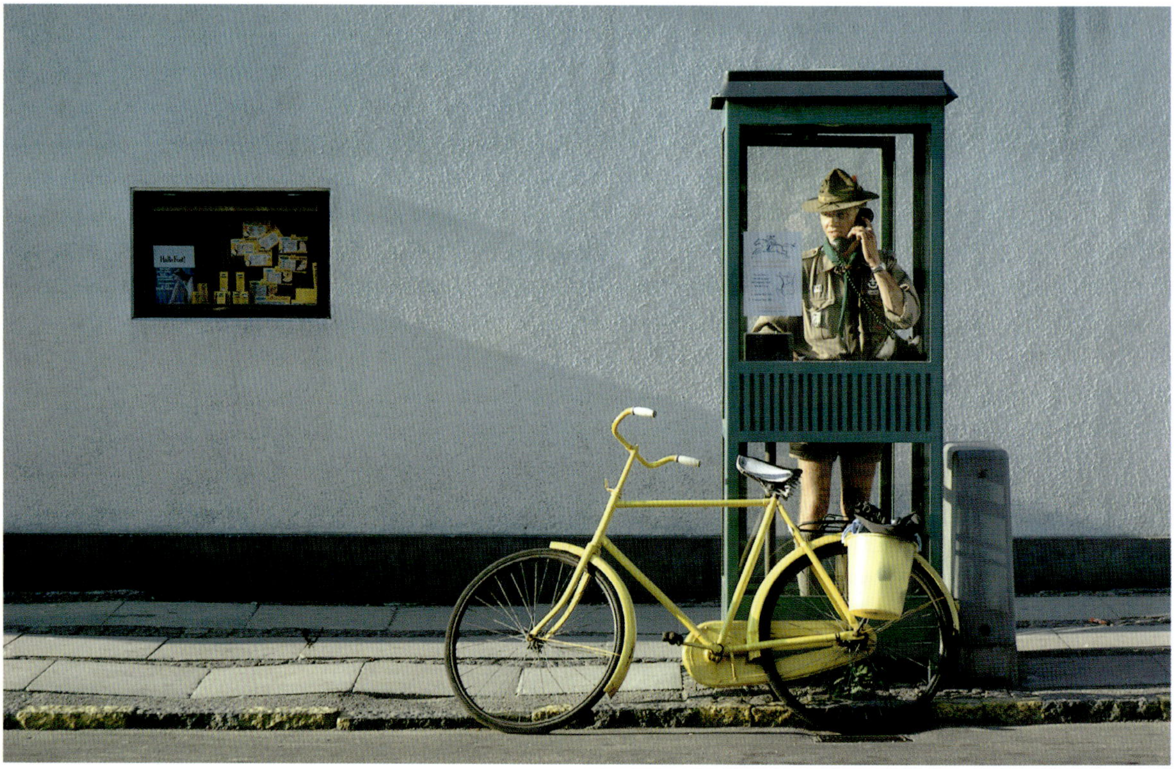

Fig. G11

Fig. G12

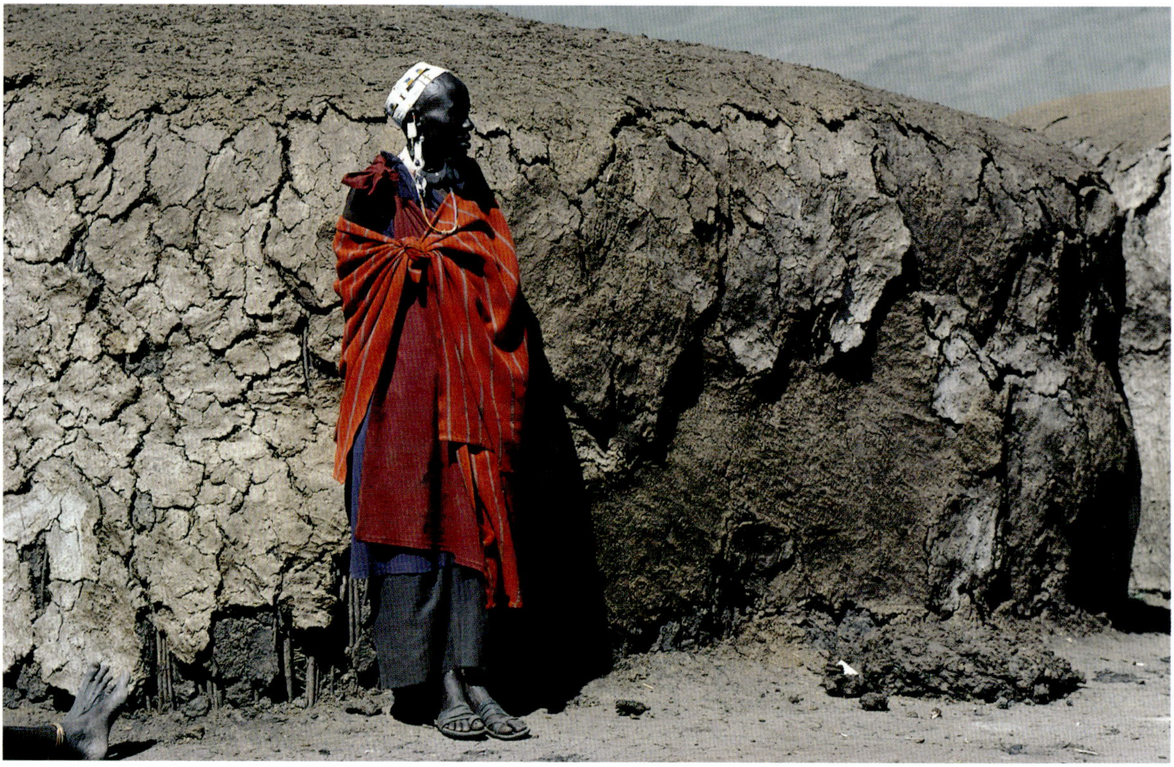

On new Leica M lenses, the focal length is engraved in large digits next to the depth-of-field scale in a very visible location, so that a desired lens can very quickly be picked out from a group of look-alike lenses. The focal length of a lens determines the size of the image of an object. The longer the focal length, the larger will an object be imaged at the same camera distance. Normal or standard lenses are lenses with focal lengths corresponding approximately to the diagonal of the picture format. For 35mm cameras (negative format 24 x 36 mm), they are the 50mm lenses. Lenses for 35mm cameras that have focal lengths longer than 50mm are called long or telephoto lenses, and those that have shorter focal lengths are called wide-angle lenses.

The designation "wide angle" alerts us to the fact that the angle of view of a lens is a function of its focal length. The larger the angle of view, the more details of our surroundings will be recorded on film. Conversely, lenses with smaller angles of view, i.e. with longer focal lengths, will cover fewer details. Since the negative size remains constant at 24 x 36 mm, it follows that, while a wide-angle lens will cover a great many details, it will also reproduce them in a very tiny size. Lenses with longer focal lengths cover fewer details, but they will reproduce them much larger. These relationships of physics and optics can be utilized deliberately as one of the creative elements in the practice of photography.

Fig. G11: *This snapshot taken across the street was very successful due to the graphic interplay of shapes and colors. The photographer shot the picture quickly before the light changed and the scene was obliterated by the traffic on the street.*

Fig. G 12: *This photo is successful due to the interplay of the strong colors and textures of the man's dark skin, the bright clothes, and the rough rocks in the background.*

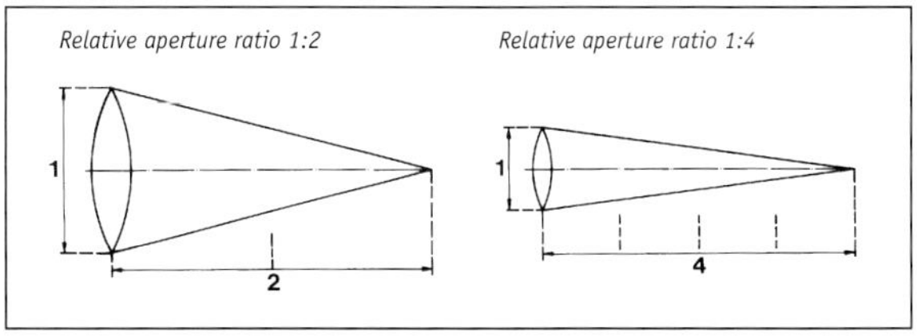

Fig. 158: *A lens' relative aperture is a measure of its light gathering power.*

Light-gathering power

The light-gathering power of a lens is expressed as the ratio of the diameter of its maximum aperture to its focal length, hence the term "relative aperture." The ratio is also engraved on the front of the lens mount as part of the full identification of the lens. In this identification, the diameter of the maximum aperture is made equal to 1. Thus, a relative aperture ratio of 1:2 (= f/2), for example, means that the focal length is twice as long as the diameter of the maximum aperture of the lens.

Aperture

In order to reduce the light-gathering power of a lens, its aperture can be continuously reduced by means of a built-in iris diaphragm. This allows less light to reach the film. Thus, by varying the aperture, one can, among other things, regulate the exact amount of light that is required for correct exposure.

The f/number indicates the relative aperture ratio that is being used, for instance, at f/5.6 the relative aperture ratio is 1:5.6, at f/8 it is 1:8, and so on. For practical reasons, the calibrations have been selected in such a way that each successive f/stop setting represents half the light-gathering ablity of the preceding one, thus requiring twice the exposure time for the same exposure. Today's lenses are calibrated with the following international sequence of f/stops:

1 – 1.4 – 2 – 2.8 – 4 – 5.6 – 8 – 11 – 16 – 22 – 32.

Leica M lenses have additional settings for half stops.

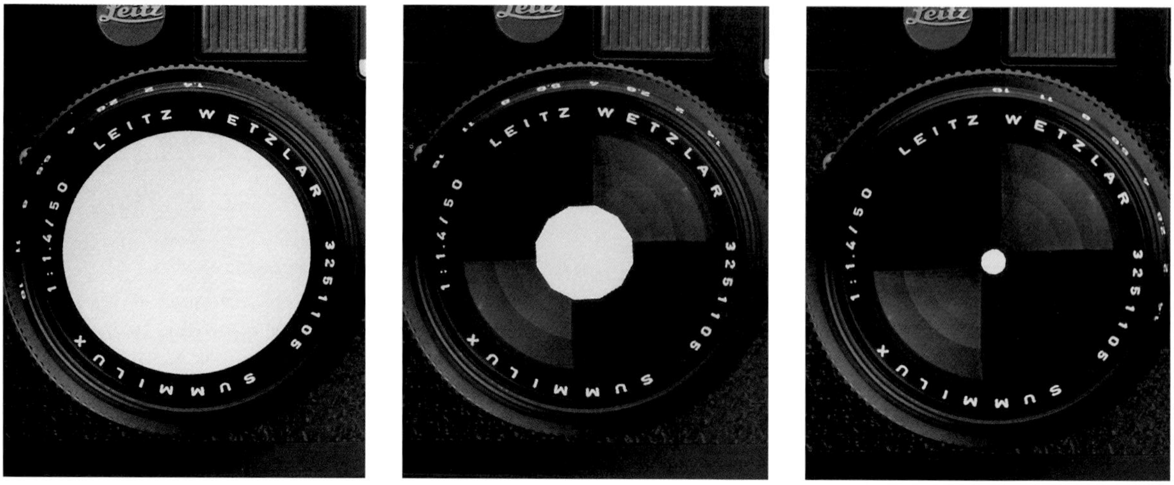

***Fig. 159:** Reducing light gathering power by stopping down. From left to right: aperture setting f/1.4, aperture setting f/4, aperture setting f/16.*

Depth of field

Based on the laws of optics, it is easy to prove that a lens will form only a sharp image of the object plane on which it has been focused. This sharp image on the corresponding image plane consists of many millions of picture elements or pixels.

On any plane in front of, or behind the image plane, a point will no longer be reproduced as a point, but as an unsharp disc, the so-called circle of confusion. But our eyes discern a deviation from a sharp (point-shaped) reproduction of a point only when the circles of confusion exceed a certain minimum size. In other words, because of the limitations of the natural acuity of our eyes, we also perceive some objects, which are actually situated just in front of, or just behind the object plane, to be sharp in the reproduction. The range from the nearest element this side of the object plane to the furthest element beyond that plane that will still not be perceived as unsharp in the photograph is called depth of field.

The two diagrams in in Fig. 160 (see page 223) show quite clearly that the size of the circle of confusion is reduced and depth of field is increased when the aperture of the lens is stopped down. Depth of field is also strongly dependent on the reproduction ratio: The larger an object is reproduced in the image, the shallower will be the depth of field. This phenomenon often leads to the erroneous assumption that wide-angle lenses have greater depth of field than telephoto lenses. By taking two separate photographs in which the object is reproduced in the same size, i.e. one photograph taken from nearby with a wide-angle lens, and the other one taken from further away with a telephoto lens, it can easily be proven that the depth of field is precisely the same for both lenses.

Making use of depth of field

The ability to control the depth of field by adjusting the aperture of the lens plays an important role in composing a photograph. By using a small depth of field, for instance, the sharp image of a face can be made to stand out from an unsharp background. Conversely, by using a large depth of field, a person that appears sharp in the foreground of a photojournalistic picture can be shown in context with events going on in a background, which has also been kept in focus. The use of depth of field in composing a picture is made easy by the depth-of-field scale on the lens. That scale shows the extent of the depth of field for a given aperture setting in relation to the distance at which the lens is focused.

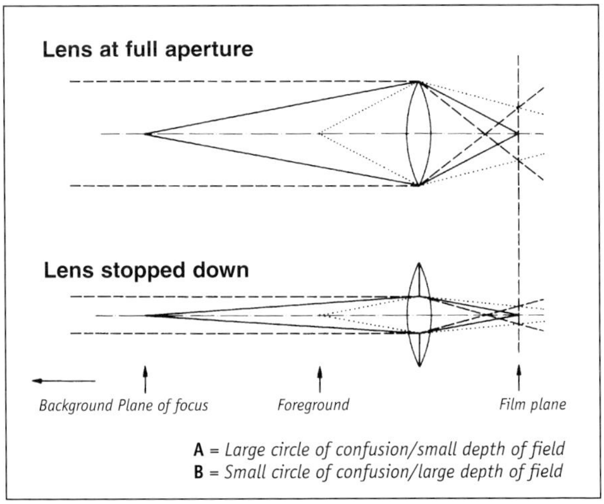

Fig. 160: *This diagram illustrates the effect of aperture on the size of the circle of confusion and thus, the amount of depth of field.*

In making conscious use of the depth-of-field scale, one will soon notice that in the normal picture-taking range of about 1 m (3 feet) to infinity (∞), one third of the depth of field is in front of the object on which the lens is focused (the object plane), and the remaining two thirds are behind that object. Only in close-up photographs is the depth of field about the same on either side of the object plane. An approximate visual evaluation of the depth of field on three-dimensional objects can be made on the ground glass of the Visoflex mirror reflex attachment by stopping the lens down to the preselected value. Since this makes the viewfinder image darker, it takes some experience to judge the effect on the depth of field accurately. This also applies to all single lens reflex cameras.

Leica camera models M2 and M3 have an optical depth of field indicator for 50mm lenses in their viewfinders. The rectangular measuring field of the rangefinder that appears in the center of the viewfinder image has a notch in its top edge and one in its bottom edge. By using these notches, it is easy to determine whether an object in front of, or behind the subject on which the lens is focused, i.e. in front of, or behind the plane of focus, will still be sharp in the reproduction. The upper notch indicates the maximum separation between double contours that an object can generate in the measuring field while still remaining within the depth of field for an aperture of f/16. The lower notch does the same for an aperture of f/5.6 (see Fig. 162).

Exact values for depth of field as a function of focal length, aperture, and focus distance can be found in a depth-of-field table. The depth-of-field values used in this table and on the depth-of-field scales of Leica M lenses, and the width of the notches in the measuring fields in the viewfinders of Leica M2 and M3 cameras are based on a circle of confusion with a diameter of 1/30 mm (0.0013"). If a very high degree of sharpness is required, as it would be for giant enlargements or for projection on large screens, these values would be too generous. In that case it is advisable to select 1/60 mm (0.0007") as the diameter of an acceptable circle of confusion. The depth of field will then be smaller, of course. The new values, based on a smaller circle of confusion, can also be determined from the depth-of-field tables or scales simply by reading the distances opposite the indices for the f/stop with the number that is half as large as the number of the f/stop for which the lens is actually set. For example, if the lens is set at f/16, read the distances for f/8 on the depth-of-field scale.

Note: As a rule, Leica M lenses reach their optimum performance when they are stopped down only two stops from full aperture. Stopping down further only expands the depth of field and increases the danger of unsharp images that may result from camera shake with longer shutter speeds. Therefore, it is wise to stop the lens down just enough to obtain the depth of field that is needed for the composition of the photograph. Using the very smallest apertures may introduce the effects of diffraction (bending of light), which can seriously impair the optical performance of a lens.

Shutter speeds

The amount of light that reaches the film is also regulated by the camera's shutter. The shutter speed can also be an important creative tool in photography. Fast motion, for instance, can be frozen with a fast

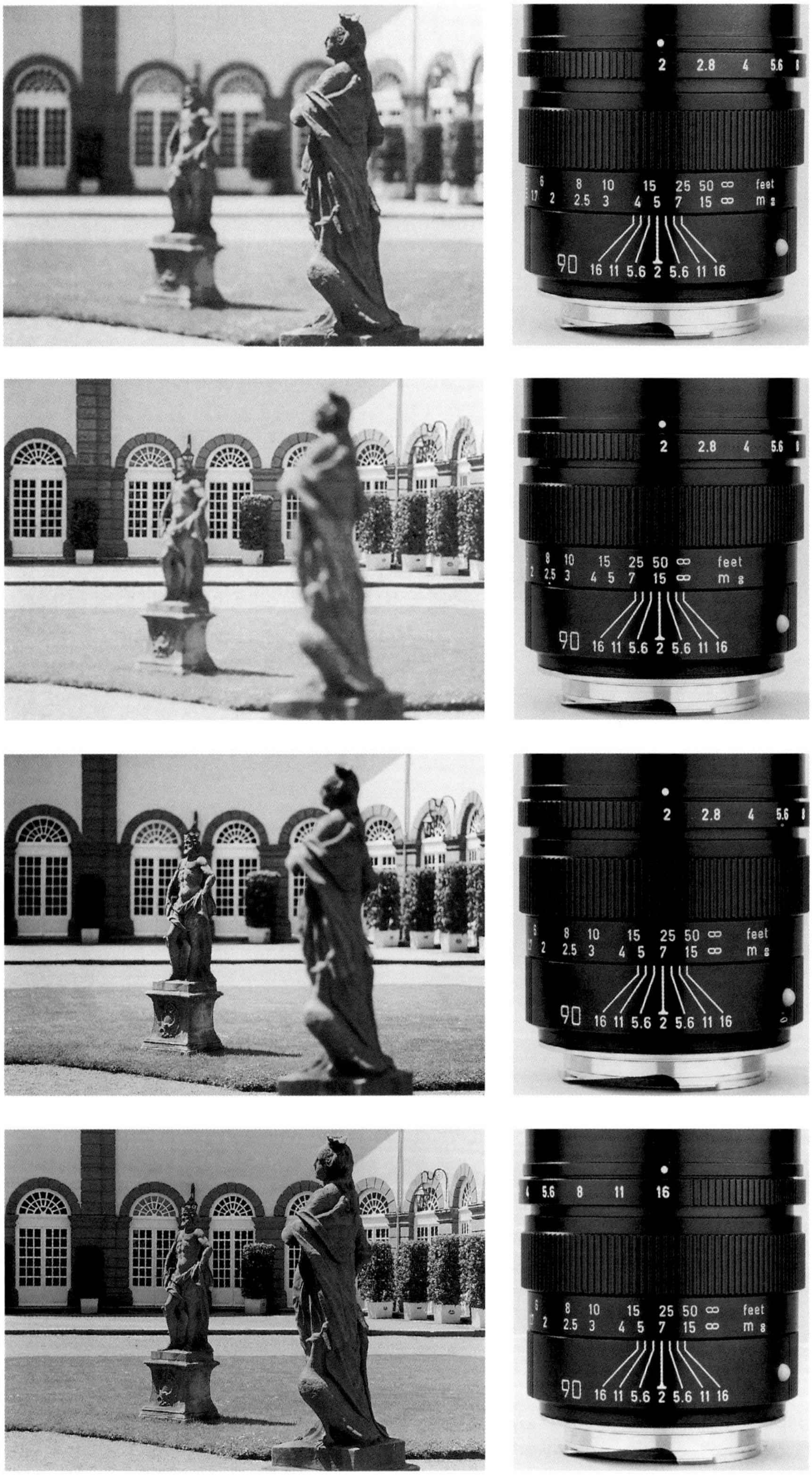

Fig. 161 a – h: *The depth-of-field scale to the left and the right of the focusing index an the lens mount shows approximately how far the depth of field extends in both directions for each aperture setting:*

In this case the lens is focused on the sculpture of a woman in the foreground, which is about 5 m (16' 5") away. The aperture is set at f/2 and the depth of field extends from approximately 4.80 m (15' 9") to 5.20m (17' 1").

The lens is focused on the windowpanes in the doors of the building in the background, which are about 15 m (49' 1") away. The aperture is still set at f/2 and the depth of field extends from approximately 13.5 m (44' 3") to 17 m (55' 9").

The lens is focused on the sculpture of the man, which is about 7.5 m (24' 7") away. The aperture still set at f/2 and depth of field extends from approximately 7. 10 m (23' 4") to 7.95 m (26' 1").

The lens still focused on the sculpture of a man that is about 7.5 m (24' 7") away, but the aperture has been stopped down to f/16. The depth of field has increased approximately 5 m (16' 5") to 15 m (49'1").

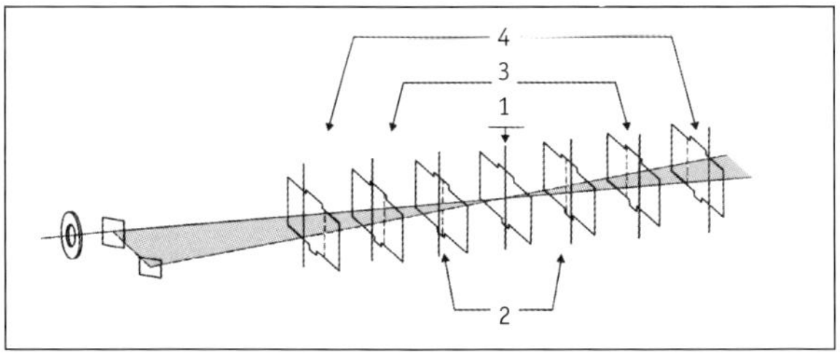

Fig. 162: Optical depth of field indicator. The measuring fields in the range-viewfinders of M2 and M3 cameras can be used to determine whether objects in front of or behind the focused object will appear sharp. 1-Plane of focus, no double contours visible; 2 - Double contours fit within the narrow lower notch in the measuring field: The image will still be sharp when the lens is set at f/5.6; 3-Double contours fit within the wider upper notch in the measuring field. The image will be sharp when the lens is set at f/16; 4 -The separation within double contours is greater than the width of either of the notches: These objects are located outside of the depth of field for either f/5.6 or f/16.

shutter speed, or it can be accentuated through motion blur produced by slow shutter speeds. Unlike lenses with built-in blade shutters, all Leica M cameras have focal-plane shutters. The latter are positioned right next to the film plane, providing a relatively light-tight cover. Lenses and accessories can, therefore, be exchanged conveniently in subdued light with out the risk of fogging the film. A focal-plane shutter consists of two curtains that travel across the film plane, one after the other. The first curtain uncovers the film for the exposure. With fast shutter speeds, the second curtain follows very shortly after the first one, forming a slit that travels across the film plane. The negative is exposed in one continuous sweep from one end to the other. The width of the slit determines the shutter speed. The shutter speeds, which are set by turning the shutter speed dial clockwise, are arranged in such a way that each succeeding one is twice as fast as the preceding one, or half as fast going the other way. One step on the shutter speed dial is equivalent to one stop on the aperture scale.

Therefore several combinations of shutter speed and f/stop can be used to produce equivalent exposures, for example: 1/1000 second at f/4, 1/500 second at f/5.6, or 1/250 second at f/8, and so on. It is up to the photographer to select the combination that best suits his or her creative intentions. Great depth of field, for instance, which is normally needed for landscape photography, requires small apertures and therefore slow shutter speeds; a sports photograph, on the other hand, usually requires a fast shutter speed and a correspondingly larger aperture. The faster a subject moves, the faster the shutter speed has to be if that subject is to be recorded without motion blur in the photograph.

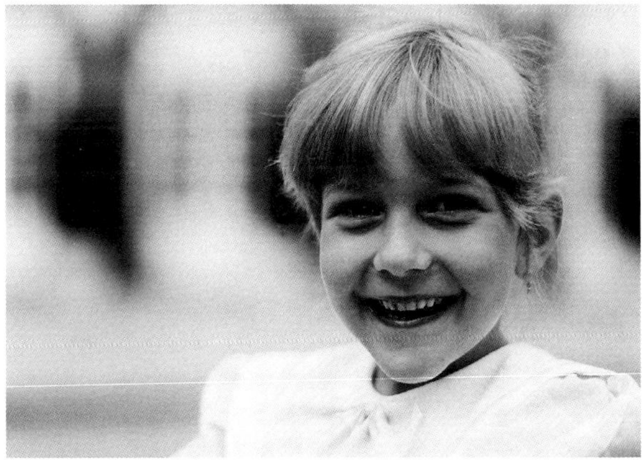

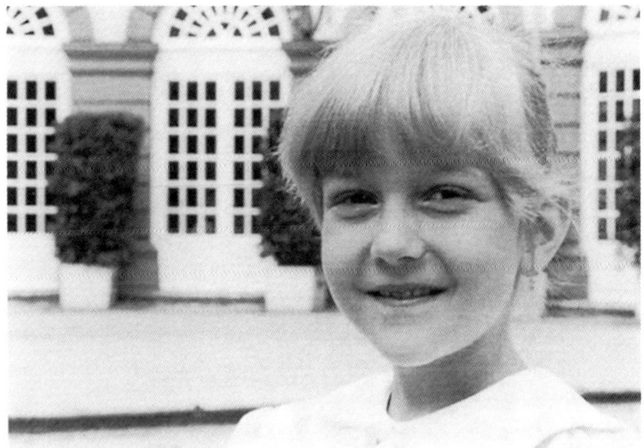

Fig. 163 a and b: *Depth of field is an important creative tool in photography. If it is shallow, for example, it can serve to accentuate the subject in the picture. A large depth of field, on the other hand, permits us to see the surroundings behind the main subject, thus establishing a certain relationship between the subject and its environment.*

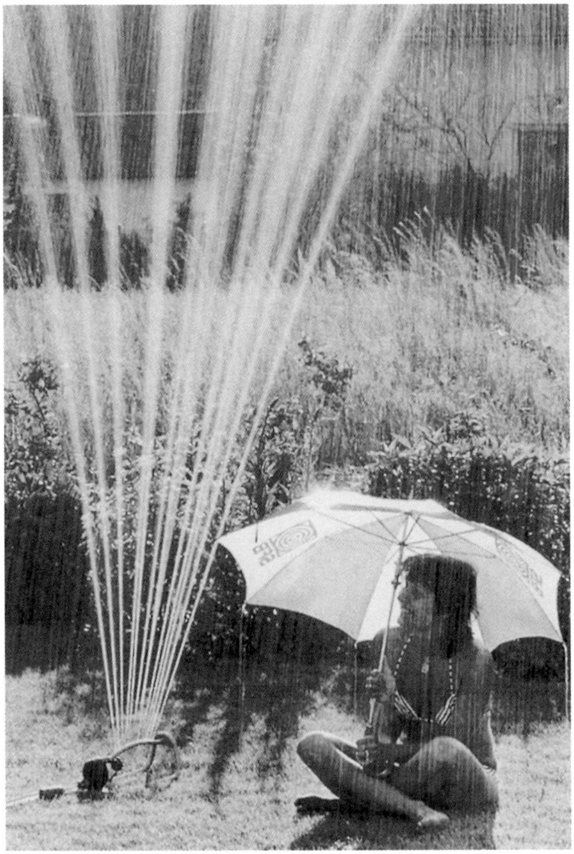

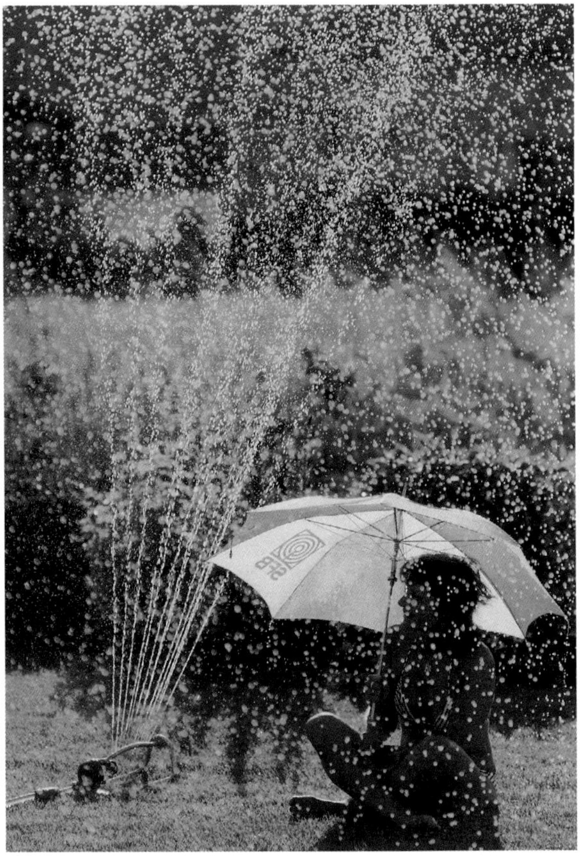

Fig. 164 a and b: *Very high shutter speeds freeze movement. Slower shutter speeds, on the other hand, enhance the impression of movement. Therefore, it is a creative choice of photographers and the effect they wish to create that determines the best choice of a shutter speed. Left: 1/8 second, Right: 1/1000 second.*

The shutter speed that will freeze action depends on:

- the focal length
- the speed of the subject motion
- the subject distance
- the relationship of the angle of view to the direction of motion
- the permissible degree of unsharpness in the photograph (circle of unsharpness = circle of confusion).

For a movement that takes place at a right angle to the optical axis, the slowest shutter speed can be calculated in accordance with the following formula:

$$\text{Shutter Speed} = \frac{\text{Distance from the subject}}{\text{Focal length X Speed of the subject (m/sec.)}} \text{ X circle of confusion}$$

This can best be explained by means of an example. If a cyclist traveling at a speed of 3 m (10 feet) per second passes in front of the camera at a distance of 5 m (16 1/2 feet) and is to be photographed with a 50mm lens, the shutter speed has to be at least

$$\frac{5}{50 \cdot 3} \cdot \frac{1}{30} = \frac{1}{900} \text{ Second}$$

if subject motion blur is to be avoided in the resulting picture. The nearest shutter speed available on the camera is 1/1000 second. If the subject is moving at an angle of 60° to the direction of the camera, the shutter speed can be slower by a factor of 1.2, at 45°, by 1.4, and at 30° by 2, which, in this example, would reduce the shutter speed to 1/500 second. If

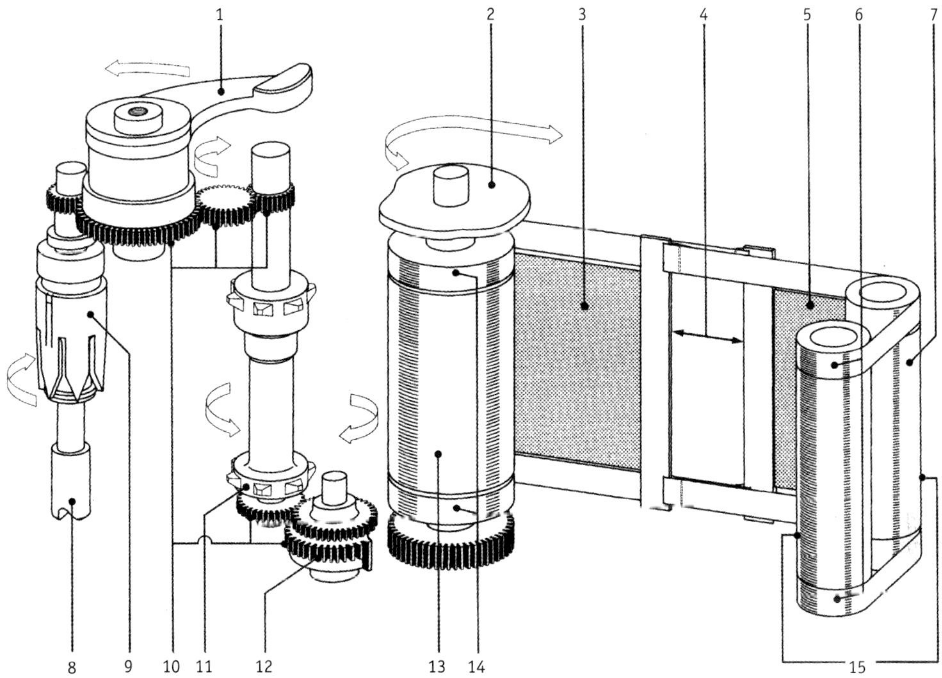

Fig. 165: The rubberized cloth focal-plane shutter of the Leica M2
1=Rapid film advance and shutter wind lever; 2=Cam for fast shutter speeds from 1/30 to 1/1000 second; 3=2nd rubberized-cloth shutter curtain; 4=Variable slit width; 5=1st rubberized-cloth shutter curtain; 6=Drums for coiling up the 2nd shutter curtain; 7=Drum for rolling up the 1st shutter curtain; 8=Coupler for Leicavit and Leica Motor; 9=Spring-loaded shaft for film take-up spool; 10=Gear train for winding the shutter and advancing the film; 11=Sprocket wheel with 8 sprockets (1 turn per frame); 12=Sector gear; 13=Large drum for 2nd shutter curtain; 14=Drum for coiling up the 1st shutter curtain; 15=Small cylinders containing tension springs.

the subject is moving directly towards the camera or directly away from it, the shutter speed can be 3 to 4 times slower than the one calculated with the above formula. In an actual situations, these calculations only represent guidelines. For instance, this calculation does not take into account the cyclist's rapidly moving legs, which may consequently not be quite sharp in the photograph.

The table that follows lists examples of shutter speeds that would be necessary to photograph subjects moving at various speeds and at various distances from the camera at a right angle to the direction of a standard lens.

The shutter speeds below correspond to conventional international geometric shutter speed calibrations.

Subject	Speed (m/s)	Distance from the camera 5 m	10 m	30 m	60 m
Pedestrian	1.25	1/500	1/250	1/60	1/30
Playing children	2.50	1/1000	1/500	1/125	1/60
City traffic	14.00	1/4000	1/2000	1/1000	1/500
Fast train	30.00	1/8000	1/4000	1/2000	1/1000

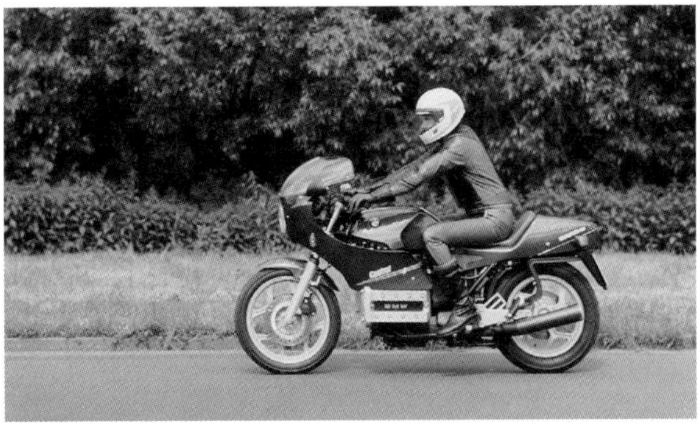

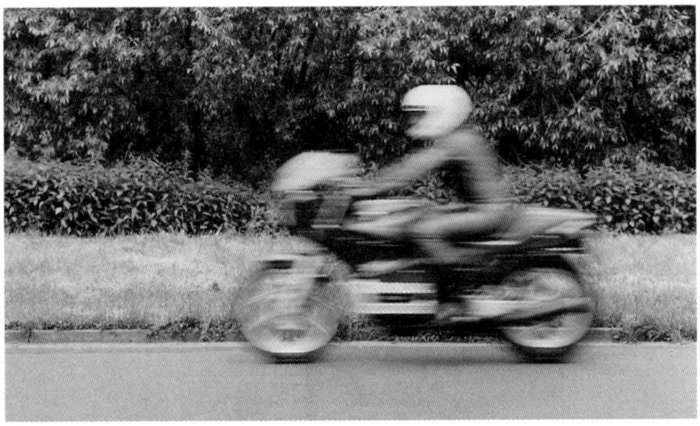

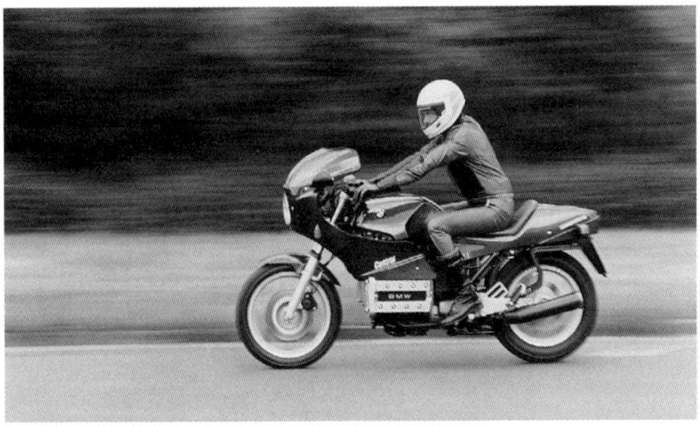

Fig. 166 a – c: *Camera handling, reaction time, and control of the viewfinder image can be optimized with simple exercises. Top and center: With the camera in a fixed position, the motorcycle drove into the picture area. With the large area surrounding bright-line frame in the viewfinder image of a Leica M camera, it was easy to anticipate the approaching motorcycle and to release the shutter at precisely the right moment. Because of the fast shutter speed of 1/1000 second, the motorcycle appears to stand still. However, at 1/60 second it becomes obvious that it was moving. By "panning" the camera along with the fast-moving motorcycle, even the relatively slow shutter speed of 1/30 second is sufficient to produce a sharp image of the vehicle. The blurred background accentuates the impression of speed.*

In actual photographic practice, such calculations would only be performed in very special photographic situations. Normally, after a little practice with the camera, one soon becomes familiar enough with one's equipment to make such calculations unnecessary. Shutter speed calibrations are engraved on the camera's shutter speed dial without the numerator and the fraction line. Therefore, "60" means 1/60 second.

The shutter speed dial on Leica cameras has the following calibrations: B, 1, 2, 4, 8, 15, 30, 60, 125, 250, 500, 1000. The Leica M7 also has "2s" and "4s" for two and four seconds, respectively. With the shutter speed dial set at "B" the shutter remains open as long as the shutter release button is depressed. The flash symbol stands for the shortest flash synchronization time of 1/50 second. The Leica M TTL features the additional engraving "OFF;" the M7 features the additional engraving "AUTO."

Proper handholding of Leica M cameras

Most of the activities that we engage in have been acquired through practice. For special activities we subject ourselves to long learning courses and strict schedules. This applies to professions and to hobbies alike. For example, there is no driver who has not taken a driving course, hardly a skier who has not spent long hours with a skiing instructor to practice conquering the slopes, and potters and amateur painters too, take appropriate courses at their local schools.

A famous musician once said, "If you buy an organ, you should also take the trouble to learn how to play it. Otherwise it is easier to make tolerable music by cranking a barrel organ or by playing a record player." The same applies to photography. If you want to use a camera for photography, you must first learn how to take photographs. Technical features mentioned in the advertisements, such as the various automatic modes and costly electronic components do not change that at all. They cannot, even with all the advances in this field, replace missing qualifications of the photographer, they generally serve only to enhance convenience.

Now as before, it continues to be valid that a photographer should know a camera so well that he should be able to operate it in his sleep. Focusing, setting exposure, and film changing, for instance, should require mere moments, even under adverse conditions. The respective movements should be practiced until they become instinctive. Only after having mastered the technique, can one devote oneself completely to observation of the subject and to creativity. Provided these creative activities have been examined beforehand.

A photographer has to be willing to pursue things. It is rare that something will turn up spontaneously in front of the camera. Sometimes there will be enormous challenges to patience before an objective is achieved. A sixth sense and an open mind, coupled with mobility are characteristics of a good 35mm photographer.

Holding the camera correctly

An important requirement for technically excellent photographs is a steady hold on the camera and a smooth release of the shutter. A large number of photographs are blurred by improper camera handling and by releasing the shutter carelessly. Leica M cameras should always be grasped firmly and, whenever possible, they should be steadied against something. That is normally the head, more specifically the eyebrow and the nose of the photographer. The right round end of the baseplate rests in the palm of the photographer's right hand. The thumb of that hand hooks into the camera's swung-out rapid wind lever, and the index finger rests on the shutter release button. The left hand holds the lens from below in such a way that its palm faces up. The left thumb then automatically rests on the left side of the lens as seen from the photographer's side. This firm way of holding the camera prevents fingers from obstructing the light path to the viewfinder and to the rangefinder.

The same way of holding the camera is recommended for eyeglass wearers and for photographers who look through the viewfinder with their left eye. Even though these photographers are at a slight disadvantage when looking through the viewfinder, they should strive to rest their right hand against their head in such a way that the Leica M camera will be well-braced. The eye should always be as close to the viewfinder eyepiece as possible. Looking through the viewfinder at a slight angle - but through its center - may sometimes be more convenient. With horizontal photographs, both upper arms of the photographer should be rested firmly (but not pressed) against the body. For vertical pictures, the camera is first held horizontally for focusing and then turned into the vertical position. The right hand continues to hold the camera in the same way and rests against the forehead, while the left hand is best moved from the lens to grasp the camera body. In addition, a particularly convenient way of holding the camera can be used for very long exposures in the vertical position: in this position, the thumb rests on the shutter release bowl, while the index finger holds the baseplate approximately where the tripod socket is located. To release the shutter, the thumb and the index finger are pressed towards each other as in a grip. Because of this pressure from both sides, which inherently occurs simultaneously, the camera can be supported very steadily. To change to the vertical format, however, both hands have to change their grip.

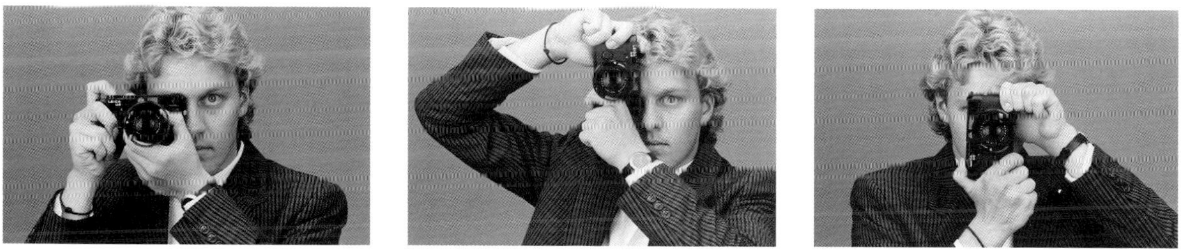

Fig. 167 a – c: *Proper handholding technique for horizontal and vertical compositions.*

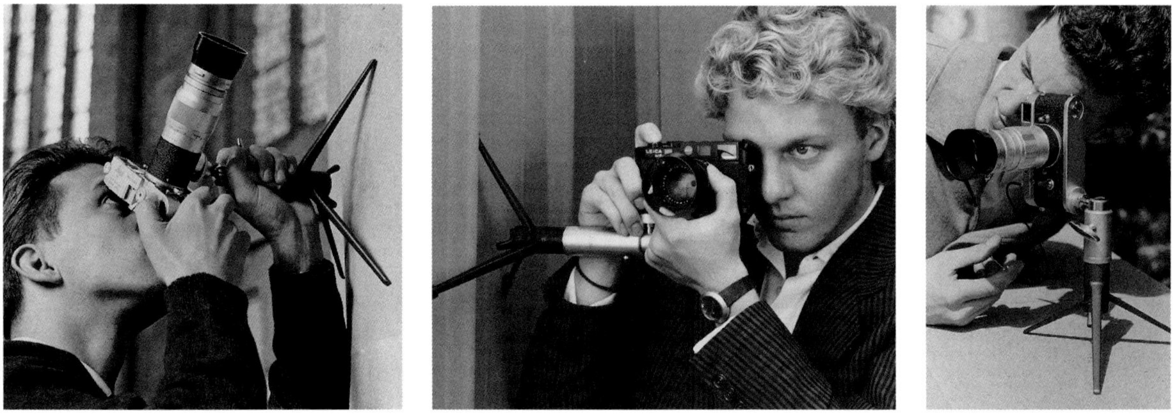

Fig. 168 a – c: A tabletop tripod is a handy tool for preventing camera shake.

The handle of the M camera is not intended exclusively for convenience, it allows the photographer to hold the Leica M in a steady manner. In particular if a photographer requires the second hand for something else, e.g., holding on to something or, for better illumination, "guides" the flash with an extended arm.

When the camera is in an eveready case, the front cover of the case has to be held out of the way during vertical exposures, so that parts of it will not cover the front element of the lens. Thus, It is better to unsnap the front part of the case to begin with. When the opportunity presents itself, one should rest one's elbows on a solid surface or use a small Leica tripod, which can be used not only to stand on a table, but it can also be pressed against flat vertical surfaces, like walls, columns and trees. The illustrations on pages 170 and 229 show examples of good camera-holding techniques.

The shutter should always be released gently, never abruptly. The index finger should be bent. Only the tip of the index finger should rest on the shutter release button and the finger should not rest on the camera. One should devote special attention to this technique in the beginning. Holding the camera correctly and releasing the shutter smoothly permits easy picture-taking with a standard lens at shutter speeds as low as 1/15 second without camera shake.

Good posture is important

The posture of the photographer has not been mentioned up to now. No one can take sharp pictures at long shutter speeds while standing on one leg or on tiptoes. In most cases, a steady position is achieved by assuming the basic stance taught in gymnastics, which is relaxed and with legs slightly spread apart.

When photographing with a Visoflex 2 or 3 and lenses with long focal lengths, the best posture is that of a rifleman, with the left leg and the left shoulder moved slightly forward. This enables the left hand to support and to manipulate the lens conveniently while the right index finger operates the shutter release.

Leaning against door frames, trees, walls, or light posts while taking a picture is not a sign of laziness—quite the contrary, it shows good form in reducing the danger of camera movement. On the other hand, one should never lean against anything while taking pictures from a moving ship, bus, train or airplane, because the many vibrations would inevitably be transmitted to the camera. This also applies to bridges with heavy traffic and to certain staircases when they are in heavy use. In those situations the best precaution is to bend the knees slightly in order to absorb the vibrations like a spring.

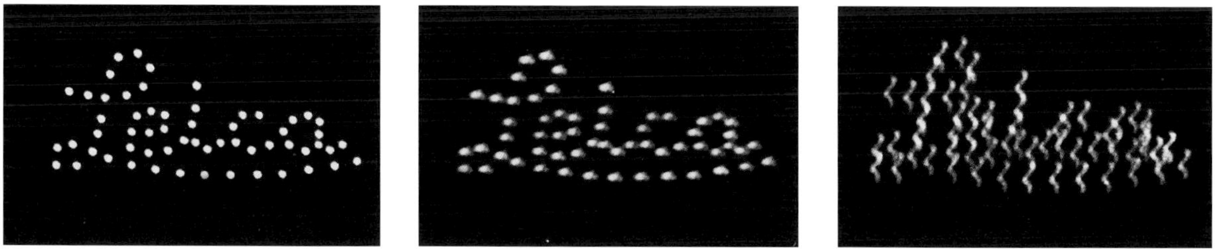

Fig. 169 a – c: Photographing an opaque piece of cardboard with tiny needle holes, which has been fastened to the inside of a window, is a good way to evaluate camera shake. The ability to hold the camera steady depends on the photographer. (a) 1/15 second = unnoticeable camera shake; (b) 1/8 second = moderate camera shake; (c) 1/2 second = major camera shake.

The camera motion test

All photographers should conduct a camera motion test in order to determine which technique of holding a camera works best for them, and also to discover their own limitations. To perform this test, take a piece of matte black cardboard about 30 x 40 cm (12" x 16") in size and punch a dozen holes in its center, using a darning needle or a thin nail with a diameter of approximately 1 mm (roughly 1/32"). Place this cardboard in front of a bright light source such as a desk lamp, or attach it to the inside of a window, so that the holes will be illuminated from behind.

The central portion of that cardboard is then photographed with black-and-white film at different distances, depending on the focal length of the lens being used. With a 50mm lens, for example, the distance should be about 1 m (3'3"), and with a 135mm lens it should be slightly more than 1.5 m (5 feet). All shutter speeds from 1/4 to 1/250 second should used two or three times with their corresponding apertures.

Note: It is easy to determine the correct combinations of shutter speed and aperture simply by making a meter reading of the light source without the cardboard (selectively) in place, and by then multiplying the exposure time by 4.

Looking at the processed negatives with a magnifier, you can determine—from the shape of the images of the holes—whether or not the camera moved during the exposure. Only if those holes appear perfectly round, can one claim to have a steady hand (see Fig. 169). The evaluation of these images is much easier when the negatives are mounted like regular slides and projected on a large screen. This camera motion test can also be used to study the photographer's breathing technique. For long exposure times, one should hold one's breath after exhaling first. This test also proves that the claim that better results can be obtained with the selftimer when the camera is on a wobbly tripod is an old wives' tale.

Become familiar with your equipment

Handling photographic equipment can often be practiced without the use of film. But sometimes the subsequent evaluation of results by means of actual photographs is indispensable. Inexpensive black-and-white films can be used for this purpose, and they need not be enlarged after processing, because they can be examined directly with a magnifier. Standard Leica M lenses can be used as magnifiers, but caution must be exercised, because the eye of the observer has to be very close to the lens, and this creates the danger of eyelashes smudging the glass surface.

Recognize sharp focus

Focusing with the long-base rangefinder of a Leica M camera can only be performed within the rangefinder

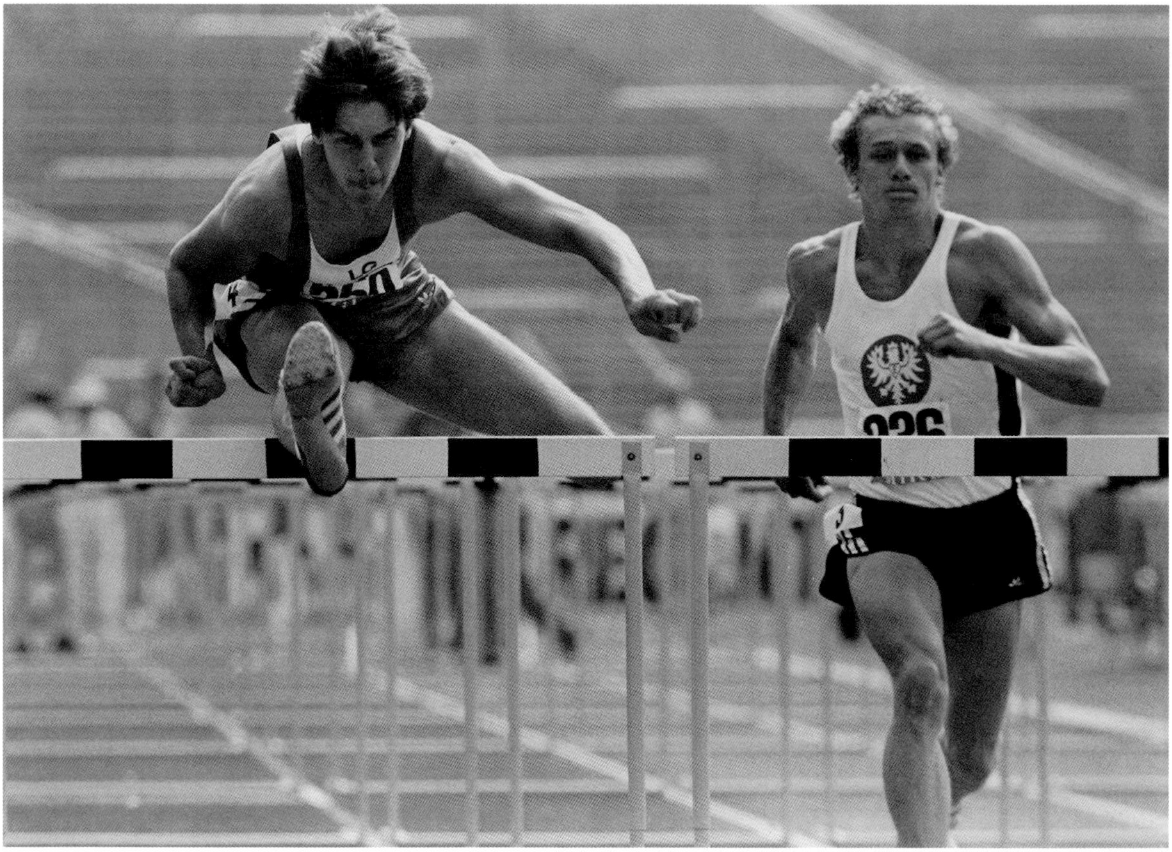

***Fig. 170:** When the subject distance changes rapidly, as it does during a nearly head-on view of a hurdle race, there is not enough time to focus accurately. The solution is to set the distance at a certain plane of focus in advance of the arrival of the hurdlers. Photograph by Bruno Walter*

field in the center of the viewfinder image (see page 46). Accurate focusing also depends on the vision of the eye with which the photographer looks through the viewfinder. Many individuals have relatively small eyesight deficiencies, which normally are not disruptive. However, the eye should be optimally "adapted" to the viewfinder of the Leica M.

If there are difficulties in focusing, the use of appropriate Leica corrective lenses is recommended, unless glasses are usually worn when looking through the viewfinder (see page 48).

Greater focusing accuracy is achieved by greater viewfinder magnification when focusing takes place. Because the newer Leica M cameras are offered with different viewfinder magnifications, this should be given consideration at the time a camera model is chosen. However, the ease of use of the viewfinder is affected by viewfinder magnification. A significant viewfinder magnification and a large angle of view to be able to see the bright line frame for wide-angle lenses in the viewfinder can unfortunately not be implemented. A good alternative is offered by the viewfinder magnifier M 1.25x which can optionally be screwed into the viewfinder eyepiece mount (see page 48), e.g., when longer focal lengths and larger apertures are used for taking pictures. This 25% (approximate) increase of the viewfinder magnification through the magnifier can considerably improve the accuracy, as well as the speed during a focusing operation.

Focus in advance

Once the right cropping has been selected by means of the appropriate bright-line frame in the viewfinder, and if there is no difficulty in focusing because of poor vision, then accurate focusing is generally not a problem and can be accomplished in a matter of seconds. Difficulties may occur while photographing slowly moving subjects at close range, with the lens set at a large aperture, i.e. with shallow depth of field. Attempts to adjust the focus continuously are usually not successful, It is much better to set the focus once and then not to change it, but to compensate for the motion of the subject by bending your own body at the hip. With this method you can take portraits even of wildly gesticulating persons With subjects like a plant swaying in the breeze, or when you yourself are standing on a rocking platform, the preset focus distance should also not be changed. The moving subject is observed continuously in the rangefinder field of the viewfinder, and when it reaches the pre-selected plane of focus again, only then should the shutter be released.

In a situation with a lot of fast action, it is impossible to focus accurately on a rapidly moving subject. Here too, it is best therefore to set the focus distance in advance. To photograph a lion leaping through a hoop held high by its trainer, for instance, one would pre-focus on the hoop, during a marathon race, one would pre-focus on a small pebble in the path of the runners. Now, all that needs to be done is to wait for the lion's head to enter the hoop, or for the runner to reach the pre-selected pebble, and then release the shutter. If we know how big the image of the runner must be in the viewfinder when he reaches the plane of focus, then we could also release the shutter when the image reaches that size.

Those who practice the photography of fast-moving subjects soon discover that one always has to release the shutter just a little earlier in order to compensate for one's own reaction time and for the time parallax between the pressing of the shutter release button and the actual exposure. The Leica M camera makes this task particularly easy for the photographer. First, because the viewfinder image, unlike that of single lens reflex cameras, always remains fully vis-ible during the exposure, and second, because the time parallax between the pressing of the shutter release button and the actual exposure is only 20 milliseconds, which is significantly faster than any modern single lens reflex camera.

Use the full frame

In addition to precise focusing, one of the most important requirements for good pictorial quality in a 35mm photograph is a picture that fills the entire frame. As simple as this requirement may seem, it is nevertheless seldom satisfied skillfully. The easiest way to accomplish this by first approaching the subject very closely, then raising the camera to the eye and backing off until the subject fills the frame completely. The reverse method, i.e. approaching the subject with the camera at eye-level and releasing the shutter when it fills the frame, brings the same results, only after a great deal of practice. Why not try it yourself?

While looking through the viewfinder, the photographer should also watch for converging verticals and slanted horizons and male certain that the camera is not tilted. Experienced photographers will also keep in mind that the angle of coverage of a lens decreases slightly as the lens is focused at shorter distances (see page 37).

Practice makes perfect

Judicious amounts of motion blur in a picture are an important creative tool in photography for suggesting speed and motion. If the results are not to be left to chance, then it is important to practice beforehand. First, attempt to capture the moving subject at the right moment, i.e. when it fills the frame in a pleasing manner. The easiest way to do this is to set up a camera with a standard lens on a tripod placed near a road that is used by cars. The distance to the nearest lane of traffic should be about 15 m (nearly 50 feet). The lens should be focused on a spot on the road where the cars will pass. A moving car is then "frozen" on film with a shutter speed of 1/500 or 1/1000 second. This exercise provides a "feel" for the moment when the shutter has to be released if the car is to be positioned in a specific part of the photograph.

Subsequent exposures are then made with relatively slow shutter speeds of 1/15 to 1/250 second. Based on the results of these tests, it can be determined which amount of motion blur, i.e. which shutter speed, best conveys the impression of speed.

The third experiment is also made with the relatively slow shutter speeds, except that the camera is now removed from the tripod and the moving car is followed by panning the camera while keeping its image in the viewfinder. This should begin when the car is still approaching, but the shutter is released only when the car has reached a preselected spot. Panning should continue, however, keeping the car in sight through the viewfinder until it is out of range. When panning is done with the hips, one can sense when the car is passing directly in front. With this technique, the car can also be recorded precisely when it is passing in front of a very specific section of the blurred background. This can be important for good color composition, for instance when the sides of white buildings, which would be reproduced as grayish-white areas, would disturb that composition.

The results of these tests will show how well you succeeded in capturing the car at the right moment, and which shutter speed produces the right amount of blur in the background. It is very important, however, that the vehicle appear absolutely sharp. Once the technique of panning has been mastered, concentration may be turned to other creative possibilities. For example, one can let the car "drive in" or "out" of the picture by placing it near the left or the right margin of the frame, or one can record a runner in a very specific, typical phase of his motion. In rhythmical sports such as running, one can simply count along, for instance: left leg = 1 ... right leg = 2 ... 1 ... 2... 1 ... 2 ... and release the shutter at the "right" moment. Optionally, one can even decide which leg of the runner should be "in front" in the picture.

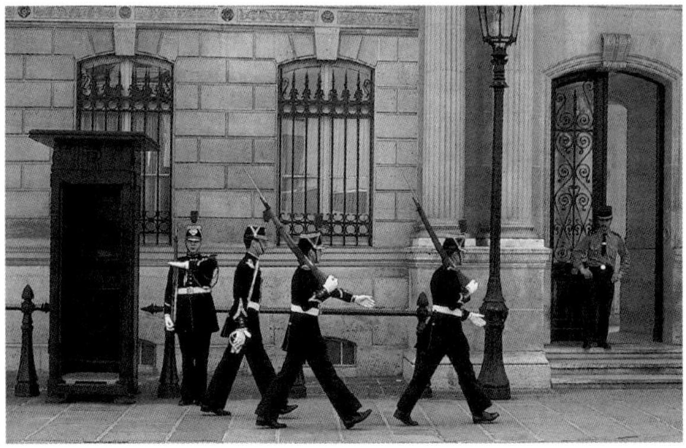

Fig. 171: *Rhythmical movements, such as jogging or marching, can be recorded at a typical point in their cycles simply by counting along (1 – 2, 1 – 2, etc.).*

All of the above exercises can also be performed with lenses with different focal lengths, and with subjects moving at different angles relative to the direction of the camera. This quickly helps to gain the necessary experience to judge what shutter speed is needed to freeze certain types of movement, or how to move the camera to achieve just the right amount of blur in the image. The Austrian-American photographer Ernst Haas developed this technique of photographing motion to perfection, and his pictures made him world-famous.

Spontaneity is important

It cannot be said often enough: Even experts have to practice constantly in order to remain proficient. This is why race drivers never forego their practice rounds, and very famous piano virtuosos consider daily finger exercises indispensable. The same principle applies to good photographers: Practice does make perfect! Naturally, training has to be tailored to the respective working style and specialty. Since a "living" 35 mm photograph depends primarily on the spontaneity of the moment, photographers cannot afford to leave anything to chance. They must always be prepared to

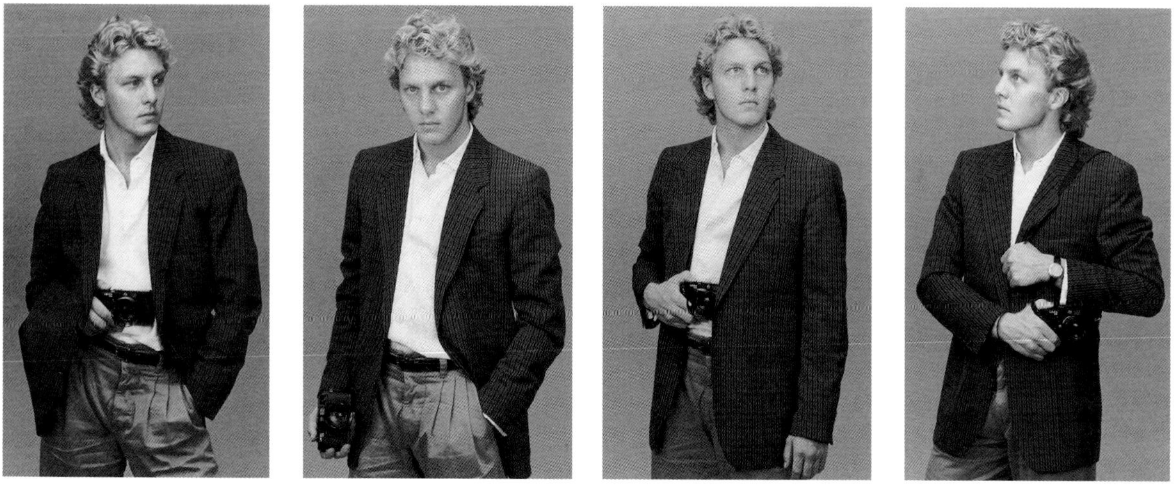

Fig. 172 a – d: *There are many ways to take pictures without being noticed.*

capture the right composition by pressing the shutter release button of the camera at the right moment, in the right place. This requires that they always be alert and active. In this context, it is most important that they develop a natural readiness to recognize picture opportunities, to observe surroundings attentively, and to acquire the ability of foreseeing when an action is about to reach a photographic peak. These exercises do not require a camera. All that is necessary is a pair of eyes, common sense and imagination to visualize the pictures in the photographer's mind. The camera merely serves to record those pictures.

Taking pictures without being noticed

In order to take pictures as discreetly as possible, the photographer must not keep the camera at eyelevel for very long. With that in mind, photographers first estimate the subject distance and the angle of view, and then they select and attach the lens with the appropriate focal length and sets the distance. Only then does one raise the camera to eye-level to check the image in the viewfinder. Fig. 172, above, depicts a method of taking pictures without looking through the viewfinder while still knowing what will be in those pictures. The bright line frame selector lever on Leica M cameras is very useful for these purposes. It enables the left index finger to actuate the frame lines for various focal lengths with lightning speed – without changing lenses!

If aperture and shutter speed have also been estimated and set ahead of time, only minor adjustments remain to be made when the camera is raised to eye-level. Becoming adept at this technique increases photographic productivity. Success then follows almost automatically. Even when a Leica M7 with automatic exposure is used, the aperture is chosen beforehand, so that the automatically created exposure time will not be too long or too short and thus necessitate extended exposure time corrections. Thus "estimate first, then measure" is the secret of a quick photographer. As this technique is perfected, the photographic yield is increased. Success will occur almost automatically. Once the Leica M camera has been raised to the photographers eye and small adjustments have been made, the right moment for the exposure can be selected. In many cases the additional area of the subject that can be seen in the viewfinder outside the field outlined by the bright line frame can be very useful, because it gives the photographer an early warning of certain events occurring in that area that may affect the picture. For example, if someone is about to walk into the picture, the photographer will not be taken by surprise, instead he will notice it in time to decide whether to release the shutter just before or after the intruder is in the picture area. Of course, another option is to release the shutter while running. But not at the very instant one foot is about to touch the ground. Release the shutter while one of your legs is swinging forward. This will avoid jarring the camera. This type of unnoticed photography is sure to produce unique pictures. When necessary, even the quiet sound of a Leica M shutter can be muffled by coughing.

Even experienced photographers will discover from the exercises described above that there are additional possibilities for sharpening their skills. Those striving for perfection may even develop additional experiments!

Exposure measurement

The image formed by the lens is recorded on the film by the exposure. This is the conclusion of a sequence of events that are necessary for creating a picture. With the exposure the photographer also largely finalizes his concept of a picture. Not only is the moment of exposure decisively important in this process, but also its length or the shutter speed. There are two reasons for this: the length of the exposure can be a creative element in making the photograph, and the amount of light that is necessary for the film to be able to be developed can be controlled precisely by means of the exposure time. The amount of light determines whether or not a photograph is usable, whether it is overexposed, underexposed, or correctly exposed.

How exposure meters work

Leitz and Leica have decisively influenced and shaped the evolution of exposure meters to their present state. Correct exposure, in the sense of controlling the amount of light, has been the main problem with which all photographers have had to come to grips since the beginning of photography and during the more than 75-year history of the Leica camera. The efforts of Oskar Barnack to determine the correct exposure for motion picture film ultimately led to the concept of the Leica camera. When the Leica was placed in production and introduced to the market, appropriate aids were designed to determine the exposure time and the aperture. Starting with exposure tables, followed by optical exposure meters, they progressed to photoelectric meters. The attachable exposure meters designed to couple with Leica M cameras were a groundbreaking development. The last model of that exposure meter, the Leicameter MR, is still available and has offered photographers the option of selective metering since 1963. By the end of the Seventies, Japanese competitors of Leica had introduced the partial metering mode in some of their cameras, billing it as the "latest achievement" and as "particularly application-oriented." This exposure-metering mode was introduced with the Leicaflex SL camera as far back as 1965 and first appeared on a range-viewfinder camera with the introduction of the Leica M5 in 1972.

Selenium cell exposure meters

The first photoelectric exposure meters for Leica M cameras, the Leicameters M and MC, were equipped with selenium metering cells. In contact with other metals, this light-sensitive element has the property of generating a very weak electrical current when it is struck by light.

Fig. H1 – H3: *Grazing light enhances structures and texture. Landscape photographs also become more dramatic with grazing light. These pictures were made on two successive days. The top and middle photos were made on the same day, first with an overcast sky at noon (top), and then in sunshine (center). The photograph at the bottom was made early in the morning on the next day.*

Fig. H4 – H7: *These pictures of changing moods created by light – from sunlight in the afternoon lighting at night – were taken in 1999. The exposures of Fig. H4 – H6 were taken with a focal length of 50mm; Fig. H7 was taken with a 90mm lens. All exposures are on daylight reversal film ISO 100.*

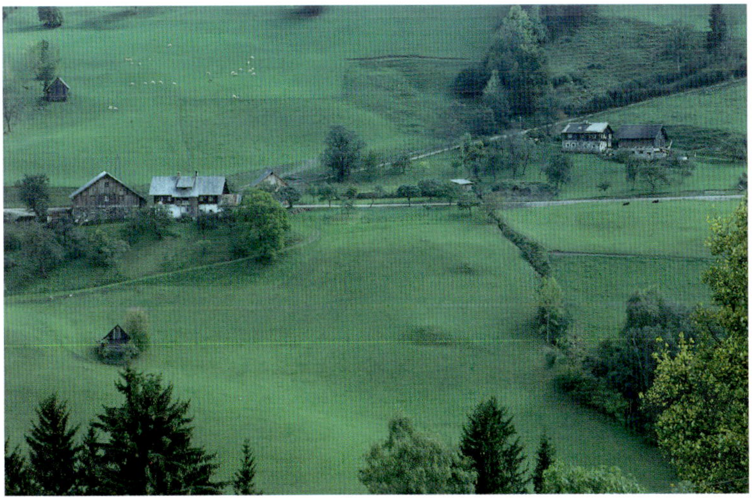

Fig. H1

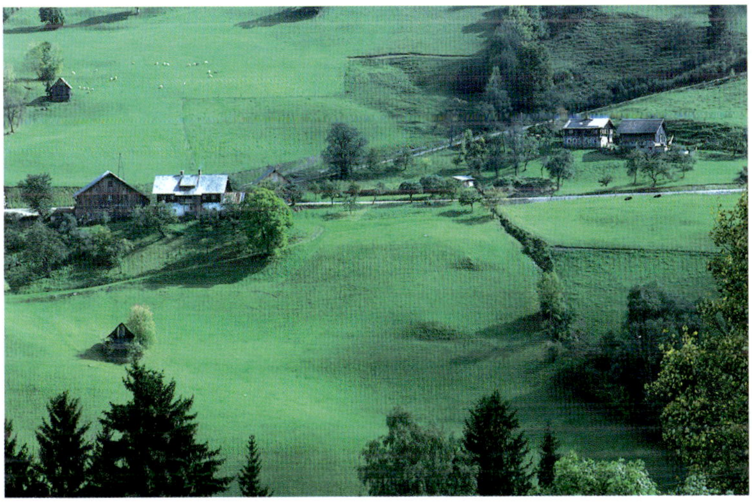

Fig. H2

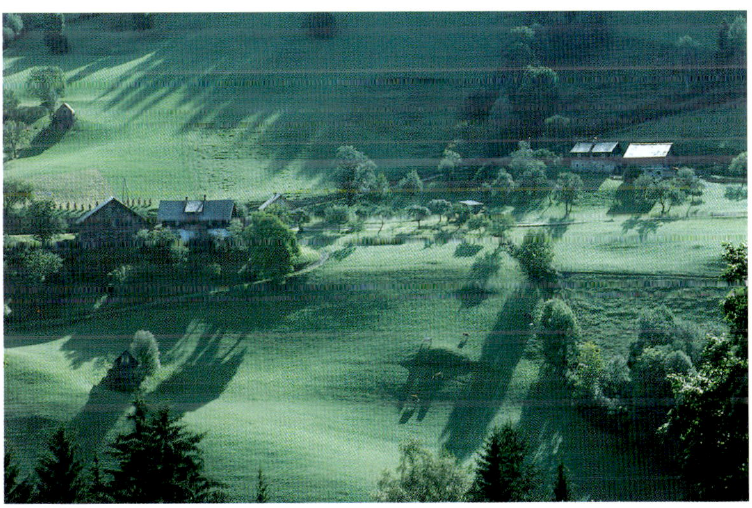

Fig. H3

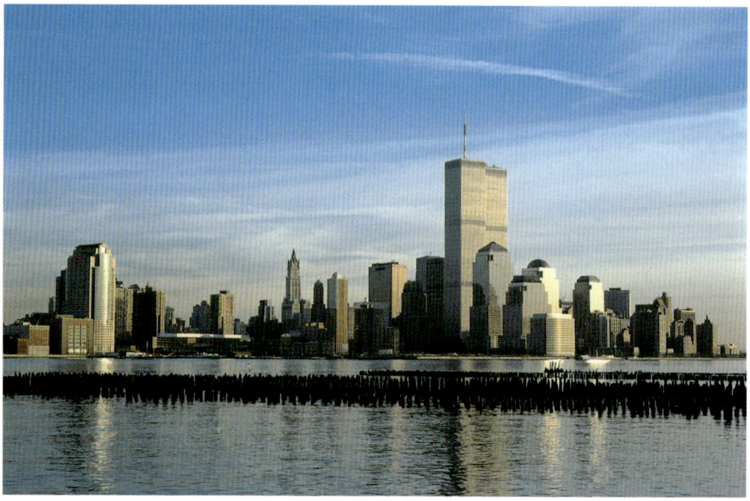
Fig. H4

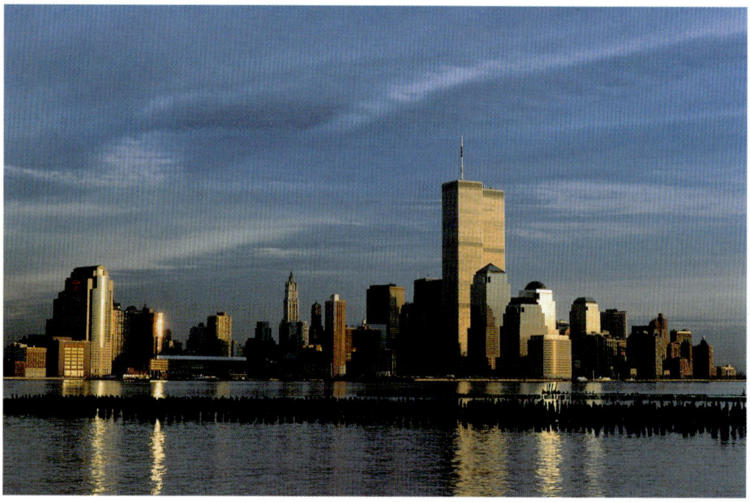
Fig. H5

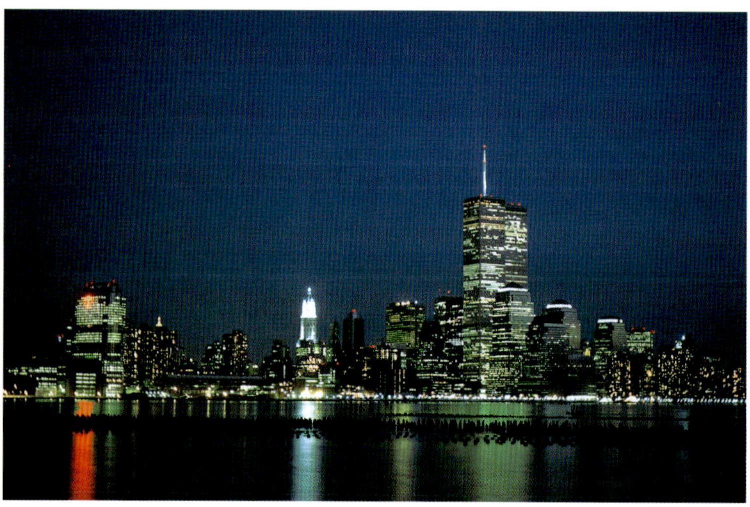
Fig. H6

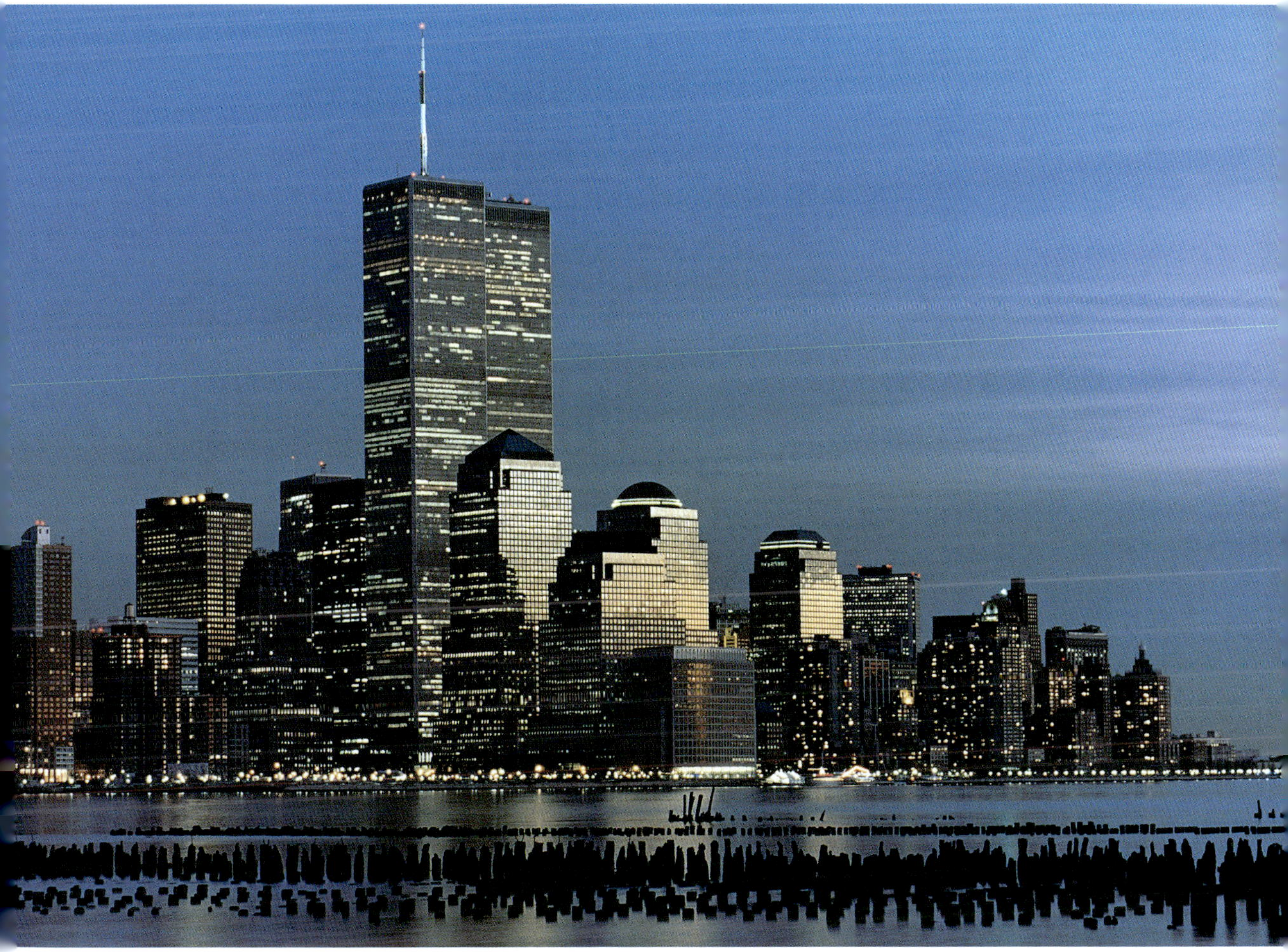

Fig. H7

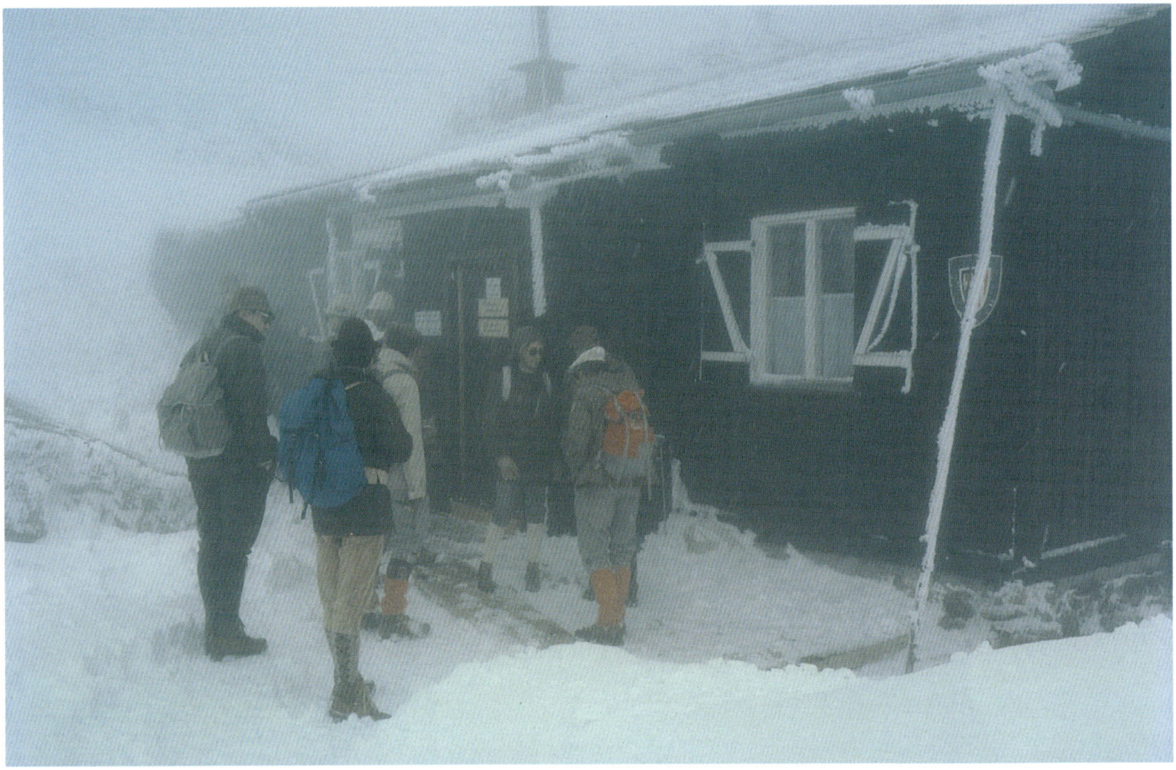

Fig. H8

Fig. H9

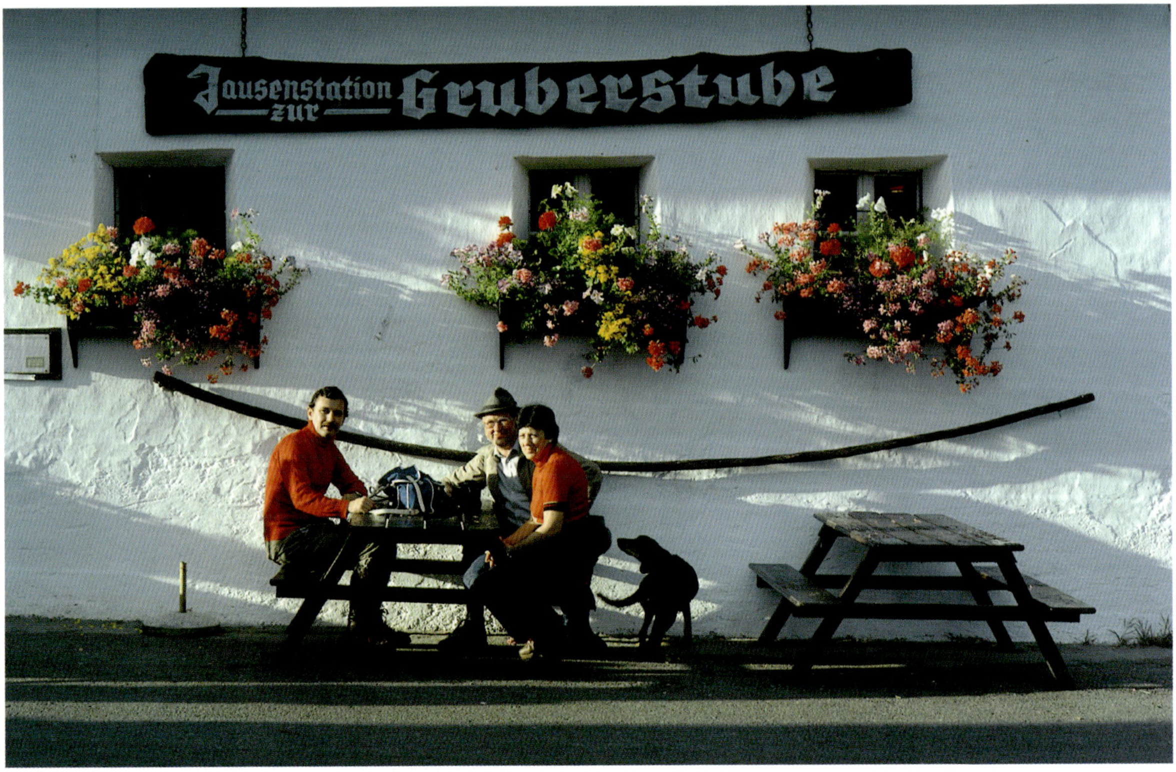

This current can be measured with a highly sensitive galvanometer. The intensity of the electrical current is directly proportional to the intensity of the light that strikes the cell. In order to receive enough light for a reading, even in poor lighting conditions, a selenium cell has to be relatively large.

The measuring angle of these exposure meters is tailored to the angle of view of a standard lens by means of a honeycomb configuration. In certain situations, this relatively large measuring angle is disadvantageous. For an exposure measurement of a landscape with a dominant bright sky, for example, the meter has to be turned slightly downward. And subjects illuminated by spotlights can only be measured at close range.

But even today, selenium cell exposure meters still have one great advantage over the latest and most modern models of exposure meters: They continue to operate even in very low temperatures, when the batteries of more modern meters have long ceased to function.

Cadmium sulfide photoresistors

The large measuring angle and the relatively weak electrical current generated by selenium cells were compelling reasons for the development of new exposure meters with photoresistors. With this principle, the intensity of an electrical current supplied by a battery is modulated by a photoresistor in proportion to the intensity of light that strikes it.

Fig. H8: *There are no poor weather conditions! Only protective clothing and suitable subjects are required. Unfortunately, photographers rarely go subject hunting on overcast days, in rain or fog.*

Fig. H9: *Even simple souvenir photos can be made interesting by grazing light.*

Since the electrical current emitted by a battery is considerably stronger than the current generated by a selenium cell, the metering angle and the light-sensitive surface of cadmium sulfide cells can be much smaller yet the sensitivity, as well as the ruggedness of the instrument, can be increased. The first generation of this type of exposure meter, which includes the Leicameter MR, was equipped with cadmium sulfide (CdS) cells of the kind that is still in use today. The Leica M5 camera is also equipped with a CdS exposure meter.

Silicon and gallium-arsenide-phosphide photodiodes

The same principle used in CdS exposure meters is also employed in exposure meters with new types of measuring cells, such as silicon (Si) and gallium-arsenide-phosphide cells. The special advantage of these new cells is their extremely fast reaction time to changing light conditions. The temporary "blinding" that occurs with CdS exposure meters when they are first exposed to strong light sources and then to darker subjects, does not occur with these new types of measuring cells.

Both of the new kinds of cells are even capable of measuring the light of an electronic flash unit within a few ten thousandths of a second. That is why they are also used for controlling the amount of light emitted by such units. In motor-driven cameras, built-in Si and GaAsP cells make accurate light measurements during the short period between exposures. The Leica M6 camera is equipped with a silicon photodiode exposure meter.

Spectral sensitivity

The spectral sensitivity of all exposure meters in the Leica M System is largely adapted to that of the human eye and thus to the spectral sensitivity of color films. The small excess sensitivity to red of the silicon photodiode in the Leica M camera is attenuated by a blue filter on the measuring cell.

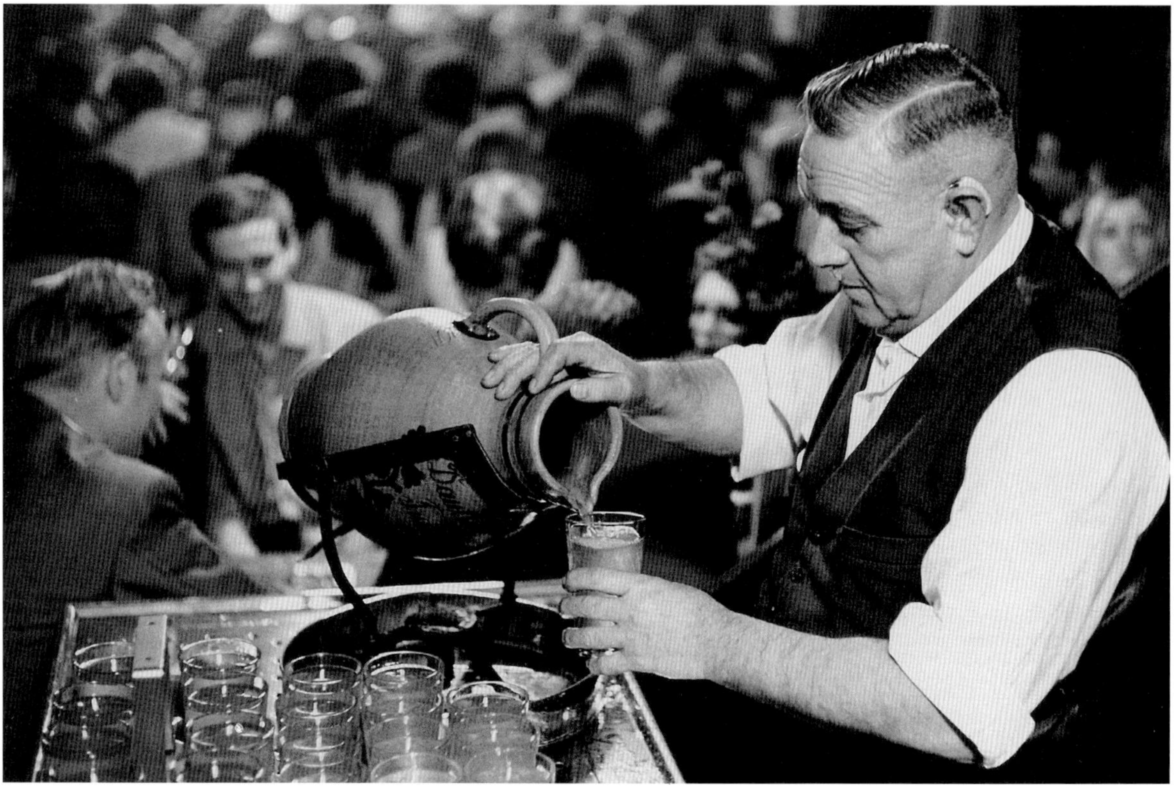

Fig. 173: *Careful exposure metering with a Leicameter MR or with the camera's built-in meter enables the photographer to determine the correct exposure conveniently. With today's superior light meters, fast lenses, and high-speed films, virtually any situation can be successfully photographed. In this case the photographer captured the unmistakable atmosphere of a Frankfurt tavern during hard cider season.*

This characteristic is typical of all silicon cells, but its effects in photographic practice are negligible. When black-and-white films are used, which have a different spectral sensitivity that furthermore may vary from brand to brand, small measuring errors of up to half an exposure value may occur in (reddish) artificial illumination. Measuring errors and consequently wrong exposures may also occur when photographs are made through reddish color filters.

A few test exposures will show whether any corrections are necessary and, if so, to what extent.

Incident and reflected light measurement

There are two basic types of light measurement—incident and reflected. Incident metering refers to the measurement of light that is impinging on the subject. With this type of metering the exposure meter is position neat the subject and aimed towards the camera. Reflected light measurement refers to the measurement of the light that is reflected by the subject, and the exposure meter is aimed from the camera towards the subject.

For incident light measurements, the exposure meter requires an accessory that can capture light coming in

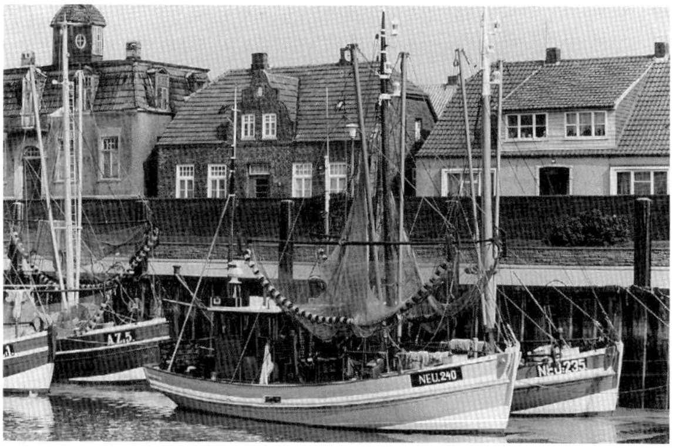

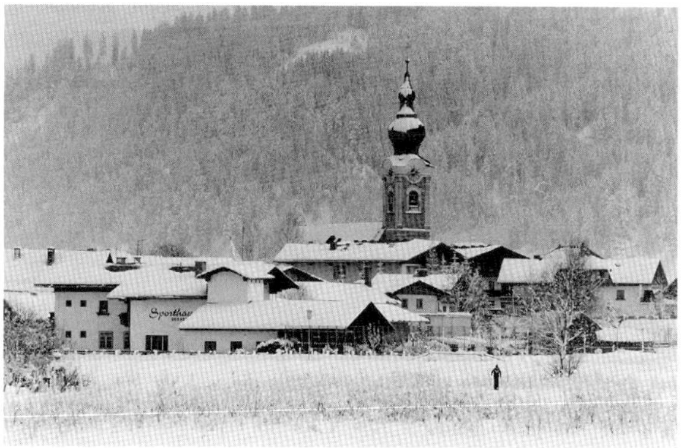

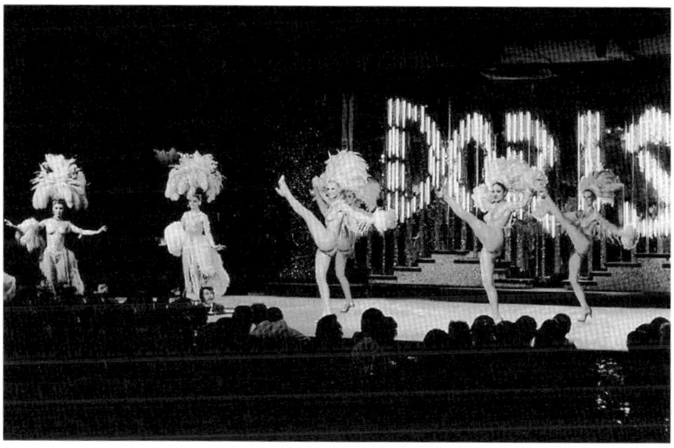

Fig. 174 a – c: *With recent Leica M cameras, average scenes with normal reflectance (upper left) are simple to meter. However, compensation is often necessary with unusual subjects. Predominantly bright details (upper right), such as snow scenes and white beaches, reflect much more light so that they may be under-exposed if the exposure is not corrected. Predominantly dark subjects (lower left), on the other hand, will tend to be over-exposed if proper adjustments are not made.*

from all sides. An appropriate diffuser was available for Leicameters M and MC, which could be inserted over the honeycomb cell for taking incident light readings. One also had to be able to take readings from the immediate vicinity of the subject in the direction of the camera. That is why nowadays this kind of exposure measurement is made only with manual exposure meters, and it is practiced almost exclusively in studios. Incident light measurement is used less for the determination of shutter speed and aperture, but mostly for checking the evenness of the illumination of the foreground, middle ground, and background. Studio photographers and motion picture and television cameramen are the main users of this measuring method.

Reflected light measurement has the advantage that the exposure can be determined from the camera position. With this method, the exposure meter has to presume the intensity of the light source based on the intensity of the light that is reflected by the subject in order to determine the exposure value, i.e. the shutter speed and aperture. Cameras with through-the-lens (TTL) exposure meters, thus, make reflected light measurements. This method is particularly advantageous for dynamic photography, for photography with long focal length lenses and for candid photography, i.e. for most fields of application of Leica M cameras.

When exposure measurement is mentioned, it normally means reflected light measurement. That is why all the discussions that follow are based on that type of measurement.

Normal subjects

Our environment normally presents itself to us full of colors and full of contrasts. Our photographic subjects therefore consist of many details of different colors and of various degrees of brightness.

The exposure measurement, or the metering of reflected light, covers all the various reflections from those details. The exposure meter thus measures the sum of all the brightnesses, and this is referred to as integrated metering.

Extensive experiments have shown that the most common photographic subjects have an average reflection that corresponds to an 18% reflective gray value. All conventional international exposure meters are based on this degree of reflectivity or this reflective gray value. This includes the Leica M cameras and all Leicameters.

Integrated metering

It is evident from the preceding discussions that integrated exposure metering assures the correct exposure in the majority of cases. This especially true when the measurement is made through the lens of the camera (TTL metering). Ingenious systems on many camera models provide additional helpful aids: Since the important part of most pictures is usually in the center of the frame, the metering system is designed to favor the central portion of the picture.

This practice-oriented, center-weighting very quickly gives the photographer the confidence that he is exposing the majority of normal subjects accurately and without problems. Thus, this type of metering is appropriate for all subjects that do not have high lighting contrasts, which is usually the case with front lighting, when there are no strong shadows, there is an even distribution of light and dark areas, and there are no extreme color contrasts. Integrated metering, for example, is ideal for landscape photography.

Caution has to be exercised, however, when too much sky is included in the metering field. Selenium cell meters, which have inherently large measuring angles, should therefore be tilted slightly downwards when metering a landscape scene. This is also recommended for TTL measurements with a super wide-angle lens.

Modern CdS exposure meters, like the Leicameter MR, for instance, have a measuring angle of less than 30°. This usually assures the coverage of a section of the subject without a bright sky (if the landscape is being metered correctly), so that an accurate exposure value will be determined. The selective metering feature of Leica M7, M6, and Leica M5 cameras is even more appropriate for this purpose.

Corrections for unusual reflection

Sooner or later every photographer will be confronted with a landscape that not only has a bright sky but very bright subject areas as well. A person who for the very first time takes a meter reading of a winter scene in the mountains in glorious sunshine will probably trust the reading of the exposure meter in good faith. The small apertures and fast shutter speeds indicated by the exposure meter would seem appropriate for such blinding brightness. With all that light, one might be tempted to stop the lens down even further or to use even faster shutter speeds. However, when the processed film comes back from the lab, the results are usually disappointing—nothing but underexposed pictures!

The reason for these poor results is easily explained: The exposure meter, which has been set for a given film speed, does not know that only the reflection in the scene is greater than normal, not the intensity of the light source. Calibrated for a normal reflection of 18% (medium gray value), the meter concludes from the amount of light it received that the light source must have a great intensity. The shutter speed it recommends is fast by a factor that is the same as the factor by which the reflectivity of the snow is greater than the reflectivity of 18% medium gray. Since white snow surfaces reflect 80 to 90% of the light, i.e. more than 4 times as much as a "normal" subject, the shutter speed indicated by the meter is also more than 4 times as fast as that indicated for a "normal" subject. Therefore this must be corrected accordingly. It should be multiplied by a factor of 4, or the aperture should be opened by two stops to increase the exposure.

On the other hand, if the subject consists mostly of dark elements, then the opposite has to be done—a faster shutter speed has to be selected to reduce the

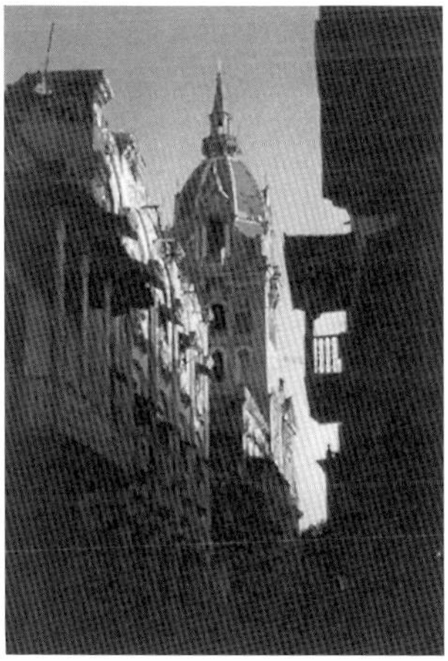 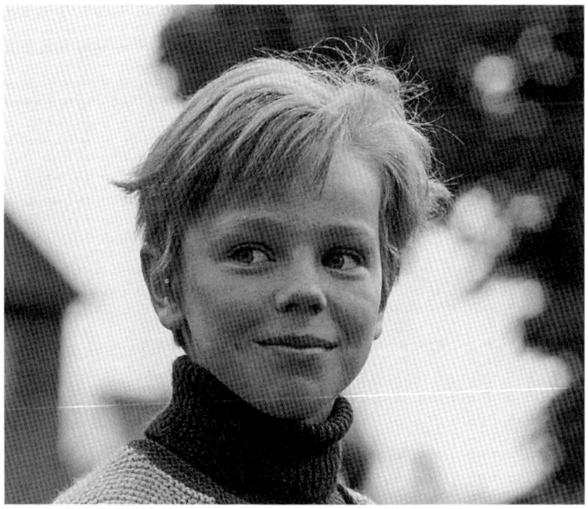 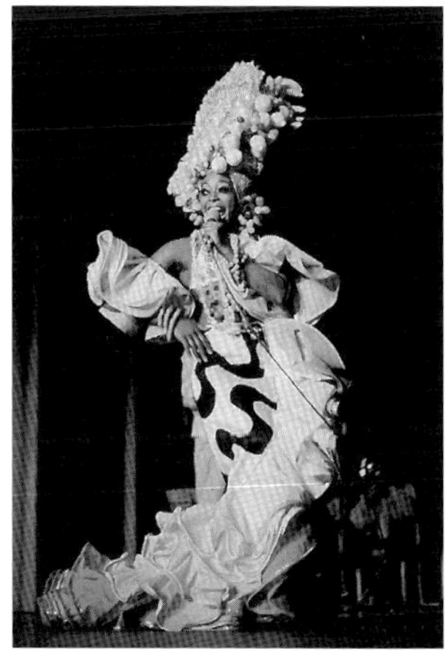

Fig. 175 a – c: *Buildings in a narrow street disappearing into deep shade, a portrait in front of a bright sky, or an actor with a dark stage backdrop all require close-up or selective metering of the subject.*

exposure. This also applies to photographs at night or in the theater, where only a few elements or persons are well illuminated, while everything else is cloaked in darkness. Again, in these situations, meter readings lead to over-exposures if they are not corrected first.

When the shutter speed and aperture are set manually, corrections must be made manually as described. However, with its aperture priority automatic exposure control, the Leica M7 has an "override" on the rear of the camera. As a result, the automatic exposure control can be corrected up to ±2 EV in 1/3 step increments. However, be aware that these corrections are only based on estimated values so that they cannot guarantee accurate exposures.

Close-up metering

In most instances, however, unusually bright or unusually dark subjects do not consist exclusively of bright or dark details. In the snowy landscape mentioned above, for example, there are trees, bushes, and/or houses. There may be skiers moving by or strong shadows, all of which stand out well from the white snow. If this were not the case, all we would see would be a uniformly white surface—hardly worth a photograph.

The objects or other elements that stand out from the snow, in turn, generally possess a normal reflectivity of 18%. If we were to just measure the light that is reflected by these more normal elements—the face of the skier, for example—we will obtain a more accurate exposure. The same applies to spotlighted actors on stage and to the illuminated parts of nighttime scenes.

Since it is necessary to get close to the "normal" elements of such scenes in order to make an exposure measurement, this is called close-up metering.

Because of the large measuring angle of selenium cell exposure meters such as Leicameters M and MC, it is necessary to get very close to the subject for an accurate close-up measurement (due to the large measuring angle). Aside from the fact that this is often unwelcome by some subjects, there is also the risk that the exposure meter itself (as well as the Leica M camera and the head of the photographer) might cast a shadow on the subject, and this would, of course, result in a false reading.

With the Leicameter MR's narrow measuring angle, however, an accurate meter reading from a comfortable distance is no problem. This is even more the case because the exposure meter's coverage can be controlled especially well through the viewfinder of a Leica M camera (see page 59).

Selective metering

Often it is difficult, even with a Leicameter MR, to get close enough to a subject to meter just an area with normal reflectance. Leitz wanted to find a solution to this problem that would also permit exact "close-up measurements" from reasonable distances. The solution was Leica selective metering. With this method, only a relatively small section of the subject area covered by the lens is used for an exposure metering.

In Leica M cameras with TTL metering, the circular metering field is positioned in the center of the picture area, and its size can be estimated very easily in the viewfinders of these cameras.

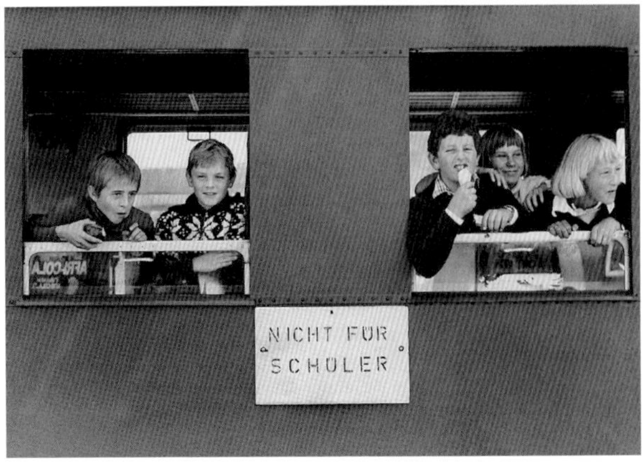

Fig. 176 For this photo of students in an off-limits railway coach, the photographer focused and metered the student standing in the right corner of the left window. He then recomposed, to create the desired composition, and took the picture.

The diameter of the metering field varies, depending on the focused distance, because of image field reduction. With the use of Leica M models and the Leica M7 it is possible to make a (selective) exposure reading of a human face through a 90mm lens from a distance of 2 m (6-1/2 feet). For a close-up reading with the integrated metering method, one would have to approach a subject at less than 1 m (3-1/4 feet).

Selective exposure metering in actual practice

Starting with the Leica M6TTL, all models feature selective exposure metering through the lens. This system was especially tailored to the applications of dynamic 35mm photography. When this camera is raised to the eye, we immediately notice the great and pleasing brightness of the viewfinder image. Then we notice the clean, uncluttered and thus highly practical layout of the viewfinder image. Dyed-in-the-wool single-lens-reflex photographers as well as theoreticians will probably miss the information that is a matter-of-course in single-lens-reflex cameras such as the Leica R8.

There are no readouts of the shutter speed and aperture setting in the viewfinder of any Leica camera; the set exposure time can be read only in the Leica M5, and in the Leica M7 only the automatically created exposure time. Of course Leica is consistently searching for options of incorporating such readouts in the viewfinder, however, not at the expense of the size and the design of a camera housing, the ease of use of the viewfinder, the handling of the camera and lens, and the compatibility of available lenses. Due to the established dimensions of the Leica M models, new components can be accommodated in the housing only when these components can be appropriately "miniaturized."

It was only in 2002 that the automatic exposure control and the required displays were successfully integrated in the viewfinder—after the appropriate technologies were developed.

The production of a 0.7 x 2.3 mm display, which was to have 33 display components, had been contemplated. However, it could be designed and manufactured only after new technology permitted. The analysis of feedback sent to Leica Camera AG by amateur and professional photographers from all over the world proved how important it is not to lose the typical features of the Leica. And Leica has committed itself to do this.

Those who use the Leica M camera for photojournalism or dynamic photography welcome this decision. Because this requires speed, experienced photogra-

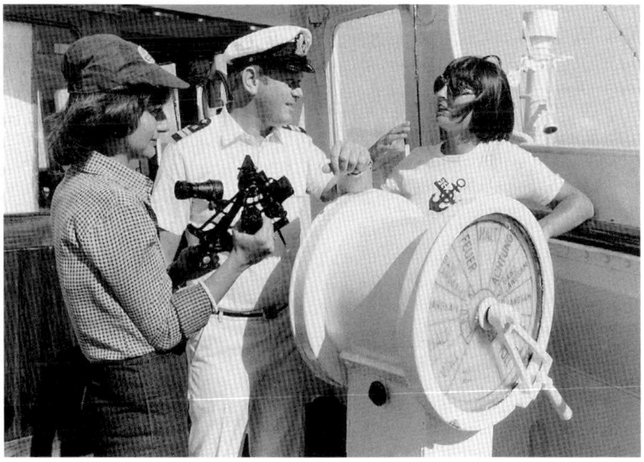

Fig. 177

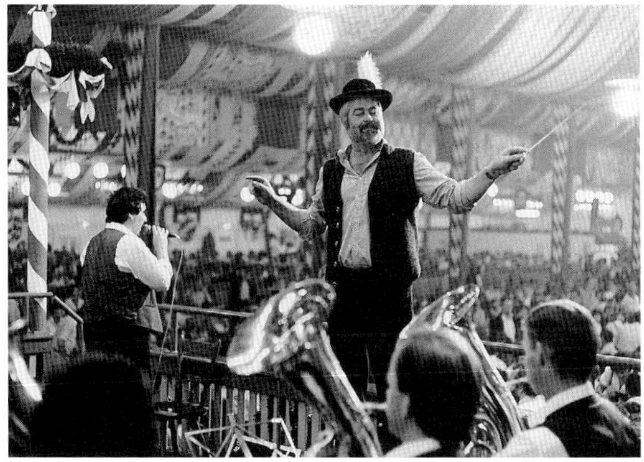

Fig. 178

phers will usually estimate and set the distance and aperture before raising the camera to their eye (see also "Taking pictures without being noticed," page 235). Estimating and setting these values (like using the clutch and changing gears while driving) should be virtually instinctive. The small residual adjustments that may still be needed after looking through the viewfinder—on the focusing mount of the lens for the correct distance and on the aperture ring for the exposure measurement—can then be executed in a quick moment.

This leaves practically no time for reading the actual values of these settings in the viewfinder. There is also no time left for aiming the exposure meter very precisely at the subject, so that a correspondingly exact readout can also be omitted. Excellent exposures made with the Leica M7, M6 TTL, or M6 will fully confirm this. The statement that the diameter of the round metering spot is equivalent to about two thirds of the short dimension of the lens' bright-line frame should work for all practical applications.

This becomes understandable and it is also proven by practical experience when one visualizes the following situation: We usually turn the camera in several directions while we decide how to frame a composition. Even for quick snapshots, it is easy to ascertain whether light and dark subject details are distributed evenly enough for a correct meter reading. A distinctive subject detail should also be used for focusing. If such a detail cannot be found in the center of an interesting composition, the view should be adjusted for accurate focusing and then the picture should be recomposed. Figures 176 and 177 were photographed in this manner.

The picture of the students in a section of a railway coach that is off-limits to them, for example, was taken by focusing and metering on the student standing in the right corner of the left window. The camera was then readjusted for the desired composition, the exposure was quickly rechecked, and the shutter was released.

The photograph on the bridge of a ship was taken by focusing and metering on the young lady standing at the left and then turning the camera back to the desired composition. The exposure measurement field of the exposure meter now covers the predominantly white subject areas. The exposure measurement was repeated with the camera turned far to the left and downward (the measurement field of the exposure meter is already partly outside of the desired composition.). Turn the camera back to the desired composition and release the shutter.

With a little practice this can be done quite quickly. The exposure meter of the Leica M is of course, calibrated for the same 18% reflectance as other exposure meters. For subjects with predominantly dark areas, like a black steam locomotive, for instance, or a dark gray slate roof, or the dark blue uniform of a ship's captain, less light than normal is reflected, so that the exposure meter will indicate too slow a shutter speed, or too large an aperture (over-exposure). In such cases, the metered exposure value has to be corrected to achieve a perfect exposure.

In a wedding, for example, it would be best to meter the face of the bride, not her white wedding gown. In landscape photographs with a wide-angle lens, the camera should be turned down far enough so that the metering field of the Leica M camera will not include the bright portions of the sky. For the photograph taken inside a festival tent, (see Fig. 178), the camera was turned slightly downward and to the left, so that the disturbing light source directly above the conductor's head would not be included in the readout of the exposure meter.

A rule of thumb for selective exposure metering is to measure the detail on which you focus. On the Leica M camera, for example, the measuring field of the exposure meter can be used as an "aiming device." Do not measure extremes. In other words, don't measure subject details like deep shadows, dark colors or bright clouds and white walls. This always leads to over- and under-exposures, respectively. Measure sections of the overall subject that are composed of many different subject brightnesses. Measure a subject within a subject. Nearly all subjects have such areas.

Strong contrasts

Photographic textbooks often advise that for subjects with high contrasts, the brightest and the darkest areas should be selectively metered and an average of these two readings used to determine the correct exposure.

Unfortunately, the result is usually not satisfactory, because the contrast is too great in most cases. It must not be higher than 4:1 or two aperture stops for color transparency film, and 7:1 or nearly three aperture stops for color print and black-and-white film. Greater contrasts cannot be reproduced in a photograph, if the highlights (the bright areas) and the shadows (dark areas) are still to contain detail.

Black-and-white film can accommodate a slightly higher brightness range if they are given "soft" development (see pages 188-190).

If the subject has too great a contrast range, we have to decide which area of the subject is most important to the photograph. This area should be measured using selective metering. Many good photographs result from high contrast lighting. Just think of backlighted photographs and photographs in which the sun illuminates certain sections of the subject like a spotlight.

The picture of the Brazilian singer (see Fig. 175 c) was also shot in an especially high contrast situation. Similar situations occur in interiors in which pictures are taken against bright window areas, or when pictures are taken through arches, and with pictures that include strong light sources in the photograph.

With close-up or selective exposure metering, the subject details that are important to the composition and that represent a medium gray value should be metered.

Close-up or selective metering, or targeted exposure measurement, requires that the photographer be familiar with the particular characteristics of films or film development, and lighting. If a photographer has mastered the rules, the composition options offered by the light with the use of these types of exposure measurement can be utilized fully.

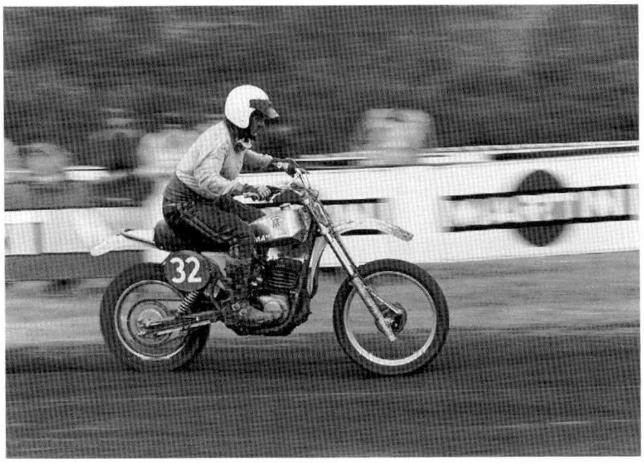

Fig. 179: *With certain subjects, there simply is not enough time to meterwhile the action is taking place. In these cases, it is usually best if the exposure can be determined ahead of time.*

Substitute metering

In the course of photographic activities, there are occasional situations when a close-up or selective measurement cannot be used to determine the exposure of the subject field, which reflects 18% of the light with accuracy. The image of the subject to be measured may be too small, one may not be able to approach it, or there may not be enough time to meter a moving subject when it appears in the viewfinder.

In situations like these, the solution is to take a substitute meter reading. This involves taking a reading of a replacement object under the same lighting conditions.

Experienced photographers like to use the palms of their hands as a replacement object. This method is excellent for side lighting, when shadows are formed on the surface of the palm.

In direct lighting, however, when no shadows are formed, a correction of plus one-half a stop should be made (the aperture should be opened by half a stop), because skin tones reflect a little more than 18%. If the reading is taken of a face, then the correction will not be necessary, because lips, eyebrows and eyelashes reflect less light than the skin, so that the reading is balanced and the meter reading can be applied directly.

Of course it is even better to use an "object" that is designed to have the exact reflectance to which exposure meters are calibrated. Photographic dealers offer "Gray Cards" for this purpose. These have a gray side with precisely 18% reflectance.

The white side of that card reflects 90% of the light, in other words it is 5 times brighter than a "normal" subject. In very dim light, it may still produce a reading in an exposure meter that might otherwise not react. Naturally, the white side of this card, or any other matte white card (or drawing paper) can also be used routinely for substitute metering. Since white has a greater reflectance, a correction has to be applied to the measured value:

Suggested metering corrections with gray or white cards

Subject brightness	Kodak Neutral Test Card (Gray side)	White card (matte)
bright	-1/2 stop	× 3
normal	Expose as metered	× 4 – 5
dark	+1/2 stop	× 6

This table also takes into account that bright subjects should be exposed a little less and dark subjects a little longer than "normal" subjects under the same lighting conditions. Projected slides will have more brilliance, and negatives will be easier to enlarge.

Metering through photographic filters

When color filters are used in conjunction with through-the-lens exposure metering, the filter's exposure factor is generally accommodated automatically. But different films have different sensitivities in certain regions of the spectrum. With very intense filters, deviations may therefore occur with respect to metered exposure values. Orange filters, for example, require an increase of about one stop, red filters generally about two. Polarizing filters (including circular polarization filters) can be used like normal filters without adjusting the TTL-meter reading.

Metering does not replace thinking

For each meter reading, one should verify whether or not the subject corresponds to the standard 18% reflectance, whether the exposure meter reading can be used directly, or whether a correction should be applied to compensate for a peculiarity of the subject. The type of film that is being used, negative or reversal, is also significant (see pages 191 to 194). Measuring the exposure requires thought. "Blind trust" in difficult lighting situations can lead to disappointing results.

Estimate, then measure

For pictures in bright sunlight, here is a practical rule of thumb that is worth remembering:

$$\text{Shutter speed for aperture f/16} = \frac{1}{\text{ISO}}$$

For example, if a film with a speed of ISO 50is being used, this would mean 1/50 sec. at f/16. With a film speed of ISO 25, applying the above formula would result in an exposure of 1/25 sec. at f/16. Other combinations of shutter speed and aperture can easily be derived from that exposure value. In actual use, the following would apply to Kodachrome 64 film (ISO 64) in bright sunlight: 1/125 second at f/11, 1/250 second at f/8, 1/500 second at f/5.6, and so on. If the actual meter readings do not match the estimated values approximately, then it should be checked whether or not the subject being measured corresponds to a medium gray value, one forgot to set the right film speed on the camera, the batteries of the exposure meter are weak, etc. A photographer should gain experience by exposing at least one film exactly according to the manufacturer's instructions, without using the exposure meter. As long as weather conditions are not extreme, and if the pictures are not taken very early in the morning or very late in the evening, most of the photographs taken in accordance with those instructions will be excellently exposed. Those who abide by the values mentioned above and by the experience gained with them, those who first estimate the exposure and then measure it, quickly gain a feeling for "the right exposure" and with it enormous confidence in any lighting situation. Thus "a bell rings" with seasoned photographers every time the exposure meter shows an unusual (erroneous) reading.

The exercises that have been mentioned will also considerably increase the agility in taking pictures under unusual circumstances. Furthermore, the experience gained in the process enables a photographer to continue working successfully with the mechanically generated shutter speeds of a Leica M camera when the batteries of the exposure meter fail and when fresh ones cannot be obtained readily, or when there is not enough time to change batteries.

Correct does not mean ideal

The correct exposure does not necessarily have to be the ideal exposure. That may sound like a paradox, but it has been confirmed by experience. Judicious over-exposures and under-exposures can reinforce the mood of a photograph and thus strengthen its message. With transparencies this also depends a little on their in-

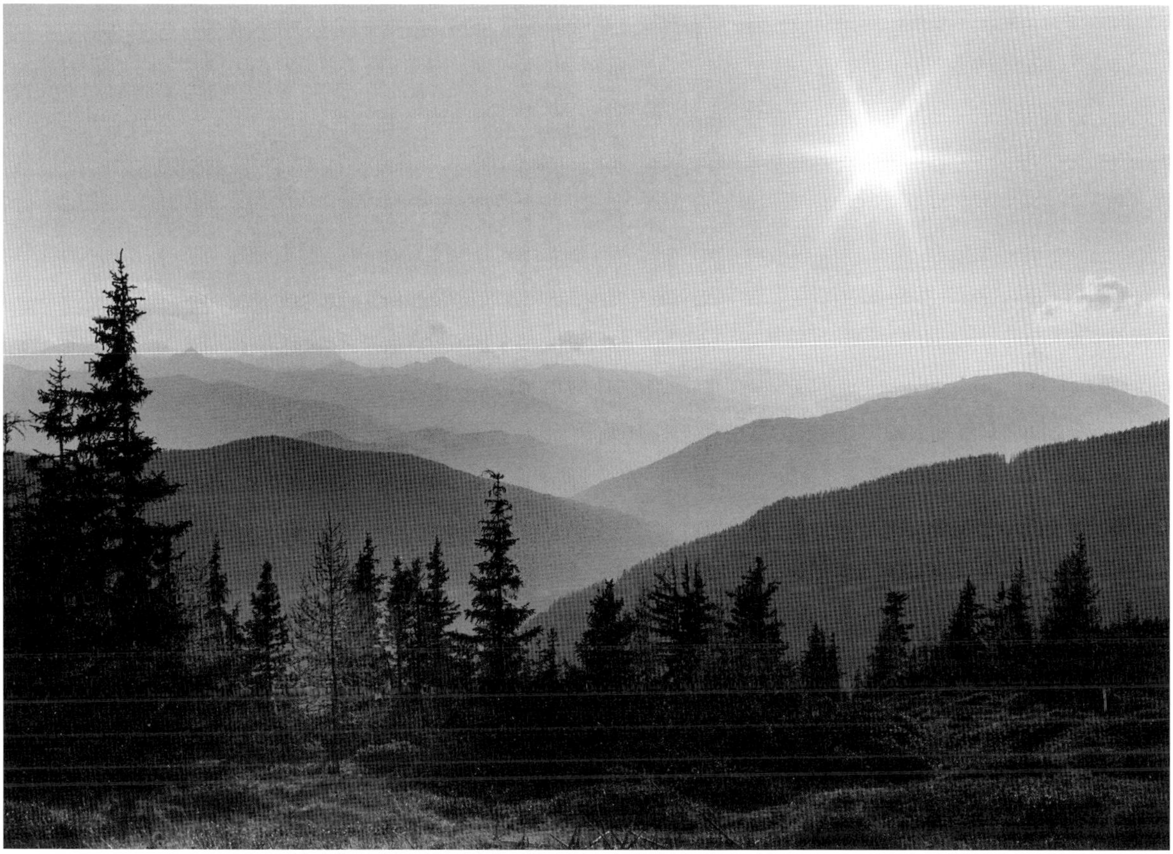

Fig. 180: *The emotional impact of a photograph can be strengthened by judiciously decreasing or increasing the exposure. Deliberate over- and under-exposures thereby become effective creative tools. In this photograph, an exposure meter reading was taken of the pines and mountain ridges an the left side (without the sky) and the film was then deliberately under-exposed by two stops.*

tended use. Slides intended for large projection on screens wider than 3 m (10 feet) appear more brilliant when they are just a little over-exposed.

Printers, on the other hand, prefer slides that are slightly underexposed, in order to produce more saturated colors in the print. The amount of over-exposure or under-exposure that is acceptable depends on the type of film and on the contrast of the subject. Therefore, test exposures are indispensable when the results have to satisfy stringent demands.

Photographers have to become familiar with their equipment, their film and their processing lab. With that approach, there is no reason for complaining to the manufacturer because of the camera or the exposure meter, when the latter has to be set for a film speed that differs by plus/minus 1 to 2 steps from the official exposure index of the film.

Perfection in black-and-white

Because black-and-white photography never lost its appeal to serious photographers and because today it is gaining importance again as a creative tool for extremely powerful photographs, the zone system should not be omitted in a discussion on exposure. This is true, even if this system requires that certain photographs must be processed in a very specific manner, whereby the 35mm film has to be developed in short lengths, or in strips, i.e. piece by piece. The pieces that have to be treated differently can easily be marked by the method described on page 201.

The internationally known American photographer Ansel Adams developed a system for black-and-white photographs that standardizes the individual steps in taking the photographs and in making the reproductions. According to this system, all colors and brightnesses in the subject are classified into nine shades of gray, which Adams called "zones" and which he identified with Roman numerals.

The range of this scale of tonal values extends from zone 1, which is a black that is only a hint away from the deepest black (maximum density) of the photographic paper, over seven shades of gray to Zone IX, which is a white without detail, such as snow in hazy light, which in a photograph only very delicately stands out from the unexposed (white) border of the print. Zone V of the Zone System is precisely in the center of the scale and it corresponds to a medium gray value with an 18% reflectance.

With the Zone System, one can already determine at the time the photograph is taken, to what gray value a particular subject brightness should correspond in the enlargement. Of course, even Ansel Adams cannot remodel photographic chemistry and physics, but the Zone System enables a photographer to control tonal value shifts in the photographs, as well as the richness and brilliance of tones in the finished enlargements. Exposure and the determination of contrast, as well as film processing tailored to those values are the cornerstones of this system. With the individual development of each negative, this technique is intended primarily for photographs on sheet film.

That, plus the general trend to color photography, may well be reasons why this perfect method of black-and-white photography never became popular in Europe. Those who still would like to learn more about this system can find appropriate publications at bookstores and camera shops.

Workshops on this topic offered by Leica Academy are even more effective because they are tailored to the special concerns of 35mm photography.

Leica

Light and Shadows

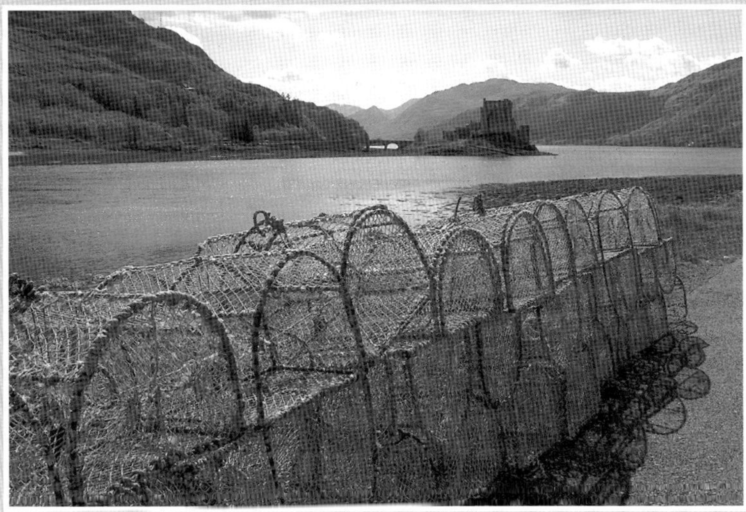

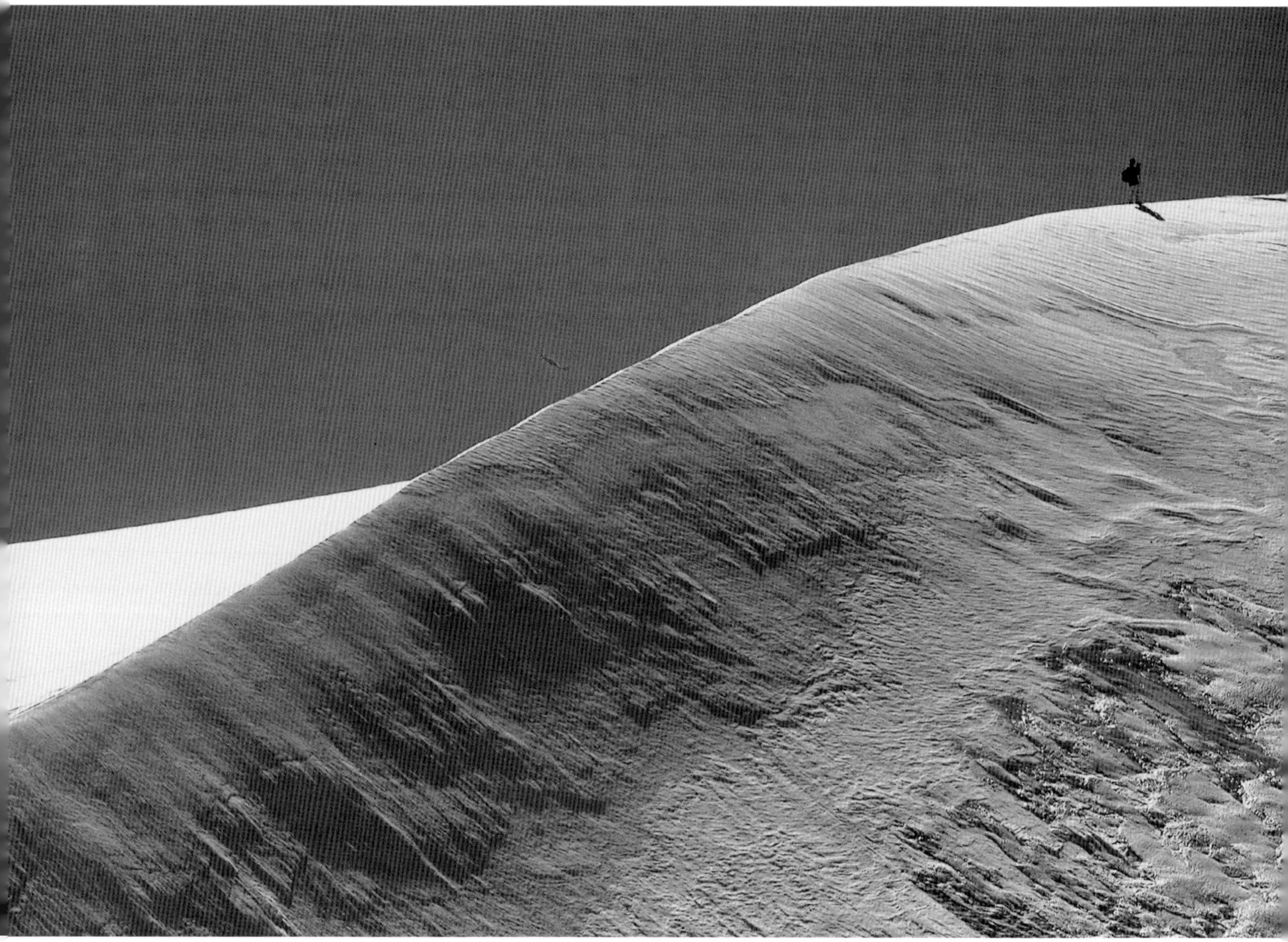

Fig. 181: *Without light grazing the walls, this waterhole would be the boring white area of ice shown on the left of this picture. Such lighting effects – caused by the changes of the position of the sun – can be observed only for a few minutes. This requires quick action on the part of the photographer. 135mm f/3.4 Apo-Telyt-M lens, 1/250 second, f/5.6 – 8, polarizing filter, medium-speed film.*

Light and shadows

"Where there is light, there are shadows." This well-known saying could have come from a photographer. Photographers depend on both—more so than nearly everyone else. Together with perspective, light and shadows increase the representation of spatial depth, the third dimension in a two-dimensional photograph, because light by itself is merely a prerequisite for photography. Light and shadows create an impression of distances in a picture. Thus, light and shadows are major creative tools for photographers.

Good photographers distinguish themselves by, among other things, knowing how to evaluate light correctly and by judging shadows confidently. Light distribution and the proportion of shadows in a photograph often determine its character. To manipulate light distribution and shadows expertly—to evaluate and control them, and to place the subject in the correct light—is the photographer's objective.

Artificial light has the advantage that the photographer can usually manipulate it, so that it can be adapted to specific needs. The large variety of artificial light sources that is available to the photographer additionally enables him to select the one that is right for a given task. For soft lighting in a portrait studio, for example, photographers will choose a so-called french-fryer, and for situations in photojournalism when even high-speed films and super-fast lenses no longer suffice, they will use portable electronic flash. If photographs are being taken in rooms with available light, it is important to recognize and evaluate the effect of light and shadows as it changes with the camera position. If pictures are being taken of people, and the Leica M camera is predestined for this like no other camera, they should not be recorded on film in only one specific position, for example, standing, lying, running or sitting. The person's environment is also important.

We usually take pictures of people because we find them interesting. We like to document their habits and record the mood of the occasion at which we meet them. Harsh flash can totally destroy the special character of such unique moments.

It is better to use available light. But what is its effect? Where can we identify distracting shadows, how can they be avoided: would it be better if we waited until the person moved a little further to the left, or should we change our own position? Could we hope for a light fringe on the blonde hair of the young woman if we ask for the wall lights to be turned on? These are but a few of the questions a photographer has to address.

With photography in daylight, we are able to wait more patiently when we know in advance what effects the light will have on landscape and architectural subjects. Frontal lighting, grazing light, transmitted light, and backlighting play a major role in exterior photographs. What are the effects of these kinds of illumination and how can photographers recognize and control them, or how can they generate these effects and use them well for a given purpose?

Those who study the effects of light and shadows will soon discover that there are no hard-and-fast rules for illumination that tell us, like a cookbook, when to use which light source, at what distance, and at what angle. There are, however, a few principles and procedures that constitute the basis for the technique of illumination. Those who become familiar with them will be better equipped to find the right solution for their lighting problems and achieve better photographs. This applies to interior and to exterior situations and, of course, to Leica M cameras as well, in spite of the fact that range-viewfinder cameras are used primarily for candid photography, rather than studio photography with a large array of lights.

Since available light can, of course, be utilized much more effectively when the reciprocal relationships between light and shadows are understood, the most important aspects of illumination technique will be described below.

What you have to keep in mind

The impression of depth in a photograph is created by light and shadows. With shiny objects, such as glass, chrome, lacquer, etc., surfaces are characterized by reflections of light sources. Surface textures can also be emphasized with appropriate lighting. The important factor is the angle at which the light strikes the object.

For good lighting technique, it is also important to be guided by the fact that we are all conditioned to certain light angles or directions. The sun, for example, as a natural "light source," generally shines on all earthly objects from above and shadows are cast downwards. Because of this natural conditioning, we subconsciously expect a certain order of things when we view a photograph. When the light source is positioned below the object (footlights), so that shadows are cast upwards, we often get a misleading impression of the shape of the object. Optical illusions are sometimes based on this phenomenon. Even familiar things can look eerie with this type of lighting. This effect is utilized deliberately in the theater and in television, for instance, when the face of the actor who plays the role of the bad guy is purposely illuminated from below. A portrait with this type of illumination has a demonic effect on us.

Having been conditioned to read from left to right and from top to bottom, we also initially subconsciously scan every picture in these directions with our eyes. This establishes the direction from which we can usually direct light most advantageously: namely from the left. Portraits on our bank notes and postage stamps are usually created according to this rule. When we depart from the conditions to which we are accustomed, however, the change has to be implemented in a very calculated manner, and the reason for making that change should be clearly evident in the photograph.

Light path and shadow formation

The shape and the size of a light source, as well as the distance from the light source to the subject, are major factors in well-balanced lighting. The discussions that follow are based on normal photolamps and electronic flash units, which are not directed by special optical devices. For the sake of simplicity, a reflector will be considered as the light source, rather than the glowing filament of the photolamps. The same applies to electronic flash units and to the sun, and since artificial light and daylight generally obey the same laws of physics, experience that has been gained with one light source can usually be applied to the other.

Fig. I1 and I2: *Striking faces demand light and shadows—not necessarily sunlight. Dark skin tones require soft light, which covers skin as a cohesive reflection.*
Fig. I1: *This older gentleman was asked to stand under an archway where light fell on him from the left and right in different intensities.*
Fig. I2: *Small and efficient electronic flash units make a photographer nearly independent of available light. Focusing is sometimes difficult but usually there is a bright spot in the scene that can be used with the camera's rangefinder.*

Fig. I3: *Compact, high performance electronic flash units are also excellent adjuncts for existing light. When used as fill flash outdoors, electronic flash lowers the overall contrast in the scene bringing it more in line with the exposure latitude of transparency film. Here, flash was used to fill in the left side of the man's face for an improved overall exposure of the side-lit subject.*

Fig. I4 and I5: *If a flash must be used, a longer exposure time and/or a larger aperture will give the picture a more natural, moody atmosphere because existing light will also influence the exposure.*
Fig. I4: *The shortest shutter speed for flash synchronization is 1/50 second.*
Fig. I5: *Shutter speed, 1/8 second with flash override.*

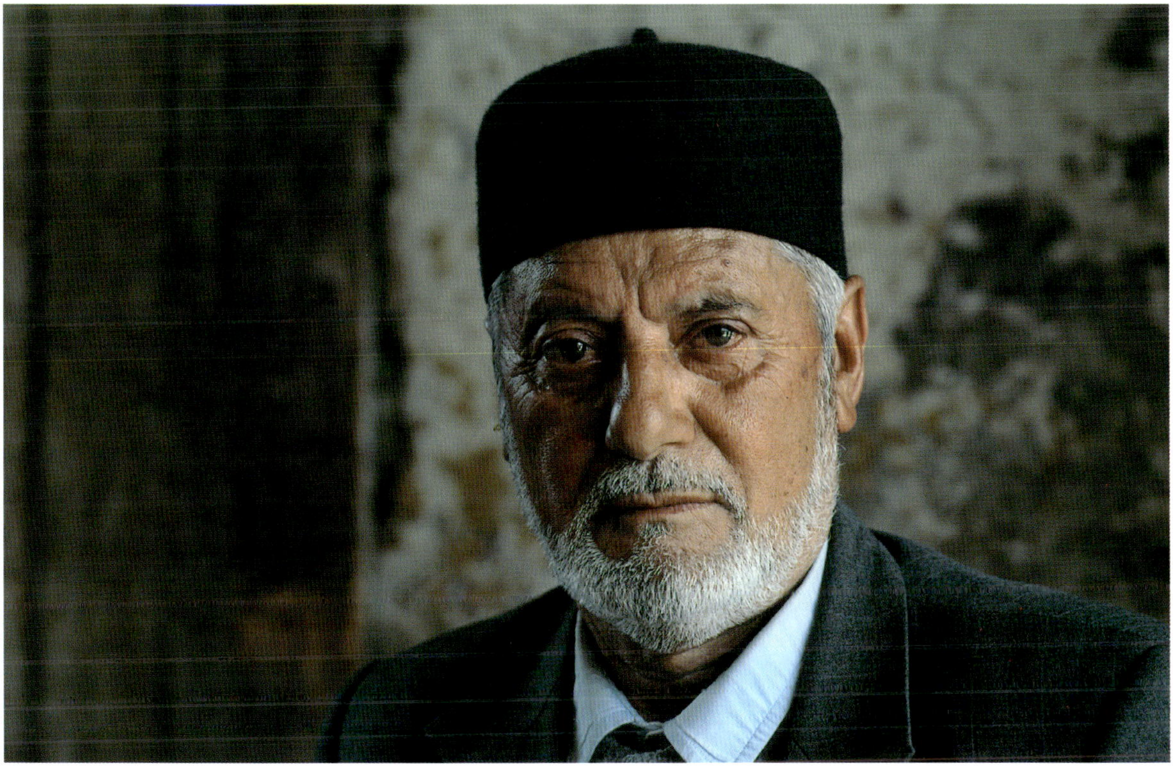

Fig. I1

Fig. I2

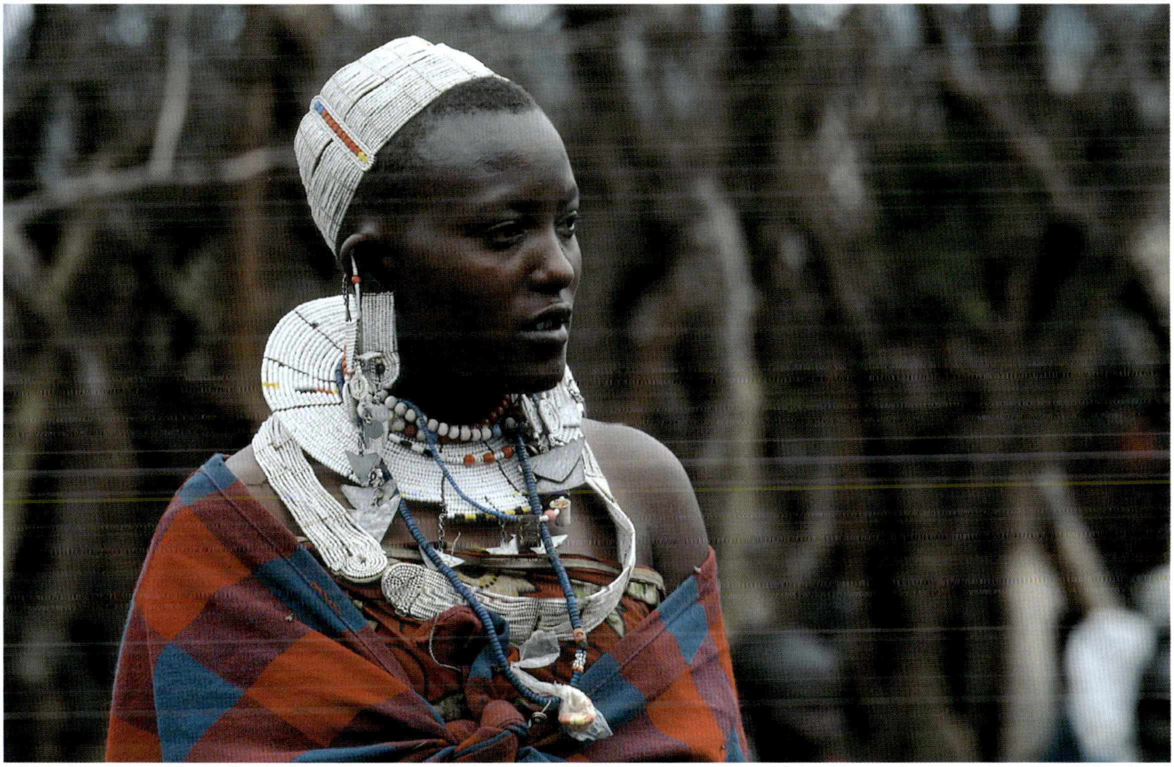

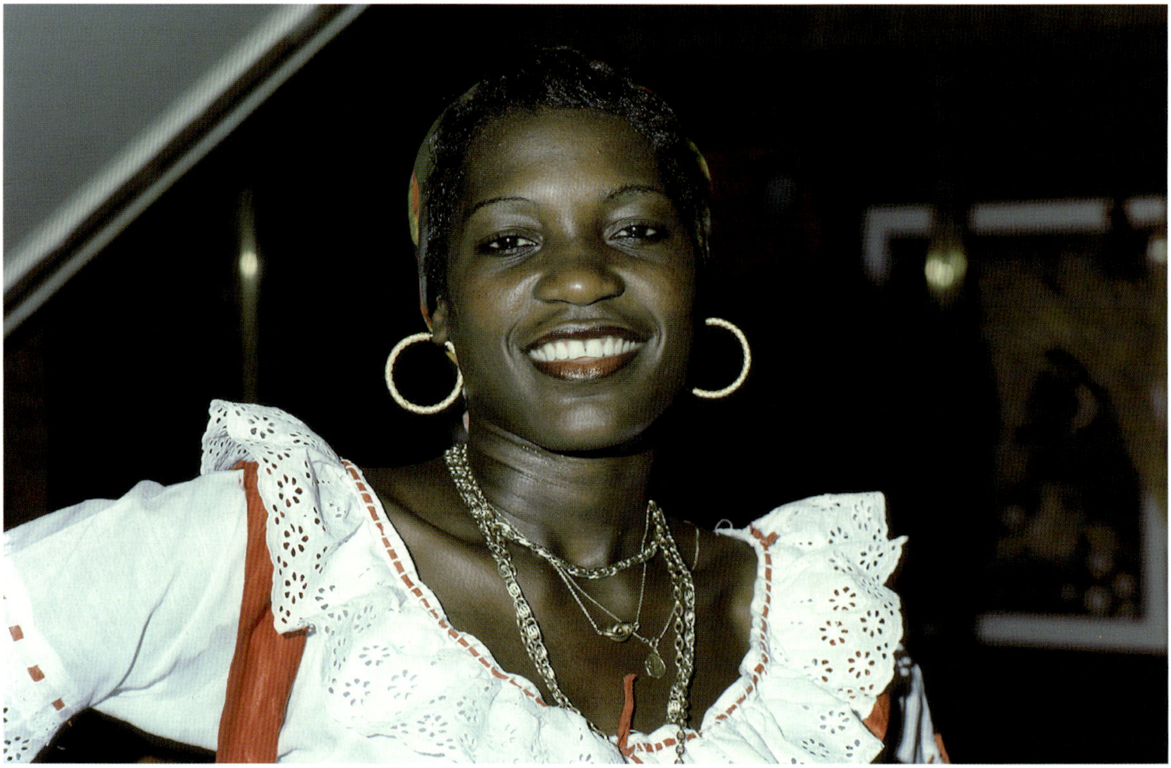

Fig. I3

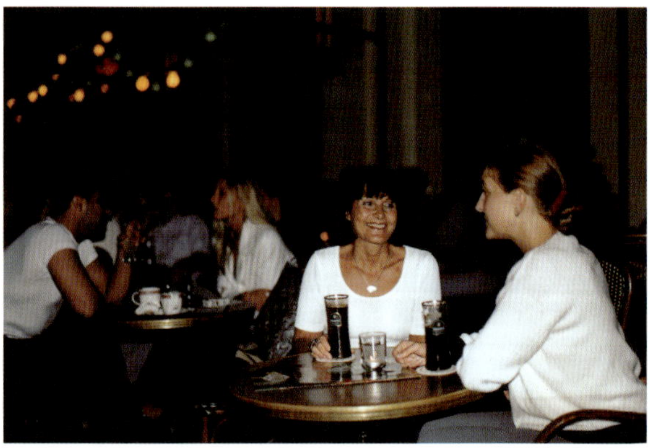

Fig. I4

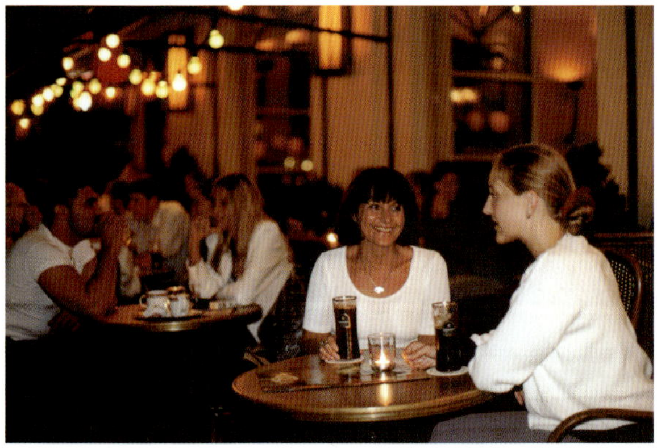

Fig. I5

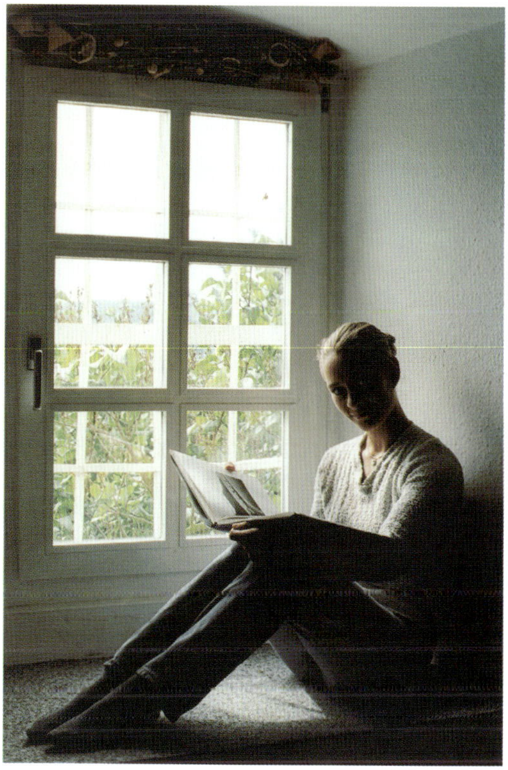

Fig. I6

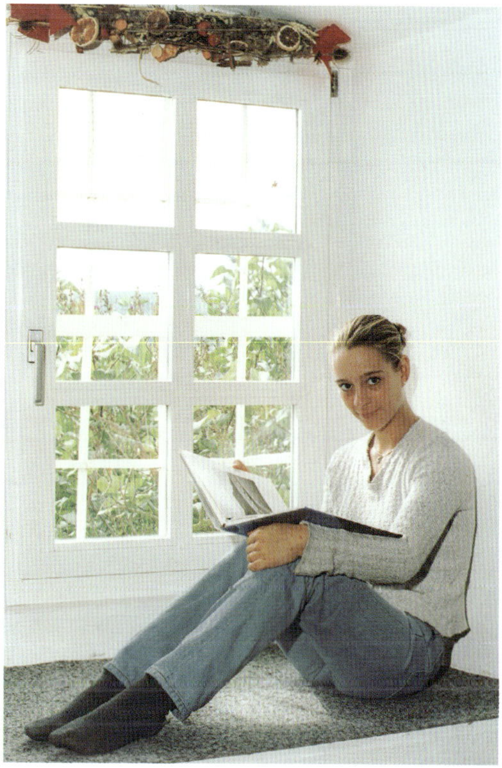

Fig. I7

Fig. I8

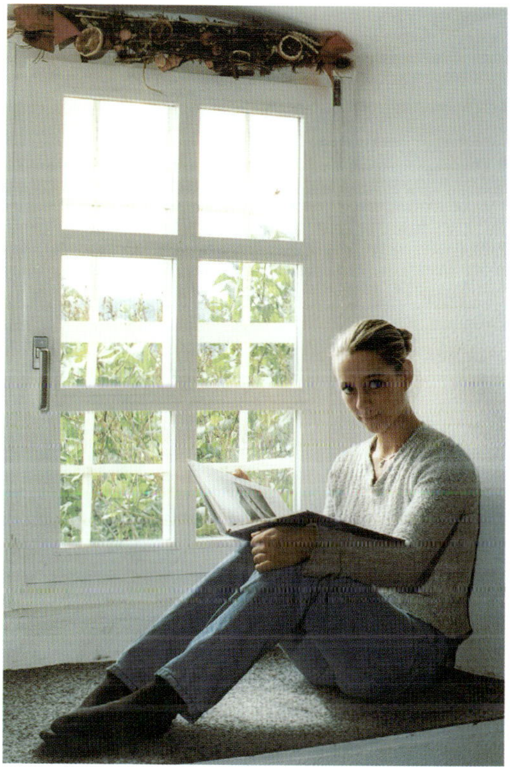

Fig. I9

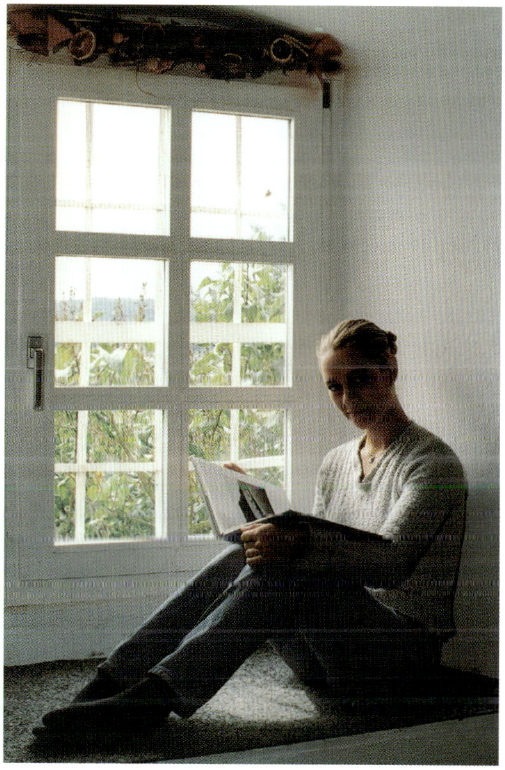

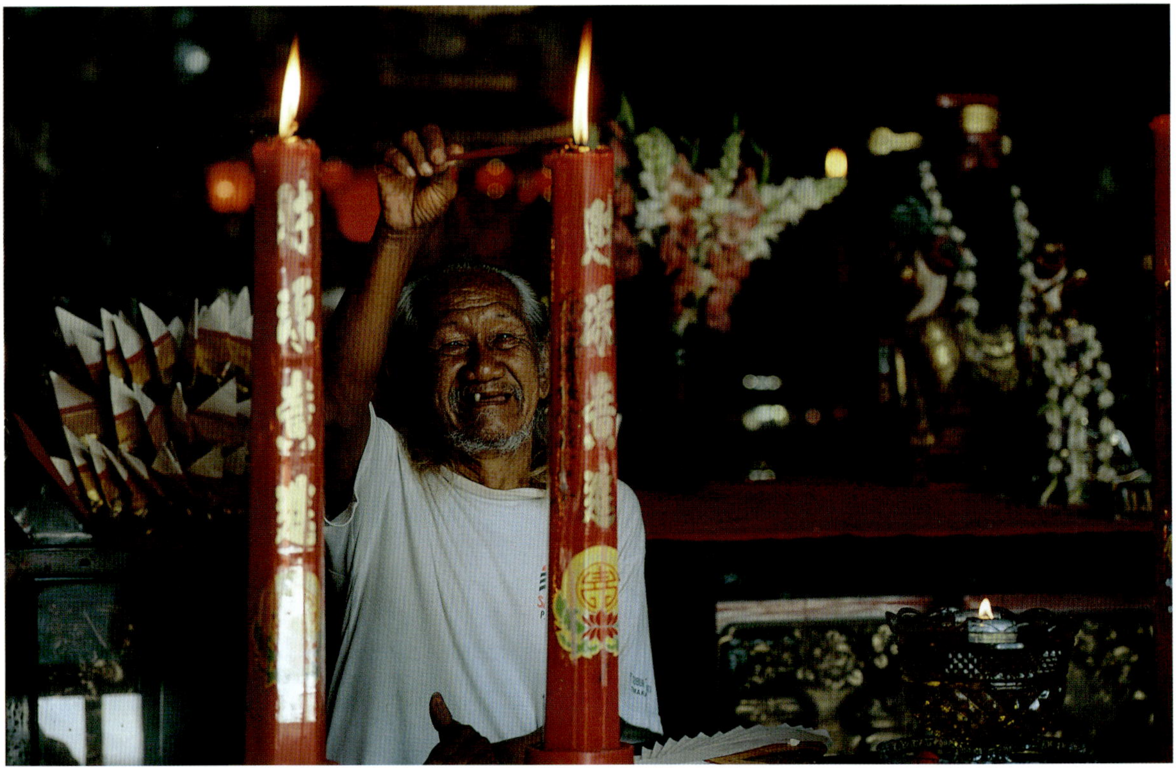

Fig. I10

Fig. I11

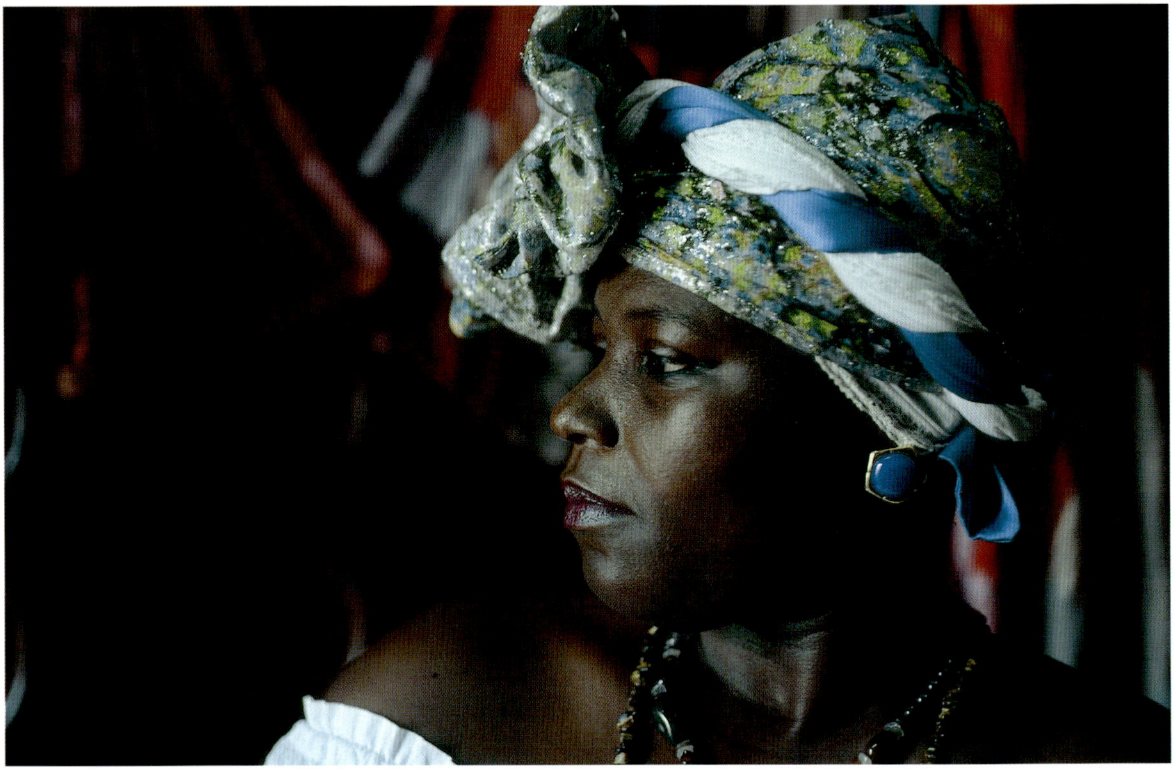

This also means that, without making a large investment, we can set up our own experiments that allow us to acquire additional experience.

It is easy to prove that the shaded portion of a sphere is the same size as its illuminated portion when the light source is the same diameter as the sphere. If the light source is smaller, the shaded area grows larger. If it is larger, the area struck by the light also becomes larger. When large light sources are placed at sufficiently long distances from the object, they produce nearly the same lighting effects as small light sources do at shorter distances. These observations generally apply to all three-dimensional objects.

Depending on the size of the light source, the transition from the lighted to the shaded portion of a sphere can be gradual or abrupt. Gradual transitions usually lead to better results in photographs. As a rule, an abrupt transition is preferable only for special effects or the detail in surface texture are to be shown.

Fig. I6 – I9: *A flash unit may be used to lighten all dark parts of a subject. These examples, photographed at the window with backlighting, show a few different options.*
Fig. I6: *Exposure without flash.*
Fig. I7: *Normal flash exposure.*
Fig. I8: *Fill flash with –1-2/3 EV.*
Fig. I9: *Fill flash with –2 EV.*
As is shown in practical applications, usually fill flash with –1-2/3 EV will produce the best result.

Fig. I10 and I11: *Any photographer who uses the Leica M should consider flash to be a useful accessory. Whenever possible, however, the photographer should use the existing light which encouraged him, or moved him, to take a picture. Highly powerful Leica M lenses and precise focusing of the Leica M camera help to achieve this. Both pictures were taken with the 75mm f/1.4 Summilux-M lens at full aperture. The picture in the Chinese temple was taken at 1/60 second, the lady with the imaginative headdress at only 1/15 second. The camera was stabilized by supporting the elbows on the table.*

Shadows on the background can distract attention from the subject or the relevant part of the picture. This formation of shadows depends on the size of the light source. With large light sources, the core of the shadow—the area that receives no direct light at all from the source—disappears completely when the background is far enough away. Even though a soft edge shadow remains, it will be brightened by the light source and will, therefore, not be as obvious. When the distance from the subject to the background is large enough, the shadow will not be obtrusive.

The smaller the light source, the smaller the edge shadow that will be formed, and the more distinct the core shadows. With a point source, no soft edge will be formed around the core shadow and the core shadow will no longer disappear. Quite the contrary, it will become larger as the distance from the subject increases. This effect can be observed often with flash photography. Because modern electronic flash units have small reflectors, they are small light sources.

This effect can be softened with the use of appropriate accessories such as a piece of translucent paper that is placed in front of the flash unit. This produces approximately the same effect as a large light source. Naturally there is a loss of light intensity that has to be taken into account. Large light sources, such as photolamps and studio flash units with large reflectors or with reflecting umbrellas are called "soft lights."

In daylight, the character of the light depends on the clouds. In sunlight with a clear sky, abrupt transitions from light to shade are unavoidable. But this effect is often softened when shadows are lightened, for instance, by reflecting walls (as it also occurs with flash pictures in a room), snow surfaces, white sand, and clouds. When a cloud formation moves in front of the sun, the character of the light can be compared to that of a large light source or a soft light.

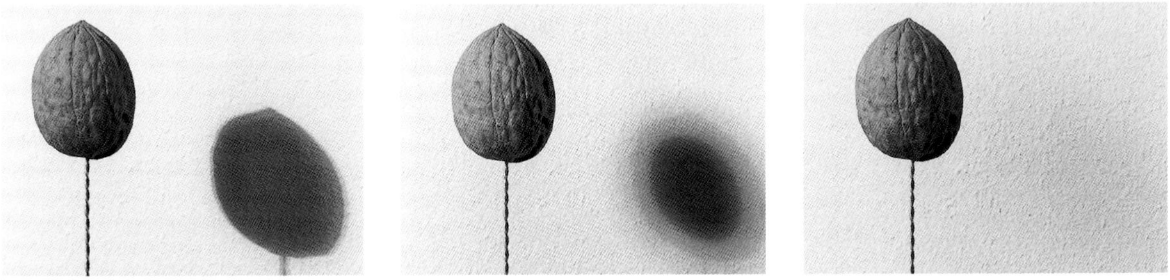

Fig. 182 a – c: *The formation of a shadow depends an the size of the light source in relation to the size of the subject, and on the distance of the light source from the subject. Basically, the following rule applies: the larger the light source, the softer the shadow. From left to right, figures 182 a – c depict shadows formed from small, medium, and large light sources.*

Light creates reflections

Shiny surfaces reflect all light sources. Large light sources form large reflections and small ones form small reflections. Often a large overall reflection is needed, one that covers the entire surface of the subject, in order to make that subject and its surface characteristics visible.

A practical way to create large reflections is to build a light tent using large pieces of translucent white paper. The overcast sky or light reflected from a large surface like the side of a white house, can also serve this purpose. Of course, light, dark, or colored surroundings will also be reflected on shiny surfaces, and this can be employed creatively in the composition of a photograph.

If all reflections are to be eliminated from shiny, uneven surfaces, polarizing filters must be attached both to the light source and the lens. Then their planes of polarization must be angled at 90° to each other. When several light sources are used, a polarizing filter must be attached to each one of them. Their planes of polarization must be parallel to each other and at a 90° angle to the polarization plane of the filter on the lens (see also page 206).

Reflections on polished metal surfaces can also be largely eliminated in this manner. But this entails a considerable loss of light. Exposures have to be approximately nine times longer; with flash the aperture has to be increased by about 3-1/2 stops.

Light has to be controlled

Frontal light does not create a three-dimensional impression of the subject, neither does diffuse or flat illumination. Grazing light, however, makes even the most delicate surface textures or alterations stand out. There are many variations between these two extremes in lighting set-ups. The angle at which the light should impinge on the subject depends on the nature of that subject; therefore this should be determined for each situation.

In architectural and in landscape photography, this often puts the photographers' patience to the test. They have to inspect a subject thoroughly many times or wait a long time until the lighting is just right.

Shadows created by side lighting must be brightened if a reasonable amount of shadow detail is to be reproduced. A secondary light source can be used for this purpose. Since this can produce objectionable additional shadows in the opposite direction, the use of umbrella lighting is often preferable for more pleasing results. Umbrella reflectors are now available at better photo dealers in a variety of sizes and from several manufacturers. A white wall can serve to brighten shadows outdoors, for instance; indoors a

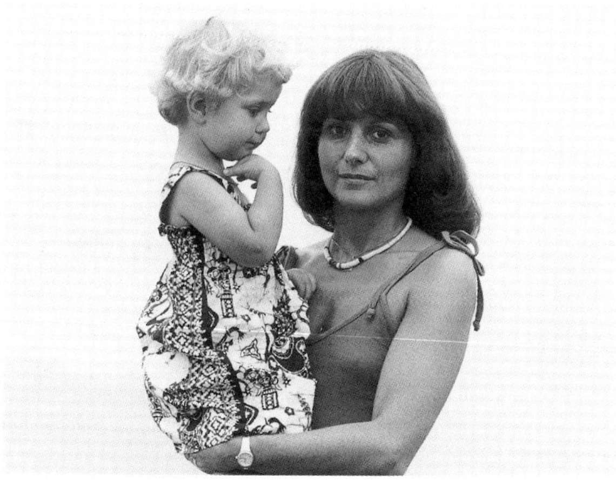

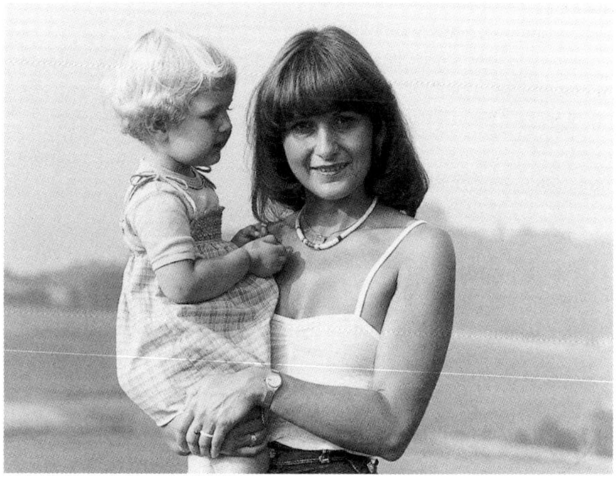

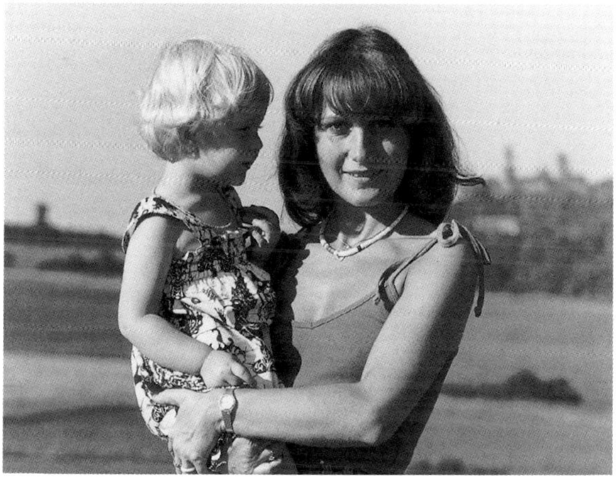

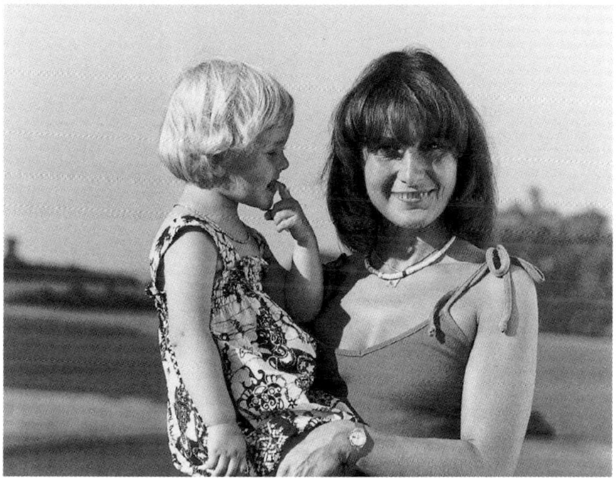

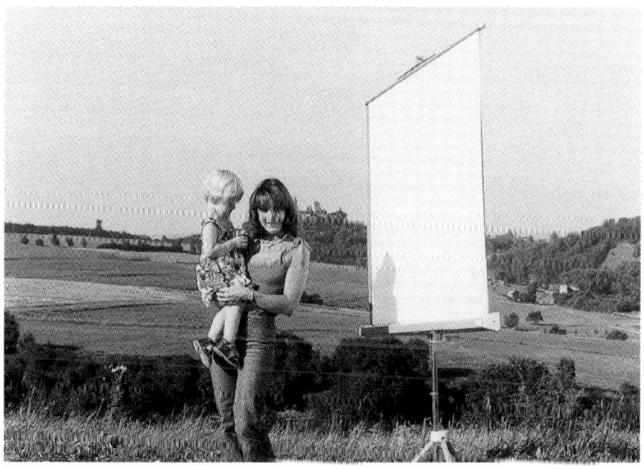

Fig. 183 a – e: *With natural light, the size of the light source determines the formation of shadows. The density of shadows is influenced by reflected natural light.*

Top left: *An overcast sky acts like a large light source and provides nearly shadowless illumination.*

Top right: *A hazy sun and scattered clouds provide soft, light shadows, which are ideal for portraits and close-up photography.*

Center left: *A cloudless sky and bright sunshine cause deep harsh shadows with little or no detail.*

Center right: *Reflecting light into harsh shadows will brighten them.*

Bottom right: *A white cardboard, a bright wall, or, as shown here, a projection screen are ideal "reflectors."*

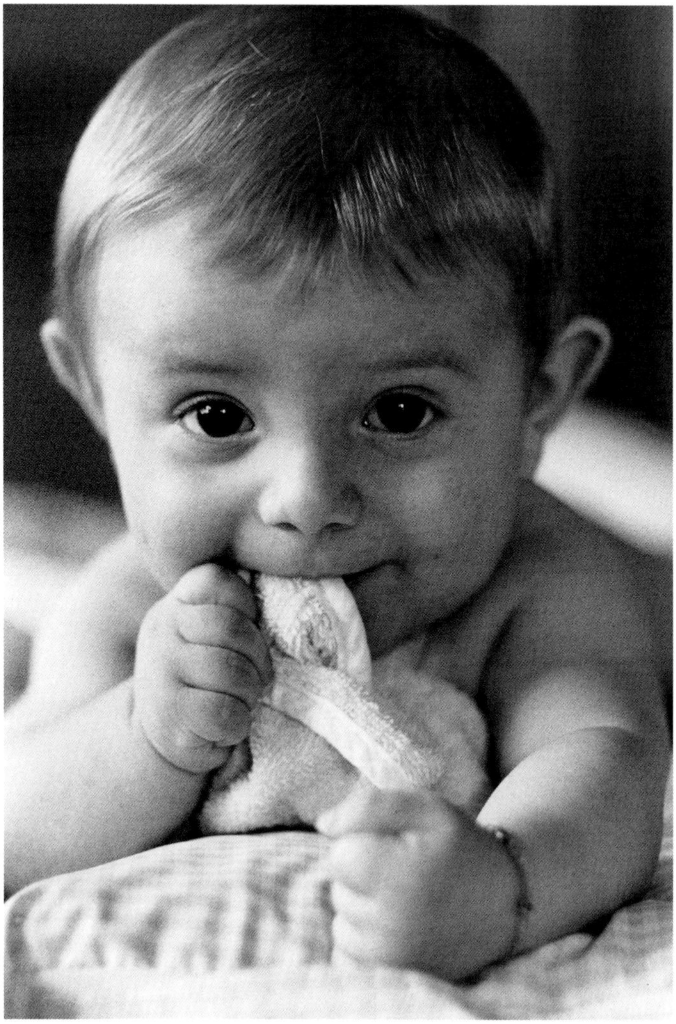

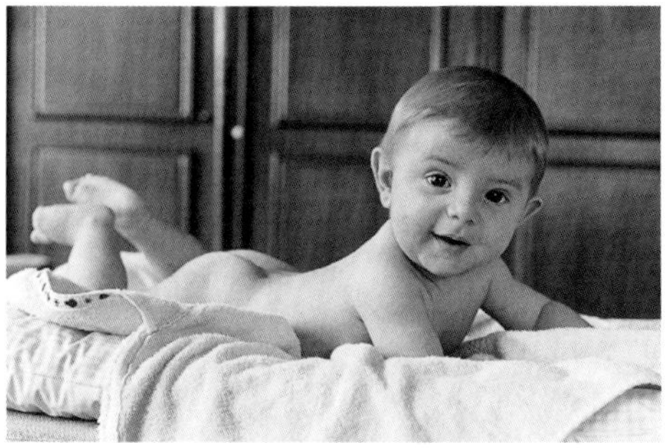

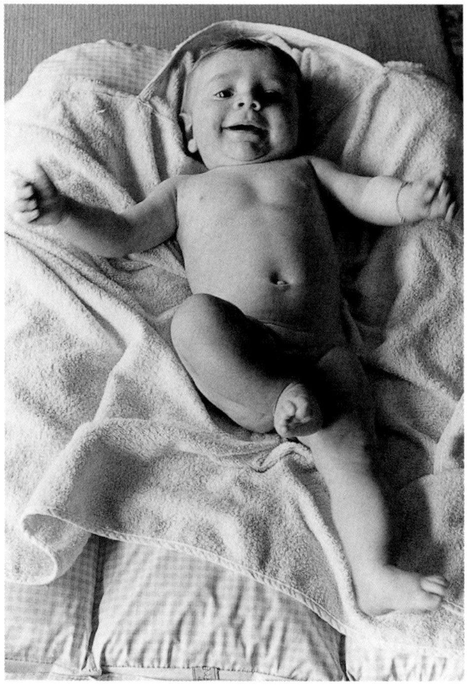

***Fig. 184 a – c:** We should also place higher standards on pictures and snapshots of pleasant memories than is generally the case. The portrait of the baby (left) was made without a major effort, simply by using a projection screen to light up shaded areas by reflecting daylight coming in through a window. All photographs were made with a 75mm f/1.4 Summilux-M lens, 1/60 second at f/2.8, high-speed film, and a tripod.*

sheet of white drafting paper or a projection screen can perform this function. Small pieces of white cardboard can serve as reflectors in close-up and macro photography.

As a rule, the contrast between light and shade (the lighting ratio) should not be greater than 4:1 if details are still to be discernible in shadow areas. With continuous lighting, this ratio can be measured with an exposure meter. The difference in brightness between light and shadows should not exceed two aperture stops.

For flash exposures, where exposure measurement has only recently become possible, the following rule applies: The light path from the light source to the subject via the reflecting surface should be longer than the light path from the light source directly to the subject by a factor of 1.4.

Transmitted light creates luminosity

The various types of lighting arrangements mentioned thus far involve only incident light. Translucent subjects can often be photographed well with transmitted light. This reveals their special character, fine textures become visible, and colors begin to "glow."

Basically, transmitted-light illumination can be set up according to two principles. If the subject is positioned directly between the camera and the light source, so that it is illuminated directly from behind, it will absorb a greater or a smaller portion of the light that is passing through, depending on its density or transmittance.

If the subject is completely transparent, or when its position is changed, the result will be a bright subject field. This principle is therefore called bright field illumination. This type of lighting is used for subjects whose details are well differentiated by their varying densities. Classic examples of this are stained glass windows in churches when they are photographed from the inside.

In dark field illumination, on the other hand, the subject is also illuminated from behind, but at an angle to the direction of the lens. If the subject has a refractive index that is different from that of the surrounding medium, such as air, or if it has no planoparallel surfaces, then the rays of light will be refracted or reflected at angles that lead them into the lens of the camera. The bright subject will become visible against a dark background. Individual water droplets of a fountain can be shown very dramatically with this type of lighting.

The most effective angle for the lateral light beam in transmitted dark field illumination is best determined experimentally. Minor changes in that angle or in the camera position often have a major effect. That effect can only be evaluated accurately by observing it from the camera position, preferably through the viewfinder. In this case it is important that the light source does not impinge directly on the front lens of the lens system.

Flash as a portable sun

Flash techniques have replaced conventional artificial illumination in many fields of photography. There are professional studio flash setups that offer all sorts of flexibility. A built-in modeling light is used for judging the lighting effect. The character of the light and the formation of shadows can be controlled by different types of interchangeable reflectors, by light banks, and by optical attachments.

For the most popular uses of Leica M cameras, such as candid snapshots and fast photojournalistic photography, accessory electronic flash units have become standard equipment. Their principal advantages are their compact size, light weight and the constant color temperature of their light, coupled with a relatively high light output. The latter is measured in watt-seconds (joules).

More common, and more useful for practical applications is their output rating by guide number. As a rule, it is indicated for a film speed of ISO 100. Guide numbers are expressed in either meters or feet, so when comparing flash units, make sure that all of the guide numbers are expressed in the same measuring system. In some flash units the guide number maybe part of the model number. For example the Leica flash unit "SF 20" uses the guide number for identification. "SF" is the abbreviation for System Flash. A flash unit with a zoom-head matches the image angles of different lenses, usually by motor-driven adjustment. This is highly practical, but does change the effective guide number depending on the position of the zoom head.

In order to fully utilize the options of the Leica M flash technology and recognize its limits, various functions of the camera, flash unit and any accessory adapters must be known. Together, these offer a number of options of utilizing existing, ambient light and the rapid burst of the flash, either alone or in combination. In this case both the camera and the flash unit affect the amount of light required for a correct exposure on the film. However, this is achieved in different ways.

In the camera, light is always controlled by the shutter speed and the lens aperture. In the flash unit, however, the flash duration is controlled by the computer operation and the TTL flash meter or by the lens aperture, when the flash unit operates at full power or constant partial power. With dedicated flash systems these control circuits are coupled with each other, i.e. the camera and the flash unit exchange information and enable different functions.

Unfortunately, the performance of a flash unit is not a measure of its effectiveness in a photograph. Although modern computer flash units have made the use of flash a great deal more convenient, and usually guarantees correctly exposed films, they do not allow the photographer to accurately evaluate the effect of the lighting in advance. Experienced Leica M photographers therefore use electronic flash units very judiciously, for example for lighting up shadows or when fast lenses and high speed films are no longer sufficient for short exposures. Those who are more interested in their lighting than in merely the amount of it needed for correct exposure should devote a little time to the theory of flash technique. With a little practice, remarkable improvements in lighting skills and even in special effects can be achieved.

Know the guide number

Unless otherwise indicated, the guide number stated in the instructions of the flash unit is based on a film speed of ISO 100 and is expressed in either feet or meters. The guide number increases with higher film speeds and it decreases with lower film speeds. Doubling or halving the ISO number results in a change in the guide number by a factor of 1.4 as shown in the table below:

Film speed		Guide number		
ISO	25	11	20	34
ISO	50	16	28	48
ISO	100	22	40	68
ISO	200	32	56	96
ISO	400	45	80	136

The guide number is used to determine the correct aperture when the distance between flash and subject is known. Conversely, the correct distance can easily be calculated when the aperture is fixed:

$$\text{Aperture} = \frac{\text{Guide number}}{\text{Distance}} \qquad \text{Distance} = \frac{\text{Guide number}}{\text{Aperture}}$$

Note: First you must check whether the guide number is based on meters or feet, because this makes a big difference. To convert a metric guide number for use with feet, multiply it by 3.28; to convert a guide number based on feet for use with meters, divide it by 3.28.

Example: With a (metric) guide number of 24 and a distance of 3 m, the required aperture would be 24/3 = f/8. In regions where distances are measured in feet, the guide number for the same combination of flash and film would be approximately 80. Therefore at the same distance, which is equivalent to 10 feet, the aperture would be 80/10 = f/8.

Older flash units are usually equipped with aperture calculators or tables, which make guide number calculations unnecessary. Modern flash units usually indicate the required information on an electronic display. Guide numbers and information on the display are valid for rooms of average size, with walls that have normal reflectance. Deviations from such "normal" conditions, such as large halls with dark wood paneling, or small bathrooms with white tiles, require an increase or a decrease, respectively, of the aperture by an amount between half a stop and a full stop. Of course, modern computerized flash units automatically compensate for such deviations.

Guide numbers and displays provide values that are valid only for frontal flash, when the angle between the optical axis of the flash reflector and that of the photographic lens is no greater than approximately 30°. If that angle is larger, the aperture has to be increased.

Aperture correction for lateral flash illumination:
45° = increase by 1/2 stop
60° = increase by 1 stop
70° = increase by 1/2 stop
90° = the light from a flash at this angle is practically negligible for determining the aperture; it merely serves as an accent light.

A correction can also be made by changing the distance from flash to subject. If that distance is increased by a factor of 1.4, the effective light intensity on the subject is reduced by one half; if the distance is decreased by a factor of 1.4, the intensity of the light on the subject is doubled.

Flash synchronization

With flash illumination, the exposure of the film is usually determined by the duration of the flash. In conventional flash units, that duration varies from approximately 1/250 to 1/50,000 second. In darkness, for instance, the shutter of a camera mounted on a tripod can be set on "B" and then opened, and the flash can then be fired when necessary. With this set-up and an infrared triggering device, a bat can be photographed in flight with maximum sharpness. A few decades ago, this open flash method was the only method with which persons could be photographed with flash in a darkened room. Open flash is still used effectively today for illuminating very large rooms (see page 284).

This technique is not suitable, however, for photographing moving subjects in light surroundings, or for making hand-held photographs. That is why flash is normally used with relatively fast shutter speeds, so that the weaker ambient light is least likely to affect the film.

As a result of the mode of operation of the focal plane shutter, not all shutter speeds can be used for flash exposures. Only when the first shutter curtain has completely cleared the film gate and the second shutter curtain has not yet begun to cover it again, is it possible for flash to expose the full format of the film. The shortest shutter speed in which this possible is called the flash synchronization speed.

Most portable electronic flash units have a foot, which can be inserted in the Leica M's accessory shoe. The center contact is used to establish the synchronous connection. If there is no center contact on the camera as is the case, earlier Leica M models, up to the M4, this connection is established by plugging a synchronization cable into a flash contact on the camera's top plate. Synchronization cables from the accessory shoe to the flash contact are generally required if a flash unit mounted to a flash bracket. Studio flash units can even be triggered by remote infrared control. To achieve this, the tiny IR emitter is slid in the accessory shoe of the camera and activated through the center contact or the synchronization lead.

The focal-plane shutters of all Leica M models use an electronic flash synchronization of 1/50 second. This is indicated on the shutter-speed dial with the symbol of a flash (⚡). The flash synchronization is ensured with all Leica M models, even with longer shutter speeds and when the camera is set to "B."

Any commercially available flash unit and studio flash system, which is thyristor-controlled or complies with the ISO 10330 standard can be connected to Leica M models, either by means of the accessory shoe's center contact or by means of a standard flash connector.

With the Leica M7 and M6 TTL, the use of older flash units may result in the disruption of functions or even damage the camera's electronic system. With some older units, when the flash is fired, peak currents of 20 Amps are possible, depending on the manufacturer. These power surges are couple electromagnetically with the camera's electronic system and may result in an exposure time that is too long or too short or could even destroy the camera's electronic system. Therefore, the use of these flash units is not recommended. However, flash systems or studio flash may be used with IR control for firing the flash.

Table 15: Flash Synchronization Leica M cameras

Type of flash		Leica M7	all Leica M6 models	all Leica M cameras with serial numbers above Nr. 854 001		Leica M3 cameras with serial numbers above Nr. 854 000	
		X	X	⚡ or X	💡 or M	⚡ = X contact	💡 = M contact
Electronic flash		B → ⚡(= 1/50)	B → ⚡(= 1/50)	B → ⚡(= 1/50) B → • (= 1/50)	–	B → 1/50	–
Dedicated SCA 3002 Adapter SCA 3502 M2		High Speed Synchronization 1/250, 1/500, 1/1000	–	–	–	–	–
Flash bulb	AG 1 AG 3 Flash cube M2	B → 1/30	B → 1/30	B → 1/30	–	B → 1/125	–
Flash bulb	XM 1 B PF 1	B → 1/30	B → 1/30	–	B → 1/60	–	B → 1/50
Flash bulb	PF 5	B → 1/30	B → 1/30	–	B → 1/60	–	B → 1/100
Flash bulb	M 3	B → 1/30	B → 1/30	–	B → 1/125	–	–
Flash bulb	GE 5 B Press 25	B → 1/30	B → 1/30	–	B → 1/500	–	B → 1/500
Flash bulb	Press 40 2	B → 1/30	B → 1/30	–	–	–	–
Flash bulb	FP 26 PF 6 3	B → 1/15	B → 1/15	–	–	–	–

⚡ or X = Flash contact for electronic flash units and hot shoe
💡 or M = Flash contact for flash bulb units

In the Leica M7 and M6 TTL, batteries must be loaded in the camera in order to fire and control connected flash units, and exposure metering must be activated by a slight depression of the shutter release button. This applies also when a studio flash is to be fired remote by an IR emitter. If this does not occur, as a result of fast complete depression of the release button, it is possible that the flash will fail to fire.

M and X contacts

Flashbulbs and electronic flash units have different flash durations. Whereas the electronic flash delivers its maximum brightness in a very brief burst, flashbulbs require a comparatively long time to reach their full brightness. This brightness is maintained for a moment, and then it subsides relatively slowly. To accommodate these diverse characteristics, all Leica M cameras up to the Leica M4-P are equipped with two flash contacts, into which the connectors of the cables from the respective flash units are inserted. The “M” contact is used with flashbulbs and the “X” contact is used with electronic flash. Some flashbulbs can be used with either the “M” or the “X” contact. The shutter speeds and which flash contact should be used are usually listed on the package. Since large, powerful flashbulbs have disappeared from the market, the M contact has become superfluous, and therefore this contact does not appear on the Leica M6 camera.

The earlier Leica M models up to the Leica M4 had special flash contacts, which were larger than today's customary concentric 3-mm sockets. Appropriate adapters that permit the use of all standard flash connecting cables on older Leica M cameras are readily available at Leica dealers.

Hot shoe

Most portable electronic flash units have a foot that can be inserted in the accessory shoe of Leica M cameras. A pin in the center of that foot completes a connection with a contact in the center of the accessory shoe (the so-called "hot shoe") of all Leica M models starting with the Leica M5 camera, thus establishing the synchronizing circuit. The "hot shoe" corresponds to the X contact. Studio flash units can thus be fired without connecting cables by using an infrared control and by inserting the infrared trigger in the hot shoe of a Leica M camera.

Checking flash synchronization

There is a convenient way to check the flash synchronization of Leica M cameras: The flash unit is attached in accordance with the instructions (using a connecting cable), the base plate is removed from the camera, the back cover is opened and a piece of enlarging paper is placed on the film gate in subdued light. The cover is closed again, the lens is removed, and the flash is then set off directly in front of the lens opening of the camera. By looking through the camera' the effect of the flash can be seen directly on the paper, even without processing. If the synchronization is accurate, when the paper is processed, the intense light of the flash will have uniformly darkened a 24 x 36 mm area of the paper.

Computerized flash units

Modern, portable electronic flash units are capable of automatically controlling the amount of light that they emit. By means of the sensor on the unit, the flash light reflected by the subject is measured and the duration of the flash is stopped immediately by a computerized control when the amount of light emitted by the flash is sufficient for a correct exposure. The duration of the flash varies between 1/250 second and 1/50,000 second, depending on the distance, aperture and film speed. Because the amount of light is controlled by the flash unit's computer, the amount of light released should produce an exact exposure. In older models, the residual energy is "discharged" with out being used. With the current generation of flash units, which uses thyristor-controlled illumination, the unused energy is stored for the subsequent exposure. Consequently, these flash units have several advantages: The flash uses only as much energy as is required and, as a result, the number of flashes per bat-

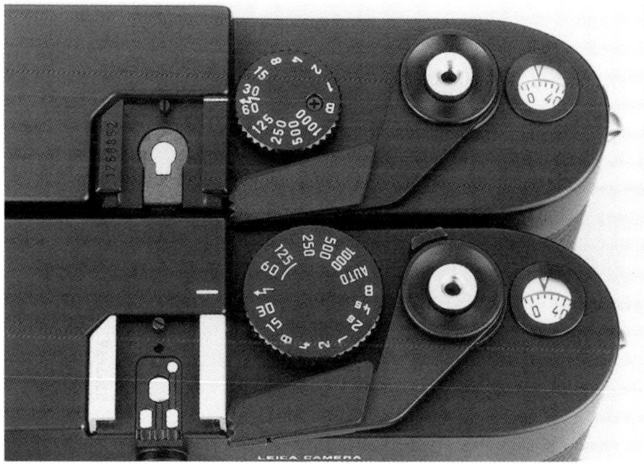

Fig. 185: *Since the introduction of the M5, Leica has included a hot shoe with a middle X-sync contact on all Leica M models, such as the one on this Leica M6 (top). The hot shoe contact triggers the flash and synchronizes it with the opening of the first shutter curtain on the camera. The hot shoes on the Leica M6 TTL and Leica M7 include other dedicated contacts for communication between the camera and flash units that are compatible with the SCA system. With flash units in this dedicated system TTL flash, and other features such as high-speed synchronization are possible depending on the flash unit.*

tery charge or battery pack is increased. Also, the unit will be ready for the next exposure in much less time if the first flash discharged did not use all of the stored energy. With appropriate light metering such an electronic flash unit can fire two, three, or even more flashes per second. Therefore, it can be used also with a motorized Leica M camera. Here, a distinction must be made between two options. The first option is to use light-dosage as usual, i.e. by measuring the flash-light or by pre-selecting the amount of energy to be released per flash. The second option offers more freedom for composition; however, it requires computation with the guide number.

Most of the measuring systems of modern computerized flash units can be pre-programmed for different apertures. Some of them can be controlled with an external sensor, which can be connected with the flash unit by a cable and operated in this manner. This is particularly advantageous when the flash is not mounted on the camera. This external sensor is mounted on the accessory shoe of the camera and it measures the light from the flash in the exact direction that is used for taking the picture. If a remote sensor is not available and the flash is to be used away from the camera, it should be set for manual operation and the proper aperture determined by means of the guide-number formula.

System-compliant flash units

Accessory flash units are offered in various sizes, featuring different performance data and technical features. With the use of appropriate adapters, many can be integrated in the camera's dedicated system, whereby the camera and flash unit control each other and various functions. Also, the amount of light can be controlled by means of metering through the camera lens (TTL flash exposure measurement) if the camera offers this feature. The dedicated flash units featuring these options are referred to as being system-compliant. These include the SF 20 by Leica and many different flash units by Metz and others with appropriate adapters for the Leica M system. The adapter system for coupling these system-compliant flash units with the Leica M7 and the Leica M6 TTL is called the SCA, which stands for "Special Camera Adaptation." Corresponding to their "flash options," the Leica M models and flash units are used with various SCA systems and adapters:

- System SCA 3000 with adapter SCA 3501 M1 for the Leica M7 and M6 TTL.
- System SCA 3002 with the adapter SCA 3502 M2 for the Leica M7 and M6 TTL.

Considering the differences of these SCA systems, there are a few common features. These include the flash readiness indicator and the flash success indicator in the viewfinder of all Leica M models.

Important: If color reversal film is used for flash exposures, it is important to know that the flash readiness indicator and the automatic switching to flash synchronization time from 1/50 sec. (X synchronization)—with the use of the Leica M7's aperture-priority automatic exposure control—occurs when the flash unit is at 70% charge, and full energy in the case of a few flash units. In accordance with the German DIN standard this is acceptable and does not need to be specifically identified. If, however, these flash units are used for exposures immediately after the flash readiness indication and 100% of flash energy is required, this may result in a noticeable underexposure of color transparencies. In these situations, the flash exposure should be made only after a few seconds of additional charge time has transpired.

TTL flash exposure

TTL (through-the-lens) flash exposure is an integral feature of the Leica M7 and Leica M6 TTL. In this case, the light reflected by the film is received by a silicon photodiode with a collecting lens, which is located on the lower right side of the camera, behind the bayonet. Because, despite their appearance, the film layers of most normal 35mm films have almost the same reflection properties, these exposures are correct. In exceptional cases an exposure correction may be made by using the override on the flash unit or the SCA adapter. In Polaroid instant slide films, for example, a correction should be made of "-1.5" or "-1-2/3."

Of course, TTL flash metering does not negate the usual laws of physics, which are applicable to general photography. For instance, flash exposure metering occurs through the lens and, as with all light meters, a correct exposure result can be expected only when the flash-exposed subjects exhibit a (normal) reflectance of close to 18%. Particularly light or dark objects, or a portrait taken with flash outdoors at night without a close background to reflect the light, will require compensation. Likewise, the rules of lighting technique retain their validity. Only with flash they are only more difficult to assess in advance than with the use of ambient light.

A special advantage of through-the-lens flash exposure metering is the (nearly) unrestricted selection of lens apertures. In general, these are limited merely by the range of the flash unit. Other advantages are that the particularly significant absorption of light by zoom lenses and the extension factor for close-up shots are automatically taken into account. TTL flash is also advantageous when the flash unit cannot be located in the immediate vicinity of the camera because of various subject limitations.

The electrical connection of the flash unit and the camera is established with an appropriate adapter by way of the accessory shoe on the camera, which, includes, in addition to the center contact, three other contacts (see Fig. 185). Flash unit manufacturers who offer the SCA system include Metz and Cullmann.

The many other advantages of TTL flash exposure measurement also include automatic switching to X synchronization in the Leica M7 when automatic exposure control is used.

Flash exposures with the Leica M7

Two options of flash exposure metering ensure that the Leica M7 will achieve excellent exposure results even when different flash units are used.

TTL flash exposure can be performed with flash units that are included in systems SCA 3002 or SCA 3000 and with adapters for the Leica M7:

Adapter SCA 3502 M2 for system SCA 3002.
Adapter SCA 3501 M1 for system SCA 3000.

The flash unit SF 20 offered by Leica as an accessory is compatible with system SCA 3000. However, an adapter is not necessary for this flash unit because its functions are integrated in the housing of the SF 20.

Another option for controlling the amount of light emitted by the flash offered by the flash units themselves is the automatic computer flash. In this case the light reflected by the subject is not measured by the Leica M7 but by a sensor on the flash unit. The amount of light required for correct exposure is then controlled by the duration of the flash. However, the absorption of light, by filters attached to the lens, and other conditions is not taken into account as it is with TTL flash metering.

Leica flash SF 20

Today, Leica offers a particularly compact flash unit for the Leica M and R systems. It incorporates all dedicated functions within the unit so there is no need for the foot of the flash to be interchangeable. Also, the reflector is located in the upper part of the elongated body, not low, as with some compact flash units. As a result, the distance between the lens and flash reflector is increased considerably. Thus the risk of red eye in flash exposures of people is reduced dramatically (see also page 282).

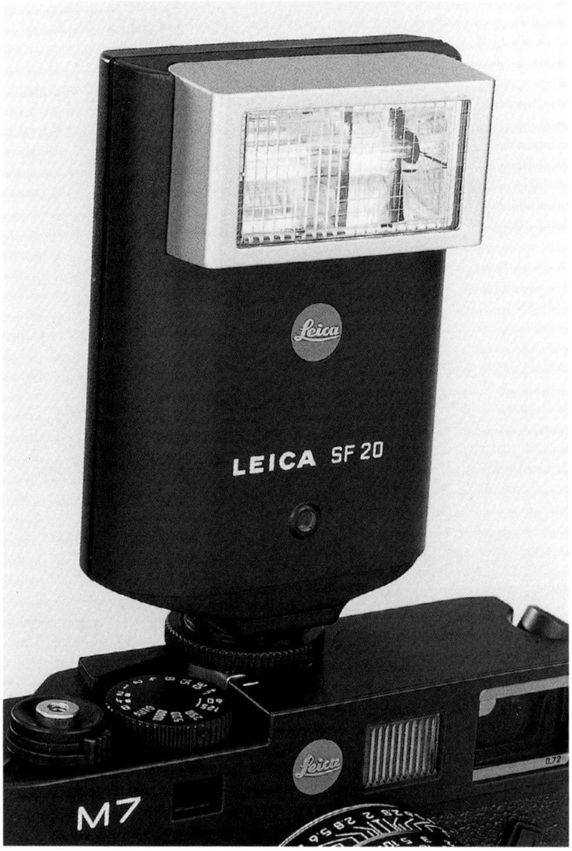

Fig. 186: *The Leica SF 20 compact dedicated flash unit for the Leica M.*

The angle of coverage of the SF 20 illuminates exposures with lenses as wide as 35mm. For shorter focal lengths of up to at most 24 mm, a diffuser can be attached in front of the reflector. The LCD on the back of the unit can be illuminated and indicates the data required for flash exposures such as shooting distance and any set exposure compensation. Also the unit provides dedicated flash status information for the displays in the viewfinder of the Leica M7 and the M6 TTL. This features includes flash readiness and flash exposure confirmation.

The SF 20 can also be used with other Leica M models and cameras of other manufacturers, however not in conjunction with a TTL flash exposure. Manual flash and sensor autoflash are possible. However, it does not supply viewfinder information. The power supply consists of two lithium batteries, type DL123A. The number of flashes on a set of batteries is approximately 250.

Adapter SCA 3502 M2

This adapter connects flash units, which are compatible with the SCA 3002 system by means of the Leica M7's accessory shoe. The adapter is secured in the accessory shoe of the camera by means of a locking ring and by a small pin, which slides into a corresponding hole in the accessory shoe. When the ring is tightened, it is held absolutely securely in place. Depending on the selected mode of operation (automatic exposure control or manual setting), the camera and flash unit automatically perform different functions or leave the photographer sufficient creative space to compose flash exposures as desired:

- TTL flash exposure metering of the subject.
- Automatic setting of the flash synchronization speed of 1/50 second with aperture-priority automatic exposure control, when the flash is charged.
- Manual selection of exposure times from 4 seconds to 1/50 second and B.
- Manual selection of all apertures.
- Automatic transfer of film speed.
- Information displays in the viewfinder of the Leica M7:
  - Flash symbol blinks slowly = flash is switched on, charging in progress.
  - Flash symbol is constantly visible = flash is ready to fire.
  - Flash symbol stays constantly visible after flash is fired, other displays are extinguished = flash exposure was OK; flash remains ready for next exposure.
  - Flash symbol blinks rapidly after release, other displays are extinguished = flash exposure was OK but the flash is not yet ready for next exposure.

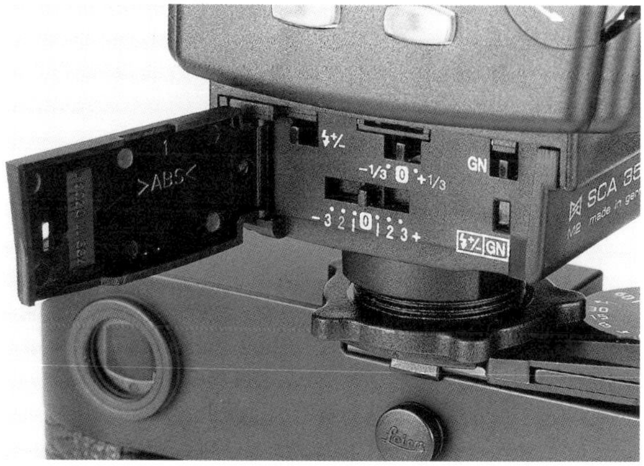

Fig. 187: *The SCA 3502 M2 adapter has on its back, hidden under a small door, the switches for flash override. These switches are used when a setting cannot be adjusted on the flash unit itself. The usually required correction for a fill flash of –1-2/3 EV is indicated in "red," can be pre-selected and activated only when required.*

- Flash symbol and other displays are extinguished after release = underexposure.
- Flash symbol not visible even though the flash is enabled and ready = set shutter speed is less than 1/50 second (flash is locked and will not fire when the shutter release is pressed).

• Flash exposure compensation of +3-1/3 EV to –3-1/3 EV. The setting for normal fill flash is marked in red.
• If autoflash mode is selected, the sensor on the front of the unit controls the flash exposure.
• Automatic adaptation to the required slower shutter speed for stroboscopic exposures.

By using appropriate adapters, multiple SCA 3002-compatible flash units may be simultaneously controlled without cables.

In conjunction with the SCA 3002-compatible flash unit and adapter SCA 3502, the Leica M7 uses integral flash exposure metering through the lens. As soon as the required amount of light has reached the film, the flash is stopped. Light from a flash that is twice as far from its source is spread over four times the area and, thus, has 1/4th the intensity. Thus, the distance between the flash and subject determines the duration of the flash. The greater the distance, the longer is the flash duration.

With very short distances the control range for the flash duration (up to 1/10,000 second or less) may not be sufficiently short, thus an over-exposure would be the result. On the other hand, if greater distances have to be covered, the entire energy output of the flash may not be sufficient to provide a proper exposure. In this case, an under-exposure would result. Therefore, the display of the flash unit indicates probable flash shooting distances. These are independent of the film speed and the selected lens aperture. If this range is exceeded and an under-exposure is the result, this will be indicated in the viewfinder of the Leica M7.

The SCA 3502 M2 adapter features an override. If, for example, deep shadows are to be eliminated in a backlighted exposure, a fill-flash setting of –1-2/3 EV is selected. Because this setting is well established in photographic practice, it has been specially identified.

Also, other settings can be selected and are necessary. For example, when an object such as a white blossom in front of a deep background is to be photographed with backlighting. Then a correction of at least –2-1/3 EV is useful because, otherwise, due to the dark, non-reflecting background, the flash would release too much light and would wash out the light blossom. Because the separate flash override of –3-1/3 EV to +3-1/3 EV can be set in one-third step increments, the photographer is given the necessary freedom to adapt the flash unit to the most varied lighting and illumination situations.

A few flash units that are part of the SCA 3002 system such as, e.g., the Mecablitz 54 MZ-3, offer functions, which also expand the photographic possibilities of the Leica M7.

Second-curtain sync

With cameras that have focal-plane shutters, the flash is usually triggered the split-second the first shutter curtain is fully open. This is called front-curtain or first-curtain synchronization. If the flash is triggered the split-second before the second shutter curtain begins to close, it is called rear-curtain or second-curtain sync. With the use of a Metz flash unit, such as the 54 MZ-3, this triggering operation may be assigned selectively to either the first or the second shutter curtain. This offers the option of moving the short-duration flash burst to the beginning or to the end of the long ambient-light exposure. For normal flash exposures with a relatively short exposure time of 1/50 second, this is of little importance because the triggering time of the first shutter curtain and that of the second virtually coincide. The reason for this is that with such a short exposure time, the first curtain has just cleared the film gate while the second curtain is just starting to cover it again. Even with extended exposure times, this triggering time is of little importance if the subjects are static and a tripod is used. As long as the contours of the image obtained by the flash exposure and those obtained with existing light exposure are superimposed in the photograph, the flash firing time is of little or no consequence. However, when extended-motion exposures are combined with flash, the ambient-light image, which is out of focus due to motion blur and the sharp image, which has been "frozen" by the burst of the flash are superimposed. If the flash exposure occurs directly before the end of the long-term exposure, the sharp image will appear to be ahead of the motion trails (which were exposed first on the film), which appears more natural to the viewer.

Flash as the main light source

Flash may act as main light source (full flash) and illuminate the subject. In the development of new flash units this has always been a most important goal. However, there are two features in particular which impair the otherwise enormous advantages of independent flash illumination:

- Due to the short duration of the flash, an evaluation of light control and the distribution of light and shadows on the subject and in the scene are not immediately possible. As a rule, one has to wait to see the processed film.
- Because of their different distances from the flash objects staggered in a scene are affected by a significant light decrease from the foreground toward the background when normal or wide-angle lenses are used. At worst, everything in the foreground of the picture will be overexposed by flash while everything that is farther away will be dark. Better illumination of the depth of a room will be achieved when the same subject is photographed at a greater distances with a longer focal length. This is explained by a simple example: A group of persons who sit at a large table is first photographed with a 35mm wide-angle lens. The distance from the flash and the camera to the closest person is approximately 1.30 m (c. 5 feet); the distance to the person who is the farthest away is approximately 4 m (c. 18 feet). Because light decreases by the square of the distance, the person who is the farthest receives only 1/4th of the light of the person who is the closest. This is a difference of two EV, or two f/stops, which is too much for a balanced illumination. If a 90mm focal length is used, the same subject at a distance of flash and camera to the closest person is captured at slightly more than 3 m (c. 13 feet). The lighting of the person who is the farthest away (approx. 6m or c. 21 feet) is decreased only by 1/2. This corresponds to one exposure value, or one f/stop. Color negative films, for instance, can easily handle this decrease in light.

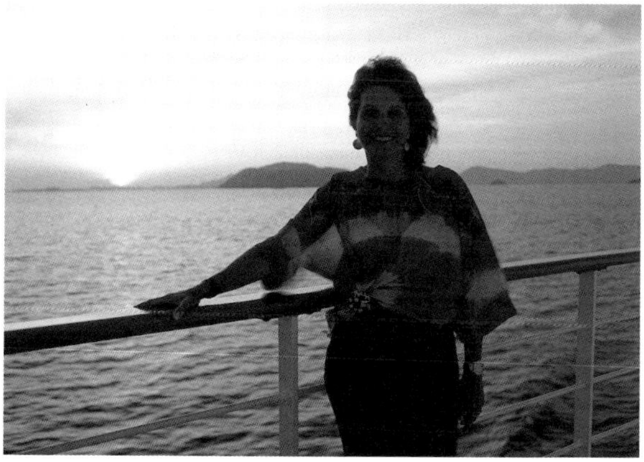

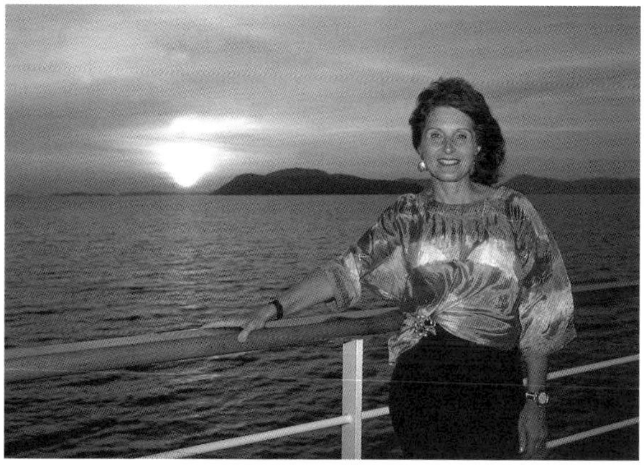

Fig. 188 a and b: *Great brightness differences between foreground and background, as in this sunset, produce an unsatisfactory result (left) when the foreground is not lightened. This significant contrast can be corrected by fill flash. If the ambient exposure remains set for the background, the mood of the sunset is retained (right). The picture on the left was taken at 1/50 second at f/4, the right at 1/50 second at f/5.6 – 8 with Leica SF 20 with a compensation of –1 EV.*

Flash as fill light

Fill flash often improves exposures but isn't utilized as often as it should be, considering how easy to use thanks to modern computerized flash units. Using fill flash reduces strong contrasts by "opening up" deep shadows caused by high contrast lighting or backlighting. For best results the effect of daylight and flash should be weighted in such a manner that the shadow areas facing the camera are exposed by 1 EV to 2 EV less than those illuminated by full daylight.

This is achieved by setting compensation on flash units, which offer this feature, such as Mecablitz models 54 MZ-3, 70 MZ-4, and 70 MZ-t. With flash units of SCA 3002 system, the adjustments are made on the SCA 3502 M2 adapter. In this case, as a rule, the required correction for the fill flash of –1-2/3 EV is highlighted in "red." All correction settings on the adapter can be pre-selected and activated as needed.

The Leica SF 20 also permits flash compensation. As in the case of the Mecablitz models, exposure values are in 1/3 steps. Also in this case, the selected normal fill flash is –1-2/3 EV.
In order to lighten deep shadow areas in the foreground to make the picture more effective or achieve more balanced illumination and more brilliant colors in overcast weather, it is advisable to work with a slightly less exposure than was determined by the exposure meter for the ambient light background.

However, the fill flash technique very quickly reaches its limits in sunlight when the Leica M is used. One reason is that the shortest flash synchronization speed of 1/50 second results in over-exposure even at f/16 when a film of ISO 100 is used. Another reason is that this shutter speed is frequently "too slow" to avoid motion blur.

Linear flash technique

Focal-plane shutters like the ones in the Leica M7 permit electronic flash synchronization only with shutter speeds that allow the film gate of the camera to be fully opened when the flash fires. In the Leica M these are shutter speeds of up to 1/50 second.

With faster shutter speeds part of the first or second shutter curtain will be covering the film gate so that the flash cannot illuminate the entire film frame.

If high shutter speeds are used and the flash pulses in very short intervals, the tight sequencing of the flash bursts acts like a continuous light source. This type of linear flash is able to synchronize with shutter speeds of up to 1/250 second. The camera will fire the linear flash at the start of the first shutter curtain if the flash unit has the required electronic control and sufficient energy for this feature. This is true of the Leica M7 and a few SCA 3002 system flash units. In this High Speed Synchronization (HSS) mode, the shutter speed and the aperture of the Leica M7 are set manually. Likewise, the flash operation is manual. Flash exposure metering is not possible. The duration of the linear flash, the light angle of the reflector, as well as the film speed in use, determine the guide number of this flash. The selected aperture, which depends on the subject distance, is indicated in the display of the flash unit. It must be substantially larger than during normal flash operation. For example, in the case of the Mecablitz 54 MZ-3 it is 4 m (c. 18 feet) at f/2 and 1/250 second for an ISO film speed of 100. Because this mode does not use flash exposure metering incorrect exposures can occur with different subject distances or if the flash output is not sufficient.

Because fill flash requires less light (-1-2/3 EV), with this technique the shooting range increases. Under the same conditions as above, the distance from the flash to the subject increases to 7.2 m (c. 24 feet). On the Leica M7, the corresponding correction is made by means of the exposure compensation setting. The output of the flash can also be reduced, however this will cut the shooting distance almost in half.

Fig. J1 and J2: *What is the message to be conveyed by your photo? That in Scotland people live in pretty white houses even in remote areas? Or that people have not yet taken over this magnificent Scottish landscape? Both are certainly right. Different accents were placed in these pictures in order to document one statement or the other.*
Fig. J1: *24mm f/2.8 Elmarit-M ASPH lens with polarizing filter.*
Fig. J2: *90mm f/2.8 Elmarit-M lens with polarizing filter. Both exposures are on daylight reversal film, ISO 64.*

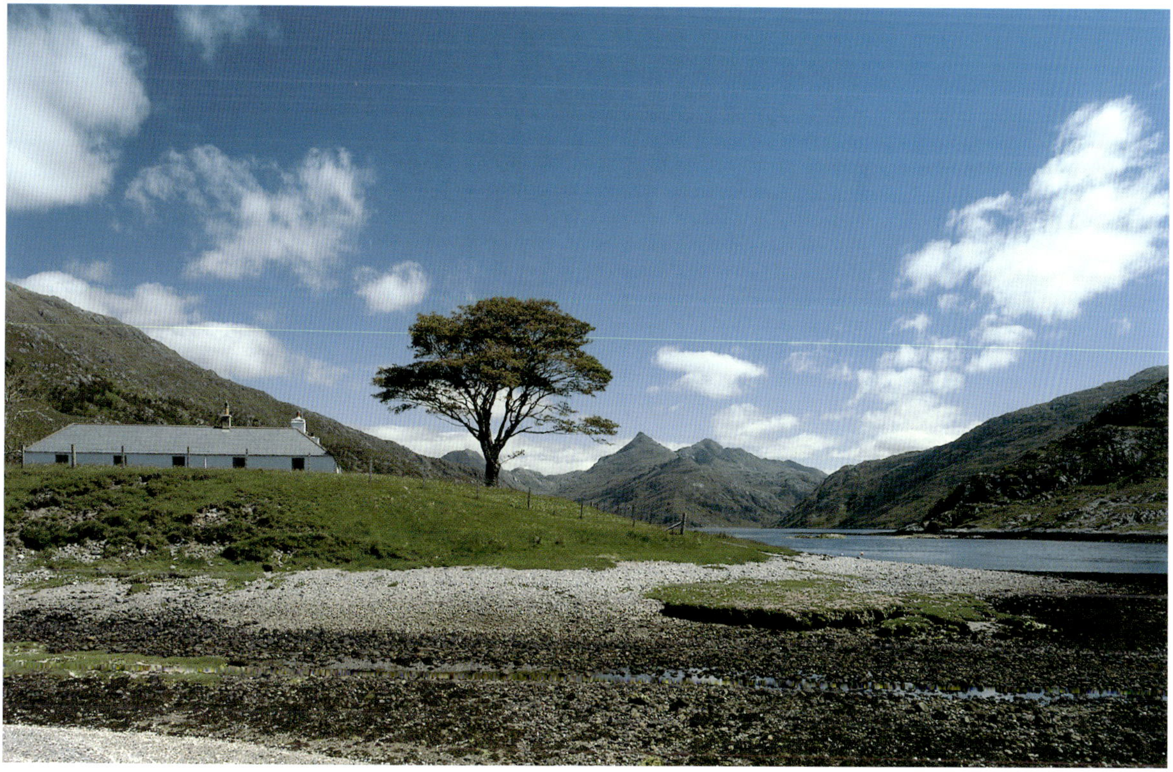

Fig. J1

Fig. J2

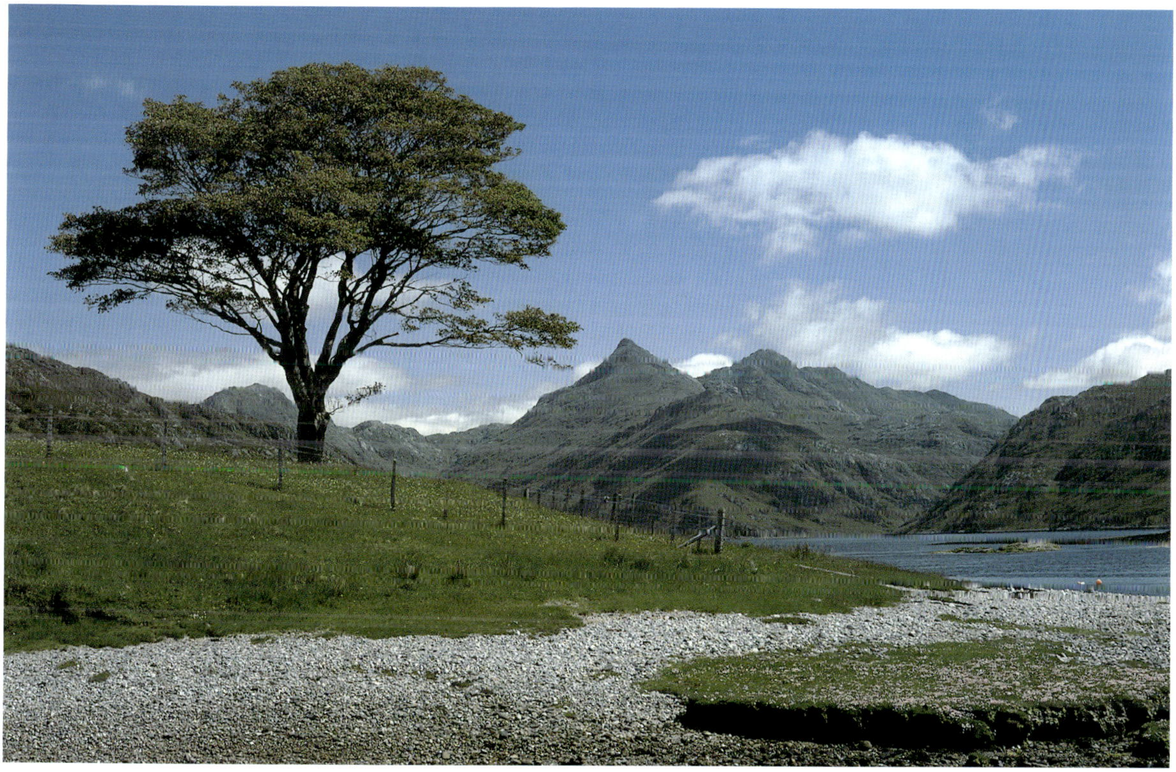

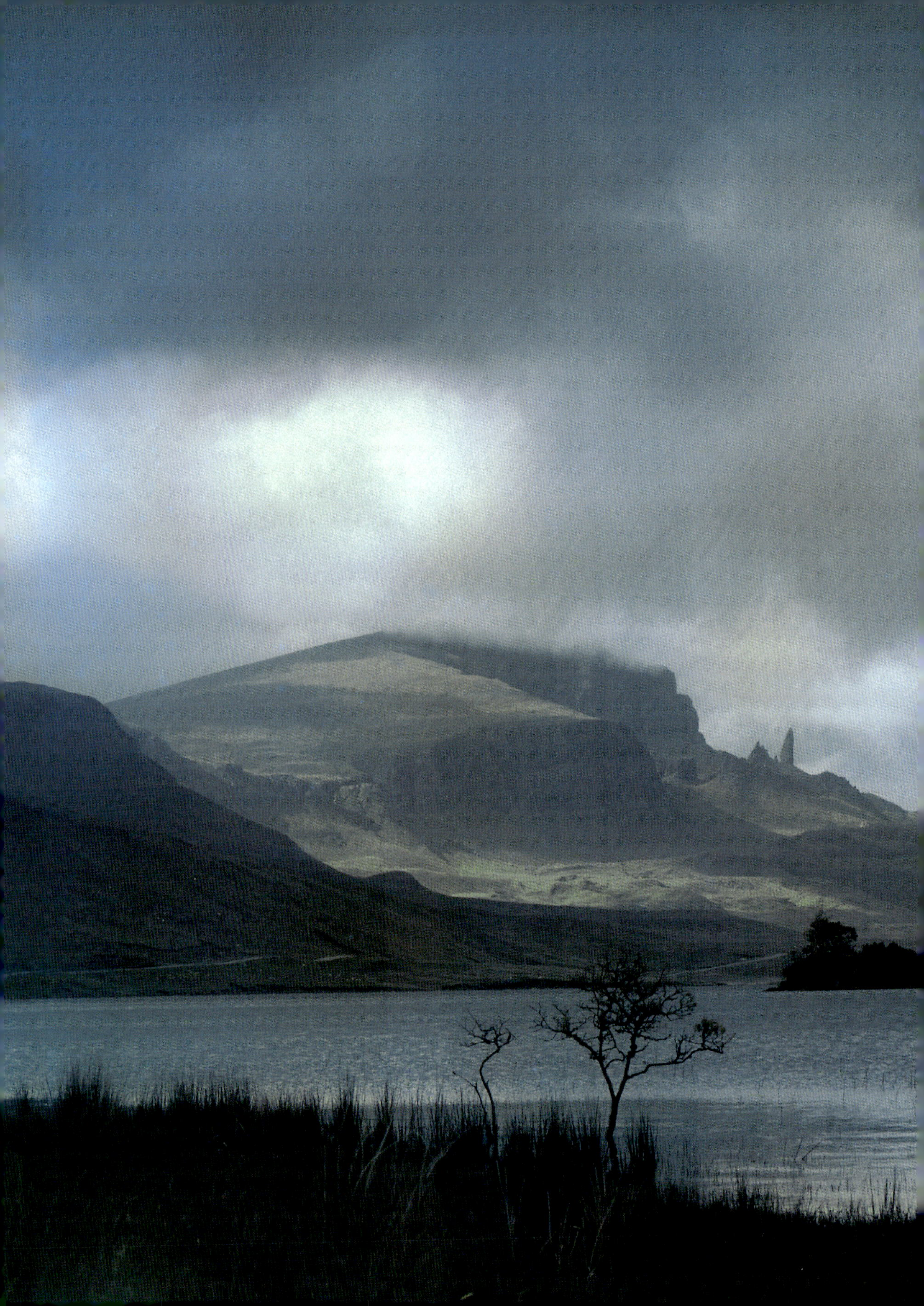

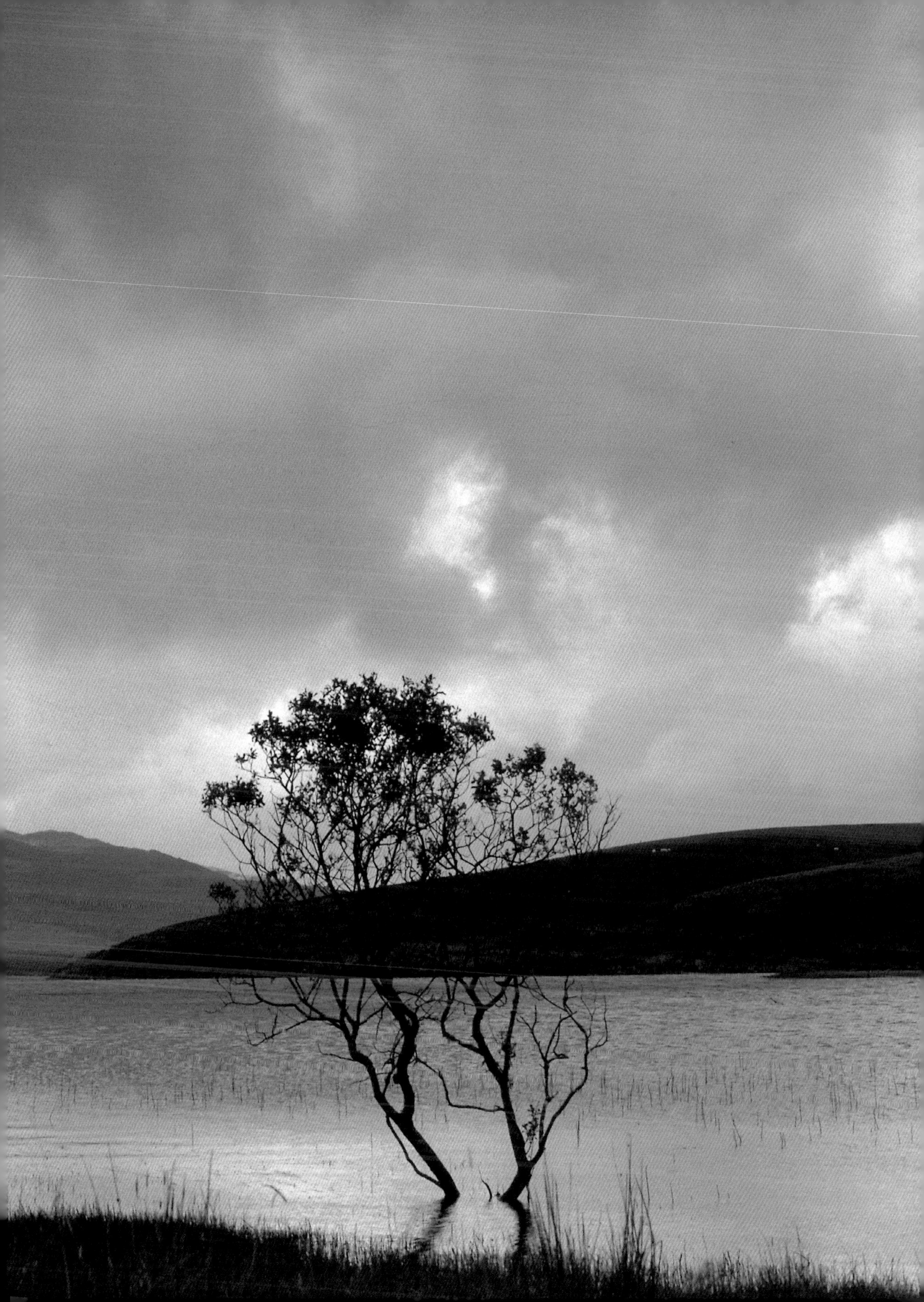

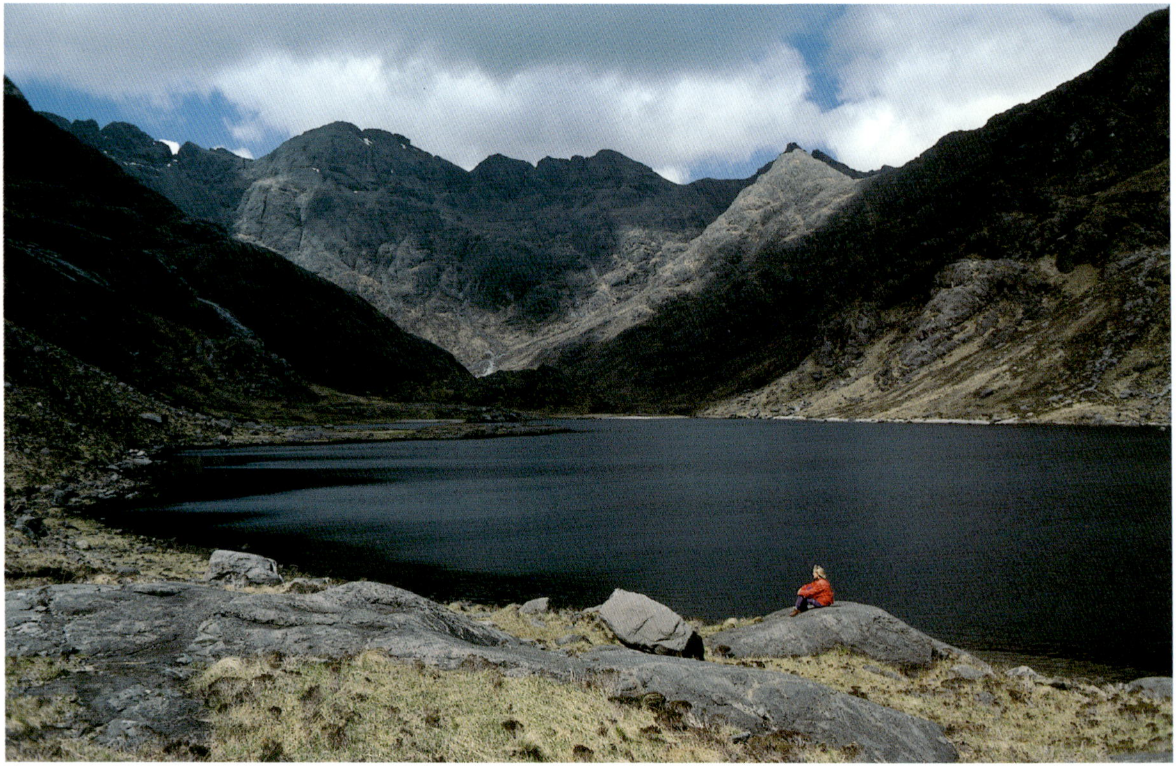

Fig. J4

Fig. J5

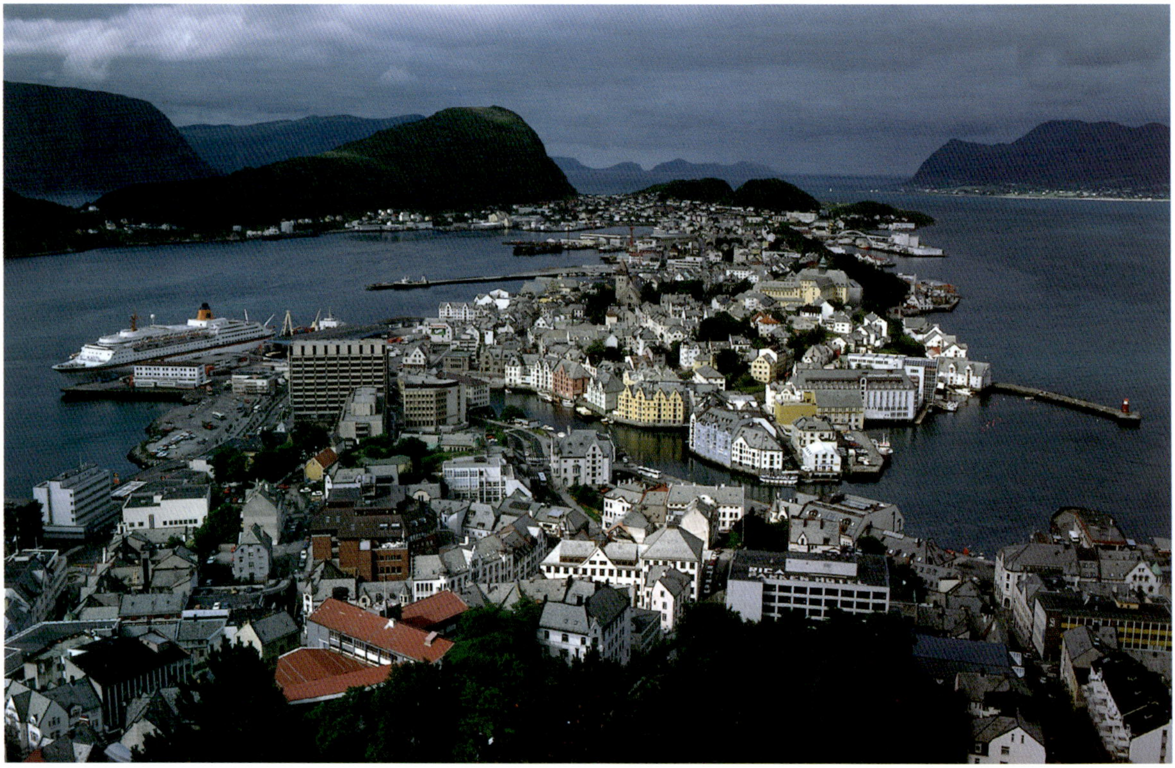

Automatic flash exposure bracketing

The possibility of being able to take several different flash exposures automatically is a practical option. Called "flash bracketing," this involves a series of three successive automatic flash exposures, which include a normal exposure, and under-exposure and an over-exposure. The correction values can be entered in 1/3 EV brackets. Because there is no correction for ambient light, automatic bracketing of the flash exposure is particularly useful with fill-flash.

Stroboscopic flash

A few flash units that are part of the SCA 3002 system may fire several rapid, successive flashes, when the shutter of the camera is open. As a result of this, rapid motion sequences may be captured and clarified or used for a motion analysis. Multiple exposures of this type are referred to as stroboscopic exposures.

Fig. J3 – J5: *Landscape shots frequently require the photographer to wait for the "right light" and to be fit enough to reach the right location. Sometimes bright sunlight and blue skies are not always desirable. A beautiful landscape photo can also be defined by heavy rain clouds or by areas lit by patchy sun.*

This is a photo of a landmark of Skye Island, an eroded basalt monolith named "The Old Man of Storr." The exposure was made in changing weather with a focal length of 28mm.

This picture was created with a focal length of 24mm when shadows created by clouds shaped the Cuilin Hills at Loch Coruisk.

The Norwegian town of Alesund was captured on a rainy Sunday morning with a focal length of 21mm. The wait for the brief moment when the cloud cover broke a little and building walls were struck by brighter light took 20 minutes.

Strobe flash exposures are most successful in weak ambient light in front of a dark background. In order to be able to fire many flashes within a short period of time, the flash unit must work with partial light performance – therefore each individual flash uses a relatively small guide number. Correspondingly, the shooting distance is minimal. The number of flashes and the frequency with which flashes are fired may be pre-selected on the flash unit.

The number and frequency determine the length of time that the shutter of the Leica M7 needs to remain open (fastest-possible shutter speed = 1/50 second). Manual settings are listed in a table in the instructions for the flash unit. However, it is computed by the flash unit itself so that the exposure meter of the Leica M7 can be controlled in this mode to determine whether the set shutter speed is sufficient for the number of flashes and whether an over-exposure by potential present ambient light might be risked.

In autoflash mode the shutter speed computed by the flash unit is automatically picked up by the camera, independent of the prevailing lighting conditions.

The required distance between subject and flash is also determined by the flash unit and indicated on the display as a function of the number and frequency of the flashes, of the film speed, as well as of the set lens aperture.

SCA 3501 M1 adapter

The predecessor of the SCA 3502 M2 adapter, its functions are adapted to flash units of the SCA 3000 system. Still, its applications, even with flash units of the SCA 3002 system, are largely identical with those of the newer adapter. This excludes the automatic switch to X synchronization, the linear flash technique, and the automatic flash exposure series.

Flash exposures with the Leica M6 TTL

Apart from two exceptions, the options and modes offered by the M6 TTL technology are identical with those of the Leica M7. This also applies to the displays in the viewfinder. Exceptions include the automatic switching to X synchronization (the Leica M6 TTL does not have automatic exposure control) and the linear flash technology, or High Speed Synchronization.

Flash tips

In photojournalistic photography, the most convenient technique is to attach the flash unit directly to the camera. But this greatly limits options in lighting control. While it is convenient, this technique also has its drawbacks: frontal flash photos of people often exhibit the "red-eye" effect. This occurs when the flash reflector is too close to the lens of the camera, so that the camera "sees" the reflection of the flash on the retinas of the person's eyes. The effect is more pronounced when a direct flash picture is taken in dim light because the pupils of the eyes are wide open. Since the effect is reduced considerably in bright surroundings, as many lights as possible should be turned on when flash pictures are being taken indoors. It is better yet to use indirect flash (bounce flash) with the unit attached directly to the camera or to mount the flash unit on a bracket so that it will be further away from the lens.

Cigarette smoke and dust in the air light up brightly with flash illumination, considerably reducing image contrast when the flash unit is mounted very close to the camera. Under these conditions, raindrops and snowflakes are reproduced as brilliant light discs (iris spots). This problem can usually be corrected simply by using the flash at arm's length. Off-camera flash is definitely necessary in close-ups of up to 3 or 4 m (approximately 10 to 14 feet) in order to create a three-dimensional effect with light and shadows. Placing the index finger on the back of the reflector helps to "feel" the approximate direction of the flash, thereby allowing the photographer to aim the flash without taking his eye away from the camera's viewfinder.

Indirect or bounce flash

The reflectors on standard flash units are designed so that their coverage matches the field of regular 35mm wide-angle lenses. For shorter focal lengths down to 28mm, there are attachments that diffuse the flash to cover the wider field of view. These can be placed over the flash reflector. If a scene is to be photographed with flash and a 21mm super wide-angle lens, uniform lighting will only be achieved with indirect flash. With this technique, the flash is pointed at a large reflecting surface, such as a white ceiling or a bright wall outside the lens' field of view. The reflected light beam is very broad and, because the reflecting surface is so large, the lighting is very soft. Many electronic flash units have tilting heads that facilitate this technique. The tilting head allows the sensor to remain aimed at the subject being photographed, accurately measuring the amount of light required for correct exposure. The intensity of that light will have been weakened by the reflection. With color film, photographs made with bounce flash will have an overall color cast if the reflecting surface is not white, neutral gray, or silver-colored. The effect can also be used deliberately, for example by using colored cardboard to reflect the flash.

In order to make photographers independent of ceilings or walls, special reflecting attachments are available for some flash units. Their variety ranges from small clip-on cards to large collapsible umbrellas with their own stands. At home, white poster cardboard or projection screens can also be used effectively. White "Styrofoam" insulating sheets, available where construction materials are sold, also work very well.

Tele-flash

The relatively large beam spread of electronic flash units can be reduced for certain applications, either with the adjustable zoom reflectors on some units or with appropriate attachments. Fresnel lenses are used most often to narrow the beam of light emitted by the flash unit in order to adapt it to the smaller angle of

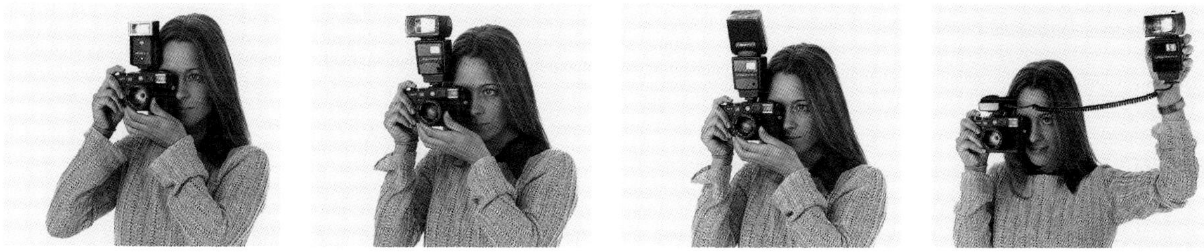

Fig. 189 a – d: *A large variety of portable electronic flash units are available for many photo applications. One very compact dedicated flash unit is the Leica SF 20. The Mecablitz 54 MZ-3 includes a tiltable zoom reflector and a second, smaller reflector for bounce flash. If the flash is triggered from the camera, flash illumination can be adapted to the individual subject. In this case, the direction of the flash is "felt" by placing the forefinger behind the reflector.*

view of longer focal lengths. This concentrates the entire output of light energy into a narrow beam that can brightly illuminate distant subjects, much like the high beams of automobile headlights. This narrow beam illuminates a subject area that usually matches telephoto lenses with focal lengths of about 135mm.

Naturally, it is important that the beam of the flash unit be accurately aligned with the angle of view of the lens. This can easily be checked through the viewfinder of a Leica M camera by firing the flash at a surface that is not too near, such as the side of a house across the street. For uniform illumination of a distant subject to be photographed with a long focal length lens, the area that will be briefly illuminated by the flash must be visible exactly in the center of the viewfinder image. Photographs should only be taken after the flash unit and the camera have been accurately aligned.

With a tele-flash attachments and high-speed films, subjects more than 100 m (328 feet) away can be covered satisfactorily. Calculators on the attachments indicate the appropriate aperture setting. Experience has shown that long-distance flash only works well in very clean air (clear weather). Even when conditions appear to be ideal, it may be desirable to develop black-and-white films a little longer to make the image as contrasty as possible.

Tele-flash has one particular advantage: at longer distances, a given depth can be illuminated more evenly than it can at closer distances with regular flash. Since light intensity decreases at a rate equal to the square of the rate at which the distance increases, the full 15 m (50 feet) depth of a theater stage, for example, cannot be illuminated from the first row (5 m or 16 feet away) without considerable light fall-off. In this example, the fall-off in brightness from the front of the stage to the backdrop amounts to four f/stops. Photographed with a longer lens and tele-flash from the first balcony (about 50 m or 164 feet away from edge of the stage), the light fall-off on the stage amounts to only one f/stop.

But tele-flash is interesting not just for photography with long focal length lenses. It can also be used creatively for a spotlight effect with lenses of normal or short focal lengths.

Focusing and cropping can be performed without difficulty through the range-viewfinder of Leica M cameras, even in darkness. Especially in this type of situation, a range-viewfinder camera is clearly superior to a single lens reflex camera, even when the latter is equipped with an autofocus system.

Warning: Because the intensity of a narrowed light beam is very high, special care must be taken not to aim it at human eyes at short distances.

Invisible light

If a glaring flash is undesirable because it might be disruptive in situations such as the theater, sports, or traffic, pictures can still be taken by using infrared film and by placing appropriate filter gels over the flash reflector. Since the infrared component of the flash output varies among the different brands of flash units, individual tests should be conducted to determine the correct guide number. Focusing must also be adjusted, because conventional photographic lenses are not corrected for infrared radiation (see page 198).

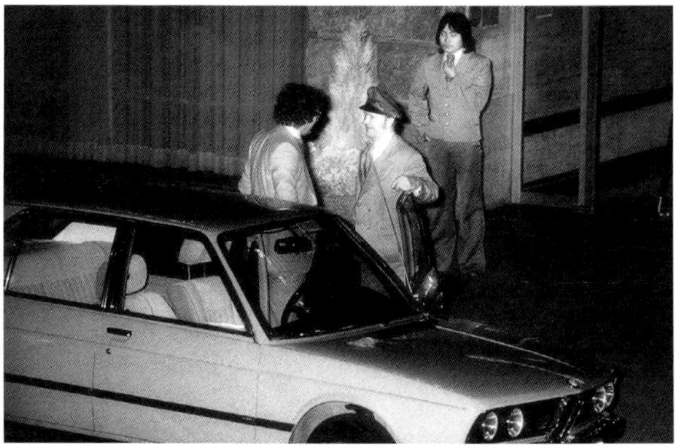

Fig. 190: *Many flash units are equipped with adapters, which accept filters and filter gels. With an IR filter gel placed over the reflector (for instance a Kodak Wratten Filter No. 87), flash pictures can be made on infrared film without detection. This photograph was taken across a busy street with a 135mm lens. Neither the three man being photographed nor the people passing by in cars noticed that the flash just fired.*

The open flash method

For certain photographic tasks like the illumination of a large hall, or in the extreme close-up range, the performance of a single flash unit is often inadequate. Especially when very small apertures are required. With stationary (static) subjects, this problem can be solved by triggering the same flash repeatedly. The camera is placed on a tripod and the shutter is kept open. The automatic computer on the flash is turned off and the guide number is used instead.

The following rule applies: as long as the position of the flash remains unchanged, two flashes double the amount of light, four flashes triple it, eight flashes quadruple it, and so on. The aperture can be reduced accordingly. The correct aperture can be computed with the following formula:

$$\text{Guide number for a single flash} \times \sqrt{\text{Number of flash heads}}$$

Using more than one flash head

One can, of course, also use multiple flash units instead of flashing a single unit repeatedly. With the modern flash units of the SCA 3000 and SCA 3002 systems, this actually works in a rather simple way. TTL exposure occurs as usual, whereby the flash unit is connected directly with the Leica M7 or M6 TTL by means of an SCA 3502 M2 or 3501 M1 adapters and takes over the control of the amount of light for all flash units. And all of this without cables!

Earlier Leica M models and older flash units this is a little more complicated. The guidelines mentioned earlier apply here as well, as long as frontal flash is used and as long as every flash unit has the same guide number. When flash units with different guide numbers are to be used together, a new collective guide number must first be calculated. Individual guide numbers are first multiplied by themselves (i.e. squared), then all the squares are added and the square root is taken of the sum, yielding the new guide number (GN):

$$GN = \sqrt{GN12 + GN22 + GN32 + GN4}$$

Since the effect of each flash depends on its position and cannot be predicted accurately, some testing will be necessary. The safest way to determine the exposure precisely is to use a special flash meter. The hot shoe and the rear flash contacts on Leica M models can be used simultaneously to trigger two electronic flash units synchronously by so-called slave triggers.

Leica

Photographic excursions

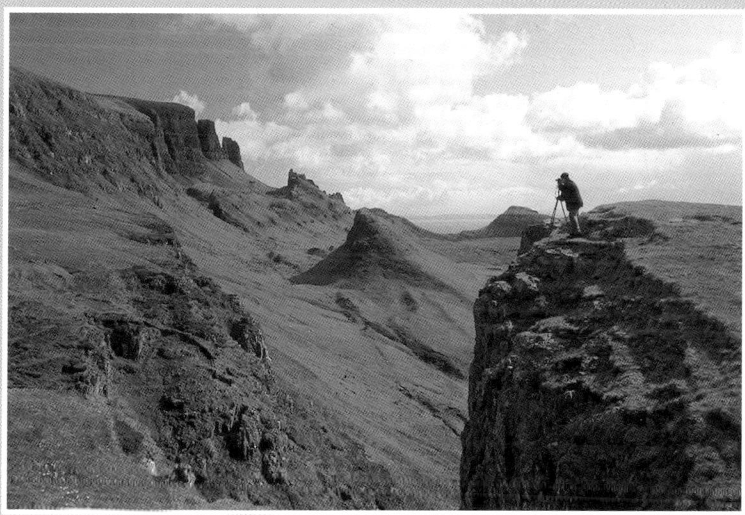

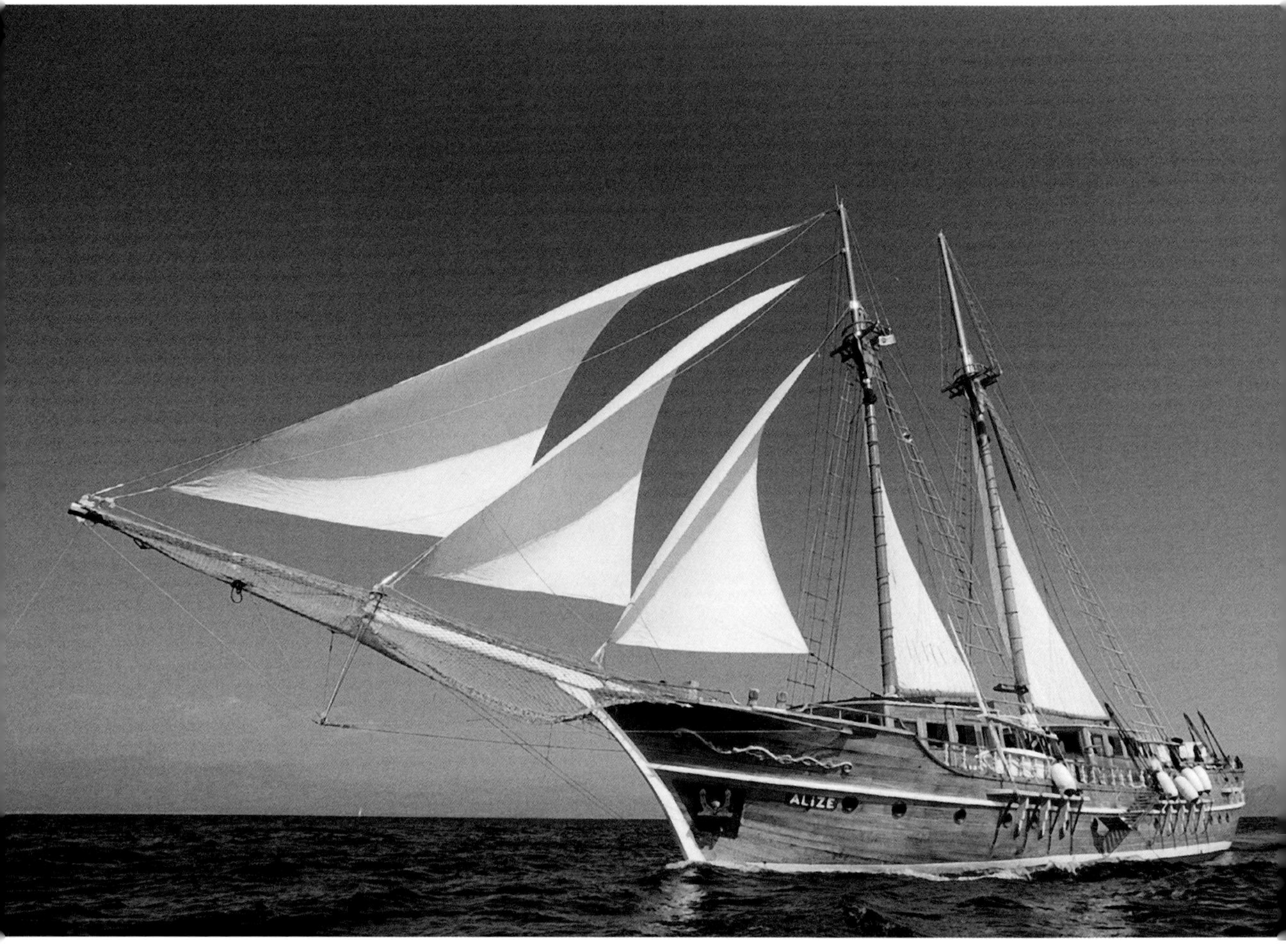

Fig. 191: *The photographic documentation of a trip should also include an attractive picture of the transportation used. Here it was a Turkish sailboat with a powerful jib boom. To give this picture character, it was taken at close range with a super wide-angle lens from a dinghy. 21mm f/2.8 Elmarit ASPH lens, 1/1000 second, f/5.6, medium-speed film ISO 100.*

Photographic excursions

A trip is not just an experience that provides a subject for good storytelling, it is also an opportunity for a lot of photography. Traveling and taking pictures therefore belong together. Yet the quality of the photographs is not a factor of the distance and the duration of a trip. Those who are interested in their surroundings and observe them with a photographic eye are able to turn even a one-hour hike into a photo trip and into a special experience. Those who take photographs with care get more out of life because they see more. Not in terms of quantity, but in terms of details. In order to photograph what is relevant, one has to know the complete subject. It does not make any difference whether we photograph people in distant lands, take portraits of fans of a football team on a weekend, or make a photographic record of the crafts of our community. Every photographic trip creates special demands on the photo-grapher and the photographic equipment.

It has been shown again and again that a traveler with a camera has to deal with more difficulties the farther away the photographer is from home and a familiar environment. The more distant the trip, the more carefully the photographic outfit has to be assembled. Weight and volume alone may force a limit on a trip as short as a Sunday afternoon hike. Journeys into tropical and desert-like areas and into regions with eternal ice present very different kinds of problems. Special attention must definitely be paid to the fact that camera, accessories, and films will be subjected to different kinds of challenges. Even though every trip requires individual preparation, the tips and suggestions that follow may be helpful in planning the next trip more effectively, so that picture taking along the way will be easier.

Inform yourself thoroughly

Compromises will have to be made in putting together a photographic outfit to be taken along on a trip. Too much equipment impairs freedom of movement and too little may lead to disappointing results. A good knowledge of the subjects that are likely to be encountered, awareness of possible restrictions, and local taboos are essential for making the right decisions concerning the accessories to be taken along. Many a photographic tour turned into torture simply because the photographer was not well enough informed to select the right clothes. Then there is the matter of customs regulations in far-off countries, which may have limits for the amount of equipment and films that may be brought in duty-free: the customs office and your travel agent should be able to provide guidance. Reputable insurance companies should be pleased to recommend the right kind of insurance.

Start planning early

Photographic equipment should be checked well ahead of a big trip, preferably about two months before departure, so that there will be enough time to make any repairs that may be needed. Leica maintains a stock of 16,000 replacement parts in order to service a variety of Leica models. The Technical Service can still repair all models of the Leica M camera. Therefore, 40 years of use are not enough of a reason for retiring a Leica M camera. All service technicians are factory-trained in Solms, so that competent repairs are available at almost any time almost everywhere. Leica maintains its own representatives in many countries, and most of them have service departments that are specialized in Leica repairs. This virtually uninterrupted worldwide service network functions smoothly even when the client and the technician do not speak the same language. The technician in an authorized repair shop will know how to correct a malfunction. Upon request, Leica Camera can supply the appropriate addresses of authorized repair shops.

New cameras and lenses should be tested well before a trip begins, along with the films that will be taken along. It is also advisable to buy all color reversal films with the same emulsion number. That ensures a uniform color balance in all slides, avoiding disturbing color changes from slide to slide during projection.

Take along proven accessories

To this day, many photographers consider the classic Leica M travel kit that consists of a Leica M body, a 35mm wide-angle lens, and a 90mm lens as the ideal outfit. This combination of lenses completely satisfies a very large number of photographic needs. But which lens speed should be given preference? The same question comes up again when additional focal lengths are being considered. The standard focal lengths for Leica M lenses, for instance, are a good example to demonstrate why each photographer must answer that question individually. Without claiming to have covered every conceivable aspect, here are some considerations that are important in making the selection:

The choice of a lens should be guided primarily by the intended range of applications and by the working habits of the photographer. It is also important to take into account whether the Leica M is to be used as a complement to a single lens reflex system, or whether it is the only system that is going to be used.

As a complement to an existing photographic outfit, a Leica M camera with a standard lens is probably adequate. As an alternative to using a single-lens-reflex camera in poor light, a Leica M camera with a 50mm f/1.4 Summilux-M or even a 50mm f/1 Noctilux-M lens is ideal. But those who often work in the close-focusing range will probably prefer the performance and the closer-focusing capability of the 50mm f/2 Summicron-M lens (0.7 m or 27-1/2 inches instead of 1 m or 39-3/8 inches).

If the Leica M system is going to be used exclusively, at least two different lenses are needed: perhaps one with the standard focal length to begin with, and later on the 135mm lens and/or the 28mm wide-angle lens. The 50mm Summilux-M lens with its maximum aperture of f/1.4 is an excellent "high-speed complement" for these two f/2.8 lenses. But those who already opted for the "mini travel kit" mentioned earlier that might consist of a 35mm f/2 Summicron-M ASPH lens and a 90mm f/2.8 Tele-Elmarit-M lens will find the Noctilux-M to be a welcome alternative.

These few examples already show that many factors can influence the choice of a particular lens. And those who have trouble deciding which lens is "the right one" for them and who are plagued by doubts can rest assured that outstanding photographs can be made with any one of the three normal Leica M lenses.

Every outfit should definitely include certain filters and a cable release. Also recommended is a small electronic flash unit that's either battery-operated or has a battery charger that can be connected to different voltages. A tabletop tripod with a ball-and-socket head is useful. Set on top of a wall, rested on the fender of an automobile or pressed against a vertical surface, it often provides a steadier support than a larger tripod that is built too lightly. Every basic outfit should, of course, include replacement batteries for the exposure meter.

Maintenance needs

Every photographic outfit should also include a “care kit” consisting of a soft camel's-hair brush, a microfiber cloth or a piece of chamois leather, a watchmaker's screwdriver set, small scissors and tweezers. These “tools” are useful for cleaning lenses, for removing debris and dust, as well as bits of film from the inside of the camera, and for tightening a screw on the tripod. Black cloth adhesive tape is also useful for temporary repairs, and a changing bag permits the camera to be opened in sunlight while it is still loaded with film.

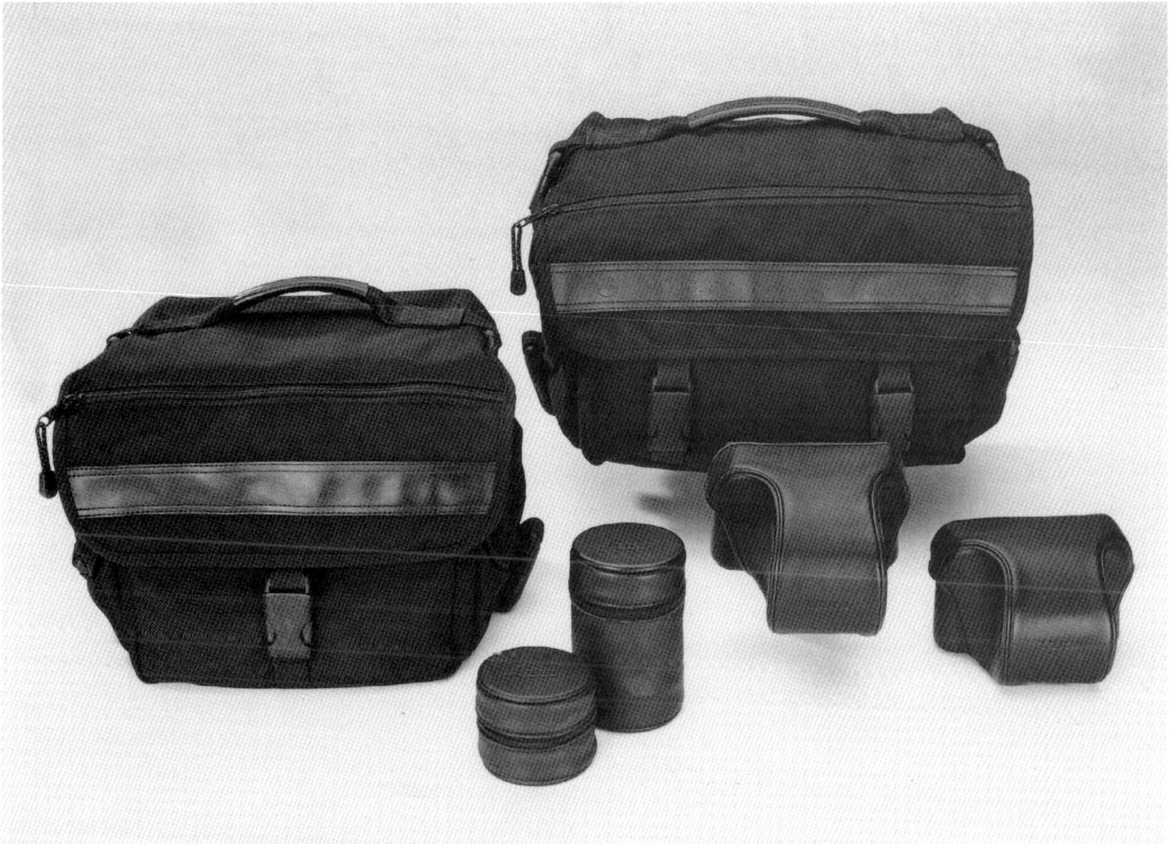

Fig. 192: *Camera cases for the Leica M.*

Camera cases for Leica M cameras

Those who want to take full advantage of the fast-action capability of the Leica M camera will use it with a carrying strap worn around the neck. But this way of carrying the camera is not without risk when traveling, whether it is by car, train, or plane. Where do you put it while you are checking in your luggage? How do you protect it from getting scuffed in a crowd, or how do you protect it while hailing a cab in a snowstorm? Leica provides the solutions with its handsome, practical and sturdy cases for Leica M cameras. Naturally, the selection that is available immediately prompts the question as to which case is best suited for accommodating the equipment that is needed, protecting if effectively, and transporting it conveniently. Or would a special hard case be more advantageous? And what about the "X" case made by the "Y" company? After countless discussions during photographic excursions, courses, and trade shows, it became evident that 100 photographers have 101 different opinions on the matter. No wonder, when one considers that individual photographers want to stow their own personal selection of accessories, and that each one has a different photographic interest, and that each one has his own particular traveling habits.

Most of the expectations of a camera bag are satisfied by the exceedingly well thought-out line of cases that Leica offers for Leica M cameras and their accessories.

Ever-ready cases

The close-fitting bottom parts of the Leica M ever-ready case are fitted to the camera from below and they are secured by means of snap fasteners on two small straps that fit around the eyelets of the camera. The normal carrying strap does not have to be removed and it remains functional. A fastening screw with a tripod socket was deliberately omitted from these ever-ready cases for two reasons. A completely rigid connection to a tripod cannot be ensured with such a screw because the compressible leather of the ever-ready case would be between that screw and the base plate of the camera. When a photographer carries two Leica M cameras with their carrying straps around the neck, the fastening screw of the ever-ready case of the upper camera may damage the top plate or the attached lightmeter of the lower camera.

The ever-ready case M is made of the finest supple cowhide and fits the Leica M7 and M6 TTL camera body with any one of the following Leica M lenses: 21mm, 24mm, 28mm, 35mm, 50mm f/2 or 50mm f/1.4. Its large front compartment even holds the Noctilux M or the Tri-Elmar-M lens.

The soft nappa leather case is designed for the particularly compact combination of a Leica M with a collapsible 50mm f/2.8 Elmar-M lens. It can be conveniently carried on the wrist by a hand strap. Wide padding provided at the level of the back of the hand makes this particularly luxurious. A wider, sturdier loop can be used to fasten the case to a waist belt.

"Outdoor" combination cases

Combination cases are made of waterproof ballistic nylon and offer maximum protection for the Leica outfit, even under the most adverse conditions. The fittings are made of sturdy leather and make this case almost indestructible. Because of its black color it always retains its clean appearance—dirt and wear spots are virtually invisible.

The main compartments of the combination cases are padded with foam rubber so that the equipment will not be scratched. In order to protect the camera and the lenses from shock and impact, the plastic bottom of the case is again reinforced with foam padding.

The external compartment is made waterproof by a zipper and the gray nylon lining of the case. All seams are sewn with a water-repellent and extremely sturdy nylon thread and the seams have been specially reinforced in order to provide additional protection for particularly stressed areas. The quick-release buckles and the welded metal rings increase the practical convenience of the combination cases. The tailored carrying strap is padded to make carrying comfortable—a suede pad on the inside provides non-slip support.

The inside of the "Outdoor" combination case has a system of flexible pads to protect the outfit from inadvertently swaying back and forth. The "lens-bride divider-system" which has been patented in the U.S.A. still permits a rapid removal of the camera and the lenses.

Because of the many separate stowing options the photographer can stow camera accessories and other items that need to be carried along in a clear and convenient manner. The underside of the case cover has an inside pocket of clear material in which filters and small accessory parts can be placed orderly and thus are always ready for use. The large front pocket is divided in several compartments in which personal items and small accessory parts can be stowed conveniently. The front side of the case has an additional small zippered pocket, which is ideal for tickets, identification documents or maps. A larger zippered pocket is on the rear side facing the body; it offers additional space for useful accessories. The large side pockets have a Velcro closure, as well as quick-release buckles to allow quick access.

The "Outdoor" combination case is available in two different-size models. Therefore, they can be adapted to differing demands made by photographers or the size of their equipment.

Large "Outdoor" combination case

External dimensions (WxHxD): 42x23x24 cm (16.5x9x9.5 inches)
Useful internal dimensions (WxHxD): 30x20x15 cm (11.8x7.8x6 inches)

Weight: 1500 g. (3.3 pounds)

Small "Outdoor" combination case

External dimensions (WxHxD): 33x23x24 cm (13x9x9.5 inches)
Useful internal dimensions (WxHxD): 25x20x15 cm (9.8x7.8x6 inches)

Weight: 1300 g. (2.8 pounds)

Case tips

Virtually all special needs for transporting equipment can be met by the extensive assortment offered by manufacturers of photographic bags and cases. Backpacks are recommended for long hikes, especially in the mountains. Hard cases should also be attached to backpack frames, not just for convenience, but also for safety reasons, because nothing can cause photographers to lose their balance faster than swinging camera bags.

Cameras and lenses are wrapped in lint-free cloths and thus protected well. Equally suitable are nappa soft leather lens cases, which are part of the lens packaging but are also available individually.

Skiers best carry their cameras under their ski jackets, and their lenses and extra film in zippered fanny-packs worn around the waist like belts. Of course there are also watertight containers for wild-water boaters, sailors and for expeditions.

Extreme climate – no problem

Modern tourism has allowed us to travel to regions with extreme climatic conditions. Situations of extreme heat, humidity, or extremely cold temperatures occur for just a few hours or for days. With only a few precautionary measures, which are not too different from those that every photographer takes for trips, a Leica M camera outfit will continue to perform reliably. But those who spend time in regions away from the usual tourist areas, do not sleep in air-conditioned rooms, and are exposed for weeks and months at a time to extreme climatic conditions, must make more thorough preparations in order to come home with outstanding photographic results.

Photographing at high temperatures

Photographic problems are most often caused by heat. With the intense sunshine on a beach or in a desert, camera bags, cameras, lenses and films can heat up to 50°C (122°F). The temperature inside a car parked in the sun can even rise to 70°C (158°F). These are actual readings, measured under these kinds of circumstances. Yet this does not harm Leica cameras and lenses of modern manufacture. Film, on the other hand, is affected quite severely when it has to "simmer" for prolonged periods of time, because heat causes color casts both on unexposed, as well as on exposed films. Heat also causes changes in rated film speeds. Films and outfits containing films should therefore be stored in ventilated shady places, and camera bags and equipment should be covered with white cloth to reflect the sunlight.

The safest way is to transport the entire outfit in aluminum cases (which also reflect sunlight) or better yet, in insulated bags. Additional cooling can be achieved by placing wet towels over these containers. Drops of perspiration should be removed immediately from metal and glass surfaces of the equipment by using lint-free tissues, which every photographer should always have on hand in ample supply. Don't be shy about placing a towel around your neck when the weather is hot and sticky, so that you can constantly wipe your face and hands. Ordinary plastic bags can protect the equipment from dust and sand. The soft plastic underwater camera cases, which also protect against dust and sand, are generally not practical for Leica M cameras because their viewfinder ports are positioned for single-lens-reflex cameras. Things become especially difficult when heat is accompanied by high humidity.

Photography in the tropics

Long visits to areas with a hot and humid climate expose the entire photographic outfit to the risk of fungus growth. Film, lenses, leather cases, all of them can be damaged by fungus. The more frequently we expose cameras, lenses, and accessories to fresh air, the lower the risk of fungus formation. Fungus growth is much more likely to occur when the equipment is not used very often. The following recommendations should be observed:

- Remove cameras from leather cases; place cameras and lenses on an open shelf and protect them against dust by covering them with a linen cloth. Move the equipment around as often as possible. Remove front and rear caps from the lenses.
- Do not leave film in the camera for more than two days. Remove the lens opening cover from the camera and open the back cover, so that air can circulate in the interior of the camera.
- Cameras that are not used for a long period of time should be stored in an exsiccator, such as a metal container that can be closed airtight, enclosing a package of the well-known drying agent silica gel.
- If the above container has to be opened in humid weather, it is advisable to replace or regenerate the silica gel; otherwise conditions may be created that actually foster fungus growth when the container is resealed, because it will trap ambient humid air and there will be no air circulation inside.
- Leather cases are especially susceptible to fungus growth in hot and humid climates. This also applies to accessories that are stored in leather containers. Cases and equipment should not be stored in drawers or cartons that also contain books, papers or textiles.
- After removing the cameras, suspend leather cases in an airy room and wipe them frequently with a dry cloth. Expose them to sunshine with moderation. Treatment with good leather conditioners is recommended.
- Whenever possible, the photographic outfit should be exposed to circulating fresh air.

Films react even more sensitively to a hot and humid tropical climate than cameras and lenses. Problems result from the absorption of humidity by the film, causing it to swell and to stick to the inside of its cartridge, for example, or to the take-up spool of the camera. The emulsion may then be torn from its support during the winding or rewinding operation, destroying any pictures that may have been taken on it. Bits of emulsion that remain behind (mostly in the vicinity of the pressure plate) will foster the growth of fungus. This is another reason for cleaning the interior of the camera frequently. Film manufacturers make the following recommendations:

- Use only films that are supplied in packages that are hermetically sealed against humidity (brand name films are sealed in foil or placed in small cans with tightly fitting lids). You should protect your film supply from heat.
- Use watertight containers and silica gel. Cold storage of exposed films in a refrigerator should only take place if these films have been wrapped in watertight materials, after first having been dried out with silica gel or after first having been left to dry out while wrapped in a porous, air-breathing material.

Photographing when it is wet

A clever thing to do when it is raining is to put on a raincoat that is several sizes too large, so that there is enough room underneath for the camera bag. Lens hoods on all lenses protect them from raindrops, which often cause unsharp pictures. A large umbrella is still the best protection while taking pictures in the rain. But it requires acrobatic talents to hold the umbrella and to take pictures at the same time.

At times like these, the assistance of a traveling companion is most useful. Good protection of cameras from rain is provided by plastic rain covers offered by several manufacturers (ask your photographic dealer about them). Of course, when the work is done, water droplets should be gently wiped off with a lint-free cloth (like a clean handkerchief), and the camera and its accessories should be allowed to dry out in a ventilated place. Metal parts of the camera react strongly to salt water. For that reason the protective measures described above are even more important near the ocean or in a boat than they are in rainy weather. Any help at all is usually too late for cameras that have been exposed to too much salt water or that have even been dropped in the ocean. Occasionally there is some hope if the camera and lens are rinsed in fresh water and quickly dried with a hair drier and then sent to Leica customer service in Solms. Even so, the usual result is an expensive repair.

Photographing when it is cold

Leica cameras and lenses operate at temperatures ranging from +70°C to -20°C (+158°F to -4°F), provided the lubricants have not deteriorated, which may be the case after many years. If the equipment is to be used for prolonged periods of time at temperatures below -20°C (-4°F), the Leica's technical service can even cold-proof Leica M cameras down to -40°C (-40° F). Here too, it is more advantageous to order an appropriately conditioned (new) camera through your photographic dealer than it is to have an existing Leica M camera treated for that purpose at a later time. But cold-proof cameras are only conditionally suited for photography in normal temperatures, as the shutter speeds will no longer be accurate because of the irregular travel of the rubberized focal plane shutter curtains. Likewise, lenses that have been cold-proofed should not be used at normal temperatures because their helical mounts will have too much play for accurate focusing at these warmer temperatures. When batteries for the exposure meter are fresh, they are also good for operation at temperatures down to -20°C (-4°F). That means that they have to be protected as much as possible against the effects of extremely low temperatures. Leica M7 and Leica M6 cameras should therefore be carried under warm clothing and close to the warm body as long as possible. With other Leica M models, the Leicameter should be removed and simply carried in a pants pocket.

How do films react to extreme cold? They become brittle and then they break easily. The rapid film advance lever and the rewinding crank should therefore be operated with "sensitivity," i.e. gently. In addition, if the film is wound too rapidly, it may also build up charges of static electricity. Tiny sparks then discharge that build-up into the camera body, creating designs on the film like branches or flakes with fine branch-like lines, which, unfortunately, can only be detected after the film has been processed.

While a Leica M camera can still be operated well with regular gloves, the bulky mittens normally used in expeditions permit only very limited manipulation. In that situation, a second pair of relatively thin cotton gloves with fingers should be worn under the big mittens. The latter can then be slipped off long enough to operate the camera. Warming the hands may become necessary, and so-called pocket heaters that operate on lighter fluid or on special "solid fuels" are ideal for this purpose.

Great care must be taken at extremely low temperatures to avoid direct contact between bare skin and metal parts, because skin will instantly freeze to the metal, and this may lead to serious injuries. Parts of the camera that may come into contact with the skin (around the eyepiece) should be covered with foam rubber.

In addition, photographic equipment should always be given enough time to cool down when it is taken from a warm environment into a bitter cold one. Otherwise snowflakes may melt when they fall on a warm camera and then freeze solid: camera and lens can ice up. On a cold camera, however, snowflakes can easily be removed with a brush. Breath that coats the eyepiece and then freezes can make it practically impossible to work with that camera.

The problems are even greater when the equipment is brought from the cold outdoors into a strongly heated room. Cameras and lenses will immediately steam up, both inside and out. It may take hours until they are absolutely dry and ready for use again. If the camera is taken outside again too soon, the tiny water droplets inside the mechanism may freeze and jam the camera.

To prevent all this, place the camera and its accessories in plastic bags before entering warm rooms. When these bags are properly sealed, they will steam up on the outside, but the objects inside the bags will remain absolutely dry.

A severe temperature shock may even cause the front element of the lens to crack. That is the case, for example, when a camera that has cooled down to -30°C (-22°F) outdoors is quickly taken indoors into a room where the temperature is a pleasant +20°C (+68°F).

Be brave - don't hesitate!

The many accessories and aids that are needed, and the listing of extensive precautions that are necessary for protection against the powers of nature may easily lead to the assumption that a camera should only be used on warm summer days, in bright sunshine, and outdoors. But that would be fundamentally wrong. Hazards that are recognized can nearly always be mastered. Most of the precautionary measures for the protection of the equipment that have been mentioned here are needed only under extreme conditions, and they can furthermore be executed quite easily. Only one thing is indispensable—consistency. And experience teaches us that the very pictures that were taken under unfavorable, even harsh conditions are often the most beautiful ones.

Seeing subjects – composing pictures

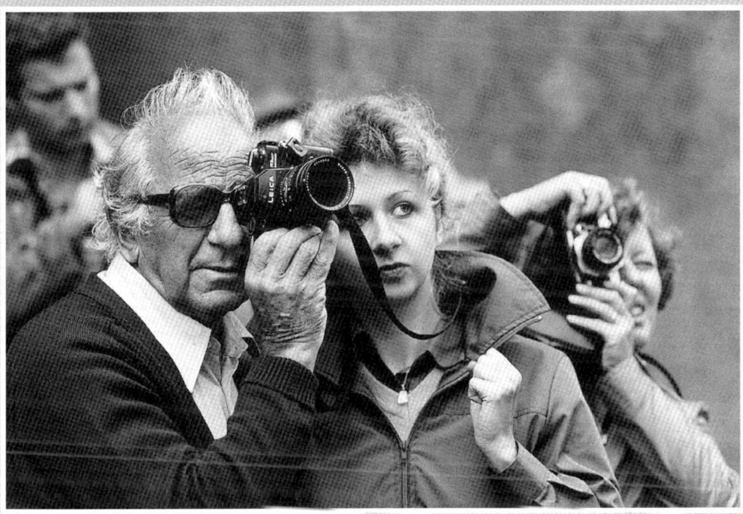

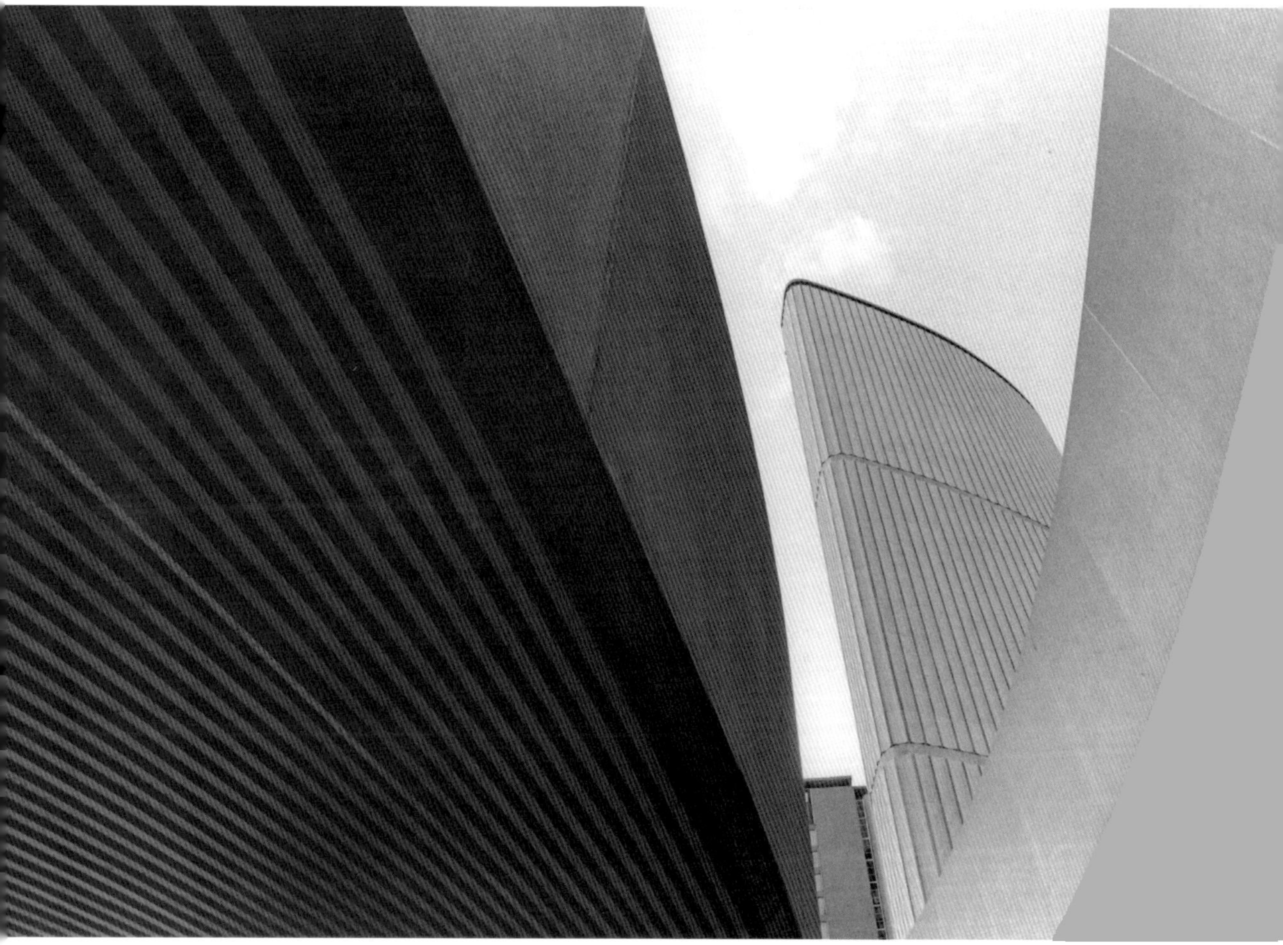

Fig. 193: *Lines, forms, surfaces, and colors can be found in every subject. Arranging these into a composition is one of the main tasks of photographers when they create a picture. 21mm f/2.8 Elmarit-M, 1/30 second at f/11, medium-speed film.*

Seeing subjects – composing pictures

Outstanding photographs are often the result of a series of creative steps made by the photographer. If just one link in this chain has a weakness, the end result will usually not be as good as it could have been. That is why a camera by itself can never guarantee great photographs, no matter what the advertisements may claim. A well-known photographer once said, "No camera is capable of making a bad photograph, only photographers can do that." Even if you are so thoroughly familiar with your camera that you can operate it in your sleep, this does not make you a good photographer, not by a long shot. It is a mistake for photographers to think they have mastered photography, once they have mastered their cameras.

From the snapshot to the composed photograph

By far the majority of photographs are made to preserve memories. They serve, and this does not at all make them less valuable, to help us to remember an "event." This kind of photograph usually only benefits the photographer or those who were directly involved. Even if a decorated Christmas tree in the picture evokes memories of Christmas, outsiders still do not know the who, what, when, and where of the scene, nor can they appreciate the emotions and feelings of the moment.

The keepsake snapshot is a short, very personal, handwritten note. It lets the "inner eye" relive events from the past. The keepsake photograph will have achieved its purpose, for example, if a person who appears very small in the picture is perceived in full size again by the viewer, who can even "recognize" a cake stain on the white floral dress. The viewer remembers and he actually "sees" the snapshot that way: "Oh yes, that was the time when uncle Patrick, the old charmer, told Julie the hilarious story about cousin John, and she laughed so hard that the cake slid right off her plate ..." Precious memories are evoked, visions are rekindled by a picture in which an outsider would see nothing but ordinary people and possibly a small darkish spot!

The keepsake photograph, the snapshot, usually cannot meet the criteria for a good photograph, which would have general appeal and interest. To examine these criteria in detail, however, would be far beyond the scope of this book. Therefore, only the most important criteria for a well-composed photograph will be described—the fact, for instance, that a good photograph conveys information, and/or appeals to our aesthetic feelings or stirs our emotions. If none of these three elements is present in a photograph, it will not draw our attention. Thus, the decision whether or not a picture appeals to us already occurs in the first 1/100 of a second of viewing.

Seeing and photographing

The old proverb, "A picture is worth a thousand words," is often cited in conjunction with photography. What is usually not said is whether or not it is really telling the truth, or in other words, whether or not it appears to contain manipulated information, or if the graphic statement that the photographer intended to make is indeed conveyed by the photograph. The notion that everything that can be seen can be photographed is widespread, as is the idea that a photographic lens creates an image the same way the human eye does.

However, neither concept quite hits the mark. No wonder then, that often many explanatory words have to be added to a photograph, in spite of the fact that all details are clearly discernible in the subject itself. If we explore the reasons for this, we discover that there are distinct differences between "seeing" and "photographing." The three most significant ones are that we see things spatially, or in three dimensions, and photograph them in two dimensions, and that the visual information captured by our eyes only becomes a picture after being "processed" by our brain. In the process, "visual errors" of our eyes, like those caused by an incorrect way of viewing, are compared with experiences stored in our memory and, if necessary, corrected. Probably the most pronounced difference between the human eye and the camera lens is that we have a subconscious ability to see selectively. We see only what interests us, and even though a myriad of details are present, we evaluate only a few individual ones.

The photographic lens, on the other hand, faithfully records everything within its angle of view, without emphasizing or selecting any particular detail. In other words, the images that are formed by the lens in our eyes and by the lens of a camera are largely identical, but we humans "see" a picture that is different from the one recorded by a camera. The unessential and the essential are recorded with equal importance. Therefore, it is very important for a photographer to become instinctively conscious of his camera's "way of seeing." In doing so, the photographer should pay particular attention to irrelevant and disturbing elements in the scene, i.e. the photographer should record only that which is really important. If photographers succeed in doing this, they will have virtually no difficulties of representing genuine and not misleading information in a photographic picture and maximize the impact of the picture. Only that kind of photograph fits the venerable saying that a picture is worth a thousand words.

Camera position and perspective

Two conditions are particularly important for a good photograph:

- The position from which the picture is taken.
- The angle of view that is covered by using a lens with an appropriate focal length.

Perspective is determined by camera position. It manifests itself through the difference in sizes of similar objects located at different distances from the camera. The farther away an object is situated from the camera, the smaller will it be reproduced in the photograph. Parallel lines that come together in the distance, at the point of convergence, like railroad tracks, for instance, are typical examples of this.

Our impression of the perspective reproduced in a photograph also depends on the size of the photograph and on the viewing distance. In order to recreate the very same viewing conditions for our eyes that the camera had when the picture was taken, we must view the original 24x36 mm photograph (35mm format) from a distance that corresponds to the focal length of the lens that was used for taking that picture. The ideal way should be to view a 21mm wide-angle photograph from a distance of 21 mm, the contact print of a picture taken with a 90mm lens from a distance of 90 mm. But that is impossible, because those viewing distances are too small, so that such photographs are necessarily viewed from greater distances. But if the same impression of perspective is to be preserved, the size of the picture has to be increased proportionately. The corresponding degree of enlargement can be determined by dividing the viewing distance by the focal length of the lens.

The normal viewing distance is 25 cm (about 10 inches). If the focal length of the lens with which the picture was taken is known, the magnification factor for an enlargement that conveys the right perspective at this viewing distance can be calculated as follows:

Exposure with 21mm f/2.8 Elmarit-M ASPH

Viewing distance: 250 mm (about 10 inches)

Enlargement factor: $\frac{250}{21} = 11.9\times$

Therefore, image format: 28.5 × 42.8cm
(about 11 x 17 inches)

Exposure with 90mm f/2 Apo-Summicron ASPH

Viewing distance: 250 mm (about 10 inches)

Enlargement factor: $\frac{250}{90} = 2.77\times$

Therefore, image format: 6.65 x 9.97 cm
(about 2-2/3 x 4 inches)

The last example also explains why in earlier days the 90mm focal length was regarded as the "ideal focal length" for Leica M lenses. With the print sizes of 6 x 9 cm (2-1/2 x 3-1/2 inches) or 7 x 10 cm (2-1/2 x 4 inches), which were customary at the time, pictures taken with a 90mm lens were enlarged to just about the ideal size for correct viewing. The photographer perceived the reproduction as being "very natural."

It is central perspective, to use the proper term, which mainly conveys the depth of a subject in a two-dimensional photograph, or the impression of space. But the direction of light and shadows is used by our brain to create spatial relationships while viewing a two-dimensional picture, as is the lack of sharpness in the background.

By taking a photograph from way down, from a worm's eye view, or from way up, from a bird's eye view, the impression of depth in a picture can sometimes be enhanced even further. In distant views, a light haze produces aerial perspective, which serves to replace the missing third dimension or depth in a photograph. An object does not necessarily show its characteristic form from all sides. The photographer has to find the "right" camera position. A teapot, for example, is generally shown from its side. Handle and spout, which give the pot its characteristic appearance, are clearly recognizable from that direction (see Fig. 199). Naturally the photographer is not bound to that viewpoint, but if he shows the teapot from a different angle, creating an unconventional view, then he has to be conscious of the unorthodox result, and he has to have a creative or technical reason for photographing it in that manner.

The right camera position is extremely important. To determine that position often requires patience, skillful observation, imagination and experience on the part of the photographer. And sometimes it also helps to have a little courage to try something new. The correct camera position is nearly always the decisive factor that determines whether or not the photographer will succeed in capturing the desired impact in the picture.

Good cropping

Any photograph can only show a section of what we actually see. The photographer must strive to capture the essence of the subject within the format of the film, and, very importantly, arrange or compose this essence within the format in such a way that the result is a good picture.

As far as photographic technique is concerned, determining the "right" framing for the best camera position does not present a problem. It is desirable to limit the picture content to the relevant part of a scene, or to fill the frame to its corners, not just for formal reasons, but also because it is important for good reproduction quality. Outstanding reproduction quality from the 35mm format can only be achieved when as much of the complete negative area of the frame is utilized for enlarging. Only a minimal amount of cropping should be necessary for the last fine-tuning of the composition! With transparency film, it is even indispensable to fill the frame correctly, because it is quite laborious to change the cropping later.

With focal lengths are carefully spaced in relation to each other and based on practical experience, the selection of Leica M lenses ranges from a super wide-angle lens to a medium telephoto lens. This enables the photographer to photograph different-size sections of the same scene from the same camera position simply by changing lenses. Remember: perspective does not change when lenses are changed! Only moving the camera to another position changes perspective. If the camera is not moved, a change of lenses serves only to fine-tune the cropping.

Learn to see photographically

Seeing how the photographic lens creates an image or composes a picture must be practiced. These exercises are also performed by aspiring painters and sketchers. Visual artists must discover how to represent the depth of a space by staggered objects in proportion relative to each other on a two-dimensional in order to create the impression of three-dimensional space.

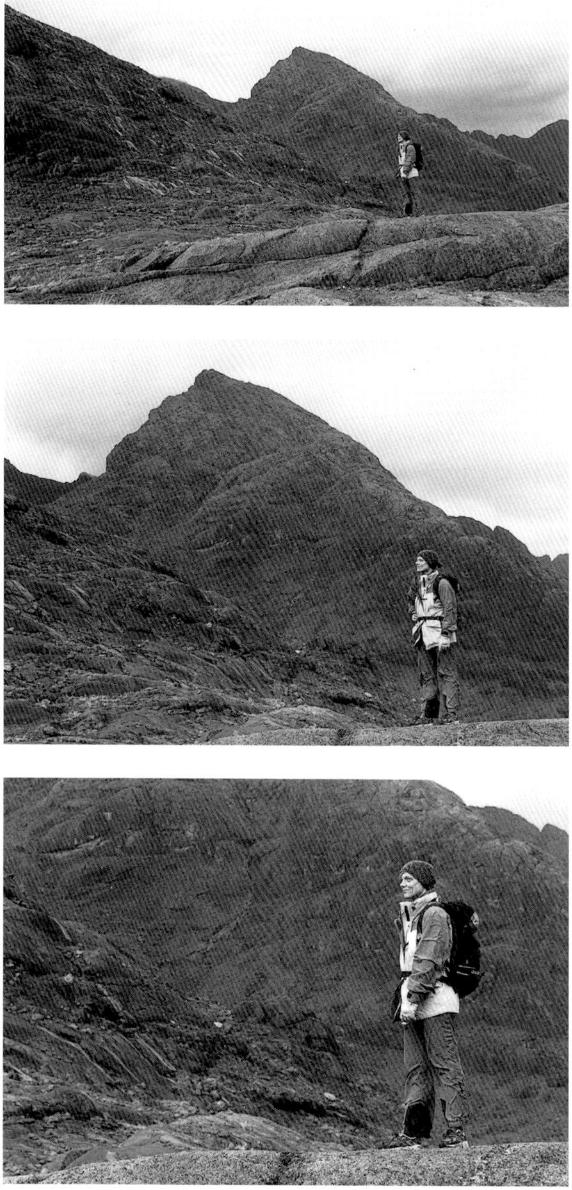

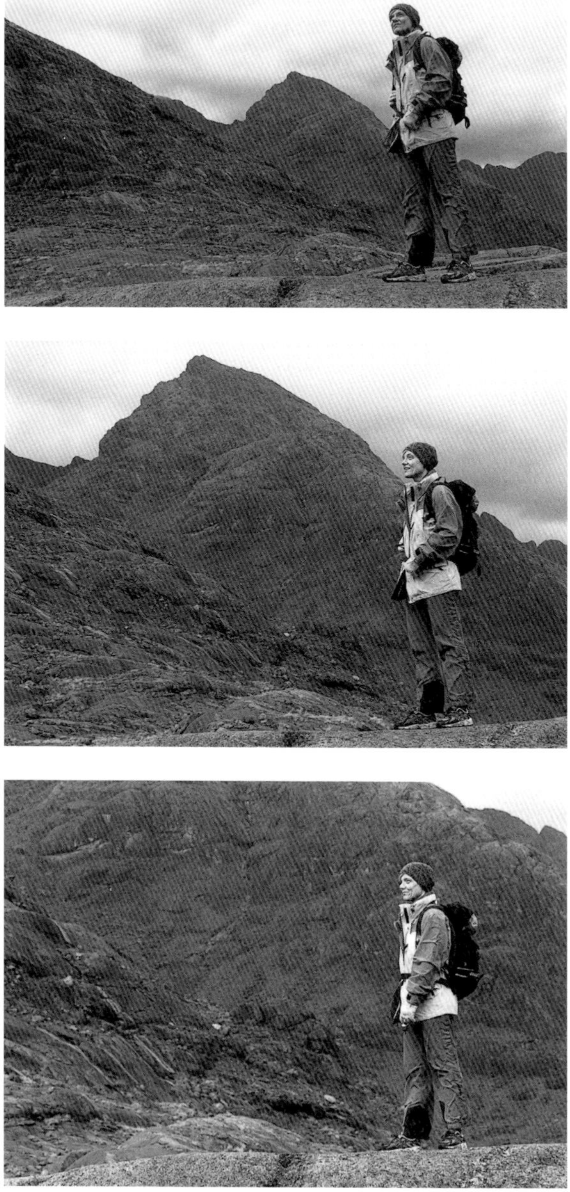

Fig. 194 a – c: *Comparison of focal lengths.*
The focal length in use determines cropping but never perspective. Advantageous cropping is one of the most important requirements for a high-quality rendition—to best position the subject within the frame. The same camera location was used; the distance to the person was approximately 9.5 m (31 feet). The focal lengths, which are illustrated, are 28, 50, and 90mm.

Fig. 195 a – c: *Comparison of perspectives.*
The selection of the camera location determines the perspective not the focal length. The person was photographed with a focal length of 28mm at a distance of approximately 3 m (13 feet), with a focal length of 50mm at a distance of approximately 5 m (16-1/2 feet), and with a focal length of 90mm at a distance of approximately 9.5 m (31 feet).

Fig. 194 – 196: *Comparison of focal lengths and perspectives. In the focal length comparison, two different focal lengths were used to take pictures from the same camera location when the subject was framed differently (Fig. 194 a – c). Therefore the sizes with which the mountain hiker and the mountain are represented are different. However, each picture shows the size ratio of the hiker in the foreground to the mountain in the background as being the same. In other words: The perspective is the same in all of the photos.*

If cropping could be performed after exposure without loss of quality in the picture, different focal lengths would be unnecessary. The desired perspective could be achieved by camera location alone, cropping could be done later in the darkroom or determined during projection. The comparison on these pages illustrates these relationships. On one hand it shows that the perspective is determined by the camera location and not by the focal length. On the other hand it becomes obvious that a subsequent enlargement of the framed image area will not satisfy normal quality expectations (Fig. below).

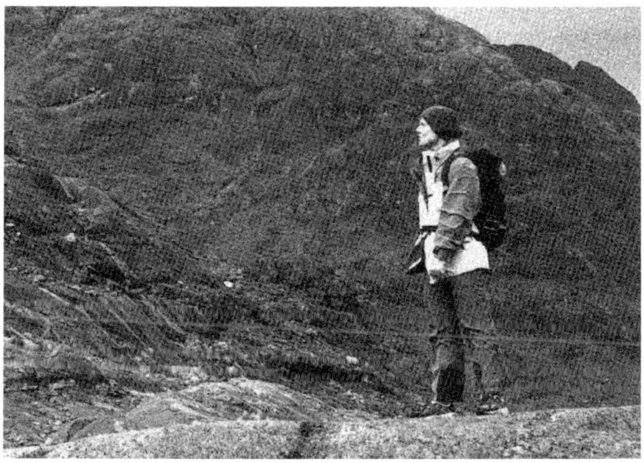

Fig. 196: *Enlarged framing.*
When an exposure made with a 28mm lens is enlarged significantly, the perspective and framing are the same as in the exposure made from the same camera location with a focal length of 90mm (Fig. 194 c and 195 c), however, reproduction suffers. That is why lenses with different focal lengths are so important!

To do this, they measure these objects by holding the shaft of a paintbrush or a sketching pencil at arm's length. It is much more important to ascertain the sizes of individual subject details relative to each other. Perspective determined in this manner is easy to transfer to canvas or paper. Photographers can perform the same experiments with the aid of an empty slide mount. By looking through the opening of the slide mount with one eye, it is easy to establish the field of view. Using the edges of that opening, i.e. with the short and the long borders of the format, the object can be measured and their relationship can be recognized easily. The distance of the slide mount from the eye represents the focal length. At a distance of 5 cm (2 inches), the coverage is that of a standard lens with a focal length of 50 mm. A shorter distance produces the effect of a wide-angle lens, a greater distance that of a lens with a focal length. With the aid of a slide mount, it is also easy to observe how composition and impact change when the camera position and/or when the field of view is changed. In actual use, the Leica M camera's viewfinder and its various bright-line frames will assume the rote of the slide mount held at various distances from the eye.

Once the photographer masters the manipulation of perspective and field of view, he can enhance the power and the impact of a photograph. He can use this to emphasize peculiarities of the subject, he can make optical adaptations to suit unconventional subjects, and he can also compensate for circumstantial problems. He can symbolically exaggerate the picture content or make it more artistically ab-stract. In plain words, he can work on creating a picture.

Judging lighting

Photographers should develop a "lighting sense." Through constant observation of light and its effect, and also from looking at photographs, they will soon learn that the world looks different in the early morning from the way it looks at midday. In the glow of the summer sun, things do not look the same as they do on a misty day in the fall or in the mild light of winter. Because a photograph cannot be made without light, the evaluation of light is more important than any other consideration. Accuracy in the judging of light requires experience. And experience comes with practice. Light and shadows can also be evaluated and reflections can be observed without the use of a camera. Photographers should take advantage of the lighting conditions, which constantly surround them, as opportunities to practice and to learn from them virtually on an ongoing basis.

In addition to aspects relating strictly to lighting and photographic technology, which certainly play an important part in the evaluation of a photograph, the aesthetic impact of the picture is of decisive importance. Therefore, it is imperative that photographers familiarize themselves with the perception of what is beautiful in order to perfect their technique.

Even though aesthetics are rarely discussed in books on photography and photographic journals, it is certainly true that "beauty" is highly important. It is not only true among those interested in photography that discussions about the "beauty" pictures frequently end with the argument "that tastes vary and different viewpoints produce different results." However, no one contests that certain rules and prerequisites must be taken into consideration when something is to become "beautiful."

One of the best-known rules for the composition of landscape pictures says that the horizon (of course perfectly horizontal) should not run through the center of the picture. In order to avoid a tension-free, usually boring division of the picture into two halves, it is recommended that the horizon be located in the upper or lower third of the frame. This recommendation follows the principle of the Golden Section.

The Golden Section or Golden Mean

The Golden Section represents a proportional relationship in mathematics. The Focal Encyclopedia of Photography, edited by Leslie Stroebel and Richard Zakia, defines the Golden Section as, "A proportional relationship obtained by dividing a line so that the

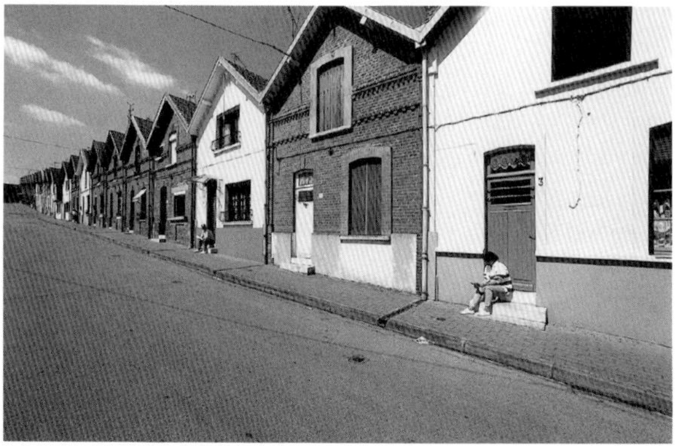

shorter part is to the longer part as the longer part is to the whole." With the use of a ruler and a compass, any line can be divided in accordance with the Golden Section and, of course, be computed based on a mathematical formula. Even if it seems far-fetched, "beauty" can, to some extent, be designed and mathematically determined. This is because we perceive that a thing is beautiful if the proportions are represented in such a manner that the shorter part is to the longer part as the longer part is to the whole. An approximation that is quite adequate for practical applications can be expressed in numbers having the following proportions: 3:5, 5:8, 8:13, 13:21, etc. In photographic terms, this means we find a photograph of a human subject appealing if that person is not set in the center of the picture, i.e. its distance from the right and left edge of the picture is in a proportion of about 3:5. Of course the relationship may be changed from the right to the left, or from the left to the right, and also from the top to the bottom, and vice versa. Therefore, any picture format offers the possibility of positioning an object in four different positions within the frame.

The old masters of painting have already have grappled with the phenomenon of the Golden Section. They knew that, as opposed to strict symmetry in a picture, the asymmetrical division in the composition of a picture appears to be alive and arranged as if by chance, and that the viewer perceives as harmonious, nevertheless. Why? They said that our ability to judge is rooted in relationships into which we humans are born—a finished world with finished forms of appearance. In this world, e.g., the distances between the planets are 3:5 or 5:8 or 8:13. Likewise,

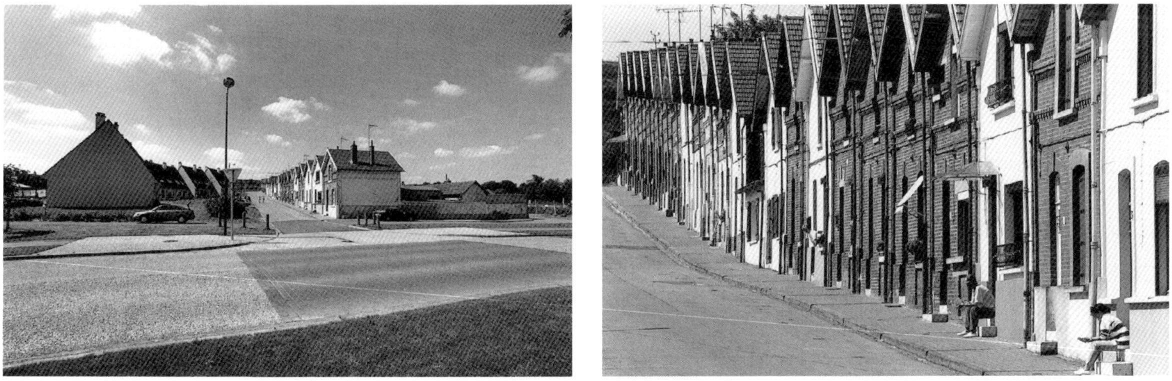

Fig. 197 a – c: *In order to represent a row of same-size houses in a photographically effective manner, a wide-angle exposure is not sufficient. Of course it shows the entire row of houses but the characteristic feature that the houses were built closely next to each other is lost because the house fronts in this photograph are reproduced in very different sizes (extreme left).*

At a greater distance with the same lens, the proportions in the picture approach reality—all the houses have the same size. Still, the actual subject, the row of houses, makes up for only a fraction of the picture (center). Without a more detailed explanation, the viewer will not understand why the photographer took this picture.

Using the same camera location and a longer focal length, the photographer has illustrated what is of importance here, namely the uniformity of the houses, which were built by a French industrialist for his workers: they all have the same size and there are lined up closely together. These pictures were taken with focal lengths or 21 and 135mm.

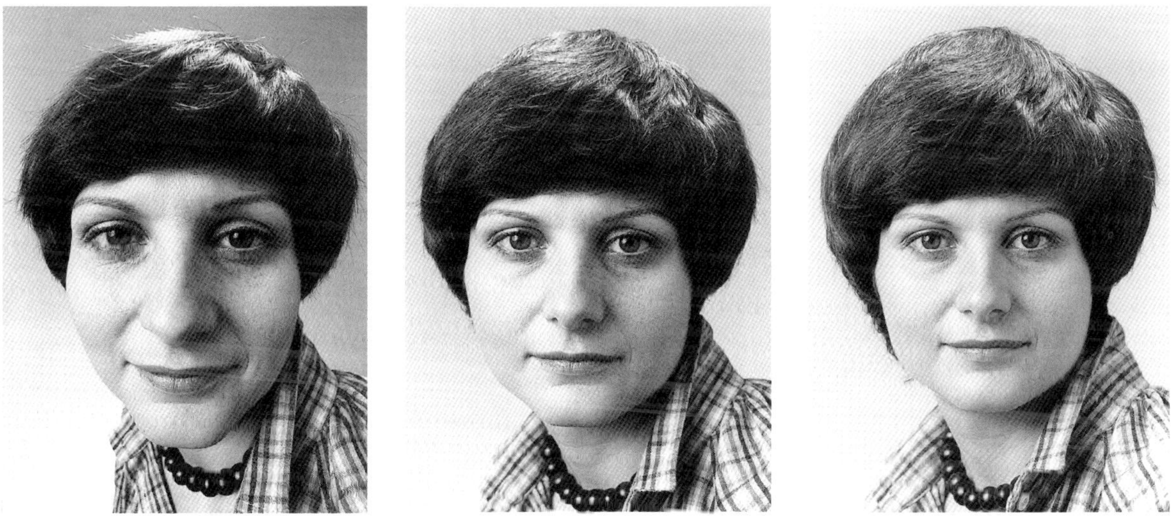

Fig. 198 a – c: *A portrait taken with a 21mm lens becomes a caricature (left) due to distortion of the proportions of the face. Even with a normal lens of 50mm, the photograph does not exhibit natural proportions: the nose is depicted too large in relation to the eyes (center). The photograph on the right, which was made with a 135mm lens, shows the correct proportions.*

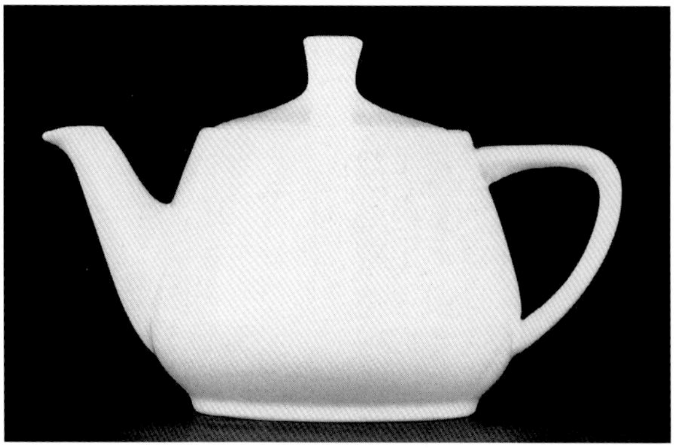

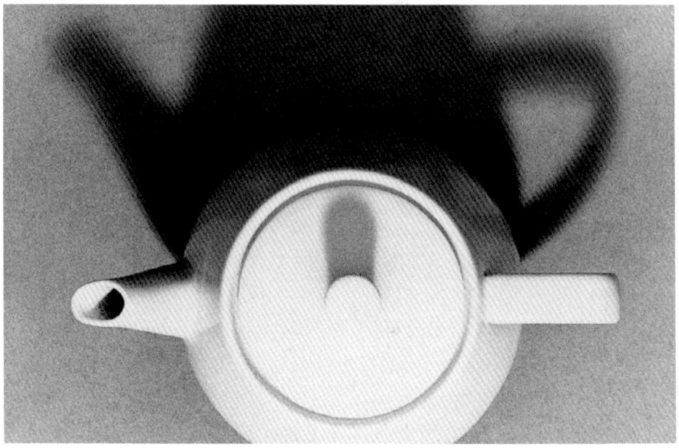

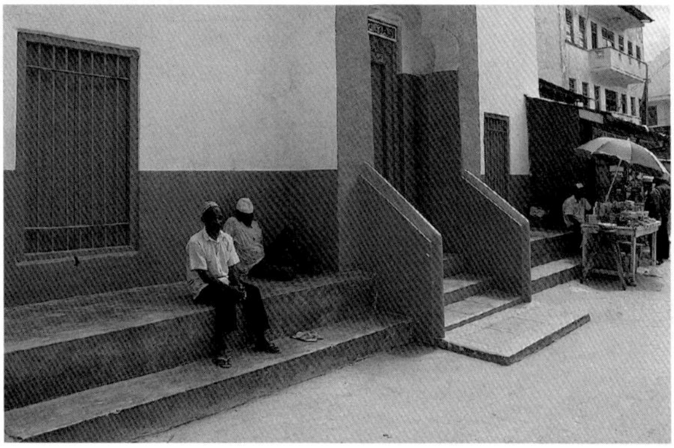

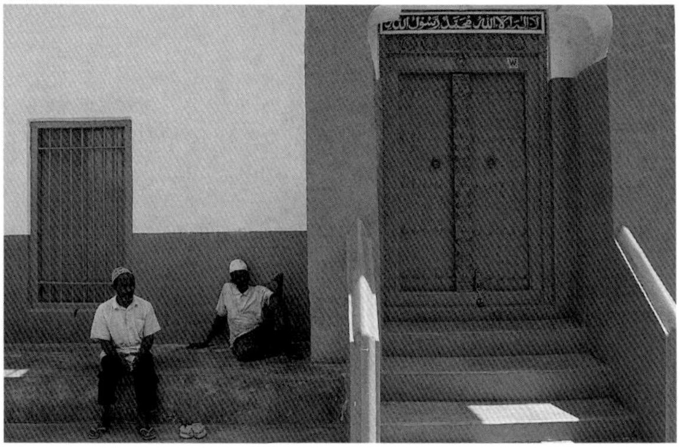

the human body has the same proportions. For instance, the abdomen is in the same proportional relationship to the torso as the torso is to the entire height of the body. For instance, the calf relates to the thigh like the thigh to the entire leg. This reality has influenced what we find appealing in art and design.

Independent of how we perceive beauty and the philosophy regarding the Golden Section, we should at least try to consciously use this composition tool in our next photographs. But, as is true in many situations, this requires a little practice because the viewfinder and the operation of any camera will initially counteract our endeavors! Because all adjustment aids for distance measurement and lighting are located in the center of the viewfinder and, as a rule, are aligned with respect to the essence of the picture, the operation almost automatically influences framing. Therefore, it is important not to forget—after taking the required measurements (and after storing the measured values) to pan the camera and observe the image composition. The tendency of the Golden Section to be away from the center of the picture is promising and in most instances leads to a more beautiful and more interesting picture.

Composing photographs

The transition from a snapshot to a composed photograph leads to simplicity, to the uncontrived. Famous photographers and creative artists have proven again and again that a powerful photograph is usually characterized by the sparse application of all the means that are available. By excluding everything that is unimportant and therefore everything that is superfluous, the photograph gains a symbolic character, it becomes representative, it appears typical. By means of appropriate creative means, the typical can be idealized, beautified, characterized and depicted.

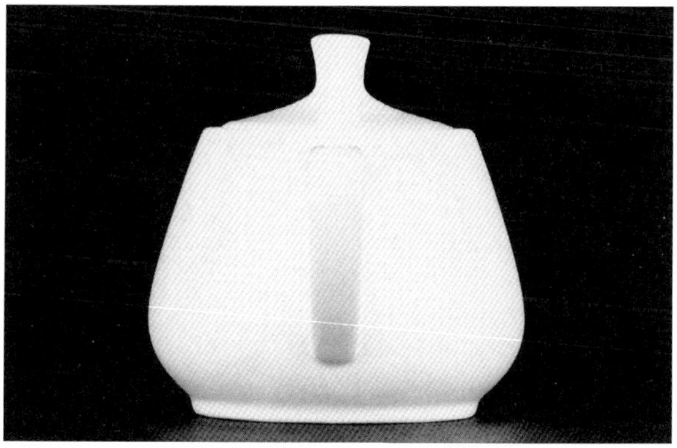

Fig. 199 a – c: *Every object has its characteristic features. On a teapot, for instance, they are the handle and the spout. When such features cannot be easily recognized in a photograph, the identity of the object is generally lost (right).*

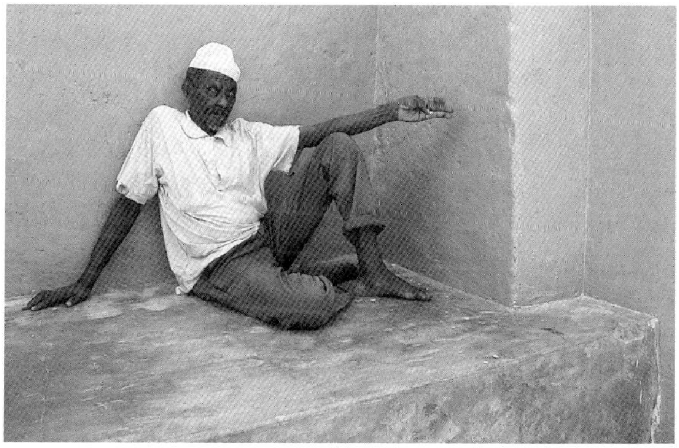

Fig. 200 a – c: *To discover pictures within a picture is particularly interesting for photographers. To achieve this, the camera location and/or the focal length may be changed. Frequently, short stories may be told photographically, or the search leads to a single picture, which describes everything that is worth mentioning. These photographs were taken in the searing midday heat in Zanzibar with the 35mm f/2 Summicron-M ASPH lens.*

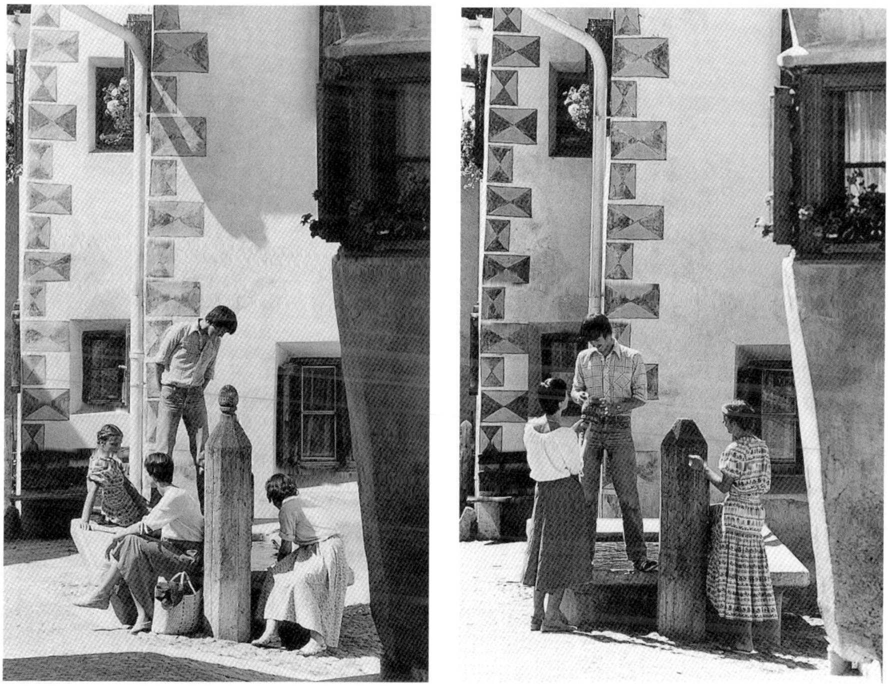

Fig. 201 a and b: *A serious photographer will devote his utmost attention to the lighting and the changing relationships between light and shadows; bright sunshine and cloudy skies; early morning, noon, or late afternoon light; grazing light or frontal illumination. These two photographs were taken at an interval of about one hour. The movement of the sun and the corresponding movement of the shadows created two very different photographs.*

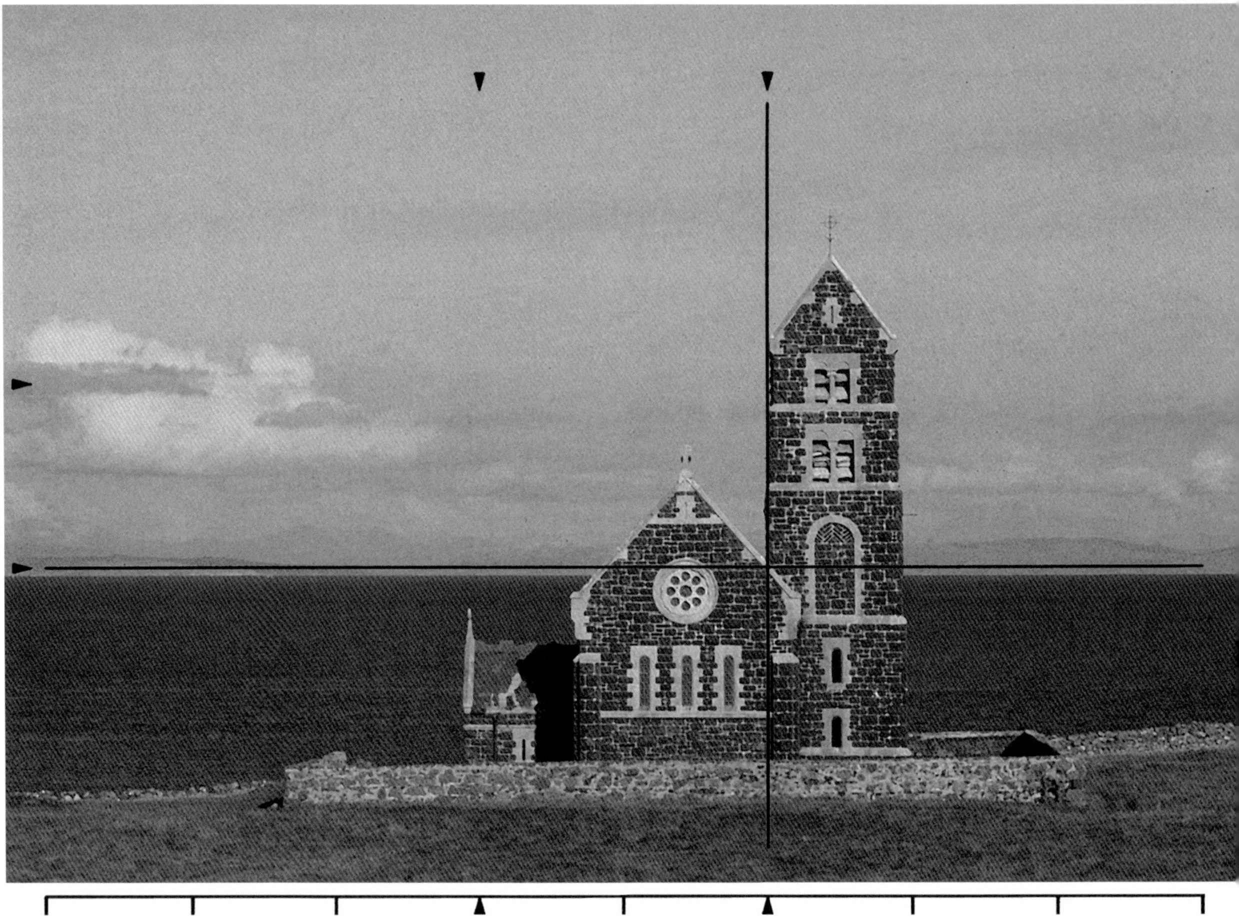

***Fig. 202:** The width and height of the frame are used to determine the location of the Golden Section by dividing the framing in proportions of 3:5 or 5:3. Both possible positions on the horizontal and the vertical outside the picture are marked by small triangles. In this picture the external edge of the church tower is located in the Golden Section of the longer picture frame (vertical line) whereas the horizon was aligned in accordance with the Golden Section in the height of the picture (horizontal line).*

Photographers have many techniques at their disposal for this purpose. Significant, for instance, are the contrasts between light and dark, between light and shadow, between foreground and background, as well as between sharpness and unsharpness. But the possibilities that vigorous as well as subdued, warm as well as cold colors offer for pictorial composition are enormous. Parallel, ascending and descending, vertical, horizontal and diagonal lines are additional creative elements.

Planes – forms - colors – lines – light: there is a series of composition rules for them, but there is also a series of opposing views. Those who seek to create more effective photographs should always do so with a very large dose of self-criticism and a clear understanding of accepted examples. In the course of time, specific areas of photography involving particular subjects will emerge, in which the photographer will specialize. Some may be particularly fond of the snapshot, because it can pictorially describe an event in a short and pertinent manner. Others may prefer photojournalism in order to be able to do interesting small picture essays, even about ordinary events. Some impart moods to their photographs in order to appeal to our emotions. Some will give preference to the objectivity of a technical photograph. Still others are unable to classify their preferences, because in

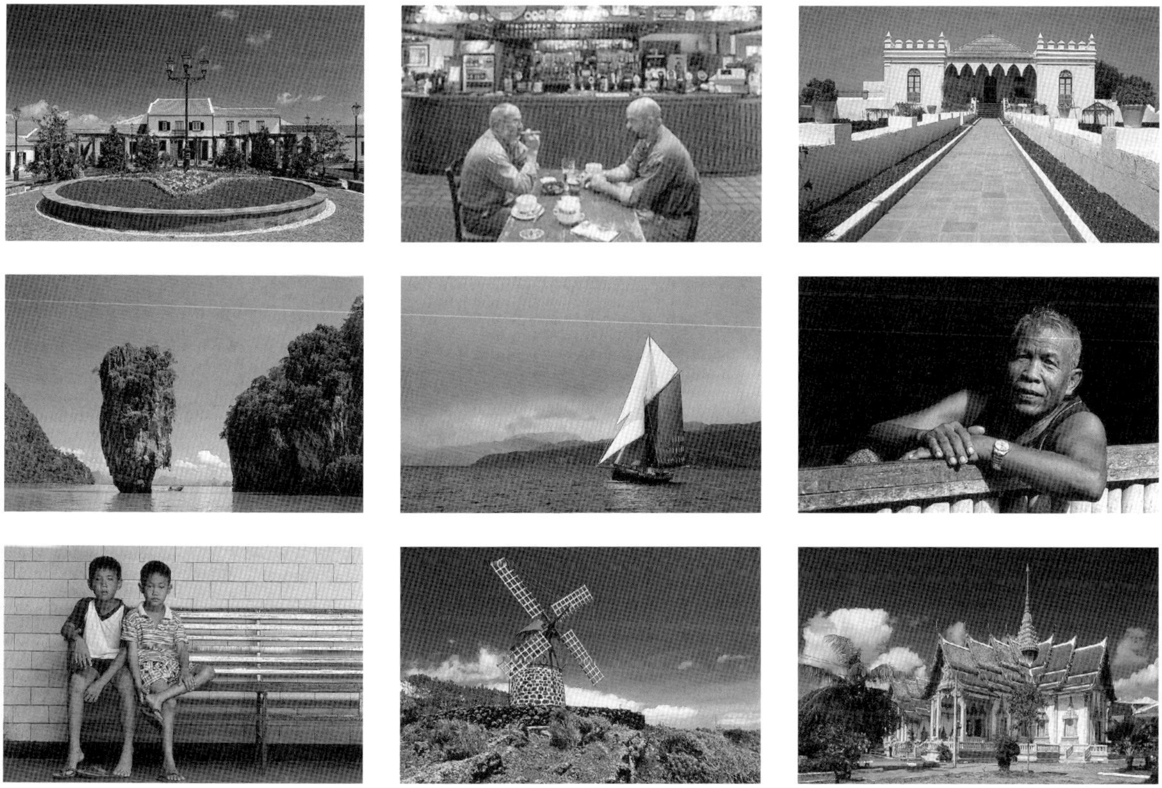

Fig. 203 a – i: *Be it a snapshot or a posed photograph, a portrait or a landscape, an architectural or close-up photograph, the image composition is usually more pleasing if the rules of the Golden Section are observed (center and lower row of pictures)*

practice the different categories of photography cannot be segregated precisely, as they often overlap.

Whichever path photographers choose in pursuing the goal of ever more perfect pictures, their personality will be molded by it. And the more distinctive a personality becomes, the more evident the photographer's own style will become in the photographs. It will become possible to recognize the photographers as their style, without ever having actually met them.

Fig. 204 a and b: *When photographing people, shoot as many frames as possible and don't worry about conserving film. As you can see in these contact prints, the tiniest nuances in the subject's expression, the position of the hands, or the blinking of the eyes can make all the difference. Only a few of the pictures are acceptable and just one is truly superb. 90mm f/2 Summicron-M, 1/125 second at f/4, high-speed film.*

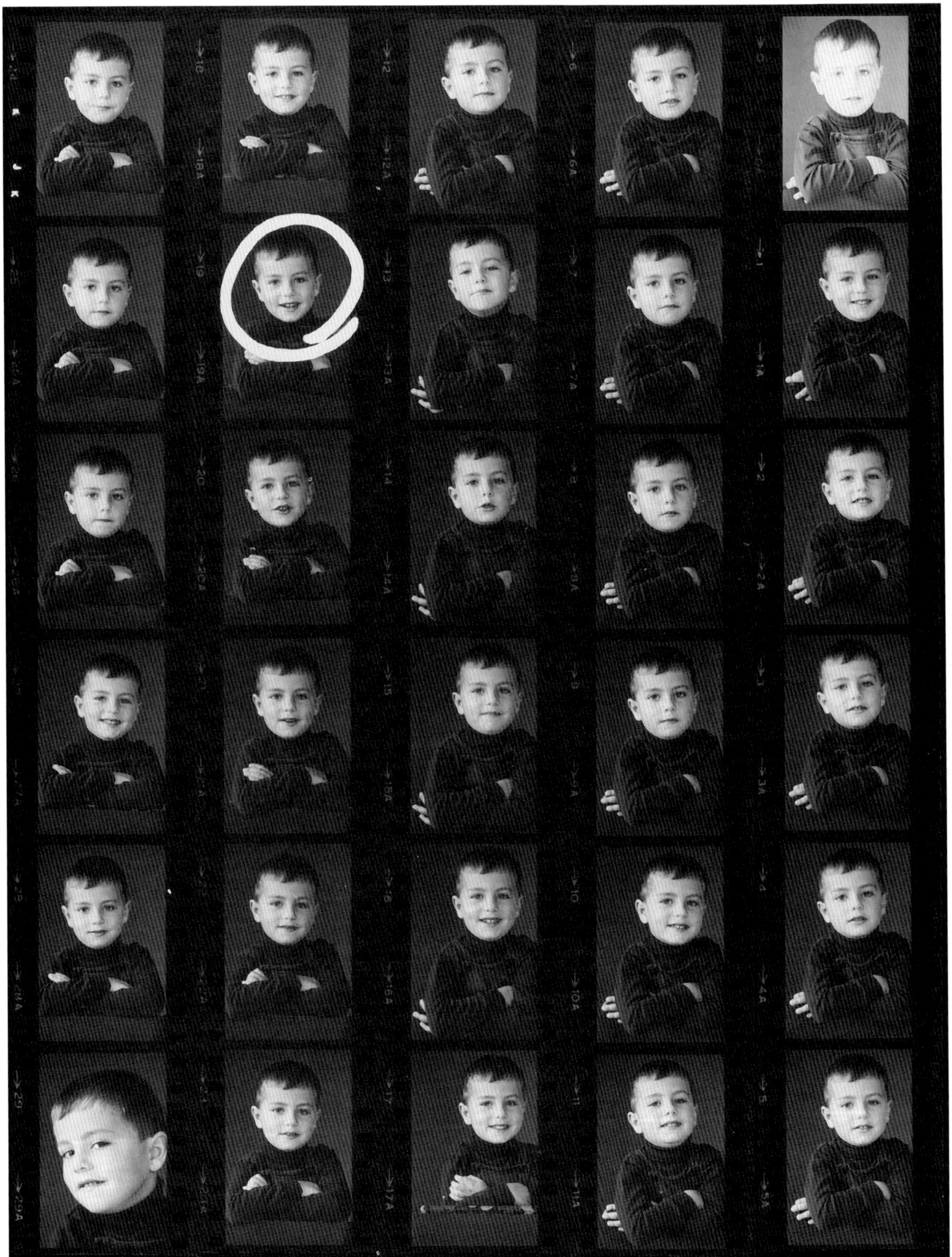

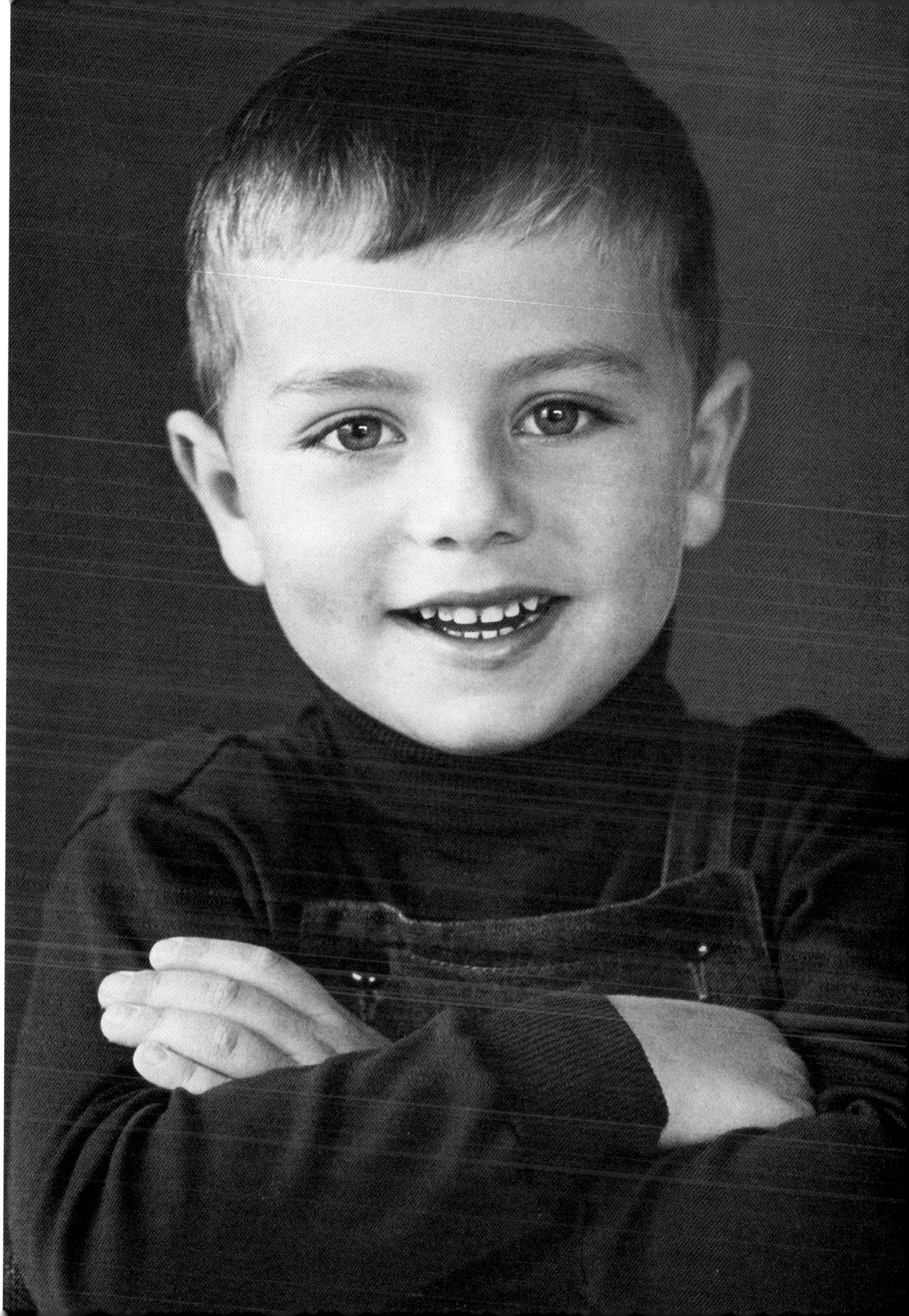

Perfect reproduction

Leica projectors

Usually, the perfect photograph is not the product of a coincidence but the result of a long chain of ideas and most diverse programmed processes. Those who want to fully utilize the advantages of the Leica M and its lenses will therefore direct their attention to each link of this long process – from before the picture is taken to the point when the finished picture is viewed – because the entire chain can only be as strong as its weakest link!

Projectors have been around for a long time, even before the first Leica was built. The Laterna Magica, which dates from the year 1659, is probably the best-known example in the centuries-old history of projectors. The 35mm still projector, however, was introduced in 1926. Of course, this projector came from Leitz, and of course it was also designed by Oskar Barnack, the inventor of the Leica camera. He realized how critically the results of his Leica photography were influenced by the quality of the devices with which they were reproduced, it was clear to him that only a high quality enlargement of a 35mm negative or high quality projection of a 35mm transparency could do justice to the extraordinary quality of a Leica photograph. That was true then and it is equally true today.

Today, Leica offers a product line of different project models, which, despite their differences in performance and design, have a few features in common. These include, among other things, excellent optical systems for lighting control and interchangeable high-power projection lenses. For example, for decades the Colorplan and the 90mm f/2.5 Super-Colorplan lenses have been considered the "kings" of projection lenses. As regards their brilliance and sharpness, they are absolutely comparable with the Leica M lenses.

The smallest projector is the Pradovit P150. It is designed for longitudinal trays and uses a 24V/150W halogen lamp (Fig. 205). The largest and most powerful model is a round-tray projector with an 85V/300W halogen cold-light mirror lamp (Fig. 206).

Together with the two longitudinal-tray projectors, Leica Pradovit P300 and P600, which are equipped with 24V/250W halogen lamps and have different equipment features, a line of projectors is offered which is optimally adapted to the most diverse demands, tasks and situations. This product line is completed by comprehensive accessories, which also include control devices for lap-dissolve projection.

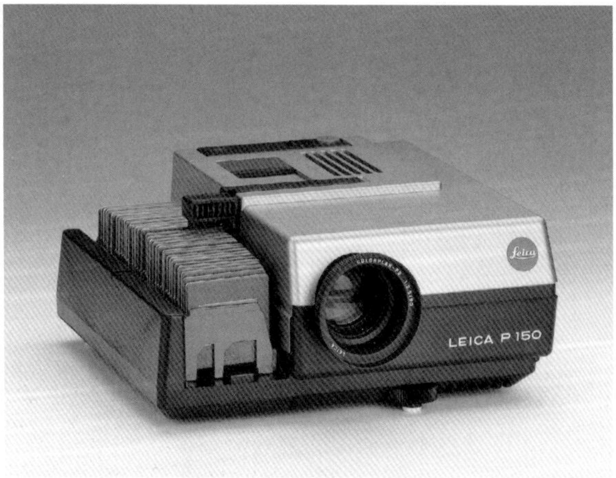

Fig. 205: *Leica Pradovit P150*

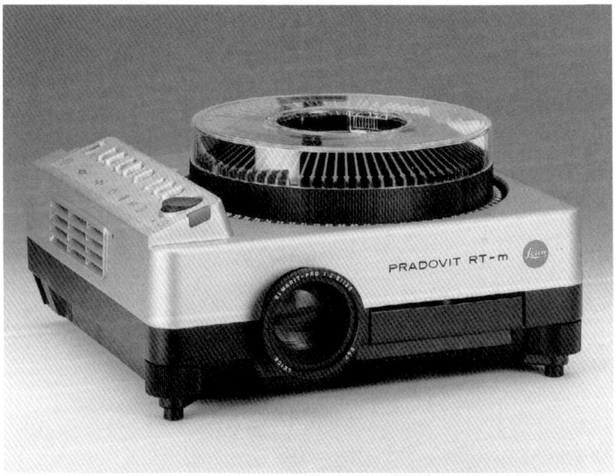

Fig. 206: *Leica Pradovit RT*

Leica

A bit of history

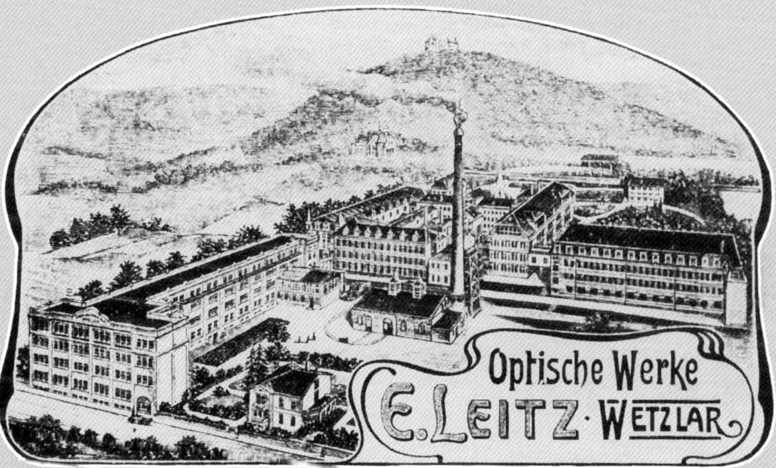

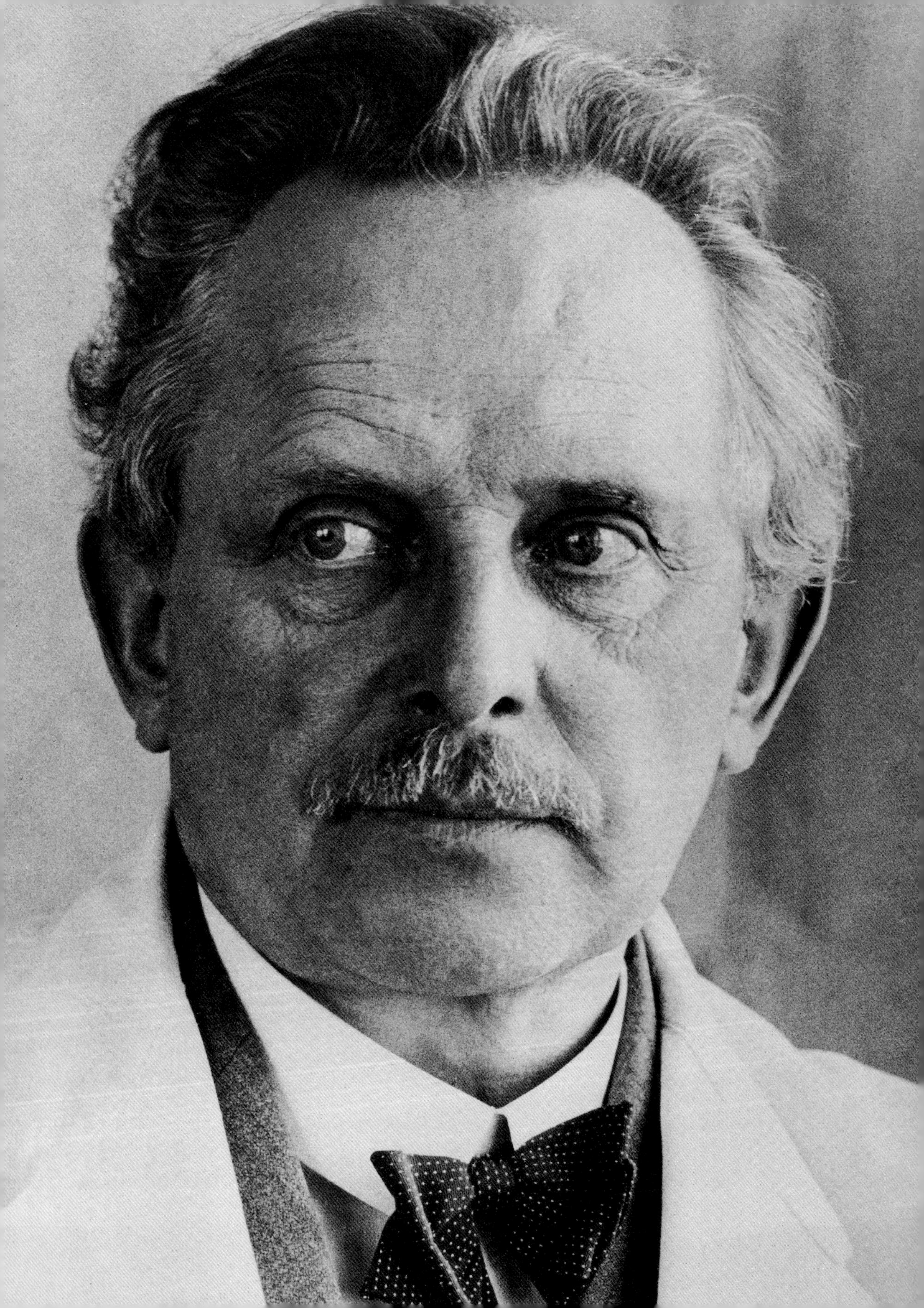

A bit of history

Oskar Barnack

When Oskar Barnack, the inventor of the Leica camera, was born on November 1, 1879 in Lynow, Germany, the firm of Ernst Leitz, which specialized in the manufacture of microscopes had already been in existence for 30 years in the free imperial City of Wetzlar. At that time, the Ernst Leitz works had 40 employees and a yearly production of 350 microscopes. The quality of Leitz microscopes had become recognized beyond the borders of Germany. Between the turn of the century and the beginning of World War I, the Ernst Leitz works became a major employer and an important source of exports for Wetzlar and the surrounding area. By 1911 the firm had grown to more than 950 employees and annual production had risen to 9,000 microscopes. At least thirty types of microscopes were produced. Scientists and researchers everywhere in the world were using Leitz microscopes. Microscope No. 150.000 was completed and presented to Nobel Prize winner Professor Dr. Paul Ehrlich in 1912.

Until 1911, Leitz had little to do with photography, apart from a few attachments that had been manufactured for its microscopes for several decades. A large horizontal camera for photomicrography had been available since 1885. In 1890, a drawing attachment with a camera was added, followed in 1900 by a device for micro-positive and transparency projection. For the photographic trade, Leitz supplied lenses of various focal lengths, designed for use with large-format plate cameras produced by other manufacturers. Beyond that, the Leitz Company had never shown any ambitions in the photographic sector and thus, photographers and photographic dealers were not among its clients. However, the first step towards the expansion of the products offered by Leitz occurred in early in 1911 when Oskar Barnack joined the company as foreman of the experimental microtesting department.

__Fig. 207:__ Oskar Barnack (1879 – 1936), inventor of the Leica camera.

Pioneer of 35mm photography – inventor of the Leica camera

Not much is known about Oskar Barnack's youth, except that his parents moved from Lynow to Berlin where Oskar attended school and later completed his apprenticeship as a machinist in a workshop for astronomical instruments. As a young man he was interested in mathematics and technical subjects, especially photography. It is said that he often used his leisure time to go on hikes, taking along his camera to photograph the countryside around his home. Perhaps it was his artistic inclination (originally he wanted to become a painter) that influenced his love for the creative media of photography and motion pictures.

He wrote in 1905 that he pursued his hobby on weekends by hiking through the woods of Thuringia carrying an unwieldy 13 x 18 cm (5 x 7 inch) plate camera, a backpack full of plates and a heavy tripod. This must have sparked the idea of creating a smaller camera, which could be taken anywhere without effort and used for making pictures with greater spontaneity.

But his first efforts in this direction were unsuccessful. The photographic plates available at that time were unsuitable for a small-format camera because they could not be enlarged satisfactorily. Even during his journeyman years, which he spent in Saxony, Vienna, Tyrol, and Jena, Barnack continued to think about inventing a small camera, albeit without practical results.

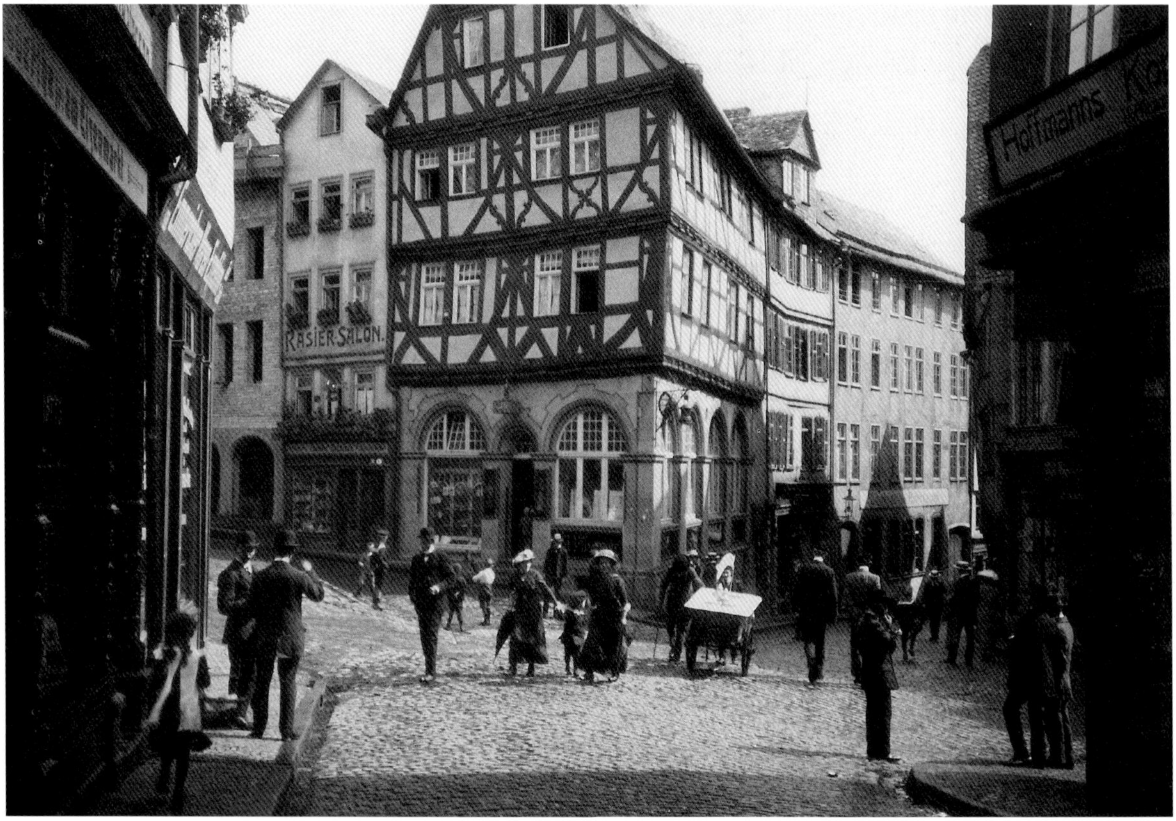

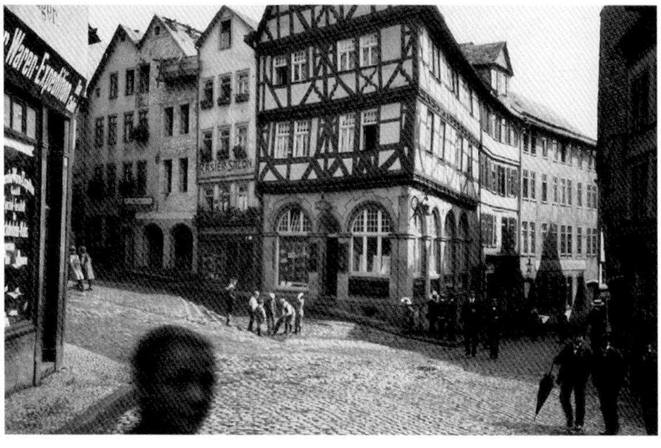

Fig. 208 a and b: *Early photographs by Oskar Barnack show the spontaneous nature of 35mm photography, which would later become characteristic of a new photographic style. He also frequently bracketed his exposures—a common practice nowadays—to see additional variations in the image. This well-known photograph of the Eisenmarkt square in Wetzlar (top) was the second exposure Barnack made of that subject. A child walked into the picture during the first exposure (bottom).*

Problems of an amateur movie maker

It was only after he joined the Leitz firm in Wetzlar that Barnack was able to devote himself to this idea again, and in 1912 he began working on the design of a motion-picture camera. It was an all-metal camera made of aluminum—a technical concept that was well ahead of its time. Pursuing his earlier interests, he conducted experiments by enlarging negatives made on motion picture film. The grain was relatively small compared to that of large-format photographic plates, which encouraged him to pursue a new direction.

Oskar Barnack had already made a number of movies around Wetzlar, which were called "Leitz Movies" and which were well received by the public when they were shown in a movie theater. But often there were scenes in the 60 m (c. 200 feet) long film that were either over-exposed or under-exposed. With the high film prices of the time, this was quite costly for

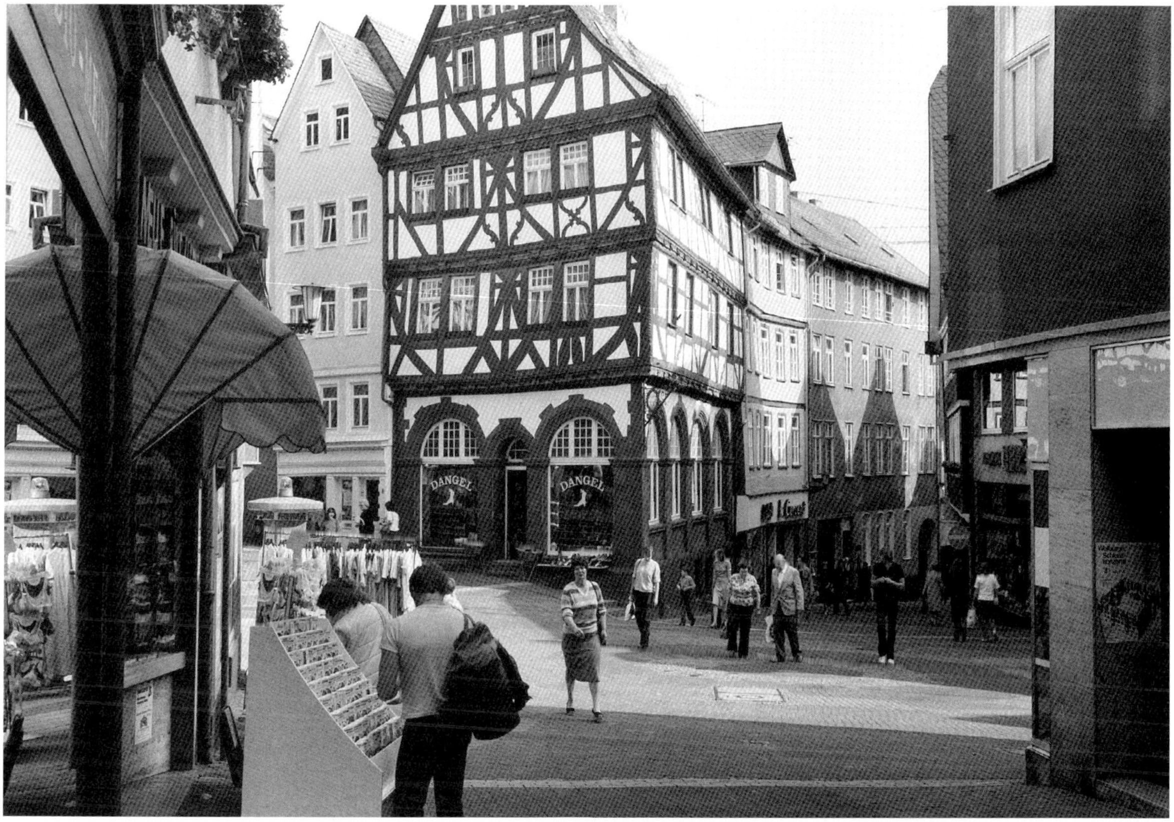

Fig. 209: *Just as the appearance of the Eisenmarkt square in Wetzlar—the subject of Barnack's early photographs of 1913—has not changed to this day, the principle of the Leica has also remained the same. This photograph was made in 1983 with a Leica M4-P camera with a 50mm f/2 Summicron lens.*

Barnack. Another concern was the amount of time lost in editing out and re-shooting the poorly exposed scenes. What he needed was an accurate exposure meter. But the selenium cells, cadmium sulfide photoresistors and silicon photodiodes that are familiar today were unheard of then. Optical aids, such as grease-spot photometers, were used for measuring the intensity of light.

So, Oskar Barnack became interested in designing an exposure meter for use with motion pictures. He went about doing this in typical Barnack fashion, that is, his approach was unconventional and innovative. Why, in fact, should he measure the exposure optically and control it mechanically? The photochemical method of exposing a test length of the actual motion picture film at various aperture settings and quickly processing it would be much more accurate for determining the correct exposure. Therefore, it seemed logical to build a small metering chamber for determining exposures and equipping it with a lens that corresponded to the lens on the motion picture camera and a shutter that provided the same exposure time as the motion-picture camera. So, Barnack went about constructing this, and in doing so, discovered two applications at the same time. Since this small measuring chamber, which was nothing more than a small still camera, made actual exposures on motion-picture film, couldn't these test exposures also be used as photographs in their own right? Wasn't this also the answer to his desire to have a small photographic still camera?

The Ur-Leica is born

Oskar Barnack, therefore, built a small metal camera that he could conveniently carry in his pocket. It was equipped with a focal-plane shutter with a fixed speed of 1/40 second. The film advance was coupled with the winding of the shutter, preventing double exposures. The optics consisted of a lens that could be collapsed like an early telescope.

Barnack decided to use the width of two motion picture frames for his still photographs, in other words he exposed negatives that were 24 mm wide and 36 mm long. This decision was not the result of lengthy ponderings like those that he often went through later for even minor camera details. The choice of that format simply corresponded to his feeling that a ratio of 2:3 was the most pleasing and the most practical. Thus the "Ur-Leica" (prototype Leica) was born. It was a roll film camera that was loaded with a strip of perforated motion-picture film, 2 m (about 6-1/2 feet) long.

For three years Barnack worked on improving the design of this new camera, which he had originally intended to use as an exposure device. Its first photographs, made in 1913 and 1914, are still preserved today.

In the meantime, Oskar Barnack built a second model of his prototype Leica, which was tested by his boss, Ernst Leitz, during trips abroad. At the time, there were no plans to develop the camera into a novel Leitz product for the marketplace. Although, Ernst Leitz did say, "Keep it in mind," World War I broke out and the work on the small camera stopped. Occasionally, Oskar Barnack would use his prototype to take pictures, a useful experiment for later on. It was only in the early 1920s that he was again able to devote himself to his original ideas. He used his unusual camera, which he had improved in the meantime, to photograph a major flood in Wetzlar, recording real action scenes much like today's news photos. This kind of photography—shooting a series of pictures of the same general subject was typical of Barnack's work, but it was not typical for amateur or professional photographers of that period. It was not until many years later that this style was championed by renowned photographers such as Erich Salomon and eventually became a regular technique of photojournalists.

The camera becomes ready for series production

However, the camera's single shutter speed of 1/40 second was not adequate for this type of photography. A new shutter that Barnack had developed, in the meantime, was incorporated into the camera. It was a self-capping shutter with a variable slit width that permitted shorter exposures. In addition, Barnack designed a separate rangefinder—an indispensable necessity for a small camera without a ground-glass focusing screen.

After building a telescopic viewfinder and designing a new type of cassette that allowed the camera to be loaded in daylight, there was only one problem left for Barnack to solve: He needed to find a lens with exactly the right focal length for the small format. It would have to be of excellent quality in order to permit at least a ten times linear enlargement of the negatives.

This is where the lens design skill of Dr. Max Berek came in. He designed an anastigmatic lens with a maximum aperture of f/3.5 and a focal length of 50mm, which corresponds approximately to the diagonal of the 35mm format. With these refinements, Barnack's small camera was finally ready to be marketed.

In the meantime, however, an external obstacle to the production of the camera had arisen—a period of great distress and runaway inflation plagued Germany. Prices were no longer stated in hundreds of Marks, but thousands, millions, billions, and even trillions became everyday occurrences. A regular letter required postage at first of 25,000 Marks, then 1 billion, and eventually 20 billion Marks. A salary received on one day would barely pay for a small loaf of bread on the very next day. To introduce a new camera to the market at this particular time would have been suicidal for any enterprise. But currency reform brought inflation to a halt, only to be followed by a period of extremely high unemployment.

Dr. Ernst Leitz II, who had taken over the company after the death of his father, was confronted with an extremely difficult decision: Should he actually build the camera?

The Leica is produced

Many businesses were critically short of orders. It was difficult to keep the workforce busy, and the German optical industry was also seriously affected by the economic crisis. There were huge lines for job applicants and for unemployment compensation everywhere. These external circumstances influenced the decision that Dr. Ernst Leitz II made, which was to have an enormous bearing on the future of his organization: he decided to expand his factory and to start the production of a camera. Not with reluctance, nor with reservation, but with the decisiveness of a modern manager, he initiated the manufacture of the first Barnack camera, which had been thoroughly tested during the inflation year of 1923.

The first 35mm cameras from Leitz were made by hand and they were numbered from No. 100 to No. 125. They were used for testing the market. Up to that time, the Leitz works had mainly produced microscopes, and the meticulous precision that was essential for the manufacture of such instruments and for the production of microscope objectives now benefited the fabrication of the camera. During the year 1924, the first samples of this new type of precision camera were entrusted to selected photographers and scientists for testing. While some were enthusiastic about the new camera and the pictures it produced, there were also quite a few professional photographers who were skeptical about the small camera. They were accustomed to large cameras, they worked with tripods and they focused on large ground glass screens. But now, there was this small gadget. Very simply, they did not trust this tiny camera. Even within the Leitz company, there were those who resisted the new product.

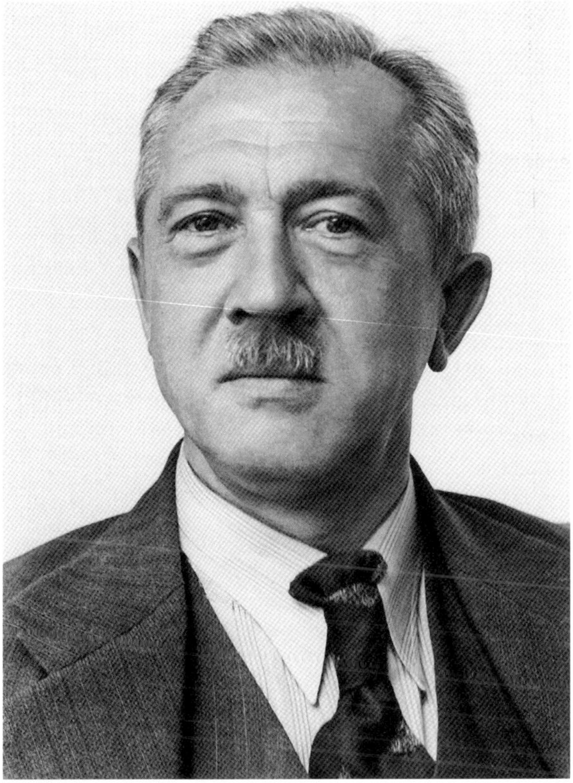

Fig. 210: *Professor Max Berek, who designed the 50mm f/3.5 Leitz Anastigmat lens at the request of Oskar Barnack, played a significant role in the success of the Leica camera.*

Nevertheless, Dr. Leitz ordered production of the first 500 cameras to begin in 1924-1925. At the same time, an application for the trademark registration of the name "Leica" was entered. However, both the first application as well as the second one in 1930 were rejected. The third application achieved the desired result in 1937, and along with it, the protection of the trademark. The name, was easy to pronounce in any language, was derived from the words "Leitz camera." It was destined to be known around the world.

Fig. 211 a and b: *How similar these pictures are—a flood in Wetzlar, taken by Oskar Barnack with his Ur-Leica in 1914 (top), and another flood in Wetzlar, taken in 1984 with a prototype of the Leica M6 camera (bottom).* ▶

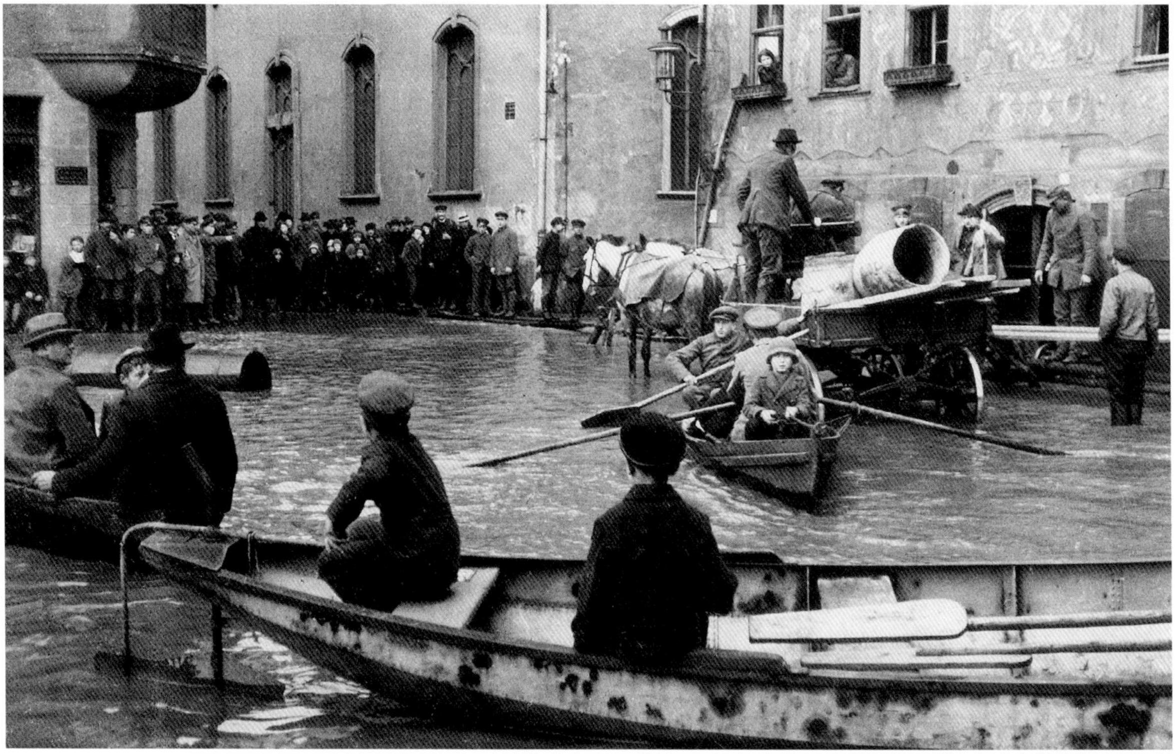

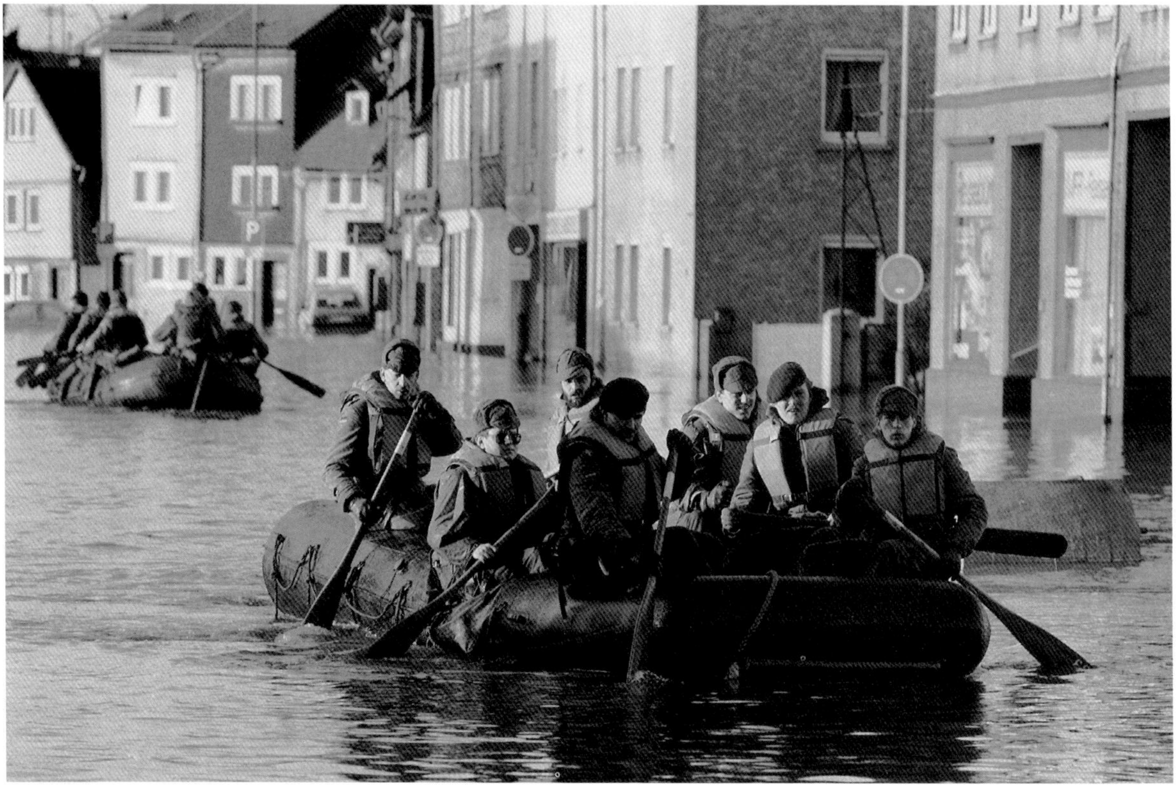

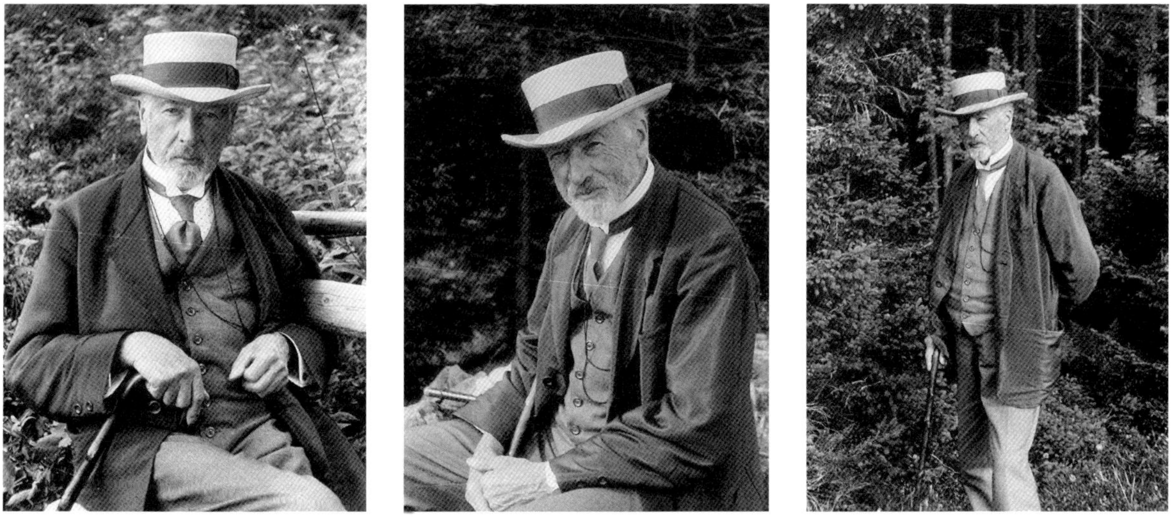

***Fig. 212 a – c:** Dr. Ernst Leitz II, son of the original Ernst Leitz who took over the small optical company in 1869, made the histor-ic decision: "Barnack's small camera shall be produced!" Oskar Barnack used the Ur-Leica to photograph Ernst Leitz I in the Black forest in the year 1914.*

An idea takes hold

The Leica camera was officially announced to the world at the 1925 Leipzig Spring Fair. The first advertisement heralded the camera as a "revolution in photography." Compared to all other cameras that were available up to that time, the Leica, beginning with this first model, was the fastest to be ready for the next shot. Double exposures were prevented and photographers were able to take 36 pictures in rapid succession without having to reload the camera between exposures. The price of film too, was an advantage, since a photographer could take 12 pictures for the price of a single 9x12 cm (approximately 3-1/2 x 4 inch) photograph.

With the new Leica camera, a photographer could compose the picture at eye level, thus achieving a surprisingly realistic perspective. Even relatively slow shutter speeds, which until 1925 generally required the use of a tripod and limited photography to rather static subjects, could now be used with a hand-held Leica camera. This is because of its handiness, its smooth shutter, and the short focal length of its lens. What this meant to photographers was that they finally had a camera, the Leica, which could be used under poor lighting conditions. Thus, the Leica gave 35mm photography the push it needed for launching a new era in photography.

The Leica camera attracted a great deal of attention. News of this innovative, new camera and its new small format spread rapidly around the world. By the end of 1925, more than 1,000 Leica A cameras (later called Leica I cameras in Germany) had been produced. The first batch of about 200 cameras was equipped with 50mm f/3.5 Leitz Anastigmat lenses; another batch of around 1,000 to 1,100 cameras had 50mm f/3.5 Leitz Elmax lenses. Later models were equipped with the 50mm f/3.5 Leitz Elmar lens that is still famous to this day.

Barely one year after the introduction of the very first model, the Leica B went into production (commonly known as the "Compur Leica"). This series would continue, with many models based on it, for the next 75-plus years. The latest model is the Leica M7, which Leica introduced at Photokina 2002.

Currently, millions of 35mm cameras are produced around the world every year. By comparison, Leica manufactures only a relatively small percentage, but it has made the conviction that their cameras meet the strict, high standards that Oskar Barnack and others established with the first Leica cameras. The photographic world owes a great deal to Oskar Barnack, because many applications of photography in business, science, technology, and administration, as well as in humanitarian, medical, and creative fields go back to ideas that inspired Barnack to create the Leica camera. With his invention Barnack created unencumbered snapshot photography and as a result, modern candid photography, contemporary photojournalism, scientific, and industrial photography all owe their roots to Barnack's belief in the 35mm format. These facts certainly are reason enough once more to pay homage to the work of Oskar Barnack and to the history of the Leica camera.

The Leica family tree

The main lobby of the Leica works in Solms houses the Leica Gallery and the Leica Museum. In the reception area of the Leica Academy, interesting Leica models are on display. The Leica family tree shows the important cameras from more than 75 years of production. Even though small variations of the same model are not necessarily included, more than 90 pieces are on exhibit.

A poster of the Leica Family Tree is also available from Leica Camera and a book, "A Brief Leica Chronicle," which provides information about the more interesting models of cameras, projectors, enlargers, and accessories. Beyond that, there is a large amount of literature in every major language available in bookshops and photographic stores, containing extensive information about every conceivable detail of each model of the Leica camera, interchangeable lenses, and the accessories (see page 345-346).

As so often happens with ingenious ideas, the original concept for the Leica was simple and logical. The principle is as valid today as it was 77 years ago when the first Leica appeared on the market. There are photographic historians and collectors everywhere in the world who specialize in the many different models of the Leica camera. Naturally, those models of which there are only a few in existence are of particular interest. There are also collectors who have several cameras with the same model designation, but none is exactly like the other in every detail. Changes in design and in manufacturing technology have brought about a large number of variations during the years of production of a given model. The chronology on these pages covers only the Ur-Leica and the most important Leica camera models that were manufactured by Leitz and Leica Camera.

Ur-Leica

Oskar Barnack built his first working prototype of a camera for 35mm motion picture film in 1914. It consisted of an all-metal body with a collapsible lens and it had a focal plane shutter that was not yet

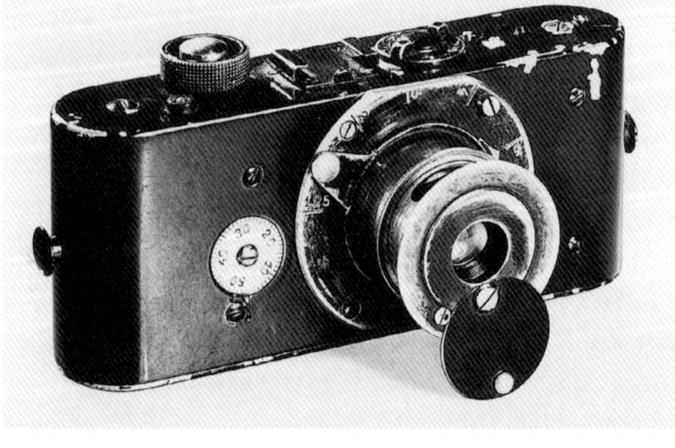

Ur-Leica

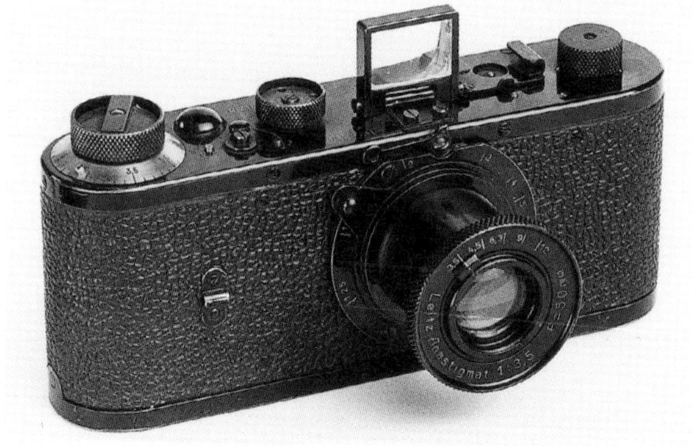

Leica 0 series

self-capping. A hinged cover had to be swung over the lens before the film was advanced in order to prevent fogging. This camera, known as the "Ur-Leica," which means the original, the very first Leica, became one of the landmarks in the history of photography.

Leica 0 series

In 1923 the first hand-made cameras were produced. These pre-series models were used to "test" the market and the manufacturing. The cameras' non-self-capping focal-plane shutter has an adjustable slit width and allows the selection of shutter speeds from 1/20 to 1/50 second. A specially constructed cassette holds the film and can be changed in daylight. The 0 series largely corresponds to the later factory manufactured Leica I. According to what we know today, only 25 cameras having the serial numbers 101 to 125 were manufactured (see also page 85).

Leica I with non-interchangeable lens

The Leica model A, also known as the Leica I, was introduced in 1925 with non-interchangeable lens. At first, this model was supplied with a 50mm f/3.5 Leitz Anastigmat lens or a 50mm f/3.5 Leitz Elmax lens. Later it was offered with the famous 50mm f/3.5 Elmar lens. A spring on the front of the camera served as the infinity latch for the lenses. The focal-plane shutter was calibrated for speeds from 1/20 to

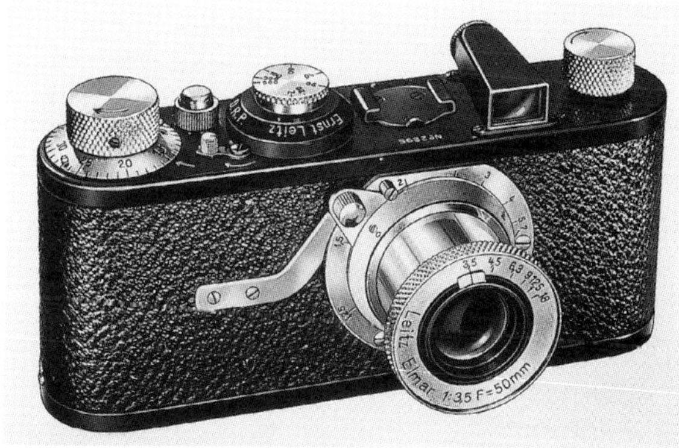

Leica I with non-interchangeable lens

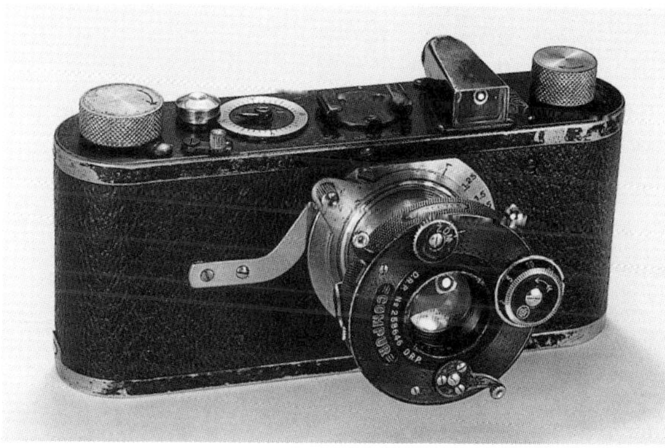

Compur Leica

1/500 second, plus time exposures. A separate rangefinder could be slipped into the accessory shoe.

Compur Leica

In 1926, Leitz introduced a black-enameled camera with a non-interchangeable 50mm f/3.5 Leitz Elmar lens and a Compur shutter instead of the customary focal plane shutter. They called the camera Leica model B. Among collectors, this camera is known as the Compur Leica. The early version of this model had a shutter with two dials on the front (therefore referred to as "dial-set"). One of the dials had settings for "B" and "T" for time exposures plus "M" for shutter speeds from 1 to 1/300 second. These had to be selected with the second dial. A later version of the

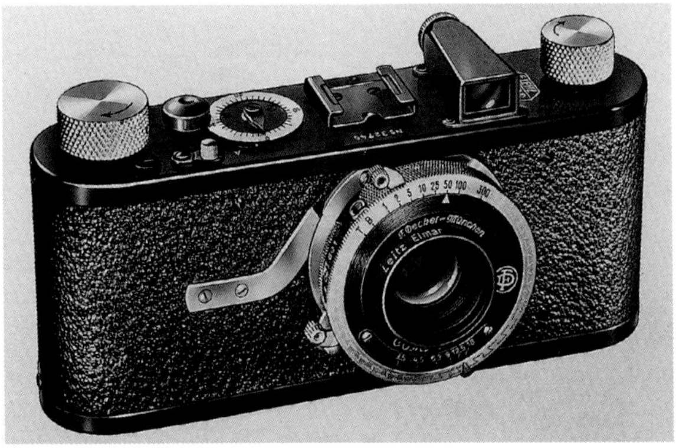

Compur Leica

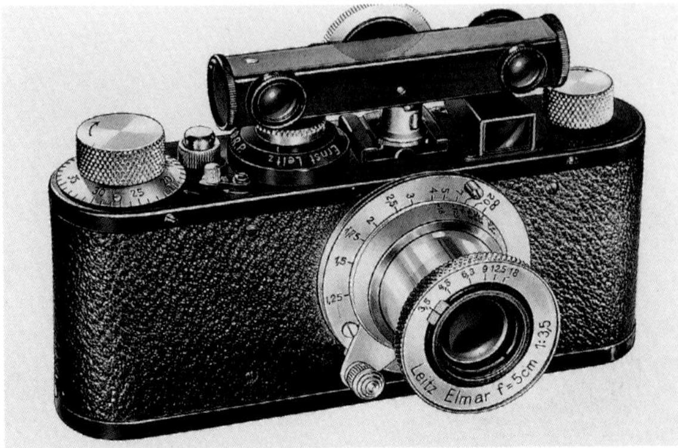

Leica I for interchangeable lenses

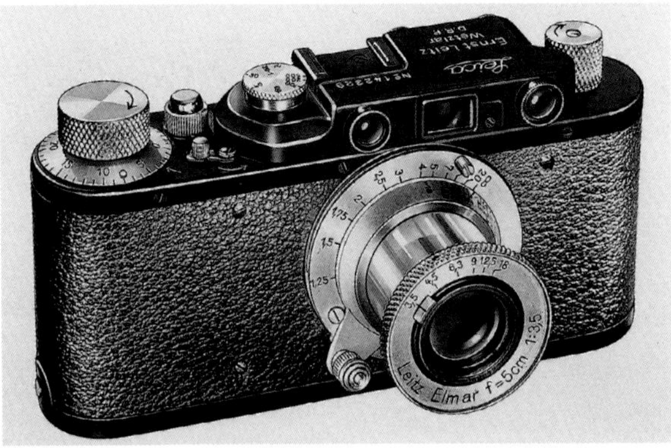

Leica II

Compur shutter (beginning in 1929) had only one dial along the outer rim of the shutter (therefore referred to as "rim-set"). It was calibrated for shutter speeds of 1, 112, 1/5, 1/10, 1/25, 1/50, 1/100, and 1/300 second, plus "B" and "T." Shutter cocking and film advance were not coupled.

Leica I for interchangeable lenses

The first Leica with a flange for interchangeable screwmount lenses, the Leica model C (also known as Leica I for interchangeable lenses). It went into production in 1930. The flange-to-film distance on these cameras was not standardized, requiring each lens to be calibrated for a specific camera. In 1931 this distance was standardized both on the camera as well as the lenses. These cameras were identified by a "0" engraved on the top, front of the lens flange.

The following three lenses were available for this model: the wide-angle 35mm f/3.5 Elmar lens, the normal 50mm f/3.5 lens, and the telephoto 135mm f/4.5 Elmar lens. Other than the interchangeable lenses, the Leica model C was similar to the Leica model A.

Leica II

The important innovation on the Leica II introduced in 1932 was the built-in coupled rangefinder for use with a larger family of lenses. Along with this new model, the lightweight, slender 105mm f/6.3 Elmar lens was announced, which later was to become famous under the name "Mountain Elmar".

The Leica had become a genuine system camera with seven interchangeable lenses with standardized mounts that couple with the rangefinder. The lenses were the following:

The Lenses:

35mm f/3.5 Elmar	90mm f/4 Elmar
50mm f/3.5 Elmar	105mm f/6.3 Elmar
50mm f/2.5 Hektor	135mm f/4.5 Elmar
73mm f/1.9 Hektor	

Three close-up attachments for magnifications up to 1:1 became available as additional accessories.

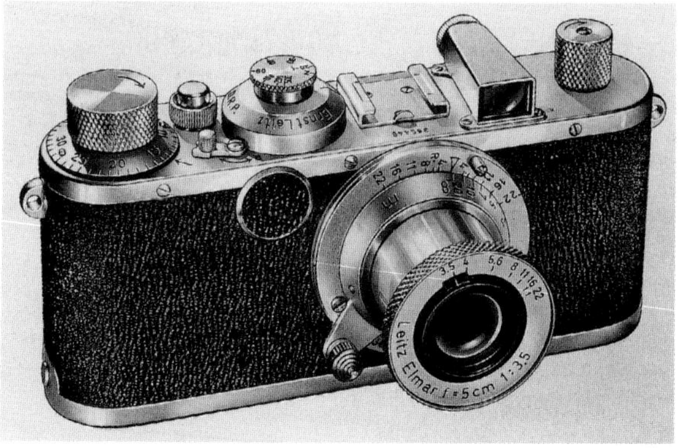

Leica Standard

Leica Standard

The Leica Standard was first introduced in 1932 in a black-enameled version, followed in 1933 by a chrome version. It looks deceivingly similar to the Leica I, except that it has a pull-up rewind knob that makes it easier to rewind the film.

Leica III

In 1933, the Leica III was added to the Leica system, offering shutter speeds from 1 to 1/500 second. Its slow shutter speeds from 1 to 20 seconds are selected by means of a slow-speed dial on the front of the camera. The family of lenses was also expanded. Leica cameras are now equipped with lateral eyelets.

Leica 250

1934 was the year of the introduction of the Leica 250, also known as the Leica Reporter, the Leica FF (1/500 second), and the Leica GG (1/1000 second). Its unusual body shape accommodated two cassettes for 10 m (33 feet) of film, which was enough for 250 exposures. The film was wound from one cassette into the other, but it could also be cut in the camera with a special knife and the cassette with the exposed part of the film could be removed in daylight. The shutter was the same as in the Leica III. The fastest shutter speed was 1/500 second. In 1936 the fastest shutter speed became 1/1000 second.

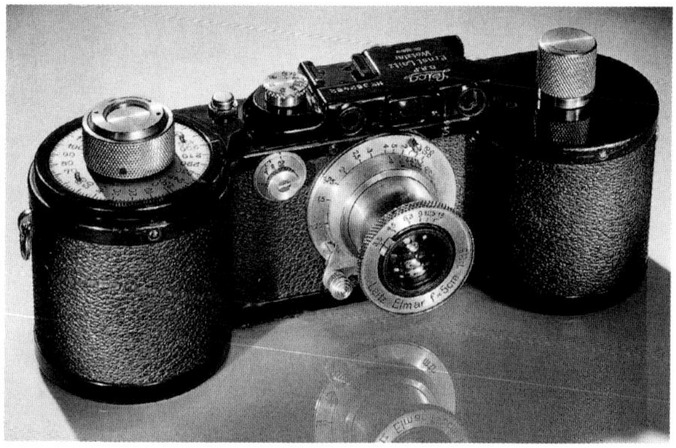

Leica 250

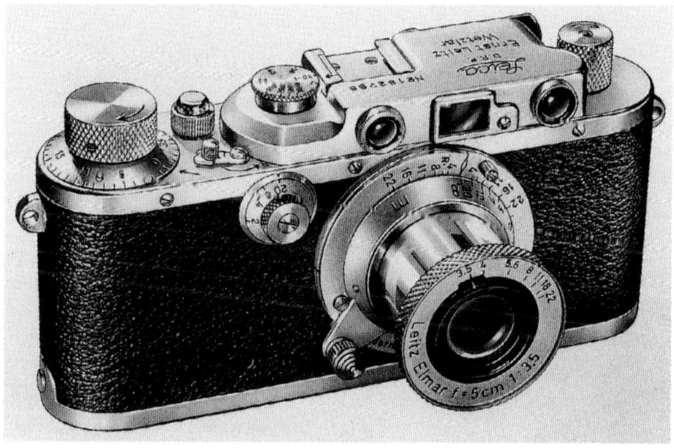

Leica IIIa

A small series of Leica 250 cameras was also equipped with an electric motor.

Leica IIIa

This variation of the Leica III, which was introduced in 1935, had an additional shutter speed of 1/1000 second.

Leica IIIb

Additional improvements were incorporated into the Leica camera in 1938. On this model, the eyepieces for the rangefinder and the viewfinder are closer together. The focusing lever for the

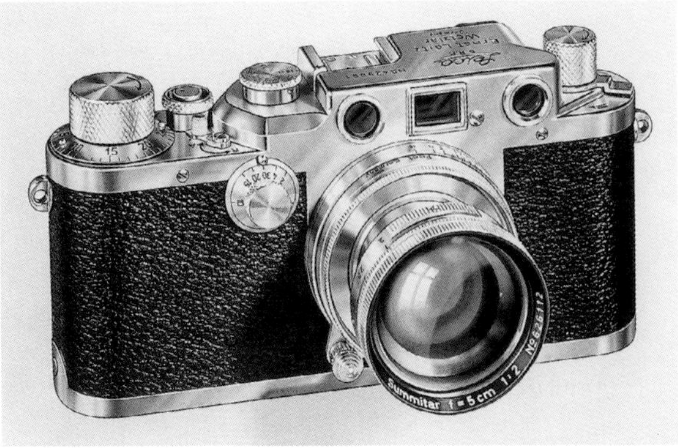

Leica IIIc

rangefinder is under the rewind knob (more user-friendly). The top plate is 1 mm (nearly 3/64") taller than on previous models.

Leica IIIc

In 1940, Leitz introduced a variation of the Leica IIIb with an exterior appearance very similar to that of its predecessor. Its improvements were mostly the result of new manufacturing technologies adopted by Leitz at the time. The body is made of die-cast aluminum, and the top plate was fabricated from a single sheet of brass instead of two. At 136 mm (5-1/2 inches), the camera is 3 mm (nearly 1/8 inch) longer than previous models.

Leica IIc

In 1948, after World War II, Leitz introduced a simplified version of the Leica IIIc in which they eliminated the slow shutter speeds.

Leica Ic

Also in 1948, the Leica Ic replaced the Leica Standard that was being produced up to that time. The camera was intended primarily for photography in science and technology, where a viewfinder and a

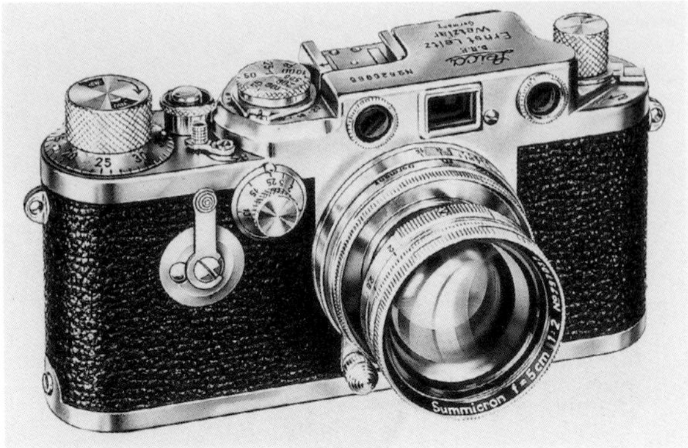

Leica IIIf

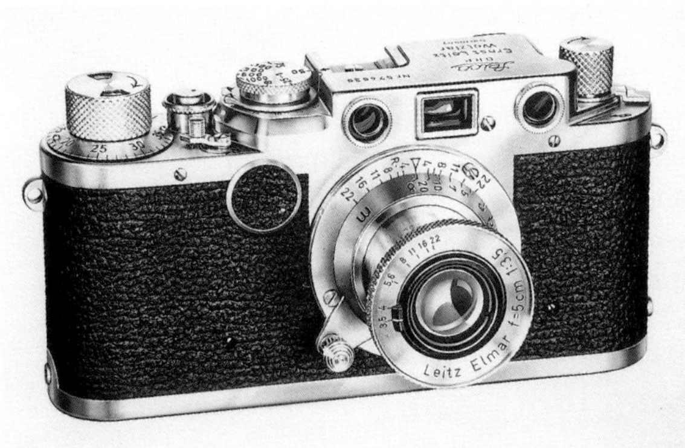

Leica IIf

rangefinder were not needed. In conjunction with a reflex housing, the Leica Ic could be used without limitations for close-up as well as distant photography. Like the Leica IIc, it had shutter speeds from 1/30 to 1/500 second.

Leica IIIf

The first new camera designed by Leitz after World War II was the Leica IIIf, which was introduced in 1950. Its external appearance was very similar to that of the Leica IIIc. In previous models, special adaptations were necessary to use flash with a Leica camera. The new Leica IIIf was synchronized for flashbulbs as well as for electronic flash units. The Leica Illf had a time-delay selector for flash

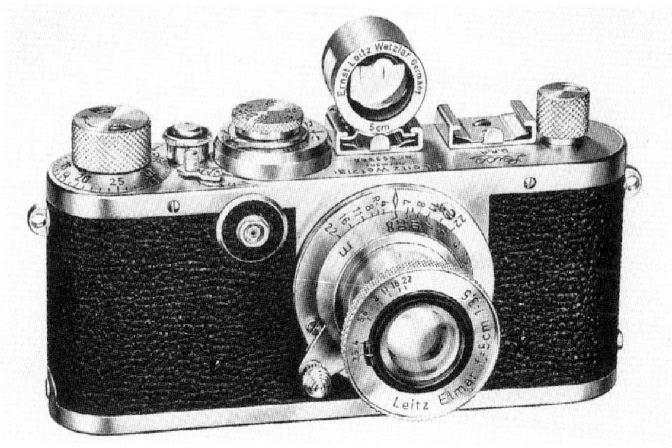

Leica If

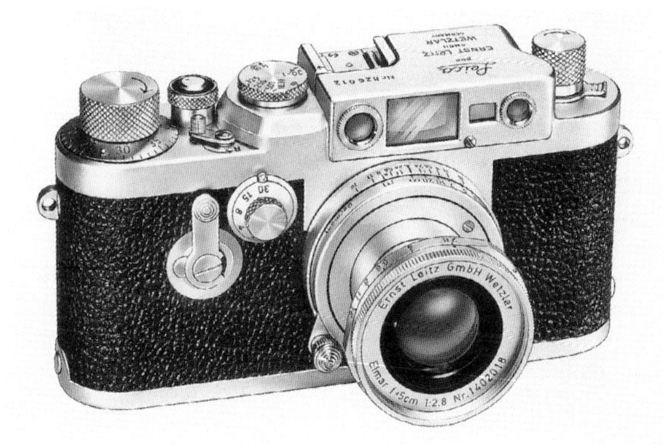

Leica IIIg

synchronization under the upper shutter speed dial, and it had a film reminder in the film advance knob.

There are many variations of the Leica IIIf, for example those with black time delay numbers and later ones with red time delay numbers, and models with and without a self-timer, and cameras with the new international sequence of shutter speeds, etc. The 500,000th Leica camera, a model IIIc, was produced during this same year.

Leica IIf

This model was added in 1952 to complement the Leica IIIf line of cameras. The Leica IIf was also available first with black time delay numbers, and later with red time delay numbers. It does not have any slow shutter speeds.

Leica If

Also in 1952, the Leica If, which had no viewfinder and no rangefinder, replaced the Leica Ic that was being produced up to that time. The flash contact on the Leica If is positioned where the slow speed dial is located on the Leica IIIf. As was the case with the Leica IIf, there were also several variations of the Leica If camera.

Leica M3

A new era of 35mm photography dawned in 1954 when Leitz introduced the Leica M3 camera with bayonet mount lenses. This radically new camera is equipped with a luminous range-viewfinder. The respective bright-line frames are activated automatically when the 50, 90 and 135mm lenses are attached to the camera body. 35mm wide-angle lenses with viewfinder attachments can also be used. A detailed description of this camera and of all other Leica M models can be found beginning on page 16.

The "Leicameter," an exposure meter that slips into the accessory shoe and couples to the shutter speed dial of the Leica M3 was introduced at the same time. Eleven different Leica lenses are now available to the photographer.

Leica IIIg

Along with the Leica Ig, which was introduced simultaneously, the last Leica model for screwmount lenses was announced in 1957. Called the Leica IIIg, it is similar to the Leica IIIf, except that it has a large bright-line viewfinder for 50 and 90mm lenses, and automatic parallax correction. The Leica IIIg is fully synchronized and thus, has no external time-delay selector. Like other Leica M cameras, it has a film reminder on the back.

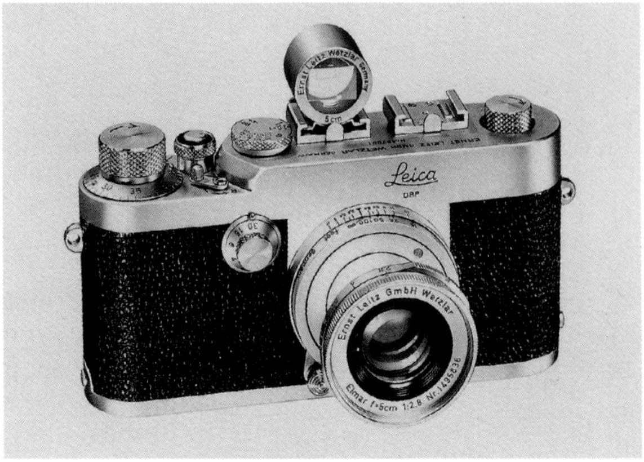

Leica Ig

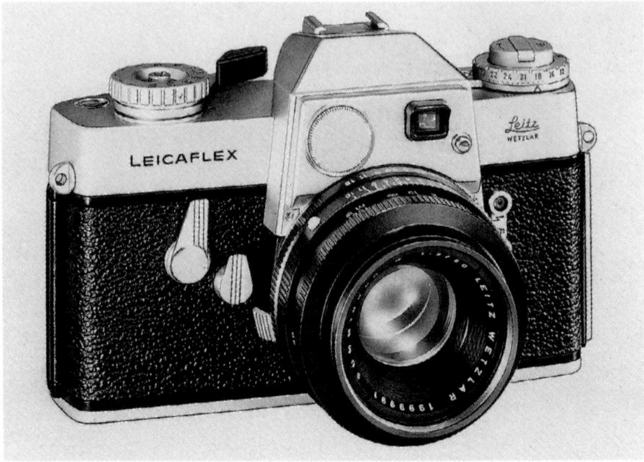

Leicaflex

Leica Ig

The Leica Ig was announced in 1957, at the same time that the Leica IIIg was introduced. It corresponds to the Leica IIIg, except that it has neither a viewfinder nor a rangefinder, and there is no self-timer. The pull-up rewind knob is partially recessed into the top plate. The Leica logo is positioned conspicuously on the upper front of the camera. The era of Leitz screwmount cameras ended in 1960.

Leicaflex

The long awaited single-lens-reflex (SLR) camera from Leitz—the Leicaflex camera—was introduced on March 1,1965. The line Leicaflex cameras, and after 1960, the Leica R cameras, constitute a second main branch of the Leica family tree. The book "Applied Leica Technique" by this author is devoted to these cameras in great detail.

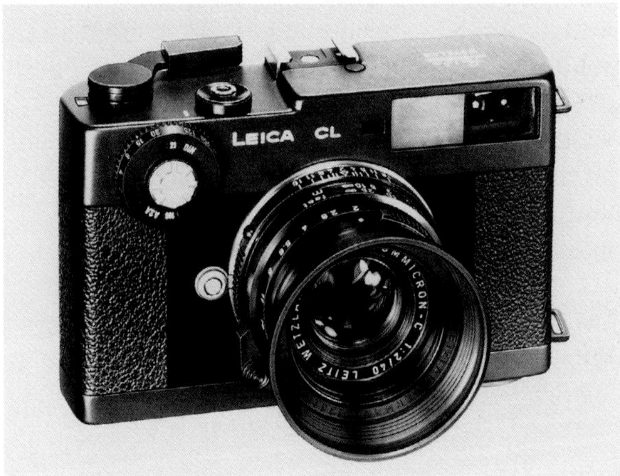

Leica CL

Leica CL

The "Compact Leica" was announced in 1973. It was the first product that resulted from the new cooperative agreement between Leitz and Minolta. The Leica CL has a luminous frame range-viewfinder with automatic parallax correction, a set of bright-line frames for 40 and 50mm lenses, and a separate bright-line frame for 90mm lenses. These frames are activated automatically when their respective lenses are mounted. The Leica CL camera is equipped with a Leica M quick-change bayonet lens mount that permits the use of Leica M lenses. The effective rangefinder base of this camera, however, is only 19.5 mm (23/32"). This severely restricts the use of several Leica M lenses. The 40mm f/2 Summicron-C and the 90mm f/4 Elmar-C lenses were designed especially for the Leica CL system. Like the Leica M5, the Leica CL has a built-in exposure meter with a hinged CdS measuring cell for selective exposure metering through the lens. The rubberized cloth focal-plane shutter runs vertically, with speeds from 1/1000 to 1 second, plus B. The entire back cover can be removed for convenient film loading.

The history of Leica is closely connected with the history of Leitz Works. It begins in the summer of 1849, when the then 23-year old mathematician Carl Kellner from Hirzenhain founded his "Optical Institute" in Wetzlar for the purpose of applying his scientific expertise to the improvement of optical devices. His father and grandfather had been active in the management of steel mills near home. He attended the Latin School in Braunfels near Wetzlar, where he showed a strong interest in mathematics and physics. In his spare time, he researched optical problems. He left school at age 17 and moved to nearby Giessen in order to supplement his theoretical knowledge with practical experience in the workshop of a mechanic named Sartorius. He continued his studies of mathematics with Dr. Stein, a teacher and later director of the Giessen high school. After two years of intensive study in Giessen, he spent a year in Hamburg learning about the construction of astronomical instruments. He further expanded his knowledge in during two years of personal study in Braunfels before moving to Wetzlar where the proximity of universities in Giessen and in Marburg may have attracted him.

Kellner's workshop was the foundation for the development of the economy of Wetzlar. While other shops were still using the old trial-and-error method for making lenses for telescopes and microscopes, Kellner performed optical calculations and precisely adjusted his lenses. In 1851 he marketed lenses and microscopes of his own design. These soon achieved a reputation for being the best products of their kind in Germany and all of Europe. In 1850 he had initially submitted his famous Orthoscopic Ocular to renowned mathematician Carl Friedrich Gauss for approval, and the latter promptly retained it for the astronomical observatory in Göttingen.

Ernst Leitz becomes an entrepreneur

After the early death of Carl Kellner, at age 29, on May 13, 1855 his young widow carried on the management of the business and its 12 employees. Precision mechanic Ernst Leitz I took over the company in 1869 and expanded it under his own name. Leitz was born in the small town of Sulzburg in the Black Forest, in the southern part of the state of Baden, where his father was a teacher. His parents wanted him to become a theologian, but driven by his intensely practical nature, he left school at age 15 in order to become an apprentice of instrument maker Christian Ludwig Oechsle, a friend of his father's in Pforzheim.

The "Workskop for Physical and Chemical Instruments and Apparatus and Machines of Mechanic Oechsle, Gold Controller of the Grand Duchy of Baden" was an ideal place for the eager and dexterous apprentice to acquire knowledge in the field of mechanics. The firm's reputation had been enhanced considerably by two of its inventions, "Oechsle's Wine Gage" and by its Gold Alloy Gage. After a lengthy period with the Swiss watch industry, where he was introduced to the art of managing people and became acquainted with the problems of labor distribution and assembly-line production, Ernst Leitz returned to Germany, arriving in Wetzlar early in 1864. On October 7, 1865, at the age of 22, he became a partner in Kellner's firm. With his skills, enterprising spirit, and optimism, he was able to lift the company from a position of weakness. In spite of tough competition, by cultivating contacts with scientists and researchers, he was able to develop instruments required by the times. In 1869 Ernst Leitz I became the sole manager of the company. His most outstanding innovation was the binocular microscope. By early 1887, the 10,000th microscope was produced and the number of employees at the firm had risen to 120. Many new types of microscopes followed.

By the end of the 19th century, the Leitz works had already garnered a worldwide reputation in the field of microscope manufacture. The social policies of the company were also remarkable: at the turn of the century, Ernst Leitz had already introduced the eight-hour workday in his company, and had founded a health insurance association.

The Leica is being built

In 1923 the aftermath of World War I and the massive postwar inflation had a severe economic impact on the company. Once again, it was a daring idea that brought about another upswing. Ernst Leitz I had died in July of 1920, and his son Ernst Leitz II (1871-1956) took over the helm of the company. In 1924 he made a farsighted decision, "The novel camera designed by Oskar Barnack is to be produced in quantity." During those years of economic depression, this decision was made to preserve and create new jobs, but it was contrary to the advice of professionals in the photographic trade. At the time, the company already had 1,000 employees. In 1925, at the Spring Fair in Leipzig, an 800-year old trade show for goods and merchandise from many countries, the Leica camera was introduced to the public for the very first time, launching it on its road to success around the world. This success made it the “blockbuster” product of the 1930s since it generated 60% of the firm's gross income.

Ernst Leitz Wetzlar GmbH

In the meantime, the three sons of Ernst Leitz II had joined the business: Ernst Leitz III (1906-1979), Ludwig Leitz (born in 1907), and Günther Leitz (1914-1969). After the death of their father in 1956, they shared the management of the firm. The fact that the factory was not destroyed during World War II was a major good fortune. Initially, postwar production was reserved for export to America. But the laws of free trade gradually became effective. As Director of Economics, Ludwig Erhard instituted policies that broke the chains of a captive economy, and the ensuing recovery sparked an upswing at Leitz.

Leitz was the first lens manufacturer to create its own glass research laboratory in 1948. A short time later the laboratory achieved major world success by developing a high-refraction glass without thorium, which is a radioactive substance. LaK9 (Lanthanum Crown Glass 9) was tone of the first thorium-free lanthanum, optical glass formulas, which Leitz licensed to nearly all European glass manufacturers. It is still used today in practically all medium- to high-speed lenses.

Fig. K1 and K2: *Strictly speaking, these pictures were staged because the sheep were driven into the frame and the young shop assistant was directed to move between the balloons for a better composition. In order to obtain a better picture, this type of direction is useful if the results do not look too contrived. In addition, grazing light and a polarizing filter added a three-dimensional appearance to the picturesque landscape while the weathered window provided an interesting frame for the portrait.*

Fig. K3 – K6: *The creative tasks of the photographer include the elimination of anything distracting and unnecessary from the picture. Because the white box distracts the viewer’s eyes from the actual subject, the fisherman, it was removed from the scene with the fisherman’s permission and the camera position was changed. As a result, disturbing details were removed from the background of the picture. Finally, the right moment had to be captured to create this pleasing environmental portrait of a fisherman repairing his nets (Fig. K6).*

Fig. K7 – K10: *Very light objects in a picture attract the viewer’s attention. No, matter how small they are. If this disturbs the composition of a picture, every attempt should be made to eliminate the objects. However, light subjects can also be used skillfully to enhance the composition of the picture, as is illustrated by these examples.*

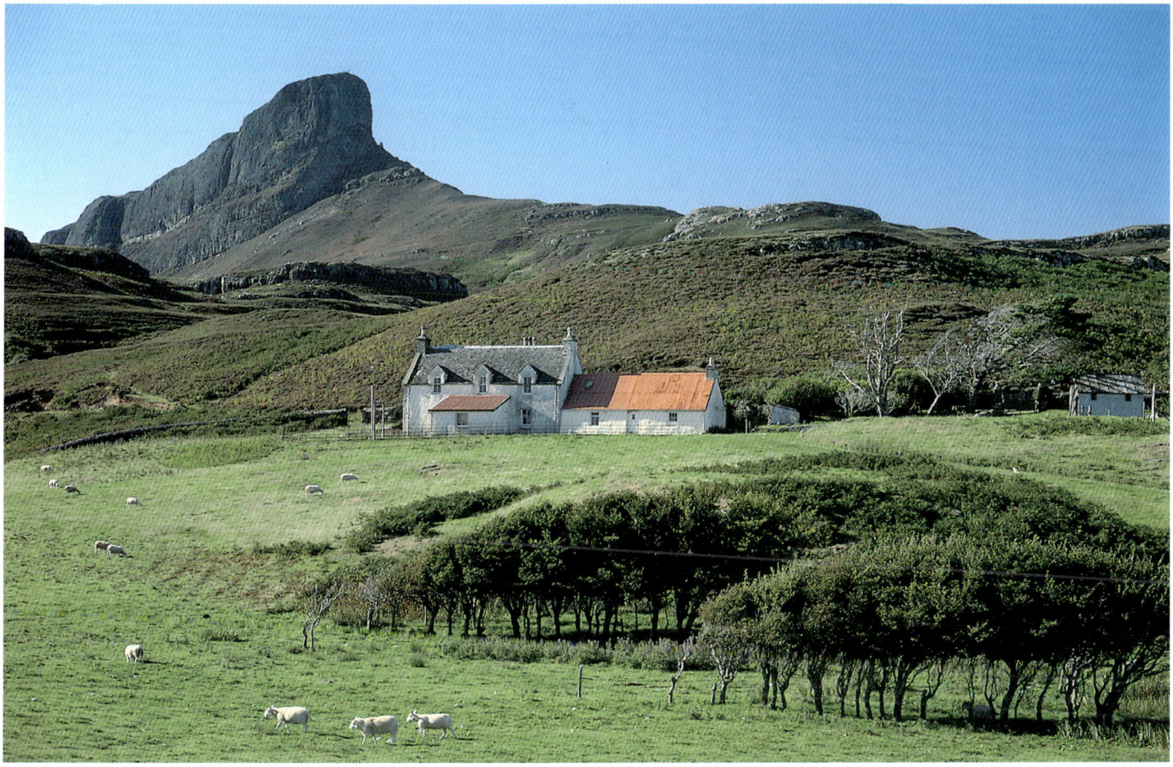

Fig. K1

Fig. K2

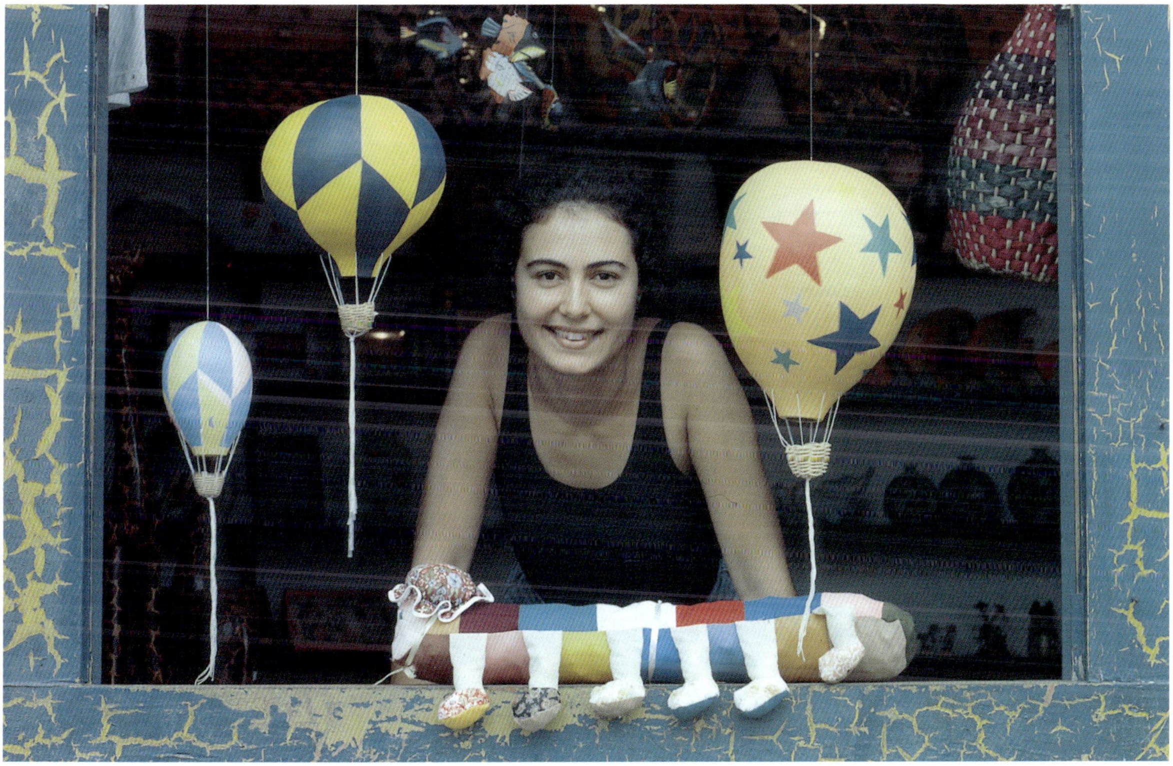

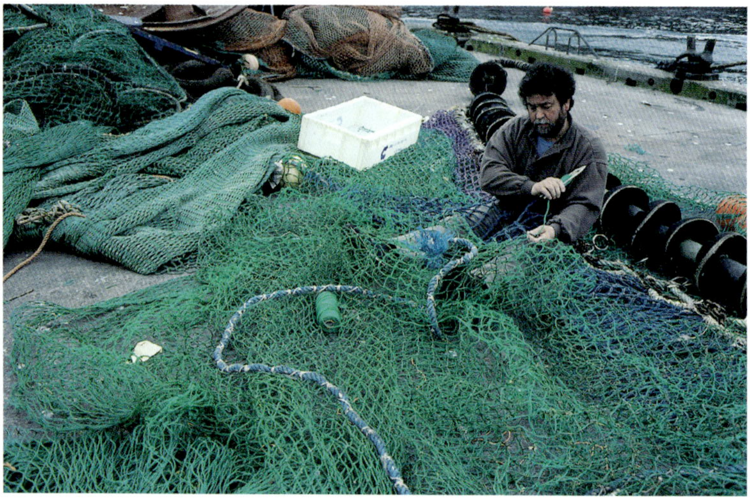

Fig. K3

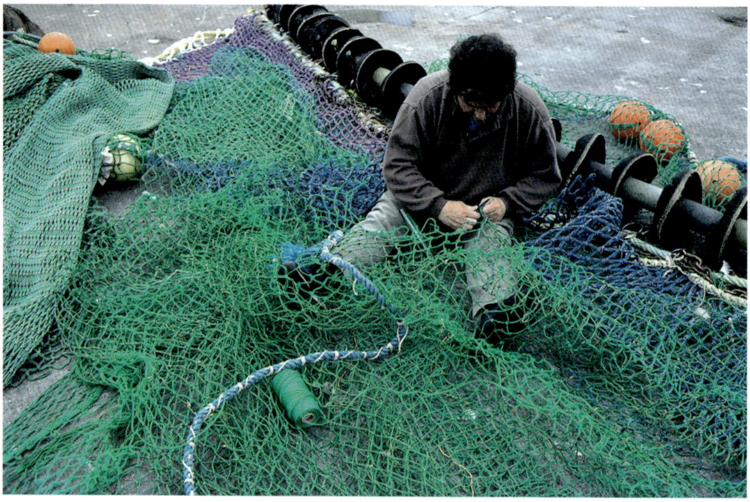

Fig. K4

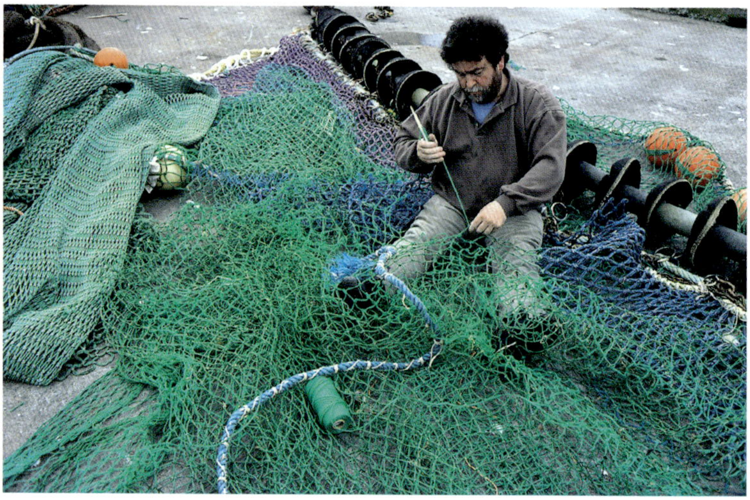

Fig. K5

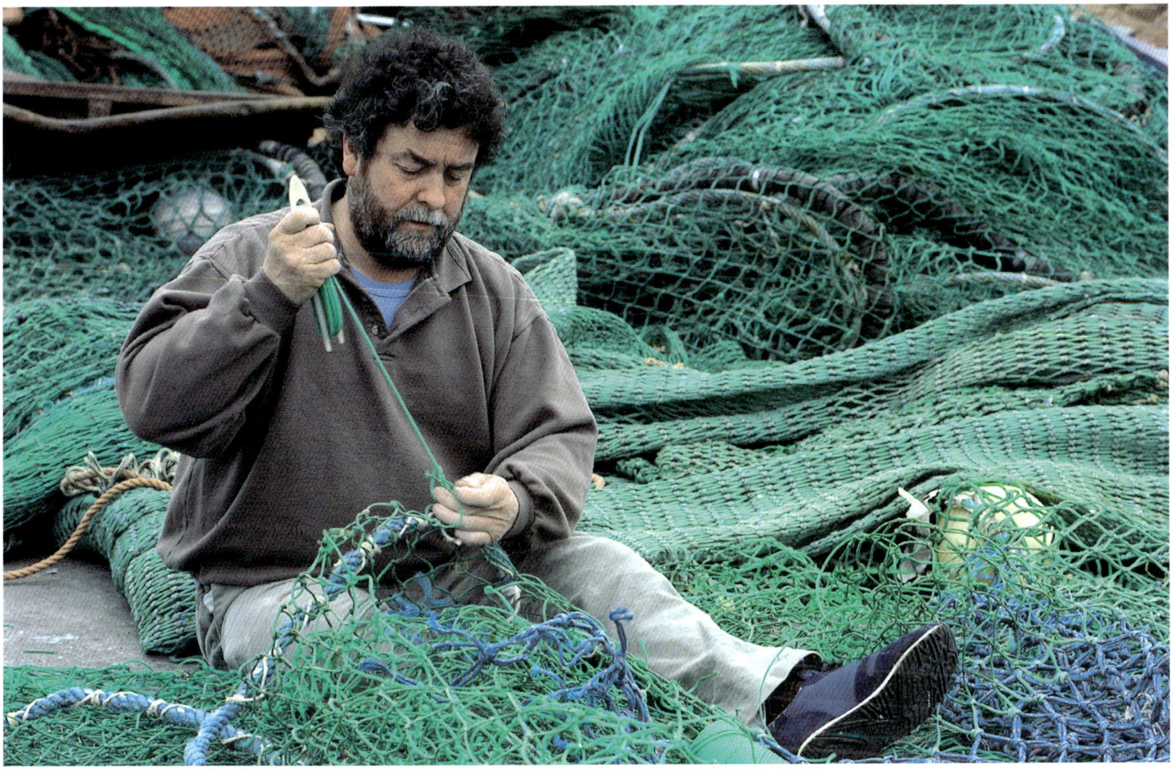

Fig. K6

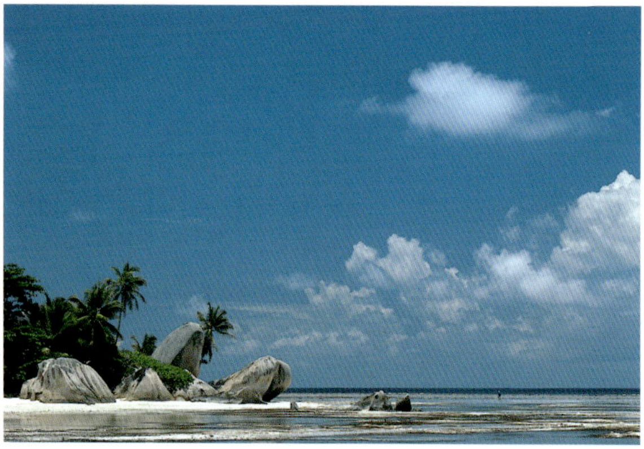

Fig.K7

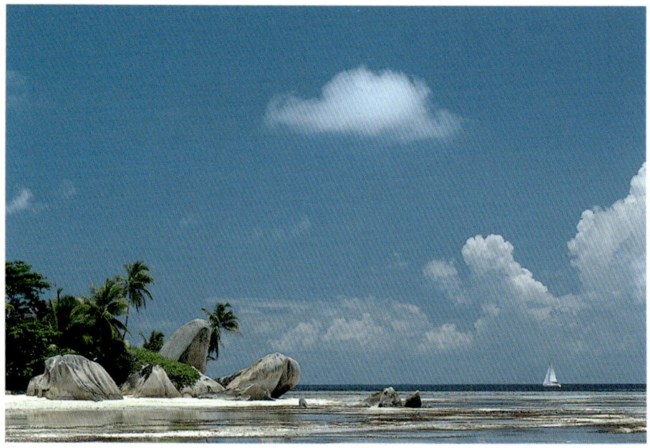

Fig. K8

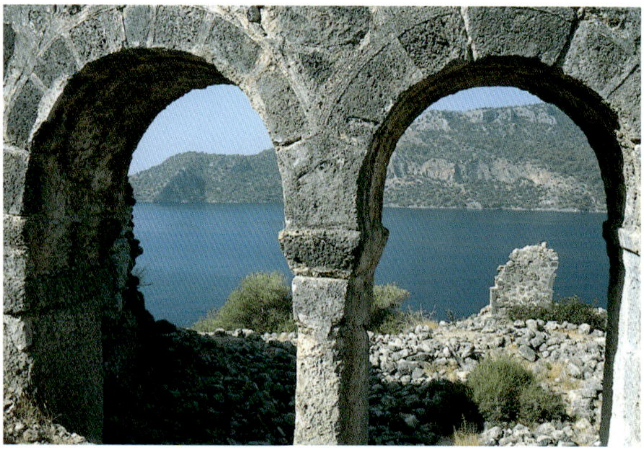

Fig.K9

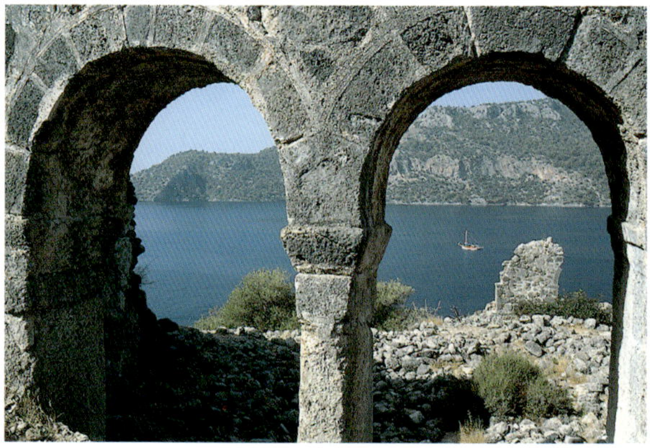

Fig. K10

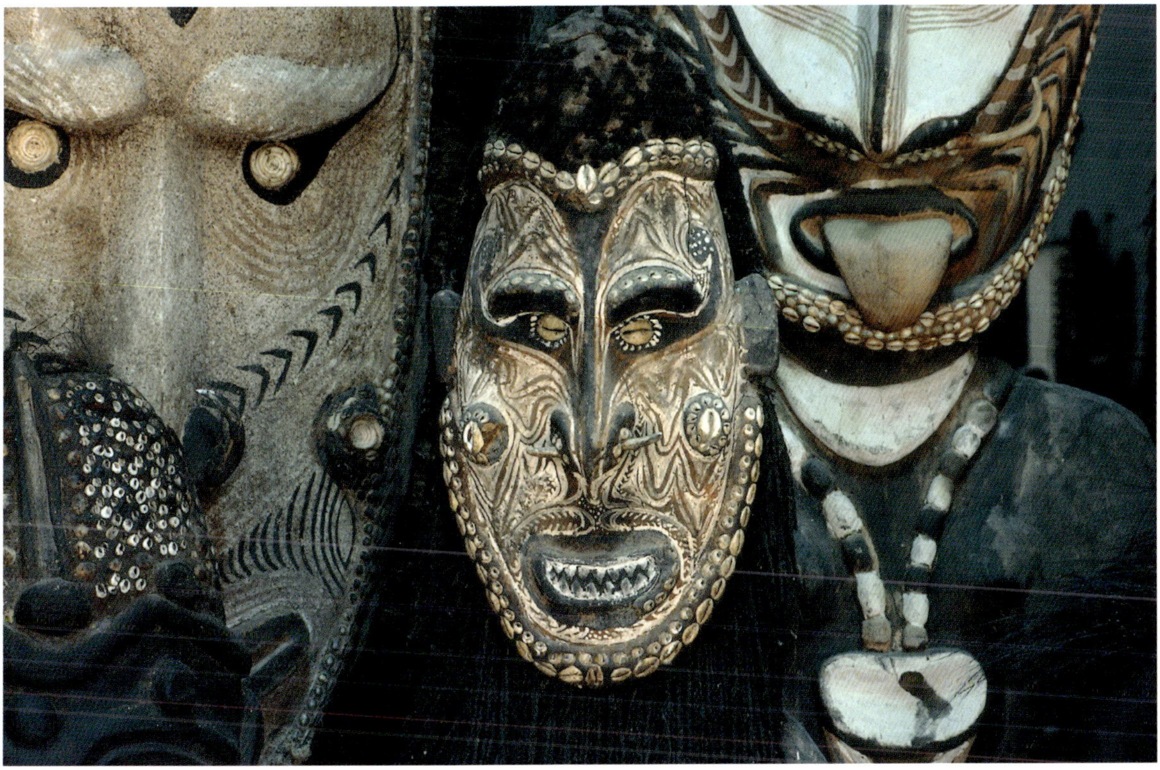

Fig. L1

Fig. L2

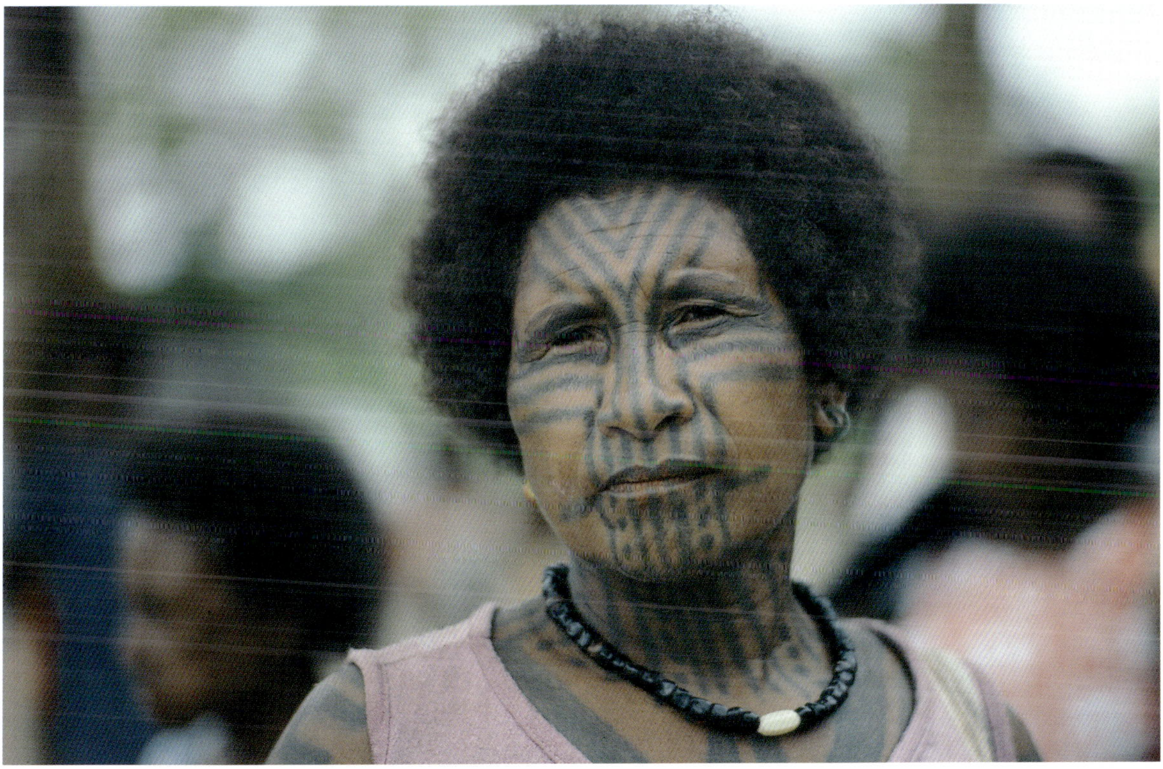

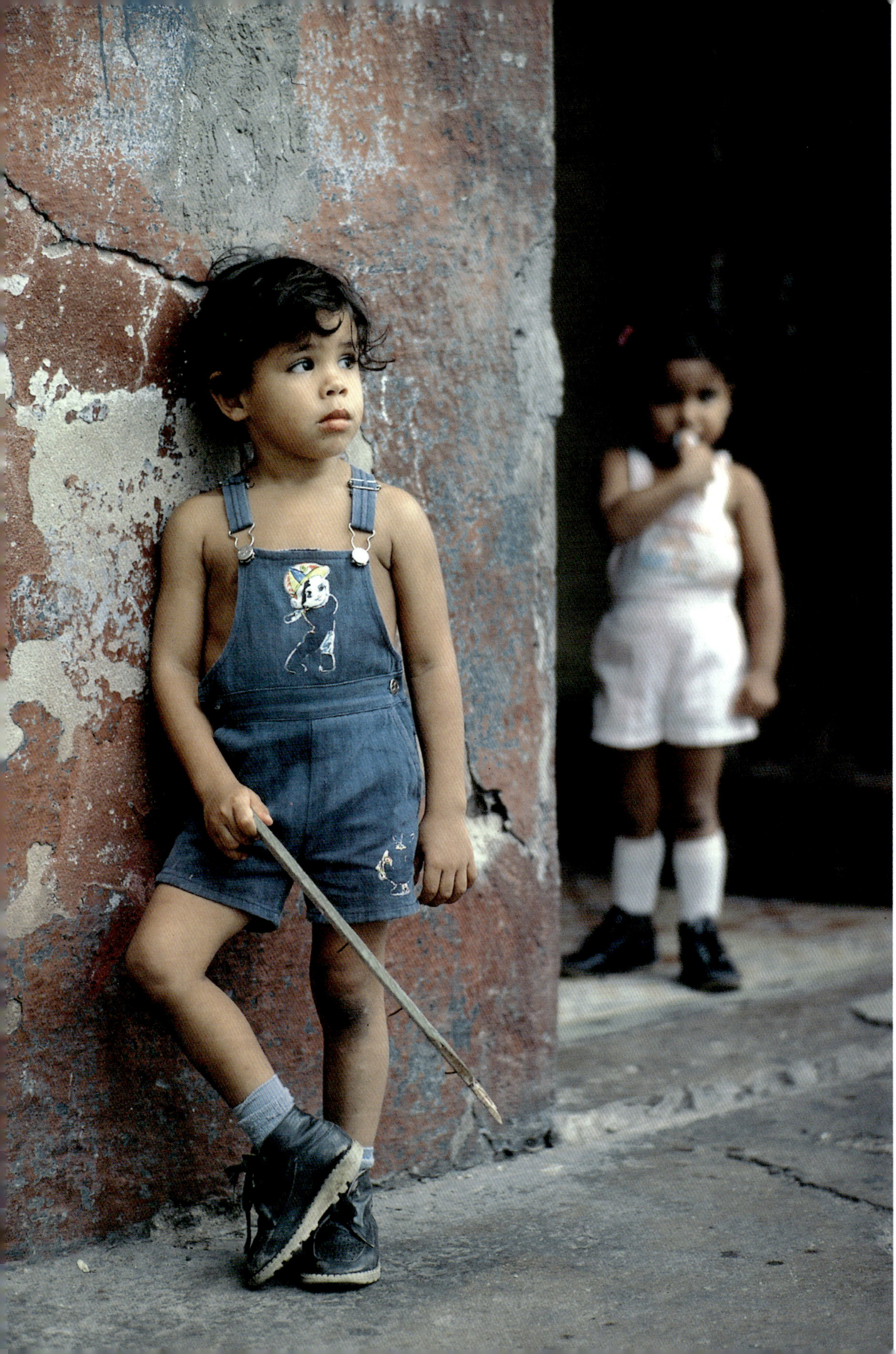

Fig.

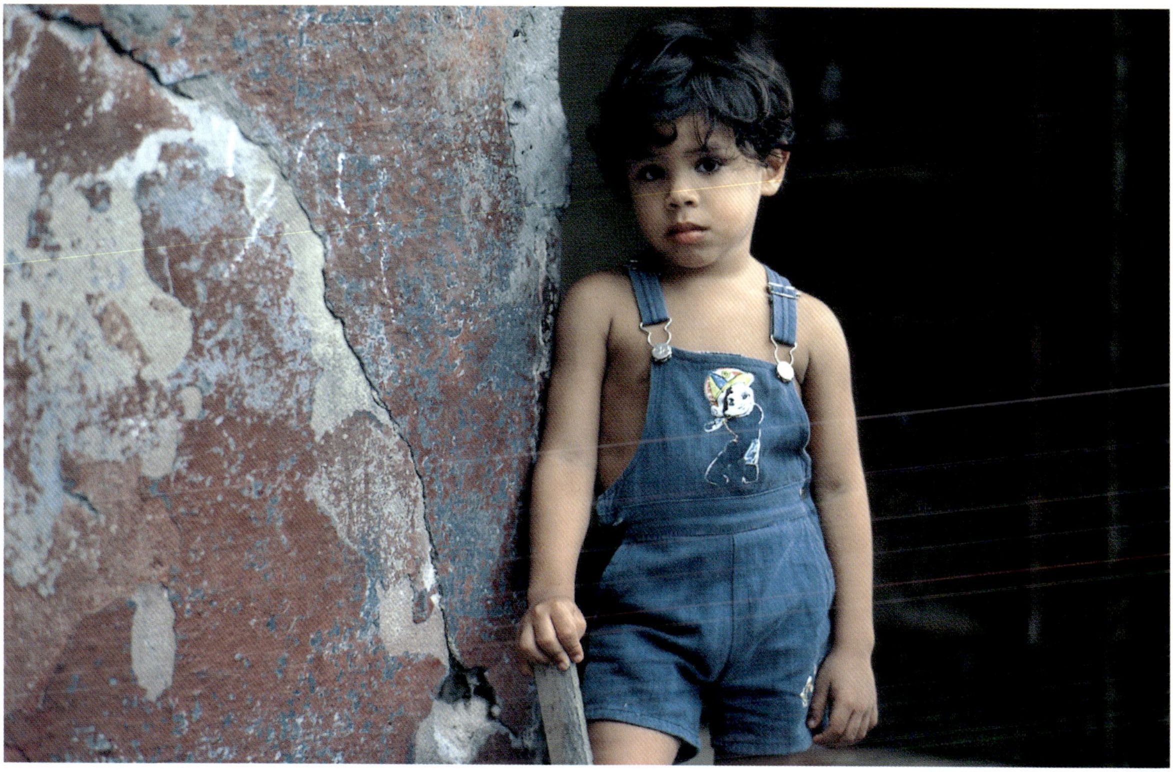

Fig. L4

Fig. L5

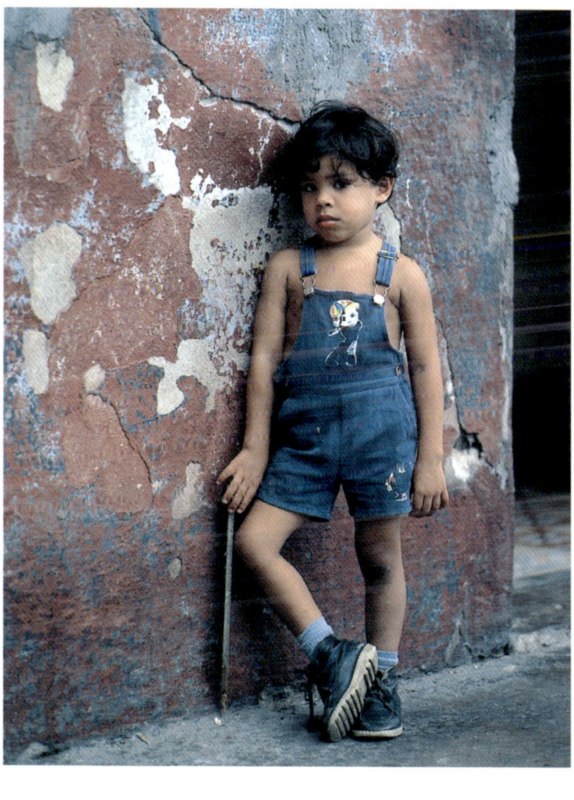

Fig. L6

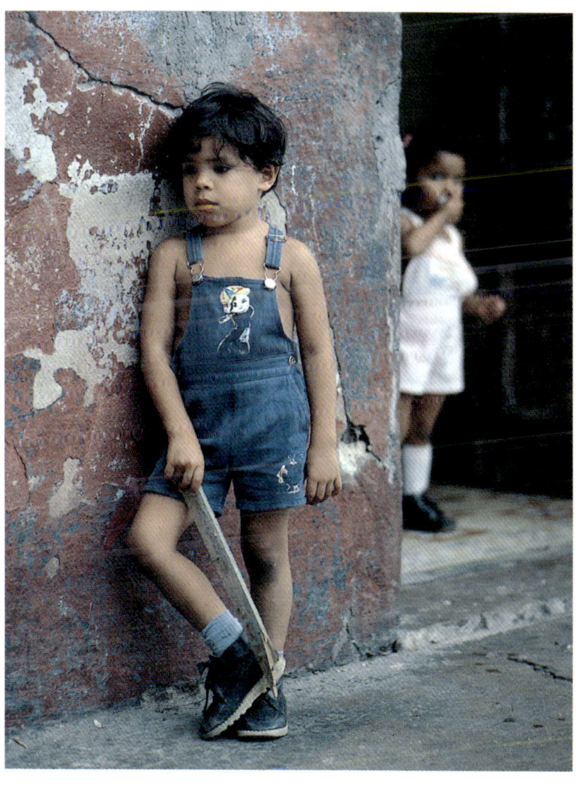

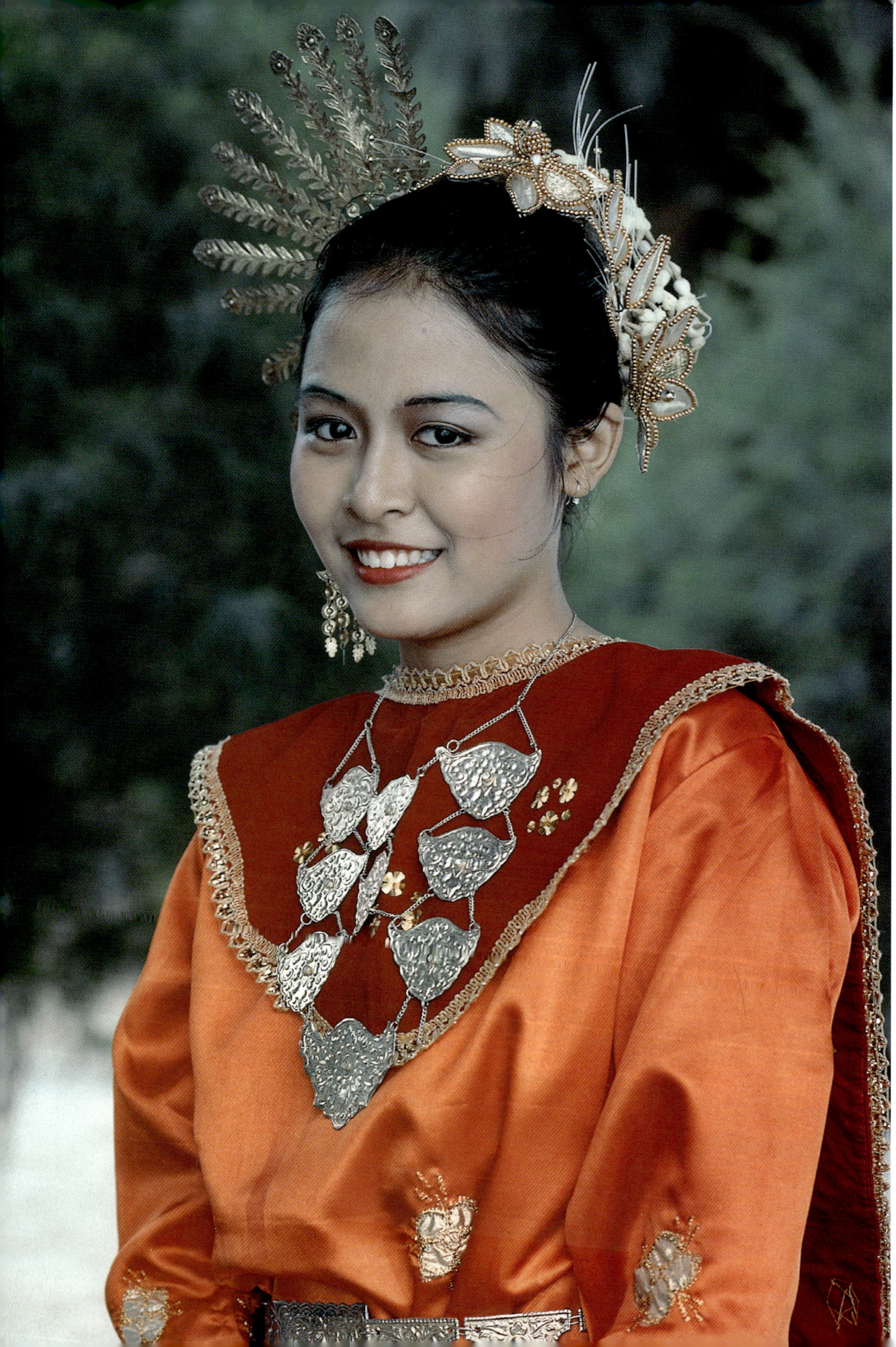

Fig.

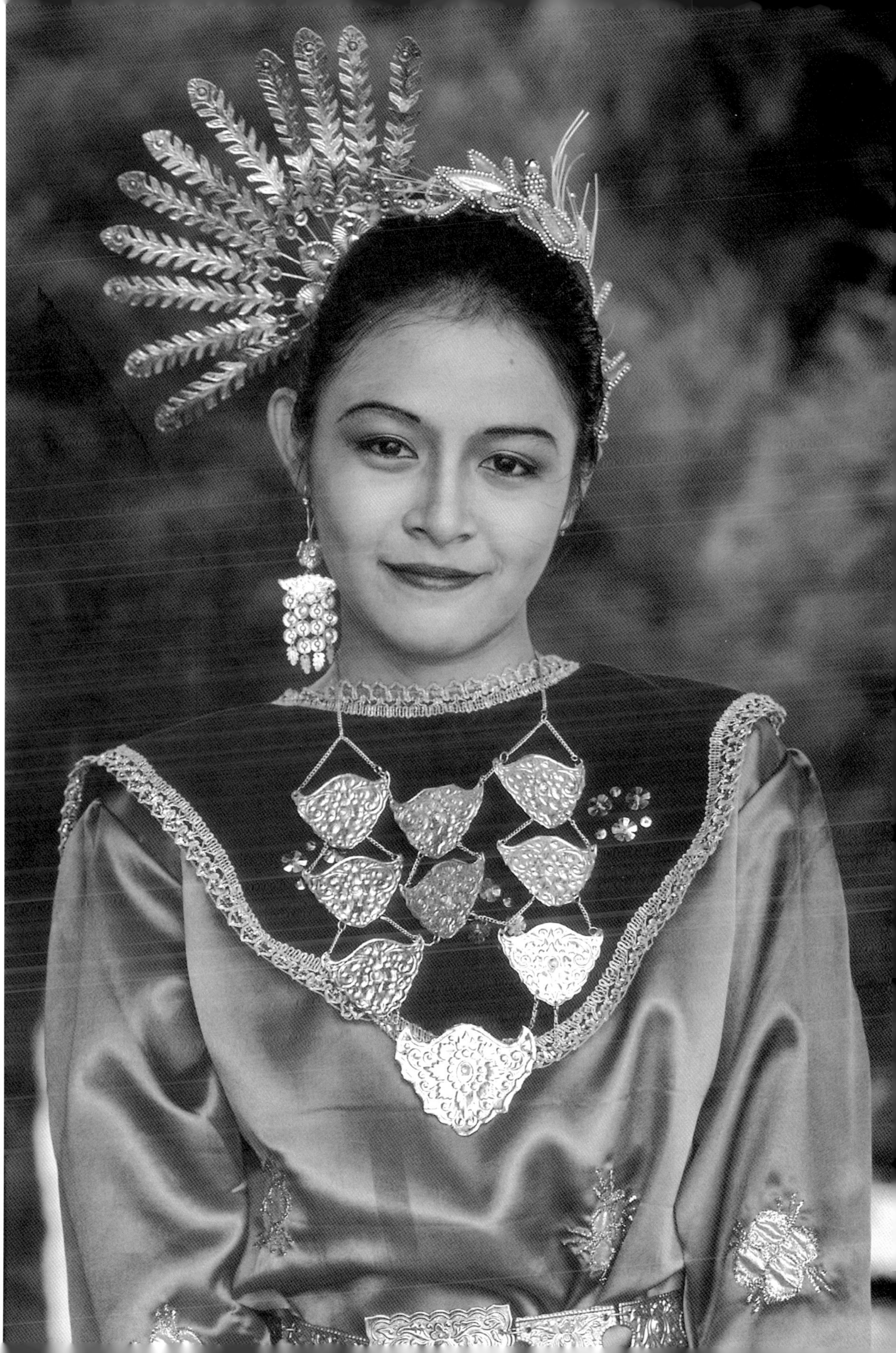

g. L8

LaK9 glass is a component that made Summicron lenses famous. During their development Leitz obtained about 50 patents. Since then, numerous additional new types of glass with different characteristics have been developed, but their production has largely been licensed to other glass manufacturers. To this day, Leitz itself produces only relatively small amounts of special types of optical glass. Among them are glass with anomalous partial dispersion that posses the characteristics of crystals, and which are used primarily in long focal-length Apo lenses for Leica cameras. In order to improve environmental protection in glass production, investments in the millions would have been necessary by 1990. However, because the relative small amounts of glass did not appear to make economic sense, Corning Glassworks in France was granted licenses and given technical knowledge. Now the special types of optical glass developed by Leitz are manufactured there. The quality is the same as earlier glass from the company's own glass laboratories.

Fig. L1 and L2: *To "tell" a story with pictures is a challenge for any photographer. Whether they are large prints on the wall, in an album from the photographer's last trip, or in a slide show. These two photographs were taken in Port Moresby on Papua, New Guinea. They show the tattooed face of a market woman and the masks that her husband makes for her to sell.*

Fig. L3 – L6: *When photographers have made the decision to take a picture in portrait or landscape format, one of many available creative components has been determined. The most exciting aspect of photography is to think of the opportunities offered by a subject. What is the effect of light and shadows? Has everything that is not essential been removed from the frame? How far does the depth of field extend? What happens in the background? Are facial expressions and poses appropriate for the situation? These questions are all the more relevant because a "picture-perfect" subject can be photographed in many ways. All exposures were taken with a 75mm f/1.4 Summilux lens, 1/125 second, f/2.8, daylight reversal film ISO 64.*

Fig. L7: *For more than 70 years Leitz/Leica has offered a line of high-quality products that meet the needs of 35mm photographers, whether they work in color or black-and-white, or both. Both pictures were taken at a focal length of 90mm.*
Left: Color negative film, ISO 100.
Right: Medium-speed black-and-white film

In the early 1970s a new regional reform was initiated, its objective was to unite the independent cities of Wetzlar and Giessen to form "Lahn City." In anticipation, Ernst Leitz GmbH changed its company name to "Ernst Leitz Wetzlar GmbH." This was done as a precautionary measure by the company to save the Wetzlar name, which was recognized worldwide as the origin for precision mechanics and high-performance optics.

However, at the time of this initiative, the population and local business voiced serious criticism and the plans were never implemented. Thus, after a brief "Lahn City" period, the two city names, Wetzlar and Giessen, were retained.

During the first half of the 1980s, approximately 60% of Leitz products were produced for the instruments market. These were microscopes for research, laboratories and teaching applications, two-dimensional and three-dimensional measuring devices for industrial measuring technology, optical measuring and inspection devices for the semi-conductor industry, as well as systems for image-processing and sample-recognition.

The photographic sector comprised about 40% of the business. This included the entire manufacturing program for two camera systems, Leica R and Leica M; the Pradovit projectors; the Focomat enlargers; and the Trinovid binoculars.

In the 1980s, approximately 4,000 salable units consisting of 77,000 individual components made up the supply program of Ernst Leitz Wetzlar GmbH. Together with the replacement parts for customer service, approximately 120,000 individual components must be planned and bought or manufactured in the appropriate numbers.

The company is considered one of the pioneers in the field of quantitative microscopy in which the application of the microscope goes way beyond its original function – the expansion of human visual capacity –

Fig. 213:
The headquarters of Ernest Leitz Wetzler GmbH, photographed in 1985.

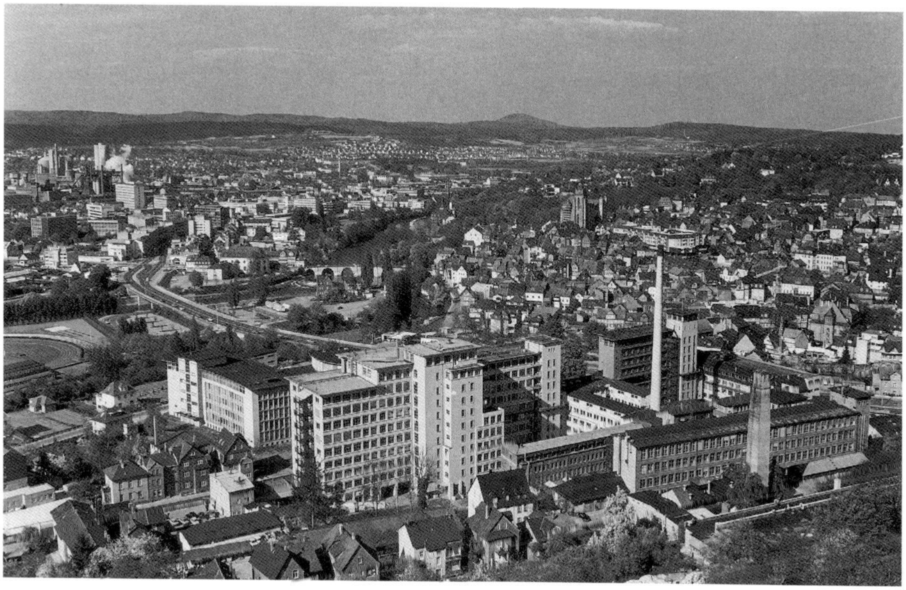

by becoming a maximum-precision measuring and analytical device for analyzing microscopic objects. New developments in this field represent a combination of optics, precision mechanics and electronics, which also includes computer technology.

Ernst Leitz (Canada) Ltd.

Ernst Leitz Canada Limited with headquarters in Midland, north of Toronto, in the province of Ontario, was founded in 1952. This plant manufactured the Leica M4-2 camera and almost the entire line of Leica M lenses. In 1990 it was taken over by the North American Hughes Corporation and continues to doe business under the name Hughes Leitz Optical Technologies Ltd.

This subsidiary produces optics assemblies and lenses, e.g., the 180mm f/34. Apo-Telyt-R lens for Leica Camera GmbH.

Leitz Portugal S.A.

The factory in Vila Nova de Famalicao, located 30 km (18 3/4 miles) north of Porto, Portugal, was founded in 1971 began operating in 1973 in rented space. Construction of a new factory building began at the same time, and the first part began operating in 1975. Since 1989 the factory belongs to Leica Camera AG and is incorporated under the name Leica Portugal. The plant currently employs approximately 800 people. Its main products are subassemblies for the Leica R and Leica M, Kompact binoculars, projection and enlarging lenses, as well as assemblies for binoculars. Development and design of all assemblies and apparatus, including the fabrication of pilot models, take at Leica Camera AG. Specialists supervise final inspection and quality control.

Leica GmbH – Leitz's photography group becomes independent

Toward the end of the 1960s, international cooperation was also increasingly important at Leitz. The first result of the Leitz/Minolta joint venture was the Leica CL (Compact Leica) in 1973. The joint venture with the noted Swiss company Wild Herbrugg AG began in 1972 and led to the take-over of additional capital shares at Leitz in 1974. At the end of 1985 the newly founded Wild Leitz Holding AG took over the remaining corporate shares for Ernst Leitz Wetzlar GmbH.

On the 1st of January 1987, Wild Heerbrugg AG and Ernst Leitz GmbH, as well as its subsidiaries and production sites worldwide, were merged into Wild Leitz Corporation. This gave them a uniform strategic direction, among other things, in order to use the potential of 9,000 employees in such a manner that the challenges of the worldwide marketplace could be optimally met in the future. In the course of this strategic alignment of the Wild Leitz corporation the decision was made to make the Leitz photographic division independent in order to continue to ensure and develop the highest-quality Leica cameras, projectors, enlargers, and binoculars. The core business of the newly created corporation was grouped in business units in the investment product field, while the photographic field of Ernst Leitz Wetzlar GmbH represented the consumer goods business.

This decision encouraged an independent, forward-looking photographic strategy—a visible sign of the corporation's readiness to be more flexible and to take greater risks. In addition to the investment product business, product lines, different types of business, ideas and innovation potential are to be promoted and developed. This allows the photographic group to be more agile and more flexible in its responses, to operate more closely to the market and respond to its demands. By making the photographic group into its own, independent company, the market-sensitive strategic and operational management of the photographic business has been ensured in the long term.

The founding of Leica GmbH at the end of 1986 and the availability of the required financial allowed the state-of-the-art expansion of the factory in nearby Solms.

This new factory combines development, production and quality assurance, together with administration, marketing, distribution, the Leica Academy, and customer service. Only the finished goods warehouse and shipping continue to be located in a shipping and service center in Wetzlar. Currently Leica Camera GmbH employs approximately 460 employees.

The Leica Camera Group is formed

On the 1st of January 1989 the Leica Camera Group was created as a legally independent corporate group of Wiled Leitz Holding AG. This group included Leica GmbH in Solms, Leitz Portugal S. A., as well as the Leica distributorships in Germany, Switzerland and the US. The Leica Camera Group has approximately 1000 employees, half of them in Germany. During the following year, Wild Leitz Holding AG and The Cambridge Instrument Company plc merged and took the corporate name Leica plc, Leica GmbH became Leica Camera GmbH.

Leica Projektion GmbH

In 1990 the Leica Camera Group acquired the Zett projector works in Braunschweig, Germany, from Ikon AG. In the same year, the projectors of the newly founded Leica Projektion GmbH, which were developed and produced in this plant, were introduced at Photokina. Until 1995, Leica projectors, as well as the world-famous Zett projectors, were designed, manufactured and distributed through the company's sales force

Feinwerktechnik GmbH Wetzlar

In the course of restructuring Leica Corporation, the Traubenstein works, which used to belong to Leitz were renamed into Feinwerktechnik GmbH Wetzlar. This production site is now a supplier specializing in lathing, milling, punching and polishing components. The base plate and the top plate of the titanium-plated Leica M6 are fabricated and finished in this plant. Also, the bayonet rings, as well as extrusion-molded components such as the dials of the Leica R models, are produced in this plant. In addition, tools and molds are designed and built here. In September 1992 the Feinwerktechnik GmbH Wetzlar with its approximately 75 employees became part of the Leica Camera Group.

Fig. 214:
The Leica Works in Solms.

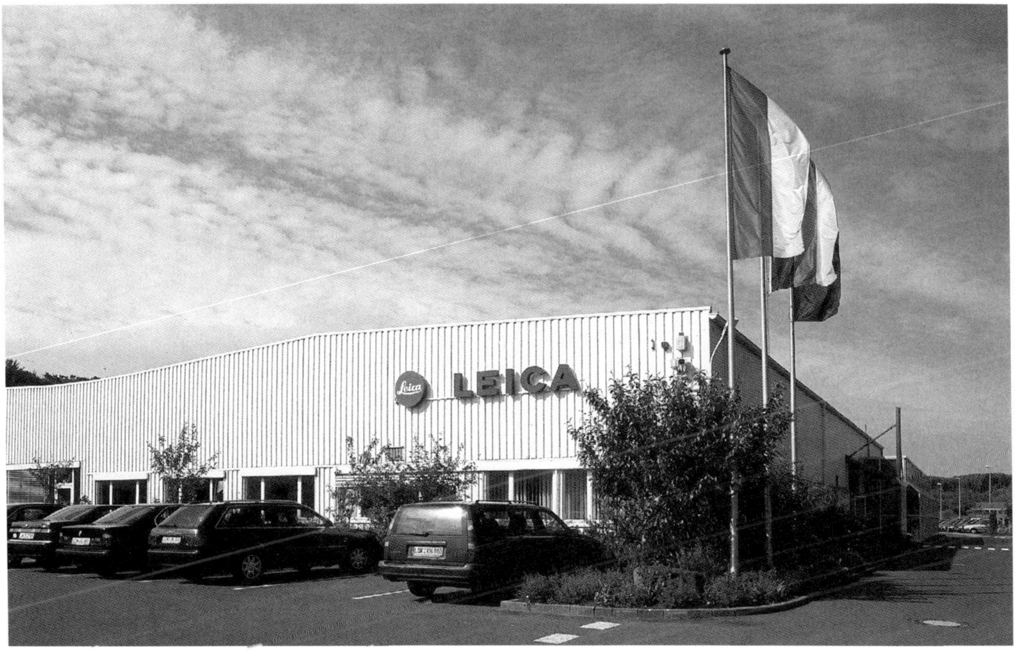

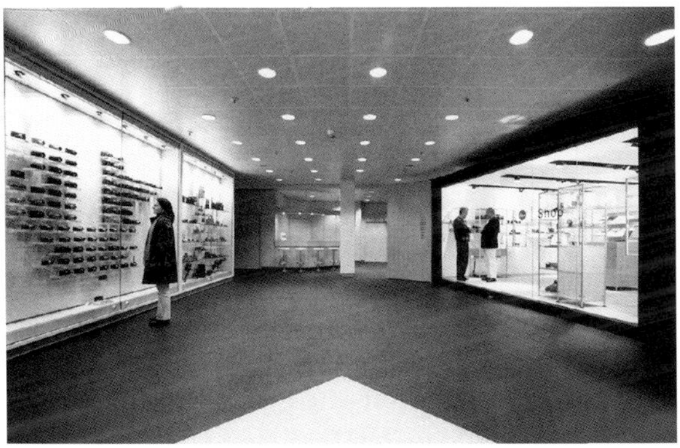

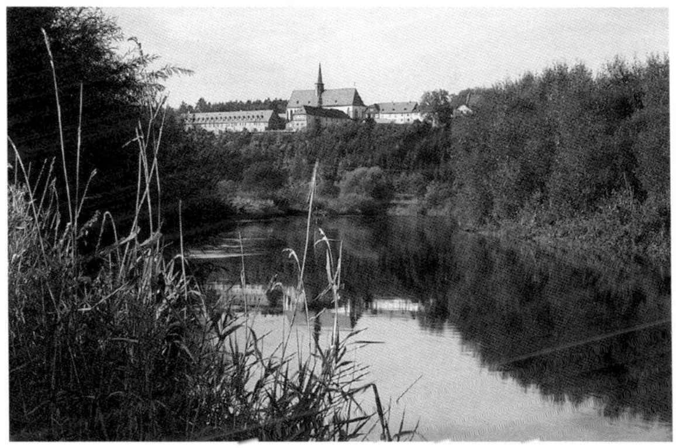

Fig. 215: *The foyer at Leica Camera AG in Solms, showing the Leica Family Tree exhibit. Opposite this, current Leica products are offered for sale at the Leica Shop. The Leica Gallery features monthly exhibits and workshops are taught at the Leica Academy by a team of experts. Program information is available upon request.*

Fig. 216: *High above the Lahn River, between Solms and Wetzlar, is the Altenberg Monastery. The Leica Academy Altenberg is housed on the monastery's estate.*

Change to Leica Camera AG

Today, the Leica Camera Group includes additional independent distribution organizations in France, Great Britain, and the United States. The Group employees approximately 1,400 employees worldwide, approximately 650 of which are in Germany. On July 22, 1996 the change from Leica Camera GmbH to Leica Camera AG was entered in the trade register. Economic development grew with the expansion of the Leica Camera Group.

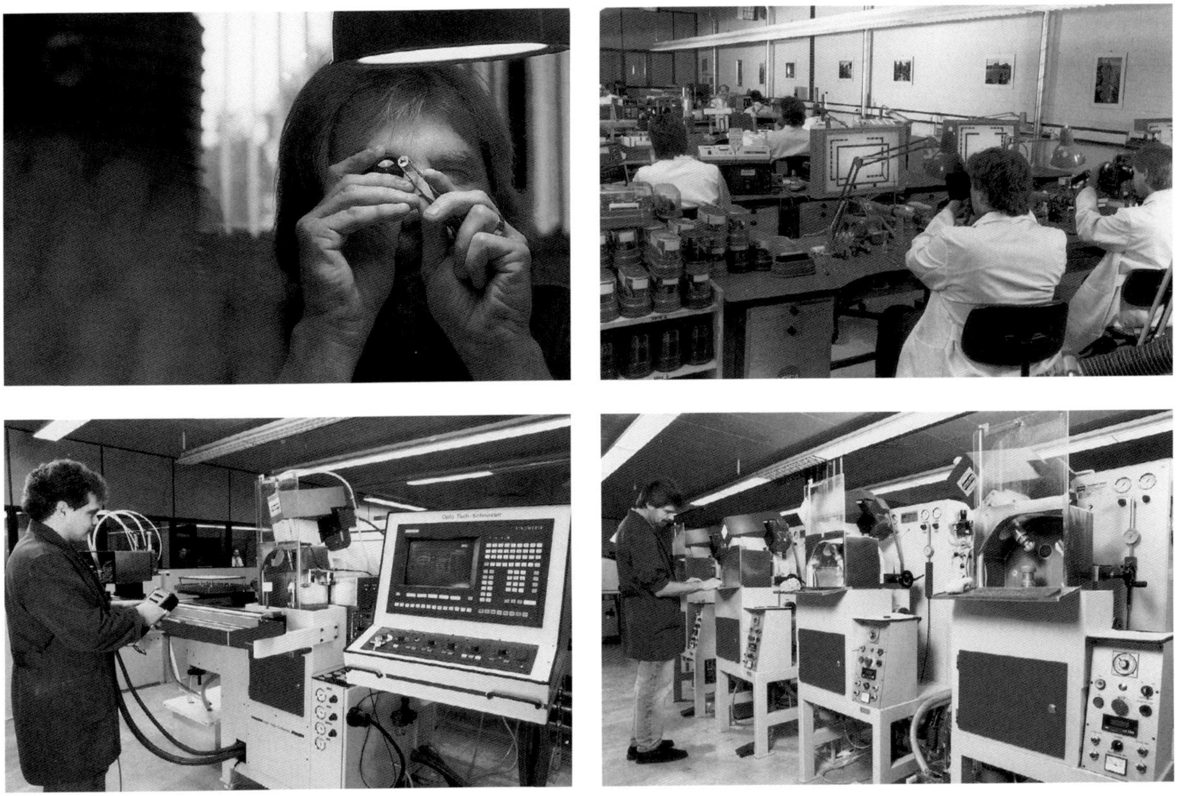

Fig. 217 a – d: *The production of Leica cameras and Leica lenses is still largely defined by skilled manual finishing. As in the past, people are the most important part of the process. Years of experience and the skill of highly qualified employees guarantee Leica quality: maximum optical performance and precise mechanics for a long life. Wherever required, of course, the most modern processes and computer-controlled tools and machines are used.*

Top left: The surface of a small lens is inspected for flaws.
Top right: Assembly of the Leica M.

Bottom left: The state-of-the-art, fully automated SM-80-CNC pre-grinding machines work accurately to tolerances within 1/1000 mm. It can be set up for 2D and 3D processes for finishing the lens blank. After programming, the machine is started via the handling system.
Bottom right: Final polishing of the lenses is done with oscillation machines. As a result of the pivoting movement of the machining head, the micro-structure of the surface becomes significantly finer and more uniform. Depending on the lens diameter, it is machined with an accuracy of up to 3/60,000 mm.

In 1988, sales amounted to DM 121 million. Four years later (1992) sales reached DM 200 million for the first time. At the end of the business year, namely on the 31st of March 2002, they reached Euro 139.8 million.

For more information

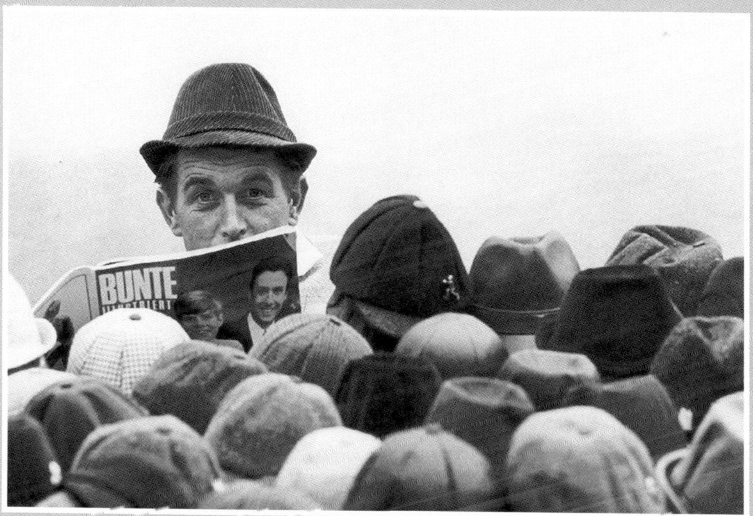

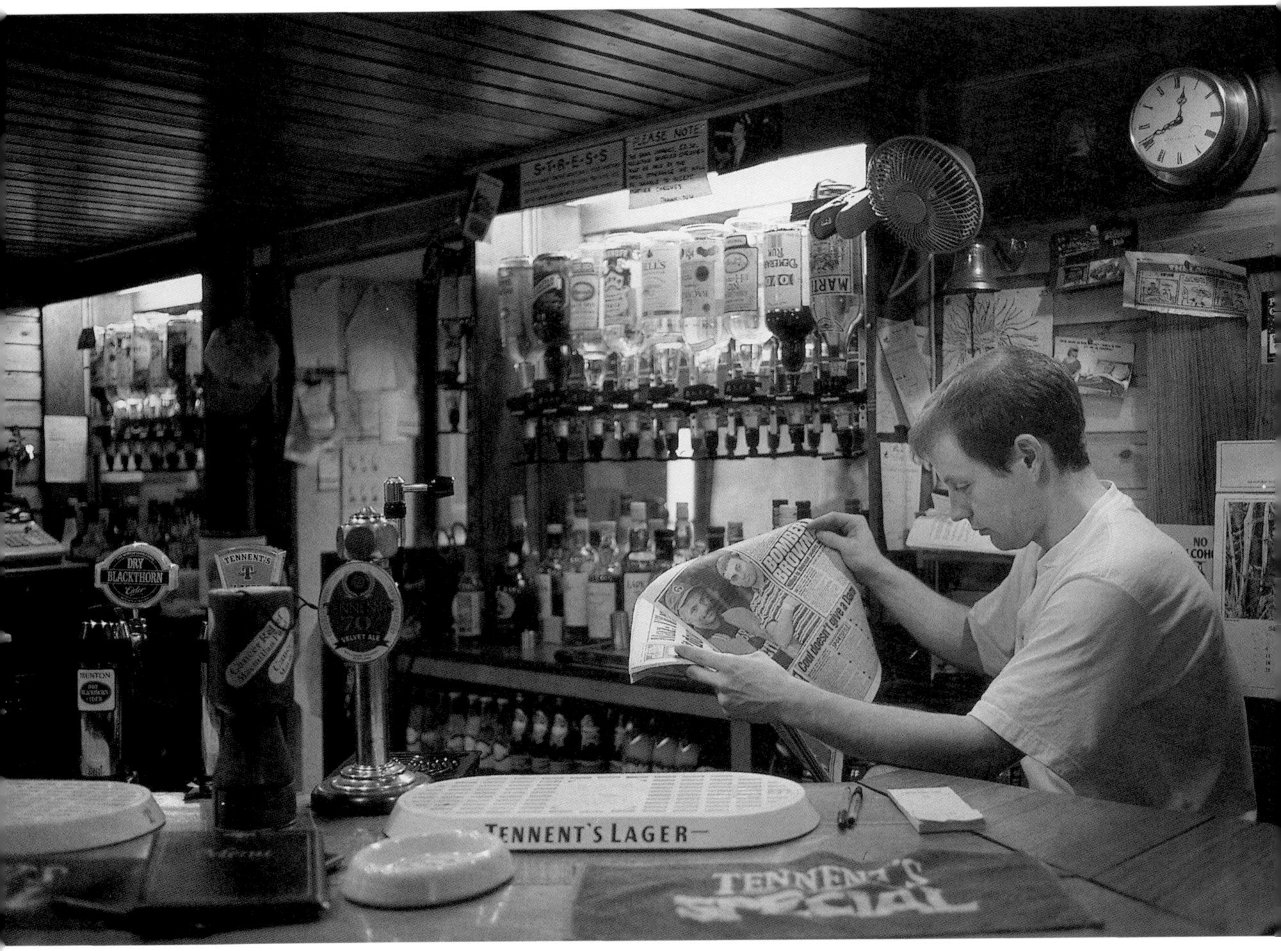

Fig. 218: *Photographic literature and photography books are definitely as important as photographic workshops for continuing your education. However, just reading and listening will not be enough to acquire the necessary experience that is crucial for successful picture-taking. You still need hands-on experience to practice your skills.*
50mm f/1.4 Summilux-M lens, 1/30 second, f/2, high-speed film.

For more information

Recommended photographic literature

There is hardly a field in our life that is not affected by photography, directly or indirectly. Accordingly, there is a myriad of opportunities to become photographically active. Ongoing advances ensure that new products and techniques allow better results in a more convenient manner. Those who wish to improve their photographic technique and expand their knowledge should use current photographic journals and established photographic literature.

Currently, thousands of photographic and picture books on the most diverse topics are available, as well as dozens of photographic journals. Those who wish to obtain information on the work of famous photographers may want to use monographs.

Those who are interested in the most recent work may wish to use annually released photography books for reference. There are a number of informative books on photographic history, as well as good information for photographers who are more interested in the fundaments of photographic theory. Literature is available at bookstores or camera shops. Also, photographic journals are available at newsstands. The author of this book recommends the following titles as supplementary reading.

Photographic journals

Leica Fotografie International
Published by IDC Corporate Publishing GmbH, Hamburg. This international magazine for 35mm photography is dedicated to Leica users in particular. Well-known amateur and professional photographers from around the world describe their practical experiences, show their best photography, and give solid technical advice—even including special situations and possibilities. It contains a wealth of photographic examples with commentaries and suggestions.
Internet: www.lfi-online.com

Leica World
Leica Camera AG
"Leica World," has received many awards for it's artistic design and coverage of topics of interest to Leica owners. Published twice a year as a large-format magazine that introduces famous Leica photographers and their work, it is dedicated to creative photography, offering interviews, reports, and journalistic articles. Also, it carries an internationally acclaimed series on great art directors. Up-to-date information from Leica Camera AG round off the program put together by the editors. Chief editor, Hans-Michael Koetzle views Leica World as "an opportunity to prevent the disappearance of great photojournalism magazines, at least on a modest level."

The care with which pictures are selected is reflected by thoroughly researched text, as well by a deliberately studied layout adhering to classic ideas. The art director of this large-format journal is Horst Moser. The publication is acclaimed for its outstanding reproduction and excellent printing.
Internet: www.leica-camera.com

Photographic technique

ANSEL ADAMS:
Ansel Adams Photography Series
Three volumes: "The Camera," "The Negative," and the "The Print" reflect the entire knowledge of this master of black-and-white photography. His Zone System is exemplary of excellence in photographic technology. It is, however, of limited use to the 35mm photographer.

Each volume has many black-and-white pictures. Publisher: Bulfinch, reprint edition 1995.

Collecting cameras

PAUL-HENRY VAN HASBROECK:
The Leica: A History Illustrating Every Model and Accessory
325 pages with illustrations.
Publisher: Sotheby Parke Bernet, 1984.

DENNIS LANEY:
Leica Collectors Guide
392 pages, illustrated with color and black-and-white pictures, and drawings.
Publisher: Hove Books, 2004.

G. ROGLIATTI:
Leica: The First 70 Years
240 pages with many black-and-white and color pictures.
Publisher: Hove Books, 2002.

Reference books

GÜNTER OSTERLOH:
Applied Leica Technique
The Leica R handbook for the practitioner.
304 pages with black-and-white and color illustrations.
Publisher: Umschau Verlag/Seven Hills Books, 1984.

Handbook of the Leica System 2002/2003
Comprehensive catalog published by Leica Camera AG covers Leica cameras, lenses, projectors, enlargers, binoculars, and accessories, available in German and English. May be purchased from Leica Camera AG, Vertrieb Deutschland, Oskar-Barnack-Strasse 11, 35606 Solms, Germany, or from Leica agencies.

Important addresses

Leica Academy

The internationally renowned Leica Academy is one of the services provided by Leica Camera AG.

Many committed photographers see this school as the fulfillment of a wish for in-depth continuing education in the areas of high-quality photography, projectors, and enlargements.

In seminars, workshops and on photographic trips, participants are familiarized in a hands-on, up-to-date manner with Leica's world of ideas and the fascinating and skilled handling of Leica products. The course subjects are applications-specific and offer a wealth of information, encouragement, and suggestions for practical applications.

The participation in photographic seminars, workshops, and trips does not require ownership of a Leica.

A detailed brochure listing all the programs and dates when they are offered is published once a year. Upon request, it may be obtained from:

Leica Camera AG, Leica Akademie
Oskar-Barnack-Str. 11
35606 Solms
Germany
Tel.: +49 (0)64 42-208-421
Fax: +49 (0)64 42-208-425
e-mail: la@leica-camera.com
Internet: http://www.leica-camera.com

Leica Customer Service

Should repairs become necessary, please have your Leica equipment repaired by authorized contract services only or by Leica Customer Service:

Leica Camera AG
Customer Service

Oskar-Barnack-Str. 11
35606 Solms
Germany
Tel.: +49 (0)64 42-208-189
Fax: +49 (0)64 42-208-339
e-mail: ts@leica-camera.com

Leica on the Internet

http://www.leica-camera.com

Leica Information Service

Questions relating to picture-taking, reproduction and observation techniques will be answered in writing, by telephone or by e-mail by:

Leica Camera AG
Leica Informationsdienst
Postfach 11 80
35599 Solms
Germany
Tel.: +49 (0)64 42-208-111
Fax: +49 (0)64 42-208-339
e-mail: info@leica-camera.com

Leica Professional Service
Leica Camera AG
Marketing Communication
Oskar-Barnack-Strasse 11
35606 Solms
Tel. +49 (0)6442 208 -406
Fax. +49 (0)6442 208 -455

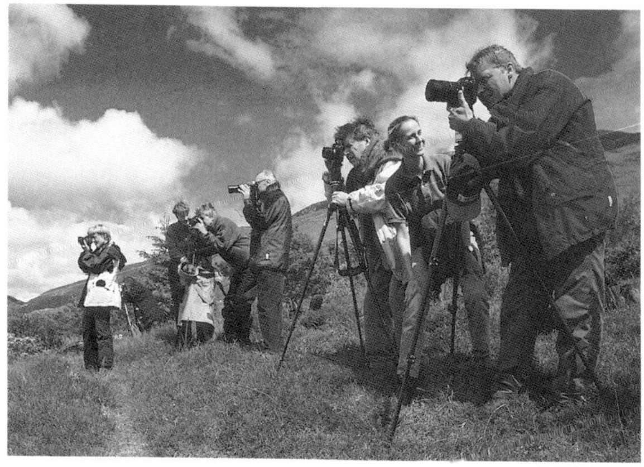

Leica Visitor and Factory Tours

Call ahead of time to make sure a tour is taking place on the date you wish to visit.
Tel.: +49 (0)64 41-200-909 9
Fax: +49 (0)64 41-200-908 8

Leica Gallery

670 Broadway, Suite 500, New York, NY 10012, U.S.A. The gallery features eight major exhibitions of Leica photographers per year. It has one of the world's largest collections of signed monographs as well as many books on Leica history and photography.

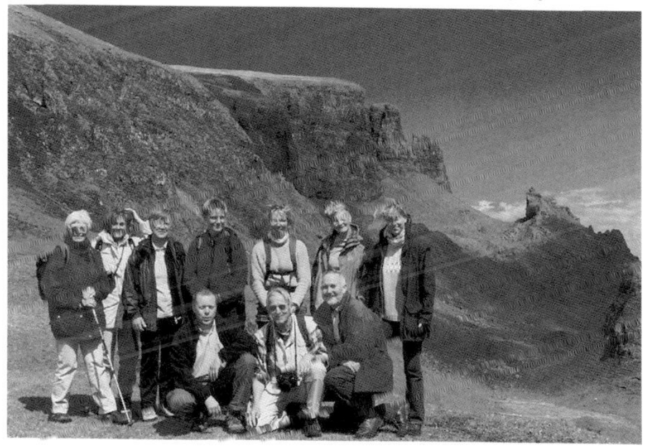

Do you still have unanswered questions? Would you like to go on a photographic excursion guided by the author? Please contact:
Günter Osterloh
Telefon: +49 (0)64 45-16 12
Telefax: +49 (0)64 45-6 12 05 31
e-mail: g.osterloh@freenet.de

Leica agencies

Germany
Leica Camera AG
Oskar-Barnack-Strasse 11
D-35606 Solms
Tel.:+49 (0)64 42-208-0
Fax:+49 (0)64 42-208-333
email:info@leica-camera.com
Internet: http://www.leica-camera.com

United States & Canada
Leica Camera Inc.
156 Ludlow Avenue
Northvale, New Jersey 07647
Tel.: +1 (201) 767-7500
Fax: +1 (201) 767-8666
email: repair@leicacamerausa.com
Internet: http://www.leicacamerausa.com

Great Britain
Leica Camera Ltd.
Davy Avenue
Knowlhill
GB-Milton Keynes MK 5 8LB
Tel.: 0044 1908 66 66 63
Fax: 0044 1908 67 13 16
email: info@leica-camera.co.uk

Netherlands
Odin B.V.
Maxwellstraat 21
P.O. Box 428
6716 BX Ede
Tel.: 0031 318 64 20 00
Fax: 0031 318 64 20 63
email: Leicanl@xs4all.nl

Japan
Nihon SiberHegner, K.K.
SiberHegner Mita Building, 6F
3-4-19 Mita
Minato-ku, Tokyo 108-8360
Tel.: +81 3-5441-4515
Fax: +81 3-5441-4524
Internet: http://www.nshcgj.jp

Hong Kong
Schmidt Marketing (H.K.) Ltd.
9/F, North Somerset House
Taikoo Place
979 King's Road
Quarry Bay, Hong Kong
Tel.: 00852 2507 0369
Fax: 00852 2968 0682
email: infohk@schmidtmarketing.com

Australia
Adeal Pty. Ltd.
2 Baldwin Road
Altona North
AUS-Vic 3025
Tel.: +61 (3) 93 69 78 11
Fax: +61 (3) 93 69 52 11
email: david@adeal.com.au

New Zealand
Lacklands Photographic Ltd.
48 George Street, Mt. Eden
P.O. Box 56-036
NZ-Aukland 3
Tel.: +64 (9) 63 00 753
Fax: +64 (9) 63 88 421
email: info@leica.co.nz
Internet: http://www.lacklands.co.nz

South Africa
Precision Photo Systems
P.O. Box 785
Fontainebleau
Randburg 2032
Johannesburg
Tel.: +27 (11) 791 08 90
Fax: +27 (11) 791 15 65
email: dechaves@iafrica.com

Index